T0305280

THE GLOBAL FACTORY

NEW HORIZONS IN INTERNATIONAL BUSINESS

Series Editor: Peter J. Buckley, *Centre for International Business, University of Leeds (CIBUL), UK*

The New Horizons in International Business series has established itself as the world's leading forum for the presentation of new ideas in international business research. It offers pre-eminent contributions in the areas of multinational enterprise – including foreign direct investment, business strategy and corporate alliances, global competitive strategies, and entrepreneurship. In short, this series constitutes essential reading for academics, business strategists and policy makers alike.

Titles in the series include:

The Global Factory

Networked Multinational Enterprises in the Modern Global Economy

Peter J. Buckley, OBE, FBA

Professor of International Business
Centre for International Business, University of Leeds (CIBUL), UK

NEW HORIZONS IN INTERNATIONAL BUSINESS

 Edward Elgar
PUBLISHING

Cheltenham, UK • Northampton, MA, USA

© Peter J. Buckley 2018

All rights reserved. No part of this publication may be reproduced, stored in a retrieval system or transmitted in any form or by any means, electronic, mechanical or photocopying, recording, or otherwise without the prior permission of the publisher.

Published by
Edward Elgar Publishing Limited
The Lypiatts
15 Lansdown Road
Cheltenham
Glos GL50 2JA
UK

Edward Elgar Publishing, Inc.
William Pratt House
9 Dewey Court
Northampton
Massachusetts 01060
USA

A catalogue record for this book
is available from the British Library

Library of Congress Control Number: 2017953157

This book is available electronically in the **Elgar**online
Business subject collection
DOI 10.4337/9781786431332

ISBN 978 1 78643 132 5 (cased)
ISBN 978 1 78643 133 2 (eBook)

Printed by CPI Group (UK) Ltd, Croydon CR0 4YY

Contents

PART III   EMERGING MARKET MULTINATIONAL ENTERPRISES

PART IV   THE GLOBAL FACTORY

Acknowledgements

The editor and publishers wish to thank the authors and the following publishers who have kindly given permission for the use of copyright material.

Academy of Management for articles: Peter J. Buckley and Roger Strange (2015), 'The Governance of the Global Factory: Location and Control of World Economic Activity', *Academy of Management Perspectives*, **29** (2), May, 237–49; Peter J. Buckley and Shameen Prashantham (2016), 'Global Interfirm Networks: The Division of Entrepreneurial Labor between MNEs and SMEs', *Academy of Management Perspectives: Symposium*, **30** (1), February, 40–58.

Elsevier Ltd for articles: Peter J. Buckley and Niron Hashai (2014), 'The Role of Technological Catch Up and Domestic Market Growth in the Genesis of Emerging Country Based Multinationals', *Research Policy*, **43** (2), March, 423–37; Peter J. Buckley, Stefano Elia and Mario Kafouros (2014), 'Acquisitions by Emerging Market Multinationals: Implications for Firm Performance', *Journal of World Business*, **49** (4), October, 611–32; Peter J. Buckley, Adam Cross and Claudio De Mattos (2015), 'The Principle of Congruity in the Analysis of International Business Cooperation', *International Business Review*, **24** (6), December, 1048–60; Peter J. Buckley, Surender Munjal, Peter Enderwick and Nicolas Forsans (2016), 'Do Foreign Resources Assist or Impede Internationalisation? Evidence from Internationalisation of Indian Multinational Enterprises', *International Business Review*, **25** (1A), February, 130–40; Peter J. Buckley, Surender Munjal, Peter Enderwick and Nicolas Forsans (2016), 'Cross-Border Acquisitions by Indian Multinationals: Asset Exploitation or Asset Augmentation?', *International Business Review*, **25** (4), August, 986–96.

Emerald Group Publishing for articles: Peter J. Buckley (2014), 'Forty Years of Internalisation Theory and the Multinational Enterprise', *Multinational Business Review, Special Issue: Advances in IB Theory*, **22** (3), 227–45; Peter J. Buckley and Jean J. Boddewyn (2015), 'The Internalization of Societal Failures by Multinational Enterprises', *Multinational Business Review*, **23** (3), 170–87.

Oxford University Press via the Copyright Clearance Center's RightsLink service for article: Peter J. Buckley, Dylan Sutherland, Hinrich Voss and Ahmad El-Gohari (2015), 'The Economic Geography of Offshore Incorporation in Tax Havens and Offshore Financial Centres: The Case of Chinese MNEs', *Journal of Economic Geography*, **15** (1), January, 103–28.

SAGE Publications, Inc. for article: Niron Hashai, Mario Kafouros and Peter J. Buckley (2015), 'The Performance Implications of Speed, Regularity, and Duration in Alliance Portfolio Expansion', *Journal of Management*, 1–25.

Springer via the Copyright Clearance Center's RightsLink service for articles: Peter J. Buckley (2014), 'Adam Smith's Theory of Knowledge and International Business Theory and Practice', *Journal of International Business Studies*, **45** (1), January, 102–9; Peter J. Buckley, Malcolm Chapman, Jeremy Clegg and Hanna Gajewska-De Mattos (2014), 'A Linguistic and Philosophical Analysis of Emic and Etic and their Use in International Business Research', *Management International Review*, **54** (3), June, 307–24; Peter J. Buckley (2016), 'Historical Research Approaches to the Analysis of Internationalisation', *Management International Review*, **56** (6), December, 879–900.

Strategic Management Society, with permission of John Wiley & Sons Ltd, for articles: Niron Hashai and Peter J. Buckley (2014), 'Is Competitive Advantage a Necessary Condition for the Emergence of the Multinational Enterprise?', *Global Strategy Journal*, **4** (1), February, 35–48; Ulf Andersson, Peter J. Buckley and Henrik Dellestrand (2015), 'In the Right Place at the Right Time!: The Influence of Knowledge Governance Tools on Knowledge Transfer and Utilization in MNEs', *Global Strategy Journal*, **5** (1), February, 27–47.

Taylor and Francis Group (www.tandfonline.com) for article: Peter J. Buckley (2014), 'The Applied Economics of (International) Business: A Personal Perspective', *International Journal of the Economics of Business*, **21** (1), 3–6.

Every effort has been made to trace all the copyright holders but if any have been inadvertently overlooked the publishers will be pleased to make the necessary arrangement at the first opportunity.

Foreword

This volume is a collection of 17 journal articles written by Peter Buckley either alone or with co-authors, and published between 2014 and 2016. It is a useful compilation because it is otherwise very difficult to keep up to date with Professor Buckley's prodigious output. The 17 articles were published in 11 different journals, and are among the 630 discrete links on Google Scholar to his writings.

The focus of the collection, as the title suggests, is 'the global factory'. For readers who are unfamiliar with Buckley's use of this term, it is intended to be 'a theoretical characterization of the modern, networked MNE, derived from internalisation theory'.

Most of the papers are organized within three sections of 3–7 papers. The first section deals with the internalisation theory of the MNE. I found the most intriguing paper to be the one with Jean Boddewyn. It examined the role of the MNE in providing public goods. This proposed 'radical extension of the internalisation theory of the MNE' is controversial.

The second section focuses on emerging market MNEs, from both empirical and theoretical perspectives. A particularly interesting paper in this section, originally published in the *Journal of Economic Geography*, looked at the high proportion of outward investment by Chinese MNEs that goes to the tax havens and offshore financial centres.

The final section, titled 'The Global Factory', contains three papers. Each examines different aspects of the governance process: 'location and control, knowledge transfer, and the performance implications of the global alliance portfolio expansion'. Of particular interest was the final paper with its emphasis on 'the impact of speed, rhythm and duration of entries'. This is indeed an underexplored and important area of study.

I am hard pressed to think of any scholar in the international business space who has been as prolific as Peter Buckley. Like many others, I look forward to seeing his further insights, ideally including consideration of the global factory in a post-Brexit, more protectionist context.

Paul W. Beamish
Canada Research Chair in International Business
Ivey Business School, Western University

Introduction

Peter J. Buckley

The first paper in this volume (Chapter 1) is a commissioned piece on research in managerial and business economics. The occasion of this paper was the twenty-first anniversary of the founding of the *International Journal of the Economics of Business* where its founding editorial board were asked to submit personal reflections on the development of this specialist field. Consequently, this paper emphasises the applied economics of international business. The piece has a note of regret in that international business has not had more influence on applied economics but points to internalisation theory as an area that has achieved some traction in the economics domain. It further points out that achievements in the international business field – in examining the role of time, in its use of economic geography, in multi-disciplinary successes such as the integration of culture into the analysis, its innovative analysis of joint ventures and collaboration, and its acknowledgement of spatial issues – could, with profit, be introduced more widely into applied economics.

The remainder of this volume emphasises those developments in examining the multinational enterprises' role as the entrepreneurial orchestrator of global networks, the analysis of technological development, economic geography and acquisitions in the new salience of emerging country multinationals, and in the governance and performance implications of the global factory as a competitive organisational form.

The theory of international business

Internalisation theory is a theory that actually works. The simple core principles – that a firm exists in those spaces where organisation is superior to market and that activities are located in a network where the nodes are in the least cost location – are fundamental but flexible (Buckley and Casson 1976, 2009; Buckley and Ghauri 2004; Buckley 2009, 2011a, 2011b). Part II of this volume examines the development of internalisation theory, its role in global interfirm networks and its extension to 'societal failures'. Other theoretical perspectives are introduced, too. The principle of congruity is used to analyse joint ventures and alliances, Adam Smith's theory of knowledge is related to international business theory and practice and historical approaches to the analysis of internationalisation are evaluated. Finally, linguistic and philosophical concepts are applied to 'emic versus etic' research in the international business field.

Chapter 2 looks back over forty years of internalisation theory as it has been applied to the multinational enterprise. It reviews the key analytical principles of internalisation theory as a general theory of the multinational enterprise (MNE). It traces the development of the theory from its origin in Coase's classic (1937) paper 'The Nature of the Firm' to its application to the MNE by Mark Casson and myself in 1976 and through its subsequent incarnations until its application to modern, networked multinationals – the global factory. The long-term aspects of the theory were emphasised by Buckley and Casson (1976, p.2) and the theory has proved itself to be a long-term survivor, equally applicable to emerging market multinational enterprises (EMNEs) and strategies such as fine-slicing, outsourcing and offshoring as to conventional MNEs of the last century. Concern for the external impact of the MNE, in development issues for instance, and for the theory as a guide to public policy remain critical research issues. The theory lives up to Kurt Lewin's (1951, p.169) aphorism that 'There is nothing more practical than a good theory'.

Chapter 3 examines the novel concept of the division of entrepreneurial labour between MNEs and small and medium sized enterprises (SMEs). This chapter analyses the differential capabilities of SMEs and MNEs (who carries out an activity), the relationships between principals and outsourcing firms (the who) and the context of the participants – specifically the spatial context (the where). The relationships within the global factory are analysed by capabilities, connectivity and contextuality. The concept of the division of entrepreneurial activity is ripe for future development.

Chapter 4 is a radical extension of the internalisation theory of the MNE. It examines the potential of MNEs to substitute for failing non-market institutions by creating intermediate markets, largely in services that are conventionally performed by the state, or, often, are completely missing in certain countries. The role of MNEs in the provision of public goods raises issues of legitimacy and is frequently controversial. The circumstances of non-performance or suboptimal performance of institutions in providing public goods (education, power supplies, local government functions, law and order, communication and transport systems) presents the opportunities for MNEs to substitute for other forms of provision. Such an extension of theory is controversial and drew a critical response (Hillemann and Verbeke 2015) and a response (Buckley and Boddewyn 2016). Internalisation theory remains interesting!

The analysis of cooperation in international business – particularly in international joint ventures (IJVs) and strategic alliances – has been a major area of success in international business theorising. Chapter 5 examines the principle of congruity in the analysis of international business cooperation. A micro-dynamic analysis of parties involved in cooperation shows their attitudes to their (prospective) partner depend on the initial (mis-) match between their mutual evaluations, their wish intensity (to cooperate) and the speed to reach congruity. Applications to different cultural backgrounds and mindsets are developed and the chapter shows that further applications are possible. The integration of the principle of congruity with the analysis of mutual forbearance (Buckley and Casson 1988) in IJVs and strategic alliances is an interesting future research avenue.

Chapter 6 argues that the reasoning and insights of Adam Smith's theory of knowledge can improve international business theory. Smith's work sheds light on decision making in MNEs and on cultural distance (Smith has a set of penetrating insights into what the current literature terms 'liability of foreignness' (Zaheer 1995)) derived from limits to Smith's concept of 'sympathy' (modern 'empathy'). The combination of these analyses yields new insights into multinationals from emerging countries and fits with Smith's depiction of the (global) economy as a complex adoptive system (Hashai and Buckley 2014).

My long-standing interest in history research, and its methods, is reflected in Chapter 7. Internationalisation is a process, and process implies a time dimension, therefore the methods of history should be a good fit in the understanding of the global growth of firms. The chapter defines the internationalisation process as a sequenced set of decisions in time and space, path dependent to some degree but subject to managerial discretion. Research on the internationalisation of firms, it argues, can benefit from historical research methods including a careful analysis of source material, time series elements, using comparative evidence across time and space and the (not uncontroversial) use of the 'alternative position' or counterfactual analysis.

Chapter 8 examines cross-cultural research in international business – 'custom' and 'culture' are the 'king of all' in the opinion of Pindar, quoted by Herodotus in the opening passage of the chapter. Distinguishing the universal from the particular is a critical task in cross-cultural research and this can be approached through the emic–etic dichotomy. The paper examines the linguistic underpinning of this contrast, and looks at issues of language translation and borrowings from social anthropology that can aid international business research. This is applied to a particular business case – German acquisitions of Polish companies and the cultural issues faced by both sides. Issues such as 'punctuality' are shown to reflect deep cultural distinctions to which 'emic calculus' versus 'etic measurement' are different responses which managers need to understand if progress is to be made.

This section on theory is wider ranging and illustrates the virtues of a core theory (internalisation) that can be supplemented by other theoretical approaches that share similar assumptions – theories of entrepreneurship, cooperation and spatial and temporal theories deriving from geography and history. The following section (Part III) applies this core theory to emerging market multinationals – a key phenomenon in twenty-first century globalisation.

Emerging market multinational enterprises

The foreign direct investment behaviour of multinational enterprises from emerging markets has become one of the foci, if not the primary focus, of international business research. The rise of the BRICs and their impact on the global economy has energised the international business research field. Of particular interest is the question as to whether outward foreign direct investment from emerging countries can be explained utilising the tried and tested theoretical rubric that has been used to explain FDI from 'advanced' countries. In fact, the challenge of explaining FDI from emerging countries has been met by refinements in, rather than the replacement of, internalisation theory (Buckley et al. 2007; Hennart, 2012). It is a severe test of a theory originally set up to explain Western private, largely manufacturing multinationals to apply the theory to firms that are often none of these. The structure of the theory, having an overarching general structure that firms internalise markets until the costs of further internalisation outweigh the benefits, plus least cost location of activities controlled by the firm, but also a number of nested special theories – for knowledge-intensive firms for instance – has facilitated the ease of application of an unchanged core theory to 'new cases'. However this requires considerable adaptation to context.

The first two chapters take a radical look at theories purporting to explain OFDI by EMNEs. Chapters 9 and 10 present the global system view of the world economy whereby the global economy is represented by a general equilibrium approach in which all participants aim to maximise the overall utility created by all players in the system. Essentially, this approach predicts the location and ownership of all firms in the global system.

Using this approach, Chapter 9 challenges the view that firm-specific competitive advantage is a necessary condition for the emergency of multinational firms. This represents a view of emerging market MNEs that accords with much casual empiricism – that EMNEs do not have technological, marketing or brand advantages and yet manage to successfully internationalise.

The global system view obviates the (often rather desperate) search for attributes that can be labelled 'competitive advantages'. The size of the domestic home economy, leading to a large number of home country entrepreneurs, asymmetric liabilities of foreignness and the ability of location and internalisation advantages substituting for ownership advantages sufficiently explain outward FDI from emerging economies.

Chapter 10 analyses how the upgrading of technological capabilities of EMNEs and increases in domestic market size impacts on value chain location choices and the relative competitiveness of EMNEs versus conventional EMNEs. Again, the existence of firm-specific advantages is not necessary for EMNEs to emerge. The model can predict the location choices of MNEs from large advanced *and* emerging economies.

One salient feature of OFDI by emerging market multinationals is the high proportion of this investment that goes (in the first instance) to tax havens and offshore financial centres. Chapter 11 analyses the investment of Chinese MNEs in these centres. There are a number of motivations for this investment – avoidance of taxation is one but so too are the escape from a weak institutional environment to stronger ones, the desire to raise offshore funds to reinvest elsewhere (capital augmentation) and 'round tripping' (investing back into the home country, often in a different province). This institutional arbitrage combines with firm-level financing decisions. Investment in tax havens and offshore financial centres is unsettling for international business analysts because the final destination of investment is unclear. This distorts the measurement of FDI flows and conceals changes of ownership en route. Of particular concern is privatisation of state-owned assets. There is much more work to do in this area not only to obtain a clearer picture of FDI sources and destinations but also from a policy point of view with regard to 'Base Erosion and Profit Shifting' (BEPS) that bedevils international taxation and fiscal policies.

The role of acquisitions by EMNEs looms large in Chapters 12, 13 and 14. Chapter 12 is one of very few extant pieces of research to assess the implications for performances in acquisitions by EMNEs. The paper shows that takeover of target firms by EMNEs often enhances the performance of the acquired firm. Not all resource inputs from EMNEs are equally beneficial for performance and some types of prior experience even have a negative effect on post-acquisition performance. The results are suggestive of a more fine-grained approach to predicting the success of a takeover by an EMNE.

Chapter 13 is one of a series of empirical studies of cross-border acquisitions by Indian MNEs – a favoured form of international operation by Indian firms. This paper is interesting because (like the previous chapter) it shows that foreign resource inputs can impede, as well as assist cross-border acquisitions. It is the *interaction* of foreign and internally owned resources within EMNEs that is critical.

Chapter 14 asks whether cross-border acquisitions by Indian MNEs are asset exploiting or asset augmenting. Internal financial and technological resources are important explanatory variables as is the presence of an asset seeking (brands, technology, market access) motivation. Interestingly, the paper shows that the experience of Indian firms in managing a culturally diverse home market helps to develop asset bundling skills.

The global factory

The development of internalisation theory to explain the networked multinational enterprise is the basis for Part IV which examines location and control, knowledge transfer and the performance implications of global alliance portfolio expansion. The governance theme links these three papers. The orchestration of activities, which may be wholly or partly owned or governed by contractual relationships, is a key skill of top managers of global factories. The role of knowledge in these processes is central and these papers examine different aspects of the governance process.

The 'global factory' as a theoretical characterisation of the modern, networked MNE derives from internalisation theory and, as such, has governance implications (Chapter 15). Internal transaction costs associated with the governance of the MNE arise from its internal architecture (Buckley and Carter 1996, 2002, 2003) and can be contrasted with external transaction costs to determine the scope of the firm (Teece 1983). This chapter considers also the risk propensity of the MNE and suggests that a future research agenda should explicitly focus on the process of strategy formation by MNE managers taking into account risk propensity.

The utilisation of knowledge transferred between units of the MNE is the subject of Chapter 16. The efficacy of knowledge utilisation is examined in terms of hierarchical governance relationships and 'lateral' relationships between subsidiaries. Lateral relationships are found to be powerful stimuli in building subsidiary relationships. This is powerful evidence of network effects within multinational enterprises.

Chapter 17 is the first paper in a strand of research on the speed of strategic moves by MNEs – examining the trajectory of firms' international alliance portfolios. It starts from the funding from extant research that faster speed in undertaking new strategic alliances has negative effects on profitability. The paper advances theory by examining both costs and revenues and the ways in which speed affects managerial costs and revenues. The negative effects on profitability from speed arise from a greater effect on costs than revenues. A more regular rhythm of expansion and a longer duration of existing alliances reduces negative profitability by moderating the increase in managerial costs. The impact of speed, rhythm and duration of entries is a fascinating and relatively unexplored aspect of the expansion of global factories. Further investigation of these aspects of internationalisation is likely to pay dividends in the understanding of key processes of globalisation by MNEs.

References

Buckley, P.J. (2009), 'Internalisation thinking – from the multinational enterprise to the global factory', *International Business Review*, **18** (3), 224–35.

Buckley, P.J. (2011a), 'International integration and coordination in the global factory', *Management International Review*, **51** (2), 269–83.

Buckley, P.J. (2011b), *Globalization and the Global Factory*, Cheltenham, UK and Northampton, MA, USA: Edward Elgar Publishing.

Buckley, P.J. and J.J. Boddewyn (2016), 'A manifesto for the widening of internalisation theory, being a reply to Hillemann and Vebeke', *Multinational Business Review*, **24** (1), 2–7.

Buckley, P.J. and M.J. Carter (1996), 'The economics of business process design', *International Journal of the Economics of Business*, **3** (1), 5–25.

Buckley, P.J. and M.J. Carter (2002), 'Process and structure in knowledge management practices of British and US multinational enterprises', *Journal of International Management*, **8** (1), 29–48.

Buckley, P.J. and M.J. Carter (2003), 'Governing knowledge sharing in multinational enterprises', *Management International Review*, **43** (3), 7–25.

Buckley, P.J. and M.C. Casson (1976), *The Future of the Multinational Enterprise*, London: Macmillan.

Buckley, P.J. and M.C. Casson (1988), 'A theory of cooperation in international business', in F.J. Contractor and P. Lorange (eds), *Cooperative Strategies in International Business*, Lexington, MA: Lexington Books, D.C. Heath & Co, pp. 31–53.

Buckley, P.J. and M.C. Casson (2009), 'The internalisation theory of the multinational enterprise – a review of the progress of a research agenda after 30 years', *Journal of International Business Studies*, **40** (9), 1563–80.

Buckley, P.J. and P.N. Ghauri (2004), 'Globalisation, economic geography and the strategy of multinational enterprises', *Journal of International Business Studies*, **35** (2), 81–98.

Buckley, P.J., J. Clegg, A. Cross, H. Voss, Xin Liu and P. Zheng (2007), 'The determinants of Chinese outward foreign direct investment', *Journal of International Business Studies*, **38** (4), 499–518.

Coase, R.H. (1937), 'The nature of the firm', *Economica*, **4** (16), 386–405.

Hashai, N. and P.J. Buckley (2014), 'Is competitive advantage a necessary condition for the emergence of the multinational enterprise?', *Global Strategy Journal*, **4** (1), 35–48.

Hennart, J.-F. (2012), 'Emerging market multinationals and the theory of the multinational enterprise', *Global Strategy Journal*, **2** (3), 168–87.

Hillemann, J. and A. Verbeke (2015), 'Efficiency-driven, comparative institutional analysis in international business', *Multinational Business Review*, **23** (3), 188–99.

Lewin, K. (1951), 'Frontiers in group dynamics', in D. Cartwright (ed.), *Field Theory in Social Science: Selected Theoretical Papers by Kurt Lewin*, New York: Harper & Row, pp. 188–237.

Teece, D. (1983), 'Technological and organizational factors in the theory of the multinational enterprise', in M.C. Casson (ed.), *The Growth of the International Business*, London: Macmillan.

Zaheer, S. (1995), 'Overcoming the liability of foreignness', *Academy of Management Journal*, **38** (2), 341–63.

PART I

A PERSONAL PERSPECTIVE

PART I

[1]

Int. J. of the Economics of Business, 2014
Vol. 21, No. 1, 3–6, http://dx.doi.org/10.1080/13571516.2013.864114

The Applied Economics of (International) Business: A Personal Perspective

PETER J. BUCKLEY

ABSTRACT   *The applied economics of international business (IB) has been successful in explaining foreign direct investment, the existence and growth of multinational enterprises (MNEs) and in integrating new concepts such as trust in the analysis of joint ventures. It now needs to face challenges in fully integrating culture into the rubric and into a comprehensive analysis of the varied phenomena of globalisation.*

Key Words: International Business; Foreign Direct Investment; Multinational Enterprise; Globalisation; Applied Economics.

JEL classifications: L2, L14, F23, F6.

International Business Research

Research in international business (IB) is relatively recent, being conventionally dated to 1960 (Stephen Hymer's thesis, 1976) or John Dunning's (1958) *American Investment in British Industry*. Much of the early pioneering work was carried out by economists, notably Kindleberger (Hymer's supervisor) and Ray Vernon in addition to the long-running contribution of John Dunning (to 2009). IB has drawn on many other influences and is genuinely interdisciplinary – a fact highlighted by Dunning's theoretical apparatus, the eclectic paradigm. Influences from geography, history, sociology, political science, anthropology and management are all evident in the development of IB research, and this makes it an excellent focus for the study of the development of applied economics as it interacts with its near neighbours.

IB research is largely empirically (or problem) focused. It has tackled several "big issues" in its progress since 1958. Initially, the focus was on international flows of foreign direct investment, then on the existence, nature and power of multinational enterprises (MNEs), on the strategies of MNEs (notably their foreign-market entry and development strategies) and on the progress of globalisation. It has produced particularly insightful research in the area of joint ventures, drawing on a wide range of perspectives, and in the analysis of cultures, cultural difference and the role and meaning of "cultural distance" in business (Buckley, 2002). A strict criterion of "research success" of

Peter J. Buckley, Centre for International Business, Leeds University Business School, University of Leeds, Maurice Keyworth Building, Leeds LS2 9JT, United Kingdom; and University of International Business and Economics (UIBE), Beijing; e-mail: pjb@lubs.leeds.ac.uk.

© 2014 International Journal of the Economics of Business

4   *P.J. Buckley*

an area of endeavour is the extent to which that area exports ideas to neigh-bouring areas – to economics more broadly defined, for instance. There have been periods and sub-areas where this has happened – the internalisation the-ory of the (multinational) firm (Buckley and Casson, 1976), aspects of interna-tionalisation theory including process theory (Johanson and Vahlne, 1977), the role of (national) culture in strategy formulation, borrowings from the analysis of joint ventures – and (marginally) location theory aspects of the MNE have, at times, spilled over into disciplines. However, this has not been as frequent as could have been expected (Buckley and Lessard, 2005), and for long periods IB has been an importer of theory and methods from other disciplines.

The Applied Economics of International Business

Hymer (1960) made the crucial distinction between foreign *direct* investment (FDI), which implies control by the investor, and foreign *portfolio* investment, which is simply diversifying by adding foreign assets in a holding. This focused attention on the investor – the firm – and moved IB away from international trade theory, where goods move but factors do not, into the theory of the firm. Similarly, Dunning's (1958) research further highlighted the differentiated nature of capital flows and FDI's special status as international conduit of technology. Buckley and Casson (1976) made the multinational enterprise the organisational focus of innovation, internalised together with production and marketing to maximise returns from the initial "patent". The growth of markets as a result of technological (electronic commerce and communication) and political (liberalisa-tion) changes has altered the Coasian balance towards outsourcing, and the emergence of new (national) locations has fostered offshoring, leading to newer forms of networked international companies. The rise of MNEs from emerging countries has led to debates as to whether "new MNEs" require new theories, but the flexible nature of internalisation theory has continued to provide satisfac-tory theoretical understanding. Globalisation is variously perceived as "partial", uneven and unequal and remains contested as to the most appropriate theoreti-cal lens of understanding (applied economics vs. political and social foci).

The future of IB remains interdisciplinary. Context is critical for IB, and there is dissent as to whether a single overarching framework is appropriate across these, largely national, contextual differences. The emergence of China in particular has led to calls for "Chinese management theories" in deliberate contradistinction to prevailing "Western" approaches. The challenge therefore is to show that applied economics can work in radically different contexts. The question should be put in terms of general and special theories. General theory is context free – "firms internalise markets up to the point where the costs of further internalisation outweigh the benefits". Special theories account for con-text – "internalisation pressures are strongest in the presence of tacit knowl-edge so we expect firms in knowledge intensive industries to pursue internalisation in core knowledge areas". Propositions about availability of cap-ital, imperfections in key markets in the source country and differing attitudes to risk aversion are all liable to suggest that special theories for certain nation-alities (or other groups) of firms are appropriate because the preconditions or assumptions of the operation of the theory will be thereby affected.

Care must also be taken with categorizing when building theory across different national contexts. Anthropologists have shown that "native categories" differ across cultures. For instance, the meaning of "policeman" is not invariant to cultural understanding. It therefore behoves the applied IB economist to understand context, avoid category errors and to ground general theory in special circumstances. This is perhaps the most profound borrowing that applied economics can take from IB.

Methods

Because international business is comparative across nations, the comparative method is core to IB research. Three key comparators are operative in IB: across time (history), across space (geography) and against a carefully specified counterfactual. The MNE is an excellent experimental locus for applied economics because it holds organisation (the firm) constant and allows the analyst to vary place and time. The comparison of national units (subsidiaries) of the same firm allows insights into the impact of different national economies, organisations and cultures. Business histories of MNEs allow the focus to be on changes over time. Counterfactual methods are means of examining alternative states of the world in accordance with the thought experiment and have been used to assess the impact of FDI (as against a local firm alternative, exports from the source country or no investment at all). Applied economists perhaps regard this as uncontroversial given that all economic costs are opportunity costs in terms of the best alternative forgone.

IB researchers constantly seek new methods to understand the evolving new data produced by IB actors. These are not only quantitative, where economics has been a prime source, but also qualitative. Case-study research at the level of the firm and research on the decision making of individual managers is frequently combined with the quantitative analysis of secondary data in "mixed methods" IB. This mix is also fruitful for applied economists in general who are usually biased towards quantitative methods.

Several areas where both IB and applied economics may innovate are individual perceptions and expectations and (from Adam Smith) "sentiment" or morality. The integration of firm-level and managerial-level decision making is imperfect in both disciplines and is in need of integration. The role of non-pecuniary rewards – morality, sentiment, solidarity, cooperation – are not factored in to most modelling (exceptions are some analyses of joint ventures; Buckley and Casson, 1988), and this is overdue.

The Nature and Form of New Research in International Business

A big research issue – the future structure of the global economy – is central to IB research. The division of the global economy between large and small firms, state-owned and private, national and global is changing, and not unidirection-ally, across countries, industries and polities. The "balance of (economic) power" between the United States and China or Europe, Asia and North America or between the EU, NAFTA and ASEAN, the emergence of Trans-Pacific economic communities, the resource requirements of continued growth, the struggle against poverty, the impact on the climate of continued

6   *P.J. Buckley*

industrialisation and urbanisation are all issues researchable under the banner
of applied economics IB research. So too, in principle, are issues of cultural
change, of managerial process and decision making and the (optimal) structure
of organisations and institutions, including NGOs, international bodies,
pressure groups and governmental organisations that are not traditionally the
preserve of economists. The use of (in this case) internalisation theory to
analyse the growth and decline of empires (Casson, Dark, and Gulamhussen,
2009) is an illustration that applied economics is capable of a wider remit than
practitioners have heretofore allowed (Buckley and Casson, 1993). The context
and interdisciplinary heritage of IB research can infuse applied economies with
a new lease of life and improve its explanatory power. Similarly, IB research
can continue to benefit from the continued importation of theory and method
from applied economics, but this must be in the context of interdisciplinarity.

References

Buckley, P. J. 2002. Is the International Business Research Agenda Running Out of Steam? *Journal of International Business Studies* 33 (2): 365–373.
Buckley, P. J., and M. Casson. 1976. *The Future of the Multinational Enterprise.* London: Macmillan.
Buckley, P. J., and M. Casson, 1988. A Theory of Cooperation in International Business. In *Cooperative Strategies in International Business*, edited by F. J. Contractor and P. Lorange, 31–53. Lexington, MA: Lexington Books, D. C. Heath & Co.
Buckley, P. J., and M. Casson. 1993. Economics as an Imperialist Social Science. *Human Relations* 46 (9): 1035–1052.
Buckley, P. J., and D. R. Lessard. 2005. Regaining the Edge for International Business Research. *Journal of International Business Studies* 36 (6): 595–599.
Casson, M. C., K. Dark, and M. A. Gulamhussen. 2009. Extending Internalization Theory: From the Multinational Enterprise to the Knowledge Based Empire. *International Business Review* 18 (3): 236–256.
Dunning, J. H. 1958. *American Investment in British Manufacturing Industry.* London: George Allen & Unwin.
Hymer, S. 1976. *The International Operations of National Firms: A Study of Direct Foreign Investment.* Cambridge, MA: MIT Press. Original dissertation written in 1960.
Johanson, J., and J.-E. Vahlne. 1977. The Internationalisation Process of the Firm: A Model of Knowledge Development and Increasing Foreign Market Commitments. *Journal of International Business Studies* 8 (1): 23–32.

PART II

THE THEORY OF
INTERNATIONAL BUSINESS

2

Forty years of internalisation theory and the multinational enterprise

Peter J. Buckley
Centre for International Business, University of Leeds, Leeds, UK

Abstract

Purpose – The purpose of this paper is to review the key analytical principles of internalisation theory as a general theory of the multinational enterprise (MNE). It illustrates the vitality, relevance and flexibility of the approach in explaining the continued evolution of the MNE. As a grounded social science theory, it provides, in combination with history and economic geography, satisfying and novel explanations of the key phenomena of the modern globalising economy.

Design/methodology/approach – This paper examines the origins and principles of internalisation theory as the foundation theory of the MNE. It considers internalisation theory in the context of current and mainstream theories and concepts in the field of international business.

Findings – Internalisation theory is equally valid for the MNEs of yesteryear as it is for those today. The theory continues to have strong explanatory power for MNE activity. Current research areas, such as multiple embeddedness, fine-slicing of the value chain, etc., and other theories, such as dynamic capabilities and the resource-based view, either are subsets of internalisation and thus explained by the theory, or contain weakness and/or inconsistencies not found in internalisation theory.

Originality/value – This paper coherently synthesises internalisation theory, its origins and evolution. It shows how commonly held and current concepts and theories are related to internalisation theory or have weaknesses, thus making internalisation theory a superior theory to explain the MNE, and identifies potential applications of the theory to novel research areas in the field of international business.

Keywords Networks, Innovation, Internalisation theory, Multinational enterprise, Market imperfection

Paper type Research paper

Introduction

The purpose of this paper is to highlight the contributions of internalisation theory to the understanding of the existence, persistence and strategy of multinational enterprises (MNEs). It emphasises strengths of internalisation theory that have been either ignored or undervalued. Over the past 40 years, MNEs have changed dramatically, and internalisation theory explains these changes and remains relevant to understanding "networked, knowledge-intensive MNEs" (Buckley, 2007). The paper re-examines Buckley and Casson's (1976) exposition of internalisation theory and demonstrates how the theory has evolved to explain subsequent developments in the management, structure and evolution of MNEs, with special reference to outsourcing, offshoring, "fine slicing" and interface competence. The analytic principles of the theory are shown to remain robust.

The author would like to thank Mark Casson for comments on earlier versions of this paper.

Multinational Business Review
Vol. 22 No. 3, 2014
pp. 227-245
© Emerald Group Publishing Limited
1525-383X
DOI 10.1108/MBR-06-2014-0022

MBR
22,3

228

Origins of the theory

"It is the object of *The Future of the Multinational Enterprise* to provide a theory of the MNE which is sufficiently powerful to afford long-term projections of the future growth and structure of MNEs. It is hoped that the theory can be used as the basis for a rational economic policy toward the MNE, which will preserve the benefits conferred by these giant firms, while restoring effective social and political control over their operations" (Buckley and Casson, 1976, p. 2).

The first and second parts of that objective (providing a theory and affording long-term projections) have been recognised rather more than the final part – the policy prescriptions for "restoring effective social and political control" – and it is the first two parts that are the focus of this paper.

Buckley and Casson (1976) point out that there are several potential levels of analysis in international business research: the firm, industry, region and nation. These were later listed as: country, manager, firm, industry, plus networks and subsidiary (Buckley and Lessard, 2005). In Buckley and Casson (1976), national firms are treated as a special case of MNEs. A national firm is simply one that has grown by internalising markets that are purely domestic.

The dynamics of the theory come from the integration of research and development (R&D) with other activities, notably marketing and production. It is thus within firms or alliances that fundamental changes occur which affect the location of the leading centres of growth, although market competition has a role as well.

Key arguments of the theory

In internalisation theory, following Coase (1937), a firm is defined as the alternative to markets. It is, therefore, delineated by the replacement and suppression of (external) markets and their replacement or enhancement (in the case of newly created internal markets) by an organisational alternative.

An MNE may be defined as an enterprise that owns and controls activities in different countries (Buckley and Casson, 1976). A useful extension is "An MNE is a firm that internalises imperfect markets across national frontiers in the services of an intermediate product owned or controlled by the firm" (Buckley and Casson, 1976, p. 1). Eight issues are taken up in this paper. Internalisation is discussed in Section 2, imperfect markets in Section 3, national frontiers in Section 4, intermediate product flows in Section 5, ownership and control in Section 6 and the firm in Section 7. The future of internalisation theory in relation to emerging research issues is discussed in Section 8, while Section 9 concludes the paper.

An important special case of this definition of an MNE is where the intermediate product is a knowledge-intensive flow arising from an intangible asset. In this case, the MNE can be viewed as a firm that builds a system to exploit a temporary monopoly arising from an innovation. It does so by internalising markets in relevant intermediate goods and services to maximise the private returns from the exploitation of the innovation. It substitutes for a theoretically perfect external market a system of knowledge creation and dissemination, as described below.

The locational elements of the theory similarly emphasise the responses of MNEs to external changes in factor endowments, transport costs, trade barriers, and so on, and their role in developing locational advantages (Dunning, 1998). The spatial configuration of the MNE often means that the headquarters (and the key decision makers) are remote from the activities that cause friction with host country institutions – negative externalities in "remote" operations can remain uncorrected in this scenario. Attention has been paid to the role of headquarters in modern networked multinationals (Buckley, 2010, 2011), but this issue is in need of further research. The current practice of "inversion" – moving headquarters for tax reasons by international mergers and acquisitions – is an example of a phenomenon requiring further investigation.

There is a reaction across international business research against "methodological nationalism" (Yeung, 2009a), which takes "the country", "the economy" or "the nation" as a homogenous entity – the country is taken as "flat". Recent research emphasises differences between provinces (e.g. China) or states (e.g. India and the USA) and focuses on cities as primary location nodes. Location factors include not only "places" (the location in the city or region) but also "spaces" (the distance between the target city and other cities and the target city and its hinterland).

This combination of internalisation theory, with new approaches to location developed in economic geography, is an exciting direction which promises substantial synergies – another is the analytics of the global value chain, as explained below.

Internationalisation – benefits and costs
The general theory examines the costs and benefits of internal versus external markets. These interact with the optimal location of activities across which markets are internalised. The firm is naturally international where market links are cross-border. As political borders do not coincide with markets, the firm extends beyond its home country. The general theory contains several "nested" special theories, which are context-rooted. Firms will grow in specific situations as they are surrounded with particular markets in which it is profitable to internalise.

The advantages of internalising a market
The advantages of internalising a market are the obverse of outsourcing. They arise where control of intermediate goods and services markets bestows benefits on the firm by avoiding risks, giving control of knowledge and eliminating instabilities. Internalisation, in certain circumstances, will confer market power and enable the use of internal transfer prices across fiscal boundaries (including international ones) that increase profits over the alternative arm's-length trading. (Buckley and Casson, 1976). A classification of motives for internalisation (vertical integration) is given in Table I, from Casson (1986).

The key internalisation factors in this exhaustive list are:

* coordination of multistage processes in which time lags exist but futures markets are lacking;
* efficient exploitation of market power through discriminatory pricing;
* eliminating instability caused by bilateral concentrations of market power in intermediate product markets;
* overcoming information asymmetries between buyer and seller ("buyer uncertainty"); and
* exploiting lack of harmonisation in international tax rates, by using internal transfer pricing to reduce overall corporate tax liability.

MBR
22,3

230

Factors affecting the level of vertical integration	Positive or negative effect	Relevance to international intra-firm trade
Factors technical		
High fixed costs	+	*
Large non-recoverable investments	+	*
Use of continuous-flow technology	+	
Perishable intermediate product	+	*
Quality variability, coupled with a natural asymmetry of information	+	*
Flexible use of working capital	+	
Inventories widely distributed over space	+	*
Efficient scales at adjacent stages of production vary, and their lowest common multiple is large	–	*
Multiplicity of joint inputs and joint outputs	–	*
Economies of scope in the utilization of indivisible assets	–	*
Market power		
Monopolist faces downstream substitution, or monopsonist faces upstream substitution	+	*
Multi-stage monopoly or monopsony	+	*
Entry-deterrence by dominant firm	+	*
Dynamic		
Novelty of the division of labour	+	*
Fiscal		
Incentives for transfer pricing: differential rates of profit taxation, *ad valorem* tariffs, or exchange controls	+	*
Statutory intervention in intermediate product markets, e.g. price regulation	+	*
Restrictions on foreign equity participation, local value added requirements, and the expropriation risk of foreign direct investment	–	*

Table I.
Factors affecting the level of vertical integration in an industry

Notes: These factors apply mainly in the context of a *closed* internal market for the intermediate product; * signify the factor applies to international intra-firm trade

The costs of internalising a market

In every case, the costs of internalising a market must be set against the benefits. These include communications costs (which will vary with cultural distance), management costs (also variable according to context) and resource costs of separating a single external market into several internal ones. There may also be political problems of foreign ownership, now conceptualised as the "liability of foreignness" (Zaheer, 1995). Managing and coordinating a multi-plant, multi-currency and multi-cultural enterprise with increasing complexity is likely to set a limit to internalised operations. External non-equity modes can be a means of avoiding regulation, as explained below.

The changing net benefits of internalisation mean that the boundaries of the firm change over time. The combination of the changing balance between outsourcing and internalisation and the reaction of MNEs to constantly shifting location costs mean that the MNE is a moving target for analysts.

The general theory generates nested "special theories" where specific forces apply particularly strongly (e.g. knowledge-intensive goods and services). Examples of extensions of the theory include an application to Chinese outward foreign direct investment (FDI) (Buckley *et al.*, 2007b). If the theory can apply, over thirty years later, to largely state-owned FDI from an emerging economy, then it still retains its considerable predictive and explanatory power.

Forty years of
internalisation
theory

231

Imperfect markets
There is no advantage in internalising a perfect market. "Buyer" and "seller" in an internalised market are the same firm, giving rise to international transfer pricing, as explained above. As external markets change and become "more perfect", outsourcing replaces internalisation. The possibility of outsourcing becomes easier and more efficient with an increasing market for outsourced activities (Liesch *et al.*, 2012). This needs to be balanced by the increasing ability of firms to manage information and to communicate it internationally at a low cost. The "internet of things", whereby products from clothing to household appliances are interconnected, and technology-enabled to transmit data, has increased knowledge internalisation economies. Thus, MNEs increasingly internalise knowledge but outsource operations. Therefore, the balance and the boundaries of firms are subject, as always, to conflicting pressures.

History, process and contingency

"History details the differences among events, whereas the sciences focus on similarities" (Berlin, 1960, p. 1). Gaddis (2002) suggests that the contrast between history and social science is that history insists on the interdependency of variables whilst social science methods rely on identifying the "independent variable," which affects (causes changes in) the dependent variable. This also implies continuity over time – the independent variable has to persist in its causative effect(s). Social sciences state that in history, everything is endogenous.

Internalisation theory offers a satisfying compromise. Recognising dependence on initial conditions – the state of external markets – brings together "narrative" and "analytical" approaches, as does periodization – "short-term" versus "long-term" changes. Causality, contingency and moderating variables become manageable when the time frame is defined:

"The new institutional economics of Coasian heritage has had considerable influence on the rise of organisational economics, which is certainly more historical than orthodox neoclassical economics" (Clark and Rowlinson, 2004, p. 331).

Managerial discretion – the role of agency – is well integrated into internalisation theory. The role of managers has been explored explicitly (Buckley, 1996; Buckley *et al.*, 2007a), and the theory of entrepreneurship is accommodated within the internalisation framework (Casson, 1982). The role of the iconic (or heroic) entrepreneur is analogous to the "great man theory of history" (it usually is a man). The exploration of outliers – innovative entrepreneurs, creative (or destructive) individuals, great leaders and iconic brands – is accommodated by both decisions within the rules of the game, and those that change the rules. It is also necessary to

MBR
22,3

not only examine growth and dynamism but also decline, failure and aborted innovation. The notion of life cycles (from Vernon, 1966, and onwards) is an important adjunct to internalisation theory. The balance between the individual judgement of managers and the impersonal forces around them (the environment) is a key aspect of constructive and successful theorising.

232

Internalisation of markets across national frontiers
Fine-slicing and the global factory

Recent applications of the theory (Buckley, 2009, 2011; Buckley and Ghauri, 2004) have led to the conceptualisation of the "global factory" – a network of firms centred on a key orchestrator (Hinterhuber, 2002) or brand owner. The global factory uses a network structure and incorporates outsourcing and offshoring as alternatives to internalisation and central location (Mudambi and Swift, 2011, 2012, 2014). The key decisions remain the location and internalisation/externalisation of the principal activities in the system, but the application of the principles has changed and the scope for market transactions has expanded. Key developments include the managerial technique of "fine slicing" (cutting the activities into discrete modules, the location and control of which can be optimised) and the critical skills of "interface competence". The management and coordination of activities even beyond the traditional company boundaries is critical in such modern multinationals. There are also influences from other cognate areas such as accounting with "mark to market" conventions. A schematic diagram of the global factory is shown in Figure 1.

Three summary narratives of the growth and development of MNEs are provided in the list below, showing different types of MNEs and the way that the theory predicts and explains their genesis and future development.

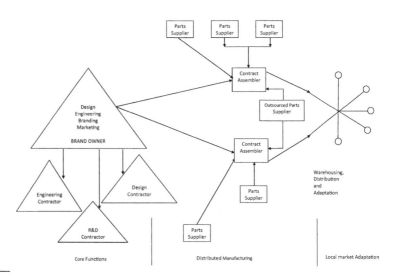

Figure 1.
Global factory

Three "Buckley and Casson" narratives are:

(1)   An innovator (innovating firm) achieves a breakthrough ("a patent"). To commercialise the idea the firm has to internalise productive assets because it cannot hire these facilities. To obtain a return it has to own and control these assets because buyer uncertainty prevents the competitive auction of the idea ("patent") that would be most efficient. It is often difficult to protect knowledge via a patent so internalisation (and continued innovation) is the best protection. This further incentivises the use of internal market and the consolidation of the firm. Productive facilities are acquired at home and abroad because no foreign licensee can be found. This enables discriminatory pricing to take place in different markets and segments. Inputs are owned and controlled to ensure a secure supply that cannot be relied upon because of missing futures markets. The resultant MNE is constrained by costs of recruiting, training and extending its management team (the "Penrose effect"). FDI is the second-best substitute for a competitive auction of the rights, the imperfect supply of inputs and a competitive independent distribution channel Offshoring and outsourcing are now closer substitutes for perfect external markets.

(2)   An entrepreneur spots an opportunity to supply the (domestic) market with products intensive in a foreign source of raw materials (oil, tobacco and copper). Raising funds from the domestic capital market against this "patent", he sets up a firm to own and control the supply source, rather than engage in arm's length trade in the key inputs. He may also be aided by superior extractive technology. The MNE is created in the home country because the entrepreneur who sees the opportunity and the raw material supply are in different countries and capital is supplied in the source country.

(3)   A state-owned Chinese firm has access to capital below market rates. This imperfect capital market enables the firm to acquire foreign assets even though the price paid may be above market value. The continued supply of cheap finance enables this MNE to buy brand names, technology and skills, including managerial skills to enable the firm to compete in international markets. This represents a temporal race between the continued supply of cheap capital and the consolidation of the acquired intangible assets into a viable competitive MNE with the requisite skilled management and an internationally recognised brand name.

These narratives illustrate the classic international business nostrum that "context matters". The direction of growth by internalisation is determined not only by the imperfections in "neighbouring" markets but also by the cultural, social and political context in which the firm is embedded. This provides an invaluable link with qualitative studies. It is notable that many internalisation theorists also carry out qualitative studies based on questionnaires, interviews, case studies and business history evidence. In testing internalisation theory, both quantitative and qualitative studies using both longitudinal and historical evidence are valuable.

The example of Apple's iPhone as a global factory could not be a more perfect match of theory and empirical reality. The knowledge-intensive, high-value elements of the value chain ("U curve" or "smile curve") are internalised and located at head office. The next level of activities down each arm of the "U curve" are externalised by contract and

MBR
22,3

located in skills-rich locations. The lowest value-adding activity, assembly, is outsourced to a Taiwanese company and further offshored in southern China – a cheap labour area with a dextrous, diligent and disciplined workforce.

Embeddedness

Much is made in current international business theorising about "embeddedness" (Forsgren *et al.*, 2007; Meyer *et al.*, 2011). Multinationals are said to benefit from "multiple embeddedness" – essentially being engaged with host and source country institutions and resources. This fuzzy concept can be better understood from the viewpoint of internalisation theory. Embeddness is the degree to which the MNE has internalised, or quasi-internalised, intermediate markets in resource flows, information or political influence. This may be as acquisitions, joint venture or alliance partnerships, or looser forms of association. It may include "political quasi-internalisation", whereby the MNE captures rents by quasi-internalising regulatory rules or even political actors (see above).

It is evident that embeddedness has costs as well as benefits. Internalisation incurs costs especially in information and management time, which differ across countries. These costs have to be traded off against the benefits of resource access, knowledge acquisition and political influence. For each individual country, there is an optimal degree of embeddedness that will vary according to the country's resources and institutions. More embeddedness is not always the right strategy and disembedding particular units may increase profitability in certain circumstances.

Intermediate knowledge-based flows: are ownership "advantages" or "dynamic capabilities" necessary in theory or in practice?
When internalisation theory is combined with other theories, it is necessary to ensure that these other theories are consistent with internalisation theory in their methodological approaches. The resulting synthesis will otherwise become a confusing concoction of incompatible ideas. In particular, complementary theories must be consistent with rational action principles. Trade theory satisfies this condition, since its economics pedigree means that it has followed rational action principles from the outset. Neo-classical economic theories of innovation also satisfy this condition. In certain areas, such as strategic management, it is sometimes unclear whether rationality is postulated or not, and even where it is postulated, it is not always clear that the postulates are consistently applied. For these reasons, internalisation theorists have been circumspect in combining the internalisation principle with other bodies of theory. Rather than seeking to explain every conceivable phenomenon in international business through liaisons with other branches of theory, they have focused on explaining those phenomena, which internalisation theory and other rational action theories explain best.

The analytics of MNE growth by innovation versus growth by product diversification was developed by Penrose (1959), and Wolf (1977), and was formalised in Buckley and Casson (2007). Ownership advantages (O) are necessarily temporary – they can be copied, stolen, replicated or competed away. For this reason, the rest of the MNE is built through internalisation to extend and protect the returns from innovation (Rugman and Verbeke, 2003). There is a divergence from the "dynamic capabilities" literature (Teece *et al.*, 1997), which purports to show that capabilities can go on being perpetuated over the long run. The definition of dynamic capabilities is problematic

(Teece *et al.*, 1997) and the separate addition of this variable is questionable. Occam's razor would suggest that it is an unnecessary addition to the theory.

In short, to capture the rent from innovation (to appropriate the returns), firms (MNEs) need to internalise the output of innovation in an integrated fashion with marketing and production. Thus, FDI, with its associated control (of knowledge) is needed to protect the value of the "patent" (the internal Intellectual Property Rights or IPR). FDI is therefore a proxy for the supporting assets needed to protect and appropriate the value of the original "idea".

The resource-based view of the firm
The resource-based view of the firm derives from several special and restrictive assumptions. Barney (1986) argues that a necessary condition for competitive advantages is imperfect factor markets. In these special circumstances, firms can appropriate the difference between the price of a factor and its value to the firm. Other contributions go on to show that it is the creation and protection of rents that drive strategy – again the creature of imperfect markets. A further special set of conditions reinforces this approach. Barriers to entry are claimed to be essentially informational in their nature. The firm must develop, and take advantage of, natural "isolating mechanisms" (Rumelt, 1984) that perpetuate the rents and fix them to the firm. Decisions regarding value-creating resources can be considered "critical" as distinct from routine (business as usual) decisions (Selznick, 1957; Nelson and Winter, 1982). If properly formulated, the resource-based view could be considered as a special variant of internalisation theory in which key resources are opportunely internalised within the firm. The firm operates in imperfect factor markets and then protects its rent-earning assets through internalisation to create a long lasting "distinctive competence" that often exhibits economies of scale and scope. Only when all the appropriate assumptions hold, and only for as long as they hold, the resource-based view will be an accurate representation of a sub-set of firm strategies. The attention to dynamics (Langlois, 1991) highlights the reinvestments that firms must make to sustain these distinctive competencies – either by exploiting increasing returns, financing R&D, marketing expenditure or building barriers to entry. This is reflected in internalisation theory by the integration of R&D within the firm (Figure 2). However, the resource-based view is not presented in these terms.

Resource-based theorists correctly draw attention to the tacitness of knowledge, but the conclusions they derive from this depend on some crucial assumptions that are questionable, and are not always made explicit. In principle, tacitness of knowledge makes knowledge transfer difficult, whether it is external to the firm or internal to it. Therefore, to link knowledge transfer to internalisation through FDI, further assumptions are needed. Tacitness may make it difficult to market knowledge because potential licensees cannot understand the knowledge. If tacitness increases the cost of marketing a license, it does indeed become a factor in internalisation. This is the classic "buyer uncertainty" issue (Buckley and Casson, 1976; Casson, 1979). Resource-based theorists propose that the firm is a social and cultural unit, so that it is cheaper to transfer knowledge to a wholly owned subsidiary because it shares "the corporate culture". But does this necessarily apply to a new subsidiary established using locally recruited staff? An even stronger assumption is sometimes utilised by resource-based theorists, which is that the differential cost of internal and external knowledge transfer

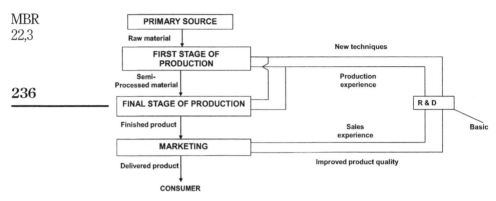

Figure 2.
Information flows in the
multinational firm

Notes: Successive stages of production are linked by flows of semi-processed materials. Production and marketing are linked by a flow of finished goods ready for distribution. Production and marketing on one hand are linked to R&D on the other hand by two-way flows of information and expertise
Source: Reproduced from Buckley and Casson (1976)

(if it exists) is the *only* determinant of internalisation decisions, ignoring IPRs and the threat of imitation and imperfections in the market for knowledge. This is contrary to long-standing evidence that these "omitted factors" are important in linking knowledge transfer to FDI.

Ownership and control
From the beginning of theorising on FDI and the MNE, "control" has been the defining feature of FDI. This is illustrated in the following quote:

> [...] *the market* and *the factory* [...] [represent] the two different methods of coordinating the division of labour. In the factory, entrepreneurs consciously plan and organise cooperation, and relationships are hierarchical and authoritarian: in the market, coordination is achieved through a decentralised, unconscious, competitive process (Hymer, 1972, citing Coase, 1937).

Here, Hymer clearly equates internal control ("the factory") with "hierarchical and authoritarian" decision-making. This aligns with the work of Williamson (1985). Williamson's approach to transaction costs was applied to the MNE by Hennart (1982, 2009) in a sustained theoretical programme. Buckley and Casson's (1976) approach to internalisation differs from the Williamson/Hennart version in that it is agnostic about the nature of internal control. Buckley and Casson take the view that the internal processes of the MNE will attempt to mimic a perfect market, and thereby appropriate the returns from removing externalities. This may involve the firm running an "internal market", which allocates resources to the most profitable internal projects, or using heuristic methods to approximate the allocation mechanisms of a market. These heuristic methods may have elements of "hierarchy" (internal monitoring, sifting and sorting out projects) or they may involve internal bidding for funds and resources from a putative "central bank".

These issues are also clouded by definition issues – what exactly is meant by control and how can it be objectively measured? The usual working definition of control (as adopted by Organisation for Economic Co-operation and Development and The United Nations Conference on Trade and Development [UNCTAD]) is 10 per cent ownership (of the voting equity if that can be ascertained). This clearly leaves a grey area of "ultimate control". In practice, it is further complicated by "pass through" investment ("round tripping" is a form of this problem) when a firm from country A invests in country B to invest in country C (if C = A, this is round tripping). Statisticians are currently grappling with this problem, as it clearly has taxation and decision-making implications for states.

Currently theorists are researching whether a subsidiary is necessarily more controlled by its parent than an offshore outsourced company subject to a tightly written contractual agreement. In many cases the answer is "no"; a parent will often require a subsidiary to innovate to improve products or services for local or global needs through a "subsidiary mandate" (Rugman and Verbeke, 2001). The last thing that a principal wants an outsourced agent to do is to innovate – the agent may appropriate the return and deprive the principal of competitive advantage.

In other words, you do not have to own something to control it. This extension of the reach and power of the MNE beyond what it owns through "non-equity modes" of foreign operation is at the forefront of research on the "global factory", on global value chains, and on the control and location of international productive activity (UNCTAD, 2011, 2013).

The firm

The boundaries of the firm

Internalisation theory has always paid attention to the boundaries of the firm. The growth of quasi-internalisation through non-equity modes, alliances, outsourcing and other cooperative activities has raised several key issues. Notable among these is the question of how far we can speak of the "strategy" of the focal firm as if it represented the whole of the global factory or value chain. Clearly, such entities represent a constellation of independent firms, each possessing (at least in principle) its own strategy and objective function. The orchestrating, focal, flagship or brand-owning firm is clearly dominant in many aspects of decision-making, and these strategies and outcomes are well-researched and understood. However, the role of smaller firms is less understood.

The efficiency and efficacy of the MNE

The approach to assessing the efficiency and efficacy of the MNE in Buckley and Casson (1976) was twofold. The first was to compare the internal solution with the external solution in the real world of imperfect markets. The second was to compare the internal solution in a world of imperfect markets with the external solution in a world of perfect markets. The first comparison is fundamental to explaining why firms internalise: they appropriate a share of the social benefits of internalisation. The second comparison is relevant to policy-making – in particular, the policy of "perfecting" markets by strengthening IPRs and encouraging the formation of forward markets. The first comparison has been examined in detail above, and the second comparison is the focus here.

Forty years of internalisation theory

237

In this comparison, the replication of knowledge-producing activities (including R&D) by competing MNEs is inefficient, as efficiency demands only one actual producer of knowledge. Given the public good nature of knowledge, once it is produced, knowledge can be communicated at the marginal cost of transmission. Social efficiency demands that it should be diffused to all who are willing to bear the marginal cost of transmission. It is then possible to compare the competitive auctioning of the acquisition and exploitation of knowledge with the (actual) operations of the MNE. In this platonic sense, the MNE is a "second best" solution. However, if we take an Aristotelian approach to the efficacy of the MNE as an institution, accounting "remediableness" for the practicality of alternative institutional solutions, we may, with Williamson (1991, 2005a, 2005b), be examining the "remediableness" of the original imperfections in the market for knowledge. This may include such solutions as allowing discriminatory pricing of knowledge, improving the patent system, and improving the external market for knowledge (i.e. facilitating licensing) (Casson, 1979).

Another question is why arbitrage activities in financial markets do not remove anomalies such as supernormal profits of MNEs. If there were a large supply of potential MNEs seeking to profit from opportunities, these gains would be quickly eliminated. However, the world supply of MNEs is inherently limited by the existence of entrepreneurs, cost of capital and the entry barriers possessed by incumbent firms. Consequently, host country locations supply their labour and resources in an increasingly competitive global market to the advantage of a relatively small set of very imperfectly competitive MNEs. This situation is exacerbated by the increasing entry of new locations (China and others) into the market (Liesch *et al.*, 2012). Local entrepreneurs are, thus, confronted by a development problem. As small businesses, they cannot compete with large MNEs, and so they need to either achieve MNE status themselves or to cooperate with existing global factories (Buckley, 2009). The achievement of global reach is a difficult, incremental process with many pitfalls. Buying an MNE (possible through the vehicle of a Sovereign Wealth Fund) is a possibility, but given that share prices will normally incorporate firm prospects, this will not yield more than normal returns. Buying a failing MNE may also prove expensive. Very deep pockets and a lot of patience may be the answer to competing in the globalised market, but this may be politically risky for host country governments.

Internalisation theory for the 2020s
There are four relatively new applications of internalisation theory that are likely to endure into the next decade. They are:

(1) networked multinationals and the global factory;

(2) emerging country MNEs (EMNEs);

(3) the increasing importance of location and economic geography; and

(4) implications for growth, development and welfare of the evolution of the MNE.

Networked multinationals
The key strategic imperatives of modern multinationals are the outsourcing of operations and the internalisation of knowledge. Locations and internalisation decisions are more closely bound than ever with a routine formula of "peripheral

location: outsourced; central location: internalised" being the norm. Of course, what is a "central location" varies over time, partly as a result of the decisions of MNEs – hence the concern with "co-evolution" of firms and states of firms and location-bound institutions (Lewin and Volberda, 1999, Lewin *et al.*, 1999). The types of knowledge that are internalised also change over time. As in Apple's iPhone example above, it is not necessarily technological knowledge that is crucial but marketing knowledge and knowledge around the customer interface. This is encapsulated in the analysis of branding, where brands are surrogates for knowledge capture by MNEs and for the returns to internalised knowledge.

These changes are felt and measured at various different points. Advanced countries have increased their service sectors (notably finance, real estate and business services) at the expense of manufacturing, while some emerging countries, notably China, have seen a massive rise in their role as manufacturing locations. Neither national accounts statistics, nor trade and industry statistics based on outmoded "industries" or "sectors", can track these changes properly. Hence, the concern to map "value chains". This, too, will not reach the essence of the changes unless the controlling intelligence and strategic decision-making of the global factory is put at the centre of enquiries.

Emerging-country MNEs
Multinationals that originate from EMNEs, particularly those from China and India, have been a major research focus in international business this century. They provide an excellent test case for any theory of the MNE. Given that most MNE theories, including internalisation theory, were developed mainly to explain investments by private Western manufacturing firms, testing internalisation theory on EMNEs is a rigorous test. Internalisation theory has stood up well to this challenge (Buckley *et al.*, 2012; Buckley *et al.*, 2007b). There are special factors that need to be accounted for, and these are best dealt with by examining the precise markets that EMNEs internalise – in the case of China, imperfections in the capital market are crucial (Buckley *et al.*, 2007b). EMNEs often seek to go abroad to acquire assets, and this requires explanation of their ability to mount foreign takeovers. A careful analysis of market imperfections is the key here, as Chinese and Indian firms have mechanisms in the home market that allow them to channel capital (and knowledge) to firms (or units of firms) to enable takeovers to be mounted. This is highly context-specific, and illustrates the importance of home (source) country institutions and market structure.

Economic geography
The integration of concepts from economic geography into international business theory has represented a welcome move away from "methodological nationalism" (Yeung, 2009a). MNEs choose not only a country in which to locate, but also a particular geographical space, usually a city. Competition between cities (including those in the same country) is a key aspect of attracting inward FDI. Competing for headquarters of MNEs is equally fierce.

This illustrates the development of a more fine-grained approach to locational aspects of FDI. It also illustrates a widening conceptual approach in which "space" is not something simply acted upon by the MNE as an *ex-cathedra* institution, but the MNE itself is seen as a constituent of geographic space. This can help us see the essence of the MNE as a spatial network interacting with other networks of firms, states, cities and other institutions, as part of a richer picture than the traditional one in which the MNE is prime mover, or even sole mover, in the system.

Economic geography and internalisation theory share a focus on the interaction of institutions (firms) and places (locations) (Mudambi, 2008). This is exemplified by the focus of both disciplines on the historical development of the division of labour. As the following quote shows, the growth of "modern central-place hierarchies" depends on both the evolution of the division of labour and the evolution of institutions – among which the firm is a key actor:

> Neither local nor long distance trade disturbed the subsistence base of peasant societies. The role of modern central-place hierarchies is, on the other hand, predicated upon the extreme division of labour and the absence of household self-sufficiency in necessities (Berry, 1967).

Internalisation theory is, by its nature, comparative (internal versus external, location A versus location B). It, therefore, possesses a close affinity with history – including business history (Buckley, 2009), where the key comparison is the change over time. It also has an affinity with regional studies, where the key comparisons are across geographic space. The MNE is important because the analyst can hold "the form" constant while varying the context – the same firm across time, or geographically separate parts of the same firm at the same time. There is much to be expected in the future from internalisation theory in concert with history and geography research, to the benefit of both (Yeung, 2009b).

The global factory and development
The relationship between MNEs and the development of less-developed countries has been at the centre of international business research since its inception. At the time of writing *The Future of the Multinational Enterprise* (Buckley and Casson, 1976), opinion and policy was largely anti-MNE as exploiters of poor countries, appropriators of scarce natural resources and as wielders of power ("small countries, large firms"). Internalisation theory, transmitted through the publications of John Dunning and his close working relationship with UNCTAD, led to a major shift in host country attitudes because it became widely understood that MNEs transferred knowledge internationally rather than just "capital" and its associated control. MNEs took (and continue to take) equity shares in their subsidiaries largely to defend their property rights to generate rents that covered the costs of their R&D. The real issue was (and remains) the appropriate contractual arrangements to protect the interests of both MNEs and host countries. As successive publications of UNCTAD have shown, in the 1990s, opinion and policy swung back towards a pro-FDI stance, and under the "Washington Consensus" (a US interpretation of the new position), host countries competed against each other to attract inward FDI.

In the twenty-first century, a more nuanced policy response has emerged because of a more balanced view of the benefits and costs of inward FDI suggested by a more careful application of internalisation theory (Rugman and Verbeke, 1998). More attention is now being paid to the comparative costs of different types of contractual arrangements (wholly owned subsidiaries, subcontractors, joint ventures and non-equity alliances) and the importance of matching appropriate contractual arrangements to specific types of activity (as exemplified by Chinese EMNEs).

Case studies of the development successes in particular contexts and spectacular failures and negative externalities in other contexts (collapsing factories and environmental disasters) have focused attention on the importance of matching strategy to context. A formidable body of case law is now demonstrating that careful analysis of the type of activity and context will lead to more successful finer-grained policies. Two examples are controversial – "footloose MNEs" and the use of child labour.

The argument that much FDI is "footloose" is a partial equilibrium result (using the single factor of labour cost as the location trigger) rather than a general equilibrium solution. If changes in labour cost are the most significant and predictable change, and all other factors do not change (or it is legitimate to assume that all else can be held constant), then the result of footloose MNEs chasing cheap labour holds. However, these assumptions are becoming less tenable as changes in technology further reduce the labour content of large swathes of production (robots and printing technologies); indeed, re-shoring (north-shoring) has diverted previously cheap labour-seeking FDI back to richer countries. Reliance on cheap labour as a stimulus to development through attracting FDI seems increasingly less viable. This may pose serious future issues for the least developed countries with excess labour.

The child labour issue is emotive and has brought opprobrium down on salient foreign MNEs that use under-age labour, often in subcontracted factories. One way of examining this is to use a historical lens. In the long-term, it is clearly optimal for children to go to school. However, in the short-term, child workers are often children of uneducated parents and they have to go to work to maintain the family income, albeit a low level of income. If children in the least developed countries do not work, they often die (alternative forms of employment such as prostitution may be less acceptable than factory work). How to then reach the optimal goal? Work in global factories, especially if it is part-time and combined with schoolwork, may provide a transitional path towards the goal. In poverty situations, the best strategy in the short-term may well be for the global factory to provide employment and to combine this with educational investment. In the long-term, proceeds from this activity can be reinvested into educational provision to phase out transitional child employment. Monitoring of the progress of this transition is vital – schooling and part-time work must be complements, not substitutes. From an internalisation viewpoint, the key issue is whether subcontracting is a method by which MNEs protect their consumer brands from contamination from the child labour opprobrium. The global factory perspective suggests that, although outsourced, control of the whole value chain reflects ultimate responsibility on MNEs for their contracted-out activities. Observation suggests that MNEs that claim "these are not our factories" are neither winning the practical nor the moral argument. The quasi-internalisation of product flows also confers responsibility onto the brand owners.

The neglected policy prescriptions of Buckley and Casson (1976) need to be revisited and focused on this development agenda with the new tools at our disposal.

Conclusion

Because of its secure social science base, internalisation theory has vast potential for integrating with other social sciences, and particularly geography and history. It is unlikely to run out of steam because of these secure connections. In taking an unnecessarily narrow view of internalisation as a technical issue, critics have failed

MBR
22,3

242

to appreciate its diversity of applications and its utility. As Lewin (1951, p. 169) famously said, "There is nothing more practical as a good theory."

The internalisation theory of the MNE is practical because it works to explain the strategic decisions of MNEs, to understand them and to predict them. By having a clear idea of the changing locational costs of different activities, the links between activities (through flows of intermediate products and services), and the optimal configuration of locations and flows, the direction of growth of MNEs can be predicted (Buckley and Hashai, 2004, 2005, 2009). By analysing the opportunities to internalise markets in knowledge-intensive products and services, and the counter-balancing attributes of productive outsourcing, the strategic decisions of MNEs can be explained. This, of course, requires technical and entrepreneurial skills as well as theoretical comprehension. I contend that this is, and has been, a far sounder basis for "strategizing" than its potential competitors:

> The theory may have lots of unanswered questions […] and it is still interesting! (Davis, 1971).

References

Barney, J. (1986), "Strategic factor markets: expectations, luck and business strategy", *Management Science*, Vol. 32 No. 10, pp. 1231-1241.

Berlin, I. (1960), "History and theory, the concept of scientific history", *History and Theory*, Vol. 1 No. 1, pp. 1-31.

Berry, B.J.L. (1967), *Geography of Market Centres and Retail Distribution*, Prentice-Hall, Englewood Cliffs, NJ.

Buckley, P.J. (1996), "The role of management in international business theory: a meta-analysis and integration of literature on international business and international management", *Management International Review*, Vol. 36 No. 1.1, pp. 7-54.

Buckley, P.J. (2007), "The strategy of multinational enterprises in the light of the rise of China", *Scandinavian Journal of Management*, Vol. 23 No. 2, pp. 107-126.

Buckley, P.J. (2009), "The impact of the global factory on economic development", *Journal of World Business*, Vol. 44 No. 2, pp. 131-143.

Buckley, P.J. (2010), "The role of headquarters in the global factory", in Andersson, U. and Holm, U. (Eds), *Managing the Contemporary Multinational*, Edward Elgar, Cheltenham, pp. 60-84.

Buckley, P.J. (2011), "International integration and coordination in the global factory", *Management International Review*, Vol. 51 No. 2, pp. 269-283.

Buckley, P.J. and Casson, M.C. (1976), *The Future of the Multinational Enterprise*, Macmillan, London.

Buckley, P.J. and Casson, M.C. (2007), "Edith Penrose's theory of the growth of the firm and the strategic management of multinational enterprises", *Management International Review*, Vol. 47 No. 2, pp. 151-173.

Buckley, P.J. and Ghauri, P.N. (2004), "Globalisation, economic geography and the strategy of multinational enterprises", *Journal of International Business Studies*, Vol. 35 No. 2, pp. 81-98.

Buckley, P.J. and Hashai, N. (2004), "A global system view of firm boundaries", *Journal of International Business Studies*, Vol. 35 No. 1, pp. 33-45.

Buckley, P.J. and Hashai, N. (2005), "Firm configuration and internationalisation: a model", *International Business Review*, Vol. 14 No. 6, pp. 655-675.

Buckley, P.J. and Hashai, N. (2009), "Formalizing internationalization in the eclectic paradigm", *Journal of International Business Studies*, Vol. 40 No. 1, pp. 58-70.

Buckley, P.J. and Lessard, D.R. (2005), "Regaining the edge for international business research", *Journal of International Business Studies*, Vol. 36 No. 6, pp. 595-599.

Buckley, P.J., Devinney, T.M. and Louviere, J.J. (2007a), "Do managers behave the way theory suggests? A choice-theoretic examination of foreign direct investment location decision-making", *Journal of International Business Studies*, Vol. 38 No. 7, pp. 1069-1094.

Buckley, P.J., Clegg, J., Cross, A., Liu, X., Voss, H. and Zheng, P. (2007b), "The determinants of Chinese outward foreign direct investment", *Journal of International Business Studies*, Vol. 38 No. 4, pp. 499-518.

Buckley, P.J., Forsans, N. and Munjal, S. (2012), "Host-home country linkages and host-home country specific advantages as determinants of foreign acquisitions by Indian firms", *International Business Review*, Vol. 21 No. 5, pp. 878-890.

Casson, M. (1979), *Alternatives to the Multinational Enterprise*. Macmillan London.

Casson, M. (1982), *The Entrepreneur*, Martin Robertson, Oxford.

Casson, M.C. (1986), "Vertical integration and intra-firm trade", in Casson, M.C. and Associates (Eds), *Multinationals and World Trade*, George Allen & Unwin, London, pp. 103-140.

Clark, P. and Rowlinson, M. (2004), "The treatment of history in organisation studies: towards an 'historic turn'?", *Business History*, Vol. 46 No. 3, pp. 331-352.

Coase, R.H. (1937), "The nature of the firm", *Economica*, Vol. 4 No. 16, pp. 386-405.

Davis, M.S. (1971), "That's interesting! Towards a phenomenology of sociology and a sociology of phenomenology", *Philosophy of Social Science*, Vol. 1 No. 2, pp. 309-344.

Dunning, J.H. (1998), "Location and the multinational enterprise: a neglected factor?", *Journal of International Business Studies*, Vol. 29 No. 1, pp. 45-66.

Forsgren, M., Holm, U. and Johnson, J. (2007), *Managing the Embedded Multinational—A Business Network View*, Edward Elgar, Cheltenham.

Gaddis, J.L. (2002), *The Landscape of History: How Historians Map the Past*, Oxford University Press, Oxford.

Hennart, J.F. (1982), *A Theory of Multinational Enterprise*, University of Michigan Press, Ann Arbor, MI.

Hennart, J.F. (2009), "Down with MNE centric theories! Market entry and expansion as the bundling of MNE and local assets", *Journal of International Business Studies*, Vol. 40 No. 9, pp. 1432-1454.

Hinterhuber, A. (2002), "Value chain orchestration in action and the case of the global agrochemical industry", *Long Range Planning*, Vol. 35 No. 6, pp. 615-635.

Hymer, S. (1972), "The multinational corporation and the law of uneven development", in Bhagwati, J.N. (Ed.), *Economics and World Order*, Macmillan, London.

Langlois, R.N. (1991), "Transaction-cost economics in real time", *Industrial and Corporate Change*, Vol. 1 No. 1, pp. 99-127.

Lewin, A.Y. and Volberda, H.W. (1999), "Prolegomena on coevolution: a framework for research on strategy and new organizational forms," *Organization Science*, Vol. 10 No. 5, pp. 519-534.

Lewin, A.Y., Long, C.P. and Carroll, T.N. (1999), "The coevolution of new organization forms", *Organization Science*, Vol. 10 No. 5, pp. 535-550.

MBR
22,3

Lewin, K. (1951), "Field theory in social science: selected theoretical papers", in Cartwright, D. (Ed.), *Organization Science*, Harper & Row, New York, NY.

Liesch, P.S., Buckley, P.J., Simonin, B.L. and Knight, G. (2012), "Organizing the modern firm in the worldwide market for market transactions", *Management International Review*, Vol. 52 No. 1, pp. 3-21.

Meyer, K.E., Mudambi, R. and Narula, R. (2011), "Multinational enterprises and local contexts: the opportunities and challenges of multiple embeddedness", *Journal of Management Studies*, Vol. 48 No. 2, pp. 235-252.

Mudambi, R. (2008), "Location, control and innovation in knowledge-intensive industries", *Journal of Economic Geography*, Vol. 8 No. 5, pp. 699-725.

Mudambi, R. and Swift, T. (2011), "Leveraging knowledge and competencies across space: the next frontier in international business", *Journal of International Management*, Vol. 17 No. 3, pp. 186-189.

Mudambi, R. and Swift, T. (2012), "Multinational enterprises and the geographical clustering of innovation", *Industry and Innovation*, Vol. 19 No. 1, pp. 1-21.

Mudambi, R. and Swift, T. (2014), "Knowing when to leap: transitioning between exploitative and explorative R&D", *Strategic Management Journal*, Vol. 35 No. 1, pp. 126-145.

Nelson, R.R. and Winter, S. (1982), *An Evolutionary Theory of Economic Change*, Belknap Press, Cambridge, MA.

Penrose, E. (1959), *Theory of the Growth of the Firm*, Blackwell, Oxford.

Rugman, A.M. and Verbeke, A. (1998), "Multinational enterprises and public policy", *Journal of International Business Studies*, Vol. 29 No. 1, pp. 115-136.

Rugman, A.M. and Verbeke, A. (2001), "Subsidiary-specific advantages in multinational enterprises", *Strategic Management Journal*, Vol. 22 No. 3, pp. 237-250.

Rugman, A.M. and Verbeke, A. (2003), "Extending the theory of the multinational enterprise: internalization and strategic management perspectives", *Journal of International Business Studies*, Vol. 34 No. 2, pp. 125-137.

Rumelt, R.P. (1984), "Towards a strategic theory of the firm", in Lamb, R. (Ed.), *Competitive Strategic Management*, Prentice Hall, Englewood Cliffs, NJ, pp. 556-570.

Selznick, P. (1957), *Leadership in Administration: A Sociological Interpretation*, Row, Peterson, Evanston, IL.

Teece, D.J., Pisano, G. and Shuen, A. (1997), "Dynamic capabilities and strategic management", *Strategic Management Journal*, Vol. 18 No. 7, pp. 509-533.

UNCTAD (2011), *World Investment Report: Non-Equity Modes of International Production and Development*, United Nations, New York, NY, Geneva.

UNCTAD (2013), *World Investment Report: Global Value Chains: Investment and Trade for Development*, United Nations, New York, NY, Geneva.

Vernon, R. (1966), "International trade and international investment in the product cycle", *Quarterly Journal of Economics*, Vol. 80 No. 2, pp. 190-207.

Williamson, O.E. (1985), *The Economic Institutions of Capitalism*, The Free Press, New York, NY.

Williamson, O.E. (1991), "Comparative economic organization: the analysis of discrete structural alternatives", *Administrative Science Quarterly*, Vol. 36 No. 2, pp. 269-296.

Williamson, O.E. (2005a), "The economics of governance", *American Economic Review*, Vol. 95 No. 2, pp. 1-18.

Williamson, O.E. (2005b), "Transaction cost economics and business administration", *Scandinavian Journal of Management*, Vol. 21 No. 1, pp. 19-40.

Wolf, B.M. (1977), "Industrial diversification and internationalization: some empirical evidence", *The Journal of Industrial Economics*, Vol. 26 No. 2, pp. 177-191.

Yeung, H.W.-C. (2009a), "Transnational corporations, global production networks and urban and regional development: a geographer's perspective on multinational enterprises and the global economy", *Growth and Change*, Vol. 40 No. 2, pp. 197-226.

Yeung, H.W.-C. (2009b), "Transnationalizing entrepreneurship: a critical agenda for economic geography", *Progress in Human Geography*, Vol. 33 No. 2, pp. 210-235.

Zaheer, S. (1995), "Overcoming the liability of foreignness", *Academy of Management Journal*, Vol. 38 No. 2, pp. 341-363.

About the author
Peter J. Buckley is Professor of International Business and Founder Director of the Centre for International Business, University of Leeds (CIBUL). Peter J. Buckley is a corresponding author and can be contacted at: pjb@lubs.leeds.ac.uk

Forty years of
internalisation
theory

245

To purchase reprints of this article please e-mail: **reprints@emeraldinsight.com**
Or visit our web site for further details: **www.emeraldinsight.com/reprints**

3

© *Academy of Management Perspectives*
2016, Vol. 30, No. 1, 40–58.
http://dx.doi.org/10.5465/amp.2013.0144

S Y M P O S I U M

GLOBAL INTERFIRM NETWORKS:
THE DIVISION OF ENTREPRENEURIAL LABOR BETWEEN
MNEs AND SMEs

PETER J. BUCKLEY
University of Leeds

SHAMEEN PRASHANTHAM
China Europe International Business School

We advance a multifaceted and spatially anchored account of the who, the how, and the where of global interfirm networks through our novel conceptualization of the *division of entrepreneurial labor* between multinational enterprises (MNEs) and small and medium-size enterprises (SMEs). The capability dimension pertains to the differential capability sets of SMEs and MNEs in exploration and exploitation, respectively (the who). The connectivity dimension posits network orchestration/participation and dialogue as differentially addressing the distinct facets of interdependence—viz., mutual dependence and power imbalance, respectively (the how). The contextuality dimension concerns the differential approaches adopted in advanced versus emerging economies (the where).

In the 21st century, research in international management has taken a decisive turn away from a unitary view of the multinational enterprise (MNE) to focus on *global interfirm networks* in which MNEs participate (Buckley & Strange, 2015; Cantwell, 2013; Johanson & Vahlne, 2009). This turn in international management research mirrors the wider literature on interfirm networks and innovation. The shift in emphasis from monolithic MNEs to global interfirm networks orchestrated by MNEs reflects the veracity of Nambisan and Sawhney's (2011, p. 40) insightful observation: "A hub firm's orchestration activities occur in a dual context—an innovation context and an interfirm network context."

However, while prior work (Dhanaraj & Parkhe, 2006; Nambisan & Sawhney, 2011) provides valuable insight into the orchestration processes of large hub firms, there is scope for a more integrative account that explicitly (1) takes into account co-specialization of MNEs *and* SMEs, which are typically overlooked

Our work has benefited from constructive suggestions from Stephen Young, Shaker Zahra, and participants at the 2013 Academy of International Business (India Chapter) conference, where an earlier draft of the paper received the Runner-up Award for Best Paper.

peripheral actors (Zahra & Nambisan, 2011, 2012), (2) unpacks different facets of interdependence, such as mutual dependence and power imbalance (Emerson, 1962), and (3) factors in spatial heterogeneity, such as that between advanced and emerging economies as venues for MNE–SME engagement, which is of course highly relevant in the context of global (as distinct from local) interfirm networks.

Therefore, the purpose of our paper is to incorporate prior research to produce a more complete and enhanced analysis of global interfirm networks. We do so by producing a multifaceted and spatially anchored account of the who, the how, and the where of global business networks. Previous work has focused on orchestration by the large focal firm in global networks; our novel conceptualization of the *division of entrepreneurial labor* encompasses the participation of smaller firms in global business networks. The division of entrepreneurial labor is a concept that allows the strategies of *all* the firms in the network to be analyzed, and further integrates spatial perspectives (place and space) that are crucial in comprehending the global nature of modern business networks. The division of entrepreneurial labor highlights the contribution of all participants in global business networks, replacing excessive

Copyright of the Academy of Management, all rights reserved. Contents may not be copied, emailed, posted to a listserv, or otherwise transmitted without the copyright holder's express written permission. Users may print, download, or email articles for individual use only.

concentration on the focal firm. The orchestrator role in global business networks is enhanced by the novel concept that the division of entrepreneurial labor allows all participants to have an active role in strategy; markets are self-organizing only with this effortful entrepreneurship. It also recognizes the spatial element in global interfirm networks.

Our central argument is this:

- Differentiation between SMEs and MNEs (the who), predominantly in terms of exploration and exploitation capabilities, respectively, creates potential for value creation in global interfirm networks.
- This potential is realized through interdependence (the how); mutual dependence is facilitated by network orchestration (and participation), whereas power imbalance is redressed through MNE–SME dialogue.
- To be globally effective, adaptation across space (the where) is typically warranted such that institutional support for entrepreneurship in advanced economies is complemented, whereas deficits in such support are substituted for in emerging economies.

We refer to these, respectively, as the capability, connectivity, and contextuality dimensions of the division of entrepreneurial labor between MNEs and SMEs in global interfirm networks.

We extend the literature by (1) shedding light on how differentiation between MNEs and SMEs sets up the potential for division of entrepreneurial labor between these disparate sets of actors, (2) clarifying differential mechanisms for different dimensions of interdependence, which helps realize efficacious MNE–SME division of entrepreneurial labor, and (3) highlighting the importance of more fine-grained spatial analyses that distinguish between MNE–SME partnering efforts in emerging versus advanced economies.

Our paper is structured as follows: We next explain the concept of the division of entrepreneurial labor. This is followed by three sections that, respectively, deal with the who, the how, and the where of the division of entrepreneurial labor, and in each we look at how *both* MNEs and SMEs contribute to joint activity in terms of proactiveness, innovativeness, and risk-taking. Thereafter we present a discussion of our contributions to research and some future research directions. Finally, we outline some implications for practitioners.

THE DIVISION OF ENTREPRENEURIAL LABOR

Making judgmental decisions about the coordination of scarce resources is the main work (or labor) of entrepreneurs, who are rewarded for making uncertain investments (Casson, 1982). Entrepreneurs exist in both small and large firms, and entrepreneurial labor (as distinct from managerial labor) involves delegated strategic decision making—for instance, introducing new ideas or plans for expansion—on behalf of the firm's owners or senior managers (Penrose, 1959; Ross, 2014). The key function of the entrepreneur is to exercise judgment in the face of uncertainty (Casson, 1982; Knight, 1921). Incomplete contracts have a positive effect on the exercise of entrepreneurship—they allow firms to adapt sequentially to changing circumstances in an uncertain world. The firm is thus the institution in which the entrepreneur (whose services are the most difficult to measure or evaluate) combines her assets (judgment) with physical assets. The firm enables previously segmented areas of judgment and skills to be blended together, and thus individual entrepreneurship becomes part of a collective organization. Individuals with entrepreneurial judgment can thus coalesce within the organization and combine their skills. Because of the noncontractibility of these skills (or rather the extremely high costs of contracting them), this coalition becomes embedded in the firm, thus giving a transactions-cost rationale for competencies residing for a finite period of time in certain companies.

The division of labor, a concept dating back to Adam Smith in 1776, is primarily used to analyze normal labor, following Smith's celebrated example of the pin factory (Smith, 1976/1776). This paper introduces the notion of a division of entrepreneurial labor where the specialization is not of task, as in manual labor, but of competence and judgment between the decision makers in different organizations. This involves two innovations—examining decision making as an activity to be analyzed analogously to task in conventional approaches to the division of labor, and examining between-organization specialization paralleling conventional in-house specialization.[1] This

---

[1] Our approach differs from that of Foss and Klein (2012), who focused on a division of entrepreneurial labor within a given firm whereby different members of the same organization attend to different aspects (discovery vs. evaluation vs. exploitation) of a given opportunity. By contrast, our approach focuses on the division of entrepreneurial labor across firms where different firms focus on different opportunities per se—for instance, opportunities relating to exploration (SME) and exploitation (MNE). Furthermore, we incorporate the "labor" involved in building interdependence between these sets of firms from the perspective of *both* sets of actors.

enables us to understand not only specialized decision making (by those most fitted and often close to the decision) but also the structure of the world economy as it is divided by organizations (firms).

Specialization in judgmental decisions entails proactiveness, innovativeness, and risk-taking, characteristics identified as foundational dimensions of entrepreneurial attitude and behavior (Khandwalla, 1977). The division of entrepreneurial labor, then, involves specialization of judgments about (1) what to be proactive about, (2) what to be innovative in, and (3) when and how to undertake risks. The division of entrepreneurial labor lies at the heart of firms' innovation strategies, not only within firms (ambidexterity challenge) but also across firms.

In this paper we focus on the division of entrepreneurial labor between MNEs and SMEs by considering how meaningful MNE–SME engagement occurs despite the considerable barriers to cooperative behavior between these disparate organizations (Doz, 1988). The optimum areas of operation of individual firm units are set by the entrepreneurial decisions of each unit over its scale and scope. These myriad decisions determine the boundaries of the firm and the market (Buckley & Casson, 1976; Coase, 1937) and between individual firms. The division of entrepreneurial labor between broad groups, such as that between MNEs and SMEs, reflects those areas of activity best served by large, global multinational firms and those suited to small, specialized, local SMEs. Generally speaking MNEs attempt to reduce their horizontal spillovers, but they often have "self-interest in creating low-cost reliable-quality suppliers in the host market" (Moran, 2014, p. 22). There are many examples (Moran gives the entry of Walmart stores into Mexico and the Indian auto sector as exemplars) where the entry of MNEs has led to crowding out and crowding in: The shock of entry reconfigures domestic supply and reorients domestic entrepreneurs toward the new opportunities, forcing domestic entrepreneurs to reevaluate their capabilities. This can sometimes lead to consolidation in domestic supply, with mergers or dropouts among less successful local companies.

Thus, a crucial aspect of developing country policy is the integration of local firms into international supply chains. The division of entrepreneurial labor substitutes for imperfect host government policy and information asymmetries between global interfirm networks and SMEs. As Moran (2014, p. 7) put it, "The middle—or higher—skill intensive investor wants reassurance ... [that] the new production site can be seamlessly woven into the global network on which the parent's competitive position in international market depends. The prospective host must therefore focus on ensuring smooth integration and reducing the likelihood of disruptions." It is precisely this reassurance and smooth integration that is the local entrepreneur's most significant offering in the division of labor between SMEs and MNEs. The SME plays a crucial role in reducing imperfections in information markets—about local supply conditions, labor availability, employment law, and all the other types of tacit knowledge a local entrepreneur possesses. The division of entrepreneurial labor reduces crowding out of local businesses and fosters crowding in.

The genesis of the division of entrepreneurial labor arises out of the asymmetry in the market for entrepreneurs between global factories—that is, interfirm networks (Buckley & Strange, 2015) and small firms. The global factory has access to a global market of mobile executives that it trains and acculturates in the mores of the company. Entrepreneurs who set up and run SMEs are more locally focused and are more likely to be untrained and part of local networks. Their particular skills will be more in demand in local networks than by global factories. This provides an excellent opportunity for symbiosis between the two noncompeting groups of entrepreneurs. We emphasize the fact that entrepreneurship occurs in large MNEs too, as well as SMEs, hence the division of entrepreneurial labor.

THE WHO: DIFFERENTIATION BETWEEN MNEs AND SMEs

SMEs[2] contrast starkly with the focal orchestrating MNE in terms of organizational attributes such as size, scale, and resource base (Prashantham & Birkinshaw, 2008). The stark differences between these actors mean that there is scope for differentiation in the expertise of MNEs and SMEs, which represents a necessary condition for the division of entrepreneurial labor. *Differentiation* in the entrepreneurial foci of SMEs and MNEs on, respectively,

---

[2] Our focus is on SMEs—that is, *genuinely* small firms. We also note that while some scholars focus on the "smallness" of entrepreneurial firms vis-à-vis large MNEs (e.g., Lu & Beamish, 2001), others emphasize the "newness" of a subset of SMEs, viz., new ventures (e.g., McDougall & Oviatt, 2000). Our arguments in this paper hold for new ventures as well as for SMEs more generally. We acknowledge also that these phenomena may be more evident in platform-based high-technology contexts.

exploration and exploitation (Geroski & Markides, 2004; March 1991) provides the basis for the potential for meaningful engagement at the MNE–SME interface.

In terms of proactiveness, SMEs and MNEs anticipate opportunities in new niches and established markets (comprising multiple, integrated niches), respectively, and this entails making judgments concerning the extent of the market opportunity (Smith, 1976/1776). In the case of SMEs, the extent of the niche reflects derived demand, whereas in the case of MNEs, the extent of the market is a function of the integration of multiple niches. An important function of entrepreneurs is creating markets where none previously existed. The entrepreneur sees an opportunity and steps in to create a new activity, which may involve coordination by one firm or by more than one trading in the new market opportunity (Casson, 1982, 1987).

Schumpeter's (1934) early work highlights explorative innovation by smaller ventures; his later work (Schumpeter, 1942) refers to the systematic exploitation of innovation by established firms. In general, MNEs have greater wherewithal to strengthen their position in extant markets, while SMEs tend to have greater entrepreneurial alertness (Kirzner, 1978) to identify and target new market niches. Potentially, then, MNEs and SMEs play complementary roles (Acs, Morck, Shaver, & Yeung, 1997; Bhide, 2000; Ceccagnoli, Forman, Huang, & Wu, 2012; Sharma, 1999; Yang, Zheng, & Zhao, 2014).

In terms of innovation, different value chain activities suit the traditional strengths of MNEs and SMEs. As evident in alliances between small biotech ventures and large pharmaceutical multinationals, highly capable SMEs are likely to contribute disproportionately to upstream activities and MNEs to downstream activities. As Acs et al. (1997, p. 10) pointed out, "A large multinational can begin marketing an innovation around the world almost immediately." This is not to discount the considerable research and development efforts of MNEs in increasingly spatially dispersed settings (Cantwell, 2009; Dhanaraj & Parkhe, 2006). Rather, we seek to make the point that the division of entrepreneurial labor may be driven by the view that SMEs can advance new product development with an agility and frugality that a large MNE cannot match. This agility is cited by Baumol (2004, p. 9), who observed that "the revolutionary breakthroughs continue to come predominantly from small entrepreneurial enterprises, with large industry providing streams of incremental improvements that also add up to major contributions." In a similar vein, Kuemmerle (2006, p. 312) observed that "as firms grow larger they tend to lose much of their flexibility and agility," whereas SMEs are renowned for their "flexibility, nimbleness, ability to seek new openings" (Buckley, 2006, p. 687). This is partly why technological innovation originating within an MNE may be "spun off" into a new venture (a subset of the SME population) with a hands-off approach by the large corporation (Chesbrough, 2003).

In terms of risk-taking, our perspective goes beyond the leveraging of complementary capabilities to highlight the scope for SMEs and MNEs to *compensate* for the deficiencies of the other. Typically, weakness emanates from the very source of strength: SMEs' smallness (and often newness) facilitates flexibility but is associated with a paucity of legitimacy, and MNEs' largeness (and often oldness) means greater resources but less flexibility. Potentially, SMEs' legitimacy deficit could be mitigated by engaging high-status MNEs, and MNEs could increase flexibility in the face of risk by partnering with agile SMEs (Buckley & Casson, 1998). These useful antidotes—which MNEs and SMEs might well anticipate while making judgments about the extent of the market or niche of interest—are an important aspect of the division of entrepreneurial labor between MNEs and SMEs.

The who of the division of entrepreneurial labor, summarized in Table 1, thus indicates that balancing exploration and exploitation (March 1991) need not be a solely intraorganizational endeavor, but could also involve *inter*organizational engagement. Also, while entrepreneurship studies "implicitly favor the need for exploration" (Dess & Lumpkin, 2005, p. 154), our approach suggests that from an interfirm network perspective, even exploitation—to which MNEs contribute disproportionately—entails entrepreneurial labor.

Synthesizing the above arguments leads to our first observation:

Observation 1: The potential for the division of entrepreneurial labor between SMEs and MNEs results from these actors leveraging their assets and mitigating their liabilities of smallness/newness and largeness/oldness, respectively. Specifically, this occurs by SMEs and MNEs:

(a) proactively anticipating the extent of niches and markets, respectively;

(b) innovatively leveraging upstream and downstream capability (assets), respectively; and

44   *Academy of Management Perspectives*   February

TABLE 1
The Who: Differentiation Between MNEs and SMEs

	MNE (Focus: exploitation)	SME (Focus: exploration)
Proactiveness	Exploiting an existing market	Exploring a new niche
	Primarily geared toward building existing markets; a greater focus on exploitation than exploration	Primarily geared toward identifying (new) market niches—at least in highly innovative SMEs; a greater focus on exploration
Innovation	Asset of largeness/oldness: Downstream	Asset of smallness/newness: Upstream
	As firms become larger their greater bureaucracy impedes radical innovation, but greater scale and streamlined processes render technical improvements and commercialization more efficient	Smaller entrepreneurial firms have greater nimbleness and agility to pursue new-to-market technologies
Risk-taking	Liability of largeness/oldness: Flexibility deficit	Liability of smallness/newness: Legitimacy deficit
	Antidote: status enhancement by acquiring reputation for attracting nimble, innovative SMEs	Antidote: Status attainment through association with a reputable MNE

(c) taking risks anticipating that these can be mitigated by the other's capacity to compensate for the focal actor's deficits (liabilities) in legitimacy and flexibility, respectively.

THE HOW: INTERDEPENDENCE BETWEEN MNEs AND SMEs

While MNE–SME differentiation results in the potential for joint value creation, interdependence is required to realize that potential. This is not straightforward in the case of asymmetric MNE–SME partnerships because although the division of entrepreneurial labor offers possibilities for valuable interorganizational activity, it also leads to certain vulnerabilities (Katila et al., 2008). This is due to a "missing markets" problem: There is a vacuum at the interface of MNEs and SMEs caused by high transaction costs, information asymmetry, and low levels of trust. The prospect of malfeasance by the more powerful MNE could be a concern for SMEs (Alvarez & Barney, 2001), whereas for MNEs, identifying high-quality SME partners (the "lemon" problem) can be difficult. These vulnerabilities are symptomatic of deficits in distinct types of trust: structural and social (Madhok, 1995). As Madhok (2006, p. 7) explained it, "The structural basis of trust is ... synergistic complementarities, and social trust has more to do with the relationship process." Social trust deficits account for SMEs' concerns regarding MNE intentions; structural trust deficits are reflected in MNEs' concerns regarding SME competence.

In this section we explicate *how* these trust deficits might be (differentially) addressed to engender interdependence. We follow Emerson (1962) in distinguishing between two facets of interdependence:

mutual dependence and power imbalance. Mutual dependence refers to the sum of dependencies between two organizations; in the context of a given dyad it connotes bilateral dependencies. Power imbalance refers to the difference in actors' dependencies on each other; this depicts the power an actor has over another. This power differential between organizations is, in effect, the ratio of the more powerful actor's power to that of the less powerful actor. While some SMEs have greater bargaining power vis-à-vis an MNE than others through, for instance, access to innovation that is vital to the latter, all things being equal, MNEs possess greater power than their SME partners due to their greater resource base and status (Katila et al., 2008). Key to Emerson's (1962) conceptualization is that mutual dependence may exist irrespective of the extent of (im)balance between actors' power levels.

In global interfirm networks involving MNEs and SMEs, each of these two distinct facets of interdependence must be addressed in its own right without assuming away or blurring this distinction. This is a theoretically important distinction because, ceteris paribus, they lead to opposing instincts on the part of high-power actors—viz., to be cooperative and (overly) demanding, respectively (Casciaro & Piskorski, 2005). The latter can thus impede the process of fostering the division of entrepreneurial labor within interfirm networks—and so in addition to enabling mutual dependence we need to *also* consider efforts that address power imbalance. Although aspects of this have been considered in previous studies, to the best of our knowledge prior work has not established the theoretical link that we do in relation to these different aspects of the how. Addressing these issues requires a different missing market problem to be addressed—viz., information asymmetries that impede the identification of technical synergy (structural trust) on one hand, and the development of positive expectations and confidence via actual interaction between partners (social trust) on the other (Madhok, 1995).

From the perspective of power-disadvantaged actors, the main concern pertains to the level of value appropriation that they can realistically achieve. This is highly relevant in the context of MNE–SME relationships; bargaining over value appropriation is an area of strategic stress as entrepreneurs are in conflict over the allocation of residual rewards (Alvarez & Barney, 2001). Accomplishing mutual dependence does not preclude the prospect of power imbalance. Conceivably, high levels of mutual dependence exacerbate power imbalance–induced obstacles by undermining harmonious negotiation, which enhances the risk that, by failing to agree to terms, the firms will achieve nothing productive because power imbalance "reduces the frequency of exchange among social actors by hindering conflict resolution" and "increases the frequency of confrontational behaviors," resulting in actors being "less likely to develop mutually satisfactory exchange relationships" (Casciaro & Piskorski, 2005, p. 175).

We identify differential manifestations of the division of entrepreneurial labor to address these challenges: network orchestration/participation and network dialogue, respectively. We conceptualize dialogue as distinct from orchestration as the set of efforts that "increases the weaker member's power … through increasing the [more powerful member's] motivational investment in the relation" (Emerson, 1962, p. 39). Implicit in the notion of dialogue is a logic of embeddedness predicated on the "infusion of sentiment" and "the more calculative rationale of actors who now have a higher stake in maintaining a smooth relationship," which leads to "effective symbiotic coexistence," notwithstanding power dynamics (Gulati & Sytch, 2007, pp. 33, 34). Such an orientation "results in each partner's giving heightened attention to the responses and attitudes of the other, such that the quality of the relationship becomes one of the main determinants of a satisfactory business tie" (Gulati & Sytch, 2007, p. 37).

Although these issues have been treated in the literature by previous authors, to the best of our knowledge these are either conflated or have not been conceptualized in the distinctive yet integrative manner we propose as responses to achieving mutual dependence and redressing power imbalance, respectively.

Achieving Mutual Dependence: MNE Orchestration and SME Participation

In terms of proactiveness, orchestrators of MNE global interfirm networks have begun to play the role of "ecosystem developers"—involving innovation integration and platform leadership (Nambisan & Sawhney, 2011)—while SMEs play the role of "ecosystem participants." Clearly, in the case of MNEs, building an ecosystem requires proactive effort and may entail going beyond its existing business network (Forsgren, Holm, & Johanson, 2005). Dhanaraj and Parkhe (2006) identified important activities that an MNE orchestrator undertakes: managing knowledge mobility, managing innovation appropriation, and managing network stability. Nambisan and Sawhney (2011) conceptualized the orchestration processes of managing innovation coherence, leverage, and—in common with Dhanaraj and Parkhe (2006)—appropriation as resulting from facets of innovation design (modularity) and network design (network openness and embeddedness).

Such activities reflect the evolving policies of MNEs to forge a range of horizontal links in addition to their traditional vertical links within their global value chain (Buckley & Strange, 2015). Proactive efforts are required on the part of SMEs as well to determine whether to participate in an MNE ecosystem and if so, which one(s). An important aspect of these decisions is whether to identify an MNE orchestrator ex ante or ex post. That is, the SME could decide a priori to build its offering to be compatible with a particular MNE's platform technology—or to build an offering first and then determine which MNE ecosystem to associate itself with. In either case, an SME ecosystem participant has to undertake the important activities that Schreiner, Kale, and Corsten (2009) identified: coordination, communication, and bonding in order for them to effectively navigate the ecosystem orchestrated by a hub MNE.

In terms of innovation, consistent with Nambisan and Sawhney's (2011) notions of innovation integration and platform leadership, respectively, MNE orchestrators have begun to undertake two important innovations: (1) in the technological realm, building platforms on which external firms (including SMEs) can build their own complementary offerings (Gawer, 2014; Gawer & Cusumano, 2002, 2014; Iansiti & Levien, 2004; Teece, 2007; Thomas, Autio, & Gann, 2014), and (2) in the organizational realm, developing systematic network entry points through, for example, the establishment of partner programs (Prashantham & McNaughton,

46   *Academy of Management Perspectives*   February

2006). MNE orchestrators use partner "services" both to attract SMEs to develop technology offerings using their underlying platform and to enable SME partners to enhance sales (through, for instance, online marketing support) of their complements (Nambisan & Sawhney, 2007). Such initiatives can be viewed as a form of "management innovation" on the part of the MNE (Birkinshaw, Hamel, & Mol, 2008).

For SME ecosystem participants, taking advantage of an MNE's partner services reduces the barriers to gaining access to updated information about the MNE's technology and business plans. This potentially results in the SME's efforts taking place under conditions of reduced asymmetric information between the two parties than has traditionally been the case. The SME's innovation may result in complements with respect to the MNE's technology platform—for instance, in the form of an app for Apple's iPhone or value-adding business process management software solution that runs on Microsoft's collaboration-software platform (Ceccagnoli, Forman, Huang, & Wu, 2012; Iansiti & Levien, 2004). As noted, the SME could decide a priori to build its offering to be compatible with a particular MNE's platform technology—or decide to build an offering first and then determine which MNE ecosystem to associate itself with (Boudreau & Lakhani, 2009). In either case, proactively leveraging the MNE's partner services makes de-duplication of innovative effort possible.

In terms of risk-taking, MNEs and SMEs bear distinct but interdependent risks: For MNE orchestrators the risks relate to undertaking ecosystem-building, which might fail due to high transaction costs and potential opportunism of partners, and to the potential that a disproportionately low value may be appropriated by the orchestrator. For SME participants there is a risk that their proactive partner selection choices prove to be ineffective—that is, they "bet the farm" on an ecosystem that proves to be unsuccessful (Iansiti & Levien, 2004). Alternatively the hub MNE may well be successful but appropriate the lion's share of created value (Alvarez & Barney, 2001). Another risk relates to the prospect that the MNE orchestrator diversifies into the SME's domain of activity, resulting in duplication (Gawer & Cusumano, 2002). This results in the SME's once-complementary offering becoming a substitute vis-à-vis the offering of the MNE orchestrator, thereby undoing the initial benefits of reduced information asymmetry through the MNE's partnering services.

Perhaps this is why expressions used to describe MNE–SME interaction, such as "swimming with sharks" (Diestre & Rajagopalan, 2012; Katila et al., 2008), "dancing with gorillas" (Prashantham & Birkinshaw, 2008), and "surviving bear hugs" (Vandaie & Zaheer, 2014), convey more than a hint of danger for the SME. It is conceivable that SMEs could be "eaten," "trampled," or "crushed" by powerful MNE partners. Thus, the prospect of a shift from cooperation to competition is one that SMEs within a global interfirm network must contend with.

Redressing Power Imbalance: Dialogue Between MNEs and SMEs

Although enabling engagement through orchestration/participation fosters mutual dependence, redressing power imbalance requires ensuring high-quality interactions that foster social trust. The structural trust associated with mutual dependence renders plausible (but is not sufficient in itself to fully realize) the potential for value creation through the division of entrepreneurial labor, whereas social trust stemming from mitigating power imbalance is vital to "the actual realization of the potential for value creation" (Madhok, 2006, p. 7) in interorganizational collaborations. The division of entrepreneurial labor in global interfirm networks is more likely to be effective when low-power actors such as SMEs are given—and of course themselves find—a voice within global interfirm networks.

However, the literature remains skewed toward the hub firm's "central, orchestrating role" (Gawer, 2014, p. 1239), and even when the SME's perspective is considered, the focus tends to be narrow, such as on sharing technical decision rights (Tiwana, Konsynski, & Bush, 2010) or on characteristics of SMEs themselves (e.g., their own safeguards and capabilities; see Ceccagnoli et al., 2012) rather than on those of the network as a whole. Our perspective is consistent with Geroski and Markides' (2004, p. 58) suggestion that "established firms must create, sustain, and *nurture* a network of young entrepreneurial companies [emphasis added]." This is important due not only to the vulnerability of the SME but also to the inevitable fragility of the interface—notwithstanding contemporary improvements noted earlier—between highly asymmetrical actors (Doz, 1988). Engagement within global interfirm networks must take into account the aspirations and apprehensions of all actors, including SMEs, through effective dialogue.

In terms of proactiveness, a key challenge for MNEs is the one-to-many approach taken in ecosystem-orchestrating processes owing to the sheer numbers of participants, especially SMEs, in interfirm ecosystems. Creating a dialogue in programmatic network initiatives is often practically infeasible. And yet there are weak signals of efforts to go the extra mile through, for instance, using sophisticated textual analysis software[3] to analyze audience feedback from both managed and unmanaged SME partners. Another proactive approach relates to the cooption of local trusted allies, including nonmarket actors (e.g., the local economic development agency), to provide the handholding for SMEs that would alleviate concerns regarding a lack of fairness and equity while dealing with a powerful MNE (Terjesen, O'Gorman, & Acs, 2008). Sun Microsystems' instigation of partnering support from regional institutions for local SMEs in Scotland illustrates this (Prashantham & McNaughton, 2006). For their part, some SMEs are also demonstrating suitable proactiveness in actively leveraging local allies including private intermediaries, such as the recently launched David & Goliath networking event series (Garland, 2014). Furthermore, they may cultivate internal champions among sympathetic MNE managers (some of whom might themselves have been previously associated with smaller ventures).

In terms of innovativeness, some MNEs supplement their one-to-many initiatives with one-to-few initiatives such as corporate incubators and other programs for highly innovative ventures that represent potential high-value partners of the future (Weiblen & Chesbrough, 2015). Microsoft is illustrative. It established a program called BizSpark One for a select group of 100 ventures around the world that could work with dedicated account managers for a 12-month period, and have since created accelerators in various parts of the world that provide selected start-ups an opportunity to be resident in these facilities for about four months and receive mentoring from internal executives and external advisors (one-to-few).[4] Practical constraints mean

that these are time-bound engagements, and yet the value for the venture can be considerable.

Importantly, the venture has a say in its own growth and development. For their part, SMEs may exhibit innovative ways of gaining greater visibility and a voice through, for instance, marshaling their limited resources to set up relationship management functions dedicated to the focal MNE relationship as a signal of commitment, and to build mini-partner networks of their own among peer firms within the interfirm network. Prashantham and Dhanaraj (2015, p. 15) described the efforts of Skelta, a venture partnering with Microsoft:

> [As] Skelta's international expansion gained momentum, the venture began building its own worldwide network of partners who acted as resellers in more than 20 countries. These included major markets like the US, the UK, Germany, France, Spain, and Portugal. These companies were typically, like Skelta, smaller firms that were deeply entrenched within the Microsoft ecosystem.

In terms of risk-taking, MNEs need to manage the potential fallout from SME partners, on occasion, defecting to competing ecosystems. However, the possibility of today's collaborator becoming tomorrow's competitor even among evenly matched actors (witness Samsung and Google's recent tensions) is well established, and so MNEs exhibit the willingness to take calculated risks by enabling, as seen previously, the participation of SME partners in their ecosystems. However, it must be recognized that occasionally renegade SME partners may have to be disciplined, even expelled; fostering greater dialogue does not provide license for abuse of trust. But ecosystems characterized by a dialogue-based approach are less likely to suffer the risk of ecosystem participants innovating in ways that are competitive to the platform in the first place (Gawer, 2014), as they win the hearts and minds of SME partners, which is important given the often fierce competition between interfirm ecosystems. Equally, SMEs must recognize that ultimately they are responsible for their own well-being through, for instance, safeguards of intellectual property protection and, less formally, through choosing how and when to disclose sensitive information to external parties (Ceccagnoli et al., 2012; Katila et al., 2008). Furthermore, they need to be thoughtful in dealing with the multiple competing goals they may face (e.g., seeking opportunities within versus outside ecosystems) when participating in interfirm networks (Nambisan & Baron, 2013). However, a key

---

[3] We thank informants at the U.K. subsidiary of a well-known American MNE; confidentiality agreements prevent us from sharing further details of this process of "listening," undertaken at a large scale.

[4] Over time, Microsoft incubators have evolved from an exclusive focus on proprietary technologies (e.g., Azure, a cloud computing platform) to a more "technology-agnostic" approach. Remarkably, a few of the incubatees that one of us visited were developing software on Apple Macintosh computers within that Microsoft facility!

point here is that when the division of entrepreneurial labor is well established and efficaciously managed by MNEs and SMEs, then risk is mitigated for all parties.

In summary (see Table 2), we make the following observation:

Observation 2: Realizing the potential for the division of entrepreneurial labor between SMEs and MNEs results from building interdependence in two ways: MNE orchestration and SME participation leads to mutual dependence, and MNE–SME dialogue to redressing power imbalances. Specifically, orchestration/participation and dialogue require distinct forms of entrepreneurial labor in the form of:

(a) proactive ecosystem engagement and voice-giving/finding, respectively,

(b) innovative platforms and communication process, respectively, and

(c) ecosystem risk management and dyadic safeguards, respectively.

THE WHERE: ADAPTATION OF MNE–SME ENGAGEMENT

Given that there are "profound variations of space" (Yeung, 2009, p. 218), we also consider the where of the division of entrepreneurial labor, which is influenced by the division of skills and competencies between the entrepreneurial pools—global and local—that global factories and SMEs draw from. The existence of localized pockets of entrepreneurial endeavor—entrepreneurial communities—is a location

TABLE 2
The How: Interdependence Between MNEs and SMEs—Two Distinct Facets

	Achieving mutual dependence	Redressing power imbalance
Missing market addressed	Information asymmetry impeding structural trust (Madhok, 1995)	Information asymmetry impeding social trust (Madhok, 1995)
Proactiveness	MNE: Creating an ecosystem - Managing knowledge mobility	MNE: Giving voice Creating a dialogue at both one-to-many and one-to-few settings, which may require being proactively initiated by the SME in the absence of readily available mechanisms for fostering dialogue
	- Managing network stability - Managing innovation coherence - Managing innovation leverage - Managing innovation appropriation (Dhanaraj & Parkhe, 2006; Nambisan & Sawhney, 2011) SME: Participating in an ecosystem - Coordination - Communication - Bonding (Schreiner et al., 2009)	SME: Finding voice Gaining visibility through, for example, cultivating internal champions and gaining traction for their innovative ideas
Innovativeness	MNE: Building technology *platforms* conducive to augmentation with complements developed by network members	MNE: Introducing innovative processes including corporate technologically neutral incubators to allow select new ventures to have an active say in their own growth and development
	Developing *management* innovations in partner structures to allow systematic entry points into ecosystem	In so doing "going the extra mile" beyond the hub MNE's platform leadership and innovation integration roles (Nambisan & Sawhney, 2011)
	SME: Building complements to MNE's existing platform(s) Doing so under lower information asymmetries due to MNE partner services	SME: Introducing innovative organizational processes, even within the constraints of their small resource base, such as creating an MNE relationship management function or building a mini-ecosystem comprising other SME partners of the MNE
Risk-taking	MNE: Risks related to undertaking ecosystem building; high transaction costs and potential opportunism; inability to appropriate the value that is created in the MNE network SME: Risk based on partner selection choices; "betting farm" on an ecosystem that may prove to be unsuccessful; risk of building complements if focal MNE enters the same product-market space, rendering it a substitute	MNE: Managing the fallout of potential rebels; the risk of collaborators turning competitors lessens given an empathetic posture toward SME partners SME: Adopting safeguards in terms of intellectual property protection and, more informally, maintaining suitable secrecy; additionally, managing risk by enhancing own capabilities

factor for the appropriate stages of global value chains. The existence of a local entrepreneurial culture is an attraction for global factories (Buckley & Casson, 1991).

An important insight we add is that global interfirm networks may have subtle differences in advanced versus emerging economies. Emerging economies possess weaker institutions than their advanced-economy counterparts. In the context of entrepreneurship this may be manifested in scarcer risk capital, weaker property rights, and fewer role models. Thus, although emerging economies have certain advantages over advanced economies, notably in terms of the costs at which entrepreneurs can access assets (Hashai & Buckley, 2014), missing markets are more acute in these settings. MNE–SME engagement in an emerging economy context may therefore witness some significant differences compared to what occurs in advanced economies—the context that accounts for the bulk of the research on this topic and related issues such as interfirm networks.

In relation to proactiveness, in a market like the United Kingdom an MNE seeking high-quality SME partners can leverage robust public policy initiatives to access partners via a reliable intermediary (Prashantham & McNaughton, 2006). By contrast, in an emerging economy like India, an MNE may have to create or strengthen intermediaries, such as Google's sponsorship of the 10,000 Start-Up Program launched by NASSCOM, the Indian software trade association. While Google may well support such initiatives in an advanced economy as well, these efforts make a more fundamental impact on the local entrepreneurial ecosystem in emerging economies.

From the perspective of SMEs, similarly, participation in MNE ecosystems in emerging economies may require nonobvious intermediaries. For instance, we have found Chinese SMEs partnering with IBM by cleverly leveraging Smart City initiatives to create enhanced services for urban residents using information technology—which on the face of it are not concerned with facilitating MNE–SME partnering but nevertheless do provide the opportunity to conduct joint activity with an MNE under the aegis of the local municipal government. This is in contrast to the more straightforward experience of Irish software SMEs attending Microsoft's worldwide partner conference as part of an Enterprise Ireland–sponsored delegation. Clearly, in both situations nonmarket actors play a particularly significant role.

In relation to innovativeness, partnering innovations such as corporate accelerators for start-ups play a more fundamental role in identifying and nurturing high-potential nascent ventures in emerging economies. Differences can be found in, for instance, the manner in which Microsoft accelerators in Seattle and London are able to feed off the robust local venture capital networks to identify interesting start-ups, whereas in similar Microsoft accelerators in Bangalore and Beijing, venture capitalists may leverage these accelerators to identify potential investments. In other words, this MNE feeds ventures to the entrepreneurial ecosystem in emerging economies rather than the other way around, as it does in advanced economies. From the perspective of SMEs, efforts to gain an MNE's attention in emerging economies will have to be more creative than in advanced economies because, more often than not, they lack the legitimacy or resources that stem from gaining an initial boost from a dynamic venture capital infrastructure.

In relation to risk-taking, in advanced economies the primary risk to engaging in technological innovation stems from failure to persuade the market of its merits and build a vibrant interfirm ecosystem, as in the case of Research in Motion (RIM), maker of the once-successful Canadian smartphone Blackberry. In emerging economies, by contrast, a rather more basic challenge lurks in the form of potentially dysfunctional competition—that is, the absence of fair play and property protection. Thus, the risk of being unable to fully appropriate value created is greater for MNEs and SMEs alike in emerging economies compared to advanced economies. From the perspective of MNEs, this creates additional constraints on the extent of the market. From the perspective of SMEs, this similarly means fewer incentives to engage in and benefit from MNE networks because the uncertainty surrounding the prospect of earning rents is magnified.

Based on the above and summarized in Table 3, we make the following observation:

Observation 3: Realizing the potential for division of entrepreneurial labor between SMEs and MNEs in emerging economies requires addressing accentuated missing markets in these settings; effective MNE–SME engagement typically substitutes for weaker institutions in emerging economies, but complements existing (well-functioning) institutions in advanced economies. Specifically, this calls for differential approaches in advanced and emerging economies to:

(a) proactive utilization of allies,

(b) innovation in partnering (e.g., accelerators), and

(c) risk-taking vis-à-vis the competition.

RESEARCH IMPLICATIONS

Contributions to Research

Our work integrates three key dimensions of the division of entrepreneurial labor between MNEs and SMEs in global networks—capability, connectivity, and contextuality—which helps to advance prior insightful work on innovation ecosystems in a number of ways, as we discuss below and summarize in Table 4.

First, analyzing MNEs and SMEs in the context of the *who* of global interfirm networks throws into relief the *capability* dimension of the division of entrepreneurial labor. We synthesize prior literature to highlight differential capability sets of SMEs and MNEs that are, broadly speaking, better suited to exploration and exploitation, respectively, and add to this the Smithian insight that the extent of specialization is associated with (expectations of) the extent of the market, which may help explain the sophisticated division of entrepreneurial labor witnessed in platform-based networks. Of course, each set of firms needs to deal with both exploration and exploitation, but nimble smaller firms are typically more adept at exploring new niches, whereas large

multinationals have the wherewithal to commercialize innovations at scale.

We provide conceptual enrichment of what is already an impressive set of perspectives (Boudreau & Lakhani, 2009; Dhanaraj & Parkhe, 2006; Iansiti & Levien, 2004; Nambisan & Sawhney, 2007) to place entrepreneurship—including actors' judgments about the fundamental scope of their business activities (Casson, 1982)—at the core of the global interfirm networks that MNEs orchestrate. While the competencies (Penrose, 1959) and dynamic capabilities (Teece, 2007) literatures seek to explain linkages by complementarities in capabilities, the differentiation of entrepreneurial labor goes further to offer a more comprehensive explanation because we can analyze proactiveness, innovation, and risk-taking as complementary characteristics of firms that cooperate across a division of labor. This differentiation-based division of entrepreneurial labor represents potential for value creation in global interfirm networks.

Second, our analysis of the *how* of global interfirm networks draws attention to what we might term the *connectivity* dimension of the division of entrepreneurial labor, which helps to realize the potential for

TABLE 3
The Where: Adaptation of MNE–SME Engagement in Advanced vs. Emerging Economies

	Advanced economy	Emerging economy
Nature of engagement	Complementing extant institutional support in local entrepreneurial ecosystems	Substituting for voids in institutional support for local entrepreneurship
Proactiveness	Engagement via readily available intermediaries an option	Hand-holding intermediaries or tapping nonobvious intermediaries
	MNE: Could proactively tap intermediaries for access to innovative SMEs that are screened (e.g., Scottish Technology and Collaboration Initiative)	MNE: Could proactively co-create screening processes to help intermediaries identify high-potential SMEs (e.g., certification program with India's NASSCOM)
	SMEs: Could use intermediaries that facilitate gaining a presence at MNE forums (e.g., Enterprise Ireland's SME delegation to Microsoft partner conference)	SMEs: Could obliquely leverage intermediaries with a different mandate to get at MNE partnering opportunities (e.g., the Smart City initiative in Ningbo, China)
Innovativeness	Partnering innovations such as accelerators that *feed off of* existing venture capital and other support	Partnering innovations such as accelerators that *feed into* nascent venture capital and other support
	MNE: Could narrow search to seed-funded ventures and accelerate their development (e.g., Microsoft accelerator in Seattle)	MNE: Typically broaden search to identify ventures and facilitate risk capital (e.g., Microsoft accelerators in Bangalore and Zhongguancun)
	SME: Gain entry into incubators, in part, to enhance the chance of gaining MNE attention	SME: Target partnering efforts at MNEs, in part, as quasi-VCs to compensate for scarce risk capital
Risk-taking	Intense (legitimate) competition may restrict market potential	Intense dysfunctional competition may restrict market potential
	MNE: Attracting partners becomes challenging when not perceived as successful, but competition is fair	MNE: Part of partnering efforts may include strenuous safeguards for intellectual property protection
	SME: Concerns about likely MNE success may lead to withholding wholehearted network participation (e.g., ventures with affinity to challenged Blackberry)	SME: Concerns about intellectual property loss may inhibit pursuit of greater visibility, close partnering (e.g., unknown ventures with sound bottom-of-the-pyramid offerings)

TABLE 4
The Division of Entrepreneurial Labor: Dimensions and Contributions

Focus	Dimension of division of entrepreneurial labor	Value addition to the literature
The who: differentiation	Capability dimension Differential capability sets of MNEs and SMEs that are better suited for exploitation and exploration, respectively; results in value-creation potential given positive expectations of the extent of the market	Analytical insight We build upon the Smithian insight that MNE–SME differentiation is shaped by expectations regarding the extent of the market to highlight the scope for MNEs and SMEs to both leverage their assets and compensate for their liabilities.
The how: interdependence	Connectivity dimension Differential approaches to establishing connections—orchestration/participation and dialogue—address different aspects of interdependence—viz., mutual dependence and power imbalance, respectively—and help realize the potential for value creation.	Clarity The insight that power imbalance warrants differential treatment—and is in fact exacerbated when there is mutual imbalance—helps add clarity by highlighting the unique importance and value of MNE–SME dialogue.
The where: adaptation	Contextuality dimension Differential approaches—acting as a complement versus substitute to the local entrepreneurial ecosystem—are required in advanced versus emerging economies, respectively.	Extension To the best of our knowledge, prior literature does not offer a sophisticated treatment of spatial differences in MNE–SME engagement, yet this is critical when considering *global* interfirm networks.

value creation in global interfirm networks. We clarify the differential entrepreneurial labor involved in different facets of interdependence: achieving mutual dependence (orchestration/participation) and redressing power imbalance (dialogue). Previous work has tended not to explicitly consider the possibility that the obstacle imposed by power imbalance may be even greater when mutual dependence exists (Casciaro & Piskorski, 2005). Unwittingly, then, despite fostering structural trust, orchestration/participation may enhance the vulnerability of power imbalance–induced obstacles leading to perceived unfairness on the part of low-power network participants (lack of social trust).

When it comes to fully realizing the potential for MNE–SME division of entrepreneurial labor, orchestration/participation represents a necessary condition, whereas dialogue is the sufficient condition. We go beyond considerations such as modularity and granularity as the architecture of participation (Nambisan & Sawhney, 2007) to emphasize dialogue that could (effortfully) yield other principles that Nambisan and Sawhney highlight but that cannot really be taken as a given: shared goals and objectives, a shared worldview, and social knowledge creation. Ours is a relationally holistic perspective that recognizes that although MNEs may be the primary orchestrators of global interfirm networks, smaller network members—notably SMEs—are not inert but rather active participants whose perspective should also be taken into account.

Third, by explicitly including the where of global interfirm networks we include the *contextuality* dimension of the division of entrepreneurial labor. Specifically, we extend the literature by highlighting the distinction between advanced and emerging economies, which demand differential approaches in terms of complementing versus substituting for, respectively, institutional support for entrepreneurship. Recognizing the division of entrepreneurial labor between MNEs and local SMEs is an important determinant of flows of capital, the development of the world economy, and individual economies within the global system (Buckley & Hashai, 2004). A careful analysis of the division of entrepreneurial activity across the boundaries of the firm is a satisfactory way of resolving the classic integration–responsiveness dilemma (Bartlett & Ghoshal, 1989) that eliminates duplication: What can locally orchestrated resources provide for us as an expanding MNE?

Our approach considers access to assets controlled by entrepreneurs outside the boundaries of the focal firm but does not concern ownership of these assets by the focal firm. Rather, it concerns coordination across the boundaries of the firm by division of entrepreneurial labor. Equity ownership, even shared in a joint venture, is only one form of cooperation, and it is one where entrepreneurial labor is joint rather than interdependent. Our analysis is concordant with Hennart's (2009, p.1448), which acknowledges the importance of the actions of "owners of local complementary assets." But in our analysis, these owners do not necessarily forgo (even part-) ownership to the MNE. As such, by focusing on the division of entrepreneurial labor in global interfirm networks, we offer a spatially sensitive account of MNE–SME engagement.

Future Research Directions

Our work suggests multiple research directions. First, our work could usefully stimulate research on innovation ecosystems (Autio, 2015; Nambisan & Baron, 2013; Thomas et al., 2014) in many ways. For example, in-depth case studies could explore how global ecosystems are created and nurtured by MNEs. Also, large-sample research could test the effects of architectural innovation to yield more precise understandings of how the design features of ecosystems affect outcomes for the hub orchestrator as well as more peripheral participants such as SMEs. Ecosystem dynamics is another promising area; longitudinal research could usefully attempt to explore the evolution of global interfirm innovation ecosystems. For instance, an interesting issue to consider is whether effective MNE–SME dialogue leads to the business model underpinning a global interfirm network becoming one with input from multiple participants rather than one that is dictated by a single MNE hub. If so, this would lead to a more holistic understanding of MNE-orchestrated interfirm ecosystems as entailing negotiated business models, rather than entirely imposed business models. That is, while the innovation integrator and platform leadership roles identified by Nambisan and Sawhney (2011) are certainly aspects of architectural innovation on the part of the hub MNE, distinction can be made between the ownership of the architecture (typically by the orchestrating MNE) and the ownership of the components (which will likely include participant SMEs). This might have interesting implications for business model innovation.

Second, our work holds relevance to internationalization process research (Johanson & Vahlne, 1977, 2009) and to research on international new ventures (Jones, Coviello, & Tang, 2011; McDougall & Oviatt, 2000; Mudambi & Zahra, 2007). By factoring in the division of entrepreneurial labor, we may be able to understand not only sequential internationalization—which countries are entered in what order—but also the gradual deepening of involvement in any given country. The first factor can be explained by the MNE's (biased) search

for complementary entrepreneurship, the second by increasing engagement with local entrepreneurs over time, involving mutual learning and possibly joint innovation. Our work renews calls for directing research at symbiotic relationships between MNEs and SMEs (Etemad, Wright, & Dana, 2001; Prashantham & McNaughton, 2006). Future research on the scope for MNE networks to act as pathways for smaller entrepreneurial firms to internationalize is a topic that merits greater attention from international business scholars (Prashantham, 2015).

Third, our focus on the division of entrepreneurial labor helps to break down the endemic methodological nationalism of traditional international business studies (Yeung, 1994). The global networks research stream enforces a much more fine-grained locational analysis focusing on cities and their hinterlands rather than a location in an undifferentiated country or territory. This brings the research much closer to the work on clusters. Not only is "place" important to entrepreneurs (i.e., the key location to operate), so too is "space"—the distance from key markets, key suppliers, or head office of collaborators, for example. Future developments of the division of entrepreneurial labor will emphasize location as a function of both place and space (Yeung & Coe, 2015).

Finally, the analysis of entrepreneurial complementarities also offers us a novel means of explaining the rise of multinationals from emerging economies. It has frequently been stated that such firms lack ownership or firm-specific advantages (Meyer, 2004; Pant & Ramachandran, 2012). However, they may be simply seeking foreign entrepreneurs with whom they can cooperate in the foreign country, possibly to serve as a launch pad for further internationalization. The analysis of the division of entrepreneurial labor thus affords an explanation of the internationalization of MNEs without competitive advantages. This fits well with the analysis of Chinese MNEs (Buckley et al., 2007; Hashai & Buckley, 2014) that are cash rich but lacking firm-specific advantages. The cash-rich nature of these firms enables them to purchase assets in foreign countries and to establish a base so they can cooperate with local entrepreneurs whose skills, knowledge, and experience then provide a springboard for global expansion.

PRACTITIONER IMPLICATIONS

The division of entrepreneurial labor described above calls for new managerial skills on the part of

MNEs and SMEs. Buckley (2012, p. 83) observed that "'Interface competence'—the ability to coordinate external organizations into the strategy of the focal firm, to liaise with external bodies and governments and to cohere these into a grand strategy—is at the heart of the skills necessary to organize a successful global factory." Juxtaposing the how and where dimensions can help to identify various interfacing skills of relevance to both MNEs and SMEs. In our conceptualization, the how can be thought of in terms of orchestration/partnering and dialogue, while the where can be categorized in terms of advanced and emerging economies. Taking advanced economies as the default location of firms, the starting point for most MNEs and SMEs is orchestration/partnering in local and proximate economies. Useful insight already exists on how this might be undertaken (Dhanaraj & Parkhe, 2006; Nambisan & Sawhney, 2007, 2011). Building from this base we highlight three processes: network deepening, network broadening, and network synergizing (see Figure 1).

Network Deepening

This entails moving beyond orchestration/participation to include dialogue in the core advanced economies in which MNEs and their SME partners operate. The ability to introduce partnering innovations that facilitate closer interfirm communication is key. An example we have previously touched on is the introduction of accelerators by various MNEs. It is intriguing that notwithstanding the rise of virtual digitized activities, the benefits of physical co-location among nascent ventures remain considerable, and interfirm networks increasingly recognize this. When executed well, both sets of firms are more likely to experience a sense of fair play in their dealings, which increases the likelihood that trust and goodwill are engendered in MNE–SME relationships.

Network Broadening

This involves expanding the geographic scope of orchestration/participation activities from advanced to emerging economies. This process may require significant adaptation because the deficits of local milieus in these settings will have to be compensated for. Mobile MNE executives based in advanced economies, some of whom have cultural ties to emerging economies such as China and India, may have a particularly salient role to play as

FIGURE 1
Network Processes Arising From the Division of Entrepreneurial Labor

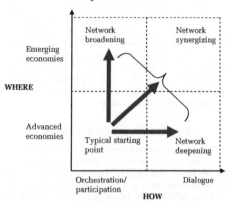

boundary-spanners not only in helping to transfer knowledge and practices to subsidiaries in emerging economies but also in acting as bridges that enable the MNE to understand the particular needs of local entrepreneurs and accordingly reconfigure orchestration activities as appropriate.

Network Synergizing

As network initiatives proliferate and dialoguing activities eventually make their way to emerging economies, it is plausible that an interfirm network possesses a suboptimally disparate set of partnering activities that must be better coordinated to ensure that they work synergistically together. At this point, a more top-down approach might be warranted to collate different bottom-up initiatives and create an organizational system, such as Google for Entrepreneurs, that enables efficient deployment of partnering practices to where they are most required. SMEs can also play their part by comprehending the MNE's partnering organizational system, which may well be located in the MNE's global headquarters to signal the seriousness being attached to such partnering.

That said, synergizing must not equate to rigid management because, of course, it is important to engage in network deepening, broadening, and (especially) synergizing without quelling entrepreneurial spirit within the network. Therefore, managers should not expect solutions to managing

54   *Academy of Management Perspectives*   February

the interface with other firms to be neat and tidy. That is, in strategic terms, global interfirm networks need not be coherent (or analytically neat). In the constellation of firms that make up a global interfirm network, each entrepreneur takes judgmental decisions about the allocation of the firm's own resources based on local knowledge and circumstances. Flexibility is definitely required on the part of both the MNE hub firm and the SMEs. The division of entrepreneurial labor will represent a shifting frontier between the firms; inflexibility is the enemy of a successful accommodation.

SYNTHESIS AND CONCLUSION

The capabilities required to ensure that the most value-enhancing division of entrepreneurial labor is effectuated are largely cognitive but subject to resource constraints. Our approach recognizes that the information input required is localized and costly. These two elements bring together our who and where as the entrepreneurs bring new order to dispersed pieces of information in new combinations (Schumpeter, 1934). Entrepreneurs explore their immediate environment—hence our emphasis on localized and sometimes culturally specific information. This exploration for information and its synthesis and incorporation into action (such as forming a firm, creating a market, selling a product) is the essence of entrepreneurship. In addition, profits accrue to those who preempt real opportunities in putting together new combinations of resources, giving us a partial answer to the how.

To exploit opportunities it is necessary to seek complementary resources, and here real asymmetries exist between SMEs and MNEs. The preexisting control of complementary assets provides a barrier to entry for SMEs and often sets the boundaries beyond which local entrepreneurs cannot venture, in part fixing our observed division of entrepreneurial labor. The entrepreneur, having identified an opportunity, needs to amass the resources to exploit it, and, crucially, to preempt other entrepreneurs who might also have identified the opportunity. This may lead to the creation of monopoly by tying up crucial resources by purchase or long-term contract (or by creating a new product). Restricting information by preventing dissemination is another strategy of preemption (Casson, 1985). The how, therefore, centers not only on resources but also on the acquisition and protection of valuable information and its synthesis into an entrepreneurial opportunity. Local and culturally specific knowledge will provide an area of monopoly for local entrepreneurs.

The division of capabilities to ensure the most productive division of entrepreneurial labor is therefore set by the following key factors:

- The relative entrepreneurial skills of SMEs and MNEs, including the ability to spot opportunities (which may have significant local and culturally specific dimensions).
- The relative ability to amass and control complementary assets (which may favor the MNE).
- The relative ability to acquire relevant knowledge and to protect it.
- The relative ability to preempt competition, which may favor the "deep pockets" of MNEs but which may be redressed by targeted local legislation or by local cultural practices.

These processes are cumulative; control of information, building a monopoly (or quasi-monopoly) position, and control of critical complementary assets all have a dynamic aspect, and may well eventually squeeze SMEs into only those areas requiring local and cultural tacit knowledge. This is not, however, an inevitable process across all global markets. These are clearly asymmetric, but over time they are not insuperable except where long-established monopoly positions control essential complementary assets.

To conclude, recognizing the role of entrepreneurship throughout the system, and not just in the focal firm, is an important step forward in the conceptualization of the global interfirm network. This contrasts with global value chain analysis (Gereffi, Humphrey, & Sturgeon, 2005), which all too frequently portrays local partners as inert and simply as price and quality takers. We call for an integrative—and possibly collaborative—scholarly effort to examine closely the division of entrepreneurial labor between MNEs and SMEs. Forming research teams involving both international business and entrepreneurship scholars may well be a practical solution to realizing the potential for making sense of intriguing issues—such as decision making; knowledge; management skills; and exclusion, collusion, and bargaining power—at the MNE–SME interface. The integrative research focus we call for addresses the concern that "an exclusive focus on the MNE makes little sense at a time when small and entrepreneurial firms are increasingly involved in international activities" (Shenkar, 2004, p. 165). Our ideas suggest that studying MNEs and SMEs need not be a case of either/or but rather of both/and. Both SMEs and MNEs can understand and identify the interdependencies in their entrepreneurial capabilities to achieve their strategic goals.

REFERENCES

Acs, Z., Morck, R., Shaver, J. M., & Yeung, B. (1997). The internationalization of small and medium-sized enterprises: A policy perspective. *Small Business Economics, 9*(1), 7–20.

Alvarez, S. A., & Barney, J. B. (2001). How entrepreneurial firms can benefit from alliances with large partners. *Academy of Management Executive, 15*(1), 139–148.

Autio, E. (2015, June). *Innovation ecosystems, architectural leverage and INV-MNE relationships.* Panel presentation at the AIB Conference, Bangalore, India. Video available at http://aib.msu.edu/publications/videos/conferencevideos.asp#year2015

Bartlett, C. A., & Ghoshal, S. (1989). *Managing across borders: The transnational solution.* Boston: Harvard Business School Press.

Baumol, W. J. (2004). Entrepreneurial enterprises, large established firms and other components of the free-market growth machine. *Small Business Economics, 23*, 9–21.

Bhide, A. V. (2000). *The origin and evolution of new business.* New York: Oxford University Press.

Birkinshaw, J., Hamel, G., & Mol, M. J. (2008). Management innovation. *Academy of Management Review, 33*(4), 825–845.

Boudreau, K. J., & Lakhani, K. R. (2009). How to manage outside innovation. *MIT Sloan Management Review, 50*(4), 69–76.

Buckley, P. J. (2006). International expansion: Foreign direct investment by small- and medium-sized enterprises. In M. Casson, B. Yeung, A. Basu, & N. Wadeson (Eds.), *Oxford handbook of entrepreneurship* (pp. 671–692). New York: Oxford University Press.

Buckley, P. J. (2012). The multinational enterprise as a global factory. In A. Verbeke & H. Merchant (Eds.), *Handbook of research on international strategic management* (pp. 77–92). New York: Oxford University Press.

Buckley, P. J., & Casson, M. C. (1976). *The future of the multinational enterprise* (Vol. 1). London: Homes & Meier.

Buckley, P. J., & Casson, M. C. (1991). Multinational enterprises in less developed countries: Cultural and economic interactions. In P. J. Buckley & J. Clegg (Eds.), *Multinational enterprises in less developed countries* (pp. 27–55). London: Macmillan.

Buckley, P. J., & Casson, M. C. (1998). Models of the multinational enterprise. *Journal of International Business Studies, 29*(1), 21–44.

Buckley, P. J., Clegg, L. J., Cross, A. R., Liu, X., Voss, H., & Zheng, P. (2007). The determinants of Chinese outward foreign direct investment. *Journal of International Business Studies, 38*(4), 499–518.

Buckley, P. J., & Hashai, N. (2004). A global system view of firm boundaries. *Journal of International Business Studies, 35*(1), 33–45.

Buckley, P. J., & Strange, R. (2015). The governance of the global factory: Location and control of world economic activity. *Academy of Management Perspectives, 29*, 237–249.

Cantwell, J. (2009). Location and the multinational enterprise. *Journal of International Business Studies, 40*(1), 35–41.

Cantwell, J. (2013). Blurred boundaries between firms, and new boundaries within (large multinational) firms: The impact of decentralized networks for innovation. *Seoul Journal of Economics, 26*(1), 1–32.

Casciaro, T., & Piskorski, M. J. (2005). Power imbalance, mutual dependence, and constraint absorption: A closer look at resource dependence theory. *Administrative Science Quarterly, 50*(2), 167–199.

Casson, M. (1982). *The entrepreneur: An economic theory.* Totowa, NJ: Barnes & Noble Books.

Casson, M. (1985). The theory of foreign direct investment. In P. J. Buckley & M. Casson (Eds.), *The economic theory of the multinational enterprise.* London: Macmillan.

Casson, M. (1987). *The firm and the market.* Oxford, UK: Basil Blackwell.

Ceccagnoli, M., Forman, C., Huang, P., & Wu, D. (2012). Cocreation of value in a platform ecosystem: The case of enterprise software. *Management Information Systems Quarterly, 36*(1), 263–290.

Chesbrough, H. W. (2003). *Open innovation: The new imperative for creating and profiting from technology.* Boston: Harvard Business Press.

Coase, R. H. (1937). The nature of the firm. *Economica, 4*(16), 386–405.

Dess, G. G., & Lumpkin, G. T. (2005). The role of entrepreneurial orientation in stimulating effective corporate entrepreneurship. *Academy of Management Executive, 19*(1), 147–156.

Dhanaraj, C., & Parkhe, A. (2006). Orchestrating innovation networks. *Academy of Management Review, 31*(3), 659–669.

Diestre, L., & Rajagopalan, N. (2012). Are all "sharks" dangerous? New biotechnology ventures and partner selection in R&D alliances. *Strategic Management Journal, 33*, 1115–1134.

Doz, Y. L. (1988). Technology partnerships between larger and smaller firms: Some critical issues. *International Studies of Management & Organization, 17*(4), 31–57.

Emerson, R. M. (1962). Power-dependence relations. *American Sociological Review, 27*, 31–41.

Etemad, H., Wright, R. W., & Dana, L. P. (2001). Symbiotic international business networks: Collaboration between small and large firms. *Thunderbird International Business Review, 43*(4), 481–499.

Forsgren, M., Holm, U., & Johanson, J. (2005). *Managing the embedded multinational: A business network view.* Northampton, MA: Edward Elgar.

Foss, N. J., & Klein, P. G. (2012). *Organizing entrepreneurial judgment: A new approach to the firm.* Cambridge, New York: Cambridge University Press.

Garland, E. (2014). David & Goliath dinner series. *Entrepreneur Country Global.* Retrieved March 24, 2015, from http://www.entrepreneurcountryglobal.com/united-kingdom/ecosystem-economics/item/fintech-dinner

Gawer, A. (2014). Bridging differing perspectives on technological platforms: Toward an integrative framework. *Research Policy, 43*(7), 1239–1249.

Gawer, A., & Cusumano, M. A. (2002). *Platform leadership: How Intel, Microsoft, and Cisco drive industry innovation.* Boston: Harvard Business School Press.

Gawer, A., & Cusumano, M. A. (2014). Industry platforms and ecosystem innovation. *Journal of Product Innovation Management, 31*(3), 417–433.

Gereffi, G., Humphrey, J., & Sturgeon, T. (2005). The governance of global value chains. *Review of International Political Economy, 12*(1), 78–104.

Geroski, P., & Markides, C. (2004). The art of scale: How to turn someone else's idea into a big business. *Strategy + Business, 35*(Summer), 51–59.

Gulati, R., & Sytch, M. (2007). Dependence asymmetry and joint dependence in interorganizational relationships: Effects of embeddedness on a manufacturer's performance in procurement relationships. *Administrative Science Quarterly, 52*(1), 32–69.

Hashai, N., & Buckley, P. J. (2014). Is competitive advantage a necessary condition for the emergence of the multinational enterprise? *Global Strategy Journal, 4*(1), 35–48.

Hennart, J.-F. (2009). Down with MNE-centric theories! Market entry and expansion as the bundling of MNE

and local assets. *Journal of International Business Studies, 40*(9), 1432–1454.

Iansiti, M., & Levien, R. (2004). Strategy as ecology. *Harvard Business Review, 82*(3), 68–81.

Johanson, J., & Vahlne, J.-E. (1977). The internationalization process of the firm—a model of knowledge development and increasing foreign market commitments. *Journal of International Business Studies, 8*(1), 23–32.

Johanson, J., & Vahlne, J.-E. (2009). The Uppsala internationalization process model revisited: From liability of foreignness to liability of outsidership. *Journal of International Business Studies, 40*(9), 1411–1431.

Jones, M. V., Coviello, N. E., & Tang, Y. K. (2011). International entrepreneurship research (1989–2009): A domain ontology and thematic analysis. *Journal of Business Venturing, 26*, 632–659.

Katila, R., Rosenberger, J. D., & Eisenhardt, K. M. (2008). Swimming with sharks: Technology ventures, defense mechanisms and corporate relationships. *Administrative Science Quarterly, 53*(2), 295–332.

Khandwalla, P. N. (1977). *The design of organizations.* New York: Harcourt Brace Jovanovich.

Kirzner, I. M. (1978). *Competition and entrepreneurship.* Chicago: University of Chicago Press.

Knight, F. (1921). *Risk, uncertainty and profit.* Boston: Houghton Mifflin.

Kuemmerle, W. (2006). Innovation in large firms. In M. Casson, B. Yeung, A. Basu, & N. Wadeson (Eds.), *Oxford handbook of entrepreneurship* (pp. 311–331). New York: Oxford University Press.

Lu, J. W., & Beamish, P. W. (2001). The internationalization and performance of SMEs. *Strategic Management Journal, 22*(6-7), 565–586.

Madhok, A. (1995). Revisiting multinational firms' tolerance for joint ventures: A trust-based approach. *Journal of International Business Studies, 26*, 117–138.

Madhok, A. (2006). How much does ownership really matter? Equity and trust relations in joint venture relationships. *Journal of International Business Studies, 37*, 4–11.

March, J. G. (1991). Exploration and exploitation in organizational learning. *Organization Science, 2*(1), 71–87.

McDougall, P. P., & Oviatt, B. M. (2000). International entrepreneurship: The intersection of two research paths. *Academy of Management Journal, 43*(5), 902–906.

Meyer, K. E. (2004). Perspectives on multinational enterprises in emerging economies. *Journal of International Business Studies, 35*(4), 259–276.

Moran, T. (2014). *Foreign investment and supply chains in emerging markets: Recurring problems and demonstrated solutions* (Working Paper 14-12, December). Washington, DC: Peterson Institute for International Economics.

Mudambi, R., & Zahra, S. (2007). The survival of international new ventures. *Journal of International Business Studies, 38*(2), 333–352.

Nambisan, S., & Baron, R. A. (2013). Entrepreneurship in innovation ecosystems: Entrepreneurs' self-regulatory processes and their implications for new venture success. *Entrepreneurship Theory and Practice, 37,* 1071–1097.

Nambisan, S., & Sawhney, M. (2007). *The global brain: Your roadmap for innovating faster and smarter in a networked world.* Philadelphia: Wharton School Publishing.

Nambisan, S., & Sawhney, M. (2011). Orchestration processes in network-centric innovation: Evidence from the field. *Academy of Management Perspectives, 25*(3), 40–57.

Pant, A., & Ramachandran, J. (2012). Legitimacy beyond borders: Indian software services firms in the United States, 1984 to 2004. *Global Strategy Journal, 2*(3), 224–243.

Penrose, E. T. (1959). *The theory of the growth of the firm.* Oxford, UK: Basil Blackwell.

Prashantham, S. (2015). *Born globals, networks and the large multinational enterprise.* London: Routledge.

Prashantham, S., & Birkinshaw, J. (2008). Dancing with gorillas: How small companies can partner effectively with MNCs. *California Management Review, 51*(1), 6–23.

Prashantham, S., & Dhanaraj, C. (2015). MNE ties and new venture internationalization: Exploratory insights from India. *Asia Pacific Journal of Management, 32*(4), 901–924.

Prashantham, S., & McNaughton, R. B. (2006). Facilitating links between MNC subsidiaries and SMEs: The Scottish Technology and Collaboration (STAC) initiative. *International Business Review, 15,* 447–462.

Ross, D. G. (2014). An agency theory of the division of managerial labor. *Organization Science, 25*(2), 494–508.

Schreiner, M., Kale, P., & Corsten, D. (2009). What really is alliance management capability and how does it impact alliance outcomes and success? *Strategic Management Journal, 30*(13), 1395–1419.

Schumpeter, J. A. (1934). *The theory of economic development.* New York: Oxford University Press.

Schumpeter, J. A. (1942). *Socialism, capitalism and democracy.* London: Allen & Unwin.

Sharma, A. (1999). Central dilemmas of managing innovation in large firms. *California Management Review, 41*(3), 146–164.

Shenkar, O. (2004). One more time: International business in a global economy. *Journal of International Business Studies, 35*(2), 161–171.

Smith, A. (1976). *An inquiry into the nature and causes of the wealth of nations.* Oxford, UK: Oxford University Press. (Original work published 1776).

Teece, D. J. (2007). Explicating dynamic capabilities: The nature and microfoundations of (sustainable) enterprise performance. *Strategic Management Journal, 28*(13), 1319–1350.

Terjesen, S., O'Gorman, C., & Acs, Z. (2008). Intermediated mode of internationalization: New software ventures in Ireland and India. *Entrepreneurship and Regional Development, 20*(1), 89–109.

Thomas, L. D., Autio, E., & Gann, D. M. (2014). Architectural leverage: Putting platforms in context. *Academy of Management Perspectives, 28*(2), 198–219.

Tiwana, A., Konsynski, B., & Bush, A. A. (2010). Research commentary—Platform evolution: Coevolution of platform architecture, governance, and environmental dynamics. *Information Systems Research, 21*(4), 675–687.

Vandaie, R., & Zaheer, A. (2014). Surviving bear hugs: Firm capability, large partner alliances, and growth. *Strategic Management Journal, 35,* 566–577.

Weiblen, T., & Chesbrough, H. W. (2015). Engaging with startups to enhance corporate innovation. *California Management Review, 57*(2), 66–90.

Yang, H., Zheng, Y., & Zhao, X. (2014). Exploration or exploitation? Small firms' alliance strategies with large firms. *Strategic Management Journal, 35*(1), 146–157.

Yeung, H. W.-c. (1994). Critical reviews of geographical perspectives on business organizations and the organization of production: Towards a network approach. *Progress in Human Geography, 18*(4), 460–490.

Yeung, H. W.-c. (2009). Transnationalizing entrepreneurship: A critical agenda for economic geography. *Progress in Human Geography, 33*(2), 210–235.

Yeung, H. W.-c., & Coe, N. M. (2015). Toward a dynamic theory of global production networks. *Economic Geography, 91*(1), 29–58.

Zahra, S. A., & Nambisan, S. (2011). Entrepreneurship in global innovation ecosystems. *AMS Review, 1*(1), 4–17.

Zahra, S. A., & Nambisan, S. (2012). Entrepreneurship and strategic thinking in business ecosystems. *Business Horizons, 55*(3), 219–229.

Peter Buckley, OBE, FBA (P.J.Buckley@lubs.leeds.ac.uk), is a professor of international business, founder director of the Centre for International Business, and founder director of the Business Confucius Institute, all at the University of Leeds, and Cheung Kong Scholar Chair Professor at the University of International Business and Economics in Beijing. He was president of the Academy of International Business from 2002 to 2004.

Shameen Prashantham (sprashantham@ceibs.edu) is an associate professor of international business and strategy at China Europe International Business School. His research focuses on new-venture internationalization, in particular how start-ups "dance with gorillas" (i.e., partner with large multinationals to improve their prospects of innovation and international expansion). He also has research interests in episodic strategy-making.

4

MBR
23,3

170

Received 20 August 2014
Revised 20 August 2014
Accepted 24 September 2014

The internalization of societal failures by multinational enterprises

Peter J. Buckley, OBE

Centre for International Business, University of Leeds, Leeds, UK, and

Jean J. Boddewyn

*Department of International Business, Baruch College,
City University of New York, New York, USA*

Abstract

Purpose – The purpose of this paper is to show that the market-internalization framework can be applied to non-economic institutions because society's non-market sub-systems – political, social and cultural – are subject to failures just like economic markets, and firms can contribute to their repair or replacement by selectively, strategically and responsibly internalizing the market and non-market arenas for these sub-systems' functions.

Design/methodology/approach – Internalization theory is applied to a new area – that of societal failures.

Findings – Internalization theory can be applied to the joint failures of economic and non-economic institutions, and this helps explain the growing "political role" of multinational enterprises in economies in transition as well as the phenomenon of increasing multinational firm activity in underdeveloped economies.

Research limitations/implications – The limits and implications of internalization are drawn in terms of theory development, legitimacy and managerial strategies.

Originality/value – This paper is the first to analyze the selective internalization of societal failures by the multinational enterprises. It extends internalization theory and examines the contested notion of "public goods".

Keywords Internalization theory, Multinational enterprises, Corporate social responsibility, Non-market strategies, Societal functions and failure

Paper type Research paper

Introduction

Public goods are normally provided by governments and not-for-profit organizations but we currently observe multinational enterprises (MNEs) substituting for failing non-market[1] institutions in a wide spectrum of societal functions (health, education, security, public utilities, roads, etc.) and geographic locations – what Scherer *et al.* (2014, p. 143) called "the business firms as a political actor". However, no comprehensive theoretical framework has been applied to analyze the important phenomenon of the MNEs substituting at times for non-market institutions, although we think it is amenable to the scrutiny of the internalization theory.

Internalization has been most successfully applied as a theory of the boundaries of the (multinational) enterprise (Buckley and Casson, 1976, following Coase, 1937). The unit of analysis is the transaction, and the firm's boundaries are set where the

The Multinational Business
Review
Vol. 23 No. 3, 2015
pp. 170-187
© Emerald Group Publishing Limited
1525-383X
DOI 10.1108/MBR-08-2014-0041

benefits of further internalization of the markets for intermediate products are offset by its costs. Overall, coordination is improved and profit accrues to the firm that beats the market in terms of transaction costs. However, this can only occur where markets have failed, so internalization theory proceeds by identifying market failures that rational managers can eliminate or perfect by absorption into the firm.

Internalization of societal failures

171

However, as Casson *et al.* (2009, p. 237) pointed out, internalization theory needs not be cast as if it applied exclusively to failing or missing markets in economic intermediate goods because it also applies to those intermediate products and services normally provided by non-firm institutions, such as the state and non-governmental organizations (NGOs). While current political economy recognizes the competition between firms and the state – as in the case of privatization – and between civil society's NGOs and firms – as in the supply of health care for workers and their dependents – it must also account for situations where state and civil society organizations are absent or grossly inefficient in providing public goods and in assuming the functions associated with the interests of all their citizen members as far as states are concerned and of those they serve at little or no charge in the case of NGOs[2].

Therefore, our analysis sets out to show the great analytical traction that can be provided by internalization theory to explain the integration of the markets for certain public goods and the assumption of particular societal functions by the MNEs in the international context of underdeveloped economies where non-market failures are more prevalent as expressed by the concept of "institutional voids" (Khanna and Palepu, 1997). Such internalization of the markets for public goods and societal functions is often necessary for the production and distribution of the private goods, which attracted the MNEs to these markets in the first place (Hillman *et al.*, 2004, p. 837). For example, referring to Gurgaon, an Indian city near New Delhi, Yardley (2011, p. A12) observed that:

> To compensate for electricity blackouts, Gurgaon's companies and real estate developers operate massive diesel generators capable of powering small towns. No water? Drill private bore-wells. No public transportation? Companies use hundreds of private buses and taxis. Worried about crime? Gurgaon has almost four times as many private security guards as police officers.

Besides, while the MNEs earn rents when markets do not function properly, they can also generate these revenues when they assume the functions of missing or inefficient non-market institutions as is revealed by the positive performance of the MNEs in various underdeveloped African nations (Henisz *et al.*, 2014) and of Indian business groups in under-serviced areas of their country (Fisman and Khanna, 2004).

Still, we need to specify the costs and benefits of internalizing societal functions and producing public goods. In addition, we must consider the limits of such integration of the markets for societal functions by the MNEs because some developmental governments in emerging markets – particularly, China – are presently re-asserting their public economic and political functions even though the MNEs will have to continue providing some infrastructural goods and services at production locations so that a new micro focus may well replace the current one on macro institutions. Based on the above issues, we will address the following research questions:

RQ1. What is the nature of societal failures – that is, what public goods and societal functions may not be adequately provided by society's main non-market institutions in underdeveloped economies?

RQ2. What factors explain that the MNEs can substitute for failing non-market institutions by transforming the missing public goods normally provided by the state and other non-market institutions into private goods supplied by the MNEs through the internalization of the markets for these institutions' non-market functions?

RQ3. What are the limits of the internalization of societal functions and how may it be compensated by the internalization of the provisioning of infrastructural goods and services at local production sites by the MNEs in emerging markets?

RQ4. What are the theoretical, managerial and legitimacy implications of this assumption by the MNEs of the functions normally assigned to the non-market institutions?

We will conclude that society's non-market sub-systems – political, social and cultural – are subject to failures just like economic markets, and the MNEs can contribute to their repair or replacement by selectively, strategically and responsibly internalizing the markets for these sub-systems' functions. This extension of the functions of the MNEs reflects their growing political role in economies in transition to a market system despite these countries' problematic distances (geographic, economic, cultural, psychic, administrative, etc.) from developed economies. While there are limits to the internalization of societal failures at the macro-national level, the MNEs can still provide public goods at the micro local production sites. The internalization of the markets for the non-market functions has strategic and legitimacy consequences for the management of the MNEs as well as theoretical implications regarding the application of internalization.

The following section examines the nature of societal failures and is followed by a discussion of the process of internalizing the markets for societal functions. The limits of this internalization are then analyzed before the theoretical, managerial and legitimacy implications of internalizing societal functions are discussed, and further research is considered.

The nature of societal failures

"Failure" refers to non-performance or sub-performance on account of factors preventing institutions, organizations and individuals from fulfilling their functions (Webster's Dictionary Including a Thesaurus, 1992). This concept has frequently been applied to market and political systems (Buchanan, 1988), but we need a classification of public goods and societal failures as well as of the mechanisms through which some form of selective internalization can occur.

The need for public goods

Public goods in such fields as utilities, education, health and security are essential for the existence, operation and performance of firms because without them, economic activity is either impossible or too expensive in terms of transaction and other costs (North, 1990, 2005). They constitute the *public* counterpart to Teece's (1998, p. 72) *private* "complementary assets" whose presence makes it possible for companies to derive economic benefits from the exploitation of their firm-specific advantages.

In well-ordered economies with secure property rights and contract enforcement, few public goods need to be produced by the MNEs, except when the provision of these goods constitutes their core activity (e.g. Blackwater's supply of security services). However, in underdeveloped economies, shortages of health and education services affect the performance of labor markets, while a lack of security and contract-enforcement mechanisms impairs local product and capital markets (Khanna and Palepu, 1997). Under such unfavorable conditions, the MNEs may have to produce or co-produce public goods as well as assist the development of local capabilities.

To date, the only treatment of the effects of the MNEs providing public goods has been in corporate social responsibility studies, which have brought up the questionable activities of private contractors hired to supply such services as security (Teegan *et al.*, 2004). These negative perceptions[3] have jeopardized these firms' legitimacy so that it is imperative to investigate what societal failures can be remedied in a responsible manner.

Societal failures' economic criteria
After World War II, the failures of some of the new nation states were commonly expressed through the economic concept of "underdevelopment" in terms of low per capita income and growth as well as deficient infra- and super-structures – hence, the use of such terms as "less-developed" and "developing" countries. Among the latter, "economies in transition" are so named because, in recent decades, they are moving away from either a centrally planned economic system or one dominated by large business group conglomerates toward economic liberalization through the privatization of state enterprises and the creation of publicly owned companies and independent intermediaries (Hoskisson *et al.*, 2000, p. 249; Khanna *et al.*, 2005; Peng, 2003). We will focus on nations still developing their economic institutions through a mixture of market means and governmental "dirigisme" but with NGOs assisting in the provision of basic necessities.

Societal failures' non-economic criteria
Nowadays, country ratings range beyond economic differences by including such "governance indicators" as political stability, government effectiveness, regulatory quality and the control of corruption, whose absence or deficiency reveals "institutional voids" – particularly, on the part of the state (Khanna *et al.*, 2005, p. 63; Kaufmann *et al.*, 2006). However, these rankings tend to overemphasize political factors at the expense of social and cultural ones, and they do not define the nature of failing societal institutions in a systematic manner but simply enumerate such evident shortcomings as weak property rights and poor contract enforcement.

In this respect, Rawls (1999, p. 23) categorized "peoples" as *liberal* if they share "a reasonably just constitutional democratic government" that serves their fundamental interests, citizens are united by "common sympathies" and they share a "moral nature". Conversely, there are *burdened* societies whose historical, social, cultural and economic circumstances make their achieving such a well-ordered liberal regime difficult if not impossible. Rawls' criteria are at once political, social, cultural and economic, and they identify the nature of societal failures, although they do not define the functions of

Internalization
of societal
failures

173

societal institutions – that is, the specific actions belonging to an institutional agent (Webster's Dictionary Including a Thesaurus, 1992).

These functions were categorized by Parsons and Smelser (1956) on the basis of general systems theory, and they pertain to the provision of *essential resources* which all societies must supply through *specialized institutions* to survive and preferably grow:

- *wealth* supplied by an economy;
- *coercion* exercised by the state and its agencies to secure law and order;
- *social integration* needed to achieve solidarity, cooperation and inter-unit conflict resolution through civil society organizations; and
- *cultural respect* (self-respect and the respect of others) necessary to generate meaning, validation, reputation and legitimacy for individuals and organizations through religious and educational organizations as well as the media.

Table I presents these institutions' functions and interchange mechanisms as well as their systemic failures which stem from the fact that all economic, political, social and cultural institutions and organizations are permanently subject to lapses from efficient, rational, law-abiding, virtuous and otherwise functional behavior (Hirschman, 1970, p. 1; North, 2005, p. 135).

Society's welfare is optimized when all institutions and organizations – those of the market, state, community and culture – cooperate and/or compete to repair their respective failures, although inefficient or ineffective organizations often remain insensitive to such interventions because they can tap other resources (market power, organizational slack, collusion, public funding, private ordering, nationalistic preferences, etc.) to survive in the face of decline. When institutional competition does not lead to the exit of inefficient organizations, political voice (petitioning, mobilizing opinion, protesting, contesting, etc.) is needed to change this situation, although internal loyalty is also available to compensate for the decline (Hirschman, 1970)[4]. We will now turn to examine the applicability of internalization theory to societal failures.

Factors affecting the internalization of markets for societal functions
Internalization theory deals with the boundary issue of why certain transactions for the provision of intermediate goods are governed in house, while others are handled in external markets or via alliances among independent suppliers. It explains why the MNE boundaries are set at the margin where the benefit of bringing further activity into the firm is just offset by the cost of supplanting external markets and alliances. Therefore, *under what conditions will the MNE's boundaries be expanded on account of the assumption of societal functions by these firms?*

The use of markets
Table I presented the major products, services and activities necessary for the functioning of contemporary societies – namely:

- the public goods (defense, transportation, education, health, security, etc.) traditionally offered by public agencies;
- the inclusion, solidarity and conflict resolution normally provided by civil society associations, societies and clubs; and

Societal subsystem	Political	Social	Cultural	Economic
Main modern institutions and their key actors	The state (governments)	Civil society[a] (associations, societies and clubs)	The culture as the validating and legitimizing community (schools, churches, media, etc.)	The market (firms)
Their key functions or contributions[b]	Authoritative decisions in the public interest and the generation of public goods	Inclusion, solidarity and inter-unit conflict resolution	Self-respect and the respect of others; validation and legitimization of self and others	Macro and micro efficiency in the use of economic resources
Their main interchange mechanisms with other sub-systems	Coercion, intimidation, control and influence	Cooperation, integration and trust	Moral commitment and the granting of legitimacy	Competition and rivalry
Their main systemic failures	Exit, avoidance and circumvention by constituents and residents	Exclusion, distrust, collusion and free-riding	Symbolic action, deceit, opportunism and fraud	No or imperfect competition and inefficiency

Notes: [a] Some definitions of "civil society" present it as an interest group mediating between firms and governments, as in the case of NGOs. Here, the emphasis is more on the social capital (*e pluribus unum*) that binds the members of a society and counters its disintegration. Thus, Brehm and Rahn (1997) defined "social capital" as the web of cooperative relationships among people that facilitates the resolution of collective action problems. The source of this modified figure is Boddewyn, 2012, p. 99); [b] these are the functions that can be internalized by MNEs

Table I.
Societal sub-systems:
Institutions,
functions,
interchange
mechanisms and
failures

- the validating behavior and legitimacy customarily supplied by cultural organizations (schools, churches, the media, etc.).

These non-market goods and services can often be obtained by the MNEs through the use of markets – that is, by the payment of taxes, fees, gifts and bribes to governments and community leaders, by purchases from private contractors when they exist and by donations to civil society organizations (NGOs, tribes, etc.) in expectation of reciprocal behavior from the recipients (Boddewyn, 2014).

For example, if the MNEs need security protection from local governments and goodwill from a local tribe, they can pay taxes, fees and bribes to public authorities and make gifts to that civil society unit. However, if these price system mechanisms fail, internalization may become necessary for securing the in-house production of these security and legitimization functions as a way of organizing the interdependence between the MNEs and the local non-market institutions. Thereby, the MNEs transform the missing or inefficient *public* goods into *private* ones, usable for improving performance and transferable within these firms.

Besides, markets may not be available because they may be suppressed by governments, supplanted by business groups or burdened with transaction costs so high that the cost of running them is less than their potential benefits. In such cases, relational contracting (Gupta, 2011) under a system of private ordering emanating from the civil society and culture allows many exchanges to take place even when the pricing is difficult, property rights are unclear or insecure, and the pursuit of self-interest is insufficient to guarantee orderly transactions free of malfeasance and opportunism (Granovetter, 1985). Deviance from approved behavior is sanctioned through ostracism from the exchange process and/or the withholding of legitimacy, which results in the denial of access to necessary resources (Ahuja and Yayavaram, 2011; Li and Filer, 2007). In any case, private ordering may co-exist with a strong government that exercises coercive force and tends to favor state enterprises – what is called "state ordering" and is evident in China.

The choice of internalization

A system based on relational exchange may exclude foreigners or be too complex and expensive for the MNEs to use so that these firms may prefer to provide by themselves the political *law and order*, the social *conflict resolution* and the cultural *validation* by internalizing the provision of these public goods and societal functions. In other words, it is the failure of the external interface which the MNEs use to transact with indigenous suppliers of public goods and societal functions that activates the internalization of the non-market intermediate functions of public coercion, social integration and cultural validation when the price system and private ordering have failed to organize the cooperation among the MNEs and the traditional host-country providers of public goods and of political, social and cultural functions. Integration is usually implemented through full ownership because equity joint ventures, mergers and acquisitions are impossible between for-profit and not-for-profit organizations (King, 2007, p. 898).

The internalization of both the market and non-market mechanisms explains why the MNEs can profitably invest in underdeveloped African countries when markets do not exist and relational exchange is either too cumbersome and expensive or unavailable to foreigners. The MNEs' boundaries are thereby selectively expanded as predicted

under internalization theory, which explains the integration of markets for both private
and public goods when private ones cannot be efficiently obtained and public ones are
missing or of inferior quality.

Internalization
of societal
failures

Internalization theory thus accounts for the assumption by the MNEs of
non-economic societal functions on account of the fact that the necessary internalizing of
market failures is impossible or very difficult when *non-market* societal failures prevent
or seriously hamper it. The MNEs thus focus on selectively internalizing the functions of
societal institutions that created the above institutional voids in the first place (Aulakh
and Kotabe, 2008, p. 212).

177

The legitimacy of assuming societal functions

Already, Drucker (1980) observed that the political system in every developed country
had become pluralist in the sense that central governments have become less potent in
the face of the growth of special purpose market and civil society institutions that have
progressively become carriers of social purpose, value and effectiveness and thereby
politicized. He stressed that business managers must also be political activists who take
the initiative, set goals and create vision instead of simply cooperating, responding and
reacting. They must build up their own constituencies and create the issues by
identifying both the societal concerns and their solutions and acting as contributors to
the common good rather than serving only the business interest. Drucker held such
activities to be legitimate because acute and widespread societal problems prevented
nation states from achieving higher levels of general development.

The recent debates about corporate social responsibility and relations with
stakeholders have converged toward a similar view. Thus, Palazzo and Scherer (2008,
p. 773) pointed to "the politicization of the corporation" that results from "the growing
positive and negative impact of corporations on democratic institutions and their
participation in global processes of governance with or without government" –
particularly, in many third world countries, where governments are either unable or
unwilling to guarantee the economic, political and social "citizenship rights" that have
provided legitimacy, solidarity and welfare to modern societies (Crane *et al.*, 2008;
Matten and Crane, 2005; Scherer *et al.*, 2006, pp. 505-506). Similarly, Hsieh (2009) argued
on the basis of Rawls' (1999) account of the Law of Peoples that the MNEs have an
obligation to fulfill a limited duty of assistance toward those living in developing
economies and a responsibility to promote well-ordered social and political institutions
in host countries that lack them.

Many scholars and activists, however, are concerned about the legitimacy of such a
strong political role for firms whose managers are neither elected nor democratically
controlled. They stress that having the MNEs design new global rules and enhancing
the administration of citizenship rights will be accepted only if these firms open up their
internal structures and processes to public scrutiny and offer transparency and full
reporting as well as participation and monitoring by outside parties to provide
"democratic accountability" (Scherer *et al.*, 2006, pp. 515-520). The moral legitimacy thus
obtained through public deliberation differs from one based on self-interest or
taken-for-granted values (Suchman, 1995).

This is, of course, a very tall order. As Williamson (2000, p. 598) observed, shocks,
threats, breakdowns, military coups and/or financial crises will "occasionally produce a
sharp break from established procedures", thereby opening "rare windows of

MBR
23,3

opportunity to effect broad reforms" of institutional arrangements. Scherer *et al.* (2006) as well as Crane *et al.* (2008) believe that we have reached such a point so that a political role for the MNEs as well as the NGOs is legitimate in the process of developing new global governance processes designed to craft order, mitigate conflict and realize mutual gains (Williamson, 2000, p. 599).

178

The limits and evolution of internalizing societal functions

Williamson (1985) also stressed that there are limits to the growth of internal markets and, therefore, of the MNEs on account of the costs and managerial difficulties of expanding a firm's internal organization beyond a certain point, and internal markets, like external ones, are subject to failures (Vining, 2003, p. 432). Consequently, internalization is always *selective* because of the resources it requires and the risks it faces – as illustrated by the difficulties encountered by the MNEs from developed countries in economies in transition where they cannot obtain market internalization's full benefits (Meyer and Peng, 2005; Peng, 2003).

Factors minimizing the need for internalizing societal failures
Actually, the need for the MNEs to internalize societal institutions' functions declines when the circumstances favoring internal integration change and/or decrease in importance. Thus, such "developmental states" as China have reinstated or reinforced their political role of making authoritative decisions in the public interest and of providing public goods (e.g. a national infrastructure of roads, ports and communication systems). Besides, in some economies in transition (e.g. India), the privatization of public agencies, the deregulation of economic activity, the liberalization of some sectors on account of globalization and the proliferation of NGOs have reduced the demand for the MNEs' interventions in the functioning or replacement of societal institutions at the national level.

In addition, the MNE investments in the provisioning of public goods in a particular country are necessarily highly site-specific, thereby precluding their use in other underdeveloped economies. Information asymmetry is acute, as it is difficult for a foreign firm to fully understand local practices, such as private ordering, and both the external and internal uncertainty surrounding the MNE investments is high because of the typical lack of stability in the host countries. The frequency of interactions necessary for internalizing societal functions is very acute, and investments are large relative to the returns that can be obtained so that both the actual risk and opportunism accompanying interactions with local institutional actors are pronounced (Rivera-Santos *et al.*, 2012, p. 1722). Such negative conditions and motivations favor *assisting* the development of existing societal actors and of private suppliers of public goods – whether for-profit intermediaries or not-for-profit NGOs (Boddewyn and Doh, 2011; Chen, 2010; Hennart, 2009) – in lieu of internalizing the provision of societal functions at the national home level.

The need to provide public goods at local production sites
Still, there is room and even necessity for the MNEs to provide public goods at local production sites rather than at the macro level of national institutions. These local public goods include:

- *the physical infrastructure*, such as roads, wells and electricity-generating equipment;
- *social services* like worker training and health as well as the provision of security in a plant's vicinity; and
- *institutional safeguards* against the market failures, inappropriate government regulations and poor contract enforcement found in emerging markets (Fisman and Khanna, 2004).

Internalization of societal failures

179

These goods, services and safeguards must be available before and during the production of the final products that originally attracted the MNEs to emerging markets.

Following Williamson (1996), we must consider the *transactional characteristics* of the provision of these infrastructural goods, social services and institutional safeguards in emerging markets. The investments needed for their supply are necessarily very *specific* because they must be provided at the plant where the production of the firm's private goods takes place, and they vary from site to site so that they cannot be leveraged anywhere else. There is practically no *external uncertainty* about the need for these public goods, as they are necessary on a continuous basis but *internal uncertainty* about the behavior of partners – particularly, their incentives to cheat, steal, hold up or leak – is high, which makes it difficult to ascertain their performance *ex post*. Thus, the host authorities can interfere with the provision of local public goods through *fiat*, while NGOs may decline to cooperate, as they are not motivated by the pursuit of profit and they may leak important MNE knowledge because of their preference for making the latter widely available (Bhanji and Oxley, 2013; Boddewyn and Doh, 2011, p. 351).

However, Geyskens *et al.* (2006), based on their meta-analysis of hundreds of transaction cost-based empirical studies, discovered that the effects of external and internal uncertainties are conditional on asset specificity being present in a non-trivial manner, in which case, a hierarchical governance mode prevents hold-up and other defections when a party's investment is exposed to control hazards (Geyskens *et al.*, 2006, pp. 520-522). In any case, the fixed costs involved in integrating transactions within the firm can only be justified if the volume of transactions is high enough – that is, if the transactions are large and recurrent (Brouthers and Hennart, 2007, p. 404). This is certainly the case with the necessary provisioning of public goods at local production sites on a continuous basis.

Ongoing and future developments
Two studies provide valuable insights about how local firms and foreign investors from developed countries handle institutional hazards in emerging markets. First, Fisman and Khanna (2004) found out that when faced with major failures in financial, labor and product markets, Indian business groups internalized the latter and developed special capabilities to leverage relationships with a variety of crucial institutions – such as obtaining Indian government subsidies and tax advantages through their superior political connections. This capacity is difficult to trade because it is embodied in an organization's knowledge, contacts and routines (Fisman and Khanna, 2004, p. 624) so that the MNEs may have to internalize the provisioning of institutional safeguards.

Second, Peng *et al.* (2005, p. 623) highlighted the lengthy transition of emerging markets to public ordering and a market system because these economies are still

MBR
23,3

180

dominated by business groups and state enterprises which perform well in institutionally underdeveloped environments – a situation conducive to private and/or state ordering (Peng *et al.* (2005, pp. 622-624). This situation favors the internalization of the production of public goods by the MNEs at local production sites as well as these firms encouraging and facilitating the transition of emerging markets toward a market economy and public ordering.

Looking further down the road, Peng (2003, pp. 286-287) envisaged that in a context of challenged privatization, liberalization and globalization, the internalization of the provision of public goods at local production sites by the MNEs will no longer be necessary, while foreign investors will tend to develop long-term relationships with local players and use indigenous managers to facilitate in-country networking and create a better fit with the institutional environment. Such a transition will take time, proceed at an uneven pace, vary by industrial sector, be affected by political and economic conditions in emerging markets and depend on the capabilities, motivations and decisions of autonomous public agencies, community leaders and NGOs (Peng *et al.*, 2005, p. 630), so that foreign investors must develop and maintain strong ties with the managers of local firms, politicians, regulators and community leaders for access to information, knowledge and resources (Acquaah, 2007; Peng and Luo, 2000).

Theoretical, managerial and legitimacy implications
We applied internalization theory to a situation seldom considered in international business research – namely, one where there is a joint failure of both economic (market) and non-economic (non-market) institutions. This situation is not uncommon in underdeveloped countries and emerging economies where key economic, political, social and cultural institutions are either missing or defective so that major public goods and fundamental societal functions have to be provided by foreign investors because, without these functions, normal business operations cannot be performed by the MNEs.

While local firms may rely on private ordering to substitute for missing market and non-market institutions, this alternative is not always open to, or manageable by, foreigners who must then do their own policing, infrastructure building, health caring for employees and the like. This is a major mission for private firms whose expanded boundaries become costly to operate so that the MNEs attempt to limit this non-market task to the sites where they operate by focusing on the provision of basic infrastructural goods (e.g. roads), social services (e.g. worker training) and some institutional safeguarding (e.g. contract enforcement via third parties).

Our analysis has shown that internalization theory can be applied to non-market institutions because the performance of non-market activities can be carried out by a range of both public and private organizations, which can use market, relational-contracting and integration arrangements for this purpose under different circumstances. Firms, such as MNEs, can take care of both market failures and institutional voids and thereby become both economic and political actors that contribute to both private and public interests in market societies and emerging economies (Scherer *et al.*, 2014, p. 148). Actually, these firms are also social and cultural actors to the extent that they assume solidarity, conflict-resolution and validating roles (Table I).

The managerial implications of our analysis are that the MNEs bring specific advantages to the task of promoting and developing well-ordered institutions – in particular, a variety of experiences and experimentations that are necessary if not sufficient to create the change in beliefs and habits that North (2005) considered essential for institutional change. The process through which new institutions are created is often initiated through the experimental actions of individual firms. In this respect, the MNEs are valued for their differences more than for their isomorphic conformity to local conditions (Kostova *et al.*, 2008), and they are change agents and social entrepreneurs that co-evolve with their institutional environment (Cantwell *et al.*, 2009).

To be sure, social entrepreneurship is an exacting task at which all-too-human executives, managers and employees will often fail – particularly, in the view of the novelty of the assignment. It requires at least a medium-term corporate commitment, which the vagaries of international business and foreign direct investment will sometimes preclude; it is a new function which short-term-oriented investors and boards of directors may not understand, and it is an initiative that entrenched interests and rivals (sometimes including NGOs) will oppose (Hsieh, 2009; Valente and Crane, 2010). In any case, it is only one of the ways by which burdened societies (Rawls, 1999) will progress toward well-ordered status, as international institutions (e.g. the World Bank), non-profit organizations (e.g. Oxfam) and local reformers also contribute to this essential project.

As Scherer *et al.* (2014, pp. 478-479) pointed out, private firms provide knowledge, resources and resolution to public issues but without democratic entitlement and control. Hence, there are legitimacy concerns regarding the provision of non-market societal functions by *private* firms that are also *foreign*. The first concerns the application of the profit motive in areas felt to be the domains of non-profit civil society and state providers. Even where public provision is failing and results in societal failures, private enterprise is resisted by those pressure groups who feel that some degree of failure (inefficiency) is preferable to the activity being performed for private gain. Health care and policing are prime examples of these areas of concern, and from this viewpoint, these public goods require public provision. Bhanji and Oxley (2013) labeled this problem "the liability of privateness".

The boundary where the private provision of public goods is politically acceptable also moves regarding the issue of foreign ownership which is often deemed illegitimate because of concerns over national security, so that policing, defense and key infrastructure provision (e.g. ports, airports, transportation) are of particular concern as expressed by *the liability of foreignness* (Zaheer, 1995). Therefore, trade-offs in efficiency versus legitimacy determine the firm's boundaries for *private* provision and more strictly for *foreign* private provision, although Palazzo and Scherer (2006) argued for communicative processes between companies and civil society to produce legitimate solutions.

Conclusion

The relevance of failures

The impetus for this inquiry was provided by the thesis of political economist Hirschman (1970) that all institutions and organizations fail at one time or another and that institutional competition and a mixture of "exit, voice and loyalty" are needed to repair their failures. Besides, our extension of the application of failures – a concept originally limited to market ones – found justification in the recent

Internalization of societal failures

181

analyses of "institutional voids" (Khanna *et al.*, 2005) and deficits (Palazzo and Scherer, 2008), although we emphasized their exploration and exploitation more than researchers who highlight them as obstacles to the development of markets in economies in transition.

On these bases, we concluded that:

- the selective internalization of societal failures is necessary for internalizing the market failures which explain the existence, operation and performance of the MNEs;

- the selective internalization of institutional voids and deficits is legitimate when accruing to the joint benefits of the MNEs and host countries as well as when democratically accounted for; and

- the remediation of societal failures provides focus and scope for non-market strategies designed to bolster the market strategies of the MNEs investing in economies in transition for their commercial opportunities.

We also noted that Buckley and Lessard (2005, pp. 598-599) deplored the current lack of "intermediate international-business theories" driven by contemporary problems – compared to the application of discipline-based theories (e.g. geographic locations and the resource-based view) that are not specific enough to explain important international issues. In this respect, our analysis has been *problem-driven* by focusing on the unexpected attractiveness of failing nation states to foreign direct investors from both developed and developing countries. Besides, relating non-market strategies to societal failures and their internalization has given theoretical substance to these strategies in lieu of simply describing them in terms of targeting non-economic institutions and organizations too often limited to governments.

The relevance of internalization theory
The handling of institutional failures in economies in transition has lacked a truly international theoretical underpinning beyond the attempts to apply universal theories of the resource-based and neo-institutional types to them (Peng, 2003). In this regard, internalization theory has proved to be provident by being already international in nature as well as applicable to a variety of market and non-market failures. This theory is relevant for handling non-economic failures precisely because being institutional in nature, it is directed at assessing the costs and benefits of alternative organizational modes – not only for the choice between external and internal exchange modes in the case of commercial products but also for the trading of new private goods (e.g. global governance processes) that corporations now supply in lieu of, or as partners of, the traditional providers of public goods when governments, civil society and culture-bearing organizations are too weak to provide them alone or at all.

Further research
Well-worth investigating is how *home institutional experience* is conducive to the positive assumption of societal functions abroad (Cuervo-Cazurra and Genc, 2008) and how different *motivations* – for instance, a feeling of moral duty on the part of firms versus their concrete need for local infrastructural goods and services – do influence the types of societal roles they are willing to assume (Scherer *et al.*, 2014, p. 152). In addition,

the use of philanthropic donations by firms to achieve institutional reform in host **Internalization** societies in lieu of internalizing societal functions there is worth a comparison. **of societal**

Through the increasingly available indices related to institutional failures, voids and **failures** deficits (Kaufmann *et al.*, 2006), it will be possible to investigate how the MNEs assess the importance of societal failures and the feasibility of their own interventions (Rondinelli, 2002, p. 409). Ghemawat's (2007) comparison of countries through his CAGE framework designed to reveal arbitrage and leverage[5] opportunities should prove useful in this regard – see also **183** Khanna *et al.* (2005) and their notion of "changing the contexts".

Our equation of societal internalization with corporate social responsibilities needs further demonstration along the lines suggested by Scherer *et al.* (2014), Scherer *et al.* (2006) and Crane *et al.* (2008). Besides, we need to better understand how the continuum between public and private goods changes over time (Doering, 2007; Kobrin, 2008; Mahoney *et al.*, 2008), thereby helping the MNEs internalize functions normally assumed by non-economic actors.

Our application of internalization theory should be compared to how various institutional, economic and organizational theories explain different types of societal failures and their internalization by the MNEs, NGOs and other societal actors (Lewin and Volberda, 1999; Meyer and Peng, 2005). Because the field of institutional entrepreneurship (Singleton, 2007) focuses on institutional change, it offers opportunities to study what factors condition, motivate and precipitate the interventions of the MNEs in the repair of societal failures (Boddewyn, 2008, pp. 5-8).

Finally, the restoration of institutions raises the issue of its impact on the market failures that underlie the existence, operation and performance of the MNEs (Heath, 2006). Reformed institutions could repair market failures and thus undermine, if not destroy, the rationale for these firms. However, the elimination of all economic and non-economic voids and deficits is improbable, so that there will always be scope for their internalization because, as Margolis and Walsh (2003, p. 296) pointed out:

> Even as business organizations may be imperfect instruments for advancing a narrowly construed wealth-maximizing objective, ironically, they may also be entities of last resort for achieving social objectives of all stripes.

Notes

1. According to Baron (1995, p. 47), "nonmarket" applies to the social, political and legal arrangements that structure interactions outside of, although in conjunction with, markets and private agreements. For Boddewyn (2003), this expression refers to the internal and external organizing, improving and correcting institutions that provide order to market and other types of organizations (including non-economic ones) so that they may function efficiently and effectively as well as repair their failures.

2. The 2008 Failed States Index produced by *Foreign Policy* and the *Fund for Peace* classified 177 countries along social, economic, political and military indicators based on data from more than 30,000 publicly available sources. Somalia ranked in first place but Israel was 58th on the list to reflect "deteriorating security in the West Bank, the country's sharp economic disparities, political stalemates, ongoing violence, and its failures to fully integrate its Arab minority" (Blitz, 2008, p. 4). Israel's surprisingly low score reveals that even democratic and market-oriented nation states can fail in institutional terms.

MBR
23,3

184

3. For example, the mishandled distribution of AIDS medications donated by the MNEs to a small African country may expose them to delegitimization challenges from local and international NGOs, that are quickly diffused everywhere by the media (Yaziji and Doh, 2009).

4. For Hirschman (1970, p. 77), *loyalty* refers to "that special attachment to an organization" which "holds exit at bay and activates voice" (p. 78) "in the hope or, rather, reasoned expectation that improvement and reform can be achieved 'from within'" (p. 79).

5. *Arbitrage* focuses on taking advantage of existing differences in national regulations, taxes, incentives and other instruments of public policy, whereas *leverage* emphasizes the creation of new advantages or the removal of old disadvantages for international firms (Kogut, 1985). Ghemawat (2007) proposed a CAGE framework based on specific distances among countries – cultural (e.g. language), administrative (e.g. regulation), geographic (e.g. proximity) and economic (e.g. purchasing power) – which can be used to compare nation states and/or evaluate them individually. The strategies he advocates (adaptation, agglomeration and arbitrage) are often designed to overcome national shortcomings.

References

Acquaah, M. (2007), "Managerial social capital, strategic orientation, and organizational performance in an emerging economy", *Strategic Management Journal*, Vol. 28 No. 12, pp. 1235-1255.

Ahuja, G. and Yayavaram, S. (2011), "Explaining influence rents: the case for an institutions-based view of strategy", *Organization Science*, Vol. 22 No. 6, pp. 1631-1652.

Aulakh, P.S. and Kotabe, M. (2008), "Institutional changes and organizational transformation in developing economies", *Journal of International Management*, Vol. 14 No. 3, pp. 209-216.

Baron, D.P. (1995), "Integrated strategy: market and non-market components", *California Management Review*, Vol. 37 No. 2, pp. 47-65.

Bhanji, Z. and Oxley, J.E. (2013), "Overcoming the dual liability of foreignness and privateness in international corporate citizenship partnerships", *Journal of International Business studies*, Vol. 44 No. 4, pp. 290-311.

Blitz, J. (2008), "Somalia tops list of world's most unstable nations", *Financial Times*, 24 June, p. 4.

Boddewyn, J.J. (2003), "Understanding and advancing the concept of 'nonmarket'", *Business & Society*, Vol. 42 No. 3, pp. 297-327.

Boddewyn, J.J. (2008), "Introduction", in Boddewyn, J.J. (Ed.), *International Business Scholarship: AIB Fellows on the First 50 Years and Beyond, Research in Global Strategic Management*, Bingley, Vol. 14, pp. 1-13.

Boddewyn, J.J. (2012), "Beyond 'the evolving discipline of public affairs'", *Journal of Public Affairs*, Vol. 12 No. 1, pp. 98-104.

Boddewyn, J.J. (2014), "Is reciprocity a market-entry mode?", Working Paper, Baruch College (CUNY), New York, NY.

Boddewyn, J.J. and Doh, J.P. (2011), "Global strategy and the collaboration of MNEs, NGOs and governments for the provision of collective goods in emerging markets", *Global Strategy Journal*, Vol. 1 Nos 3/4, pp. 345-361.

Brehm, J. and Rahn, W. (1997), "Individual-level evidence for the causes and consequences of social capital", *American Journal of Political Science*, Vol. 41 No. 3, pp. 999-1023.

Brouthers, K.D. and Hennart, J.-F. (2007), "Boundaries of the firm: insights from international entry mode research", *Journal of Management*, Vol. 33 No. 3, pp. 395-425.

Buchanan, J.M. (1988), "Market failure and political failure", *Cato Journal*, Vol. 8 No. 1, pp. 1-13.

Buckley, P.J. and Casson, M. (1976), *The Future of the Multinational Enterprise*, The Macmillan, London and New York.

Buckley, P.J. and Lessard, D.R. (2005), "Regaining the edge for international business research", *Journal of International Business Studies*, Vol. 36 No. 6, pp. 595-599.

Cantwell, J., Dunning, J.H. and Lundan, S. (2009), "An evolutionary approach to understanding international business activity: the co-evolution of MNEs and the institutional environment", *Journal of International Business Studies*, Vol. 41 No. 4, pp. 567-586.

Casson, M.C., Dark, K. and M.A. Gulamhussen, M.A. (2009), "Extending internalization theory: from the multinational enterprise to the knowledge based empire", *International Business Review*, Vol. 18 No. 3, pp. 236-256.

Chen, S.F.S. (2010), "A general TCE model of international business institutions: market failure and reciprocity", *Journal of International Business Studies*, Vol. 41 No. 6, pp. 935-959.

Coase, R.H. (1937), "The nature of the firm", *Economica*, Vol. 4 No. 16, pp. 386-405.

Crane, A., Matten, D. and Moon, J. (2008), *Corporations and Citizenship*, Cambridge University Press, New York, NY.

Cuervo-Cazurra, A. and Genc, M. (2008), "Transforming disadvantages into advantages: developing-country MNEs in the least-developed countries", *Journal of International Business Studies*, Vol. 39 No. 6, pp. 957-979.

Doering, III, O.C. (2007), "The political economy of public goods: why economists should care", *American Journal of Agricultural Economics*, Vol. 89 No. 5, pp. 1125-1133.

Drucker, P.F. (1980), *Managing in Turbulent Times*, Harper Business, New York, NY.

Fisman, R. and Khanna, T. (2004), "Facilitating development: the role of business groups". *World Development*, Vol. 32 No. 4, pp. 609-628.

Geyskens, I., Steenkamp, J.E.B.M. and Kumar, N. (2006), "Make, buy or ally: a transaction cost theory meta-analysis", *Academy of Management Journal*, Vol. 49 No. 3, pp. 519-543.

Ghemawat, P. (2007), *Redefining Global Strategy: Crossing Borders in a World Where Differences Still Matter*, Harvard Business School Press, Boston, MA.

Granovetter, M. (1985), "Economic action and social structure: the problem of embeddedness", *American Journal of Sociology*, Vol. 91 No. 33, pp. 481-510.

Gupta, A. (2011), "The relational perspective and East meets West: a commentary", *Academy of Management Perspectives*, Vol. 25 No. 3, pp. 19-27.

Heath, J. (2006), "Business ethics without stakeholders", *Business Ethics Quarterly*, Vol. 16 No. 4, pp. 533-557.

Henisz, W., Dorobantu, S. and Nartey, L. (2014), "Spinning gold: the financial and operational returns to external stakeholder engagement", *Strategic Management Journal*, Vol. 35 No. 12, pp. 1727-1748.

Hennart, J.-F. (2009), "Down with MNE-centric theories: market entry and expansion as the bundling of MNE and local assets", *Journal of International Business Studies*, Vol. 40 No. 9, pp. 1432-1454.

Hillman, A.J., Keim, G.D. and Schuler, D. (2004), "Corporate political activity: a review and research agenda", *Journal of Management*, Vol. 30 No. 6, pp. 837-857.

Hirschman, A.O. (1970), *Exit, Voice and Loyalty: Responses to Decline in Firms, Organizations and States*, Harvard University Press, Cambridge, MA.

Hoskisson, R.E., Eden, L., Lau, C.M. and Wright, M. (2000), "Strategy in emerging economies", *Academy of Management Journal*, Vol. 43 No. 2, pp. 249-267.

Internalization
of societal
failures

185

Hsieh, N-h. (2009), "Does global business have a responsibility to promote just institutions?", *Business Ethics Quarterly*, Vol. 19 No. 2, pp. 251-273.

Kaufmann, D. Kraay and Mastruzzi, M. (2006), "Governance matters v. governance indicators for 1996-2005", Working Paper 4012, The World Bank, Washington, DC.

Khanna, T. and K. Palepu (1997), "Policy shocks, market intermediaries and corporate strategy: the evolution of business groups in Chile and India", *Journal of Economics and Management Strategy*, Vol. 8 No. 2, pp. 271-310.

Khanna, T., Palepu, K. and Sinha, J. (2005), "Strategies that fit emerging markets", *Harvard Business Review*, Vol. 83 No. 6, pp. 63-76.

King, A. (2007), "Cooperation between corporations and environmental groups: a transaction-cost perspective", *Academy of Management Review*, Vol. 32 No. 3, pp. 889-900.

Kobrin, S.J. (2008), "Private political authority and public responsibility: transnational politics, transnational firms and human rights", *Business Ethics Quarterly*, Vol. 19 No. 3, pp. 349-374.

Kogut, B. (1985), "Designing global strategies", *Sloan Management Review Summer*, Summer, Vol. 26 No. 4, pp. 15-28, and Vol. 26 No. 5, pp. 27-38.

Kostova, T., Roth, K. and Dacin, T. (2008), "Institutional theory in the study of MNCs: a critique and new directions", *Academy of Management Review*, Vol. 33 No. 4, pp. 994-1007.

Lewin, A.Y. and Volberda, H.W. (1999), "Prolegomena on coevolution: a framework for research on strategy and new organizational forms", *Organization Science*, Vol. 10 No. 5, pp. 519-534.

Li, S. and Filer, L. (2007), "The effects of the governance environment on the choice of investment mode and the strategic implications", *Journal of World Business*, Vol. 42 No. 1, pp. 80-98.

Mahoney, J.T., McGahan, A.M. and Pitelis, C.N. (2008), "Innovation in the private and public interest", Working Paper, University of Illinois College of Business, Champaign, IL.

Margolis, J.D. and Walsh, J.P. (2003), "Misery loves companies: rethinking social initiatives by business", *Administrative Science Quarterly*, Vol. 48 No. 2, pp. 268-305.

Matten, D. and Crane, A. (2005), "Corporate citizenship: toward and extended theoretical conceptualization", *Academy of Management Review*, Vol. 30 No. 1, pp. 166-179.

Meyer, K.E. and Peng, M.W. (2005), "Probing theoretically into Central and Eastern Europe: transactions, resources, and institutions", *Journal of International Business Studies*, Vol. 36 No. 6, pp. 600-621.

North, D. (1990), *Institutions, Institutional Change, and Economic Performance*, Cambridge University Press, New York, NY.

North, D.C. (2005), *Understanding the Process of Economic Change*, Princeton University Press, Princeton, NJ.

Palazzo, G. and Scherer, A.G. (2006), "Corporate legitimacy as deliberation: a communicative framework", *Journal of Business Ethics*, Vol. 66 No. 1, pp. 71-88.

Palazzo, G. and Scherer, A.G. (2008), "Corporate social responsibility, democracy, and the politicization of the corporation", *Academy of Management Review*, Vol. 33 No. 3, pp. 773-775.

Parsons, T. and Smelser, N.J. (1956), *Economy and Society*, Free Press, New York, NY.

Peng, M.W. (2003), "Institutional transitions and strategic choices", *Academy of Management Review*, Vol. 28 No. 2, pp. 275-296.

Peng, M.W. and Yadong Luo (2000), "Managerial ties and firm performance in a transition economy: the nature of a micro-macro link", *Academy of Management Journal*, Vol. 43 No. 3, pp. 486-501.

Peng, M.W., Lee, S-H. and Wang, D.Y.L. (2005), "What determines the scope of the firm over time? A focus on institutional relatedness", *Academy of Management Review*, Vol. 30 No. 33, pp. 622-633.

Rawls, J. (1999), *The Law of Peoples*, Harvard University Press, Cambridge, MA.

Rivera-Santos, M., Rufin, C. and Kolk, A. (2012), "Bridging the institutional divide: partnerships in subsistence markets", *Journal of Business Research*, Vol. 65 No. 12, pp. 1721-1727.

Rondinelli, D.A. (2002), "Transnational corporations: international citizens or new sovereigns?", *Business and Society Review*, Vol. 107 No. 4, pp. 391-413.

Scherer, A.G., Palazzo, G. and Baumann, D. (2006), "Global rules and private actors: toward a new role for the transnational corporation in global governance", *Business Ethics Quarterly*, Vol. 16 No. 4, pp. 505-532.

Scherer, A.G., Palazzo, G. and Matten, D. (2014), "The business firm as a political actor: a new theory of the firm for a globalized world", *Business & Society*, Vol. 53 No. 2, pp. 143-156.

Singleton, L.G. (2007), "Institutional entrepreneurs: a comparative analysis of current empirical work", Working Paper, Boston College, Department of Organization Studies, Boston, MA.

Suchman, M.C. (1995), "Managing legitimacy: strategic and institutional approaches", *Academy of Management Review*, Vol. 20 No. 3, pp. 571-610.

Teece, D.J. (1998), "Capturing value from knowledge assets: the new economy, markets for know-how, and intangible assets", *California Management Review*, Vol. 40 No. 3, pp. 55-79.

Teegan, H., Doh, J.P. and Vachani, S. (2004), "The importance of nongovernmental organizations in global governance and value creation: an international business research agenda", *Journal of International Business Studies*, Vol. 35 No. 6, pp. 463-483.

Valente, M. and Crane, A. (2010), "Public responsibility and private enterprise in developing countries", *California Management Review*, Vol. 52 No. 3, pp. 52-78.

Vining, A.R. (2003), "Internal market failure: a framework for diagnosing firm inefficiency", *Journal of Management Studies*, Vol. 40 No. 2, pp. 431-457.

Webster's Dictionary Including a Thesaurus (1992), *Webster's Dictionary Including a Thesaurus*, J.G. Ferguson, Chicago, IL.

Williamson, O. (1985), *The Economic Institutions of Capitalism*, Free Press, New York, NY.

Williamson, O.E. (1996), *The Mechanisms of Governance*, Oxford University, Oxford.

Williamson, O.E. (2000), "The new institutional economics: taking stock, looking ahead", *Journal of Economic Literature*, Vol. 38 No. 3, pp. 595-613.

Yardley, J. (2011), "In India, dynamism wrestles with dysfunction", New York Times, 8 June, A1, A12.

Yaziji, M. and Doh, J. (2009), *NGOs & Corporations: Conflict & Collaboration*, Cambridge University Press, New York, NY.

Zaheer, S. (1995), "Overcoming the Liability of Foreignness", *Academy of Management Journal*, Vol. 38 No. 2, pp. 341-364.

Internalization of societal failures

187

Corresponding author
Peter J. Buckley, OBE can be contacted at: pjb@lubs.leeds.ac.uk

For instructions on how to order reprints of this article, please visit our website:
www.emeraldgrouppublishing.com/licensing/reprints.htm
Or contact us for further details: **permissions@emeraldinsight.com**

5

International Business Review 24 (2015) 1048–1060

Contents lists available at ScienceDirect

International Business Review

journal homepage: www.elsevier.com/locate/ibusrev

ELSEVIER

The principle of congruity in the analysis of international business cooperation

Peter J. Buckley [a,1], Adam Cross [b,2], Claudio De Mattos [c,*]

[a] Centre for International Business, Leeds University Business School, University of Leeds, Maurice Keyworth Building, Leeds LS2 9JT, United Kingdom
[b] International Business School Suzhou (IBSS), Xi'an Jiaotong-Liverpool University (XJTLU), Suzhou 215123, China
[c] University of Manchester, Manchester Business School, Booth Street West, Manchester M15 6PB, United Kingdom

A R T I C L E   I N F O

Article history:
Received 7 August 2014
Received in revised form 10 December 2014
Accepted 14 April 2015
Available online 16 May 2015

Keywords:
Alliances and joint ventures
Congruity theory
Cross-cultural behaviour
Managerial expectations
Negotiation and bargaining procedures
Strategic alliances in emerging markets

A B S T R A C T

This study investigates an under-researched topic: individual-to-individual or team-to-team interactions during the alliance pre-formation phase. We develop a general theory based on the principle of congruity for understanding the micro-dynamics of the alliance formation process. The attitudes of each party in an alliance towards their prospective partner depend on the level of mismatch between their initial evaluations of the contributions of each partner, and on their wish intensity and speed to reach congruity. The impact of different managerial cultural backgrounds (special theory) and mind-sets (special theory application) are theorised. Further applications are considered and all are presented as testable propositions.

© 2015 Elsevier Ltd. All rights reserved.

1. Introduction

Efforts to understand individual-to-individual or team-to-team interactions during the final alliance pre-formation phase are scarce. Besides game theory (e.g., Parkhe, 1993; Seale, Arend, & Phelan, 2006), a few attempts to further the theoretical understanding of the micro-dynamics of the process of forming alliances have been reported in the literature, such as theoretical models regarding the development of trust (see Bhattacharya, Devinney, & Pillutla, 1998; Fulmer & Gelfand, 2012; Jones & George, 1998; Kim, Dirks, & Cooper, 2009; Zaheer, McEvily, & Perrone, 1998). To date most alliance theories focus on the antecedents and consequences of alliance formation. Furthermore, calls for furthering understanding of the micro-aspects of intergroup interaction have been made in recent years (e.g., Ferrin, Bligh, & Kohles, 2008; Song, 2009).

In order to address these gaps, we offer an application of the principle of congruity to alliance formation. The principle of congruity (Osgood & Tannenbaum, 1955) proposes that evaluations or re-evaluations of objects by an individual tend to seek congruity with that individual's frame of reference. Subjective valuation differences have also been identified in other business contexts and models attempting to make compatible these subjective views have been put forward (e.g., Weingartner & Gavish, 1993). The exploration of alternative actions to forming a partnership is likely to increase the negotiating power of the actor (Malhotra & Gino, 2011), which in our case could mean higher disappointment with an evaluation from the other party in an alliance. In general, parties that develop a positive atmosphere or good rapport with each other are more likely to reach a mutually satisfying outcome (Jap, Robertson, & Hamilton, 2011). It has been also suggested that understanding the other party's frame of reference as well as using messages consisting of informational or relational content may help to establish a positive atmosphere (Chung, Sternquist, & Chen, 2006; Srivastava & Chakravarti, 2009). This closely parallels the ideas of Buckley and Casson (1988), who suggest 'mutual forbearance' as the key to success in joint ventures.

We organise this conceptual study into three stages. First, we develop a general theory based on the principle of congruity, and a reverse interpretation of that principle, extended to the case of alliance formation. Second, we develop a special theory considering

* Corresponding author. Tel.: +44 0 1613063413; fax: +44 0 1613063505.
E-mail addresses: pjb@lubs.leeds.ac.uk (P.J. Buckley), adam.cross@xjtlu.edu.cn (A. Cross), claudio.de-mattos@mbs.ac.uk (C. De Mattos).
[1] Tel.: +44 0 113 343 4646; fax: +44 0 113 343 4754.
[2] Tel.: + 86 512 8816 7746.

http://dx.doi.org/10.1016/j.ibusrev.2015.04.005
0969-5931/© 2015 Elsevier Ltd. All rights reserved.

P.J. Buckley et al. / International Business Review 24 (2015) 1048–1060   1049

the impact of cultural differences between the parties. Third, we present an application of the special theory—the case of different mind-sets between managers/entrepreneurs of developed countries and those from emerging economies. This novel extension of the above theory to the context of alliance formation adds to the understanding of the micro-dynamics of interactions between individuals (or between teams).

The use of alliance-based cross-border strategies has intensified in recent years in many business sectors (e.g., Gulati, Lavie, & Singh, 2009; McDermott & Corredoira, 2010). However, the success rate of transnational alliances (TAs) in general is low, with figures of 40 per cent and below commonly being cited, although in a few sectors (such as biotechnology) or in firms from a particular country (e.g., Japan) success rates are somewhat higher (see Delios & Beamish, 2004; Kale & Singh, 2009; Lunnan & Haugland, 2008). This is an issue of importance for organisations in general, since the costs of failure can be considerable (Wassmer, Dussauge, & Planellas, 2010). Moreover, in the case of TAs, it becomes even more crucial when other factors (such as cultural differences) have the potential to increase the likelihood of inter-partner conflict (see Barkema & Vermeulen, 1997; Marino, Strandholm, Steensma, & Weaver, 2002). Such situations could, for instance, increase the chances of differing evaluations of the contributions of each partner, which may lead eventually to a negative outcome. A strong relationship between partners should have positive effects on the venture's long-term results (Yan & Gray, 2001).

In our study, we propose that the attitude towards the other party is likely to be influenced by the congruence or incongruence of the parties' initial evaluations regarding the prospective contributions of each party (including one's own) to the alliance, and ultimately, this will affect the feasibility of the alliance. In other words, our theoretical framework sheds light on the micro-dynamics of the interaction between mismatched partner-contribution evaluations – a potential source of disagreement and dispute during the establishment of the alliance – and the attitudes of managers from the potential partner firms. Drawing on congruity theory, we consider a possible causal link between conflicting partner expectations regarding contributions to the alliance, together with the effect of the attitudes of the managers formalising the alliance towards each other on the one hand, and the likelihood of successful alliance formation on the other. Our theoretical approach assumes that incongruous expectations regarding partners' contributions amongst prospective partners have the potential to impact negatively upon the decision-making process of one or both parties at the time that the alliance is about to be formed and thereafter (cf. Inkpen & Currall, 2004). It may also have a cumulative effect on managerial judgement regarding the viability of such a partnership. One key factor for establishing and developing a successful TA between unrelated foreign companies is the ability to manage effectively those disputes that might later undermine the commitment of one or more of the parties to the agreement. One approach that should increase our understanding about the formation of effective alliances is to build upon a theory and framework that have originated in other domains.

The remainder of the paper is organised as follows. In the next section, we describe the principle of (in)congruity, its assumptions and prior usage. Subsequently, we develop a general theory, based on the principle of congruity, to inform understanding of the micro-dynamics of prospective partners' interactions in the alliance formation process. We go on to develop a special theory regarding the effect of cultural differences on the process of alliance formation. We then illustrate the special theory through a hypothetical illustration that highlights the effect of different mind-sets in the formation of an alliance between a firm from a developed country and a counterpart from an emerging economy

(e.g., a BRIC country). Finally, we conclude and propose implications for academics, practitioners, and policy-makers.

2. Background

2.1. Contextual issues

A key contextual issue in this study is business alliances between two firms, specifically transnational alliances (TAs). A business alliance between two firms implies a sharing of resources between the partners (Glaister & Buckley, 1996), and it is usually seen as an expansion strategy involving lower resource commitment, which in turn decreases perceptions of business risks associated with the new venture. The term covers a range of joint activities or commitments (Grant & Baden-Fuller, 2004).

A number of models have attempted to capture the intricacies of cooperative agreements, and may also be applied to alliances. Models of cooperation have drawn on a range of theoretical frameworks, from game-theory (e.g., Katz, 1986) and economics (e.g., Buckley & Casson, 1996; Contractor, 1985), resource dependency (e.g., Pfeffer, 1972; Pfeffer & Nowak, 1976; Van de Ven, 1976) transaction-costs economics (Buckley & Strange, 2010; Hennart, 1988; Ring & Van de Ven, 1992; Williamson, 1979, 1991) and strategy views (Fornell, Lorange, & Roos, 1990; Glaister & Buckley, 1996; Harrigan, 1988; Kogut, 1991), through to relational exchange (Dhanaraj, Lyles, Steensma, & Tihanyi, 2004; Kale, Singh, & Perlmutter, 2000; Zaheer & Venkatraman, 1995) and knowledge-based perspectives (Grant & Baden-Fuller, 2004; Hamel, 1991; Kogut, 1988). These theories advance the understanding of alliances by focusing on the antecedents and consequences of alliance formation. Nonetheless, they do not shed much light on the micro-level evaluations leading to micro-level tactical decisions just prior to the conclusion of the agreement.

A stream of literature associated with our topic concerns intergroup trust (e.g., Doney, Cannon, & Mullen, 1998; Lander & Kooning, 2013; Mayer, Davis, & Schoorman, 1995; McKnight, Cummings, & Chervany, 1998; Song, 2009). Our framework identifies micro-dynamic mechanisms during interactions prior to alliance formation. Those micro-interactions may lead ultimately to higher levels of trust between the parties; however, the scope of our framework does not presume initial levels of trust, nor does it attempt to predict outcomes beyond the alliance formation stage. We further argue that our framework differs from those frameworks that focus on trust, because the parties are not at risk (see Mayer et al.'s, 1995 definition of risk); the setting of pre-alliance formation assumes a voluntary process in which either party may walk away should they decide to do so (e.g., in the event of no prospective benefits being perceived from the agreement). Therefore, this condition pre-empts the notion of partner vulnerability and the associated need for trust.

Extant theorizing is less helpful in furthering our understanding of the micro-dynamics of alliances' final pre-formation stage, when the prospective partners' contributions to the alliance are evaluated, usually at team-to-team or individual-to-individual meetings, and the agreement about who is bringing what to the alliance is concluded. The expectations formed at this stage, which are the basis for the decision-making process, are influenced by different types of bias due, for instance, to the processing of information by each individual/manager involved, as well as by the interaction with other individuals/managers if they are part of a team (Carter, 1971). One of the key factors in establishing and developing a successful TA between unrelated foreign companies is the ability to manage effectively the disputes arising (Fey & Beamish, 2000) that might later undermine the commitment of one or more of the parties to the agreement.

2.2. The principle of (in)congruity

The principle of congruity (Osgood & Tannenbaum, 1955) was developed by social psychologists in the 1950s to explore instances of attitude change. Subsequently, it has been applied to or mentioned in the areas of politics (e.g., Brady & Sniderman, 1985; Kirkpatrick & McLemore, 1977; Shapiro, 1969) and consumer marketing, particularly in advertising and branding (e.g., Aaker & Keller, 1990; Olshavsky & Miller, 1972; Perkins & Forehand, 2012; Salciuviene, Ghauri, Streder, & De Mattos, 2010; Zhang, 2010). So far as we know, the present study represents the first application of congruity theory to international business cooperation. We should note here that the principle of congruity refers to individual action and it differs, therefore, from concepts of congruence or congruity at the organisation level, usually denoting strategic fit between firms (e.g., Bierly & Gallagher, 2007).

The essence of congruity theory is that changes in the evaluation of a phenomenon (or concept) by an individual are always in the direction of increased congruity with the existing frame of reference of that individual (Osgood & Tannenbaum, 1955). In other words, congruity theory predicts that a change in the attitude of one individual or party is dependent upon the degree of congruity between the assertions made by another individual or party and the former individual's frame of reference, as these assertions manifest themselves during interactions between the two. Here, the dependency of one's behaviour on the actions or behaviours of others in a negotiation parallels the concept of relational-self (see Gelfand, Major, Raver, Nishii, & O'Brien, 2006). We may assume causality in two directions. In one direction, say *positive causality*, individuals will tend to agree with those who hold similar frames of reference expressed by similar views or evaluations of objects or actors. In another direction, say *reverse causality*, individuals will tend to adjust their frames of reference to compensate for dissimilar views or evaluations of objects or actors held by others. Thus, in the former case congruity is achieved through holding similar views, whereas in the latter case (henceforth referred to as reverse interpretation) congruity is achieved by adjusting one's frame of reference to dissimilar views or evaluations regarding objects or actors.

The necessary participation of individuals (i.e., managers or executives) at the concluding stage of alliance agreements (even as part of a team) supports the use of psychology research on individual decision-making processes, such as congruity theory; this, in turn, can be expected to deepen our understanding of the final stage of the allying process. Social interaction among individuals, as well as the context in which these interactions occur, are the basis for the development of any theory in the social sciences (Bales, 1950). Our main purpose here is to hypothesise about a generalised pattern of behaviour regarding the conclusion of the alliance agreement.

Some of the general assumptions underlying theories on the psychology of individual decision-making such as congruity theory are as follows:

(a) Individuals (alone or as part of a team) will either take or influence decisions or both. In general, observable social phenomena comprise both overt interactions among individuals and the situation or context in which these interactions take place. It may include the self, other individuals and physical objects (Bales, 1950). In particular, we assume that, underlying the interactions that may be observed, there are interactions with the self which are not observable overtly, as interactions with other individuals or those with objects (Bales, 1950). We assume that interactions with the self-influence the decision-making process of individuals or, more specifically in our case, managers.

(b) Those decisions will draw on each individual's past experiences or knowledge-base and how each individual respectively processes and employs that information.

(c) Individual and/or team interactions between prospective partners will also generate information that will in turn be fed into each individual's knowledge-base as described above.

(d) If an individual is part of a team, his or her influence on the final decision regarding any item will also reflect the hierarchical structure and decision-making rules within the team. For instance, assuming a leadership structure, the attitude of individuals positioned closer to the team's decision-maker will have greater influence relative to individuals who are more distant from the decision-maker. This parallels ideas related to the effects of the homophily principle—ties between individuals brought about by perceived similarities (e.g., McPherson, Smith-Lovin, & Cook, 2001).

These assumptions lead to areas where current understanding is obscure, such as the dynamic process through which individual decisions are formed and how these influence decisions developed by the team through interactions within its members.

Although our study focuses on the micro-dynamics of interactions in the context of alliance formation, we make assumptions regarding the macro-environment in which these proposed micro-interactions take place, using existing conceptual frameworks. This should clarify the impact of critical macro-environment factors, which may significantly affect the potential testability of the propositions presented later in the paper, on our process model. It should also support the future testability of the model through empirical research. Further research should be able to systematically disentangle the proposed effects and validate the propositions outlined later in the paper. Such prior circumstances may mould the frames of reference used in managerial decision-making, thus influencing both process and outcome, and should highlight the boundary conditions and possible limitations of our proposed conceptual framework.

The context of our study considers a dyadic (two-party) alliance context rather than one associated with an alliance network (Koka & Prescott, 2002) or multi-party alliance (i.e. an alliance constellation) (Das & Teng, 2002). Within this context, we shall clarify our assumptions regarding the firms' social embeddedness (Hagedoorn, 2006), status similarity (Chung, Singh, & Lee, 2000; Podolny, 1993, 1994), the amount of inter-firm social capital (Inkpen & Tsang, 2005; Koka & Prescott, 2002), inter-relationships between organisational activities such as innovation (Stuart, 1998), and the existence of prior ties (Gulati, 1995a, 1995b).

First, considering the three levels of embeddedness of a firm as proposed by Hagedoorn (2006), and in order to keep our process framework simple, we assume with regard to environmental country-specific and industry-specific factors (i.e. environmental embeddedness) high complexity and uncertainty arising from local business practices (such as those in large emerging markets) and high-technology sector constraints and uncertainties (such as those in biotechnology sectors). Relative to the history of the parties regarding alliance attempts, (i.e., interorganisational embeddedness) as well as personal network links between individuals across organisations (i.e., dyadic embeddedness), we assume, for simplicity, the absence of any prior contact in both cases. These assumptions will adequately represent the case of firms from a developed country approaching emerging-economy counterparts in a high-technology sector for the first time.

The relative status of prospective partners is another factor that may impact alliance formation prospects. Chung et al. (2000) suggest that the relative status of prospective partners is usually assessed prior to alliance-formation attempts. The perceived quality of a firm's products is a measure of the status of such

P.J. Buckley et al./International Business Review 24 (2015) 1048–1060   1051

firms (Podolny, 1993). The simplest assumption in this case, and the one we adopt, will be of equal status between partners. One may argue, however, that status will depend on the social dynamics of a specific business environment; for instance, a local firm may have high status locally, without being known in broader contexts (e.g. the global environment). We therefore assume that whatever differences may exist in status between two firms, this will be considered as part of the potential contributions firms may offer to, or aim to retrieve as a benefit from, the partnership.

A further factor that may affect efforts to create and alliance concerns the amount of inter-firm social capital, which emphasises the benefits harvested through previous social links (Portes, 1998), highlighting rational individual decision-making and motivation within the constraints of a social environment (Coleman, 1988). Benefits accrued through social links, such as access to relevant information, may facilitate the establishment of an alliance, particularly if they support the process of generating or strengthening trust, concomitantly curbing opportunism (Inkpen & Tsang, 2005). Social capital associated with an alliance network may support, for instance, the selection of appropriate partners, skilled in relevant capabilities and resources (Gulati, 1995a); it should also positively affect knowledge transfer between partners after the alliance is established (Koka & Prescott, 2002). The perceived mutual benefits to be realised through sharing resources may in turn strengthen the positive drive towards alliance formation (Gulati, 1995a).

In this study, each area of knowledge potentially available through an alliance, such as knowledge on alliance or network management practices or novel technology (Inkpen & Tsang, 2005), may be seen as a contribution from one of the partners to the alliance and should generate expectations regarding its value and impact. Aiming to simplify our model, we assume that intra-firm social capital is non-existent, or in the initial phases of development—in other words, a situation characterised by an abundance of 'structural holes' (Burt, 1997), which increases the potential opportunities for establishing value-adding intra-firm links. We further assume that the interacting firms are aware of the limitations that each may carry into the alliance and the benefits they may achieve by accessing their partner's capabilities and resources through the alliance. Such arguments are popular among resource-dependence theorists. If each opportunity for beneficial resource-sharing is seen as a potential contribution to the alliance, what differs is the importance or value assigned to each potential contribution. This is the gap investigated in this study.

In addition, the similarity of firms' technological bases should affect alliance formation positively (Mowery, Oxley, & Silverman, 1998), as there should be a stronger mutual understanding of the technology to be shared through alliance (Stuart, 1998). Moreover, not only may technology be a potential contribution, but the firm's capacity to absorb a particular technology (Cohen & Levinthal, 1990) may be seen as a contribution to the ultimate goal of forming an effective alliance. Our assumption here is that both knowledge and the capacity to absorb it exist respectively at specified levels, and they are perceived as prospective contributions and considered as such in our process framework.

Another factor that may influence alliance formation is the level of similarity in inter-firm status (Podolny, 1994; Chung et al., 2000; Shipilov, Li, & Greve, 2011), as well as a firm's accumulation of status through links with better-known players (Shipilov & Li, 2008). Current understanding suggests that uncertain environments tend to be associated with alliance formation between firms of similar status, although this trend may only be observed if the level of economic activity in a particular market is in decline (Collet & Philippe, 2014). Considering international alliances, it is challenging to ascertain a measure of a firm's status because of the contextual importance of local versus international standing.

However, it would seem reasonable to assume that a firm will only contemplate firms above a certain status level as prospective matches, even if only considering the local context. For instance, a foreign partner will most likely consider allying with one of the top local firms, even though they may not have any significant international standing.

Finally, a history of previous alliances will also tend to affect collaboration prospects positively (Gulati, 1995b). This seems to be the case when such previous ties are conducted and concluded successfully and without major conflict. Cases where a firm is removed from consideration as a prospective partner due to conflict generated in previous interactions have not been investigated to our knowledge, although such action might reasonably be expected. For simplification, our assumption here is that there has been no business interaction prior to the attempt that serves as context to this study. Although we exclude here firms that have had previous ties, we acknowledge that some past connections of a social rather than business nature may exist, even if such connections were generated through the business-deal initiative under scrutiny. We might expect that the non-existence of prior ties could work as a deeper underlying factor regarding the level of mismatch in critical evaluation of the contributions of each partner, the magnitude and scope of the wish intensity and the speed of searching congruence.

In order to further simplify our model, we assume that each party follows a leader or decision-maker whose attitudes and opinions drive the sequence of interactions towards a possible agreement. By doing this, we focus on one individual's (the leader) decision-making process rather than that of the team. One implication of congruity theory is that individuals are likely to place greater importance or value on people who hold beliefs that are more congruent with their own belief system or frame of reference. These assumptions may be made more complex at a later stage of the theory-building process.

3. Model development

3.1. A general theory: Application of congruity theory to alliance formation

In this section we first extend congruity theory to alliance formation using a reverse interpretation. We demonstrate our proposition by making a small number of assumptions in order to simplify the model and to allow us to focus on the essence of our interpretation of the principle of congruity. Finally, we include possible mediator variables and derive a general theory. We look at the interaction between managers considering their valuation of the contributions of each partner and their attitude towards the other party. We propose that, *ceteris paribus*, different sequences of micro-interactions may lead to diverse (even opposing) likely outcomes. Our proposed approach using congruity theory addresses the knowledge gap regarding individual-to-individual or team-to-team interactions in the concluding stages of alliance pre-formation, when the final agreement regarding the partners' contributions to the alliance is reached. In other words, the congruity approach allows us to predict the micro-dynamics of the interaction of managers prior to finalising an alliance agreement.

Analysis using congruity theory can be extended to the case of dyadic (two-party) business alliance formation by considering the attitudes of both partners towards each other, together with their evaluations of the contributions they expect to bring to the alliance, as well as of those contributions they expect from the potential alliance partner. The attitude of one prospective alliance Partner (P1) (i.e. an individual or team within that firm) towards another prospective alliance Partner (P2) is dependent on the cumulative effect of the (in)congruity of P1's attitudes towards a

P.J. Buckley et al./International Business Review 24 (2015) 1048–1060

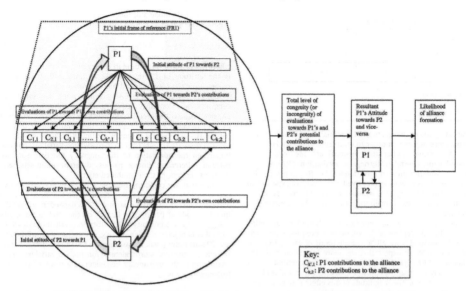

Fig. 1. Influence of congruity of evaluations/expectations regarding partner contributions and likelihood of alliance formation.

number of objects of judgement and P2's attitudes towards the same objects. Thus, we may define the initial Frame of Reference of P1 (FR1) in the context of a dyadic alliance as the initial attitude of P1 towards P2 ($A_{1,2}$), together with the original attitude (or evaluation) ($t = 0$) of P1 towards the k potential contributions (C_k) to the alliance by P2, plus the original attitude ($t = 0$) of P1 towards their own k' potential contributions ($C_{k'}$) to the alliance. Thus, FR1 comprises $A_{1,2}$ as well as $A_{t = 0,i = 1,Ck,j}$ (where A stands for attitude; "$t = 0$" for time "0" or initial attitude; "$i = 1$" for P1; and "j" takes values of "1"—relative to P1, and "2"—relative to P2) (see Fig. 1). We also define the congruity of attitudes between P1 and P2 towards the contribution k of P2 ($CA_{Ck,2}$) and the contribution k' of P1 ($CA_{Ck',1}$). The Total Attitude Congruency for a two-party alliance will be a function of the added effects of $CA_{Ck',1}$ and $CA_{Ck,2}$, that is, $CA_{total} = f(CA_{Ck',1}; CA_{Ck,2})$ or, assuming a cumulative linear effect, $CA_{total} = \sum_k CA_{Ck,1} + \sum_{k'} CA_{Ck,2}$. In other words, the attitude of P1 towards P2 at a certain point in time ($t = 1$) depends on the initial attitude of P1 towards P2 (i.e., $t = 0$) plus the effect of the (in)congruence of various attitudes (i.e., based on subjective evaluations) between P1 and P2 towards items or features linked to the deal—for simplicity in our case the prospective contributions of each partner. This can be expressed as: $A_{t = 1,1,2} = A_{t = 0,1,2} + CA_{total}$, where $CA_{total} = \sum_k CA_{Ck,1} + \sum_{k'} CA_{Ck,2}$, where: $A_{t = 1,1,2}$ is the attitude of P1 towards P2 at time $t = 1$, and $A_{t = 0,1,2}$ is the attitude of P1 towards P2 at time $t = 0$, and CA_{total} is the overall congruence between the attitudes of P1 ($A_{Ck,1}$) and P2 ($A_{Ck,2}$) regarding contributions of each partner ($C_{k'}$ and C_k) and assuming a cumulative linear effect.

Following the principle of congruity, these changes of attitude may be generated by the degree of conformity or match between P1's initial expectations regarding each partner's contribution and P2's expectations, regarding, respectively, each of those contributions. A simplified demonstration follows.

Let us further assume that the initial attitude of P1 towards P2 is neutral ($A_{1,2} = 0$)—a realistic assumption when firms attempt to

establish an alliance for the first time. Should P1 possess any negative information about P2, P1 will not proceed with the arrangement. Consider the possible attitudes of both partners regarding contribution 1 of P2 ($C_{1,2}$). Let us further consider only two possible attitudes favourable or positive (+1), and indifferent or neutral (0).[1] If P1's attitude towards P2 is initially neutral, we can focus our attention on the congruence of attitudes between P1 and P2 towards the alliance partners' contributions. Both partners could potentially bring to the alliance 'k' different contributions and each partner would have an initial expectation considering each respective contribution by each partner.

Next, we focus attention on the original attitudes towards the contributions of each partner. Table 1 illustrates possible congruity or incongruity of expectations between partners regarding Contribution 1 of P2 ($C_{1,2}$), as well as the resultant levels of congruity or incongruity. Based on the principle of congruity, we would expect that instances where there is congruence regarding the indifferent evaluation of $C_{1,2}$ (lower right cell) will not cause any change in P1's frame of reference. Instances where there is congruity about favourable perspectives (upper left cell) should affect positively P2's image in P1's frame of reference. The instances of incongruity (lower left and upper right cells) indicate conflicting perceptions or evaluations and should influence negatively P1's perception of P2 within P1's frame of reference. This procedure can be repeated for each of the k contributions of Partner 2 ($CA_{Ck,2}$), and, assuming a cumulative linear effect, will result in a Total Attitude (In)Congruence of $CA_{total} = \sum_k CA_{Ck,2}$.

According to the principle of congruity, the tendency is to reach maximum congruity with one's frame of reference. Taking as an example the situation indicated by the lower left cell (i.e., one of the incongruous instances), P2's assertion regarding $C_{1,2}$ conflicts with P1's initial frame of reference. Assuming that attitudes

---

[1] This approach simplifies the three-level approach adopted in previous studies (e.g., Tannenbaum, 1956).

Table 1
Possible congruence of evaluations in a two level model.

$CA_{1,2,C1,2}$	$A_{2,C1,2}$ [a]		
		+	0
$A_{1,C1,2}$ [b]	+	0 [c]	-1
	0	-1	0

[a] P2 attitude towards $C_{1,2}$.
[b] P1 attitude towards $C_{1,2}$.
[c] '0' = congruous, '–1' = incongruous.

towards $C_{1,2}$ do not change, then P1's evaluation of P2 will tend to become more negative in order to reach congruity (see Fig. 2 for $t = 1$). A negative (rather than neutral) attitude towards P2 counter-balances the relatively negative evaluation of P2 regarding $C_{1,2}$. Or, considering another direction for the effect, a prospective partner (evaluator) who is perceived negatively is expected to make (relatively) negative evaluations of the objects under scrutiny, in our case contribution $C_{1,2}$, and thus congruity is maintained.

If similar evaluations are put forward when P1 is examining $C_{2,2}$, then P1's perception of P2 will become even more negative. We could repeat this for all 'k' contributions of each partner. It seems reasonable to expect that the more incongruous are the evaluations of P2 regarding each of his own k contributions ($C_{k,2}$), the less likely it is that the conclusion of an alliance will lead to a successful outcome. The magnitude of this effect may be culture-dependent as we point out in the next section.

Extending this thinking to the formation of alliances between independent firms, it can be argued that incongruence concerning the contributions to a transnational alliance expected by the respective partners will influence negatively the attitudes of managers as they exchange information during the early phases of discussion and reaching agreement. Following Dreu, Weingart and Kwon (2000), this negative attitude may then affect unfavourably the atmosphere in which discussions are held and the ability for a mutually acceptable agreement to be concluded, to the detriment of current and future relationships and dealings between the firms.

Thus, based on the above discussion, a theoretical link between different perceptions regarding the potential contributions of partners of an alliance and the chances of successful alliance formation can be established.

If we include moderator functions or variables, we arrive at a general proposition as follows.

$$A_{t=1,1,2} = A_{t=0,1,2} + f_a\left(CA_{total}, \sum_m M_m\right) \quad (1)$$

where $A_{t=1,1,2}$ is the attitude of P1 towards P2 at time $t = 1$, $A_{t=0,1,2}$ is the attitude of P1 towards P2 at time $t = 0$, $f_a =$ function representing the congruity and the adaptation effects.

$CA_{total} = \sum_k CAc_{k,1} + \sum_k CAc_{k,2}$, representing the cumulative congruity or incongruity regarding the contributions of each partner. CA_{total} is the overall congruence between the Attitudes of P1 ($Ac_{k,1}$) and P2 ($Ac_{k,2}$) regarding the contributions of each partner ($C_{k'}$ and C_k) and assuming a cumulative linear effect;

M_m ($m = 1, 2, 3, \ldots, r$) refer to 'r' moderator-variables that will impact on the adaptation of the congruity function, such as, cultural differences among parties, different mind-sets, and different genders, or their combined effects.

In general, we could say that the attitude of one prospective partner (P1) (i.e., an individual or team within that firm) towards another prospective alliance partner (P2) is dependent on: (a) the initial attitude of P1 towards P2; (b) on the total (in)congruence (CA_{total}) or the (in)congruity of P1's attitudes (evaluations) towards a number of objects of judgment (e.g., the partners' contributions) and P2's attitudes (evaluations) towards the same objects; and (c) the effect of the mediator/moderator functions or variables on the adaptation of the individual's behaviour as a result of the total (in)congruity (CA_{total}).

3.2. A special theory: The impact of cultural differences on the application of congruity theory to alliance formation

In this section we consider the effect that cultural differences may have on the general model. The literature indicates that culture may influence face-to-face interactions in a number of ways. Cultural dimensions have been found to impact managers' preferences and behaviour towards business partners (Lee, Shenkar, & Li, 2008; Marshall & Boush, 2001), in particular during the negotiation process (e.g., Graham, Evenko, & Rajan, 1992; Lee, Yang, & Graham, 2006).

An illustration of the importance of culture as an important factor on international interfirm deals regards the acquisition of Volvo Cars by the Chinese car manufacturer Geely. Or in the words of Geely's chairman Mr Li Shufu regarding the post-acquisition

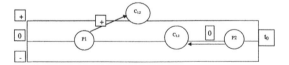

Initial setting (t=0): Attitude of P1 towards P2 is neutral, Attitude of P1 towards $C_{1,2}$ is positive, Attitude of P2 towards $C_{1,2}$ is neutral.

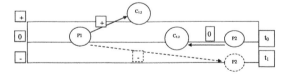

Subsequent setting (t=1): Attitude of P1 towards P2 becomes negative following the principle of congruity

Fig. 2. Change in attitude of P1 towards P2, following an incongruent evaluation of P2 regarding P2's own potential contribution 1 (C1,2).

process: "[The biggest lesson in the first year after buying Volvo is that] you really need to study and understand and respect the culture of the company and the culture of the nation and through discussion form a consensus." (Waldmeir, 2011).

It has been suggested that cross-cultural negotiations will tend to achieve lower joint gains than intra-cultural negotiations (Brett & Okumura, 1998). Moreover, different cultures may support seemingly opposite negotiation approaches, each leading to optimum outcomes under given circumstances (Graham et al., 1992). In addition, cultural differences seem to have a stronger negative effect on trust building when interacting with new business contacts as the partners do not know each other well (Marshall & Boush, 2001).

Difficulties to go across different corporate cultures may be another illustration, or in the words of a senior financial analysis (Thomas Caldwell, Caldwell Financial, Toronto) while analysing the low performance and subsequent acquisition of Merrill Lynch by the Bank of America under Mr John Thain by the end of 2008: "[Merrill Lynch is] a unique culture. If you come in as an outsider, you'd better be paying attention, because it's a tough game." (Farrell & Sender, 2009).

Lander and Kooning (2013) suggest that the development of trust is based concomitantly on a number of domains including the personal sphere and the interaction process. Another related finding refers to the long-term orientation of Japanese retailers as an antecedent to trust and satisfaction with suppliers and how, as a consequence, Japanese retailers put more effort into resolving their differences with suppliers than searching for new ones (Chung et al., 2006), which may be seen as culture-specific behaviour. Suggestions for deepening the understanding of the negotiation process, particularly in international cross-cultural settings, have been made (e.g., Brett & Okumura, 1998). More recently, the importance of understanding the motivations and constraints or alternatives of the other party has been highlighted (Malhotra, 2013). Furthermore, a number of potential sources of conflict have been identified by looking at cross-cultural business interactions as well as through comparisons across cultures. Such sources of conflict range from differences on culturally-derived or culturally-embedded values (Chen, Mannix, & Okumura, 2003; Molinsky, 2007; Tinsley & Pillutla, 1998; Tinsley, 2001) and business practices or negotiation approaches (Adler, Brahm, & Graham, 1992; Graham, 1985; Liu, Friedman, & Hong, 2012), to cognitive styles (Abramson, Lane, Nagai, & Takagi, 1993; Adler, Doktor, & Redding, 1986; Redding, 1980) and interaction behaviours (Adair, Weingart, & Brett, 2007; Adler et al., 1992; Lee et al., 2006; Liu, Chua, & Stahl, 2010).

If we compare the possible effect of a collectivistic versus individualistic culture, it seems reasonable to expect that members of collectivist cultures will tend to seek harmony faster than members of individualist cultures, as it is part of their cultural behaviour to place collective concerns above individual ones (Kim, Park, & Suzuki, 1990; Marcus & Le, 2013). This may be interpreted as affecting the speed and strength of a desire to return to congruity. In other words, a member of a collectivistic culture can be expected to desire a faster return to congruity, compared to a member of an individualistic culture. Hence, the strength to comply with the principle of congruity, is culturally dependent. The extent of incongruity is first perceived by the party or individual and, subsequently, there is time for adjustment to occur. The speed of adjustment will also be culturally dependent.

In our context, cross-cultural differences can be expected to affect the micro-dynamic stages of a sequence of interactions and, hence, the predicted outcome of the alliance formation process. More specifically, both the strength of the intention to reach congruity and the speed to take action towards that objective can be expected to be culturally dependent.

Using the general formulation from the previous section – see Formula (1) – and setting the moderator function $M_1 = C_r$, we have:

$$A_{t=1,1,2} = A_{t=0,1,2} + f_a(CA_{total}, C_r) \qquad (2)$$

where C_r represents cultural differences described by a cultural vector $C_r = g(C_{r1}, C_{r2}, \ldots, C_{rn})$, with n as the number of cultural dimensions under consideration. C_r affects both the magnitude and the speed of the incongruity adaptation effect.

It should be noted that other special theories could be derived from the general theory, for example, the effect of the gender of the participants on compliance with the principle of congruity.

3.3. An application of the special theory: Contrasting mind-sets of managers of developed countries and their counterparts in large emerging economies

Next we illustrate an application of the special theory (see previous section) to the case of alliance formation between managers of diverse mind-sets, that is, managers of firms from Developed Countries (DCs) and those of firms from Large Emerging Markets (LEMs). In this context, one potential source of disagreement and dispute concerns the contributions to the transnational alliance (TA) expected by and of the partners (Stopford & Wells, 1972). The impact of divergent expectations due to diverse objectives or mind-sets has been illustrated in the context of entrepreneurs and venture capital managers (Chua & Woodward, 1993). Underpinning this idea is the notion that early identification of misunderstandings concerning the potential contributions of the partner can increase the ability of managers to intervene and resolve any mistrust that might arise, through better communication of their respective viewpoints and objectives and through the development of joint solutions. Yan and Gray (2001) suggest that the bargaining power of the parties is determined not only by the partners' contributions but also by the context of the negotiation and the strength of the relationship. It has also been suggested that the evaluation of the other party's benefits may be linked not just to the relationship situation, but to the negotiators' personality characteristics too (Corfman & Lehmann, 1993).

Three important issues in international business studies provide the context for this application of the special theory. The first concerns the low success rates of TAs, the second the growing importance of LEMs in the global arena (De Mattos, Burgess, & Shaw, 2013), and the third the importance of commercial biotechnology for both governments and the private sector. Moreover, LEMs and high-technology sectors illustrate respectively environments of high uncertainty and high complexity. We suggest that the rapidly-changing conditions of these environments may affect the judgement of managers and therefore their mind-set. LEMs such as Brazil, China, India, Turkey, and Mexico are quickly acquiring greater prominence in the global economy (e.g., NIC, 2008; O'Neill & Stupnytska, 2009; UNCTAD, 2009, 2010; Wilson, Kelston, & Ahmed, 2010) and have consequently attracted considerable scholarly attention (e.g., Eichengreen, Gupta, & Kumar, 2010; Lu, Zhou, Bruton, & Li, 2010; Kotabe, Parente, & Murray, 2007; Meyer, Estrin, Bhaumik, & Peng, 2009; Muller & Kolk, 2010; Ramamurti & Singh, 2009; Trevino & Mixon, 2004; Wasti, 2008). This prominence is expected to grow more rapidly over the coming years as firms strive to secure first-mover advantages in LEMs, and benefit from scale economies, location advantages and other effects. In addition, contrary to some widely-held assumptions in the literature, business opportunities in LEMs are not restricted to low- and medium-technology deals. Indeed, LEM-based firms have grown their presence in markets for technology-intensive products and services (Santos, 2007; UNCTAD, 2010), particularly those from Latin America and the transition economies (see Filatotchev, Liu, Buck, & Wright, 2009; Murray, Kotabe, & Zhou, 2005; Kotabe et al., 2000, 2007; Siqueira & Bruton, 2010).

As a result, business deals between firms from LEMs and their counterparts in developed countries have increased. Recently, MNEs from LEMs have invested into developed countries to source technology and other strategic assets (UNCTAD, 2010). LEMs differ from other developing economies in that they generally possess a reasonably good industrial infrastructure and have fairly advanced scientific capabilities, even if these are limited to universities and research centers, and are generally unavailable on a commercial scale. However, LEMs share with other developing countries certain market inefficiencies, such as investment-unfriendly regulatory regimes and taxation systems, as well as policies which often stifle local entrepreneurship (Dinello & Shaoguang, 2009; Gupta, Hasan, & Kumar, 2010; World Bank, 2010). Within this context, the ability of firms – be they LEM firms looking to acquire technology and other assets from developed-country partners, or developed-country firms seeking to tap into the opportunities presented by LEMs – to devise mechanisms and tools that help potential sources of conflict to be identified at an early stage of TA formation would go a long way towards improving the probability of a successful alliance. Based on our review of the literature, we can identify four areas of potential incongruity regarding the perceptions of different groups of managers concerning the prospective contributions of the developed country partner and, thus, potential sources of conflict between alliance partners. These incongruities relate primarily to the resource-seeking strategies of the respective firms, namely access to capital, advanced technology, technical personnel, and supplementary product lines.

3.3.1. Transnational alliance partner contributions

One application of the principle of congruity is to the case of dyadic (two-party) alliances, in order to establish in theory a causal link between congruence of expectations (or evaluations) regarding the contributions from a prospective partner to the alliance and the likelihood of alliance formation.

From our discussion of the literature, we can extract two main ideas. First, managers contemplating a transnational alliance have certain prior expectations of their potential partners, especially concerning their respective contributions. Second, these expectations may differ amongst alliance partners, or, expressed another way, incongruity may be present. Should this prove to be the case, conflict is likely to ensue and the risk of failure may be heightened. For the reasons explained above, because of respective institutional and environmental differences it is likely that incongruous expectations will be observed between developed-country firms and those from emerging markets. This indicates the need for managers in such situations to be more cognisant of possible mismatches of expectations during the alliance formation process and to be better prepared to deal with them as and when they arise.

There is now a substantial literature on how firms select potential partners on the basis of the contribution that the partner can bring to the TA. A review of this literature has helped us to identify those potential contributions to a TA which, as the discussions above indicate, have the potential to provide a source of incongruity between the respective managers of the partner firms. The importance of the contributions of potential partners to an alliance will depend on the ongoing strategy of the firms involved, and on the availability of each factor under examination, including the internal resources of participating firms. Dong, Buckley, and Mirza (1997) draw attention to differences in the perceived importance of contributions between culturally-different foreign collaborators. We can infer from congruity theory thinking that it is likely that any manager involved in a potential alliance will have a frame of reference (or mind-set) against which

he or she will assess the potential contributions of a prospective TA partner, possibly allocating objective or subjective weightings to those contributions as they are evaluated (Cavusgil, Ghauri, & Akcal, 2013). However, prior literature identifying precisely what these contributions are likely to be is somewhat limited. Only a limited number of studies provide detailed lists of potential contributions, and only few of those consider contributions of developed-country partners (e.g., Beamish, 1987; De Mattos, Sanderson, & Ghauri, 2002; Dong et al., 1997; Dong, & Glaister, 2006; Erden, 1997; Geringer, 1991; Glaister & Buckley, 1997; Raveed & Renforth, 1983; Stopford & Wells, 1972; Wright, Filatotchev, Buck, & Bishop, 2002). Within this literature there is little consensus A number of other studies do consider partner contributions, but without it being their main purpose or focus (see Blodgett, 1991; Chen, Park, & Newburry, 2009; Fagre & Wells, 1982).

Having established that contributions from TA partners, in general, are expected to influence the likelihood of successful formation as well as the continuance of a transnational alliance, in the next section we turn our attention to specific contributions and the potential incongruity of perceptions between TA partners regarding those contributions and hence their potential to cause conflict and derail the TA formation process.

Considering that the general theory (1) and the special theory focusing on cultural differences (2), and defining $C_r = g(C_{r1})$, i.e., the cultural vector (C_r) is dependent on just one dimension (C_{r1}), which represents the different mind-sets of managers from DCs and their counterparts in LEMs, we have:

$$A_{t=1,1,2} = A_{t=0,1,2} + f_a(CA_{\text{total}}, C_{r1}) \qquad (3)$$

In this special case, the Attitude of P1 towards P2 at time $t = 1$ $(A_{t=1,1,2})$ is the Attitude of P1 towards P2 at time $t = 0$ $(A_{t=0,1,2})$ plus the effect of the cumulative congruity or incongruity, which in turn is affected by the different mind-sets (f_a) in what relates to determining setting the magnitude and speed of the wish to conform with the principle of congruity. Further specific propositions could be derived from variants of the special theory of cultural differences—for instance, those based on the various dimensions of culture in Hofstede's work (Hofstede, 1980). Examples include a proposition that the different speed or intensity of compliance with the principle of congruity depends on the degree of individualism/collectivism of the individuals or teams interacting in the joint venture. Similarly it could be proposed that compliance speed or intensity will vary according to the cultural distance (psychic distance) between the participants.

4. Propositions

Our approach provides a set of testable propositions at general, special and specific levels. It enhances the theoretical understanding of behaviour in joint ventures and is complementary to the approach based on 'mutual forbearance' given by Buckley and Casson (1988). Indeed, the two approaches together suggest a means of achieving success in collaborative ventures based on a commitment to understanding the culture and mind-set of partners and maximising congruity in order to increase the commitment of all partners to the venture. Such an approach can reduce the *ex ante* risk of (international) inter-cultural joint ventures.

We develop below a number of propositions to guide the necessary empirical testing. The propositions derive from the general theory as well as from further specifications of the special theory. Regarding the former, propositions may be raised regarding moderators (M_i) different from those already covered by the special theory (i.e., culture) or the application of the special theory (i.e., mind-set). An example of such a proposition drawing on the general theory is a special theory on the effect of gender differences.

Indirect recognition that there may be gender-related factors affecting women entrepreneurs are indicated by the European Commission initiatives and the 2012 report (European Commission, 2012): "The aim [of this report] is to follow the development of the number of women entrepreneurs and of gender segregated statistics and thereby make the contribution of women entrepreneurs to society more visible." The report carries on by pointing out the problems in identifying the contributions of female entrepreneurs (and by implication, female managers) because many countries do not provide business-related statistics differentiated by gender.

Proposition 1. Considering a sequence of interactions and individuals of similar cultural background, the wish intensity as well as the speed to reach congruity following incongruent initial valuations of prospective partners' contributions to an alliance will be gender-dependent.

The above proposition may give rise to a number of hypotheses that will consider different outcomes when considering, for instance, different cultural dimensions.

Or using the general theory, refer to formula (1), and defining $\sum_m M_m = M_g$, we have:

$$A_{t=1,1,2} = A_{t=0,1,2} + f_a(CA_{total}, M_g),$$

where $A_{t=1,1,2}$ is the attitude of P1 towards P2 at time $t = 1$; $A_{t=0,1,2}$ is the attitude of P1 towards P2 at time $t = 0$; f_a = function represents the congruity and adaptation effects (both speed and wish intensity to reach congruity); $CA_{total} = \sum_k CAc_{k,1} + \sum_{k'} CAc_{k,2}$, represents the cumulative congruity or incongruity regarding the contributions of each partner; and M_g represents the potential moderation of gender on the adaptation of the congruity function.

Moreover, regarding the special theory, propositions may be specified further along the lines of a number of diverse dimensions of culture, see the cultural vector presented previously, for example, Hofstede's dimensions such as collectivism/individualism, or cultural distance.

As suggested by Brett and Okumura (1998, p.496) "The linkage of goals to self as opposed to the collective and the emphasis on personal needs as opposed to social obligations suggest that individualists should be more self-interested in negotiations than collectivists." This indicates that differences between individualistic and collectivist cultures are expected to be significant in the context of cross-cultural negotiation interactions.

Below are examples of such propositions.

Proposition 2a. Considering a sequence of interactions and individuals with cultural backgrounds of varying degrees of collectivism/individualism, the wish intensity as well as the speed to reach congruity following incongruent initial evaluations of prospective partners' contributions to an alliance will differ.

Or, using the special theory, refer to Formula (2), and defining $C_r = C_{c/i}$, we have:

$$A_{t=1,1,2} = A_{t=0,1,2} + f_a(CA_{total}, C_{c/i})$$

where: $A_{t=1,1,2}$ is the attitude of P1 towards P2 at time $t = 1$; $A_{t=0,1,2}$ is the attitude of P1 towards P2 at time $t = 0$; f_a = function represents the congruity and adaptation effects (both speed and

wish intensity to reach congruity); $CA_{total} = \sum_k CAc_{k,1} + \sum_{k'} CAc_{k,2}$, represents the cumulative congruity or incongruity regarding the contributions of each partner; and $C_{c/i}$ represents the potential moderation of the cultural bi-polar dimension of collectivism/individualism on the adaptation of the congruity function.

Different expectations and procedures dependent on the local cultural environment have been indicated as determining the chances of success of business ventures (Buckley, Clegg, & Tan, 2006). Thus, considering a general culture-related construct (i.e. cultural distance):

Proposition 2b. Considering a sequence of interactions and individuals with different cultural backgrounds having a non-zero cultural distance, the wish intensity as well as the speed to reach congruity following incongruent initial valuations of prospective partners' contributions to an alliance will differ.

Or using as previously the special theory, refer to formula (2), and defining $C_r = C_{C-D}$, we have:

$$A_{t=1,1,2} = A_{t=0,1,2} + f_a(CA_{total}, C_{C-D})$$

where $A_{t=1,1,2}$ is the Attitude of P1 towards P2 at time $t = 1$; $A_{t=0,1,2}$ is the Attitude of P1 towards P2 at time $t = 0$; f_a = function represents the congruity and adaptation effects (both speed and wish intensity to reach congruity); $CA_{total} = \sum_k CAc_{k,1} + \sum_{k'} CAc_{k,2}$, represents the cumulative congruity or incongruity regarding the contributions of each partner; and C_{C-D} represents the potential moderation of the cultural distance on the adaptation of the congruity function.

The impact of discordant mindsets may be illustrated with the case of KKR (Kohlberg Kravis Roberts), the renowned corporate buy-out investor. One of the three founders split-up after over ten years of joint operations due among other factors to "differences between the hard-driving business style of the young cousins [i.e., Henry Kravis and his cousin George Roberts] and the quieter approach of their former mentor [Jerome Kohlberg]" (Sender, 2011).

An evolving mindset has been highlighted as important in todays' world. The implicit implication is that different mindsets coexist in todays' business environment and, as pointed out by Gupta and Govindarajan (2002), they operate differently, some more successfully than others. A proposition addressing this issue is suggested below.

Another dimension, paralleling the idea of mindset, is an executive's personality trait, as illustrated by the case of Wipro, the Indian giant computer services provider and their joint CEOs, Mr Suresh Vaswani and Mr Girish Paranjpe. Explaining their dissimilar approaches and its positive effect we quote Mr Paranjpe: "Since we have different personalities, we find people and clients interact differently with us. So that becomes a good tactic. Some clients respond better to me and others to Suresh [i.e., Mr Suresh Vaswani]." (Leahy, 2008).

We could create propositions to be tested for the application of the special theory regarding mind-sets, which parallels what we proposed previously regarding cultural dimensions, as follows.

Proposition 3. Considering a sequence of interactions and individuals with different mind-sets, initial valuations of prospective partners' contributions as well as the wish intensity and the speed to reach congruity following incongruent initial evaluations of prospective partners' contributions to an alliance will differ.

Or, using as previously the special theory, refer to formula (3), and defining $C_{r1} = C_{m-s}$, we have:

$$A_{t=1,1,2} = A_{t=0,1,2} + f_a(CA_{total}, C_{m-s})$$

P.J. Buckley et al./International Business Review 24 (2015) 1048–1060   1057

where $A_{t=1,1,2}$ is the Attitude of P1 towards P2 at time $t = 1$; $A_{t=0,1,2}$ is the Attitude of P1 towards P2 at time $t = 0$; f_a = function represents the congruity and adaptation effects (both speed and wish intensity to reach congruity); $CA_{total} = \sum_k CAc_{k',1} + \sum_{k'} CAc_{k,2}$, represents the cumulative congruity or incongruity regarding the contributions of each partner; and C_{m-s} represents the potential moderation of the differing mind-sets on the adaptation of the congruity function.

The above propositions may generate a number of hypotheses aimed at testing the different theoretical levels (i.e., general theory, special theory, and application of the special theory). We theorise that variations in the context as well as variations regarding the timing and order of the interactions in a sequence may lead to diverse outcomes. Both quantitative and qualitative techniques may be used to test and develop the theory. Regarding the former, simulations of business interactions seem an appropriate research instrument to achieve a better control of the parameters considered (e.g., Brett & Okumura, 1998; Graham et al., 1992). Surveys regarding cross-cultural business interaction practices may also be employed to test the theory under specific circumstances (e.g., Rao & Schmidt, 1998). The analysis of secondary panel data may provide additional insights particularly in relation to comparisons of two or more country environments and cultures. In issues that concern qualitative techniques, case studies could also be used to detail the micro-dynamic procedures used by practitioners, bringing the theory closer to questions arising from current and novel real-life managerial challenges and empirical solutions (e.g., Buckley, 2002). A multidisciplinary approach could also play an important role in developing this theory, particularly the use of disciplines such as anthropology (Buckley & Chapman, 1996).

5. Conclusions

Based on the principle of congruity, this paper seeks to advance understanding of individual-to-individual micro-dynamics of two-party interactions in the final stages of a transnational alliance (TA) formation. More specifically, using the principle of congruity we develop a general theory that considers the effect of a mismatch of expectations between prospective partners about the contributions of both partners plus the partners' attitudes towards each other on the likelihood of alliance formation. We also develop a special theory that considers cultural differences as influencing managers' wish to follow the principle of congruity, taking into account both the intensity and speed of adjustment. Finally, we present an application of the special case which reflects the effect of different mind-sets between managers of firms from developed countries (DC) and their counterparts in large emerging markets.

Recent studies propose similar paths, particularly on interpersonal interaction (e.g., Lander & Kooning, 2013). The potential for a successful TA can be significantly influenced by the perceptions and expectations of the principal parties involved, as well as by their attitudes. The reasons why misconceptions arise appear to be related, at least in part, to differences in national culture and business environments.

5.1. Managerial relevance

Our study implies that managers who enter into discussions on the formation of transnational alliances should focus on communicating clearly and explicitly what resources they intend to commit to provide, and what they expect to receive from the arrangement, since this is likely to be a significant source of misunderstanding and potential conflict; this should occur either during the allying process, or once the alliance has been agreed.

This paper also contributes by raising awareness of the importance of managers being cognisant of possible mismatches of expectations during the alliance formation process, and the importance of being better prepared to deal with any potential mismatches. Preemption or early identification of issues that could lead to misunderstandings concerning potential partner contributions can increase the ability of managers to intervene and resolve any mistrust that might arise, through better communication of respective viewpoints and objectives, and through the development of joint solutions. Therefore, if areas of high conflict-generation potential can be identified in advance during the informal stages of TA formation, and then evaluated and acted upon early by managers, such misconceptions can be addressed to minimise their effects. The use of checklists and other tools that focus attention on potential sources of misconceptions, such as the contributions expected of a partner, may complement more informal efforts to identify and take steps to mitigate the effects of misunderstandings and conflict, and to promote a self-reinforcing dynamic of mutual trust-building.

We propose that an attitude of mutual commitment and trust-building may be accomplished by unilateral or multilateral efforts by the parties involved to understand the standpoint of the other party. In so doing, managers should be able to reach a better understanding of the consequences of their respective demands that might appear, on the surface at least, to be associated with national, 'taken-for-granted', mind-sets. With this in mind, pre-alliance formation discussions with prospective collaborators could follow a step-wise approach, in which (i) the partners identify the contributions they expect to make towards and receive from the other party (perhaps using checklists), (ii) these contributions are ranked or scored by managers according to the relative importance to their firm, and (iii) these rankings are shared between the partners in order to draw attention to where any incongruity of expectation is greatest, and therefore where further dialogue is needed. One possible limitation is that culturally-embedded factors that affect business interactions can be expected to have different speeds of change (Fang, Worm, & Tung, 2008).

5.2. Relevance for policy formulation

This approach may be considered by policy-makers when they seek to promote alliances. In this context, a similar use of checklists as suggested above to managers may be helpful in seeking clarity about the respective positions of TA partners. Many governments around the world are looking to promote high-technology and high value-added sectors as a key development objective, while emerging economies not only have untapped markets for final products but can also be seen as high-demand markets for novel technologies. It is recommended that mechanisms are established that help to clarify the objectives of companies in these types of sectors regarding the establishment of TAs with foreign firms, particularly among those government agencies charged with promoting international technology transfer through the use of transnational alliances. In addition, the support of managers of small and medium-sized businesses in terms of training and increased awareness about problems that may be caused by incongruities of expectations should assist with efforts to attract foreign investors and new-technology developers to emerging economies. At the same time, the dissemination among emerging economies of innovative products deriving from new product development initiatives in advanced countries could increase the generation of revenue amongst technology-based firms.

References

Aaker, D. A., & Keller, K. L. (1990). Consumer evaluations of brand extensions. *Journal of Marketing, 54*, 27–41.

Abramson, N. R., Lane, H. W., Nagai, H., & Takagi, H. (1993). A comparison of Canadian and Japanese cognitive styles—Implications for management interaction. *Journal of International Business Studies, 24*, 575–587.
Adair, W. L., Weingart, L., & Brett, J. (2007). The timing and function of offers in US and Japanese negotiations. *Journal of Applied Psychology, 92*, 1056–1068.
Adler, N. J., Brahm, R., & Graham, J. L. (1992). Strategy implementation: A comparison of face-to-face negotiations in the People's Republic of China and the United States. *Strategic Management Journal, 13*, 449–466.
Adler, N. J., Doktor, R., & Redding, S. G. (1986). From the Atlantic to the Pacific century—Cross-cultural management reviewed. *Journal of Management, 12*, 295–318.
Bales, R. F. (1950). *Interaction process analysis: A method for the study of groups*. Chicago and London: The University of Chicago Press.
Barkema, H. G., & Vermeulen, F. (1997). What differences in the cultural backgrounds of partners are detrimental for international joint ventures? *Journal of International Business Studies, 28*, 845–864.
Beamish, P. W. (1987). Joint ventures in LDCs: Partner selection and performance. *Management International Review, 27*, 23–37.
Bhattacharya, R., Devinney, T. M., & Pillutla, M. M. (1998). A formal model of trust based on outcomes. *Academy of Management Review, 23*, 459–472.
Bierly, P. E., III, & Gallagher, S. (2007). Explaining alliance partner selection: Fit, trust and strategic expediency. *Long Range Planning, 40*, 134–153.
Blodgett, L. L. (1991). Partner contributions as predictors of equity share in international joint ventures. *Journal of International Business Studies, 22*, 63–78.
Brady, H. E., & Sniderman, P. M. (1985). Attitude attribution—A group basis for political reasoning. *American Political Science Review, 79*, 1061–1078.
Brett, J. M., & Okumura, T. (1998). Inter- and intracultural negotiation: US and Japanese negotiators. *Academy of Management Journal, 41*, 495–510.
Buckley, P. J. (2002). Is the international business research agenda running out of steam? *Journal of International Business Studies, 33*, 365–373.
Buckley, P. J., & Casson, M. (1988). A theory of cooperation in international business. In F. J. Contractor & P. Lorange (Eds.), *Cooperative strategies in international business*. Lexington, MA: Lexington Books.
Buckley, P. J., & Casson, M. (1996). An economic model of international joint venture strategy. *Journal of International Business Studies, 27*, 849–876.
Buckley, P. J., & Chapman, M. (1996). Economics and social anthropology—Reconciling differences. *Human Relations, 49*, 1123–1150.
Buckley, P. J., Clegg, J., & Tan, H. (2006). Cultural awareness in knowledge transfer to China—The role of guanxi and mianzi. *Journal of World Business, 41*, 275–288.
Buckley, P. J., & Strange, R. (2010). The governance of the multinational enterprise: Insights from internalization theory. *Journal of Management Studies, 48*, 460–470.
Burt, R. S. (1997). The contingent value of social capital. *Administrative Science Quarterly, 42*, 339–365.
Carter, E. E. (1971). Project evaluations and firm decisions. *Journal of Management Studies, 8*, 253–279.
Cavusgil, S. T., Ghauri, P. N., & Akcal, A. A. (2013). *Doing business in emerging markets* (2nd ed.). London: Sage Publications.
Chen, D., Park, S. H., & Newburry, W. (2009). Parent contribution and organizational control in international joint ventures. *Strategic Management Journal, 30*, 1133–1156.
Chen, Y. R., Mannix, E. A., & Okumura, T. (2003). The importance of who you meet: Effects of self- versus other-concerns among negotiators in the United States, the People's Republic of China, and Japan. *Journal of Experimental Social Psychology, 39*, 1–15.
Chua, J. H., & Woodward, R. S. (1993). Splitting the firm between the entrepreneur and the venture capitalist with the help of stock-options. *Journal of Business Venturing, 8*, 43–58.
Chung, J. E., Sternquist, B., & Chen, Z. Y. (2006). Retailer-buyer supplier relationships: The Japanese difference. *Journal of Retailing, 82*, 349–355.
Chung, S., Singh, H., & Lee, K. (2000). Complementarity, status similarity and social capital as drivers of alliance formation. *Strategic Management Journal, 21*, 1–22.
Cohen, W. M., & Levinthal, D. A. (1990). Absorptive-capacity—A new perspective on learning and innovation. *Administrative Science Quarterly, 35*, 128–152.
Coleman, J. S. (1988). Social capital in the creation of human-capital. *American Journal of Sociology, 94*, S95–S120.
Collet, F., & Philippe, D. (2014). From hot cakes to cold feet: A contingent perspective on the relationship between market uncertainty and status homophily in the formation of alliances. *Journal of Management Studies, 51*, 406–432.
Contractor, F. J. (1985). A generalized theorem for joint-venture and licensing negotiations. *Journal of International Business Studies, 16*, 23–50.
Corfman, K. P., & Lehmann, D. R. (1993). The importance of others welfare in evaluating bargaining outcomes. *Journal of Consumer Research, 20*, 124–137.
Das, T. K., & Teng, B. S. (2002). Alliance constellations: A social exchange perspective. *Academy of Management Review, 27*, 445–456.
De Dreu, C. K. W., Weingart, L. R., & Kwon, S. (2000). Influence of social motives on integrative negotiation: A meta-analytic review and test of two theories. *Journal of Personality and Social Psychology, 78*, 889–905.
De Mattos, C., Burgess, T. F., & Shaw, N. E. (2013). The impact of R&D-specific factors on the attractiveness of small- and medium-sized enterprises as partners vis-à-vis alliance formation in large emerging economies. *R&D Management, 43*, 1–20.
De Mattos, C., Sanderson, S., & Ghauri, P. (2002). Negotiating alliances in emerging markets—Do partners' contributions matter? *Thunderbird International Business Review, 44*, 701–728.
Delios, A., & Beamish, P. W. (2004). Joint venture performance revisited: Japanese foreign subsidiaries worldwide. *Management International Review, 44*, 69.
Dhanaraj, C., Lyles, M. A., Steensma, H. K., & Tihanyi, L. (2004). Managing tacit and explicit knowledge transfer in IJVs: The role of relational embeddedness and the impact on performance. *Journal of International Business Studies, 35*, 428–442.
Dinello, N. E., & Shaoguang, W. (2009). China, India and beyond: Development drivers and limitations. In *Global development network series*Cheltenham, UK; Northampton, MA: Edward Elgar (pp. xxxv, 254).
Doney, P. M., Cannon, J. P., & Mullen, M. R. (1998). Understanding the influence of national culture on the development of trust. *Academy of Management Review, 23*, 601–620.
Dong, H., Buckley, P. J., & Mirza, H. (1997). International joint ventures in China from a managerial perspective: A comparison between different sources of investment. In G. Chryssochoidis, C. Millar, & J. Clegg (Eds.), *Internationalisation strategies*. New York, NY: St. Martin.
Dong, L., & Glaister, K. W. (2006). Motives and partner selection criteria in international strategic alliances: Perspectives of Chinese firms. *International Business Review, 15*, 577–600.
European Commission – Enterprise & Industry Directorate General (2012). *«European Network to Promote Women's Entrepreneurship» (WES) Activity Report 2009-2010*. Brussels: European Commission – Enterprise & Industry Directorate General.
Eichengreen, B. J., Gupta, P., & Kumar, R. (2010). *Emerging giants: China and India in the world economy*. Oxford: Oxford University Press (pp. xxxi, 368).
Erden, D. (1997). Stability and satisfaction in cooperative FDI: Partnerships in Turkey. In P. W. Beamish (Ed.), *Cooperative strategies: European perspectives* (pp. 158–183). San Francisco: The New Lexington Press.
Fagre, N., & Wells, L. T. (1982). Bargaining power of multinationals and host governments. *Journal of International Business Studies, 13*, 9–23.
Fang, T., Worm, V., & Tung, R. L. (2008). Changing success and failure factors in business negotiations with the PRC. *International Business Review, 17*, 159–169.
Farrell, G., & Sender, H. (January 26, 2006). Lynched at Merrill. *Financial Times*.
Ferrin, D. L., Bligh, M. C., & Kohles, J. C. (2008). It takes two to tango: An interdependence analysis of the spiraling of perceived trustworthiness and cooperation in interpersonal and intergroup relationships. *Organizational Behavior and Human Decision Processes, 107*, 161–178.
Fey, C. F., & Beamish, P. W. (2000). Joint venture conflict: The case of Russian international joint ventures. *International Business Review, 9*, 139–162.
Filatotchev, I., Liu, X., Buck, T., & Wright, M. (2009). The export orientation and export performance of high-technology SMEs in emerging markets: The effects of knowledge transfer by returnee entrepreneurs. *Journal of International Business Studies, 40*, 1005–1021.
Fornell, C., Lorange, P., & Roos, J. (1990). The cooperative venture formation process—A latent variable structural modeling approach. *Management Science, 36*, 1246–1255.
Fulmer, C. A., & Gelfand, M. J. (2012). At what level (and in whom) we trust: Trust across multiple organizational levels. *Journal of Management, 38*, 1167–1230.
Gelfand, M. J., Major, V. S., Raver, J. L., Nishii, L. H., & O'Brien, K. (2006). Negotiating relationally: The dynamics of the relational self in negotiations. *Academy of Management Review, 31*, 427–451.
Geringer, J. M. (1991). Strategic determinants of partner selection criteria in international joint ventures. *Journal of International Business Studies, 22*, 41–62.
Glaister, K. W., & Buckley, P. J. (1996). Strategic motives for international alliance formation. *Journal of Management Studies, 33*, 301–332.
Glaister, K. W., & Buckley, P. J. (1997). Task-related and partner-related selection criteria in UK international joint ventures. *British Journal of Management, 8*, 199–222.
Graham, J. L. (1985). The influence of culture on the process of business negotiations: An exploratory study. *Journal of International Business Studies, 16*, 81–96.
Graham, J. L., Evenko, L. I., & Rajan, M. N. (1992). An empirical-comparison of Soviet and American business negotiations. *Journal of International Business Studies, 23*, 387–418.
Grant, R. M., & Baden-Fuller, C. (2004). A knowledge accessing theory of strategic alliances. *Journal of Management Studies, 41*, 61–84.
Gulati, R. (1995a). Social structure and alliance formation patterns: A longitudinal analysis. *Administrative Science Quarterly, 40*, 619–652.
Gulati, R. (1995b). Does familiarity breed trust—The implications of repeated ties for contractual choice in alliances. *Academy of Management Journal, 38*, 85–112.
Gulati, R., Lavie, D., & Singh, H. (2009). The nature of partnering experience and the gains from alliances. *Strategic Management Journal, 30*, 1213–1233.
Gupta, A. K., & Govindarajan, V. (2002). Cultivating a global mindset. *The Academy of Management Executive, 16*, 116.
Gupta, P., Hasan, R., & Kumar, U. (2010). What constrains Indian manufacturing. In B. J. Eichengreen, P. Gupta, & R. Kumar (Eds.), *Emerging giants: China and India in the world economy*. Oxford: Oxford University Press.
Hagedoorn, J. (2006). Understanding the cross-level embeddedness of interfirm partnership formation. *Academy of Management Review, 31*, 670–680.
Hamel, G. (1991). Competition for competence and inter-partner learning within international strategic alliances. *Strategic Management Journal, 12*, 83–103.
Harrigan, K. R. (1988). Joint ventures and competitive strategy. *Strategic Management Journal, 9*, 141–158.
Hennart, J.-F. (1988). A transaction costs theory of equity joint ventures. *Strategic Management Journal, 9*, 361–374.
Hofstede, G. (1980). *Culture's consequences: International differences in work related values*. Beverly Hills, CA: Sage Publications.
Inkpen, A. C., & Currall, S. C. (2004). The coevolution of trust, control, and learning in joint ventures. *Organization Science, 15*, 586–599.
Inkpen, A. C., & Tsang, E. W. K. (2005). Social capital, networks, and knowledge transfer. *Academy of Management Review, 30*, 146–165.
Jap, S., Robertson, D. C., & Hamilton, R. (2011). The dark side of rapport: Agent misbehavior face-to-face and online. *Management Science, 57*, 1610–1622.
Jones, G. R., & George, J. M. (1998). The experience and evolution of trust: Implications for cooperation and teamwork. *Academy of Management Review, 23*, 531–546.

Kale, P., & Singh, H. (2009). Managing strategic alliances: What do we know now, and where do we go from here? The Academy of Management Perspectives, 23, 45–62.

Kale, P., Singh, H., & Perlmutter, H. (2000). Learning and protection of proprietary assets in strategic alliances: Building relational capital. Strategic Management Journal, 21, 217–237.

Katz, M. L. (1986). An analysis of cooperative research-and-development. Rand Journal of Economics, 17, 527–543.

Kim, K. I., Park, H. J., & Suzuki, N. (1990). Reward allocations in the United-States Japan, and Korea—A comparison of individualistic and collectivistic cultures. Academy of Management Journal, 33, 188–198.

Kim, P. H., Dirks, K. T., & Cooper, C. D. (2009). The repair of trust: A dynamic bilateral perspective and multilevel conceptualization. Academy of Management Review, 34, 401–422.

Kirkpatrick, S. A., & McLemore, L. (1977). Perceptual and affective components of legislative norms—Social-psychological analysis of congruity. Journal of Politics, 39, 685–711.

Kogut, B. (1988). Joint ventures—Theoretical and empirical perspectives. Strategic Management Journal, 9, 319–332.

Kogut, B. (1991). Joint ventures and the option to expand and acquire. Management Science, 37, 19–33.

Koka, B. R., & Prescott, J. E. (2002). Strategic alliances as social capital: A multidimensional view. Strategic Management Journal, 23, 795–816.

Kotabe, M., Parente, R., & Murray, J. Y. (2007). Antecedents and outcomes of modular production in the Brazilian automobile industry: A grounded theory approach. Journal of International Business Studies, 38, 84–106.

Kotabe, M., Teegen, H., Aulakh, P. S., Coutinho de Arruda, M. C., Santillán-Salgado, R. J., & Greene, W. (2000). Strategic alliances in emerging Latin America: A view from Brazilian, Chilean, and Mexican companies. Journal of World Business, 35, 114–132.

Lander, M. W., & Kooning, L. (2013). Boarding the aircraft: Trust development amongst negotiators of a complex merger. Journal of Management Studies, 50, 1–30.

Leahy, J. (September 22, 2008). Management by the 'power of two'. Financial Times.

Lee, K., Yang, G., & Graham, J. L. (2006). Tension and trust in international business negotiations: American executives negotiating with Chinese executives. Journal of International Business Studies, 37, 623–641.

Lee, S. H., Shenkar, O., & Li, J. T. (2008). Cultural distance, investment flow, and control in cross-border cooperation. Strategic Management Journal, 29, 1117–1125.

Liu, L. A., Chua, C. H., & Stahl, G. K. (2010). Quality of communication experience: Definition, measurement, and implications for intercultural negotiations. Journal of Applied Psychology, 95, 469–487.

Liu, W., Friedman, R., & Hong, Y.-Y. (2012). Culture and accountability in negotiation: Recognizing the importance of in-group members. Organizational Behavior and Human Decision Processes, 117, 221–234.

Lu, Y., Zhou, L., Bruton, G., & Li, W. (2010). Capabilities as a mediator linking resources and the international performance of entrepreneurial firms in an emerging economy. Journal of International Business Studies, 41, 419–436.

Lunnan, R., & Haugland, S. (2008). Predicting and measuring alliance performance: A multidimensional analysis. Strategic Management Journal, 29, 545–556.

Malhotra, D. (2013). How to negotiate with VCs. Harvard Business Review, 91, 84–90.

Malhotra, D., & Gino, F. (2011). The pursuit of power corrupts: How investing in outside options motivates opportunism in relationships. Administrative Science Quarterly, 56, 559–592.

Marcus, A., & Le, H. (2013). Interactive effects of levels of individualism-collectivism on cooperation: A meta-analysis. Journal of Organizational Behavior, 34, 813–834.

Marino, L., Strandholm, K., Steensma, H. K., & Weaver, K. M. (2002). The moderating effect of national culture on the relationship between entrepreneurial orientation and strategic alliance portfolio extensiveness. Entrepreneurship: Theory & Practice, 26, 145–160.

Marshall, R. S., & Boush, D. M. (2001). Dynamic decision-making: A cross-cultural comparison of US and Peruvian export managers. Journal of International Business Studies, 32, 873–893.

Mayer, R. C., Davis, J. H., & Schoorman, F. D. (1995). An integrative model of organizational trust. Academy of Management Review, 20, 709–734.

McDermott, G. A., & Corredoira, R. A. (2010). Network composition, collaborative ties, and upgrading in emerging-market firms: Lessons from the Argentine autoparts sector. Journal of International Business Studies, 41, 308–329.

McPherson, M., Smith-Lovin, L., & Cook, J. M. (2001). Birds of a feather: Homophily in social networks. Annual Review of Sociology, 27, 415–444.

McKnight, D. H., Cummings, L. L., & Chervany, N. L. (1998). Initial trust formation in new organizational relationships. Academy of Management Review, 23, 473–490.

Meyer, K., Estrin, S., Bhaumik, S., & Peng, M. (2009). Institutions, resources, and entry strategies in emerging economies. Strategic Management Journal, 30, 61–80.

Molinsky, A. (2007). Cross-cultural code-switching: The psychological challenges of adapting behavior in foreign cultural interactions. Academy of Management Review, 32, 622–640.

Mowery, D. C., Oxley, J. E., & Silverman, B. S. (1998). Technological overlap and interfirm cooperation: Implications for the resource-based view of the firm. Research Policy, 27, 507–523.

Muller, A., & Kolk, A. (2010). Extrinsic and intrinsic drivers of corporate social performance: Evidence from foreign and domestic firms in Mexico. Journal of Management Studies, 47, 1–26.

Murray, J. Y., Kotabe, M., & Zhou, J. N. (2005). Strategic alliance-based sourcing and market performance: Evidence from foreign firms operating in China. Journal of International Business Studies, 36, 187–208.

NIC (2008). Global trends 2025: A transformed world. NIC, National Intelligence Council.

Olshavsky, R. W., & Miller, J. A. (1972). Consumer expectations, product performance, and perceived product quality. Journal of Marketing Research, 9, 19–21.

O'Neill, J., & Stupnytska, A. (2009). The long-term outlook for the BRICs and N-11 post crisis. In Global Economics Paper No.192. Goldman Sachs.

Osgood, C. E., & Tannenbaum, P. H. (1955). The principle of congruity in the prediction of attitude change. Psychological Review, 62, 42–55.

Parkhe, A. (1993). Partner nationality and the structure-performance relationship in strategic alliances. Organization Science, 4, 301–304.

Perkins, A. W., & Forehand, M. R. (2012). Implicit self-referencing: The effect of nonvolitional self-association on brand and product attitude. Journal of Consumer Research, 39, 142–156.

Pfeffer, J. (1972). Merger as a response to organizational interdependence. Administrative Science Quarterly, 17, 382–394.

Pfeffer, J., & Nowak, P. (1976). Joint ventures and interorganizational interdependence. Administrative Science Quarterly, 21, 398–418.

Podolny, J. M. (1993). A status-based model of market competition. American Journal of Sociology, 98, 829–872.

Podolny, J. M. (1994). Market uncertainty and the social character of economic exchange. Administrative Science Quarterly, 24, 458–483.

Portes, A. (1998). Social capital: Its origins and applications in modern sociology. Annual Review of Sociology, 24, 1–24.

Ramamurti, R., & Singh, J. V. (2009). Emerging multinationals from emerging markets. Cambridge; New York: Cambridge University Press.

Rao, A., & Schmidt, S. M. (1998). A behavioral perspective on negotiating international alliance. Journal of International Business Studies, 29, 665–693.

Raveed, S. R., & Renforth, W. (1983). State enterprise-multinational corporation joint ventures: How well do they meet both partners' needs? Management International Review, 23, 47–57.

Redding, S. G. (1980). Cognition as an aspect of culture and its relation to management processes—An exploratory view of the Chinese case. Journal of Management Studies, 17, 127–148.

Ring, P. S., & Van de Ven, A. H. (1992). Structuring cooperative relationships between organizations. Strategic Management Journal, 13, 483–498.

Sender, H. (2011 November 18). Lunch with the FT: Henry Kravis and George Roberts.

Salciuviene, L., Ghauri, P. N., Streder, R. S., & De Mattos, C. (2010). Do brand names in a foreign language lead to different brand perceptions? Journal of Marketing Management, 26, 1037–1056.

Santos, J. (2007). Strategy lessons from left field. Harvard Business Review, 85, 20–21.

Seale, D. A., Arend, R. J., & Phelan, S. (2006). Modeling alliance activity: Opportunity cost effects and manipulations in an iterated prisoner's dilemma with exit option. Organizational Behavior and Human Decision Processes, 100, 60–75.

Shapiro, M. J. (1969). Rational political man—Synthesis of economic and social-psychological perspectives. American Political Science Review, 63, 1106–1119.

Shipilov, A., & Li, S. (2008). Can you have your cake and eat it too? Structural holes' influence on status accumulation and market performance in collaborative networks. Administrative Science Quarterly, 53, 73.

Shipilov, A. V., Li, S. X., & Greve, H. R. (2011). The prince and the pauper: Search and brokerage in the initiation of status-heterophilous ties. Organization Science, 22, 1418–1434.

Siqueira, A., & Bruton, G. (2010). High-technology entrepreneurship in emerging economies: Firm informality and contextualization of resource-based theory. IEEE Transactions on Engineering Management, 57, 39–50.

Song, F. (2009). Intergroup trust and reciprocity in strategic interactions: Effects of group decision-making mechanisms. Organizational Behavior and Human Decision Processes, 108, 164–173.

Srivastava, J., & Chakravarti, D. (2009). Channel negotiations with information asymmetries: Contingent influences of communication and trustworthiness reputations. Journal of Marketing Research, 46, 557–572.

Stopford, J. M., & Wells, L. T. (1972). Managing the multinational enterprise: Organization of the firm and ownership of the subsidiaries. New York, NY: Basic Books.

Stuart, T. E. (1998). Network positions and propensities to collaborate: An investigation of strategic alliance formation in a high-technology industry. Administrative Science Quarterly, 43, 668–698.

Tannenbaum, P. H. (1956). Initial attitude toward source and concept as factors in attitude-change through communication. Public Opinion Quarterly, 20, 413–425.

Tinsley, C. H. (2001). How negotiators get to yes: Predicting the constellation of strategies used across cultures to negotiate conflict. Journal of Applied Psychology, , 583–593.

Tinsley, C. H., & Pillutla, M. M. (1998). Negotiating in the United States and Hong Kong. Journal of International Business Studies, 29, 711–727.

Trevino, L. J., & Mixon, F. G., Jr. (2004). Strategic factors affecting foreign direct investment decisions by multi-national enterprises in Latin America. Journal of World Business, 39, 233–243.

UNCTAD (2009). World investment report 2009: Transnational corporations, agricultural production and development. New York, NY and Geneva: United Nations.

UNCTAD (2010). World investment report 2010: Investing in a low-carbon economy. New York, NY and Geneva: United Nations.

Van de Ven, A. H. (1976). On the nature, formation, and maintenance of relations among organizations. Academy of Management Review, 1, 24–36.

Waldmeir, P. (April 20, 2011). Voluptuous' Volvo debuts in China. Financial Times.

Wassmer, U., Dussauge, P., & Planellas, M. (2010). How to manage alliances better than one at a time. MIT Sloan Management Review, 51, 77–84.

Wasti, S. (2008). Trust in buyer-supplier relations: The case of the Turkish automotive industry. Journal of International Business Studies, 39, 118–131.

Weingartner, H. M., & Gavish, B. (1993). How to settle an estate. Management Science, 39, 588–601.

Williamson, O. E. (1979). Transaction-cost economics: The governance of contractual relations. Journal of Law and Economics, 22, 233–261.

Williamson, O. E. (1991). Comparative economic organization: The analysis of discrete structural alternatives. *Administrative Science Quarterly, 36,* 269–296.

Wilson, D., Kelston, A. L., & Ahmed, S. (2010). *Is this the 'BRICs decade'?* Goldman Sachs.

World Bank (2010). *Doing business 2010.* World Bank.

Wright, M., Filatotchev, I., Buck, T., & Bishop, K. (2002). Foreign partners in the former Soviet Union. *Journal of World Business, 37,* 165–179.

Yan, A., & Gray, B. (2001). Antecedents and effects of parent control in international joint ventures. *Journal of Management Studies, 38,* 393–416.

Zaheer, A., McEvily, B., & Perrone, V. (1998). Does trust matter? Exploring the effects of interorganizational and interpersonal trust on performance. *Organization Science, 9,* 141–159.

Zaheer, A., & Venkatraman, N. (1995). Relational governance as an interorganizational strategy: An empirical test of the role of trust in economic exchange. *Strategic Management Journal, 16,* 373–392.

Zhang, J. (2010). The persuasiveness of individualistic and collectivistic advertising appeals among Chinese generation-X consumers. *Journal of Advertising, 39,* 69–80.

6

Journal of International Business Studies (2014) 45, 102–109
© 2014 Academy of International Business   All rights reserved 0047-2506
www.jibs.net

PERSPECTIVE

Adam Smith's theory of knowledge and international business theory and practice

Peter J Buckley[1,2]

[1]Centre for International Business, Leeds
University Business School, UK; [2]University of
International Business and Economics (UIBE),
Beijing, P.R. China

Correspondence:
PJ Buckley, Centre for International Business,
Leeds University Business School, University
of Leeds, Maurice Keyworth Building, Leeds
LS2 9JT, UK.
Tel: +44(0) 113 343 4646,
Fax: +44(0) 113 343 4754.

Abstract
This paper demonstrates that Adam Smith's insights and reasoning can improve
the theory of international business, and shed light on its academic practices.
Smith was a system builder; his theory of knowledge underpinned his entire
oeuvre, and understanding his systematic approach can help current international
business to achieve a similarly coherent body of theory. Smith's approach sheds
direct light on decision-making in multinational enterprises, and on cultural
distance (the "liability of foreignness"). Combining these two areas yields new
Smithian insights into multinational enterprises from emerging countries.
Journal of International Business Studies (2014) 45, 102–109. doi:10.1057/jibs.2013.44

Keywords: history of thought; integration of pre-existing theoretical approaches; decision-making; cultural distance; emerging-market multinationals; Adam Smith

INTRODUCTION

This paper sets out to demonstrate how some applications of Adam
Smith's insights and reasoning can significantly improve the current
analysis of international business. In particular, it builds on Smith's
underlying theory of knowledge, which is antecedent to his two
great works – *An Enquiry into the Nature and Causes of the Wealth of
Nations* (1776) (hereafter, WN) and *The Theory of Moral Sentiments*
(1759) (hereafter, TMS). Smith's theory of knowledge provides a
foundation for understanding the problematic nature of current
theories of business, and this paper shows that the system that Smith
built can help to deal with these difficulties.

Smith's theory of knowledge may be a fundamental source in
understanding complex adaptive systems (Kennedy, 2008). The
global economy is one such system, and the academic milieu in
which this system is analysed is another. This paper therefore applies
Smith's theory of knowledge both to international business practice
and to international business academia.

There are many other profound thinkers from whom we can also
learn (Shakespeare, Mill, Aristotle, Plato, Marx), and indeed many
other innovative Scottish enlightenment "economists" (Rutherford,
2012), but none of them built a system that includes economics and
business theories predicated on a fundamental theory of knowledge.
Uniquely, Smith's theory of knowledge led to applications in economics (WN) morality (TMS) and legal rights (Smith, 1762–1763,
1766, *Lectures on Jurisprudence* (hereafter, LJ)). Understanding the

Received: 9 December 2011
Revised: 20 May 2013
Accepted: 22 July 2013
Online publication date: 12 September 2013

fundamentals of Smith's thinking can point to solutions of contemporary problems, helping us to avoid making the same mistakes again and again.

SMITH'S THEORY OF KNOWLEDGE

In terms of system-building, Smith practised what he preached. He believed that a system of science had to be built from first principles, and should ideally be all-encompassing. It should depend on: "certain principles, known or proved, in the beginning, from whence we account for the several phenomena, connecting all together in the same chain" (*Lectures on Rhetoric and Belles Lettres* (LRBL), ii: 133).

This precept Smith applied in his works on economics (WN), philosophy (TMS), legal principles (Smith, 1762–63, 1766 after LJ), the history of astronomy (Smith, 1795 after HA), linguistics (Smith LRBL) and rhetoric and literature (Smith, 1762–1763, LRBL).

Smith's theory of knowledge was centrally concerned with the principles of human nature, and was deeply grounded in the study of history. The most important source of Smith's theory of knowledge is his *History of Astronomy* (HA), described in the General Introduction by its editors as "one of the best examples of theoretical history, it is perhaps most remarkable as a study of those principles of human nature which 'lead and direct' philosophical inquiry" (Raphael & Skinner, 1980: 2).

Possibly Smith's greatest contribution was to see the economy as a system, and to provide "a persuasive coherent account of coordination in a commercialized society" (Dow, 2009: 106). How far does current international business theory provide a similarly cohesive account of the global economy, or of the process of globalisation (to parallel the process of commercialisation studied by Smith)? A system, as Smith pointed out, is the science of connected principles. It is arguable that international business academia has yet to find a similar coherent general system of connected principles to theorise globalisation.

The History of Astronomy is a work of metascience. It is an analysis of the nature and causes of progress in a particular field of scientific thought. Smith is explaining the sentiments of wonder, surprise and admiration. The sentiment of wonder is a response to novelty, surprise to unexpectedness, and admiration to what is great or beautiful. Smith's central concern, therefore, is the role of the imagination in building up our beliefs about the world. Subjective feelings are important drivers of scientific and philosophical progress. There is a strong link to the

"Austrian School" of economics (Lachmann, 1986; von Mises, 1949).

Smith points to the importance of conventional knowledge in our subjective understanding of the world. "Custom" and "indolence" rule our thinking in the "normal science" of the Kuhnian analysis (Kuhn, 1962). There is, however, a difference between the philosopher (or specialist) and the ordinary man. Careful study and training increase perceptions. Disruptions in thinking give rise to surprise and wonder. As these disruptions become more frequent or salient, so there are provoked changes in sentiment, leading to revisions of world view and to a "scientific revolution". The unexpectedness of the arrival of new phenomena or observations causes a disequilibrium – the thought system becomes too complicated as it struggles to accommodate new observations, and so it is replaced by a simpler system that encompasses these novelties. Scientific development resembles successive equilibria interspersed with disruptive change – punctuated equilibria.

Smith traces the historical sequence of astronomical thought. The transitions between systems are brought about by self-consciousness. Leading thinkers modify the existing thought system until, overburdened, it is replaced by a more acceptable system. The analysis is applied by Smith to language (LRBL) and to transitions in society – for instance, from feudalism to the commercial system (WN book III) (Samuels, 2011). Smith's theory of knowledge provided the basis for his great contributions to social science. "It was his capacity for analytical history which allowed him to build up a theory of human nature and apply that to formulate a theory of the social system" (Dow, 2009: 110).

FROM FUNDAMENTALS TO THE WEALTH OF NATIONS AND THE THEORY OF MORAL SENTIMENTS

Much is made of the contrast between "sympathy" in TMS and "self-interest" in WN. Smith identifies exchange as distinctively human, and a degree of sympathy is a precondition for considering exchange as a strategy. As any specific exchange must be based on a self-conscious recognition of a differentiation of interest, an appeal to the potential trading partner's self-interest can be made only with the capacity to realise what this interest is likely to be. The advantages explored by Smith in developing an understanding of other people's motives and behaviour allow us to modify our own to facilitate the adoption of many kinds of (apparently) successful practice, without necessarily understanding why they are successful. This is an important mechanism in the diffusion of innovations (Boulding, 1966; Marschak, 1968).

The surprise result of Smith's work is that markets and benevolence are not opposed, but are actually self-reinforcing. This is a direct result of the working-out of Smith's theory of knowledge, as Otteson (2002: 291–292) puts it:

> In an effort to facilitate their respective searches for happiness, individuals spontaneously try out, and then discard or adopt various habits of behaviour. ... We have there, then, the beginnings of a process that acts as a natural cement for human society: because mutual sympathy is sought by all, each person tries to put himself in situations in which such sympathy can be obtained. (Otteson, 2002: 291–292)

This creates a social bond and provides the mechanism by which self-interest can be combined with sympathy for others.

> Hence, contrary to what one might have expected, according to Smith's account, allowing the extension of self-interested behaviour (within, as always, the bounds of justice) in economic markets can actually lead to an extension of natural affection for and benevolence towards others – indeed, perhaps more so than in other types of economic arrangements. (Otteson, 2002: 12)

In summary, Smith's theory of human interactions as derived from his theory of knowledge satisfactorily combines psychology, sociology and economics (as we now conceive them) into a holistic view of the development of societies.

We can now advance from Smith's theory of knowledge to its relevance to international business.

THE SMITHIAN SYSTEM AND ITS RELEVANCE TO INTERNATIONAL BUSINESS

Smith's theory of knowledge suggests that the progress of human knowledge consists of patterns that are created by imagining novel connections in response to observations that conflict with conventional systems. All systems are conjectures, which may prove to be inadequate. International business theory is one example.

Smith's search for a single, overarching system was extraordinarily ambitious. He recognised that even major subsystems required simplifications and approximations that are not appropriate for other subsystems. This is even true within single "disciplines" – those of coordination theory and development theory in economics, for instance, as recognised by Schumpeter (1911) and Penrose

(1959). Theories of business face similar problems. Knight (1921) pointed out the insufficiency of probabilistic reasoning in the face of uncertainty. Simon (1965) and Williamson (1975) have noted the limitations of human intelligence in being "boundedly rational". Control theorists have pointed out that using data generated by a system to generate a model using that system implies that one is no longer sampling from the same population, and that the applicability of the model is doubtful. This analysis can also be applied to the businesses that academics study. There is no inference from Smith's work that any theory of business success can be enduring – including reliance on "distinctive competencies", "dynamic capabilities" (Teece, Pisano, & Shuen, 1997) or "ownership advantages" (Dunning, 1977, 1995, 2000; Kindleberger, 1969). Capitalism's virtue is that "creative destruction" can happen without generating system disorder.

SMITH'S THEORY OF KNOWLEDGE AND INTERNATIONAL BUSINESS ACADEMIA

Smith's theory of knowledge can be applied to international business at two levels. The first is its application to the academic community. The second is the phenomena of study – (multinational) enterprises. The insights are multiplied when we examine the theory of knowledge together with the concept of the division of labour. Any field of scientific endeavour requires the deliberation of multiple rational individuals. The division of labour encourages several local foci of attention. This will produce not only variety within each specialism but problems of coordination between specialisms, which will often be based on incompatible hypotheses (often rendering coordinated searches impossible).

Academia's thinking on international business issues would do well to follow Smith's lead. Dow (2009: 109) remarks that:

> the principle of the division of labour can be thought of as a way of organising thought about causal powers at work in commercialised society ... while a rationalist account of society lends itself to a deductive axiomatic system, the more complex Scottish account of human behaviour, its determinants and its consequences, all referring to the peculiarities of the context in relation to the historical system, cannot be captured in a deductive system. In any case, the method of applying principles to new contexts might always lead to an evolution of theory, and thus a new mode of expression of the principles.

In other words, history matters; context matters. Testing principles against new contexts leads to new and better theories. This is precisely what international business academics preach, and occasionally practise.

> While axioms are "self-evidentially true" by introspection, principles are derived from detailed observation. While the deduction of propositions from the axioms was the end of the matter for the deductivist approach, this was only one further step for the experimental approach, requiring also adaptation to the observed characteristics of the domain of application, with the possibility always of revision of principles. (Dow, 2009: 109)

This is an excellent basis for the justification of a study of *international* business, where general principles can be applied to different national contexts, and their applicability can then be tested to destruction. This enables us to judge the generality of theories of business, and the extent to which business behaviour is context specific. The context, both geographical/spatial and historical – gives us two great comparators – over space, and over time.

Smith also distinguishes between the formulation of a theory and its communication. This is also a hot current topic in international business academia, and in academic life generally. The control of "gatekeepers" such as academic journal editors exerts a profound influence on the dissemination (communication) of academic knowledge.

SMITH'S THEORY OF KNOWLEDGE AND CURRENT INTERNATIONAL BUSINESS THEORISING

There are two key areas of current theory on which Smith's approach sheds direct light – decision-making in multinational enterprises (MNEs), and the impact of cultural distance on decisions.

Decision-Making in MNEs

In comparing the "deductivist methodology of the French enlightenment" with "the 'experimental'" approach of the Scottish enlightenment, Dow suggests that "Smith's system ultimately was a mental construct designed for psychological appeal, but also for plausibility in the light of experience" (Dow, 2009: 109). It is precisely the non-dogmatic nature of Smith's theory of knowledge that makes it appropriate for (international) business decision-making. Smith's theory of knowledge suggests that all knowledge is provisional. Many business decisions – such as the choice of entry mode in foreign markets – are contingent, and indeed "experimental". Businesses will often explicitly make choices when faced with uncertainty (like that undertaken when entering a foreign market) that are experimental in the sense

that they are designed to be flexible in the face of volatility (Buckley & Casson, 1998). The real options literature (Buckley, Casson, & Gulamhussen, 2002; Kogut & Kulatilaka, 1994) suggests that this is a motive for foreign entry via joint ventures. Other applications of this principle are "listening posts" and non-equity modes of foreign involvement (the focus of the 2011 World Investment Report; UNCTAD, 2011).

A recent empirical investigation using structured experimentation on foreign direct investment location choice illustrates these points (Buckley, Devinney, & Louviere, 2007b). The results show that, in creating sets of investments for consideration, managers of multinational firms followed fairly rational rules. However, the choice of actual investments utilised past experience, "judgement", and often impulsive decision-making. Reason and experience are twin pillars of Smith's system of thought.

Smith's idea of the economy as a system is paralleled by the connections (or lack of connections; Loasby, 2003) amongst the actors. Missing connections are part of the explanation for the existence of the firm in Coase (1937), where the firm substitutes for imperfect or missing markets. This analysis was utilised by Buckley and Casson (1976) to explain the existence of multinational firms, and a wider global system approach has been used to explain the configuration of the world economy, and its division between intra-firm and market links (Buckley & Casson, 2001; Buckley & Hashai, 2004). As we see below, the idea of missing connections, and the role of the MNE in providing them, have implications for theorising the rise of multinationals from emerging economies.

Cultural Distance

Smith also has profound insights into the issue we now see as "cultural distance" (usually between nations, but applicable to any defined groups, such as regions, religious groups or social classes; Hofstede, 1980, 1997; Shenkar, 2001) or "the liabilities of foreignness" in the explicit context of international involvement – usually applied to foreign-owned companies in a host-country context (Zaheer, 1995). We can formulate Smithian approach to psychic distance derived from the decline of sympathy with distance, both geographic and cultural, and with declining (mutual) knowledge.

Otteson suggests that Smith saw it as a fundamental characteristic of human nature that

> the natural interest that people have in the fortunes of others is informed and modulated by the knowledge they have of

one another. The degree to which I can understand and therefore sympathise with your motives and your actions depends on the degree to which I know what your circumstances, passions and interests are and whether I judge your motives and actions to be proper in light of them. (2002: 4)

From this Otteson derives Smith's familiarity principle:

Smith argues in TMS not only that the benevolence we naturally feel toward others varies directly with our level of familiarity with them – the more familiar the more benevolent; and vice versa – but also that it is morally proper that our behaviour toward others should be motivated in this way. (2002: 4)

Forman-Barzilai (2010: 137) (in a chapter entitled "Sympathy in space") suggests that Smith's account of sympathy in TMS "ranks among the subtlest accounts we have of the nature of sympathetic activity and of its prominence in human life". Smith understood the spatial complexities of sympathetic activity, and accounted for three dimensions of spatial differences in the exercise of sympathy: physical space, affective space and historical/cultural space. Any act of sympathy will be situated somewhere on each of these continua, and acts of sympathy will be a particular confluence of these three dimensions (Forman-Barzilai, 2010: 141). Geographical separation, affective connection and historical familiarity thus determine "psychic distance" or cultural distance. However, Smith's account is remarkably subtle compared with current analyses, such as Hofstede's "four dimensions" (1980, 1997). Smith's approach includes the understanding that cultural distance from A to B may differ from that from B to A, and a multidimensional approach – rather than an aggregation into "dimensions" is much more nuanced than its modern alternatives.

Smith's familiarity principle has several important implications for international business.

First, it applies to expatriate behaviour, on which there is a huge volume of work in international business (see McNulty & De Cieri, 2011). It sheds insight into the phenomenon of "going native", to which temptation expatriates and diplomats are adduced to succumb. Second, it is relevant to the role of "cultural brokers", who can play an important role in bridging cultural divides (or "limits on the bounds of sympathy" in Smith's analysis). Third, it explains the role of "experts", who because of their increased degree of familiarity often empathise with those they study (and possibly, in extreme form, with "Stockholm syndrome", where hostages sympathise with their captors' causes). Fourth, it illustrates the importance of context in all

international business research endeavours. Fifth, if focuses attention on mutual trust. As Buckley and Casson (1988) have shown, mutual forbearance plays a crucial role in joint ventures. International joint ventures may be profoundly affected by Smith's psychic distance postulate; it is harder to engender trust via mutual forbearance where sympathy declines because of a lack of familiarity between partners of different nationalities.

To return to a point made in the Introduction, Smith provided an explanation for spontaneously generated social order – an explanation that derives, fundamentally, from his theory of knowledge. The desire for mutual sympathy plus the natural drive to better our conditions in life lead to an unintended or spontaneous order. This unintended order derives from unforced everyday interactions as each seeks to satisfy their interests. Thus the economy is conceived as a complex, adaptive system, very similar to Polanyi's "spontaneous order" (Jacobs, 1999).

INSIGHTS FROM ADAM SMITH'S WORK

An important argument for researching Adam Smith's work is that it provides a new analytical lens and fresh insights. Such a new insight can be made by combining Smith's analysis of managerial decision-making and cultural distance into an examination of the most important current phenomenon in international business research – the rise of multinational firms from emerging countries.

As newcomers to internationalisation and the world economy, multinationals from emerging economies are subject to greater degrees of uncertainty than are experienced MNEs. They are likely, therefore, to make mistakes as they learn. Their approach is likely to be experimental – in Smithian terms they are operating using highly contingent, experimental knowledge. Many are likely to employ cautious, gradual entry, possibly using "Uppsala-style" cultural closeness as a bridge to enter culturally close markets (Johanson & Vahlne, 1977, 2009), and real-options-based, cautious, step-by-step entry into those markets (Buckley et al., 2002; Kogut & Kulatilaka, 1994). Other firms will follow a bold strategy, typified by large acquisition entry, largely ignoring risk and the collection of knowledge (Buckley et al., 2007b). This may be partly because, in their state of knowledge, they are unaware that they need to collect information, or even know what information they need or how to acquire it.

Much has been made of "institutional voids" in less-developed markets (Khanna & Palepu, 1997, 1999; Khanna, Palepu, & Sinha, 2005). This exactly parallels Smith's concept of the economy as a system in which some systemic links are missing. These missing market links, or institutional voids, provide opportunities for enterprises to emerge to provide these links, and thereby to appropriate profit. This is precisely the role that many emerging-market multinationals fulfil. This expertise (competitive advantage) can then provide the basis for global expansion. An example of this insight is given by the suggestion that, because emerging-market firms can cope with corruption and other imperfections in their home market, this provides an internationally transferable "ownership advantage" (Luo, 2000; Luo & Rui, 2009).

To these Smithian insights into managerial judgement we can add his insights into cultural distance, to give a satisfactory analysis of the rise of emerging-country multinationals. Smith's notion that "sympathy" declines with distance suggests that multinationals from emerging countries will have difficulty in engaging with culturally distant countries – particularly those from countries such as China and Myanmar that have been cut off from the world economy for a considerable period of time. Smith's "familiarity principle" also reminds us that cultural distance is not equidistant from A to B as from B to A. Emerging markets may be culturally closer for advanced-country firms than advanced-country markets are for emerging-market firms. Local knowledge has a different status for inexperienced, naïve firms unfamiliar with the outside world – exactly paralleling Smith's notion of the decline of sympathy with (cultural) distance. Smith claims that

our potentially true beliefs about the external world are dependent on, and thus limited by, our actual observations. If we have not observed something, we cannot know whether what we believe about it is true or not. (Otteson, 2011: 29)[1]

This leads to several results. First, there is likely to be a regional (home) bias in the operations of these firms. Second, they are likely to rely heavily on "cultural brokers" – possibly expatriates – to help with their internationalisation. Third, they are likely to rely heavily on the knowledge of their foreign partners or acquired company expertise, because of the (lack of) familiarity principle. Fourth, and directly in line with Smith's principles, they are likely to rely on historical and cultural links in their internationalisation strategies. A good example here is the bias of Indian multinationals for acquisitions in the UK (Buckley, Forsans, & Munjal, 2012).

Taken together, this Smithian analysis prefigures the "liability of outsidership" that defines the strategic difficulties of multinationals from emerging countries (Johanson & Vahlne, 2009). All these propositions are supported in the extant literature on emerging-market multinational firms (Buckley et al., 2007a; Morck, Yeung, & Zhao, 2008; Rugman & Li, 2007; Witt & Lewin, 2007). An understanding of Adam Smith's current system can thus provide insights into an important international business phenomenon. The combination of the analysis of business decision-making and cultural distance found in Smith focuses our attention on the difficulties of building mutual trust in the growth of emerging-country multinationals because of the decline of sympathy over distance, and the ability of these firms to fill institutional voids (i.e., correct market imperfections) first in the home market and then in the wider world economy.

CONCLUSION

Adam Smith's work has a timeless quality. Although expressed in archaic language, it can speak to the current difficulties of analysing international business issues, and to an understanding of the behaviour of firms and executives in the real world today. This paper has argued that in order to see the worth of Smith's oeuvre, we need to understand the system that he expounded in his theory of knowledge to trace this thinking through the current questions of economics, sociology, philosophy and law.

Smith believed that a systematic, connected view of phenomena was the basis of scientific advance "Philosophy is the science of connecting principles of nature" (Smith, 1790; Astronomy II.12). "The task of establishing a system of thought must be conducted in terms of a combination of reason and experience" (Raphael & Skinner, 1980: 1). To comprehend reason and experience, we must understand human nature and human sentiments. That done, we can relate sentiments to (the advancement of) scientific knowledge. Thus a philosophy of science arises from first principles. This is Smith's fundamental contribution. The ultimate objective is to achieve "the beauty of a systematical arrangement of different observations connected by a few common principles" (WN v.l.f.25: 768–769).

Adam Smith built a historically contingent approach to scientific knowledge. International business theory is (ought to be?) evolving a spatially or geographically contingent approach to the application of theories of business. The two in combination allow us to see the importance of historical and geographical context in the application of the principles of business analysis and business decision-making. There are lessons, too, in Smith's notion of system. International business theory has not yet built a global analogue of Smith's depiction of the economy as a complex adaptive system. Smith's theory of knowledge can challenge us to greater achievements, accuracy of prediction, and understanding of business decisions. This is illustrated by the example of a "Smithian" analysis of MNEs from emerging countries. In this, as in so much else, Adam Smith remains an exemplar and a pioneer.

NOTE

[1]This "again demonstrates Smith's privileging empirical observation as a source, perhaps *the* source, of human knowledge" (Otteson, 2011: 30).

REFERENCES

Boulding, K. E. 1966. The economics of knowledge and the knowledge of economics. *American Economic Review*, 56(2): 1–13.

Buckley, P. J., & Casson, M. C. 1976. *The future of the multinational enterprise*. London: Palgrave Macmillan.

Buckley, P. J., & Casson, M. C. 1988. A theory of cooperation in international business. In F. J. Contractor, & P. Lorange (Eds), *Cooperative strategies in international business*. Lexington, MA: Lexington Books.

Buckley, P. J., & Casson, M.C. 1998. Models of the multinational enterprise. *Journal of International Business Studies*, 29(1): 21–44.

Buckley, P. J., & Casson, M. C. 2001. Strategic complexity in international business. In A. M. Rugman, & T. L. Brewer (Eds), *The Oxford handbook of international business*. Oxford: Oxford University Press.

Buckley, P. J., & Hashai, N. 2004. A global system view of firm boundaries. *Journal of International Business Studies*, 35(1): 33–45.

Buckley, P. J., Casson, M. C., & Gulamhussen, M. A. 2002. Internationalisation – Real options, knowledge management and the Uppsala approach. In V. Havila, M. Forsgren, & H. Hakansson (Eds), *Critical perspectives on internationalisation*. Oxford: Elsevier.

Buckley, P. J., Clegg, J., Cross, A., Zheng, P., Voss, H., & Liu, X. 2007a. The determinants of Chinese outward foreign direct investment. *Journal of International Business Studies*, 38(4): 499–518.

Buckley, P. J., Devinney, T. M., & Louviere, J. J. 2007b. Do managers behave the way theory suggests? A choice-theoretic examination of foreign direct investment location decision-making. *Journal of International Business Studies*, 38(7): 1069–1094.

Buckley, P. J., Forsans, N., & Munjal, S. 2012. Host–home country linkages and host–home country specific advantages as determinants of foreign acquisitions by Indian firms. *International Business Review*, 21(5): 878–890.

Coase, R. H. 1937. The nature of the firm. *Economica*, 4(16): 386–405.

Dow, S. 2009. Smith's philosophy and economic methodology. In J. T. Young (Ed), *Elgar companion to Adam Smith*. Cheltenham: Edward Elgar.

Dunning, J. H. 1977. Trade, location of economic activity and the MNE: A search for an eclectic approach. In B. Ohlin, P. O. Hesselborn, & P. M. Wijkmon (Eds), *The international allocation of economic activity*. London: Palgrave Macmillan.

Dunning, J. H. 1995. Reappraising the eclectic paradigm in the age of alliance capitalism. *Journal of International Business Studies*, 26(3): 461–491.

Dunning, J. H. 2000. The eclectic paradigm as an envelope for economic and business theories of MNE activity. *International Business Review*, 9(2): 163–190.

Forman-Barzilai, F. 2010. *Adam Smith and the circles of sympathy*. Cambridge: Cambridge University Press.

Hofstede, G. 1980. *Culture's consequences: International differences in work related values*. Beverly Hills, CA: Sage.

Hofstede, G. 1997. *Cultures and organizations: Software of the mind*. New York: McGraw-Hill.

Jacobs, S. 1999. Michael Polanyi's theory of spontaneous orders. *Review of Austrian Economics*, 11(1–2): 111–127.

Johanson, J., & Vahlne, J. E. 1977. The internationalization process of the firm: A model of knowledge development and increasing foreign market commitments. *Journal of International Business Studies*, 8(1): 23–32.

Johanson, J., & Vahlne, J. E. 2009. The Uppsala internationalization process model revisited: From liability of foreignness to liability of outsidership. *Journal of International Business Studies*, 40(9): 1411–1431.

Kennedy, G. 2008. *Adam Smith: A moral philosopher and his political economy*. Basingstoke: Palgrave Macmillan.

Khanna, T., & Palepu, K. 1997. Why focused strategies may be wrong for emerging markets. *Harvard Business Review*, 75(4): 41–51.

Khanna, T., & Palepu, K. 1999. Policy shocks, market intermediaries, and corporate strategy: Evidence from Chile and India. *Journal of Economics and Management Strategy*, 8(2): 271–310.

Khanna, T., Palepu, K. G., & Sinha, J. 2005. Strategies that fit emerging markets. *Harvard Business Review*, 83(6): 63–76.

Knight, F. 1921. *Risk, uncertainty and profit*. George J. Stigler (Ed), Chicago: University of Chicago Press, (1971).

Kindleberger, C. P. 1969. *American business abroad*. New Haven, CT: Yale University Press.

Kogut, B., & Kulatilaka, N. 1994. Operating flexibility, global manufacturing and the option value of a multinational network. *Management Science*, 40(1): 123–139.

Kuhn, T. S. 1962. *The structure of scientific revolutions*. Chicago: University of Chicago Press.

Lachmann, L. M. 1986. *The market as an economic process*. Oxford: Blackwell.

Loasby, B. J. 2003. Closed models and open systems. *Journal of Economic Methodology*, 10(3): 285–306.

Luo, Y. 2000. Dynamic capabilities in international expansion. *Journal of World Business*, 35(4): 355–378.

Luo, Y., & Rui, H. 2009. An ambidexterity perspective towards multinational enterprises from emerging economies. *Academy of Management Perspectives*, 23(1): 49–70.

Marschak, J. 1968. Economics of inquiring, communicating, deciding. *American Economic Review*, 58(2): 1–18.

McNulty, Y., & De Cieri, H. 2011. Global mobility in the 21st century: Conceptualising expatriate return on investment in global firms. *Management International Review*, 51(6): 897–919.

Morck, R., Yeung, B., & Zhao, M. 2008. Perspectives on China's outward foreign direct investment. *Journal of International Business Studies*, 39(3): 337–350.

Otteson, J. R. 2002. *Adam Smith's market place of life*. Cambridge: Cambridge University Press.

Otteson, J. R. 2011. *Adam Smith*. New York: Continuum International Publishing Group.

Penrose, E. 1959. *Theory of the growth of the firm*. Oxford: Blackwell.

Raphael, D. D., & Skinner, A. S. 1980. "General introduction" by Adam Smith (1976–1980) Volume III. In W. P. D. Wightman, & J. C. Bryce (Eds), *Essays on philosophical subjects*. Oxford: Oxford University Press.

Rugman, A. M., & Li, J. 2007. Will China's multinationals succeed globally or regionally? *European Management Journal*, 25(5): 333–343.

Rutherford, D. 2012. *In the shadow of Adam Smith: Founders of Scottish economics 1700–1900*. London: Palgrave Macmillan.

Samuels, W. J. 2011. *Erasing the invisible hand*. Cambridge: Cambridge University Press.

Schumpeter, J. 1911. *The theory of economic development*. Translated by R. Opie. Cambridge, MA: Harvard University Press (1934).

Shenkar, O. 2001. Cultural distance revisited: Toward a more rigorous conceptualization and measurement of cultural differences. *Journal of International Business Studies*, 32(3): 519–535.

Simon, H. A. 1965. *Administrative behaviour*. New York: Free Press.

Teece, D. J., Pisano, G., & Shuen, A. 1997. Dynamic capabilities and strategic management. *Strategic Management Journal*, 18(7): 509–533.

UNCTAD. 2011. *World investment report 2011: Non-equity modes of international production and development*. Geneva: United Nations Conference on Trade and Development.

von Mises, L. 1949. *Human action: A treatise on economics*, 4th revised edn. San Francisco, CA: Fox & Wilkes, (1996).

Williamson, O. E. 1975. *Markets and hierarchies: Analysis and antitrust implications*. New York: Free Press.

Witt, M. A., & Lewin, A. Y. 2007. Outward foreign direct investment as an escape response to home country institutional constraints. *Journal of International Business Studies*, 38(4): 579–594.

Zaheer, S. 1995. Overcoming the liability of foreignness. *Academy of Management Journal*, 38(2): 341–363.

WORKS BY ADAM SMITH

TMS	The Theory of Moral Sentiments
LJ(A)	Lectures on Jurisprudence, Report of 1762-1763
LJ(B)	Lectures on Jurisprudence, Report dated 1766
HA	History of Astronomy
LRBL	Lectures on Rhetoric and Belles Lettres
WN	The Wealth of Nations

ABOUT THE AUTHOR

Peter J Buckley, OBE, is Professor of International Business and Founder Director of the Centre for International Business, University of Leeds (CIBUL). He was President of the Academy of International Business 2002–2004, and is currently Director of the Business Confucius Institute at the University of Leeds, and Cheung Kong Scholar Chair Professor in the University of International Business and Economics (UIBE), Beijing.

Accepted by John Cantwell, Editor-in-Chief, 22 July 2013. This paper has been with the author for two revisions.

7

Manag Int Rev (2016) 56:879–900
DOI 10.1007/s11575-016-0300-0

mir
Management
International Review

RESEARCH ARTICLE

Historical Research Approaches to the Analysis of Internationalisation

Peter J. Buckley[1]

Received: 31 October 2013 / Revised: 7 May 2015 / Accepted: 26 May 2015 /
Published online: 29 September 2016
© The Author(s) 2016. This article is published with open access at Springerlink.com

Abstract Historical research methods and approaches can improve understanding of the most appropriate techniques to confront data and test theories in internationalisation research. A critical analysis of all "texts" (sources), time series analyses, comparative methods across time periods and space, counterfactual analysis and the examination of outliers are shown to have the potential to improve research practices. Examples and applications are shown in these key areas of research with special reference to internationalisation processes. Examination of these methods allows us to see internationalisation processes as a sequenced set of decisions in time and space, path dependent to some extent but subject to managerial discretion. Internationalisation process research can benefit from the use of historical research methods in analysis of sources, production of time-lines, using comparative evidence across time and space and in the examination of feasible alternative choices.

Keywords Historical research methods · Internationalisation · Process research · Business history

1 Introduction

The title of this focused issue is 'About Time: Putting Process Back into Firm Internationalisation Research'. It would therefore seem obvious that historical research methods, whose primary concern is the role of time, would be at the forefront of the analysis. This is not necessarily the case, as these methods are neglected in internationalisation research, and in international business more

✉ Peter J. Buckley
  pjb@lubs.leeds.ac.uk

[1] Centre for International Business, University of Leeds (CIBUL), Leeds University Business School, University of Leeds, Leeds, England, UK

generally. Historians face many of the same research problems that business researchers do—notably questions related to the analysis of process—but they have produced different answers, particularly in relation to the nature of causation. As a field, international business researchers need to question our research approaches more deeply.

This paper seeks to examine the types of research approaches from history that might aid in a more rounded analysis of internationalisation. Issues of sequencing, path dependence, contingent choices and the evaluation of alternatives are all critical in the internationalisation process and are grist to the mill of historical research. An examination of historical research methods leads to a new approach to the concept of internationalisation itself.

1.1 Historical Research Approaches: The Challenge of Different Underlying Philosophies

It is the difference in underlying philosophy between history and social science that presents the keenest challenge in integrating the temporal dimension with international business research. The contrast between the philosophy underlying history and that of social science—an issue for over a century (e.g., Simiand 1903)—is put by Isaiah Berlin:

> History details the differences among events, whereas the sciences focus on similarities. History lacks the sciences' ideal models, whose usefulness varies inversely with the number of characteristics to which they apply. As an external observer the scientist willingly distorts the individual to make it an instance of the general, but the historian, himself an actor, renounces interest in the general in order to understand the past through the projection of his own experience upon it. It is the scientist's business to fit the facts to the theory, the historian's responsibility to place his confidence in facts over theories (Berlin 1960, p. 1 (Abstract).[1]

Gaddis (2002) suggests that a particular contrast between history and social science is that history insists on the interdependence of variables, whilst mainstream social science methods rely on identifying the 'independent variable' which affects (causes) changes in dependent variables (Gaddis 2002, particularly Chapter 4). He suggests that this parallels the distinction between a reductionist view and an ecological approach (2002, p. 54), and that this arises from the social scientists' desire to forecast the future (2002, p. 56). This also implies continuity over time—the independent variable persists in its causative effect(s). It is also connected with assumptions of rationality, which also is assumed to be time-invariant. Social scientists would counter that historians are theory resistant, at least to the kind of

---

[1] It is suggested by Cannadine (2013, p. 9) that academic histories are often responsible for emphasising divergences rather than similarities: 'Most academics are trained to look for divergences and disparities rather than for similarities and affinities, but this relentless urge to draw distinctions often results in important connections and resemblances being overlooked'. The contrast between history and social science has been an issue for over a century (see Simiand 1903).

independent variable/rationalist/context-invariant reductionist theory that (perhaps stereotypically) characterises economistic approaches.

Compromises are possible. Recognising sensitive dependence on initial conditions brings 'narrative' and 'analysis' much closer together, as does dividing time into manageable units—perhaps 'short-term and long term' or 'immediate, intermediate and distant' (Gaddis 2002, p. 95). Causality, interdependence, contingency and moderating variables are more manageable when the time-frame is defined. Research in history therefore demonstrates the importance of time, sequencing and process. It also highlights the role of individuals and their decision making. These elements are particularly important in examining entrepreneurship and individual (manager's) decisions and their outcome in contexts such as the internationalisation of the firm.[2]

How, then, would we recognise if genuinely historical work had been accomplished in internationalisation studies (or indeed in any area of the social sciences)? Tilley (1983, p. 79) gives us an answer:

> By 'genuinely historical', I mean studies assuming that the time and place in which a structure or process appears makes a difference to its character, that the sequence in which similar events occur has a substantial impact on their outcomes, and that the existing record of past structures and processes is problematic, requiring systematic investigation in its own right instead of lending itself immediately to social-scientific synthesis.

History matters—the importance of historical effects in international business—is illustrated by Chitu et al. (2013), who document a 'history effect' in which the pattern of foreign bond holdings of US investors seven decades ago continues to influence holdings today. Holdings 70 years ago explain 10–15 % of the cross-country variation in current holdings, reflecting the fixed costs of market entry and exit together with endogenous learning. They note that fixed costs need not be large to have persistent effects on the geography of bilateral asset holdings—they need only to be different across countries. Evidence was also found of a 'history effect' in trade not unlike that in finance. The history effect is twice as large for non-dollar bonds as a result of larger sunk costs for US financial investments other than the dollar. Legacy effects loom large in international finance and trade.

It is argued in this paper that time and place (context) do make a difference to the structure and process of an individual firm's internationalisation, that past structures and processes do influence outcomes and that proper acknowledgement of context is vital in understanding and theorising internationalisation. It is further argued that attention to these issues leads to a new conception of internationalisation.

2 Research Methods

Reflecting on the purpose of his methods in his book *Bloodlands*, on Eastern Europe in the period 1933–45, the historian Timothy Snyder (2010, p. xviii) states that:

---

[2]   See also the debate on the 'historic turn' in organisation studies (Clark and Rowlinson 2004).

...its three fundamental methods are simple: insistence that no past event is beyond historical understanding or beyond the reach of historical enquiry; reflection upon the possibility of alternative choices and acceptance of the irreducible reality of choice in human affairs; and chronological attention to all of the Stalinist and Nazi policies that labelled large numbers of civilians and prisoners of war.

This paper follows similar principles. These are: (1) that the methods of history are appropriate to the study of the internationalisation of firms; (2) that choices and alternatives at given points of time are central to this process; (3) that the role of sequencing and time are central; and (4) that the comparative method is an aid to comprehension of the process of internationalisation.

This paper now examines research methods widely used in history[3] that have the capability to improve international business research. These are: (1) source criticism (here it is argued that international business researchers are insufficiently aware of deficiencies in "texts"); (2) the analysis of sequences, including time series analyses and process theorising; (3) comparative methods (not exclusive to historical research); and (4) counterfactual analyses (which are currently less utilised than in previous periods of international business theorising). This followed by a proposed research agenda based on the two key methods of examining change over time and utilising comparative analysis.

2.1 Source Criticism

The use of sources is as prevalent in international business as in history but they are often accepted uncritically. Gottschalk (1950), noting that few source documents are completely reliable, suggests that, 'for each particular of a document the process of establishing credibility should be separately undertaken regardless of the general credibility of the author'. Given that reliability cannot be assumed, source criticism, as Kipping et al. (2014) argue, is fundamental to any historical research.

The trustworthiness of an author may establish a basic level of credibility for each statement, but each element must be separately evaluated. This requires questioning the provenance of the text and its internal reliability (Kipping et al. 2014)—including, importantly, attention to language translation issues if relevant. This leads to the important checks brought about by triangulating the evidence. Triangulation requires the use of at least two independent sources (Kipping et al. 2014). This principle is utilised in international business journals by the requirement that both elements of a dyadic relationship are needed to cross check each other. Examples include licensor and licensee, both partners in a joint venture, parent and subsidiary in a multinational enterprise. The question of how far these are independent sources also needs careful investigation. Documents or statements

---

[3] Stephanie Decker (2013, p. 6) identified four features that 'clearly distinguish historical from non-historical research designs'. These are: reconstruction from primary sources (empirical rigour), thick contextualisation in time and space (empirical at times, theoretical rigour), periodization (theoretical rigour when combined with strong historiography) and historical narrative (accessibility, empirical and theoretical rigours).

 Springer

addressed to different individuals and institutions may serve a variety of purposes. Those addressed to powerful individuals, groups or institutions may be intended for gain by the sender. Interviews may be designed to impress the interlocutor. The purpose of the document needs to be explicated. Documents may be designed for prestige, tax minimisation, satisfaction of guarantees (by government, sponsors or creditors) or to cover deficiencies in performance. The historian's craft is, in part at least, to expose fraud and error (Bloch 1954).

Source criticism includes evaluating what is not present in archives, not just what is. Jones (1998) points out that the company archives many analysts require often do not survive—those that involve statutory obligations often do, but those involving high-level decision making, such as Board papers, often do not. He points out that 'issues of capabilities, innovation and culture will necessitate looking at what happens "lower down" within a firm's structure' (Jones 1998, p. 19). Further,

> The study of intangibles such as the knowledge possessed within a firm, flows of information, and the corporate culture—and how all these things changes over time can involve a very wide range of historical record far removed from documents on strategies… Oral history—of staff employed at all levels—is of special use in examining issues of culture, information flows and systems (Jones 1998, p. 19).

These issues—intangible assets, strategy, culture and decision making in the face of imperfect information—are crucial in international business strategy research.

In addition to criticisms based on material that exists in 'the archive', we need to recognise that the archive is the result of a selection process and therefore that excluded material may be important.[4] The selection process may be biased towards particular nations, regions, races, classes, genders, creeds, political groupings or belief systems. This is a key theme of 'subaltern studies' growing out of South Asia, and particularly India, in imperial times (Ludden 2001). The clear implication of these studies is that the colonial era archive was compiled by the colonial (British) administrators and this presents a largely pro-Imperial bias. However, it is also true that among the dispossessed voices, some were privileged (e.g., the Congress Party spokespeople) and others selected out. The lineage of subaltern studies leads us through Gramsci (1973) to postmodern views of the text: Derrida (1994), Foucault (1965), Barthes (2005). As well as not 'hearing' particular groups, the archive records may not cover particular questions or issues[5] (see also Belich 2009[6]; Decker 2013; Moss 1997).

---

[4] For an excellent review of the use (and extension) of archive material see Wilkins and Hill (2011) 'Bibliographical Essay' pp. 445–458.

[5] See also Schwarzkopf (2012).

[6] Belich notes, of trying to identify 'emigrants' and their opinions: 'This problem of the silent majority is, of course, endemic in the social history of ideas. The standard solution, not one to be despised in the absence of alternatives, is to pile up available examples of opinions in the vague hope that these are typical. Once possible refinement is the analysis of the conceptual language of substantial groups of lesser writers who are trying to persuade their still-larger target audience to do something' (Belich 2009, p. 148 f.).

2.2 Analysing Sequences, Time Series and Processes

There are a number of important techniques in historical research which are useful to international business scholars in examining process, sequence, rhythm and speed—all of which are important in internationalisation. As Mahoney points out (2004, p. 88), 'Causation is fundamentally a matter of sequence'. This is a problem addressed in economics as 'Granger causality' (1988). The critical question is not data access, but careful theorising. Sequence and duration arguments attempt to pick up sensitivity to time and place.

Process analysis holds out the possibility of integrating the time dimension into the internationalisation of firms. Process research, which is contrasted to 'variance paradigms', pays particular attention to the sequencing of events that take place within cases (Welch and Paavilainen-Mantymaki 2014). Events, not variables, are the crucial writ of analysis and capturing multiple time points builds narrative, event studies and panel data analyses. In combination with variance approaches, process analysis has the potential to explain the effects of context (place) and time in internationalisation. The critical task is the identification of the linking mechanisms that connect cause and effect. This requires connecting qualitative data evaluation with experimental reasoning. It is also a useful check on spurious statistical relationships (Granger and Newbold 1974). Easterlin (2013) argues that cross-sectional relationships are often taken to indicate causation when they may merely reflect historical experience, i.e., similar leader–follower patterns for variables that are causally unrelated. This is particularly the case when similar geographic patterns of diffusion are captured by the data—as may well be the case when studying the internationalisation of firms. This may reflect the fact that one set of (national) firms get an early start whilst others play catch-up.

We must, however, beware of 'ingrained assumptions about historical peri-odization where mere temporal succession is insufficiently distinguished from historical explanation' (Gregory 2012, p. 9). This provides a connection to 'path dependence' and sensitivity to initial conditions. Careful examination of relevant data allows analysts to identify reactive sequences 'whereby an initial outcome triggers a chain of temporally ordered and causally connected events that lead to a final outcome of interest' (Mahoney 2004, p. 91).

Page (2006), however, shows that path dependence describes a set of models, not a single model. Forms of history dependence can be divided between those where outcomes are history dependent and those in which the equilibria depend on history. Path dependence requires 'a build-up of behavioural routines, social connections, or cognitive structures around an institution' (p. 89). Page shows that there is a variety of types of path dependence, each of which can be precisely defined, and that it is insufficient to cite 'increasing returns' as evidence of path-dependent processes. The consequences for process research on internationalisation are profound and require researchers to be as precise as possible, when asserting path dependence, to evidence its roots and specify their impact on future trajectories. Jackson and Kollman (2010) build on Page's definitions and suggest 'If social scientists use notions of path dependence, they should have clearly articulated definitions and criteria for what constitutes a path dependent process' (p. 258): 'Any such formulation must be able to explain how the effects of initial and early outcomes are maintained over long periods of time and continue to be observed in current outcomes' (p. 280). This is far stronger than a simple statement that 'history matters'. Path-dependent sequences raise important theoretical issues and thereby contribute to a further and deeper round of understanding; as with quantitative analysis we need to be constantly attentive to sources of bias (Nickell 1981).

Understanding sequences entails additional complexities. Brown (2012, p. xxii) points out that choosing the periodicity (start and end points of data collection and investigation) can risk coming to foregone conclusions and 'a deceptive teleology':

> Two aspects of history are particularly important for historians: propulsion and periodization. The first concerns the forces that promote change. The second involves mental architecture: the chronological framework within which we set out history. Since all periodization presumes a theory of change, these are linked theoretical properties (Green 1993, p. 17).

Propulsion and periodization—change and classification—are ultimately constructs and need to be placed both within a theoretical framework and a given context of time and place. This is a challenge to international business research which is often insufficiently theoretical and contextualised.

International business studies need to be sensitive to the period of study. Laidler (2012, p. 5) advises,

> The past may be the only source of data against which economic hypotheses can be tested or calibrated, but data never speak entirely for themselves. They need to be interpreted through a theory. When the only theory deemed suitable for this purpose embodies itself as part of its own structure, even on an 'as if' basis, then that structure is inevitably projected onto the past, and other perspectives on the historical record are obscured.

This suggests that a fundamental problem is that international business research is often inadequately theorised. Theories which stand up to testing in many historical periods are more robust than those that do not. Jones and Khanna (2006, p. 455) see history as an important source of time series data: 'historical variation is at least as good as contemporary cross-sectional variation in illuminating conceptual issues'. Although it should be noted that many historians are sensitive to the limits of generalisation across historical periods. Burgelman (2011) sees longitudinal qualitative research being situated between history as 'particular generalization' (Gaddis 2002) and reductionism; that is, 'general particularization'.

Longitudinal research and good process research draw on both history's narrative methods and statistical and mathematical models. Such longitudinal studies clearly need rigorous methods from both history and statistics. A relevant example is Kogut and Parkinson (1998), who examine the adoption of the multidivisional structure, testing Chandler's (1962) core thesis over a long time period, 'analysing history from the start'. Despite the difficulties of compiling archival data for a large sample of firms, the authors are able to test an innovative methodology on diffusion histories of the 'M-form' from the period beginning in 1950. They use a hazard model (of adopting the M-form) with imitation and firm covariates that predict adoption rates. The sample (62 firms) is large enough to be split into 'fast' and 'slow' adopters of this organisational innovation and a comparison of the difference between the two samples enables the authors to confirm Chandler's historical account and to point to some qualifications concerning flows of information between firms which meant that proximate firms were more likely to adopt the M-form structure. Imitation effects by firms located in the same industry and firms with links to M-form adopters also seemed significant.

The Kogut and Parkinson (1998) study is a successful example of 'History Meets Business Studies' (p. 257) and also of the application of techniques of organisational demography. This approach has also been successfully applied to the birth and death of subsidiaries and foreign market entry strategies (Kogut 2009). Historical studies have established an important precedent of 'the importance of sampling on founders rather than survivors and of the effects of age on mortality' (Kogut 2009, p. 721). Shaver (1998) pointed out that many previous studies had not accounted for endogeneity and were subject to self-selection bias but that such effects could be corrected for using a methodology that factors in the full history of entries, taking account of strategy choice based on firm attributes and industry conditions. Strategy choice is endogenous and self selected based on these conditions and modelling has to account for this. Concepts such as the 'liability of newness' (Stinchcombe 1965) and the (in International Business) celebrated 'liability of foreignness' (Zaheer 1995 after Hymer 1976) examine diffusion over time. There are, however, as Kogut (2009) points out, several unresolved challenges in the organisational demography literature. First, self-selection bias is still unresolved in that successful firms are more likely to venture abroad. Second, because of unobserved variables (such as the quality of the firm) heterogeneity remains in any sample of firms and any heterogeneous population can be shown to suffer 'liability of newness'. Controls for heterogeneity, of course, are a palliative (e.g., size of firm) but it is difficult to control all such variation. A careful specification of the growth process of firms (despite Penrose (1959) and her heirs) still eludes us.

In concluding this section, it should be mentioned that cliometrics, or the measurement of history (also called the New Economic History) is not uncontroversial (Diebolt 2012). 'Hypothetico-deductive models' (utilising the counterfactual position) using 'propositions contrary to the facts has not escaped criticism' (Diebolt 2012, p. 4), and they contrast with the inductive position of the German historical school (Grimmer-Solem 2003). The economistic tradition of 'opportunity cost' whereby the true costs of any action is the best alternative foregone, provides a firm philosophical link between economics and the counterfactual as discussed below.

2.3 Comparative Methods

The comparative method is of great importance throughout the social sciences. There are three classic comparators in social science research: across space, across time, and against a carefully specified counterfactual state of the world (Buckley et al. 1992). International business research has traditionally focused on just one of these—across space. Historical research specialises particularly in comparisons

 Springer

across time, but also has lessons in spatial comparison and in counterfactual analysis.

> Research that depends on *ex post* statistical adjustment (such as cross-country regressions) has recently come under fire; there has been a commensurate shift of focus towards design-based research—in which control over confounding variables comes primarily from research design, rather than model-based statistical adjustment (Dunning 2012, p. xvii).

The design of a randomised controlled experiment has three characteristics (Freedman et al. 2007, pp. 4–8):

1. The response of the experimental subjects assigned to receive a treatment is compared to the response of subjects assigned to a control group. This allows comparisons of outcomes across the two groups.
2. The assignment of subjects to treatment and control groups is done at random—a coin toss, for example. This establishes *ex ante* symmetry between the groups and obviates the existence of confounding variables.
3. The manipulation of the treatment or intervention is under the control of the experimental research. This establishes further evidence for a *causal* relationship between the treatment and the outcomes (Dunning 2012, p. 15).

Crucially most extant research utilises 'as if random' assignment of interventions rather than 'natural'. Its success depends upon the plausibility of 'as if random', the credibility of models and the relevance of intervention. 'Qualitative evidence plays a central role in the analysis of natural experiments' (Dunning 2012, p. 228). This is because an investigation of the causal process is critical (Collier et al. 2010) in avoiding 'selecting on the dependent' variable by analysing only those cases where causal-process observations appear to have played a productive inferential role. Indeed, Dunning (2012, p. 229) suggests that a future research agenda should focus on developing a framework that distinguishes and predicts when and what kinds of causal-process observations provide the most useful leverage for causal inference in natural experiments. Results however may be very particular and parochial because of the limited availability of natural experiment possibilities (Yin 2014). Experimental results, therefore, come at a price.

> The price for success is a focus that is too narrow and too local to tell us 'what works' in development, to design policy, or to advance scientific knowledge about development processes (Deaton 2009, p. 426).

Comparison across places by geographic area or space is frequent in international business research (across nations, cultures, regions, areas, cities). The multinational enterprise is an excellent laboratory or natural experiment because it holds constant the single institution of the firm but varies the location of study. The division, and the later unification, of Germany allowed Kogut and Zander (2000) the opportunity to conduct a natural experiment by comparing the two sections of the Zeiss Company under socialism and capitalism. The experimental design measured the dependent variable (outcome)—the technological output of the two firms proxied by

 Springer

patents—under 'treatments' offered by the different economic contexts of the two different economic systems. This unusual design substituted for a random sample by eliminating the effects of extraneous factors and isolating the effects of the treatment variable on the 'same' firm. Comparative management experiments can be done by comparing company A's subsidiary in Vietnam with its subsidiary in Virginia. This is the stock-in-trade of many international business experiments and was utilised by Hofstede (1991, 1997, 2001), whose work on culture held the host company (IBM) culture constant whilst varying the purported national cultural responses of the firm's employees.

Comparisons across time, holding place constant, are the essence of 'history'. They give rise to notions of 'growth', 'progress', 'design', 'loss'. Chandler (1984) describes his method as the comparison of detailed case studies to generate 'non historically specific generalizations'. Research in business history has challenged the Chandler thesis that managerial capitalism is universally becoming the norm (Whittington 2007; Rowlinson et al. 2007). Hannah (2007) illustrates the use of comparative historical data to challenge the received wisdom. As noted elsewhere in this piece, such comparisons are fraught with danger unless carefully conducted. Meanings of documents, words, artefacts and statements vary according to different point of time usage and must be carefully analysed as best practice historical research dictates. As Ragin says (1987, p. 27),

> many features of social life confound attempts to unravel causal complexity when experimental methods cannot be used… First, rarely does an outcome of interest to social scientists have a single cause… Second, causes rarely operate in isolation. Usually, it is the combined effect of various conditions their intersection in time and space, that produces a certain outcome… Third, a specific cause may have opposite effects depending on context.

These three factors—multiple, interacting causes, differential by context—are the very essence of international business research. Because of the difficulty of designing natural experiments International business research has emphasised statistical control in its methods. Ragin (1987) points out that statistical control is very different from experimental control.[7] Statistical control does not equate to experimental control: 'the dependent variable is not examined under all possible combinations of values of the independent variables, as is possible in experimental investigations' (Ragin 1987, p. 61). Ragin presents a Boolean approach to qualitative comparison (after George Boole (2003) [1854] and also known as the algebra of logic or algebra of sets). Kogut (2009) shows the relevance of this approach to international business research (see also Saka-Helmhout 2011). A recent development of the use of Boolean algebra in international business is the

---

[7] 'In most statistical analyses, the effect of a control variable is its average effect on the dependent variable, across all cases, not of the effects of other variables. The subtraction of effects central to statistical control is a purely mechanical operation predicted on simplifying assumptions. It is assumed in multiple regression, for example, that a variable's effect is the same in each case—that a one-unit change in an independent variable has the same effect on the dependent variable regardless of context, that is, regardless variable's effect by simple subtraction. The result is a dependent variable whose values have been "corrected" for the effects of one or more independent variables' (Ragin 1987, p. 59).

 Springer

Condition			Outcome
A	B	C	1 or 0
0	0	0	0
0	0	1	?
0	1	0	?
1	0	0	?
1	1	0	?
1	0	1	?
0	1	1	?
1	1	1	1

Fig. 1 Truth table for a three cause proposition

application of fuzzy-set qualitative comparative analysis in the assessment of different models of capitalism (Judge et al. 2014).

Qualitative comparisons are of the essence in (historical) international business research. As Kogut (2009) shows, a proposition based on a three-cause explanation in order to avoid simplifying assumptions at the outset requires a truth table of 2^3 or eight combinations as in Fig. 1. Thus, to achieve experimental control, the investigation needs eight cases with the characteristics shown in the table in order to determine which combination of causes (A, B, C) determines the outcome (1). (See Ragin 1987, particularly Chapters 7 and 8.) Thus historical comparative data can focus our attention on cases as wholes and to explore the combinatorial complexities of causation (Ragin 1987, p. 171).[8] It is also suggestive of the answer to the perennial question of how many cases are needed to satisfy a proposition. For instance, it might be suggested that the rise of Japan was due to (1) lifetime work contracts, (2) company unions and (3) the Keiretsu system. In order to prove or disprove the argument, the bottom line where all three proposed casual factors are present must be contrasted with situations where none of them are present (the top line) where only one of the proposed causes is present and where combinations of two causes are present. This enables the analyst to identify necessary and sufficient conditions. In a three cause theoretical proposal, a total of eight cases are needed.

As Mahoney (2004, p. 82) says, 'comparative-historical methodology offers tools well adapted to the analysis of necessary and sufficient causes'. This need not rely on deterministic logic because necessary and sufficient causes can be expressed in a probabilistic framework. This also aligns with expressing variables in a continuous rather than in a dichotomous fashion. These techniques are helpful, as Saka-Helmhout (2011) points out, in analysing cross-case analyses of bundles of conditions, in particular in the identification of patterns of regularities and differences. The methodological stream (and theoretical underpinnings) of comparative historical research therefore lead to the more systematic pinpointing of necessary and sufficient causes in international business case research. For applications to management research, see Oz (2004).

---

[8] For a full discussion of varieties of comparative history, see Skocpol and Somers (1980).

2.4 Counterfactual Analysis

The third classic comparator is the 'alternative position'. The counterfactual question—'what if?'—is a particular type of thought experiment designed to elucidate causality. It is widely (if sometimes unwittingly) used in economics where 'opportunity cost' (the real cost of resources) is defined as the cost of the next best alternative foregone. The 'alternative position' and its specification have long been a particular problem in international business research—classically in the analysis of foreign direct investment (FDI). What would have happened in the absence of a particular foreign investment? (Reddaway et al. 1968; Steuer 1973; Cairncross 1953; Buckley et al. 1992, p. 36). Jones and Khanna (2006, p. 464) say that a 'comparative approach also gets at the spirit of specifying counterfactuals'.

Historians have long had to face this issue. Several variously sophisticated attempts have been made to try to answer the question of what would (might) have happened had some of the crucial turning points of history turned out differently (Beatty 2011; Ferguson 1997; Cowley 1999; Lebow 2014). Lebow (2012) points out that counterfactuals are frequently used in physical and biological sciences to develop and evaluate sophisticated, non-linear models. The counterfactual has to be well defined and this requires a thorough analysis and presentation of the context of the alternative position. Such thought experiments are perhaps history's closest comparator to a laboratory experiment (Gaddis 2002, p. 100)—although see the section on natural experiments in the social sciences above. The counterfactual counteracts the static nature of much historical analysis by focusing upon dynamics and processes.

Durand and Vaara (2009, p. 1245) have examined the role of counterfactuals in explicating causality in the field of business strategy. They argue that:

> Counterfactual history can add to our understanding of the context-specific construction of resource-based competitive advantage and path dependence, and causal modelling can help to reconceptualize the relationships between resources and performance.

The role of counterfactual reasoning in organisation studies was also explored in two issues of *Management & Organizational History* [volume 3(1) 2008 and volume 4(2) 2007]. MacKay (2007) pointed out that counterfactuals can guard against path dependencies in both structure of organisations and perception. Counterfactuals illustrate that the world could be other than it is and help the analyst to evaluate different possibilities including decisions and their outcomes. Thus socio-economic and technical path dependencies can introduce rigidities and cognitive or psychological path dependencies can impair organisational learning. Toms and Beck (2007) criticise received counterfactuals (on the Lancashire cotton industry) as suffering from the problems of teleology and hindsight that occur when the counterfactual is contaminated by *ex post* knowledge of the outcome (Maielli and Booth 2008).[9] Toms and Beck (2007, p. 315) attempt to construct a history 'from the perspective of decision making entrepreneurs as embedded historical

---

[9] See Evans (2014) for a critical appraisal of counterfactuals.

actors'. This is surely the model for internationalisation researchers, when examining past decisions and their outcome.

The key, as Leunig (2010) points out, is to be explicit in specifying the counterfactual position as this provides more evidence than a simple judgement on the impact of (say) a critical innovation. Fogel (1964) in finding that agricultural land opened up by the railroads might otherwise have been undeveloped, examined the possibility of an alternative network of canals.[10] This was done not by simple perusal of a map but by examining detailed typographical maps, as a canal builder would do. A limitation of counterfactual analysis is the ability to go on to use comparative analysis because the carefully constructed counterfactual is often locationally or temporally specific. For instance, although in Fogel's counterfactual, canals could have done most of the work of railroads, he assumed away the vagaries of the weather—in the Northeast of the US at least, canals would have been frozen for at least 4 months of the year.[11] An excellent example of a carefully constructed counterfactual is Casson's construction of the (optimal) counterfactual railway network (complete with timetable) for the UK taking account of network performance, the physical geography of the UK, Victorian urbanisation and traffic, engineering constraints, regulation, institutional and political constraints (Casson 2009).

The counterfactual has an important place in the development of international business theory as analyses of the impact of FDI on host and source countries have been cast in the terms of the 'alternative position'—what would have happened in the absence of FDI. Foreshadowing the current debate an offshoring and outsourcing, earlier literature on the impact of FDI following Hufbauer and Adler (1968) identified three polar 'alternative positions' (Buckley and Artisien 1987, pp. 73, 78–79, 80).

The classical assumption assumes that FDI produces a net addition to capital formation in the host country but a similar decline in capital formation in the source country. This is equivalent to the assumption that FDI substitutes for exports. The reverse classical assumption assumes that the FDI substitutes for investment in the host country but leaves investment in the source country unchanged. This is equivalent to 'defensive investment' where the source country firm cannot penetrate the target market via exports and would lose the market to host country firms in the absence of FDI. The anti-classical assumption is that FDI does not substitute for capital investment in the source country, neither does it reduce investment by host country firms. Consequently FDI increases world capital formation (in contrast to the other two assumptions where world capital formation is unchanged).

Anticlassical conditions are most likely when host country firms are incapable of undertaking the projects fulfilled by FDI. Each of these assumptions is static and rigid—not allowing for a growth of demand, perhaps from the 'presence effect'. An organic model, postulating that FDI substitutes for exports in the short run, but in the long run substitutes for rival investment is more likely. Hood and Young (1979)

---

[10] As a referee points out, Fogel was not posing the 'what if' question but rather 'by *how much* less would the US economy have grown if there had been no railways'.

[11] I owe this point to Geoff Jones (personal communication 09.07.2013).

 Springer

pointed out that the relationship between FDI and exports needs to be fully specified in any such examination of effects of FDI.

This debate needs to be updated as it predated studies of MNEs' foreign market servicing strategies and motives other than market-seeking. A parallel move away from economic counterfactuals towards specifying alternative decision making scenarios for decision-making entrepreneurs would be a step forward here (Toms and Beck 2007). A further important question here concerns the identity of the decision maker and whether ownership (foreign versus domestic) matters. As concern with the employment impact of FDI at home and abroad grows, counterfactual analysis is useful in specifying the myriad impacts (employment among them) of modern MNEs.

The 'historical alternatives approach' (Zeitlin 2007) is a specifically business history variant of counterfactual analysis. The historical alternatives approach is promoted by Zeitlin (2007) as 'against teleology and determinism'. The approach suggests that plasticity of technology has been underrated, leading to technological determinism of a particularly narrow type. Strategic action in the face of uncertainty, mutability and hedging strategies gives a far wider range of outcomes than conventionally allowed for and 'the market' is dogmatically and narrowly the result of historical construction. Size of firms, strategic action, industry imperatives and rationality are too glibly taken as determining factors and the result is an excessively pre-determined view of business choices. While it is certainly the case that many analyses based on historical reasoning are unduly constrained in terms of other potential outcomes, alternative futures have to be specified extremely carefully and constraints that are to be lifted on outcomes must be spelled out and the degree to which they are assumed to be not binding requires extensive and meticulous research.

In internationalisation research, alternative positions are important concepts in the development of the process. The decisions that key managers make can be evaluated by presenting them with alternative scenarios, as Buckley et al. (2007) did. This is usually, for practical and cost reasons, a point-of-time rather than a continuous exercise even though, in principle, these choices could be presented to managers frequently throughout the internationalisation process. There are examples of where a single investment is considered as a 'Go/No go' decision and others where several alternative investments are simultaneously considered (Buckley et al. 1978). In many cases firms will themselves investigate alternative scenarios even if this is done informally rather than through 'scenario planning'.

3 Discussion

Table 1 shows the areas where the four key methods identified above have been successfully applied in international business.

The application of the above principles of method suggests that a new international business history is called for that relies on the two key principles of examining change over time and using the comparative method. If we accept that the study of history is about change over time, then international business history

Table 1 The use of historical research methods in international business

Historical research method	Areas of use in international business	Examples
1. Source criticism	Executive interviews	Buckley et al. (2007)
	Archival research	Jones (2000), Decker (1994, 2013)
	Company statements	Moss (1997)
	Government policy pronouncements	Buckley and Pearce 1991
2. Time series analyses	Long period investigations	Kogut and Parkinson (1998) on Chandler's multi division hypothesis
	Organisational demography	Birth and death of subsidiaries; Kogut (2009)
	Computable general equilibrium models	O'Rourke and Williamson (1999)
	Process research	Internationalisation studies—see those reviewed in Welch and Paavilainen-Mantymaki (2014)
3. Comparative methods	'Natural experiment' in a multinational company	Kogut and Zander (2000) on Zeiss company in East and West Germany
	Long run business culture	Haggerty (2012), Jones (2000) and see text
	Combining comparative data: historical, geographical sectoral	Becuwe et al. (2012) 'the first globalization'
4. Counterfactual analysis	Impact of foreign direct investment on host country	Steuer (1973), Buckley and Artisien (1987) (European hosts "South")
	Impact of FDI on source country	Cairncross (1953) (UK), Hufbauer and Adler (1968) (US), Reddaway et al. (1968) (UK), Buckley and Artisien (1987) (European investors 'North')
	Impact of railways	Fogel (1964), Casson 2009

needs to take a long-run view of change and of the role of multinational firms in large scale social and economic development. This presents a major challenge in view of the material in archives. Company archives cover the world from the point of view of the (single) company. In international business this represents only one actor in a complex drama. The roles of host and source countries are perforce omitted. It behoves the writers of international company histories to take a wider perspective than just the company's viewpoint. In approaching the comparative method, the spatial comparison encompasses the international dimension but changes over time require a longer run view than most company histories allow for. Comparing the role of a company in the eighteenth century with the nineteenth is not often possible from a single company's archives (and it can be argued, were this to be so, we would be dealing with an outlier). In short, the writing of international business history needs to be more imaginative, not only in method but also in its engagement with wider theory and technique.

It is equally the case that international business theory and methods can enrich historical research.[12] In addition to the Chitu et al. (2013) examination of 'history effects' in international finance and trade, international business can be focused on global history in the way that Bell and Dale (2011) analysed the economic and financial dimensions of the medieval pilgrimage business (using contract and network theory and the analysis of saints' shrines as business franchise, under an umbrella brand of the Universal Catholic Church).

3.1 Historical Research Approaches and the Internationalisation Process

The question of how firm internationalisation evolves over time is best answered by the careful use of historical research methods duly adapted for the context of international business research (Jones and Zeitlin 2007) . The temporal dimension of the internationalisation process needs to be centre-stage and critical decision points and turning points need to be mapped on a timeline and against feasible alternatives. As extant international business research has shown (Buckley et al. 2007), managers are only partly guided by rational processes and context and contingency play roles in determining the final decisions. If we know *when* these critical decisions are made, then it becomes much easier to understand the factors that were in play in the decision makers' minds. It is frequently remarked that key 'events' (a coup, the launch of a rival's product, a competitive market entry) were the triggers for investment (or non-investment) decisions and a timeline of events—a mapping of process—can be a key to understanding. The temporal sequencing of 'events' in the internationalisation process is clearly vital to comprehension of the firm's strategy and decisions. As well as time, at a given place, we need to add place at a given time for all these events. Thus a double comparative across time and space is necessary for a rounded understanding of outcomes.

Process research also needs to comprehend simultaneous processes as there is not just one sequence of events in internationalisation; rather, there are multiple. Selection of processes to track has to be theoretically driven. Process research cannot stand apart from the theory, it is has to be fully engaged with the appropriate theories and to feed back into them (Paavilainen-Mantymaki and Welch 2013). This is fully in accord with Pettigrew's (1997) approach to processual analysis. Moreover, as Pettigrew (1997, p. 340) says, 'The time quality of a processual analysis thereby lies in linking processes to outcomes'. Linking internationalisation processes to outcomes (performance) is a missing element in our understanding— the results of the managerial decisions form an essential element of a feedback loop to further internationalisation.

The four generic methods applied in historical research outlined here—source criticism, time series analysis, the use of comparative methods and counterfactual analysis—are all vital in constructing a proper process analysis of the internationalisation of the firm (or of a firm's internationalisation). It is fundamental that a critical appraisal of all sources be undertaken, be they company statements,

---

[12] Kobrak and Schneider (2011) make a call for a renewal of historical research methods in business history, 'reviving some basic historiographical notions' (p. 401).

 Springer

archives, documents or interviews. Wherever possible these should be triangulated against other sources. Nothing should be taken on trust and, if it has to be, this should be clearly stated. Wherever possible, a timeline of relevant events should be made in order to sequence the decision processes and outcomes. The construction of multiple timelines—of different managers, sub-units of the firm and other key actors (such as competitors, agents, customers, suppliers, governmental bodies, support agencies) should be compared and contrasted. The coincidence in time of actions by interested parties is *prima facie* evidence of joint causality. These techniques can be extended by the use of comparisons not only in time but in space. The geographical mapping of actions and outcomes gives richness to the process analysis. The transmission and impact of decisions from one geographical point (e.g., headquarters) to another (a subsidiary, a potential takeover victim), the time-lags involved and the reaction time of the recipient are all vital in understanding internationalisation. Counterfactual analysis, too, can be a useful tool. Firms often approach internationalisation decisions with a number of contingencies. If they cannot acquire foreign firm X, should they turn to Y, or to a greenfield venture instead? These alternatives are useful to know and it may be possible to construct feasible alternative internationalisation paths.

In summary, historical research methods and approaches provide a research design for internationalisation process studies that enhance the depth of understanding by incorporating concrete timelines, alternatives and decision processes.

3.2 A New Concept of Internationalisation

The new concept of internationalisation that emerges from a consideration of the light shed by historical research on managerial processes is that internationalisation is the outcome of a set of decisions, dependent on context and previous decisions, considering alternative locations, entry and development methods in a choice set of time and space. In these sequential decisions, knowledge of past decisions and their outcomes plays a part in the next round of decisions. Hence companies can create 'vicious circles' or 'virtuous circles' in their internationalisation processes. In this sense, a knowledge of history of the company making the decision and of similar companies making comparable decisions can be valuable for the manager. History matters to decision-makers as well as analysts. The question of when to take history into account and when to ignore it and 'take a chance' is the essence of managerial judgement (and of 'real options theory'—see Kogut and Kulatilaka 2001; Buckley et al. 2002). Those who make regular correct calls will develop a 'track record' and be valued accordingly. Thus both the weight of history and the judgement of successful individuals will build path dependence into the internationalisation process.

The research approach formulated in this article encompasses the Uppsala approach to internationalisation (Johanson and Vahlne 1977, 2009) as a special case. The Uppsala approach has no explicit role for time. It explains market entry as a sequence which is determined by psychic proximity to the source country in a loose path dependent fashion. A more careful specification of the relationship between market entry and psychic distance and an explicit acknowledgement of the

 Springer

role of time would allow a fully historical analysis of market entry sequencing in the Uppsala tradition.

4 Conclusion: The Response to the Challenge of Historical Research

The last sentences of Butterfield's (1965, p. 132) *The Whig Interpretation of History* encompasses the challenge of historical research methods: 'In other words, the truth of history is no simple matter, all packed and parcelled ready for handling in the market-place. And the understanding of the past is not so easy as it is sometimes made to appear'. Historical research methods can help international business researchers to be more questioning, analytical and critical and to think laterally in terms of alternative states of the world, different choices and outcomes. There is a justifiable argument that international business research is insufficiently critical of 'texts' in all their forms—company statements, official statistics, interviews with managers among them—and historical research has a number of techniques for improving the penetration of meaning behind texts, as this piece has shown.

In using research methods derived from history we must always factor in 'Contingency, choice and agency' (Clark 2012, p. 362). We should also remember that history interacts with geography—context is crucial. To quote the historian Peter Brown's work on wealth in the early Christian period, 'A true history of Latin Christianity requires an unremitting sense of place' (Brown 2012, p. xxii). A good example relevant to international business is the combined use of historical, geographical and sectoral data by Becuwe, Blancheton and Charles (2012) in analysing the decline of French trade power in the 'first globalization' of 1850–1913. A sense of place involves understanding both the global macro context and the particular location.

There is an awkward disjunction between traditional historical research and hypothetico-deductive modelling. This is paralleled by the lack of integration between quantitative and qualitative methods in international business research, arising from their philosophical bases in positivism and subjectivism. The careful integration of historical research methods into international business provides us with one channel of progress towards a more complete understanding of the phenomena of international business.

In the particular case of the analysis of the internationalisation of the firm, historical approaches place managerial judgement central to the process. Such judgement, however, is constrained by context. This context is both temporal and spatial. 'When' and 'where' matter in both an individual decision and the analysis of decisions. The use of the plural here implies sequencing and therefore a focus on process. The choice set faced by the manager is constrained by what has gone before—by history. This does not determine the next decision in the sequence but it influences it. The new concept of internationalisation is that sequence, not events, are at the heart of the international growth of the firm, that spatial issues (including psychic distance to a potential host country) must be accounted for, and that past decisions constrain outcomes.

On the importance of methodology (in international business as elsewhere) we can end with a quote from Kogut (2009, p. 711): 'It is one of the best-kept secrets of research that a methodological contribution is the most powerful engine for the replication and diffusion of an idea'.

Acknowledgments I am grateful for comments on earlier versions from Chris Clark (Cambridge), Simon Ball (Leeds), Andrew Thompson (Exeter), Niall Ferguson (Harvard), Jeremy Black (Exeter), Mark Casson (Reading), Janet Casson (Oxford), Catherine Casson (Birmingham), Jonathan Steinberg (Pennsylvania), Catherine Welch (Sydney), Adrian Bell (Reading), Peter Miskell (Reading), Stephanie Decker (Aston), Geoffrey Jones (Harvard), Mira Wilkins (Florida International University), an anonymous reviewer for the AIBUK 2013 Conference at Aston University, participants at AIBUK Aston 2013, three anonymous reviewers for AIB 2013 and participants at the AIB Conference, Istanbul, July 2013, two anonymous referees and particularly to the editors of this Focused Issue.

Open Access This article is distributed under the terms of the Creative Commons Attribution 4.0 International License (http://creativecommons.org/licenses/by/4.0/), which permits unrestricted use, distribution, and reproduction in any medium, provided you give appropriate credit to the original author(s) and the source, provide a link to the Creative Commons license, and indicate if changes were made.

References

Barthes, R. (2005). *Criticism and truth. Translated and edited by K. P. Keueman*. London: Continuum International Publishing Group.

Beatty, J. (2011). *The lost history of 1914: How the Great War was not inevitable*. London: Bloomsbury.

Becuwe, S., Blancheton, D., & Charles, L. (2012). *The decline of French trade power during the first globalization (1850–1913)* (pp. 2012–2022). Cahiers du Gretha: Université de Bordeaux.

Belich, J. (2009). *Replenishing the earth: The settler revolution and the rise of the Angle-World 1783–1939*. Oxford: Oxford University Press.

Bell, A. R., & Dale, R. S. (2011). The medieval pilgrimage business. *Enterprise and Society, 12*(3), 601–627.

Berlin, I. (1960). History and theory. The concept of scientific history. *History and Theory, 1*(1), 1–31.

Bloch, M. (1954). *The historian's craft. Translated Peter Putman*. Manchester: Manchester University Press.

Boole, G. (2003). *[1854] An investigation of the laws of thought, on which are founded the mathematical theories of logic and probabilities*. Amherst: Prometheus Books.

Brown, P. (2012). *Through the eye of a needle: Wealth, the fall of Rome and the making of Christianity in the West 350–550 AD*. Princeton: Princeton University Press.

Buckley, P. J., & Artisien, P. (1987). *North-south direct investment in the European communities: The employment impact of direct investment by British, French and German multinationals in Greece, Portugal and Spain*. Basingstoke: Macmillan.

Buckley, P. J., Casson, M. C., & Gulamhussen, M. A. (2002). Internationalisation—Real options, knowledge management and the Uppsala Approach. In V. Havila, M. Forsgren, & H. Hakansson (Eds.), *Critical perspectives on internationalisation* (pp. 229–261). Oxford: Elsevier.

Buckley, P. J., Devinney, T. M., & Louviere, J. J. (2007). Do managers behave the way theory suggests? A choice-theoretic examination of foreign direct investment location decision-making. *Journal of International Business Studies, 38*(7), 1069–1094.

Buckley, P J., Newbould, G. D., & Thurwell, J. (1978). *Going international—The experience of smaller companies overseas*. London: Associated Business Press/New York: Halsted Press.

Buckley, P. J., Pass, C. L., & Prescott, K. (1992). *Servicing international markets: Competitive strategies of firms*. Oxford: Basil Blackwell.

Buckley, P. J., & Pearce, R. D. (1991). *International aspects of UK economic activities: Reviews of UK statistical sources*. Review No 44, Volume XXVI Royal Statistical Society/Economic and Social Research Council. London: Chapman and Hall.

Burgelman, R. A. (2011). Bridging history and reductionism: A key role for longitudinal qualitative research. *Journal of International Business Studies, 42*(5), 591–601.

Butterfield, H. (1965). *The Whig interpretation of history.* New York: W. W. Norton & Company Inc. **(Original 1931).**

Cairncross, A. (1953). *Home and foreign investment.* Cambridge: Cambridge University Press.

Cannadine, D. (2013). *The undivided past: History beyond our differences.* London: Allen Lane.

Casson, M. (2009). *The world's first railway system.* Oxford: Oxford University Press.

Chandler, A. D. (1962). *Strategy and structure: Chapters in the history of the American industrial enterprise.* Cambridge: MIT Press.

Chandler, A. D. (1984). Comparative business history. In D. C. Coleman & P. Mathias (Eds.), *Enterprise and history: Essays in honour of Charles Wilson* (pp. 473–503). Cambridge: Cambridge University Press.

Chitu, L., Eichengreen, B., & Mehl, A. J. (2013). *History, gravity and international finance.* National Bureau of Economic Research Working paper 18697, Washington D.C.

Clark, C. (2012). *The sleepwalkers: How Europe went to war in 1914.* London: Allen Lane.

Clark, P., & Rowlinson, M. (2004). The treatment of history in organisation studies: Towards an 'historic turn'? *Business History, 43*(3), 331–352.

Collier, D., Brady, H. E., & Seawright, J. (2010). Sources of leverage in causal inference: Towards an alternative view of methodology. In H. E. Brady & D. Collier (Eds.), *Rethinking social enquiry: Diverse tools, shared standards* (2nd ed., pp. 229–266). New York: Rowman and Lillefield.

Cowley, R. (Ed.). (1999). *What if?.* New York: G.P. Putnam's Sons.

Deaton, A. (2009). *Instruments of development: Randomization in the tropics, and the search for the elusive keys to economic development. The Keynes Lecture.* London: British Academy.

Decker, S. (2013). The silence of the archive: Post-colonialism and the practice of historical reconstruction from archival evidence. *Management and Organisational History, 8*(2), 155–173.

Derrida, J. (1994). *Specters of Marx. Translated Peggy Kamuf.* New York: Routledge.

Diebolt, C. (2012). *The cliometric voice.* Association Française de Cliométrie. Working paper No. 12.

Dunning, T. (2012). *Natural experiments in the social sciences.* Cambridge: Cambridge University Press.

Durand, R., & Vaara, E. (2009). Causation, counterfactuals and competitive advantage. *Strategic Management Journal, 30*(12), 1245–1264.

Easterlin, R. A. (2013). *Cross sections are history.* IZA discussion paper No. 7341.

Evans, L. J. (2014). *Altered pasts: Counterfactuals in history.* London: Little, Brown.

Ferguson, N. (Ed.). (1997). *Virtual history: Alternatives and counterfactuals.* London: Picador.

Fogel, R. W. (1964). *Railroads and American economic growth: Essays in econometric history.* Baltimore, Maryland: The Johns Hopkins Press.

Foucault, M. (1965). *Madness and civilization. Translated R. Howard.* New York: Pantheon.

Freedman, D., Pisani, R., & Purves, R. (2007). *Statistics* (4th ed.). New York: W. W. Norton Inc.

Gaddis, J. L. (2002). *The landscape of history: How historians map the past.* Oxford: Oxford University Press.

Gottschalk, L. (1950). *Understanding history: A primer of historical method.* New York: Alfred A Knopf.

Gramsci, A. (1973). *Selections from the prison notebooks.* Edited by Q. Hoare and G. Nowell Smith. New York: International Publishers.

Granger, C. W. J. (1988). Causality, cointegration and control. *Journal of Economic Dynamics and Control, 12*(2), 551–559.

Granger, C. W. J., & Newbold, P. (1974). Spurious regressions in econometrics. *Journal of Econometrics, 2*(2), 111–120.

Green, W. A. (1993). *History, historians and the dynamics of change.* Westport: Praeger.

Gregory, B. S. (2012). *The unintended reformation: How a religious revolution secularized society.* Cambridge: Belking Press of Harvard University.

Grimmer-Solem, E. (2003). *The rise of historical economics and social reform in Germany 1864–1894.* Oxford: Oxford University Press.

Haggerty, S. (2012). *'Merely for money?' Business culture in the British Atlantic 1750–1815.* Liverpool: Liverpool University Press.

Hannah, L. (2007). The 'divorce' of ownership from control from 1900 onwards: Re-calibrating imagined global trends. *Business History, 49*(4), 404–438.

Hofstede, G. (1991). *Cultures and organisations: Software of the mind.* London: McGraw Hill.

Hofstede, G. (1997). *Cultures and organisations: Software of the mind.* New York: McGraw-Hill.

Hofstede, G. (2001). *Culture's consequences: Comparing values, behaviours, institutions and organisations across nations* (2d ed.). New York: Sage Publications.

Hood, N., & Young, S. (1979). *The economics of international business*. London: Longman.

Hufbauer, G. C., & Adler, F. (1968). *US manufacturing investment and the balance of payments*. Washington, DC: US Treasury Department.

Hymer, S. H. (1976). *The international operations of national firms: Study of foreign direct investment*. Cambridge: MIT Press.

Jackson, J. E., & Kollman, K. (2010). A formulation of path dependence with an empirical example. *Quarterly Journal of Political Science, 5*(3), 257–289.

Johanson, J., & Vahlne, J. E. (1977). The internationalization process of the firm: A model of knowledge development and increasing foreign market commitments. *Journal of International Business Studies, 8*(1), 23–32.

Johanson, J., & Vahlne, J. E. (2009). The Uppsala internationalization process model revisited: From liability of foreignness to liability of outsidership. *Journal of International Business Studies, 40*(9), 1411–1431.

Jones, G. (1998). *Company history and business history in the 1990s*. University of Reading discussion papers in economics and management (series A), p. 383.

Jones, G. (2000). *Merchants to multinationals. British trading companies in the nineteenth and twentieth centuries*. Oxford: Oxford University Press.

Jones, G., & Khanna, T. (2006). Bringing history (back) into international business. *Journal of International Business Studies, 37*(4), 453–468.

Jones, G., & Zeitlin, J. (Eds.). (2007). *The Oxford handbook of business history*. Oxford: Oxford University Press.

Judge, W. Q., Fainshmidt, S., & Brown, J. L. (2014). Which model of capitalism best delivers both wealth and equality? *Journal of International Business Studies, 45*(4), 363–386.

Kipping, M., Wadhwani, R. D., & Bucheli, M. (2014). Analyzing and interpreting historical sources: A basic methodology. In M. Bucheli & R. D. Wadhwani (Eds.), *Organizations in time: History, theory, methods* (pp. 305–329). Oxford: Oxford University Press.

Kobrak, C., & Schneider, A. (2011). Varieties of business history: Subject and methods for the twenty-first century. *Business History, 53*(3), 401–424.

Kogut, B. (2009). Methodological contributions in international business and the direction of academic research activity. In A. Rugman (Ed.), *The Oxford handbook of international business* (2nd ed., pp. 711–739). Oxford: Oxford University Press.

Kogut, B., & Kulatilaka, N. (2001). Capabilities as real options. *Organization Science, 12*(6), 744–758.

Kogut, B., & Parkinson, D. (1998). Adoption of the multidivisional structure: Analysing history from the start. *Industrial and Corporate Change, 7*(2), 249–273.

Kogut, B., & Zander, U. (2000). Did socialism fail to innovate? A natural experiment of the two Zeiss companies. *American Sociological Review, 65*(2), 169–190.

Laidler, D. (2012). *Today's standards and yesterday's economics—two short occasional essays—eliminating history from economic thought and Mark Blaug on the quantity theory*. Economic Policy Research Institute working paper series 2012–6, University of Western Ontario.

Lebow, R. N. (2012). Counterfactual thought experiments: A necessary teaching tool. *The History Teacher, 40*(2), 153–176.

Lebow, R. N. (2014). *Archduke Franz Ferdinand lives!*. New York: Palgrave Macmillan.

Leunig, T. (2010). Social savings. *Journal of Economic Surveys, 24*(5), 775–800.

Ludden, D. (Ed.). (2001). *Reading subaltern studies: Critical history, contested meaning and the globalization of South Asia*. London: Anthem Press.

MacKay, R. B. (2007). 'What if': Synthesising debates and advancing prospects of using virtual history in management and organization theory. *Management & Organizational History, 2*(4), 295–314.

Mahoney, J. (2004). Comparative-historical methodology. *Annual Review of Sociology, 30*, 81–101.

Maielli, G., & Booth, C. (2008). Counterfactual history, management and organizations: Reflections and new directions. *Management & Organizational History, 3*(1), 49–61.

Moss, M. (1997). Archives, the historian and the future. In M. Bentley (Ed.), *Companion to historiography* (pp. 960–973). London: Routledge.

Nickell, S. (1981). Biases in dynamic models with fixed effects. *Econometrica: Journal of the Econometric Society, 49*(6), 1417–1426.

O'Rourke, K., & Williamson, G. (1999). *Globalization and history: The evolution of a nineteenth-century Atlantic economy*. Cambridge: MIT Press.

Oz, O. (2004). Using Boolean—and fuzzy-logic-based methods to analyse multiple case study evidence in management research. *Journal of Management Inquiry, 13*(2), 166–179.

Paavilainen-Mäntymäki, E., & Welch, C. (2013). How to escape an unprocessual legacy? A viewpoint from international business research. In M. E. Hassett & E. Paavilainen-Mäntymäki (Eds.), *Handbook of longitudinal research methods in organisation and business studies* (pp. 229–248). Cheltenham: Edward Elgar.

Page, S. E. (2006). Path dependence. *Quarterly Journal of Political Science, 1*(1), 87–115.

Penrose, E. T. (1959). *The theory of the growth of the firm.* Oxford: Basil Blackwell.

Pettigrew, A. M. (1997). What is processual analysis? *Scandinavian Journal of Management, 13*(4), 337–348.

Ragin, C. C. (1987). *The comparative method: Moving beyond qualitative and quantitative strategies.* Berkeley: University of California Press.

Reddaway, W. B., et al. (1968). *Effects of UK direct investment overseas: Final report.* Cambridge: Cambridge University Press.

Rowlinson, M., Toms, S., & Wilson, J. F. (2007). Competing perspectives on the 'managerial revolution': from 'managerialist' to 'anti-managerialist'. *Business History, 49*(4), 464–482.

Saka-Helmhout, A. (2011). Comparative historical analysis in international management research. In R. Piekkari & C. Welch (Eds.), *Rethinking the case study in international business and management research* (pp. 383–407). Cheltenham: Edward Elgar.

Schwarzkopf, S. (2012). Why business historians need a constructive theory of the archive. *Business Archives, 105*(November), 1–9.

Shaver, J. M. (1998). Accounting for endogeneity when assessing strategy performance: Does entry mode choice affect FDI survival? *Management Science, 44*(4), 571–585.

Simiand, F. J. (1903). Méthode historique et sciences socials. *Revue de Synthèse Historique, 6*, 1–22.

Skocpol, T., & Somers, M. (1980). The uses of comparative history in macrosocial inquiry. *Comparative Studies in Society and History, 22*(2), 174–197.

Snyder, T. (2010). *Bloodlands: Europe between Stalin and Hitler.* London: The Bodley Head.

Steuer, M.D. et al. (1973). *The impact of foreign direct investment on the U.K.* London: HMSO.

Stinchcombe, A. L. (1965). Social structure and organisations. In J. G. March (Ed.), *Handbook of organizations* (pp. 142–193). Chicago: Rand-McNally.

Tilley, C. (1983). *Big structure, large processes, huge comparisons.* New York: Russell Sage Foundation.

Toms, S., & Beck, M. (2007). The limitations of economic counterfactuals: The case of the Lancashire textile industry. *Management & Organizational History, 2*(4), 315–330.

Welch, C., & Paavilainen-Mäntymäki, E. (2014). Putting process (back) in: Research on the internationalization process of the firm. *International Journal of Management Reviews, 16*(1), 2–23.

Whittington, R. (2007). Introduction: Comparative perspectives on the managerial revolution. *Business History, 49*(4), 399–403.

Wilkins, M., & Hill, F. E. (2011). *American business abroad: Ford on six continents.* Cambridge: Cambridge University Press **(Original edition 1964 Wayne State University Press)**.

Yin, R. K. (2014). *Case study research: Design and methods* (5th ed.). Thousand Oaks: Sage Publications.

Zaheer, S. (1995). Overcoming the liability of foreignness. *Academy of Management Journal, 38*(2), 341–363.

Zeitlin, J. (2007). The historical alternatives approach. In G. Jones & J. Zeitlin (Eds.), *The Oxford handbook of business history* (pp. 120–140). Oxford: Oxford University Press.

8

Manag Int Rev (2014) 54:307–324
DOI 10.1007/s11575-013-0193-0

RESEARCH ARTICLE

A Linguistic and Philosophical Analysis of Emic and Etic and their Use in International Business Research

Peter J. Buckley · Malcolm Chapman ·
Jeremy Clegg · Hanna Gajewska-De Mattos

Received: 19 December 2012 / Revised: 25 September 2013 / Accepted: 3 December 2013 /
Published online: 23 January 2014
© Springer-Verlag Berlin Heidelberg 2014

Abstract The purpose of this paper is to examine ways in which cross-cultural research in international business can use emic–etic approaches more effectively. The majority of research conducted in the field has been etic, while the cross-cultural data used by the researchers have been emic in nature. This resulted in producing ethnocentric results which are biased towards Western perspectives. We call for a re-evaluation of the importance of in-depth qualitative analysis in international business research. We go back to the origins of emic and etic in linguistics and conduct a linguistic and philosophical analysis of these terms to demonstrate that the emic–etic distinction is not helpful for adequately studying cross-cultural data. We provide examples from linguistics, kinship, and from international business research on German-Polish acquisitions. We demonstrate that what conventional etic cross-cultural research perceives to be a problem is often an opportunity to gain deep insight. We find that emic matters in some cases more that etic, and that the emic can often add value beyond the etic. We conclude that a research strategy employing emic and etic approaches is a vital step to enable cross-cultural researchers to obtain more adequate and meaningful results. While most of researchers have treated emic and etic as dichotomous, we demonstrate the benefits of treating them as complementary approaches.

Keywords Cultural differences · Emic and etic · Poland and Germany ·
Qualitative methodology

P. J. Buckley · M. Chapman · J. Clegg · H. Gajewska-De Mattos (✉)
Centre for International Business, Leeds University Business School,
University of Leeds, Leeds, UK
e-mail: hgdm@lubs.leeds.ac.uk

1 Introduction

Herodotus, writing in the fifth century BC, has an early account of cultural differences and their importance.

> One might recall in particular, an account told of Darius. When he was King of Persia, he summoned the Greeks who happened to be present at his court, and asked them what they would take to eat the dead bodies of their fathers. They replied that they would not do it for any money in the world. Later, in the presence of the Greeks, and through an interpreter, so that they could understand what was said, he asked some Indians, of the tribe called Callatiae, who do in fact eat their parents' dead bodies, what they would take to burn them. They uttered a cry of horror and forbade him to mention such a dreadful thing. One can see by this what custom can do, and Pindar, in my opinion, was right when he called it 'king of all' (Herodotus 1972, p. 187).

Darius did not feel it necessary to add that as a good Persian, the only way to dispose of the dead was to expose them on a high platform and let the carrion crows eat them!

This is a powerful example of the difficulty of distinguishing the universal from the particular in cross-cultural analysis. The culture-specific elements are so compelling, that they overwhelm the universal. If we try to abstract the universal from Herodotus's account, we might come up with something like 'what people do with the dead people in their society'. This is rather meaningless, and almost certainly inadequate to the different cultural specificities that we are trying to summarise. The 'dead' tangles us up immediately with theories of the afterlife, reincarnation, the spirit world, and all the rest. Our simple attempt to create a universal—the disposal of the dead—requires us to go back to the culturally specific, to cosmology, religion, diet, systems of classification of all kinds.

The distinction between universal and culture specific has often been conceptualised in international business research as an emic–etic dichotomy. This dichotomy has intuitive appeal as it has been widely used in this sense by the researchers (see e.g., Adler 1983; Sekaran 1983; Chen and Li 2005; Khatri et al. 2005; Leung et al. 2005; Ling et al. 2005; Zaheer and Zaheer 2006; Earley 2006; Pellegrini and Scandura 2006; Knight et al. 2007; Shapiro et al. 2008; Tung 2007; Hult et al. 2008; Styles et al. 2008). Etic is often used in this literature as an issue or category which is culturally 'comparable' (Berry 1980). As shown in our Herodotus example, this is problematic, as it is very difficult to identify all the culturally 'comparable' variations that can described and discussed, as their understanding and meaning will be very different in different cultural contexts.

Emic and etic perspectives, while being theoretically rather than methodologically defined, have traditionally been associated with qualitative and quantitative methods respectively (Morris et al. 1999). This association, however, is by no means absolute. As argued by Morris et al. (1999) in some cases quantitative surveys can be used within emic perspectives of indigenous constructs as well as ethnographic observation and qualitative data within etic perspectives.

 Springer

This paper examines ways in which cross-cultural research in international business can use emic–etic approaches more effectively. Sinkovics et al. (2008) argue that the emic–etic dichotomy is "a hindrance to the development of the field" of international business (p. 693). While there have been discussions in the literature as to how to overcome this tension (e.g., Helfrich 1999; Peng et al. 1991; Lonner 1999; Peterson and Pike 2002; Peterson and Quintanilla 2003), these discussions did not find application in the practice of cross-cultural research (Sinkovics et al. 2008). While international business researchers mainly deal with cross-cultural data which is emic in nature (e.g., attitudinal and behavioural phenomena), the majority of research conducted in the field has been etic. As argued by Doz (2011), while there is a lot that qualitative research methods can offer to international business, the field has largely developed without benefiting from them. As a result cross-cultural comparisons have been ethnocentric and mostly biased towards Western perspectives. This has profound implications for the future direction of international business cross-cultural research design. With the rise of the emerging economies, far more of this research is conducted on economies that have greater apparent differences. What is more, the polarity of the investment direction is reversed— emerging economy firms are now investing in advanced economies. This makes our research very timely as international business researchers are grappling with these new cross-cultural challenges.

We conduct a linguistic and philosophical analysis of emic and etic terms, and we provide examples from linguistics and international business research on German-Polish acquisitions. We make the case that the models used in social anthropology, deriving from the linguistic analogies of phonemic and phonetic analysis, deserve careful attention. We demonstrate that what conventional etic cross-cultural research perceives to be a problem is often an opportunity to gain deep insight. We argue that emic matters in some cases more that etic, and that the emic can add value beyond the etic in a large number of cases.

We conclude that a research strategy employing both emic and etic approaches is a vital step to enable cross-cultural researchers in international business to obtain more adequate and meaningful results. While most of international business researchers have treated the emic and etic approaches as dilemma, we demonstrate the benefits of treating them as equally applicable and complementary. Our conclusion points to the need for deep qualitative work in international business, with serious attention paid to 'native categories' (Buckley and Chapman 1997).

2 What do Emic and Etic Mean in International Business Studies?

Within the domain of cross-cultural business studies, it has become standard to invoke the emic–etic distinction to mean this: Emic is culture-specific and etic is universal. Adler (1983), for example, uses the terms to differentiate 'the universal from the particular', and defines them as follows:

Emic: Sounds which are specific to a particular language
Etic: Sounds which are similar in all languages (p. 36)

 Springer

   The etic category is commonly used in such literature in the context of being cross-culturally 'comparable' as opposed to emic which does not allow such comparisons (Davidson et al. 1976).

   These usages are only one interpretation of the linguistic analogies from which the terms derive. Their route into modern business studies goes through Pike (1954, 1955, 1960), through social psychology (e.g., Triandis and Berry 1980), and into the very extensive domain of North American business studies which is influenced by social psychology.

> By dropping the root (phon), the two suffixes (emics, etics) become terms which are applicable to this local versus universal distinction in any discipline. By analogy, emics apply in only a particular society; etics are culture-free or universal aspects of the world (or if not entirely universal, operate in more than one society) (Berry 1980, p. 11).

   As further argued by Berry (1980) it is very difficult to produce descriptions of behaviour that would be meaningful to members of a particular culture and at the same time comparable across different cultures. The proposed solution (Berry 1980) involves an iterative process following the initial application of extant hypotheses concerning behaviour, until an emic description can be made by progressively altering the imposed etic until it matches a purely emic point of view. This convergent methodology however begs the question of how we should know when convergence has been attained.

   Much of cross-cultural research is concerned with the search for various types of 'equivalence' (see Usunier 2009, for further discussion). Usunier and Lee (2013) distinguish between six types of equivalence: Conceptual (meaning of concepts between different social units), functional (meaning of functions of similar products and activities), translation (lexical, idiomatic, grammatical-syntactical, experiential equivalence), measure equivalence (perceptual, metric, calibration and temporal), sample equivalence (sampling unit) and data collection equivalence (respondents' cooperation) (Usunier and Lee 2013). We would argue, however, that instead of searching for equivalence, we should look carefully from one emic to another. If we keep looking for equivalence, however hard and however often we try, we will always be looking for the 'some of the etic that is left' to which Berry referred, and which is of very little importance to what it is that is being studied as much of data is 'emic', and grounded in the categories and classifications of those who are being researched.

   Let us illustrate this with an example of translation equivalence. As put by Ardener (1989):

> The paradox of total translation shows both that we do not want it, and that in life rather than in text (and here is our crucial break with high structuralism) we cannot have it. (p. 185).

   One of the techniques commonly used by cross-cultural researchers in order to find translation 'equivalence' (in particular lexical and idiomatic) is back-translation. Within this approach a text is translated from a source language into a target language by one translator, and the translated text in a target language is

Springer

then translated again, by a different translator (without prior knowledge of the source text), back into the source language. The two texts in the source language version are then compared in order to produce the final text in a target language (Usunier and Lee 2013). It is worth remarking, however, that back-translation is more of a 'band-aid' applied across the problem of equivalence (Usunier 2009) and it does not solve the fundamental incongruity of categories between systems. Back-translation may give you some clues that there are problems of incongruity, but even this outcome is not certain. Even where we have a category whose 'content' is 'the same', from one system to another, the 'sameness' is almost inevitably compromised by the different structure of the surrounding categories.

Sekaran (1983) points out the importance of experiential equivalence by giving an example of how a statement "I would like to be a florist" (p. 62), while perfectly applicable and understood in the US may be completely lost in countries which do not have flowershops. We would argue that the problem is much more complex than the presence or absence of 'flowershops'. It could potentially pertain to the existence or otherwise of an exchange economy; the medium of exchange (e.g., money); the possibility of different spheres of exchange; the existence or otherwise of shops, and what a shop is thought to be for; the existence or otherwise of patterns of gift-giving and the place of flowers in such patterns; the gender patterns of gift-giving specific to the context; the climate, seasonality and desirability of flowers in general and certain flowers in particular.

This problem is often ignored in cross-cultural management work deriving from cross-cultural psychology (Chapman 1996/1997). For example, Haire et al. (1966) argued that while large scale questionnaires prevent any in-depth exploration of respondents' attitudes, they assure the researcher that "each respondent answered exactly the same questions, and that the results are strictly comparable from one group to another" (Chapman 1996/1997, p. 2). This tradeoff between depth and breadth is an inevitable feature of social-scientific research, what is problematic here, however is a fact that the authors are insisting that it is precisely *lack* of depth that allows them to ensure comparability of results between different groups that were studied. They secure this result, in their own view, by careful attention to translation, and rephrasing and eliminating questions which meaning would be sensitive to cultural differences. This is the search for 'equivalence' in cross-cultural questionnaires.

3 The Origin of the Terms 'Emic' and 'Etic'

The emic and etic are the terms derived from the linguistic analogies of phonemic and phonetic analysis (see Saussure de 1916; Sweet 1877; Robins 1967). The initial approach to studying and annotating spoken languages was positivist: Methods were sought to recognise, describe and annotate the sounds of all languages, using an objective method of observation, and a universal system of annotation (see Sweet 1877). A good deal of progress was made, and the 'universal system of annotation' came to exist as the 'International Phonetic Alphabet' (often abbreviated to IPA; see IPA 1949). On the route to this, however, observers were obliged to notice that their own linguistic apprehension of what constituted significant sound was radically challenged by that of speakers of other languages and dialects; other people persisted in grouping together large ranges of apparently disparate sounds, or differentiating between sounds that seemed to be the same: The 'phoneme' was, perforce, discovered (for a description of this process, see Robins 1967).

Phonemic analysis is based on the phonemes of a language. A phoneme is a range of sound possibilities, produced and perceived within any one language (or dialect), as if it were a single significant sound. The phonemes exist in an artificial system of boundaries and oppositions—a system which is arbitrary, arbitrarily imposed upon physical reality. The particular phonemic structure with which we are familiar dominates our perception and our production of sounds, and thereby our understanding of language. It is not the physical reality of sound which has significance for us, but the system we impose upon it. As O'Connor (1973) says: "Our thinking is tied so very much to phonemes rather than to sounds that it is easier to see the relationship between the two in foreign languages than in our own" (p. 66). Peoples generally enjoy making fun of the way foreigners speak their languages: Much of the entertainment derives from the meeting of different and incongruent phonemic systems.

Let us go back to the emic–etic research perspective within which it is a desired and desirable outcome of research that an etic should be discovered, common across cultures. It is assumed and argued that this etic feature will be capable of generating theory and analysis of wider cross-cultural applicability than emic features alone. The researcher, within this perspective, continues to assume the capacity to make discriminations that the people under study do not make. The researcher continues to say, this part of the category is important, that part is less important. The researcher continues to maintain, as a desirable feature, a degree of objective and scientific distance from the culture under study. In this sense, it is no surprise that the research enterprise should continue to be regarded as one of the study of 'behaviour'. We have seen above that a phoneme does not exist in itself, but in a system of oppositions—it is defined by what it is not. It is this system of oppositions which determines the reality status of the phoneme, and not the relationship of the phoneme to underlying physical or material structures or manifestations. The challenge to a positivist view of the world is clear—if systems of opposition, socially constructed and arbitrary, are given the power to define the world, the securities of physicality and materiality are lost, at least in the social sphere. It is these securities which the term 'behaviour' seems to provide—behaviour, in the understanding of those that use the term, is in the external, observable, concrete realm.

4 What Can International Business Studies Learn from Social Anthropology?

A discipline which recognised that linguistics offered conjoint empirical and theoretical advances was social anthropology, which successfully applied the concepts from this field to studying cultures (e.g., Hjelmslev 1943; Leach 1961; Needham 1962; Levi-Strauss 1963; Jones 1964; Douglas 1966; Parkin 1982;

 Springer

Ardener 1971a, b, 1989). The idea of the phoneme gave rise to the idea that human and social realities were classified, by societies or cultures, into 'categories'. A phoneme groups together somewhat disparate sounds, into a unit which has significance in a particular language—within the unit, the meaning of the different sounds is the same. Each phoneme is 'opposed' to neighbouring phonemes. It is the system of opposition which gives each element within the system its significance. A social categorisation does the same thing, with material and ideological realities.

The issue was first examined using kinship examples. In English, there are series of commonly used kinship terms, which are used to talk about relationships to other people (father, mother, sister, brother, etc.). Social anthropologists began to study other kinship systems with the assumption that these English categories were self-evident. They found, however, that other cultures had kinship systems which were unintelligible when viewed through the lense of English terminology. Other languages classified together individuals which English classified apart, and classified apart individuals which English classified together. For example, the English term 'uncle' specifies (at a minimum) 'male parental siblings' and it does not distinguish between 'mother's brother' and 'father's brother' as it is the case in other languages. We discover here a range of differentiating features which can be applied to related people. The different way in which these differentiating features are played out, in social life and language, gives rise to kinship and social structures which can be dramatically different from those familiar to most of people in the modern English-speaking world. This is particularly relevant to international business research as more and more international business activity is conducted with regard to emerging economies.

Again by analogy with the phonemic example, it is not necessarily useful or helpful to look across kinship systems, observe that a particular genealogically specified individual is common to two otherwise different categories, and to conclude that this part of the category (say 'father's brother') is more real, cross-culturally valid, or etic, than the other parts of the categories (respectively, 'mother's brother' and 'father's brother's son'). This is imputing a distinction which is neither lived, nor experienced, nor understood, in the two different systems of which we are talking.

This notion that culture could be regarded as a system of classifications came to be accepted within social anthropology. A single item could not be understood, in and of itself, without an understanding of its relationships to the other items surrounding it. A system makes sense, *in its own terms*, and that there will always and necessarily be problems of translation from one system to another, from one culture to another. This is not regarded as a problem to be defined or researched away. It is, rather, the prime focus of interest and attention. Social anthropologists do not particularly expect 'equivalence' across cultures, and are suspicious of it when it seems to be apparent.

The difference in perspective between international business and social anthropology is profound. While we are examining systems which make sense internally, through opposition of elements within the system, and then trying to compare across systems, we find that it is not clear what should be compared with what. In some cases, we preserved the physical, acoustic possibility that there would

 Springer

be some common feature across all the systems. This is the exact analogy of Berry, with whom we started, saying 'if some of the etic is left', as we look across different systems, 'then a universal for that particular behaviour will be achieved'. But we have argued that this cross-system element is irrelevant, in the most profound way, to how the individual systems operate within themselves. We have some 'etic left', and it does us no good at all in analysis. Through finding the 'etic that is left', we have discovered something of very little importance, and potentially obscured many things, like a 'disposal of the dead' from our Herodotus example above. In what follows we discuss how the ideas from linguistics and social anthropology can be applied to international business research in order to use emic and emic approaches more effectively. We do so by general examples and examples from international business research on German-Polish acquisitions.

5 How Can Emic and Etic Approaches be Used More Effectively in International Business Research?

Many usages of etic and emic imply that the former concerns objective culture-independent description, and the latter knowledge informed by the culture of those under study. The second of these, the emic perspective, as conceived in cross-cultural management studies, under the influence of Pike's ideas, is not unlike the idea of 'holistic system analysis', as derived from the idea of classification and definition by opposition.

The former, however, the etic perspective, conceived as an objective and culture-free account, is in practice much more problematic than is commonly supposed. In a strict linguistic sense, the phonetic implies an objective description, fully specified in all possible dimensions, and the phonemic implies a description which is based upon the categories employed by the people under study. So, in the original linguistic examples, a complete phonetic description of how somebody says a particular vowel requires a complex description of tongue, teeth, mouth, lips, volume, timbre, pitch and so on. It is a hard thing to research and express. A phonemic description of how somebody from a particular linguistic community says a vowel can be much simpler—it summarises in one symbol the range of sounds which people speaking this language will hear and produce as appropriate. Ardener (1989) says:

> Essentially, phonemes were formulaic statements for the abstraction of significant units of speech. The analyst simplified the initial 'phonetic' data by using fewer terms but at the expense of requiring a book of rules to interpret them (p. 31).

In the standard discourse of cross-cultural business studies, it is often implied that etic studies, because they use categories that are the same across all cultures, are somehow simpler, less empirically and conceptually challenging, than emic studies, which require the use of culture-specific categories. This is generally a misconception. The research, scientific and descriptive apparatus required to discover and express *exactly* how somebody says a particular vowel is formidably complex. The use of phonemic analysis allows the infinite range of possible vowel sounds to be broken into the locally relevant categories.

We can carry the analogy into the kinship example. When you talk to people about their kinship system, they give you what we might call their emic categories—the categories that are relevant to their system. We might want to say, well, what they think does not matter; we can simply go for objective genealogical descriptions, according to who is related to whom in a consanguineal or affinal sense. Empirically, methodologically, that is when the trouble starts. How do you find out? If you ask people, they give answers according to their categories. Looked at in this way, it is clear that we are necessarily dependent upon emic accounts in a great deal of our social scientific research. Every time we ask someone a question, we get an emic answer. We often cannot reduce the variety of emic answers to etic universals, without falling into the traps already described. The etic perspective is not somehow easier or more scientific—it is often quite simply unavailable. This is often true in cross-cultural management research, and indeed in international business studies more generally; it is also usually unacknowledged.

Therefore, as argued by Buckley and Chapman (1997), taking emic ('native') categories into a consideration is a [...] "vital, step towards adequate positivist research" (p. 291). In their paper, they give an example of counting the number of policemen in a given culture, and argue that for this exercise to be meaningful a researcher should first find out how a policeman is defined by this culture, otherwise the results would be inadequate and ethnocentric. The same applies to forms of status differentiation, for example the idea of leadership as the 'big man' in the Pacific Islands is very different from what it means in the rest of the world, as in that culture it has got a permanent status (Peterson and Quintanilla 2003). Another good example is a concept of 'face' which, while universally understood as "self-awareness of social evaluation" (Qi 2011, p. 280), it has got different contextual connotations in Chinese language for example, where there are two words representing it: 'Mianzi' (social face) and 'lian' (moral face) (Qi 2011). Trying to discard this information, on the grounds of a lack of equivalence, would result in discarding what really matters for understanding these cultures, taking it into account, however, would result in a more comprehensive and adequate account of phenomena under investigation (leadership and face respectively). Also studying family firms across different cultures and only focusing on what these firms have got in common, would result in producing categories which were imposed upon cultural variety to which they were not appropriate, as the notion of family is very different in different cultures, reflecting differing kinship systems in those cultures. In rule-based countries like the USA or UK for example, kinship is limited to the immediate family, while in relation-based countries (e.g., Asia, Latin America, Southern Europe, etc.), it includes extended family of several generations. These examples demonstrate that what conventional etic cross-cultural research perceives to be a problem is often an opportunity to gain deep insight, as in many cases emic matters more that etic, and that the emic can often add value beyond the etic.

 Springer

6 Emic and Etic Aspects of German-Polish Acquisitions

In this section we apply the proposed approach to our own research. The example discussed here derives from a series of open-ended interviews with the managers from German companies that acquired companies in Poland, and with managers from these. The main focus of inquiry was the impact of cultural differences on post-acquisition integration. The study adopted a broadly qualitative, interpretive approach, in order to access an understanding and knowledge of the post-acquisition process, from the point of view of those under study (D'Iribarne 1997; Miles and Huberman 1994; Yin 1994). The data was organised by using the QSR Nvivo 7. All interview material was coded and organized first under free nodes and then under tree nodes. Free nodes were used to capture the key ideas emerging from the data without imposing any structure on them and without assuming any relationships between them, as the researchers were looking for accounts of experience of acquisition process from both German and Polish side. Subsequently tree nodes were used to organise these ideas into conceptual groups (Bazeley 2008). And it was during that process, and after a number of attempts to achieve a coding that could capture both the German and Polish accounts of the experience of acquisition, the two authors most closely involved in the coding were baffled. Codes that worked for the material from Polish informants, seemed to offer no place or sense to the material from German informants, and vice versa. This was in spite of the fact that they were talking about the same companies, the same examples of acquisition and post-acquisition integration.

The two authors carrying out the coding approached one of the other authors, and described the problem. The coded data from the Polish managers was mostly about change, progress and success. The coded data from the German managers was mostly about lack of change, barriers to progress and failure. How could this data be sensibly related to what were the *same* events?

We need to stress that the data discussed here concerns cross-national, and specifically German-Polish, acquisitions. The German-Polish specificity has some importance. It has been argued that the German/Polish interaction, in recent centuries, has typically been one where the powers of definition lay in German hands (or in the German imagination), and where the Poles and Poland have been subject to German interpretation (Chapman et al. 2004, 2008). Because of this, in recent years German/Polish interactions in the business sphere have tended to be lived as an ambition on the part of the Poles to meet German expectations, and an aspiration on the part of the Germans to bring the Poles up to their expectations. This has been particularly so since the demise of central planning in Central Europe. There is no particular problem with this. We might, as a result, readily envisage a world where the Poles were trying and succeeding to meet German expectations, and the Germans acknowledged the effort and success. We might equally envisage a world where the Poles were trying but failing to meet German expectations, and the Germans acknowledged the effort and the failure.

What we found was something rather different. The interviewed Poles and Germans give dramatically different accounts of the same events and experience. There is consistency, also, in the structure of the difference that emerges. Right

 Springer

across the range of interviews, the Poles talk of improvements and progress, and the Germans talk of obstacles and barriers to progress. They are talking about the same things. What are we to do about this?

We argue that we can go directly to the ideas that we have discussed above. Using analogies from structural linguistics and structural anthropology, we can show that 'reality' can be structured into units which are defined by (and which derive their meaning from) other surrounding units. We can say that, for those who live within realities which are structured in this way, it is often difficult to experience or perceive other realities, and to appreciate the way in which meaning is structured in these other realities (see Chapman 1992).

In the linguistic and kinship examples given above, we have seen that it is possible for the same 'objective reality' to be classified differently from one system to another. This means that the same 'objective reality' can be classified, as a unitary category, with different other 'objective realities' in one system and the other.

Figure 1, which is our etic approach, suggests that the Germans and the Poles are looking at the same continuous stretch of 'reality', but looking at it through different category systems, what Poles perceive to be progress, Germans see as barriers. We now must try to imagine that this reality is a variable organisational or social feature, which has a satisfactory/unsatisfactory, acceptable/unacceptable, normal/abnormal, or even good/bad, distinction built into it. We must also try to imagine that this feature is continuously variable, in an objective sense.

We must then try to imagine that, for the Poles and the Germans, the boundary between the satisfactory and the unsatisfactory, on this continuously variable stretch of empirical reality, is differently placed. That is what Fig. 1 illustrates. In order to better illustrate these empirical realities, we imposed values from 0 to 1 and on that scale what is between 0 and 0.3 is unsatisfactory and what is between 0.7 and 1 is satisfactory. The area between 0.3 and 0.7 is where both Polish and German 'realities' overlap. What it tells us in terms of post-acquisition integration is that this could be potential area for negotiation which would narrow down the disputes in the process. Our 'realities' in Fig. 1 highlight the potential problems in post-acquisition integration (Poles see progress and Germans see barriers), but do not yet offer explanations of these problems or indeed solutions.

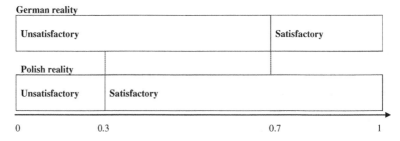

Fig. 1 German 'reality' and Polish 'reality' (etic approach)

German reality

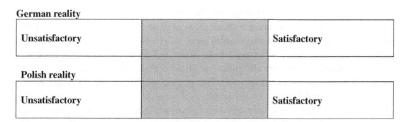

Fig. 2   The meeting of 'realities'—progress and barriers (emic approach)

If we look now at Fig. 2, representing emic approach, we can see, in the shaded area, that there is a stretch of objective reality which the Poles regard as 'satisfactory', and which the Germans regard as 'unsatisfactory'.

Imagine now that the Poles are, as a result of contact with the Germans, pushing the boundary between what they consider to be satisfactory and unsatisfactory in a German direction. They are, in their own terms, making progress. What the Germans see, however, is that the Poles are still on the wrong side of the satisfactory/unsatisfactory frontier, as this is defined by the Germans. So where the Poles perceive progress, and congratulate themselves, the Germans perceive enduring barriers to progress, and express their perceptions in this way. By adopting an emic approach we were able to explain the problem and to bring it one step closer to finding a solution. This example illustrates that doing emic allows you to do better etic.

Figures 1 and 2 are intentionally content free. Any cultural meeting, and any account of cultural meeting, is multidimensional, and there are many different empirical issues which could be discussed in the context of Figs. 1 and 2. The coding of our data, using NVivo, threw up the apparent paradox that the Poles saw 'progress', where the Germans saw 'barriers to progress'. When we looked again at the empirical domains from which these judgements emerged, we found a number of major themes.

One issue was punctuality. The Poles thought that their punctuality (in many different senses—meeting deadlines, ensuring that the workforce arrived on time, promptness in arriving at meetings, and so on) was improving. They recognised a deficiency, but considered that they had made genuine positive steps to rectifying this. The Germans, by contrast, thought that the Poles were still unpunctual.

A second issue concerned attitudes to cost and efficiency. We might broadly say that this issue concerned questions like: 'What is the company for?' 'for whose benefit should the company be managed?', and so on. Two examples emerged. The first concerned the willingness to reduce jobs and head count in pursuit of efficiency and lower costs. The Poles came to this issue with a good deal of background—the importance, within once state-owned companies, of providing not only employment but also a range of social services to the workforce; the importance, within a centrally planned system that did not work very well, of informal networks of influence, patronage and favour. The Germans came to the issue with a rather clearer idea that the first objective of the company was to make profits, and that if

Springer

jobs needed to go for this to be achieved, then the jobs should go. The Germans, of course, did not come to this issue without ideas of their own about the value of jobs, and the need to maintain stable employment where this was possible. What we might call the 'emic calculus' around these issues, however, on the part of the Poles and the Germans, led to very different conclusions about the balance of costs and benefits involved in suppressing jobs. The second example concerned the Polish willingness to spend lavishly on corporate facilities, decoration and furniture. The Poles saw this evidence that they were, as managers, successful. The Germans saw this as evidence that the Poles were incurably extravagant, and apparently incapable of grasping what real efficiency was.

A third issue concerned the Polish managerial reliance on political and family networks of trust and influence, as opposed to the German reliance on formal and contractual relationships. From a German perspective, the Polish reliance on informal networks seemed unreliable, chaotic, nepostic. From a Polish perspective, this was how things were done, and how security of outcome was achieved in an uncertain system. In important senses, the bases for decision making, for one side, were invisible to the other. Again, what we have called the 'emic calculus', as made by one side of the acquisition, occupied a concentual space that, while it involved the 'same' events, was differently structured.

A fourth issue concerned alcohol consumption. Heavy consumption of alcohol, particularly in the form of vodka, has long been recognised as a feature of the life of Slavonic speaking peoples. The drabness and frustrations of the planned economy did nothing to reduce this. Where a workforce was formally employed, but in practice generally underemployed, then a degree of alcohol consumption in the workplace was tolerable and normal. State-owned companies which were over-manned, with poorly maintained equipment and drab facilities, were not places where alcohol consumption seemed particularly out of place. The Germans came to the problem from a dramatically different perspective. For them, *any* alcohol in the workplace was a problem. This gives us perhaps the simplest empirical illustration of Fig. 2 that we are able to offer. The presence of one half-empty bottle of vodka, in a locker or hidden behind a crate, was evidence for the Germans that the entire Polish outfit occupied the space 'unacceptable' [in German terms]. From a Polish perspective, the presence of only one half-empty bottle of vodka meant that the problem was pretty much solved, and that near-German standards of sobriety were being achieved.

We have said that the meaning of materialities, even when they are apparently the same from one structure to another, can vary according to the greater 'emic' category that they occupy. The half-empty vodka bottle does not change, but the conclusions drawn from it, according to the 'emic' categories surrounding it, are dramatically different.

The examples given above are illustrations of the general tendency, discovered from the coding of the interview data within Nvivo, for Polish and German managers to perceive the 'same' events in rather different ways. Does it still make sense to say that these were the 'same' events? The Germans and the Poles come away from these events, after all, with rather different accounts of them. The process by which the two accounts can be reconciled is not, in reality, a smooth one.

 Springer

Both Germans and Poles will be aware of dissatisfaction with the other, of a sense that something uncomfortable and at least in part inexplicable is happening. We can say, in general, that the problems that occur in culture meeting are those caused by the meeting of different and incongruent category systems (see Ardener 1989; Chapman 1992; McDonald 1989). Shenkar et al. (2008) has recently argued that we should think of the problems caused by culture meeting as caused by 'friction'. We would argue that the meeting of incongruent category systems allows us to understand, in fine detail, the multi-dimensional meetings of interlocked ideas and materialities, which generate what Shenkar calls 'friction'.

Tung (2007) cites the Japanese businessman Takeo Fujisawa, to the effect that 'Japanese and American management practices are 95 % the same and differ in all important ways'. She goes on to say 'The '95 % similarity' that Fujisawa alluded to would constitute the etic component of culture, whereas they "differ in all important ways" represents the emic dimension' (p. 44). Of course Fujisawa's statement is a *bon mot*, rather than a theoretical statement, and it probably does not make much sense to put numbers to the problem in this way. Nevertheless, if we stay with these percentages, they perhaps provide us with another way of illustrating our argument. For the 5 % of difference we can regard as distributed over the other 95 %, such that *everything* is different; the 5 % of difference does not come in a different package, separable and identifiable as such, but as virtually limitless incongruences (some small, some large) between the category systems of different cultures.

We can return here to the possibility of access to the etic reality. In every case which we have discussed, the interview data give us an emic view of the events within the acquired company. Any interview, any questionnaire, would always primarily be accessing such a view. This means that the resulting data needs to be put into a holistic context, where the meaning of the categories employed is determined, or at the very least illuminated, by the surrounding categories. Where we get two different emic perspectives meeting, then we have shown that we are able, with thought, and with a bit of help from anthropological analogies, to make some sense of the outcomes of the meeting. We have also seen, however, that many researchers have imagined that they could readily leave aside the emic perspective, and take an objective etic perspective. We have also argued that in many cases this etic perspective is not available.

Looking back to the kinship analogy which was argued above, we can turn our attention to the possibility of an etic understanding of how much alcohol is consumed in a Polish workplace. An emic study of how much Poles drink, and how much Germans think they drink, can be carried out by getting the Poles and Germans to talk about this. In this way, we will discover their categories for assessing this—their emic perspective. How would we do an etic study, however? To do that (and remembering the 'phonetic' analogy) we would need to measure every bottle and glass, be inside every locker and every office, be constantly alert to every corner of the workplace and the home, and know the exact strength of the alcohol being consumed. We clearly cannot do that—we do not have the research capacity, and the level of intrusion into social life that this would require would be totally unacceptable.

Could some of the differences in perceptions in our empirical example be differences in corporate rather than national culture? If we follow Hofstede (1991) then we can treat the differences in national cultures as deeply rooted values of these cultures which will shape how people from these cultures expect for the companies to be run. Therefore, even if we distinguish between national cultures and corporate cultures these expectations are deeply rooted in national cultures. Furthermore, the different and opposing views of the protagonists' relationship found in our empirical example occur in many cultures. We also observe such inter-group dynamics within one culture. In the realm of corporate culture, common stories suggest that in merged companies members of the two previous organizations retain their own views of history and present ways of thinking and valuing for years, even decades. Research, for example, has found intergroup dynamics where two groups have quite different views of the same history and of their partnership and tend to disparage the other and make their own group more heroic are more prevalent when groups believe that they have competitive goals rather than cooperative ones (Vaara 2002). These intergroup dynamics have emic as well as etic aspects, as much of the context of the messages will depend upon the culture and aspects of the immediate situation.

The examples from our data allow us to understand both the 'socially constructed' aspects of these realities, and the 'positivist' realities which co-exist with them. There are 'categorical' features, which we can regard as the product of 'social construction' as well as 'statistical' features, which we could regard as real in a positivist sense. The 'categorical' features both generate the 'statistical' features, and are elements in their perception and relevance.

How can we actually research these? We can access 'categorical' features, which are derived from the imposition of culture-specific boundaries on reality, by getting people to talk about them. The 'statistical' features, the positivist realities, we can also access by standard scientific techniques (of counting and enumeration of various kinds). But, we need to acknowledge, to a far greater degree than has been common in international business research, that much of our data is emic, and grounded in the categories and classifications of those whom we are researching. We can then start to think, in a way that does justice to the complexity of the phenomena, about the interaction between the 'socially constructed' realities, and the 'positivist' realities.

7 Conclusion

Cross-cultural analysis in international business is faced with challenges arising from the difficulty of distinguishing the universal from the particular. We argued that the models deriving from the linguistic analogies of phonemic and phonetic analysis, successfully (and appropriately) used in social anthropology, deserve careful attention, if we are to do justice to the complexity of the phenomena we are researching. We need to acknowledge, to a far greater degree than has been common in international business research, that much of our data is 'emic', and grounded in the categories and classifications of those under research.

 Springer

8 Lessons for International Business Researchers

We have examined ways in which cross-cultural research in international business can use emic–etic approaches more effectively. Using examples from linguistics, kinship and our own research, we argued that international business researchers have to recognise the profound differences in culture, as the Herodotus example shows. In our empirical example, the categories utilised by the Polish and German managers did not match up and could not be made to match up. This was a research opportunity and not a research failure. What this means for the international business researchers, is that the search for equivalence should no longer be a prime ambition of cross-cultural research. If equivalence is there, then it can be embraced. If equivalence is not there, however, it should not be forced. There is no need to design the search for equivalence into all cross-cultural research. We have shown that what conventional cross-cultural research perceives to be a problem, should often be regarded instead as deep insight. This takes a degree of courage. We hope that this paper will empower qualitative researchers to follow such insights, rather than try to evade them or conceal them. This is not an easy thing to do. It is uncomfortable, and it is conceptually hard, both to grasp and to express. Emic and etic cannot co-exist with the notions of definition by opposition, system, value, and so on. The ideas cannot be introduced to one another in bits. The question has an 'all or nothing' aspect. This paper has taken an uncompromising approach to this difficult issue, because the stakes are so high. Employing both emic and etic approaches is a vital step to enable cross-cultural researchers in international business to obtain more adequate and meaningful results, and there are clear benefits of treating them as complementary rather than dichotomous.

References

Adler, N. J. (1983). A typology of management studies involving culture. *Journal of International Business Studies, 14*(2), 29–47.
Ardener, E. (1971a). *Social anthropology and language, introduction to social anthropology and language*. London: Tavistock.
Ardener, E. (1971b). The new anthropology and its critics. *Man, 6*(3), 449–467.
Ardener, E. (1989). *The voice of prophecy and other essays*. Oxford: Blackwell.
Bazeley, P. (2008). *Qualitative data analysis with NVIVO*. London: Sage Publications.
Berry, J. W. (1980). Acculturation as varieties of adaptation. In A. M. Padilla (Ed.), *Acculturation: theory, models, and some new findings* (pp. 9–25). Boulder: Westview.
Buckley, P. J., & Chapman, M. (1997). The use of 'native categories' in management research. *British Journal of Management, 8*(3), 283–299.
Chapman, M. (1992). *The Celts: the construction of a myth*. London: Macmillan.
Chapman, M. (1996/1997). Social anthropology, business studies and cultural issues. *International Studies of Management and Organisation, 26*(4), 3–29.
Chapman, M., Clegg, J., & Gajewska-De Mattos, H. (2004). Poles and Germans: an international business relationship. *Human Relations, 57*(8), 983–1015.
Chapman, M., Gajewska-De Mattos, H., Clegg, J., & Buckley, P. J. (2008). Close neighbours and distant friends: perceptions of cultural distance. *International Business Review, 17*(3), 217–234.

Chen, X. P., & Li, S. (2005). Cross-national differences in cooperative decision-making in mixed-motive business contexts: the mediating effect of vertical and horizontal individualism. *Journal of International Business Studies, 36*(6), 622–636.

D'Iribarne, P. (1997). The usefulness of ethnographic approach to international comparison of organisations. *International Studies of Management and Organisation, 26*(4), 30–47.

Davidson, A. R., Jaccard, J. J., Triandis, H. C., Morales, M. L., & Diaz-Guerrero, R. (1976). Cross-cultural model testing: toward a solution of the etic–emic dilemma. *International Journal of Psychology, 11*(1), 1–13.

de Saussure, F. (1916). *Cours de linguistique generale*. Paris: Payot.

Douglas, M. (1966). *Purity and danger*. London: Routledge and Kegan Paul.

Doz, Y. (2011). Qualitative research for international business (perspective). *Journal of International Business Studies, 42*(5), 582–590.

Earley, P. C. (2006). Leading cultural research in the future: a matter of paradigms and taste. *Journal of International Business Studies, 37*(6), 922–931.

Haire, M., Ghiselli, E., & Porter, L. (1966). *Managerial thinking: an international study*. New York: Wiley.

Helfrich, H. (1999). Beyond the dilemma of cross-cultural psychology: resolving the tension between etic and emic approaches. *Culture and Psychology, 5*(2), 131–153.

Herodotus (1972). *The histories*. Translated by A. de Selincourt (Revised Edition). London: Penguin.

Hjelmslev, L. (1943). *Omkring sprogteoriens grundlaeggelse*. Copenhagen: Munksgaard (translated 1963 by J. Whitfield, *Prolegomena to a theory of language*. Menasha: University of Wisconsin).

Hofstede, G. (1991). *Cultures and organisations: software of the mind*. London: McGraw-Hill.

Hult, G. T. M., Ketchen, D. J., Griffith, D. A., Finnegan, C. A., Gonzalez-Padron, T., Harmancioglu, N., Huang, Y., Talay, M. B., & Cavusgil S. T. (2008). Data equivalence in cross-cultural international business research: assessment and guidelines. *Journal of International Business Studies, 39*(6), 1027–1044.

IPA (1949). *Principles of the international phonetic association*. London: International Phonetic Association.

Jones, D. (1964). *The history and meaning of the term 'phoneme'*. London: International Phonetic Association.

Khatri, N., Tsang, E. W. K., & Begley, T. M. (2005). Cronyism: a cross-cultural analysis. *Journal of International Business Studies, 37*(1), 61–75.

Knight, J. G., Holdsworth, D. K., & Mather, D. W. (2007). Country-of-origin and choice of food imports: an in-depth study of European distribution channel gatekeepers. *Journal of International Business Studies, 38*(1), 107–125.

Leach, E. (1961). *Rethinking anthropology*. London: Athlone Press.

Leung, K., Bhagat, R., Buchan, N., Erez, M., & Gibson, C. (2005). Culture and international business: recent advances and their implications for future research. *Journal of International Business Studies, 36*(4), 357–378.

Levi-Strauss, C. (1962). *Le totemisme aujourd'hui*. Paris: Presses Universitaires de France (translated as Totemism, 1963a, by R. Needham. Boston: Beacon Press).

Levi-Strauss, C. (1963). *Structural anthropology*. New York: Basic Books.

Ling, Y., Floyd, S. W., & Baldridge, D. C. (2005). Toward a model of issue-selling by subsidiary managers in multinational organizations. *Journal of International Business Studies, 36*(6), 637–654.

Lonner, W. J. (1999). Helfrich's 'principle of triarchic resonance': a commentary on yet another perspective on the on-going and tenacious etic–emic debate. *Culture and Psychology, 5*(2), 173–181.

McDonald, M. (1989). *We are not French! Language, culture and identity in Brittany*. London: Tavistock.

Miles, M. B., & Huberman, A. M. (1994). *Qualitative data analysis: an expanded sourcebook* (2nd ed.). London: Sage Publications.

Morris, M., Leung, K., Ames, D., & Lickel, B. (1999). Views from inside and outside: integrating emic and etic insights about culture and justice judgement. *Academy of Management Review, 24*(4), 1781–1796.

Needham, R. (1962). *Structure and sentiment*. Chicago: Chicago University Press.

O'Connor, J. (1973). *Phonetics*. Harmondsworth: Penguin.

Parkin, D. (1982). *Semantic anthropology*. London: Academic.

Pellegrini, E. K., & Scandura, T. A. (2006). Leader-member exchange (LMX), paternalism, and delegation in the Turkish business culture: an empirical investigation. *Journal of International Business Studies, 37*(2), 264–279.

Peng, T. K., Peterson, M. F., & Shyi, Y.-P. (1991). Quantitative methods in cross-national management research: trends and equivalence issues. *Journal of Organizational Behavior, 12*(2), 87–107.

Peterson, M. F., & Pike, K. L. (2002). Emics and etics for organizational studies: a lesson in contrast from linguistics. *International Journal of Cross-Cultural Management, 2*(1), 5–19.

Peterson, M. F., & Quintanilla, S. A. R. (2003). Using emics and etics in cross-cultural organizational studies: universal and local, tacit and explicit. In D. Tjosvold et al. (Eds.), *Cross-cultural management: foundations and future.*

Pike, K. (1954, 1955, 1960). *Language in relation to a unified theory of the structure of human behaviour.* Glendale: Summer Institute of Linguistics.

Qi, X. (2011). Face: a Chinese concept in a global sociology. *Journal of Sociology, 47*(3), 279–295.

Robins, R. (1967). *A short history of linguistics.* Harlow: Longman.

Sekaran, U. (1983). Methodological and theoretical issues and advancements in cross-cultural research. *Journal of International Business Studies, 14*(2), 61–73.

Shapiro, J. M., Ozanne, J. L., & Saatcioglu, B. (2008). An interpretive examination of the development of cultural sensitivity in international business. *Journal of International Business Studies, 39*(1), 71–87.

Shenkar, O., Luo, Y., & Yeheskel, O. (2008). From "distance" to "friction": substituting metaphors and redirecting intercultural research. *Academy of Management Review, 33*(4), 905–923.

Sinkovics, R. R., Penz, E., & Ghauri, P. N. (2008). Enhancing the trustworthiness of qualitative research in international business. *Management International Review, 48*(6), 689–713.

Styles, C., Patterson, P. G., & Ahmed, F. (2008). A relational model of export performance. *Journal of International Business Studies, 39*(5), 880–900.

Sweet, H. (1877). *Handbook of phonetics.* Oxford: Clarendon Press.

Triandis, H., & Berry, J. (1980). *Handbook of cross-cultural psychology: methodology* (Vol. 2). Boston: Allyn and Bacon.

Tung, R. L. (2007). The cross-cultural research imperative: the need to balance cross-national and intra-national diversity. *Journal of International Business Studies, 39*(1), 41–46.

Usunier, J.-C. (2009). *Language as a key input in investigating conceptual equivalence in cross-cultural management research.* Paper presented at the workshop on language and multilingualism in management: themes, concepts and methodologies, Hanken School of Economics, Helsinki, June 2009.

Usunier, J.-C., & Lee, J. A. (2013). *Marketing across cultures* (6th ed.). Harlow: Pearson Education Limited.

Vaara, E. (2002). On the discursive construction of success/failure in narratives of post-merger integration. *Organization Studies, 23*(2), 211–248.

Yin, R. K. (1994). *Case study research: design and methods. Applied social research methods series* (2nd ed.). London: Sage Publications.

Zaheer, S., & Zaheer, A. (2006). Trust across borders. *Journal of International Business Studies, 37*(1), 21–29.

PART III

EMERGING MARKET MULTINATIONAL ENTERPRISES

9

Global Strategy Journal
Global Strat. J., **4**: 35–48 (2014)
Published online in Wiley Online Library (wileyonlinelibrary.com). DOI: 10.1111/j.2042-5805.2013.01069.x

IS COMPETITIVE ADVANTAGE A NECESSARY CONDITION FOR THE EMERGENCE OF THE MULTINATIONAL ENTERPRISE?

NIRON HASHAI[1]* and PETER J. BUCKLEY[2]
[1]*School of Business Administration, The Hebrew University of Jerusalem, Mt. Scopus, Jersusalem, Israel*
[2]*Centre for International Business, Leeds University Business School, The University of Leeds, Leeds, United Kingdom*

This article challenges the view that competitive advantage is a necessary condition for the emergence of the multinational enterprise. It formally derives the conditions under which multinational enterprises may emerge without possessing a competitive advantage vis-a-vis their rivals. This counterintuitive argument is based on three insights: (1) the ability of a larger number of disadvantaged home country entrepreneurs to enroll workers in the host country more efficiently than a smaller number of advantaged host country entrepreneurs; (2) asymmetric liability of foreignness for home and host country entrepreneurs; and (3) the ability of location and internalization advantages to substitute for ownership advantage. Copyright © 2014 Strategic Management Society.

INTRODUCTION

The view that the possession of a competitive advantage is a necessary condition for the emergence of the multinational enterprise (MNE) is a cornerstone of the international business and international strategy literatures. This dates back to Hymer's (1976) 'liability of foreignness' (LOF) concept and to Dunning's eclectic paradigm (Dunning, 1977). It makes the claim that foreign entrants must possess competitive advantages (denoted by Dunning as 'ownership advantages')—manifested by technological advantages, well recognized brands, or superior organizational practices to coordinate and control transactions efficiently (Dunning, 1988, 1993)—to compensate for the extra costs of doing business abroad and to successfully compete with

Keywords: multinational enterprise; competitive advantage; eclectic paradigm; ownership advantage; internationalization
*Correspondence to: Niron Hashai, School of Business Administration, The Hebrew University of Jerusalem, Mt. Scopus, Jerusalem, 91905, Israel. E-mail: nironh@huji.ac.il

indigenous firms and other MNEs. This view has proved robust and, over time, has become an axiom for international business and international strategy scholars in many influential studies seeking to explain the emergence of the MNE (e.g.,Kogut and Zander, 1993; Martin and Salomon, 2003; Nachum and Zaheer, 2005; Tallman, 1991; Rugman, 1981).

Yet, the recent rise of emerging country-based MNEs challenges this view. Many emerging country-based MNEs lack firm-specific competitive advantages (Amsden and Chu, 2003; Goldstein, 2007; Mathews, 2006; Ramamurti, 2009a, 2009b; Rugman, 2009), but are apparently still able to establish operations in developed countries. While some scholars have tried to reconcile this contradiction to extant wisdom by pointing to alternative competitive advantages possessed by emerging country-based firms, the debate on the existence or nonexistence of competitive advantages for these types of firms, raises a more fundamental question—*is competitive advantage a necessary condition for firms to become MNEs?* (i.e.,to own subsidiaries in two or more countries (Buckley and Casson, 1976; Caves, 1996)).

Copyright © 2014 Strategic Management Society

The current article questions the extant wisdom that competitive advantage is *required* for MNEs to exist. Indeed, at a first glance, the association of MNEs with the possession of valuable and rare firm-specific resources and capabilities is highly plausible and consistent with resource-based arguments for competitive advantage, familiar from the strategy literature (e.g., Barney, 1991; Peteraf, 1993; Wernerfelt, 1984). Yet, if a long-term general equilibrium approach, rather than a short-term single-firm point of view, is taken, this reasoning does not necessarily hold. The long-term general equilibrium approach aims to maximize the overall utility created by *all* players in the global system, rather than taking the partial view of maximizing the utility created by a single firm when operating abroad. It, therefore, implies a steady state where, as long as there is no exogenous change in the baseline parameters, no change in the preference of a given foreign operation mode over others is expected.

As we will show, the general equilibrium approach captures both domestic and foreign utility and accounts for the utility derived both from inward and outward international transactions of both entrepreneurs and workers. This point is critical because in the long run, firms and individuals that can increase their utility are bound to do so (Buckley and Hashai, 2004; Casson, 2000). Ignoring their utility when making predictions regarding the dominancy of a given foreign market operation mode over others is, therefore, likely to be faulty or, at best, yield unsustainable results. Taking a short-term approach further assumes away the likely outcome of depletion of competitive advantages and is subject to the danger of making additional unsustainable predictions. A long-term general equilibrium approach, therefore, offers a more complete account of the considerations for the emergence of MNEs.

The current article builds on the recent work of Buckley and Hashai (2009), who offer a general equilibrium model that formalizes *internationalization* within Dunning's eclectic paradigm. Since this model formulates the specific mathematical relationships that need to be satisfied in order to allow for the emergence of the MNE[1] vis-a-vis alternative operation modes, it is fairly straightforward to test—in a transparent and rigorous manner—whether these conditions hold for firms that do not possess competitive advantages.

---

[1] I.e.,the establishment of one or more foreign subsidiaries (Buckley and Casson, 1976; Caves, 1996; Dunning, 1977).

The main conclusions from this exercise are that four major conditions increase the probability of firms that possess no competitive advantages to operate abroad through wholly owned foreign subsidiaries. These conditions are: (1) a greater number of entrepreneurs in the home country relative to the host country, which allows the former to enroll host country workers more efficiently; (2) low liability of foreignness for the home country entrepreneurs operating in the host country, both in absolute terms and relative to the liability of foreignness of the host country entrepreneurs operating in the home country; (3) high transaction costs in the international markets for knowledge, stemming, for instance, from greater tacitness of knowledge; and (4) a relatively larger quantity of labor and greater labor productivity in the home country than in the host country, which allow greater utility generation for home country entrepreneurs since they are not subject to the liabilities of foreignness and international transaction costs when employing domestic workers.

To exemplify this point of view, we have implied that, for instance, a single U.S.-based firm may have some short-term competitive advantages relative to Chinese competitors, yet the Chinese firms, as a group, may still be able to successfully establish foreign operations in the U.S. because: (1) they can enroll U.S. employees more efficiently due to diminishing economies of scale of the U.S. firm; and (2) the managers of the Chinese firms had some background in the U.S. (as students or expatriates) that reduces their liability of foreignness in the U.S., while the U.S. firm managers face high liability of foreignness, which limits the overall outputs of their firm. These two factors are sufficient to allow the Chinese firms to create a greater quantity of products than their U.S. counterpart and also produce such products more cheaply; and, therefore, outcompete the U.S. firm even with no apparent competitive advantage. Hence, while competitive advantage may increase the probability for the emergence of MNEs, this not a necessary condition for it to occur. In other words, as much as firms do not need a competitive advantage to exist (they just need to be more efficient than arm's-length market transaction), they do not need a competitive advantage to become MNEs.

In the next section, we briefly survey the literature on the emergence of MNEs while focusing on the recent phenomenon of emerging country-based MNEs. Then we summarize the features of Buckley and Hashai's (2009) model that compares the

Copyright © 2014 Strategic Management Society

utilities of entrepreneurs and workers (who represent 'firms' when bundled together) in various possible foreign market operation modes, namely: domestic production, outward and inward international licensing, and outward and inward foreign direct investment (FDI). We then test under what conditions outgoing FDI is still superior to other operation modes given the existent of competitive *disadvantages* of internationalizing firms. Finally, we discuss the implications of our results on the theory of the MNE and the role of competitive advantage within it, while highlighting the theoretical and empirical challenges for future research.

LITERATURE REVIEW

The emergence of the MNE

Dunning's eclectic paradigm (Dunning, 1977, 1981, 1988, 1993, 1998) is the most straightforward articulation of the firm's strategic motivation to become an MNE. It relies on the combined impact of ownership, location, and internalization advantages. *Ownership advantage* is a firm characteristic parallel to competitive advantage.[2] It is manifested by firm-specific ownership of intangible assets such as technological, marketing or managerial knowledge as well as by superior managerial capabilities (in comparison to those of competitors) to control and coordinate international transactions. The factors constituting ownership advantages are viewed as an 'intrafirm public good,' transferable between different units of an MNE around the world. In that respect, such factors constitute scale free capabilities (Levinthal and Wu, 2010) that are a source of competitive advantage. Ownership advantage compensates for the liabilities of foreignness (Hymer, 1976; Salomon and Martin, 2008; Zaheer, 1995), reflecting the extra costs of foreign firms doing business abroad and, hence, allows firms to successfully compete with indigenous firms and other MNEs. *Location advantage* is a country-specific characteristic. Location advantage is represented by the comparative cost of country-specific inputs (e.g., materials, labor, and natural resources) accessible by enterprises operating within that country's borders or by the cost of trade barriers between countries.

The factors that constitute location advantage are country specific and are location bound—they are internationally immobile. *Internalization advantage* is a transaction attribute. It stems from the fact that the factors constituting ownership advantage become private goods once transferred outside the boundaries of the firm. Internalization advantage applies to the case where the firm prefers to exploit its ownership advantage *internally*, rather than by licensing or any other collaborative mode, in order to minimize the transaction costs associated with the interfirm transfer of proprietary knowledge and capabilities (Buckley and Casson, 1976; Rugman, 1981). This implies that the existence of ownership advantages (or competitive advantages), foreign location advantages, and internalization advantages are three necessary conditions complementing each other to justify the emergence of the MNE.[3]

In a more recent elaboration of this line of thinking greater attention was given to the role of knowledge asset seeking motivation for FDI (Almeida, 1996; Fosfuri and Motta, 1999; Kogut and Chang, 1991; Rugman and Verbeke, 2001). Knowledge asset seeking implies that the MNE's competitive advantage does not necessarily originate in a firm's home country but may be acquired and augmented abroad. Regardless of its origin, the mere existence of competitive advantages has remained an integral part of explanations for the existence of the MNE where the possession of firm-specific advantages in technological advances, brands, or managerial practices are taken to be a necessary condition for the emergence of the MNE.

Thus, the existence of a competitive advantage has become an integral part of explanations for the existence of the MNE. This view echoes resource-based arguments (Barney, 1991; Peteraf, 1993; Wernerfelt, 1984) in its perception that a firm must possess a competitive advantage in order to outcompete indigenous and other foreign competitors. This stance has not only dominated the international business and

---

[2] Another popular term for this type of advantage is 'firm-specific advantage' (Rugman, 1981; Rugman and Verbeke, 2001).

[3] It is noteworthy that the separation between ownership and internalization advantages has been criticized by several scholars viewing the two advantages as inseparable (see, for instance, Buckley, 1985: 18; Casson, 1986: 45; Eden, 2003; and Rugman, Verbeke, and Nguyen, 2011). Some of this criticism was addressed in Dunning's later work (1988, 1993) and the work of Rugman (1981) by referring to different types of 'ownership' or 'firm-specific' advantages—those that result from the exploitation of proprietary assets and those that result from the superior capability to coordinate and control transactions. Yet, it is important to note that this line of criticism still views competitive advantage as a prerequisite for the emergence of the MNE.

Copyright © 2014 Strategic Management Society

Global Strat. J., 4: 35–48 (2014)
DOI: 10.1111/j.2042-5805.2013.01069.x

international strategy literatures (e.g., Kogut and Zander, 1993; Martin and Salomon, 2003; Nachum and Zaheer, 2005; Tallman, 1991; Rugman, 1981), but has also gained popularity in recent international economics literature (e.g., Carr, Markusen, and Maskus, 2001; Helpman, Melitz, and Yeaple, 2004; Markusen, 2001).

The centrality of competitive advantages in explaining the emergence of the MNE has rarely been challenged. However, Casson (1987) states that a firm's competitive advantage: *'does not belong within the subdivision of theory that deals with choice* [i.e.,firm boundaries], *but within the subdivision that deals with success'*. Yet, this view separating firm boundaries and firm competitiveness has gained limited attention and has been mostly dismissed (for instance, see Kogut and Zander, 1993).

The rise of emerging country-based MNEs

The increased salience of emerging country-based MNEs has led many scholars to wonder how one can explain the ability of these firms to establish wholly owned subsidiaries in advanced countries, given that many emerging country-based firms lack firm-specific competitive advantages (Amsden and Chu, 2003; Goldstein, 2007; Mathews, 2006; Ramamurti, 2009a, b; Rugman, 2009). Multiple pieces of anecdotal evidence, where allegedly more advanced firms from developed countries have been acquired by less advanced firms from emerging ones, has exacerbated the confusion regarding the role of competitive advantage in explaining the emergence of emerging country-based MNEs. This evidence includes Lenovo's takeover of IBM's PC business; the successful operations of Hyundai in the U.S. and Europe; the acquisition of Arcelor by Mittal; Tata group's takeover of the Anglo-Dutch Corus Steel; Jaguar, Land Rover; and Tetley Tea and Cemex's takeover of large cement companies in Australia, the U.K., and the U.S. The absence of competitive advantages for emerging country-based MNEs, therefore, seems to contradict extant explanations for the existence of many MNEs.

Some scholars argue that emerging country-based MNEs enjoy alternative advantages such as: privileged access to country-specific advantages such as natural resources and cheap labor (Rugman, 2009) or access to cheap capital because of imperfections in domestic capital markets (Buckley *et al.*, 2007). Other explanations regarding the increased activity of emerging country-based MNEs in advanced countries are based on their desire to access superior knowledge resources in such countries (Dunning, 2006; Dunning, Kim, and Park, 2008; Goldstein, 2007; Luo and Tang, 2007; Mathews, 2002). While this is a possible motivation for emerging country-based MNEs to engage in FDI in advanced countries, it remains unclear whether firms that are less advanced can outcompete more advanced firms in their own home markets and whether less advanced firms are really able to successfully acquire and absorb the knowledge of more advanced ones.

The debate regarding the existence or nonexistence of competitive advantages for emerging country-based MNEs, therefore, raises a more general question: is the extant literature correct in assuming that competitive advantages are indeed a necessary condition for the emergence of MNEs? In theoretical terms, it is interesting to ask whether a Country A firm that is competitively disadvantaged relative to a Country B firm (and does not possess alternative firm-specific advantages to compensate for its disadvantages) may establish wholly owned subsidiaries in Country B *without* acquiring Country B firm's sources of competitive advantage.

To answer the question in a transparent and rigorous manner, the current article builds on the recent formalization of internationalization within the eclectic paradigm as presented by Buckley and Hashai (2009). Buckley and Hashai offer a simple general equilibrium model that specifies in mathematical terms the relationships that need to be satisfied in order to allow for the emergence of the MNE vis-a-vis alternative operation modes, such as domestic production (for local consumption and/or exports) and international licensing. Given the specific mathematical relationships, it is fairly straightforward to test whether the conditions for outward FDI through the establishment of wholly owned subsidiaries hold for firms that do not possess competitive advantages.

COMPETITIVE ADVANTAGE WITHIN THE ECLECTIC PARADIGM

Buckley and Hashai (2009) consider a world comprised of two countries: A and B, representing a home and a host country, respectively. A single good (g) can be produced in A and B, by using two intermediate goods: labor (l) and know-how (k). It is assumed that there are two types of 'consumer-producer' individuals in A and B: 'entrepreneurs' and

Copyright © 2014 Strategic Management Society

Global Strat. J., 4: 35–48 (2014)
DOI: 10.1111/j.2042-5805.2013.01069.x

'workers.' The entrepreneurs supply technological, marketing, or managerial know-how that is transformed by the workers into units of g. It is further assumed that there are n_A identical entrepreneurs in A and n_B identical entrepreneurs in B. This assumption is consistent with our main interest in the competitive advantage of entrepreneurs from A relative to that of entrepreneurs from B.

The production function of g is assumed to be of a Cobb-Douglas type, in the following structure: $G = aK^\alpha L^\beta$, where G is the output volume of g, and K is the required level of k to produce g. K can be thought of as the level of tacit and codified technological know-how, brands, and organizational practices to efficiently coordinate and control transactions obtained by entrepreneurs. K can, therefore, be thought of as a scale free, nondiminishable resource (Levinthal and Wu, 2010). L is the quantity of l required to produce g and α and β are productivity constants. The costs of producing a given quantity of K are assumed to be sunk costs, while L is subject to a per unit wage cost of w_i (i = A,B). Constants a, α, and β are positive, with $a > 1$, $0 < \alpha < 1$, and $0 < \beta < 1$, reflecting the diminishing returns of K and L. Know-how productivity (α) is assumed to be equal in A and in B; however, labor productivity is assumed to be different—accordingly, workers' productivity in A is denoted as β_A and workers' productivity in B is denoted as β_B.

Following classic trade theories (e.g., Heckscher, 1949; Ohlin, 1933) entrepreneurs and workers cannot permanently move between A and B, however the entrepreneurs' k can be transferred across borders.[5] Entrepreneurs may also sell know-how (k) to other entrepreneurs in the market. Since in each country entrepreneurs are assumed to be identical, the sale of k is relevant only between A and B. Thus, k is an intangible tradable intermediate good that is not freely available in the market, where entrepreneurs with higher K are said to have an ownership (or competitive) advantage. $K'i$ represents the level of k held by each entrepreneur in i (i = A,B). $te_{k,ij}$ is the transaction efficiency of the sale of know-how to other entrepreneurs, where $0 < te_k < 1$,

i,j = A,B, i ≠ j. Thus, in the case where k is traded in the market, it is subject to a transaction cost coefficient of $1-te_k$. For the sake of simplicity, intrafirm transaction costs are assumed to be zero (i.e., $te_k = 1$) and, hence, reflect the internalization advantage.

Given that workers cannot move between A and B, l is a country-specific intermediate good representing an important component of location advantage. The overall quantity of labor available in A and B is denoted by L_A and L_B, respectively.

An additional major factor in the model is the efficiency of operating in a foreign country, denoted as $te_{f,ij}$ (i,j = A,B, i ≠ j). Thus, $1-te_{f,ij}$ may be regarded as a fixed learning cost that stems from the 'liability of foreignness' (Hymer, 1976; Salomon and Martin, 2008; Zaheer, 1995). Entrepreneurs from A are foreigners in B (and vice versa) and, thus, have to pay a certain 'cost penalty' over indigenous entrepreneurs who are more familiar with the local business, legal, and political environments.

Based on the these assumptions, Buckley and Hashai (2009) calculate the utility of all firms, represented by bundles of entrepreneurs and workers in Countries A (the 'home' country) and B (the 'host' country) in five alternative operations modes: (1) domestic production which serves for exports and/or local consumption (entrepreneurs from A (B) enrolling workers from the same country); (2) international licensing from A to B (entrepreneurs from A selling their k to entrepreneurs from B who enroll workers from B); (3) international licensing from B to A (entrepreneurs from B selling their k to entrepreneurs from A who enroll workers from A); (4) FDI in B (entrepreneurs from A enroll workers from B); and (5) FDI in A (entrepreneurs from B enroll workers from A). In all cases, the general equilibrium approach dictates that the utility of A and B entrepreneurs and workers from domestic and foreign production is taken into account where both the markets for end products and production factors are cleared. The transactions involved in each operation mode, the resulting production characteristics, and the calculation of the overall utility derived for entrepreneurs and workers from each operation mode are described in detail in Buckley and Hashai (2009) and are not repeated here for the sake of brevity (a summarized description of all operation modes and their resulting overall utility appears in Table 1).

By comparing the overall utility obtained from the different operation modes, Buckley and Hashai (2009) are able to define the set of necessary and

---

[4] It is noteworthy that in the original Cobb Douglas formulation, K denotes 'capital,' whereas in our model, it denoted 'knowledge.'

[5] Following Casson (1985), the fact that capital can be considered even more mobile across countries than knowledge indicates that it has little or no impact on competitive or comparative advantages. We, therefore, do not include capital in our model.

Table 1.   Production characteristics of alternative operation modes

Operation mode	Production characteristics in A	Production characteristics in B	Overall utility
Domestic production for exports and local consumption	A's entrepreneurs use their k to produce g with L_A	B's entrepreneurs use their k to produce g with L_B	$U_{domestic} = n_A a(K'_A)^{\alpha}(L_A/n_A)^{\beta_A} + n_B a(K'_B)^{\alpha}(L_B/n_B)^{\beta_B}$
International licensing from A to B	A's entrepreneurs use their k to produce g with L_A	B's entrepreneurs use k from A's entrepreneurs to produce g with L_B	$U_{license-AtoB} = a(K'_A)^{\alpha}((te_{k,AB})^{\alpha}(L_B/n_B)^{\beta_B} n_B + n_A(L_A/n_A)^{\beta_A})$
International licensing from B to A	A's entrepreneurs use k from B's entrepreneurs to produce g with L_A	B's entrepreneurs use their k to produce g with L_B	$U_{license-BtoA} = a(K'_B)^{\alpha}((te_{k,BA})^{\alpha}(L_A/n_A)^{\beta_A} n_A + n_B(L_B/n_B)^{\beta_B})$
FDI in B	A's entrepreneurs use their k to produce g with L_A	A's entrepreneurs use their k to produce g with L_B	$U_{FDI-B} = n_A a(K'_A)^{\alpha}((L_A/n_A)^{\beta_A} + (te_{f,AB})^{\alpha}(L_B/n_B)^{\beta_B})$
FDI in A	B's entrepreneurs use their k to produce g with L_A	B's entrepreneurs use their k to produce g with L_B	$U_{FDI-A} = n_B a(K'_B)^{\alpha}((L_B/n_B)^{\beta_B} + (te_{f,BA})^{\alpha}(L_A/n_A)^{\beta_A})$

Adapted from Buckley and Hashai (2009).

sufficient conditions for the emergence of the MNE. Entrepreneurs are expected to prefer the operation mode where they obtain the highest utility. Workers, however, are expected to prefer the operation mode that yields the highest wages for their level of productivity and, thus, would prefer to work for the entrepreneur with the highest utility level. Typically, each entrepreneur has his/her own production function that can then be aggregated for all entrepreneurs in a given country. Hence, the operation mode that yields the highest overall utility will be selected in equilibrium. This approach is consistent with the traditional view in the strategic management literature whereby higher utility creation is equivocal to potentially superior performance.[6]

It is noteworthy that the approach taken by Buckley and Hashai (2009) is broader than that of Dunning and his followers because it explicitly considers the domestic utility derived by A and B entrepreneurs and the utility that B entrepreneurs derive from international licensing or FDI in A, in addition to the utility derived by the A entrepreneurs in B. This view differs from the more limited analysis, focusing only on the utility derived by the home country entrepreneurs from possible operation modes relative to host country entrepreneurs' utility from domestic production. The importance of taking this general equilibrium approach lies in the fact that, in the long run, entrepreneurs and workers who can increase their utility through alternative operation modes will do so (Buckley and Hashai, 2004; Casson, 2000). Ignoring the domestic utility of internationalizing entrepreneurs (and the resulting utility of their workers) as well as the utility from incoming licensing and incoming FDI is, therefore, likely to lead to unsustainable and erroneous conclusions regarding the dominancy of a given operation mode over others and does not offer a complete account of all possible operation modes that can emerge in the global system.

Taking the point of view of entrepreneurs in A (the 'home' country), the set of necessary and sufficient conditions for FDI in B (the 'host' country), reflecting the emergence of MNEs from A, is specified by inequalities 1a-1d, which represent the conditions under which the overall utility from FDI in B (i.e., outgoing FDI from A) is greater than the overall utility from domestic production, international

---

[6] We are in debt to an anonymous reviewer for this insight.

Copyright © 2014 Strategic Management Society

Global Strat. J., **4**: 35–48 (2014)
DOI: 10.1111/j.2042-5805.2013.01069.x

licensing from A to B, international licensing from B to A, and FDI in A,[7] respectively:

$$\frac{(K'_A)^\alpha n_A^{1-\beta_A}(L_A)^{\beta_A} + (K'_A)^\alpha n_A^{1-\beta_B}(te_{f,AB})^\alpha(L_B)^{\beta_B}}{(K'_A)^\alpha n_A^{1-\beta_A}(L_A)^{\beta_A} + n_B^{1-\beta_B}(K'_B)^\alpha(L_B)^{\beta_B}} > 1 \quad (1a)$$

$$\frac{n_A^{1-\beta_A}(L_A)^{\beta_A} + n_A^{1-\beta_B}(te_{f,AB})^\alpha(L_B)^{\beta_B}}{n_B^{1-\beta_B}(te_{k,AB})^\alpha(L_B)^{\beta_B} + n_A^{1-\beta_A}(L_A)^{\beta_A}} > 1 \quad (1b)$$

$$\frac{(K'_A)^\alpha}{(K'_B)^\alpha} \cdot \frac{n_A^{1-\beta_A}(L_A)^{\beta_A} + n_A^{1-\beta_B}(te_{f,AB})^\alpha(L_B)^{\beta_B}}{n_A^{1-\beta_A}(te_{k,BA})^\alpha(L_A)^{\beta_A} + n_B^{1-\beta_B}(L_B)^{\beta_B}} > 1 \quad (1c)$$

$$\frac{(K'_A)^\alpha}{(K'_B)^\alpha} \cdot \frac{n_A^{1-\beta_A}(L_A)^{\beta_A} + n_A^{1-\beta_B}(te_{f,AB})^\alpha(L_B)^{\beta_B}}{n_B^{1-\beta_B}(L_B)^{\beta_B} + n_B^{1-\beta_A}(te_{f,BA})^\alpha(L_A)^{\beta_A}} > 1 \quad (1d)$$

THE ROLE OF COMPETITIVE DISADVANTAGE

Equations 1a-1d enable a straightforward analysis of the research question raised in the current article. Since K'_i represents the level of k held by each entrepreneur in i ($i = A,B$), it follows that the ratio $\frac{K'_A}{K'_B}$ represents the level of knowledge held by A's entrepreneurs relative to that of B's entrepreneurs. Thus, if $\frac{K'_A}{K'_B} < 1$, it follows that B's entrepreneurs enjoy a competitive advantage over A's entrepreneurs. Assigning this inequality in equations, 1a-1d should, therefore, yield the conditions for the emergence of an MNE from A in the case where competitive advantages are absent, relative to each alternative operation mode, as will be detailed later.

Outward FDI versus domestic production

We first compare the utility from FDI in B relative to that of *domestic production in both A and B* (for

[7] Buckley and Hashai (2009) also relate to knowledge asset seeking driven FDI. We ignore this operation mode in the current article, since it is obvious that the utilization of superior knowledge in B by A's entrepreneurs will always lead to higher utility. In contrast, our specific interest in the current article focuses on whether FDI is feasible without such superior knowledge.

Copyright © 2014 Strategic Management Society

exports and/or local consumption). An investigation of Equation 1a reveals that the equation holds if the right part of its numerator is larger than the right part of its denominator. This implies that we are interested in the relative utility created in Country B by either A's or B's entrepreneurs, while assuming constant the utility created by A's entrepreneurs in their home country. A simple mathematical manipulation of the term $\frac{(K'_A)^\alpha n_A^{1-\beta_B}(te_{f,AB})^\alpha(L_B)^{\beta_B}}{n_B^{1-\beta_B}(K'_B)^\alpha(L_B)^{\beta_B}} > 1$, under our baseline condition that $\frac{K'_A}{K'_B} < 1$, leads to Equation 2a:

$$\frac{n_B^{1-\beta_B}}{n_A^{1-\beta_B}} < (te_{f,AB})^\alpha \quad (2a)$$

Equation 2a spells out the condition for FDI in B to occur without having a competitive advantage of A's entrepreneurs, rather than domestic production in A and B. Essentially it implies that the number of entrepreneurs in A should be sufficiently larger than the number of entrepreneurs in B to compensate for the liability of foreignness of A's entrepreneurs when operating in B. Equation 2a brings to the forefront the importance of taking a general equilibrium approach rather than the single firm approach taken by Dunning and his followers when articulating the conditions for the emergence of the MNE. This approach highlights, in this specific case, the importance of scale and of taking both the utility from domestic and foreign operations into account. Country A's entrepreneurs may be disadvantaged relative to those of Country B in terms of firm-specific competitive advantages and may be liable to the extra costs of operating in a foreign country; yet if there is a large enough number of entrepreneurs, the overall utility that these entrepreneurs create will be greater than that of a smaller number of more advantaged local entrepreneurs. This results from the diminishing returns to scale of the entrepreneurs' production function, implying that, in this case, the relatively few entrepreneurs from Country B may be unable to efficiently employ all the workers in B, allowing A's entrepreneurs to create greater utility when enrolling B's workers.[8] The prediction is that

[8] It can easily be shown that for the utility functions detailed in Table 1, for the same amount of workers employed, a higher number of entrepreneurs leads to greater overall utility.

Global Strat. J., **4**: 35–48 (2014)
DOI: 10.1111/j.2042-5805.2013.01069.x

large countries, which are relatively abundant with entrepreneurs, may be able to use their relative scale advantage to engage in outward FDI even in the absence of competitive advantages. So, a large group of Indian or Chinese entrepreneurs may outcompete fewer but larger American or European entrepreneurs due to the lesser diminishing effects in enrolling labor. In practical terms, the many small car manufacturers from China may outcompete General Motors in the U.S. even if the latter is more technologically advanced.

Equation 2a further allows the introduction of empirically testable propositions regarding the likelihood of FDI in B relative to domestic production. As indicated before, the greater the number of entrepreneurs in A relative to that of entrepreneurs in B, the higher the probability of FDI in B. Furthermore, Equation 2a implies that the number of entrepreneurs in A must be larger than that in B in order to allow FDI in B, since the ratio of B's entrepreneurs to A's entrepreneurs must be smaller than $te_{f,AB}$ (which is, by definition, smaller than 1). Likewise, the lower the liability of foreignness for A's entrepreneurs to operate in B (i.e., the higher the transaction efficiency of transferring knowledge from A to B), the higher the probability of FDI in B. The latter proposition is fairly intuitive and self-explanatory, yet it is different from the accepted interpretation of the liability of foreignness since here low liability of foreignness allows outward FDI in the case of a competitive *disadvantage*. Following our example regarding the group of Chinese car producers competing with General Motors, we expect Chinese firms headed by managers that have been educated or formerly posted in the U.S., to have an even greater probability of outcompeting General Motors.

Outward FDI versus outward licensing

When it comes to the relative utility of FDI in B and *international licensing from A to B*, Equation 1b indicates that the $\frac{K'_A}{K'_B}$ ratio does not play any role in this case. A mathematical manipulation of Equation 1b indicates that the condition for greater utility for FDI in B than that of international licensing from A to B is:

$$\frac{n_B^{1-\beta_B}}{n_A^{1-\beta_B}} < \frac{(te_{f,AB})^\alpha}{(te_{k,AB})^\alpha} \qquad (2b)$$

Equation 2b implies that in addition to the relative number of entrepreneurs in A and B and the extent of liability of foreignness for A's entrepreneurs to operate in B, discussed above, the transaction efficiency of the international market for know-how is another factor affecting the probability of FDI in B. In fact, the main insight of Equation 2b is that the relative transaction efficiencies of the market for know-how and that of operating in a foreign market are dominant determinants of the emergence of MNEs from A (investing in B). The greater the transaction efficiency of operating in country B for A's entrepreneurs (i.e., the lower their liability of foreignness) and the lower the transaction efficiency of the international market for know-how (i.e., the greater the international transaction costs), the greater the probability of FDI in B. This insight is perfectly consistent with the point of view of the internalization school (Buckley and Casson, 1976; Rugman, 1981) and shows that competitive advantage does not play a role in the decision whether to internalize or externalize foreign operations when compared to outward licensing.

Outward FDI versus inward licensing

When comparing the relative utility from FDI in B for MNEs with no competitive advantages and the utility from *international licensing from B to A*, mathematical manipulation of Equation 1c, under the base assumption that $\frac{K'_A}{K'_B} < 1$, leads to the following inequality:

$$n_A^{1-\beta_A}(L_A)^{\beta_A}(1-(te_{k,BA})^\alpha)$$
$$> (L_B)^{\beta_B}(n_B^{1-\beta_B} - n_A^{1-\beta_B}(te_{f,AB})^\alpha) \qquad (2c)$$

Equation 2c indicates that the probability of MNEs from A, with no competitive advantage, to engage in FDI in B increases in the following cases: (1) the transaction costs in the international market for technology (from B to A) are high; (2) the number of A's entrepreneurs (relative to the number of B's entrepreneurs) is high; (3) the liability of foreignness of A's entrepreneurs operating in B is low; and (4) the relative labor contribution to utility (as a function of the quantity of Labor, *L*, and labor productivity β), $\frac{(L_A)^{\beta_A}}{(L_B)^{\beta_B}}$, is high. Cases 1–3 were already discussed for Equations 2a and 2b. Case 4 seems counterintuitive at first sight. However, its reasoning can be explained when considering the differential effects of $te_{f,AB}$ and $te_{k,BA}$ on FDI in B and on international licensing from B to A. A's entrepreneurs are not 'taxed' on the domestic production part of the utility they gain from $(L_A)^{\beta_A}$ (as reflected by $K'_A n_A^{1-\beta_A}(L_A)^{\beta_A}$). They are taxed (in terms of the liability of foreignness), however, on the utility they gain from $(L_B)^{\beta_B}$ (see Equation 1c). But, B's entrepreneurs are not 'taxed' on the domestic production part of the utility they gain from $(L_B)^{\beta_B}$ (as reflected by $K'_B n_B^{1-\beta_B}(L_B)^{\beta_B}$), but are taxed (in terms of transaction costs) on the utility they gain from $(L_A)^{\beta_A}$ (see Equation 1c). Since in both operation modes the domestic and foreign utilities are taken into account, it follows that the higher the wedge between $(L_A)^{\beta_A}$ and $(L_B)^{\beta_B}$ the higher the utility from FDI in B relative to the utility from international licensing from B to A. In other words, the greater domestic utility created by A's entrepreneurs (who also engage in FDI in B), when $(L_A)^{\beta_A}$ is sufficiently larger than $(L_B)^{\beta_B}$, leads to the dominancy of outward FDI on inward licensing.

Outward FDI versus inward FDI

Finally, a comparison of the relative utility from FDI in B for MNEs with no competitive advantages and that of FDI in A (incoming FDI) allows the testing (of probably the most interesting case) of competing MNEs from two different nations. Equation 2d specifies the conditions for the former to exist under the base assumption that $\dfrac{K'_A}{K'_B} < 1$:

$$(L_A)^{\beta_A}(n_A^{1-\beta_A} - n_B^{1-\beta_B}(te_{f,BA})^{\alpha})$$
$$> (L_B)^{\beta_B}(n_B^{1-\beta_B} - n_A^{1-\beta_A}(te_{f,AB})^{\alpha}) \qquad (2d)$$

Equation 2d indicates that the probability of MNEs from A, with no competitive advantages, to engage in FDI in B increases in the following cases: (1) the number of A's entrepreneurs (relative to the number of B's entrepreneurs) is high; (2) the liability of foreignness of A's entrepreneurs operating in B is low, relative to the liability of foreignness of B's entrepreneurs operating in A; and (3) the relative labor contribution to utility (as a function of the quantity of Labor, L, and labor productivity β), $\dfrac{(L_A)^{\beta_A}}{(L_B)^{\beta_B}}$, is high. The first case was already identified in Equations 2a-2c. The second case is intuitive and

straightforward and demonstrates that it is not only the liability of foreignness of MNEs from a given country that matters, but actually the *relative* liability of foreignness of competing MNEs from different nations. This view is consistent with the literature on asymmetric cultural and psychic distances between countries (Shenkar, 2001; Hakanson and Ambos, 2010). Given that cultural distance is one of the major factors affecting the liability of foreignness, asymmetric cultural distance leads to differences in bidirectional liabilities of foreignness. It shows that even without the possession of a competitive advantage, a relatively lower liability of foreignness to that of competing MNEs originating from other countries may allow MNEs to engage in outgoing FDI at the expense of incoming FDI (from MNEs with a competitive advantage). Case 3 once again seems counterintuitive. However, its reasoning can be explained similarly to the approach taken for Equation 2c, while considering the effects of $te_{f,AB}$ and $te_{f,BA}$ on FDI in B and FDI in A. A's entrepreneurs are not 'taxed' on the domestic production part of the utility they gain from $(L_A)^{\beta_A}$, but are taxed (in terms of the liability of foreignness from A to B) on the utility they gain from $(L_B)^{\beta_B}$ (see Equation 1d). B's entrepreneurs are not 'taxed' on the domestic production part of the utility they gain from $(L_B)^{\beta_B}$, but are taxed (in terms of the liability of foreignness from B to A) on the utility they gain from $(L_A)^{\beta_A}$ (see Equation 1d). Taken together, it once again follows that the higher the wedge between $(L_A)^{\beta_A}$ and $(L_B)^{\beta_B}$, the higher the overall utility from FDI in B relative to the overall utility from FDI in A.

Overall, when considered *jointly*, Equations 2a-2d represent the necessary and sufficient conditions for the emergence of MNEs with no competitive advantage.[9] The equations demonstrate how internalization advantage (represented by $te_{k,ij}$ $i,j = A,B$), the liability of foreignness (as a function of $te_{f,ij}$ $i,j = A,B$), and relative location advantage (represented by $(L_A)^{\beta_A}$ and $(L_B)^{\beta_B}$) interact among themselves and with the relative number of entrepreneurs in each country (represented by n_i $i = A,B$) to allow outgoing FDI, even in cases where a competitive advantage does not exist. This insight supports the view of Buckley and Hashai (2009) that ownership (or competitive), location, and internalization advantages should be conceived as the product of

---

[9] Individually, each equation represents a necessary but insufficient condition for the emergence of MNEs with no competitive advantage.

Copyright © 2014 Strategic Management Society

Global Strat. J., 4: 35–48 (2014)
DOI: 10.1111/j.2042-5805.2013.01069.x

continuous (nonzero) variables, with the magnitude of each variable affecting the probability of the emergence of MNEs. Thus, competitive disadvantage can be counterbalanced by other factors included in the model and, therefore, MNEs with no competitive advantage emerge. Ownership, location, and internalization advantages, hence, do not only complement, but also substitute, for each other.

DISCUSSION

The existence of a competitive advantage as a precondition for the emergence of MNEs is a cornerstone of international business theory. While acknowledging that in many cases MNEs possess competitive advantages when internationalizing, this article challenges the extant wisdom that assumes competitive advantage is a *necessary* condition for the emergence of the MNE. This view, pioneered by Hymer (1976) and Dunning (1977), takes a single firm point of view to determine that firms must have a competitive advantage to successfully compete with indigenous and other foreign firms in host foreign markets. In contrast, this article compares the overall utility from outward FDI relative to the overall utility from multiple alternative operation modes.

This approach, based on the formalization of internationalization in the eclectic paradigm, recently suggested by Buckley and Hashai (2009), differs from the traditional interpretation of the eclectic paradigm in several ways. First, while the original paradigm is mostly compared with domestic production in the host country and international licensing from the home to the host country, the current approach also contrasts the utility of outgoing FDI with the utility from international licensing from the host to the home country and with incoming FDI from the host to the home country. In this respect, the approach suggested by Buckley and Hashai (2009) offers a more complete account of the feasibility of FDI than the original paradigm and is more up-to-date in capturing recent developments in the global system. Second, a general equilibrium approach takes into account both the domestic and foreign utilities of all actors in the global system, namely the entrepreneurs and the workers in the home and host countries. In contrast, the original paradigm focuses only on the utility that entrepreneurs can gain when operating in a host country and, hence, provides only a partial and potentially

misleading view on the utility consequences of the global system players. The current type of modeling is consistent with the general equilibrium approach taken by Coase (1937). In particular, the consideration of the utility of entrepreneurs from domestic production, in addition to foreign operations and the consideration of the utility from employing otherwise inefficiently employed host country workers, are important. This is because in general equilibrium terms we are interested in the overall utility created by entrepreneurs in their home and host countries and in the clearing of both the product and factor markets. Third, the general equilibrium approach takes a long-term view, whereas the partial equilibrium is short term in nature. Taking a short-term approach is subject to the danger of making unsustainable predictions. This flaw is, in fact, exacerbated, given the focus of this article, because it assumes away the likely outcome of depletion of competitive advantages over time and, hence, cannot predict long run determinants of global configurations. Finally, the approach taken by Buckley and Hashai (2009) treats ownership advantage, location advantage, and internalization advantage as continuous variables that can compensate for each other. It thereby enables outgoing FDI to occur even without the possession of ownership (or competitive) advantages. In other words, it shows that the three types of advantages do not only complement, but also substitute for, each other. Hence, firms that do not possess ownership advantages may still be able to create greater utility than those with such advantages by better exploiting labor at home (due to absence of liabilities of foreignness) and at the host country (where a group of disadvantaged foreign entrepreneurs avoid the diminishing returns to scale of a smaller group of more advantaged local entrepreneurs). In addition, firms with no competitive advantages are in particular expected to outperform more advantaged firms in industries with high transaction costs, e.g., where there is a need to extensively transfer tacit knowledge, thereby making licensing a less viable option (Kogut and Zander, 1993; Martin and Salomon, 2003).

The current article specifically tests the conditions necessary for outward FDI to occur for entrepreneurs who lack competitive advantages vis-à-vis competing host country entrepreneurs. It does so by assuming that the knowledge stock of these entrepreneurs, in terms of proprietary assets and the capability to efficiently coordinate and control transactions, is lower than that of their foreign

Global Strat. J., 4: 35–48 (2014)
DOI: 10.1111/j.2042-5805.2013.01069.x

competing entrepreneurs. The analysis reveals that, contrary to conventional wisdom, outward FDI is indeed possible even without the possession of competitive advantages and that the conditions for this to occur, when the utility from outward FDI is compared to that of alternative operation modes, are consistent.

We have identified four complementary conditions that allow for outward FDI to occur, in the absence of competitive advantages. These conditions are: (1) a sufficiently larger number of entrepreneurs in the home country relative to the host country, whose overall utility substitutes for the utility created by a smaller number of more advantaged entrepreneurs. This results stems from the diminishing returns to scale of the entrepreneurs' production function, implying that a larger number of disadvantaged entrepreneurs may more efficiently employ foreign workers than a smaller number of advantaged entrepreneurs from the host country. Thus, employing otherwise inefficiently employed foreign workers allows the former group of entrepreneurs to outcompete the latter; (2) low liability of foreignness for the home country entrepreneurs when operating in the host country, both in absolute terms and relative to the liability of foreignness of the host country entrepreneurs operating in the home country. This condition is straightforward, as it implies a smaller depreciation of the utility created by such entrepreneurs relative to that of advantaged host country entrepreneurs, thus acting as a neutralizer of the latters' advantages; (3) high transaction costs in the international markets for knowledge that indicates that the greater utility created by more advantaged entrepreneurs is compromised when externalized foreign market operation modes such as licensing are used; and (4) a higher home country labor contribution to utility (as a function of the quantity of Labor, L, and labor productivity β) than that of the host country, reflecting the importance of scale in allowing outward FDI in the absence of competitive advantages, this time with respect to labor abundance. This allows home country entrepreneurs to generate higher utility, as they are not subject to the liabilities of foreignness and international transaction costs when employing domestic workers, and this may lead to a greater overall utility (accounting for both domestic and foreign market-created utilities) of competitively disadvantaged entrepreneurs from large home countries.

It follows that scale in terms of the number of entrepreneurs and workers in the home country, low

liability of foreignness, high transaction costs, and high domestic labor productivity may compensate for the lack of competitive advantages to allow for the emergence of MNEs. This observation may further allow predicting in which countries and industries we are likely to witness the emergence of MNEs with no competitive advantages. In terms of scale, one may anticipate that the large emerging countries that are abundant with entrepreneurship and labor, but where entrepreneurs usually lack competitive advantages, may be a viable source of outward FDI. Hence, it is no surprise that firms from Brazil, Russia, India, and China (BRIC) have been internationalizing rapidly to advanced countries in the last decade. In fact, the stock of outward FDI from the BRIC countries to leading developed economies such as the United States, the United Kingdom, Japan, and Germany has increased tenfold in the last decade (OECD, 2012). In such countries, the relative abundance of entrepreneurs and workers may well be the main driver for the increasing levels of outward FDI directed toward advanced countries.

In terms of liability of foreignness, several factors are leading to the reduction in liability of foreignness for emerging countries' entrepreneurs operating in advanced countries. These include: the increasing number of students from the BRIC (and other emerging) countries who are educated in Western higher education institutions (located either in advanced countries or in emerging countries); the experience gained by emerging countries' entrepreneurs who have been working in the past for advanced countries' MNEs; and the growing trend of repatriation from advanced countries to emerging countries as the standard of living in these countries rapidly increases (Peng, Wang, and Jiang, 2008). All these factors decrease the liability of foreignness for entrepreneurs from emerging countries when operating in advanced countries. However, this process is not symmetrical where the substantially different institutional and cultural environments in emerging countries seem to keep on heavily taxing advanced countries' entrepreneurs in terms of the costs of doing business abroad (Henisz, 2005; Peng *et al.*, 2008; Hakanson and Ambos, 2010).

It is further anticipated that in countries and industries where international transaction costs are high, the probability of the emergence of MNEs with no competitive advantages will increase. This implies that countries where bilateral treaties for intellectual property protection are not settled—as is often the case where emerging and advanced countries are concerned—are natural candidates for this phenomenon. In addition, industries with higher transaction costs, which are usually high technology industries such as automotive, electronics or software, are likely to be candidates for the emergence of FDI of the type analyzed in this article. Indeed, the international rise of firms such as TATA, Infosys, Haier, and so on falls well within this category. Finally, when referring to labor productivity, recent evidence shows that the gap in productivity between emerging and advanced countries is closing rapidly (Isaksson, Ng, and Robyn, 2005). As we have argued, the contribution of domestic production to the utility of internationalizing entrepreneurs plays an important role in allowing such entrepreneurs to successfully outcompete host country entrepreneurs who possess firm-specific advantages. In fact, our approach emphasizes the importance of the home country location advantages, rather than the host country location advantages, in promoting outward FDI in the absence of competitive advantages.

CONCLUSION

The research question posed in this study should not be taken to refute the view that MNEs often do possess firm-specific competitive advantages. The current article shows formally that the existence of such advantages is actually not a necessary condition for outward FDI. This is clearly an important twist to the theory of the MNE as articulated in both the international business and international economics literatures (e.g., Carr *et al.*, 2001; Helpman *et al.*, 2004; Markusen, 2001) and allows us to think more widely about the determinants of outward FDI. Furthermore, our arguments regarding the factors allowing the emergence of MNEs that do not necessarily possess competitive advantages can be tested empirically due to the fact that we treat the different components of the eclectic paradigm separately. As discussed by Buckley and Hashai (2009), several easily accessible proxies can be found to test the validity of our view in different country and industrial settings.

It is noteworthy that the model presented in this article can be easily expanded into a multicountry model where entrepreneurs in some countries are less advantaged than entrepreneurs in others. While the current article sought to make a point by focusing on the simplest case of a two-country model, it would be interesting to test possible configurations

of the global systems where multiple countries are taken into account. In addition, we chose to take the simplifying assumption that the entrepreneurs in each country are identical. Once again, this assumption has facilitated the main argument of this article. In reality, one can expect that this would not be the case. If this assumption is relaxed, one may expect an equilibrium where competitively advantaged entrepreneurs from the host country will operate domestic firms in addition to competitively disadvantaged entrepreneurs from the home country as long as the number of workers employed by the former entrepreneurs is not outweighed by the better labor utilization of the larger number of the latter entrepreneurs. Thus, extending the current article into a multicountry model as well as allowing for some heterogeneity of entrepreneurs within each country are two promising avenues to extend our understanding of the factors that allow the emergence of MNEs.

The conclusion of this article is that the centrality that competitive advantages have gained in explaining the emergence of MNEs has been overemphasized. We suggest that the combination of: (1) location advantages originating in the international trade and economics literatures (e.g., Heckscher, 1949; Ohlin, 1933); (2) internalization advantages as articulated by Buckley and Casson (1976) and Rugman (1981) among others; and (3) the liability of foreignness (Hymer, 1976, Zaheer, 1995) provides a sufficient explanation for the phenomenon of the MNE. Competitive advantages may play an important role in specific instances but, as this article shows, MNEs may exist without their possession. Just as firms do not need a competitive advantage to exist, they do not need a competitive advantage to become MNEs.

ACKNOWLEDGEMENTS

The authors would like to thank Coeditors Stephan Tallman and Torben Pederson for their insightful comments and guidance. The article has also benefited from the comments of two anonymous GSJ referees and participants of the EIBA 38th annual conference in Sussex, U.K., as well as those of Christian Asmussen, Mark Casson, Seev Hirsch, Mario Kafouros, and Francesca Sanna-Randaccio. Niron Hashai would like to acknowledge the financial support of the Asper Center for Entrepreneurship at the Hebrew University.

Copyright © 2014 Strategic Management Society

REFERENCES

Almeida P. 1996. Knowledge sourcing by foreign multinationals: patent citation analysis in the U.S. semiconductor industry. *Strategic Management Journal*, Winter Special Issue **17**: 155–165.

Amsden AH, Chu WW. 2003. *Beyond Late Development: Taiwan's Upgrading Policies*. MIT Press: Cambridge, MA.

Barney J. 1991. Firm resources and sustained competitive advantage. *Journal of Management* **17**: 99–120.

Buckley PJ. 1985. A critical view of theories of the multinational enterprise. In *The Economic Theory of the Multinational Enterprise*, Buckley PJ, Casson M (eds). Macmillan: London, U.K.; 1–19.

Buckley PJ, Casson MC. 1976. *The Future of the Multinational Enterprise*. Macmillan: London, U.K.

Buckley PJ, Clegg LJ, Cross AR, Zheng P, Voss H, Liu X. 2007. The determinants of Chinese outward foreign direct investment. *Journal of International Business Studies* **38**(4): 499–518.

Buckley PJ, Hashai N. 2004. A global system view of firm boundaries. *Journal of International Business Studies* **35**(1): 33–45.

Buckley PJ, Hashai N. 2009. Formalizing internationalization in the eclectic paradigm. *Journal of International Business Studies* **40**(1): 58–70.

Carr D, Markusen JR, Maskus KE. 2001. Estimating the knowledge-capital model of the multinational enterprise. *American Economic Review* **93**: 693–708.

Casson M. 1985. Multinational monopolies and international cartels. In *The Economic Theory of the Multinational Enterprise*, Buckley PJ, Casson M (eds). Macmillan: London, U.K.; 60–97.

Casson M. 1986. General theories of the multinational enterprise: their relevance to business history. In *Multinationals: Theory and History*, Hertner P, Jones GG (eds). Gower: Aldershot, U.K.; 42–61.

Casson M. 1987. *The Firm and the Market*. MIT Press: Cambridge, MA.

Casson M. 2000. *The Economics of International Business*. Edward Elgar: Cheltenham, U.K.

Caves RE. 1996. *Multinational Enterprise and Economic Analysis*. Cambridge University Press: Cambridge, U.K.

Coase RH. 1937. The nature of the firm. *Economica* **4**: 386–405.

Dunning JH. 1977. Trade, location of economic activity, and the MNE: a search for an eclectic approach. In *The International Allocation of Economic Activity*, Ohlin B, Hesselborn PO, Wijkman PM (eds). Macmillan: London, U.K.; 395–418.

Dunning JH. 1981. *FDI and the Multinational Enterprise*. Allen & Unwin: London, U.K.

Dunning JH. 1988. The eclectic paradigm of FDI: a restatement and some possible extensions. *Journal of International Business Studies* **19**(1): 1–31.

Dunning JH. 1993. *Multinational Enterprises and the Global Economy*. Addison-Wesley: Reading, MA.

Dunning JH. 1998. Location and the multinational enterprise: a neglected factor? *Journal of International Business Studies* **29**(1): 45–66.

Dunning JH. 2006. Comment on dragon multinationals: new players in 21st century globalization. *Asia Pacific Journal of Management* **23**: 139–141.

Dunning JH, Kim C, Park D. 2008. Old wine in new bottles: a comparison of emerging market TNCs today and developed country TNCs thirty years ago. In *The Rise of Transnational Corporations from Emerging Markets: Threat or Opportunity?*, Sauvant KP (ed). Edward Elgar: Cheltenham, U.K.; 158–182.

Eden L. 2003. A critical reflection and some conclusions on OLI. In *International Business and the Eclectic Paradigm*, Cantwell J, Narula R (eds). Routledge: London, U.K.; 277–297.

Fosfuri A, Motta M. 1999. Multinationals without advantages. *Scandinavian Journal of Economics* **101**(4): 617–630.

Goldstein A. 2007. *Multinational Companies from Emerging Economies*. Palgrave Macmillan: London, U.K.

Hakanson L, Ambos B. 2010. The antecedents of psychic distance. *Journal of International Management* **16**(3): 195–210.

Heckscher E. 1949. The effect of foreign trade on the distribution of income. In *Readings in International Trade*, Ellis HS, Metzler LA (eds). Blakiston Company: Philadelphia, PA; 272–300.

Helpman E, Melitz MJ, Yeaple SR. 2004. Export versus FDI with heterogeneous firms. *American Economic Review* **94**(1): 300–316.

Henisz WJ. 2005. The institutional environment for international business. In *What is International Business?*, Buckley PJ (ed). Palgrave Macmillan: Hampshire, U.K.; 85–109.

Hymer SH. 1976. The international operations of national firms: a study of direct foreign investment. PhD thesis, MIT, Cambridge, MA.

Isaksson A, Ng TH, Robyn G. 2005. *Productivity in Developing Countries: Trends and Policies*. UNIDO: Vienna, Austria.

Kogut B, Chang SJ. 1991. Technological capabilities and Japanese foreign direct investment in the United States. *Review of Economics and Statistics* **73**: 401–413.

Kogut B, Zander U. 1993. Knowledge of the firm and the evolutionary theory of the multinational. *Journal of International Business Studies* **24**(4): 625–645.

Levinthal DA, Wu B. 2010. Opportunity costs and non-scale free capabilities: profit maximization, corporate scope, and profit margins. *Strategic Management Journal* **31**(7): 780–801.

Luo Y, Tang RL. 2007. International expansion of emerging market enterprises: a springboard perspective. *Journal of International Business Studies* **38**: 481–498.

Copyright © 2014 Strategic Management Society

Global Strat. J., 4: 35–48 (2014)
DOI: 10.1111/j.2042-5805.2013.01069.x

Markusen JR. 2001. International trade theory and international business. In *The Oxford Handbook of International Business*, Rugman AM, Brewer TL (eds). Oxford University Press: New York; 69–87.

Martin X, Salomon R. 2003. Tacitness, learning, and international expansion: a study of foreign direct investment in a knowledge-intensive industry. *Organization Science* **14**(3): 297–311.

Mathews JA. 2002. *Dragon Multinational: A New Model for Global Growth*. Oxford University Press: New York.

Mathews JA. 2006. Dragon multinationals: new players in 21st century globalization. *Asia Pacific Journal of Management* **23**: 5–27.

Nachum L, Zaheer S. 2005. The persistence of distance? The impact of technology on MNE motivations for foreign investments. *Strategic Management Journal* **26**(8): 747–767.

OECD. 2012. OECD Database. Available at: http://stats.oecd.org/ (accessed 1 December 2012).

Ohlin B. 1933. *Interregional and International Trade*. Harvard University Press: Cambridge, MA.

Peng MW, Wang DYL, Jiang Y. 2008. An institution-based view of international business strategy: a focus on emerging economies. *Journal of International Business Studies* **39**(5): 920–935.

Peteraf M. 1993. The cornerstones of competitive advantage: a resource-based view. *Strategic Management Journal* **14**(3): 179–191.

Ramamurti R. 2009a. Why study emerging country multinationals? In *Emerging Multinationals in Emerging Markets*, Ramamurti R, Singh JV (eds). Cambridge University Press: Cambridge, U.K.; 3–22.

Ramamurti R. 2009b. What have we learned about emerging market MNEs? In *Emerging Multinationals in Emerging Markets*, Ramamurti R, Singh JV (eds). Cambridge University Press: Cambridge, U.K.; 399–426.

Rugman AM. 1981. *Inside the Multinationals: The Economics of Internal Markets*. Columbia University Press: New York.

Rugman AM. 2009. How global are TNCs from emerging countries? In *The Rise of Transnational Corporations from Emerging Markets: Threat or Opportunity?*, Sauvant KP (ed). Edward Elgar: Cheltenham, U.K.; 86–106.

Rugman AM, Verbeke A. 2001. Subsidiary specific advantages in multinational enterprises. *Strategic Management Journal* **22**(3): 237–250.

Rugman AM, Verbeke A, Nguyen QTK. 2011. Fifty years of international business theory and beyond. *Management International Review* **51**(6): 755–786.

Salomon R, Martin X. 2008. Learning, knowledge transfer, and technology implementation performance: a study of time-to-build in the global semiconductor industry. *Management Science* **54**(7): 1266–1280.

Shenkar O. 2001. Cultural distance revisited: towards a more rigorous conceptualization and measurement of cultural differences. *Journal of International Business Studies* **32**: 519–536.

Tallman SB. 1991. Strategic management models and resource-based strategies among MNEs in a host market. *Strategic Management Journal*, Summer Special Issue **12**: 69–82.

Wernerfelt B. 1984. A resource-based view of the firm. *Strategic Management Journal* **5**(2): 171–180.

Zaheer S. 1995. Overcoming the liability of foreignness. *Academy of Management Journal* **38**(2): 341–363.

Copyright © 2014 Strategic Management Society

Global Strat. J., **4**: 35–48 (2014)
DOI: 10.1111/j.2042-5805.2013.01069.x

Research Policy 43 (2014) 423–437

Contents lists available at ScienceDirect

Research Policy

journal homepage: www.elsevier.com/locate/respol

ELSEVIER

The role of technological catch up and domestic market growth in the genesis of emerging country based multinationals

Peter J. Buckley [a,1], Niron Hashai [b,*]

[a] Centre for International Business, Leeds University Business School, University of Leeds, Maurice Keyworth Building, Leeds LS2 9JT, United Kingdom
[b] Jerusalem School of Business Administration, The Hebrew University of Jerusalem, Mount Scopus, Jerusalem 91905, Israel

ARTICLE INFO

Article history:
Received 29 March 2012
Received in revised form 16 October 2013
Accepted 5 November 2013
Available online 4 December 2013

Keywords:
Emerging country based MNCs
Technological catch up
Domestic growth
Global system view
Location choice

ABSTRACT

The paper presents a model that evaluates how upgraded technological capabilities of emerging country based multinationals (EMNCs) and an increase in the domestic market size of large emerging countries affect value chain location choices and the competitiveness of emerging country based firms versus advanced country based ones. The model shows that, even without possessing a competitive advantage in terms of technology and/or brands, EMNCs from large or rapidly technologically advancing countries can become dominant players in the global system. The model highlights the central role of firm level technological intensity and product differentiation in determining the location of value chain activities as well as defining organisational boundaries. Empirical analysis of the location choices of the world's top multinationals from large advanced and emerging countries in 2010 supports the model's predictions.

© 2013 Elsevier B.V. All rights reserved.

1. Introduction

Post World War II globalisation, in terms of Foreign Direct Investment (FDI) and international trade, has been dominated by large advanced country based multinationals (AMNCs). Such hegemony was facilitated by technological advantages, well recognised brands, superior managerial practices and production efficiency, coupled with the existence of large domestic markets as a major source of demand for products and services (Dunning, 1988, 1993; Vernon, 1966, 1971).

However, the accelerated development of countries such as Brazil, India, China and Russia has resulted in a growing number of emerging country based multinationals (EMNCs) beginning to play an important role in today's global system. The increased salience of EMNCs has been widely documented in the extant literature (e.g. Bonaglia et al., 2007; Buckley et al., 2007; Dunning, 2006; Duysters et al., 2009; Goldstein, 2007; Lall, 1983; Luo and Tang, 2007; Mathews, 2002, 2006; Niosi and Tschang, 2009; Ramamurti and Singh, 2009; Sauvant, 2008; Wells, 1983).

A recurring question in this stream of literature is how can one explain the rise of EMNCs, and especially their ability to engage in FDI in advanced countries, given that many emerging country based firms lack firm-specific competitive advantages?

(Amsden and Chu, 2003; Goldstein, 2007; Mathews, 2006; Nolan, 2004; Ramamurti, 2009a; Rugman, 2009). According to Dunning's Ownership-Location-Internalisation paradigm (Dunning, 1977, 1988) the possession of firm specific advantages, mainly in technological advance and brands, is a necessary condition for the emergence of the multinational corporation (MNC). This is because such advantages are needed to compensate for the liabilities of foreignness (Hymer, 1976), which imply a higher cost of doing business abroad for foreign firms. Hence, in the absence of such advantages, the rise of EMNCs seems to contradict extant explanations for the existence of MNCs.

Several answers were provided to this question, including: the superior ability of EMNCs to operate in harsh institutional environments in other developing countries (Cuervo-Cazzura and Genc, 2008; Dunning and Lundan, 2008), greater capability to adapt products to the specific demands of import protected developing markets (Lall, 1983; Wells, 1983), the leverage of home country advantages such as natural resources and cheap labour (Rugman, 2009; Cantwell and Barnard, 2008; Williamson and Zeng, 2009), access to cheap capital because of imperfections in the domestic capital market (Buckley et al., 2007) and the desire to engage in "knowledge asset seeking" in foreign markets (Dunning, 2006; Dunning et al., 2008; Goldstein, 2007; Hoskisson et al., 2000; Luo and Tang, 2007; Mathews, 2002). Yet, it still remains unclear if and under what conditions EMNCs are likely to compete successfully with AMNCs on a global scale (Ramamurti, 2009b).

The current paper utilises the global system view model (Buckley and Hashai, 2004; Casson, 2000) to postulate the conditions under which EMNCs will close the gap vis-à-vis AMNCs in

* Corresponding author. Tel.: +972 0 2 5883110; fax: +972 0 2 5881341.
E-mail addresses: pjb@lubs.leeds.ac.uk (P.J. Buckley), nironh@huji.ac.il (N. Hashai).
[1] Tel.: +44 0113 343 4646; fax: +44 0113 343 4754.

0048-7333/$ – see front matter © 2013 Elsevier B.V. All rights reserved.
http://dx.doi.org/10.1016/j.respol.2013.11.004

terms of dominance in serving global markets and foreign direct investment. More specifically, the model formally analyses how upgrading the technological capabilities of EMNCs and a substantial increase in domestic market size of emerging countries, are likely to project EMNCs versus AMNCs in terms of the worldwide location and ownership of Research and Development (R&D), production and marketing activities. The model specifically highlights the role of technology intensity and product differentiation in the comparative statics of a global system comprised of EMNCs and AMNCs.

The model predicts a novel phase of globalisation where EMNCs from countries where lower production costs are maintained, and that encounter rapid technological progress or possess a large and growing domestic market become dominant competitors for AMNCs. It shows that value chain location for AMNCs and EMNCs is likely to be quite different, where AMNCs are expected to locate R&D and marketing activities primarily in advanced countries, EMNCs are expected to locate R&D and production activities primarily in emerging countries. The model further shows that greater technological intensity increases the propensity of AMNCs to locate production in advanced countries, while increasing the propensity of EMNCs to locate marketing activities in emerging countries. Greater technology intensity and product differentiation further increase the propensity of both AMNCs and EMNCs to integrate activities in-house, rather than outsource them. Empirical analysis of the location choices of the world's top MNCs from large developed and developing countries in 2010 (in Gross Domestic Product terms) shows support to these value chain location and integration predictions.

A key insight of the model is that even without possessing firm specific advantages in R&D and marketing, EMNCs from large and rapidly technology advancing countries may become dominant players in the global system. Once emerging country based firms catch up on technology (while not achieving a competitive advantage) and once their domestic market size increases sufficiently (making the interaction with consumers less costly) they become able to successfully compete with advanced country based firms.

In the next section we briefly present the literature on the rise of EMNCs. In Section 3 we build on the "global system view" perspective and present a simple model that predicts the outcome of EMNCs versus AMNCs competition in terms of value chain location and integration. Section 4 presents our data, measures and methods, and results are presented in Section 5. Insights from the model and the structure of the resulting emergent global system are discussed in the concluding sections.

2. The globalisation of EMNCs

The global system at the end of the 20th century started to emerge after the Second World War (Obstfeld and Taylor, 2002).[2] This system has been characterised by the dominance of the US, Europe and Japan in terms of military power, political influence and technological advance. Foreign investments were the engine of this globalisation phase where integrated capital markets absorbed FDI outflows led by AMNCs, reaching a peak of over US$ 2 trillion in 2007 (UNCTAD, 2009).

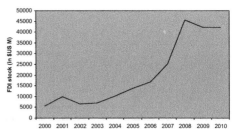

Fig. 1. Outward FDI from the BRIC countries to the United States, Japan, Germany and the United Kingdom.
Source: OECD.Stat. –

Yet, already 30 years ago a new type of multinational had emerged: emerging country based multinationals.[3] The rise of this type of multinational initially was explained by their superior ability to substitute imports in protected emerging countries in terms of scale, labour costs, skill and adapted materials (Wells, 1983). It was further argued that EMNCs often use outdated and simpler adapted technology in other emerging countries going down the ladder of the product life cycle to even less advanced countries (Ghymn, 1980; Lall, 1983). In many aspect EMNCs are still believed to enjoy the advantages of experience of operating in harsh institutional environments (Cuervo-Cazzura and Genc, 2008; Dunning and Lundan, 2008) and data indeed shows that such firms mainly establish foreign operations in other emerging countries, most often in their home region (Rugman, 2008, 2009). All in all this pattern of EMNCs investing in other emerging countries seemed to fall within the boundaries of extant FDI theories (Dunning et al., 2008).

Yet, as Fig. 1 illustrates, the outward FDI stock from large emerging countries such as Brazil, Russia, India and China (BRIC) into major advanced countries, such as Germany, Japan, the US and the UK, has increased almost tenfold in the last decade. While in terms of share out of inward FDI, FDI from emerging countries into advanced ones is still modest (about 1.2% in 2010) it is clear that a growing number of EMNCs are establishing operations in advanced countries. Multiple pieces of anecdotal evidence such as Lenovo's takeover of IBM's PC business, Tata Steel's takeover of the Anglo-Dutch Corus Steel, Jaguar, Land Rover and Tetley Tea, Cemex's takeover of large cement companies in Australia, the UK and the US provide further evidence for the growing dominance of EMNCs vis-à-vis AMNCs.

The fact that many EMNCs establish foreign operations in advanced countries seems to contradict extant international business theories. One would expect EMNCs to possess competitive advantages in terms of technology, brands or superior managerial practices (Dunning, 1977, 1988) that will compensate for their liability of foreignness (Hymer, 1976) when operating in more advanced countries. Given that many EMNCs often lack firm specific competitive advantages (Amsden and Chu, 2003; Goldstein, 2007; Nolan, 2004; Mathews, 2006; Ramamurti, 2009a,b; Rugman, 2009) alternative explanations to the rise of EMNCs were sought.

One important explanation refers to the establishment of foreign operations in advanced countries as a vehicle for knowledge

---

[2] Of course this process is not unique as the following quotation about ancient Rome illustrates. "...trading with Empires, picking up new farming techniques from them, receiving their diplomatic subsidies, copying their weaponry and ideologies, and organising yourself to fend off the worst excesses of domination, all pushed forward the sequential emergence of more developed economies and larger state structures in the Germanic and Slavic worlds in the two halves of the first millennium... particular groups in the periphery are able to take advantage of the opportunities opened up by the range of new contracts with an imperial neighbour, and this is precisely what we now call a globalization" (Heather, 2013: 294).

[3] The exact definition of EMNCs is not trivial (Goldstein, 2007, Section 2.1). In this paper we refer to multinationals that are managed from an emerging country headquarters as "EMNCs". We acknowledge the fact that this definition may not include all multinationals originating in emerging countries yet it captures the vast majority of such multinationals.

P.J. Buckley, N. Hashai / Research Policy 43 (2014) 423–437 425

asset seeking (Buckley et al., 2007; Cantwell and Barnard, 2008; Dunning, 2006; Dunning et al., 2008; Goldstein, 2007; Luo and Tang, 2007; Mathews, 2002). In other words, EMNCs do not go abroad to exploit existing firm specific advantages but rather to explore new ones (Hoskisson et al., 2000). By establishing a presence in advanced countries, EMNCs gain greater proximity to advanced country firms as means to facilitate the acquisition of superior technological knowledge, marketing advances, or managerial practices. Yet, given the inherent assumption that EMNCs are disadvantaged relative to AMNCs, this explanation falls short in explaining exactly how EMNCs suddenly become able to efficiently absorb the superior capabilities of AMNCs, acquire and in some instances outcompete them.

Other scholars argue that EMNCs build on their country specific advantages such as natural resources or cheap labour. Since access to such production factors in emerging countries is often limited and controlled, EMNCs that are granted privileged access to these factors may build on such resources to create a competitive advantage (Cantwell and Barnard, 2008; Dunning et al., 2008; Rugman, 2009; Williamson and Zeng, 2009). Access to cheap capital because of subsidies, deficiencies in the domestic banking system, family finance or conglomerate cross-subsidisation may also enable the internationalisation of EMNCs (Buckley et al., 2007). While this argument is plausible it has more to do with the ability of EMNCs to compete with AMNCs in emerging markets rather than in advanced ones, and is much less applicable to industries where technology and marketing brands are dominant determinants of competitive advantage.

Other explanations for the rise of EMNCs include: the fact that international operations provide an opportunity to diversify risks and improve flexibility especially in the case of emerging country based business groups (Amsden and Hikino, 1994; Lawrence, 1993; Ramamurti, 2009a), the greater entrepreneurial spirit of EMNCs as compared to more bureaucratic management practices of AMNCs (Amsden, 2009) and late mover advantages when operating in mature mid-tech industries (Ramamurti, 2009b). These explanations, while probably making a good case for specific EMNCs, are hardly generalisable to capture the phenomenon of increased EMNC growth in the advanced country markets.

It follows therefore that the plethora of explanations for the rise of EMNCs does not provide an adequate answer to the questions: *To what extent EMNCs are able to successfully compete with AMNCs?*; and *under which conditions are they able to do that?* In order to answer these questions one has to take into account two major phenomena that have been observed in some of the emerging countries in the recent decade: technological catch up (Perez, 2002) and the growth of domestic markets.

2.1. Technological catch up and domestic market growth in large emerging countries

The accelerated globalization of the last half century in terms of FDI and foreign trade coincided with a technological revolution: the "information revolution" (Perez, 2002). This revolution was led, from its emergence in the early 1970s, by the United States (Perez, 2002). However, in the last decade some emerging countries, such as Brazil, India, China and Russia, have gone through a rapid process of catching up in terms of their share in the world's high technology production and technological advance (Borensztein and Ostry, 1996; Mahmood and Singh, 2003; Naughton, 2007). This has not only resulted from intensive efforts for technology assimilation (Nelson and Pack, 1999) but also from innovation by EMNCs themselves and the establishment of R&D sites in these countries (Athreye and Cantwell, 2007). Large governmental spending on higher education, coupled with legal and economic reforms aimed at increasing competition and securing an effective

system of property rights (Peng et al., 2008; Yang, 2003; Yang et al., 2008) are some of the prominent reasons for this catching up process. In many cases, it was the improved technological and macro-economic infrastructure led by the incoming FDI of AMNCs that facilitated this technological catch up (Amsden and Hikino, 1994; Cantwell and Barnard, 2008; Goldstein, 2007; Khanna and Palepu, 2006; Rugman and Doh, 2008).

Table 1 lists the global capabilities (GloCap) index of technological advance (Filippetti and Peyrache, 2011) for selected emerging and advanced countries. The GloCap index is comprised of various technological indicators including: business innovation (patents, business R&D expenditures), knowledge and skills (number of researches, scientific articles published, public R&D expenditures) and infrastructure (number of PCs, internet users, broadband subscribers).[4] The Index relates to the year 2007 and the table also reports its growth rate between 1995 and 2007. Table 1 clearly reveals that while the GloCap index is lower for the selected emerging countries, its average annual growth rate in the 1995–2007 period is significantly higher than that of advanced countries.[5] Indeed, recent data (National Science Board, 2012) reveal that the rate of real growth in R&D expenditures is the highest for Asian countries, headed by China. Asian countries have actually matched the level of R&D expenditures of the US, with overall annual expenditures of about US$ 400 billion.

This catching up process is also one of the triggers for the rapid increase in the income per capita of several large emerging countries, making their domestic markets central in the world's goods markets (Cantwell and Barnard, 2008). Indeed, the differences in income per capita between advanced and emerging countries remain significant (World Bank, 2012), yet the increase in income per capita in large population countries, such as China or India, results in an overall significant increase in such countries Gross Domestic Product (GDP). Table 1 further lists 2010 GDP data (in absolute terms) and GDP growth between 2000 and 2010 for selected advanced and emerging countries. China's Gross Domestic Product (GDP) is second to the US reaching over US$ 5.9 trillion, Brazil is seventh in its ranking with a GDP of over US$ 1.7 trillion (World Bank, 2010).[6]

This trend implies that several emerging economies became attractive for foreign and local investors not only due to their relatively cheap resources but also due to their growing domestic markets. This trend has intensified following the recent financial crisis that virtually led to a halt in GDP growth in advanced countries, while only marginally slowing down the growth rate of emerging countries such as China and India (UNCTAD, 2009). Just as the large domestic markets of advanced countries have been one of the sources for the dominance of such countries' multinationals in the last half century, larger domestic markets are becoming a source of growth to EMNCs. In fact, some scholars predict that Asia's share of the world's total GDP will increase from about 23% in 1970 to 50% in 2050 (Sachs, 2008).

Given the technological catch up of large emerging countries and the growth of domestic markets, a potentially important question is therefore to what extent these factors can explain the

---

[4] The GloCap index is based on the principles guiding the construction of the ArCo index (Archibugi and Coco, 2004, 2005) but is updated.

[5] In fact, assuming that the average annual growth rates of the listed emerging and advanced countries do not change, one can estimate the time period by which the gap in the GloCap index is to be closed, via the equation: $0.117 \times (1 + 0.354)^n = 0.604 \times (1 + 0.069)^n$. In this case $n = 7$ (years) represents the timeframe where the GloCap index of the BRIC countries surpasses that of advanced countries, indicating technological catch up.

[6] Assuming that the average annual rates of GDP growth will be retained, the equation $1.7 \times (1 + 0.074)^n = 2.2 \times (1 + 0.017)^n$ reveals that the domestic market size of India, for instance, will surpass that of the UK in 5 years.

426   *P.J. Buckley, N. Hashai / Research Policy 43 (2014) 423–437*

Table 1
Technological capabilities and Gross Domestic Product (GDP) for BRIC and advanced countries.

	GloCap Index (2007)	Average annual change in GloCap Index (1995–2007)	GDP US$ trillions (2010)	Average annual GDP growth rate (2000–2010)
BRIC countries				
Brazil	0.130	30.3%	2.1	3.7%
Russia	0.182	9.5%	1.5	5.3%
India	0.039	38.1%	1.7	7.4%
China	0.078	63.8%	5.9	10.3%
Average	0.117	35.4%	2.8	6.7%
Advanced countries				
US	0.632	6.2%	14.6	1.8%
Japan	0.659	5.8%	5.5	0.9%
Germany	0.605	7.1%	3.3	1.2%
United Kingdom	0.520	8.3%	2.2	1.7%
Average	0.604	6.9%	6.4	1.4%

Sources: Filippetti and Peyrache (2011) and World Bank (2010).

rapid development of EMNCs from large emerging countries in the last two decades (Ramamurti and Singh, 2009; Sauvant, 2008) and how it affects their global value chain location and organisational boundaries.

3. Theoretical framework – global system evolution

The potential outcome and characteristics of globalisation led by EMNCs because of their technological catch up and increase in domestic market size are next demonstrated by introducing a simple model of an economic system producing products that differ in their technological intensity and differentiation. The model builds on the "global system view" perspective (Buckley and Hashai, 2004, 2009; Casson, 2000, chapter 3) and predicts the evolving dominance of advanced versus emerging country origin multinationals as well as the shifting location of R&D, marketing and production activities. Applying a global system view to the theory of internationalisation, the world is modelled as a grid of locations for value chain activities (e.g. R&D, production, and marketing) that are interconnected through knowledge flows. The basic notion of the global system view dates back to Coase's (1937) transaction cost theory. Essentially, each value adding activity can be located in any location and coordinated within a firm or through a market exchange. The number of firms that eventually exist, their location and their organisational boundaries (in terms of value chain activities) is expected to minimise the overall cost of the system as well as the cost for each firm. Equilibrium will not be achieved as long as there is a profit opportunity somewhere in the system that enables actors within it to reduce costs. At one extreme there would be as many firms as the number of potential locations multiplied by the number of relevant value chain activities. At the other extreme, a single multinational would exist and would internalise the whole world system.

The global system model, presented below, analyses optimal location and internalisation choices in the global system before and after technological catch up and a substantial increase in the domestic market size of emerging countries. It enables the prediction of the outcome in the changing dominance of advanced versus emerging country multinationals and their location and internalisation choices across the value chain.

3.1. Specification of the model

Consider an economic system that produces consumer goods. The system is comprised of an advanced country (AD) and an emerging country (EM). Four types of value chain activities are

involved: Headquarters (HQ), R&D (R), Production (P)[7] and Marketing (M). AD is assumed to be comparatively abundant with skilled labour; and hence according to the Hecksher–Ohlin–Samuelson (H–O–S) theory it is expected to have a comparative advantage in value chain activities that are "skilled labor" intensive. EM is comparatively abundant with unskilled (or cheap) labour and hence has a comparative advantage in value chain activities that are "unskilled labour" intensive[8] (Ramamurti, 2009b).

The value chain activities are linked to one another by flows of knowledge (denoted by K). Four main types of linkage are identified: K_{HQ-R} – flow of knowledge between the firm's headquarters and R&D, reflecting the role of managerial discretion. K_{R-P} – flow of know-how between R&D and production, K_{M-R} – flow of knowledge between marketing and R&D and K_{M-C} – flow of knowledge between the marketing entity and customers (C). All knowledge flows are two-way. This is because there is always feedback in knowledge flows between different value adding activities. Consistently with extant global system view models (Buckley and Hashai, 2004; Casson, 2000, chapter 3) the flow of knowledge between headquarters, production and marketing is entirely intermediated by R&D.

The location of headquarters (either in AD or EM) represents the origin of the firm (Goldstein, 2007). Each of the other value chain activities (R, P and M) can be located either in AD or EM, hence may be thought of as representing the major bulk of R&D, production and marketing activity taking place in the system. This implies 16 (2^4) alternative location options that are depicted in Fig. 2. Each location option (hereinafter – location configuration) represents a potentially optimal system that includes headquarters, R&D, production and marketing activities, connected via knowledge flows (marked in arrows), that can be located either in AD or EM. Each location configuration may include a maximum of four firms (assuming each activity is performed by an independent firm) and a minimum of one firm (assuming one multinational internalises all value chain activities).

The various cost components of the model are as follows.

3.1.1. R&D costs

The output of an R&D laboratory is an intangible good (such as a patent or technological specification) that can be transferred

---

[7] Production costs may be considered as "operation" costs making the model also suitable to relate to service (rather than product) providers.

[8] Labour is assumed to be internationally immobile whereas capital is assumed to be internationally mobile and thus has little or no impact on comparative advantage (Casson, 1985).

P.J. Buckley, N. Hashai / Research Policy 43 (2014) 423–437

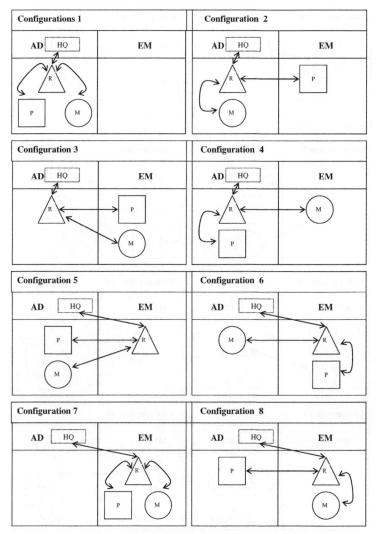

Fig. 2. Alternative location configuration.

428   *P.J. Buckley, N. Hashai / Research Policy 43 (2014) 423–437*

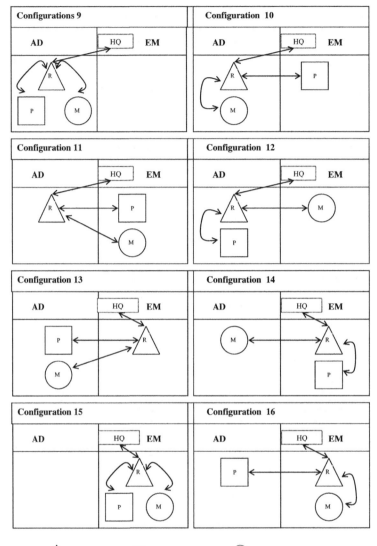

Legend: △R - R&D activities; ▢ - production activities; Ⓜ - marketing activities
▢HQ - Headquarters; AD= advanced country; EM=emerging country;

⟷ Knowledge flow; knowledge flows to customers not shown.

Fig. 2. (*Continued.*)

P.J. Buckley, N. Hashai / Research Policy 43 (2014) 423–437

via K_{R-P} to production sites around the globe. Following Buckley and Hashai (2004) and Adler and Hashai (2007), R&D activities are assumed to incur only a fixed cost. In addition since AD is comparatively abundant with skilled labour it is expected to have a comparative advantage in high value adding activity such as R&D (Mudambi, 2008). Hence, we assume that for a given level of technological output $C_{R,AD} < C_{R,EM}$ (C_R = R&D cost).[9] This assumption is consistent with recent findings on R&D location choices in advanced and emerging countries (Demirbag and Glaister, 2010).

3.1.2. Production costs

Production cost is made up of variable production cost, that is determined by the variable cost of producing and shipping one product unit to end customers (V_i, i = AD, EM), and fixed production costs (F). More specifically, one can determine that: $C_{P,i} = F_i + V_i \times x$; ($C_P$ = cost of production, i = AD, EM, x = number of produced units). Since EM is comparatively abundant with unskilled labour it has a comparative advantage in low value adding activities such as production (relative to R&D, for instance) indicating that: $C_{P,EM} < C_{P,AD}$ (Mudambi, 2008). This implies that, by and large, the cost of producing at EM and shipping products from EM to AD is expected to be lower than the cost of producing at AD and shipping products domestically (Hirsch, 1976). The latter assumption stems from the large production cost differences between AD and EM countries coupled with the sharp decline in international transportation costs and tariff barriers in the few last decades (Adler and Hashai, 2007; Aulakh et al., 2000; Hummels, 2007).

3.1.3. Marketing costs

The cost of marketing is specifically defined as the costs of the interface between the marketing personnel and consumers as well as the cost of supplying post-sale services (including travelling costs and on-going market research cost). Like production costs, marketing costs are a function of fixed and variable costs, as: $C_{M,i} = F_i' + V_i' \times x'$ (C_M = cost of marketing, F – fixed costs, V – variable costs, i = AD, EM, x' = number of units sold) where fixed costs include the baseline costs of operating sales offices and customer support centres, while the variable costs represent the fact that the larger the sales volume, the larger the number of employees that will be enrolled in marketing activities. As in the case of R&D, the fact that AD is comparatively abundant with skilled labour indicates that AD has a comparative advantage in high value adding activity such as marketing (Mudambi, 2008). Hence, we assume that $C_{M,AD} < C_{M,EM}$ (C_M = marketing cost). This assumption is consistent with classic views of the comparative advantage of developed countries in the international business and economics literatures (Dunning, 1988, 1993; Flam and Helpman, 1987; Matsuyama, 2000; Volrath, 1991).

3.1.4. Costs of knowledge flows

Geographic boundaries. Knowledge flow costs include communication costs and transaction costs, thus they might be viewed as fixed costs that are higher within the advanced (or emerging) country than across them (Casson, 2000: 67–70; Teece, 1977) because of the effect of liability of foreignness and cultural differences between countries (Contractor, 1990; Hofstede, 1980; Hymer, 1976; Kogut and Singh, 1988). Hence, if we let α denote within country knowledge flow cost and β denote across country knowledge flow cost, we assume that $\alpha < \beta$.

Organisational boundaries. Where firm boundaries are concerned we follow Kogut and Zander (1993), Martin and Salomon (2003) and many others to assume that the more complex products

are, the greater the difference between intra-firm and inter-firm knowledge transfer costs. Transaction costs are further likely to increase inter-firm knowledge transfer costs the more technology intensive and differentiated products are due to frequency and specificity effects (Williamson, 1985). On the other hand, specialisation of firms in specific value adding activities as well as the reduction of agency costs through externalisation may reduce inter-firm knowledge transfer costs for low-technology intensive and non-differentiated products (Buckley and Casson, 1976, 1998; Casson, 1994, 2000; Williamson, 1985). Letting γ denote intra-firm knowledge flow cost and δ denote inter-firm knowledge flow cost, it therefore follows that $\gamma < \delta$ for knowledge flows related to high technology intensive and/or differentiated products and $\gamma > \delta$ for knowledge flow costs related to low-technology intensive and/or non-differentiated products.

3.2. Optimal location and control configurations

3.2.1. Initial global system

A global system is determined by the location of value adding activities (location configuration) and the combination of internalised or externalised activities comprising it (referred to as the control configuration). An *optimal* global system is one that minimises the cost of operations and knowledge flows relative to all other potential systems (Casson, 2000: 65). This view corresponds with the 'economic school' view of internationalisation, explaining patterns of investment in foreign markets is explained by rational economic analysis, according to which firms choose their optimal structure by evaluating the cost of economic transactions (e.g. Buckley and Casson, 1976; Dunning, 1977, 1988, 1993; Hirsch, 1976; Morck and Yeung, 1992; Rugman, 1986), but also extends it to a global system where cost minimisation pertains to the *whole* system and not to a *single* firm (Casson, 2000: 62–63, Buckley and Hashai, 2004, 2009).

According to the above assumptions, the global system is comprised of sixteen alternative location configurations (labelled configuration 1–16 in Fig. 2).[10] Consistently with Fig. 2, configurations 1–8 include headquarters in AD while configurations 9–16 include headquarters in EM.

The total cost of each location configuration can be calculated by summing up the relevant costs of operation (for R, P and M activities) in AD or EM and the relevant knowledge flows between value chain activities and to customers. The configuration(s) with the lowest operation and knowledge flow costs represents the solution of the global system in terms of location optimality. Once the location configuration is determined, the appropriate firm boundaries (or control configuration) may also be determined according to the difference between intra- and inter-firm knowledge flow costs for high and low technologically and differentiated/non-differentiated products (Casson, 2000: 62–63, Buckley and Hashai, 2004). The origin of each firm in the system is mostly determined based on the location of headquarters (either in AD or EM). Yet, possible solutions of the system allow the separation of headquarters from value chain activities, reflecting externalisation (or outsourcing) of specific activities. In this case the location of such value chain activities identifies their home origin.

The easiest way to understand the general properties of the solution is to eliminate the configurations that are dominated by others (i.e. involve higher costs). Initially, we identify the optimal configurations for a global system where a preponderance of the world's market is assumed to be located in AD (as a base case). Taking the year 2000 as our point of departure, and given the sharp differences

---

[9] Formally, comparative advantage in this case implies that, for instance, relative to production: $C_{R,AD}/C_{P,AD} < C_{R,EM}/C_{P,EM}$ (C_R = R&D cost; C_P = production cost).

[10] Knowledge flows to customers in AD and EM are not shown in Fig. 2.

in GDP between advanced in emerging countries in this point of time (World Bank, 2000) the market in AD can be assumed to be considerably larger than that of EM.[11] In the next subsection we compare these configurations to the optimal configurations emerging after a technological catch up on behalf of EM and a substantial increase in its domestic market size have occurred. Table A1 spells out the costs of all operation and knowledge flow costs. Specifically, given that in the initial global system the market in AD is substantially larger than that of EM, in the last column of Table A1 we distinguish between knowledge flow between marketing to customers in the AD larger market (denoted by α or β) and similar knowledge flows to customers in the EM smaller market (denoted by α' or β'). Due to the substantial differences in market size it is taken that in the initial stage significantly less knowledge needs to be transferred to EM, implying that: $\alpha' \ll \alpha$ and $\beta' \ll \beta$.

Based on the assumptions made earlier on operation and knowledge flow costs, we can calculate which configurations dominate other configurations. This domination can be easily calculated from Table A1. For instance, the total cost of configuration 1 equals: $C_{R,AD} + C_{P,AD} + C_{M,AD} + 4\alpha + \beta'$. The total cost of configuration 4 equals: $C_{R,AD} + C_{P,AD} + C_{M,EM} + 2\alpha + 2\beta + \alpha'$. Given that $C_{M,AD} < C_{M,EM}$ and given that $\alpha < \beta$ and that $\alpha' \ll \alpha$ and $\beta' \ll \beta$, the total cost of configuration 1 is lower than that of configuration 4, which in turn implies that configuration 1 dominates configuration 4. The total costs of all the configurations are calculated in a similar fashion revealing that configurations 4, 5, 8, 9, 12, 13, 14 and 16 are dominated by configuration 1, and that configurations 3, 6 7, 10, 11 and 16 are dominated by configuration 2. Thus, we are left with configurations 1 and 2 as two dominant solutions of the initial global system.

The levels of technological intensity and product differentiation determine the organisational boundaries for these location configurations in terms of internalisation and externalisation due to their effect on the relative magnitude of γ and δ as discussed above. For products that are high technology intensive either a domestic AD firm with boundaries spanning {HQ$_{AD}$, R$_{AD}$, P$_{AD}$, M$_{AD}$} for configuration 1 or an AMNC with production activities in EM for configuration 2 {HQ$_{AD}$, R$_{AD}$, P$_{EM}$, M$_{AD}$} emerge as optimal solutions of the system. For products that are differentiated (but low technology intensive) three AD originating firms emerge, with the following boundaries: *firm i*: {HQ$_{AD}$}, *firm ii*: {R$_{AD}$, M$_{AD}$}, and *firm iii* which can be either {P$_{AD}$} for configuration 1 or {P$_{EM}$} for configuration 2. Finally for products that are both low-technologically intensive and non-differentiated four AD originating firms, each conducting only a single activity, emerge. These firms have the following boundaries: *firm i*: {HQ$_{AD}$}, *firm ii*: {R$_{AD}$}, *firm iii* which can be either {P$_{AD}$} for configuration 1 {P$_{EM}$} for configuration 2 and *firm iv*: {M$_{AD}$}. The latter configurations represent AD entrepreneur(s) coordinating three different value adding activities where *firm ii* supplies technology to an independent producer (*firm iii*) and *firm iv* markets the product. In all cases, the global system solutions imply that AD based firms translate the comparative advantage of AD in high technology intensive and/or differentiated products into competitive advantages (Mudambi, 2008; Porter, 1990) thus outcompeting EM based firm across the board.

3.2.2. Newly emerging global system

As discussed above two fundamental shifts are likely to change the initial global system. One is the technological catch up on behalf of EMNCs and the other is the increase in the domestic market size of large emerging countries, as a result of the increase in the standard of living in such countries coupled with

their large population. In terms of our model, the significant development of technological capabilities in EM implies that EM neutralises AD's comparative advantage in R&D, hence we assume that: $C_{R,EM} = C_{R,AD}$. This assumption is supported by the literature documenting the vast increase in R&D activities in emerging countries in the recent decade (Demirbag and Glaister, 2010; Lewin et al., 2009). Yet, it is noteworthy that this technological catch up does not imply that EM has a comparative advantage in R&D activities nor do EM based firms possess a competitive advantage in product development.

The increase in the relative size of the market in EM relative to that in AD, implies that we can no longer assume that $\alpha' \ll \alpha$ and $\beta' \ll \beta$. This implies that the knowledge flow costs, of both AMNCs and EMNCs, with consumers in EM, become similar to the knowledge flow costs to AD consumers. While in the longer term the increase in the standard of living in emerging countries may also affect the comparative advantage of AD in marketing and that of EM in production, we maintain that these effects are currently still less substantial, as evident from the sharp differences in the income per capita of emerging and advanced countries (World Bank, 2012) and the much larger number of brands possessed by advanced country based firms (Brandz, 2010; WIPO, 2012). We therefore keep our baseline assumptions regarding these value chain activities.

Repeating the comparison of total costs of all configurations, as above, one can note that, in the newly emerging global system, the following configurations are dominated by others: configurations 3, 6, 10 and 11 (by configuration 2), configurations 4, 5, 8, 9, 12 and 13 (by configuration 1) and configurations 7 and 16 (by configuration 15). Thus, we are left with configurations 1, 2, 14 and 15 as optimal solutions of the global system.

The organisational boundaries of configurations 1 and 2 remain identical to those in the initial global system. For the EMNCs (configurations 14 and 15) the levels of technological intensity and product differentiation determine organisational boundaries. For products that are high technologically intensive an EMNC with the following value chain activities: {HQ$_{EM}$, R$_{EM}$, P$_{EM}$, M$_{AD}$} for configuration 14 (where the firm is engaged in FDI in marketing) emerge as the optimal solution of the global system. Alternatively, a domestic EM firm with boundaries spanning {HQ$_{EM}$, R$_{EM}$, P$_{EM}$, M$_{EM}$} for configuration 15, may also emerge as the optimal solution of the system. For products that are differentiated (but low technology intensive) three EM originating firms emerge, with the following boundaries: *firm i*: {HQ$_{EM}$}, *firm ii*: {P$_{EM}$} and *firm iii* which can be either {R$_{EM}$, M$_{AD}$}[12] for configuration 14, or {R$_{EM}$, M$_{EM}$} for configuration 15. Finally, for products that are both low-technologically intensive and non-differentiated four EM originating firms, each conducting a single activity emerge, with the following boundaries: *firm i*: {HQ$_{EM}$}, *firm ii*: {R$_{EM}$}, *firm iii*: {P$_{EM}$} and *firm iv* which can be either {M$_{AD}$} for configuration 14, or {M$_{EM}$} for configuration 15. In all cases, the global system solutions imply that EM based firms serve their domestic markets as well as export to the AD countries as competition to the AD based firms FDI in EM. All in all, the global system that emerges, due to the change in relative market size of EM and AD and in the comparative advantage in R&D, is mainly characterised by the addition of EM based firms to the optimal solutions for the global system that was previously relatively more dominated by AD based firms.

3.2.3. Value chain location and control characteristics in the new global system

Our model is quite specific in its predictions regarding the location and control configurations in the newly emerging global

---

[11] Take for instance the US economy in 2000 with a GDP of US$ 10 trillion, relative to the Chinese economy in that year with a GDP of US$ 1 trillion.

[12] It is noteworthy that this in the only configuration for which the model cannot predict the firm's origin.

P.J. Buckley, N. Hashai / Research Policy 43 (2014) 423–437   431

system. In terms of value chain location, the prediction is that very specific location configurations will dominate others, where AMNCs and EMNCS are expect to differ in their configurations. For AMNCs, the model predicts a continuous dominancy in the location of R&D and marketing activities in advanced countries. In addition, our model predicts that high technological intensity (increasing K_{R-P}) increases the propensity of locating production activities in advanced countries as means to reduce these costs. The main idea here is that AMNCs are likely to face lower liabilities of foreignness due to lower cultural distance and lower differences in technological advance when operating in advanced countries (Hofstede, 1980; Hymer, 1976; Kogut and Singh, 1988; Teece, 1977). This implies that the more technology intensive AMNCs are, the more likely they are to prefer configuration 1 over configuration 2.

For EMNCs our model predicts dominancy in the location of R&D and production activities in emerging countries. In addition, high technological intensity increases the propensity of locating marketing activities in emerging countries, as means to reduce R&D-marketing knowledge transfer costs. The lower liabilities of foreignness EMNCs are expected to face when operating in other emerging countries are likely to drive this prediction. This implies that the more technology intensive EMNCs are, the more likely they are to prefer configuration 15 over configuration 14.

Technology intensity and product differentiation are further expected to substantially impact the control configuration (or organisational boundaries) of both AD and EM based firms. Greater technology intensity is expected to lead to fully integrated firms conducting R&D, production and marketing activities in house. Greater product differentiation is expected to increase the propensity for the emergence of firms with integrated R&D and marketing activities and outsourced production activities.

4. Empirical analysis

4.1. Data

We test the predictions for location and control configuration on data pertaining to the world's largest MNCs from large advanced and large emerging countries for the year 2010 (UNCTAD, 2011). This source contains two separate lists of the top 100 largest MNCs in general and the 100 largest TNCs originating in emerging countries. Given that a central feature of our model relates to domestic market size, we have first screened out from the two lists all MNCs that originate from countries that are not included in the world's top 15 countries in terms of GDP (World Bank, 2012). This has resulted with a list of 139 firms, 79 from advanced countries and 60 from emerging countries.

For these firms, UNCTAD (2011) includes data on total and foreign assets, total and foreign sales and total and foreign employees. We have collected additional data from multiple secondary sources, including: the DataStream and WorldScope databases, web pages and financial reports of the firms, press announcements from Lexis Nexis academics (pertaining to outsourcing and alliance announcements for the time period 2005–2010), United States Patent and Trademark Office (USPTO) (for patent data) and WIPO Global Brands database.

These sources enable us to get detailed data at the MNC level regarding: the prime locations of R&D, production and marketing activities, the extent of outsourcing R&D, production and marketing activities, R&D expenses and number of patents (as two alternative proxies for technological intensity), selling, general and administrative costs and number of brands (as two alternative proxies for product differentiation) and firm age.

4.2. Measures

4.2.1. Dependent variables

In testing predictions regarding location configurations, we use dummy variables for each MNC's main R&D facility, the location of the main production site and the main location of marketing activities. Each such variable receives a value of "0" if it represents location in an advanced country and "1" if it represents location in an emerging country.[13] For testing hypotheses regarding the location of all three value chain activities we use a three cell vector which combines the three variables.

In testing predictions regarding the externalisation or outsourcing of value chain activities, we also use a set of dummy variables for R&D, production and marketing activities. Each dummy variable receives the value "0" if a specific value chain activity (R&D, production or marketing) is mostly conducted in house and "1" if there is an extensive outsourcing or alliance activity in this value chain. Extensive outsourcing and alliance activity is defined as cases where MNCs conduct major parts of a specific value chain activity with a significant partner and/or where MNCs have at least three partners with which they are conducting their activities in a specific value chain activity.

4.2.2. Independent variables

Given the focus of the study on advanced versus emerging country MNCs, we use a dummy measure to indicate whether a given firm originates from an emerging country (receiving the value "0") or an advanced country (receiving the value "1"). The origin of each MNC was determined based on UNCTAD (2011) classifications cross checked against the location of the MNC headquarters to be consistent with our theoretical model.

Our main measure for *technological intensity* is the total number of patents of each firm. The main measure for *product differentiation* is the number of brands it possesses. We further use GDP (2010 data) as a rough proxy for *domestic market size*.

4.2.3. Control variables

We use three control variables that may affect firms' location and control configurations. The first is *firm size*, for which our main measure is the overall assets of the MNCs. The second control variable is firm level of internationalisation, as reflected by the level of *foreign assets* and the third control variable is firm *age*.

4.3. Analysis

In order to test the predictions of our model we conduct several analyses. First we compare the unconditional probabilities for occurrence of configurations 1 and 2 for the AMNCs and configurations 14 and 15 for the EMNCs. Next, we conduct a Probit analysis to determine whether the choice of different locations for R&D, production and marketing activities is correlated with the MNC origin (advanced or emerging country). We further test whether *technological intensity* and *domestic market size* affect such locations, as per our predictions. Finally, we conduct a separate Probit analysis to determine the correlation between *technological intensity* and the probability of MNCs to have fully integrated operations (i.e. internalising R&D, production and marketing) as well as the correlation between *product differentiation* on the probability of MNCs to internalise R&D and marketing activities, but outsource production.

---

[13] Generally speaking the locations of main value chain activities were determined based on the firms' own reports and represent the locations where the largest number of employees and/or assets exist. Clearly, both AMNCs and EMNCs usually have multiple sites for each value chain activity.

432   P.J. Buckley, N. Hashai / Research Policy 43 (2014) 423–437

Table 2
Descriptive statistics – top AMNCs and EMNCs, 2010 (US$ million).

	AMNCs mean (SD)	EMNCs mean (SD)
N	79	60
Assets	126,855	48,304
	(104,570)	(90,369)
Foreign assets	79,952	12,562
	(76,345)	(13,747)
Sales	85,311	29,113
	(78,258)	(42,850)
Foreign sales	52,956	13,500
	(48,187)	(19,384)
Employees (number)	167,125	102,998
	(254,096)	(207,189)
Foreign employees (number)	91,361	32,254
	(103,015)	(56,015)
Average GDP ($ billions)	4084	2101
	(4460)	(1711)
R&D expenses	1888	269
	(2479)	(1077)
Patents granted in the US	18,504	3727
(number)	(43,949)	(13,995)
Sales, general and	14,082	2833
administration and expenses	(12,535)	(4827)
Brands (number)	1896	97
	(2925)	(300)
Age (years)	81	53
	(58)	(43)

5. Results

Table 2 presents descriptive statistics of the advanced country- and emerging country MNCs. The table reveals that AMNCs are, on average larger and more international than EMNCs in terms of assets, sales and employees. Further, AMNCs are more technology intensive and more products differentiated than EMNCs and are also older.

Table 3 reports the propensity of the analysed AMNCs and EMNCs to choose specific location configuration from the 16 possible configurations detailed in Fig. 2. In order to do so, we have looked separately on the advanced- and emerging country MNCs. The table indicates that the vast majority of AMNCs choose configuration 1 (73%), while the second largest group of firms chooses configuration 2 (10%). Table 3 further indicates that the vast majority of EMNCs choose configuration 15 (66%), while the second largest group of firms chooses configuration 14 (12%). Taken together these results show support to the predictions of the model that configurations 1 and 2 are the most likely to be chosen for AMNCs whereas configurations 14 and 15 are the most likely to be chosen for EMNCs. Table A2 details the breakdown of our MNCs sample based on their chosen location configuration.

To further test the propensity of MNCs to locate their value chain activities according to the predictions of our model, Table 4 analyses the factors affecting the choice of each location configuration for AMNCs relative to EMNCs while also taking into account technological intensity, domestic market size and product differentiation and controlling for firm size, level of internationalizations

and age. The eight models in Table 4 represent the 2^3 possibilities for locating R&D, production and marketing activities in advanced versus emerging countries. The AMNC dummy represents the location of these firm's headquarters and tests it against the probability to choose a specific location configuration for R&D, production and marketing. Models 1 and 2 in Table 4 support our prediction that AMNCs are more likely than EMNCs to locate their R&D and marketing activities in advanced countries while locating their production activities either in advanced or emerging countries more than EMNCs. This can be observed by the positive and significant coefficient of the AMNC dummy variable and implies that AMNCs are significantly more likely to choose location configuration 1 or 2. Models 6 and 7 in Table 4 support the view that EMNCs are more likely than AMNCs to locate their R&D and production activities in emerging countries while locating their marketing activities either in advanced or emerging countries (i.e. choose location configuration 14 or 15), as indicated by the negative and significant sign of the AMNC dummy for these models. We did not find any significant differences between location configurations of AMNCs and EMNCs for any of the other configurations.

Models 1 and 2 in Table 4 further show that technological intensity (as measured by the number of patents) is positively and significantly correlated with production location in advanced countries (model 1) and negatively correlated with production location in emerging countries (model 2). Taken together with our previous observations, these results imply that technology intensive AMNCs are the more likely to locate their production activities in advanced countries, as per our predictions. A similar analysis of models 6 and 7 (where firms differ only in the location of their marketing activities) shows that greater technological intensity is expected to lead to the location of marketing activities in emerging countries, while less technological intensity increases the probability of locating marketing activities in advanced countries. Together with the previous result that EMNCs are more likely to choose the relevant location configurations that these models represent, it follows that knowledge intensive EMNCs are more likely to locate their marketing activities in emerging countries than other EMNCs. In addition, models 1, 2 and 7 show that domestic market size is positively associated with the probability of choosing the respective configurations. Given that AMNCs are more likely to choose the location configurations represented by models 1 and 2 and that EMNCs are more likely to choose the configuration represented by model 7, we can see the domestic market size is important for the emergence of MNCs, even within a sample consisting of large countries at the first place. It is noteworthy that domestic market size is insignificant for the second largest group of EMNCs (represented by model 6). EMNCs belonging to this group apparently rely more on export markets, making domestic market size less significant for them. These results are consistent with our predictions showing that both technological intensity and domestic market size are positively affecting the probability of firms from emerging countries to become MNCs. In terms of the control measures Table 4 shows that the firm size, level of internationalisation and firm age are correlated with the probability to choose some loca-

Table 3
Location configuration distribution of the top AMNCs and EMNCs, 2010.

Configuration no.	AMNCs (N = 79)	Configuration no.	EMNCs (N = 60)
1 (HQ$_{AD}$, R$_{AD}$, P$_{AD}$, M$_{AD}$)	73%	9 (HQ$_{EM}$, R$_{AD}$, P$_{AD}$, M$_{AD}$)	3%
2 (HQ$_{AD}$, R$_{AD}$, P$_{EM}$, M$_{AD}$)	10%	10 (HQ$_{EM}$, R$_{AD}$, P$_{EM}$, M$_{AD}$)	2%
3 (HQ$_{AD}$, R$_{AD}$, P$_{EM}$, M$_{EM}$)	8%	11 (HQ$_{EM}$, R$_{AD}$, P$_{EM}$, M$_{EM}$)	5%
4 (HQ$_{AD}$, R$_{AD}$, P$_{AD}$, M$_{EM}$)	5%	12 (HQ$_{EM}$, R$_{AD}$, P$_{AD}$, M$_{EM}$)	2%
5 (HQ$_{AD}$, R$_{EM}$, P$_{AD}$, M$_{AD}$)	0%	13 (HQ$_{EM}$, R$_{EM}$, P$_{AD}$, M$_{AD}$)	8%
6 (HQ$_{AD}$, R$_{EM}$, P$_{EM}$, M$_{AD}$)	3%	14 (HQ$_{EM}$, R$_{EM}$, P$_{EM}$, M$_{AD}$)	12%
7 (HQ$_{AD}$, R$_{EM}$, P$_{EM}$, M$_{EM}$)	1%	15 (HQ$_{EM}$, R$_{EM}$, P$_{EM}$, M$_{EM}$)	65%
8 (HQ$_{AD}$, R$_{EM}$, P$_{AD}$, M$_{EM}$)	0%	16 (HQ$_{EM}$, R$_{EM}$, P$_{AD}$, M$_{EM}$)	3%

P.J. Buckley, N. Hashai / Research Policy 43 (2014) 423–437

Table 4
Probit Analyses for value chain location configurations (N = 139).

Probability of:	{R$_{AD}$, P$_{AD}$, M$_{AD}$} Model 1	{R$_{AD}$, P$_{EM}$, M$_{AD}$} Model 2	{R$_{AD}$, P$_{EM}$, M$_{EM}$} Model 3	{R$_{AD}$, P$_{AD}$, M$_{EM}$} Model 4	{R$_{EM}$, P$_{AD}$, M$_{AD}$} Model 5	{R$_{EM}$, P$_{EM}$, M$_{AD}$} Model 6	{R$_{EM}$, P$_{EM}$, M$_{EM}$} Model 7	{R$_{EM}$, P$_{AD}$, M$_{EM}$} Model 8
AMNC	.290**	.074**	.185	.012	n.a.	−.057**	−.173**	n.a.
Number of patents	.011*	−.021*	−.032	.120	.008	−.014*	.084**	−.075
Number of brands	.064	.009	.012	.192	.312	.415	−.022	−.081
Domestic market size	.125**	.011*	.003	.005	.061	.012	.134*	.004
Assets	.212*	.018	.005*	.128*	.025*	.052*	.112*	018*
Foreign Assets	.013	.200*	.101*	.079*	.163*	.130	.046	.010*
Age	.016	.022*	.003*	.013*	.020*	.024	.013	.022*
Log likelihood	−71.33	−75.25	−57.76	−59.11	−58.19	−72.66	−77.33	−58.20

Legend: R = R&D; P = production; M = marketing; AD = location in advanced country; EM = location in emerging country. n.a. – variable unavailable (no AMNCs with this configuration).
* Significant at 5%.
** Significant at 1%.

Table 5
Probit analyses for control configurations (N = 139).

Dependent variable = probability of:	R&D externalisation (Model 1)	Production externalisation (Model 2)	Marketing externalisation (Model 3)
AMNC	.012	.167	.115
Number of patents	−.325**	−.121**	−.215**
Number of brands	−.101**	−.022	−.089**
Domestic market size	.011	.017	.015
Assets	−.139**	−.225**	−.009*
Foreign assets	−.067*	−.035*	−.012*
Age	−.023	−.005*	−.031
Log likelihood	−82.11	−79.17	−80.23

* Significant at 5%.
** Significant at 1%.

tion configurations. Overall, all the models presented in Table 4 are highly significant in terms of their log likelihood (p < 0.1%).

Finally, Table 5 tests our predictions regarding the outsourcing of value chain activities. Models 1–3 in Table 5 show that *technological intensity* significantly decreases the probability of externalising R&D, production and marketing activities while product differentiation (measured through the number of brands each firm possesses) significantly decreases the probability of externalising R&D and marketing activities. In contrast to the case of value chain activity location, domestic market size does not have a significant effect on the internalisation decision of the analysed MNCs. These results are once again consistent with our predictions. In terms of the control measures, Table 5 shows that the firm size and the level of internationalisation generally decrease the probability of externalising value chain activities. All three models presented in Table 5 are highly significant in terms of their log likelihood (p < 1%).

We have conducted several robustness tests to the analyses above. First, we have used R&D expenditures as an alternative proxy for *technological intensity*. Second, we have used sales, general and administration costs as an alternative proxy for *product differentiation*. We have further used MNC sales volume and the number of employees as alternative proxies for firm size. Foreign sales and the number of foreign employees were likewise used as alternative internationalisation measures. In all cases results remained unchanged in terms of the factors affecting MNCs' location and control configurations.

6. Discussion

The study analyses the impact of technological catch up on behalf of large emerging countries and an increase in the domestic market of such countries on the relative dominance of EMNCs versus AMNCs. This analysis is based on the observation that the global system is currently in the midst of a technological revolution – the information revolution, where large emerging countries are closing the technological gap with more advanced countries

while rapidly increasing their domestic market growth. This phase is particularly interesting given that, despite these changes, emerging countries are still far behind advanced ones in terms of their income levels, hence allegedly preserving their cost based comparative advantages in production.

To present this point of view, we introduce a model, which is empirically tested and verified, that predicts the location of value adding activities and their organisational boundaries in a world comprised of advanced and emerging countries, where the latter experience technological catch up and substantial growth of their domestic market. Essentially, the model predicts that technological catch up and/or an increase in emerging country domestic market size leads to more intensive competition for AMNCs from emerging country based firms. Overall, technological catch up and increase in the domestic market size of emerging countries result in the emergence of quite a different global system than the global system that has dominated since the Second World War – where advanced country based firms had clear hegemony. This system is jointly shared by AMNCs and EMNCs, where the latter mostly cater other advanced and emerging countries through exports.

Given this rise of EMNCs, the model predicts a greater probability of locating R&D and marketing activities in emerging market countries. In this respect, our model supports recent observations that the world's production is gradually moving to emerging countries at the expense of more advanced countries. Yet, the model further shows that an even more important trend might be the greater propensity of locating high value adding activities such as R&D and marketing in emerging countries (Gassmann and Hann, 2004; Li and Zhong, 2003; Von Zedtwitz, 2004).

In terms of firm boundaries, the model predicts that technological intensive firms are likely to choose more internalised configurations, whereas product differentiated firms will prefer to integrate R&D and marketing activities while outsourcing production. This is why we predict that that the newly emergent global system will be centred on focal brand owners that may be termed "the global factory" (Buckley, 2009; Buckley and Ghauri, 2004).

154   The Global Factory

Such brand owners will either originate in advanced countries which are expected to preserve their comparative advantage in marketing differentiated products, with strong, familiar brands or they may originate in emerging countries that will enjoy advantages in the marketing of "weaker" brands.

6.1. Main contributions of the model

While the model presented in this paper is extremely simple, it is rich in its predictions regarding the newly emergent global system. In industrial organisation terms, the model allows for the emergence of monopolies (single firm configurations) and competition (multiple firm configurations). In terms of value chain activities the model allows for fully integrated firms (conducting all value chain activities), partially integrated firms (conducting some of the value adding activities) and specialising firms (conducting only a single value adding activity). The model further acknowledges the existence of multiple types of domestic and foreign operations, including: domestic firms serving their own markets and export markets (e.g. configurations 1 and 15 for integrated firms), FDI in production activities (e.g. configuration 2 for an integrated MNC), FDI in marketing activities (e.g. configuration 14 for an integrated MNC), as well as domestic and foreign outsourcing and licensing of technology to third parties (for instance, in control configuration where each value chain activity is conducted separately).

An important insight stemming from our results is that the predicted increased dominance of emerging country based firms in the global system is achieved neither with the possession of a competitive advantage in R&D nor in marketing. This insight implies that even without gaining a competitive (or ownership) advantage (Dunning, 1988, 1993; Porter, 1990) based on technology or brands, firms from large emerging countries where technological catch-up takes place can successfully compete with advanced country based firms. This is an important observation given the fact that many scholars are sceptical regarding the ability of emerging country firms to outcompete advanced country ones because of their lack of ownership advantages (Amsden and Chu, 2003; Cuervo-Cazzura and Genc, 2008; Goldstein, 2007; Nolan, 2004; Ramamurti, 2009a; Rugman, 2009). In practical terms, our model implies that emerging country based firms become able to compete successfully with advanced country based firms when they reach a similar level of technological capability or when their domestic market size increases sufficiently and becomes another important growth source for such firms. Both phenomena do not imply a competitive advantage on behalf of emerging country based firms. Yet, as our results show, this will lead to a global system with an increased dominance of emerging country based firms.

The model presented in this paper demonstrates that while the cost advantages existing in different locations are available to domestic and foreign firms, the difference between international and domestic knowledge transfer costs and that between intra- and inter-firm knowledge transfer costs is the main factor that shapes the organisational and geographical boundaries of firms. Once emerging country based firms catch up on technology (while not achieving a competitive advantage) and once their domestic market size increases sufficiently, making the knowledge transfer from marketing activities located in emerging countries to consumers less costly, they are much better able to compete with advanced country firms. The centrality of knowledge flow costs in determining firm boundaries and competitive advantage is consistent with the view of the internalisation school (Buckley and Casson, 1976; Rugman, 1986), the view of firms as entities that are more efficient in the transfer of complex knowledge (Kogut and Zander, 1993;

Martin and Salomon, 2003) and observations regarding the costly cross border flow of knowledge (e.g. Adler and Hashai, 2007; Casson, 2000: 67–70; Fisch, 2004; Hirsch, 1976; Teece, 1977).

In a broader sense, the privileged access that EMNCs have to their home markets relative to AMNCs is also consistent with the predictions of Teece (1986) who, among other things, addressed privileged market access as a central pre-condition for gaining competitive advantage. In fact, to the extent that specific industrial policy measures in emerging countries, such as high tariffs, local content requirements or any other discriminatory measure in favour of EMNCs, are in force, we expect EMNCs originating from emerging countries with large domestic markets to be even more likely to emerge and gain dominancy when competing with AMNCs.

In that respect it is noteworthy that one can reasonably argue that EMNCs may build on their technological catch up to successfully compete with AMNCs, even in cases where their domestic markets are small, by serving foreign markets through exports. Indeed, Lee et al. (2013) show that small-size markets (e.g. Taiwan) may also grow successful MNCs. In terms of our model and empirics, we essentially argue that the ability to cater large domestic markets is complementary to firms' level of technological advance and is not a necessary condition for the emergence of EMNCs. EMNCs from smaller domestic markets will likely require the possession competitive advantages in terms of technology or brands to outcompete AMNCs. On the other hand, EMNCs originating in countries with larger markets may not require possessing such advantages, in order to outcompete AMNCs, due to their relatively more privileged access (e.g. in terms of knowledge exchange with local consumers) to their home markets.

The originality of this modelling as compared to other global system view models is twofold. First, by adding the headquarters function, the current modelling attributes specific origins to firms (in our case advanced versus emerging countries). This allows us to be more specific in our predictions regarding their relative dominance as well as empirically test these predictions. Second, the model goes beyond previous models of the global system (Buckley and Hashai, 2004, 2009; Casson, 2000) by adopting improved predictions on technological intensity and differentiation of products and their comparative statics in terms of location and control configurations.

Given that three out of the four dominant location configurations that the model identifies as dominant configurations indicate serving markets via exports,[14] our model further implies that the emerging global system is likely to be mostly based on foreign trade where exports from emerging country firms are likely to replace or compete with current FDI activities of AMNCs. This insight is important as it indicates a dramatic change in two central global phenomena: (1) the trade balance of advanced countries with emerging ones is likely to become more negative; (2) outgoing FDI from advanced countries to emerging ones is expected to significantly reduce. Taken together the two phenomena may indicate the emergence of a new equilibrium where foreign trade rather than FDI dominates.

The predicted global system is expected to be the basis for a new wave of emerging countries-led globalisation. In order to evaluate which emerging countries are likely to become the leaders, several factors should be considered. One important factor is the institutional environment in such countries. In this respect we expect that emerging countries' institutional environments that promote technological advance and intellectual property rights will be

---

[14] Note that only configuration 2 indicates FDI in production.

P.J. Buckley, N. Hashai / Research Policy 43 (2014) 423–437

Table A1
Costs of alternative location configurations.

Configuration no.	Knowledge flow HQ–R&D	R&D	Production	Knowledge flow R&D–production	Marketing	Knowledge flow R&D–marketing	Knowledge flow marketing–customers
1	α	$C_{R,AD}$	$C_{P,AD}$	α	$C_{M,AD}$	α	$\alpha + \beta'$
2	α	$C_{R,AD}$	$C_{P,EM}$	β	$C_{M,AD}$	α	$\alpha + \beta'$
3	α	$C_{R,AD}$	$C_{P,EM}$	β	$C_{M,EM}$	β	$\beta + \alpha'$
4	α	$C_{R,AD}$	$C_{P,AD}$	α	$C_{M,EM}$	β	$\beta + \alpha'$
5	β	$C_{R,EM}$	$C_{P,AD}$	β	$C_{M,AD}$	α	$\alpha + \beta'$
6	β	$C_{R,EM}$	$C_{P,EM}$	α	$C_{M,AD}$	β	$\alpha + \beta'$
7	β	$C_{R,EM}$	$C_{P,EM}$	α	$C_{M,EM}$	α	$\beta + \alpha'$
8	β	$C_{R,EM}$	$C_{P,AD}$	β	$C_{M,EM}$	α	$\beta + \alpha'$
9	β	$C_{R,AD}$	$C_{P,AD}$	α	$C_{M,AD}$	α	$\alpha + \beta'$
10	β	$C_{R,AD}$	$C_{P,EM}$	β	$C_{M,AD}$	α	$\alpha + \beta'$
11	β	$C_{R,AD}$	$C_{P,EM}$	β	$C_{M,EM}$	β	$\beta + \alpha'$
12	β	$C_{R,AD}$	$C_{P,AD}$	α	$C_{M,EM}$	β	$\beta + \alpha'$
13	α	$C_{R,EM}$	$C_{P,AD}$	β	$C_{M,AD}$	β	$\alpha + \beta'$
14	α	$C_{R,EM}$	$C_{P,EM}$	α	$C_{M,AD}$	β	$\alpha + \beta'$
15	α	$C_{R,EM}$	$C_{P,EM}$	α	$C_{M,EM}$	α	$\beta + \alpha'$
16	α	$C_{R,EM}$	$C_{P,AD}$	β	$C_{M,EM}$	α	$\beta + \alpha'$

more likely to achieve accelerated technological catch up (Peng et al., 2008; Perez, 2002; Yang, 2003; Yang et al., 2008). In addition, countries that promote economic reforms that will lead to an increase in the purchasing power of consumers in such countries (Peng et al., 2008) are more likely to be the source for global firms that become dominant players in the newly emergent global system. Importantly, is its noteworthy that a key argument here is that large domestic market size of emerging countries is a fundamental condition for these countries' EMNCs to become dominant players in the newly emerging global system.

Finally, it should be noted that the current model is limited in its key assumptions. When using the global system view, the model does not take into account possible institutional hurdles to the development of EMNCs such as the need to develop a welfare system, build a stronger intellectual property protection system and be more environmentally friendly (Dunning, 2006; Naughton, 2007). These challenges may well affect the relative costs of conducting R&D, production and marketing in emerging versus advanced countries and hence may affect the predictions of our model. Furthermore, our model assumes that since the costs of cross border transportation and tariff barriers have been reduced significantly relative to the cost of production, in the vast majority of products the cost of production in emerging countries remains lower than the cost of production in advanced countries even after overseas transportation costs and tariff barriers are taken into account. To the extent that this assumption does not hold for specific product categories the predictions of our model should be taken with caution. Our model is also limited in its predictions to firms where R&D activities are central in the intermediation of knowledge between production and marketing activities. This view is perfectly consistent with the extant global system modelling literature (Buckley and Hashai, 2004; Casson, 2000), and further acknowledges the importance of R&D activities in a high technology economy. However, it is noteworthy that different location and control configurations are likely to emerge for firms with no R&D activities or for firms where either production or marketing activities serve as such intermediators.[15] The model and empirical analysis also do not take into account the "knowledge asset seeking" activities of many EMNCs, that locate some of their R&D activities in advanced countries as means to absorb knowledge there (Buckley et al., 2007; Cantwell and Barnard, 2008; Dunning, 2006; Dunning et al., 2008; Goldstein, 2007; Luo and Tang, 2007;

Mathews, 2002). While many EMNCs are likely to retain their main R&D activities at home, future studies may expand the current model and take into account new knowledge acquisition in advanced countries as means to gain a more fine grained picture of the global dispersion of R&D (and other value chain activities) of EMNCs.

7. Conclusion

Casual empiricism suggests that emerging countries are beginning to approach advanced countries in terms of shares of world trade, FDI and technological dominance. This paper models the effects of upgraded technology and increases in relative market size of large emerging countries on the emergence of dominant MNCs based in emerging countries. The global system view is shown to be an excellent framework for the analysis of these potentially radical changes in the world economy. This application of model has profound implications for policy in both emerging and advanced countries. As long as emerging countries enjoy comparative advantages in production AMNCs need to specialise more in technologically intensive and highly differentiated products in order to compete with the newly powerful EMNCs. Emerging countries should work to attract R&D and seek to upgrade their marketing capabilities to further increase their global dominance. This paper has utilised the global system view model to trace the impact of upgrading of technological competence and increased market size in large emerging economies on ownership and location in the future global economy. Such a model enables us to take a nuanced and differentiated view of the impact of rising firms from emerging countries in contrast to straight line projections of their growth and potential power. It explains how, even without obtaining a competitive advantage in R&D and marketing, such firms are likely to become dominant players in the global system.

Acknowledgments

We wish to thank Mark Casson, Editor Keun Lee and two anonymous reviewers for comments on earlier drafts.

Appendix.

See Tables A1 and A2.

---

[15] We wish to thank an anonymous reviewer for raising this point.

Table A2
Classification of MNCs into location configurations.

Configuration 1 (HQ$_{AD}$, R$_{AD}$, P$_{AD}$, M$_{AD}$)	WPP PLC	**Configuration 14 (HQ$_{EM}$, R$_{EM}$, P$_{EM}$, M$_{AD}$)**
General Electric Co	Hitachi Ltd	Lukoil OAO
BP plc	Renault SA	Samsung Electronics Co., Ltd.
Vodafone Group Plc	The Coca-Cola Company	Yue Yuen Industrial Holdings Ltd
Toyota Motor Corporation	Alstom S.A.	Rusal
Volkswagen Group	Barrick Gold Corporation	TPV Technology Limited
EDF SA	BAE Systems plc	CITIC Group
E.ON AG	Pernod-Ricard SA	Shangri-La Asia Ltd
Enel SpA	**Configuration 2 (HQ$_{AD}$, R$_{AD}$, P$_{EM}$, M$_{AD}$)**	**Configuration 15 (HQ$_{EM}$, R$_{EM}$, P$_{EM}$, M$_{EM}$)**
Siemens AG	Royal Dutch Shell plc	Vale SA
Deutsche Telekom AG	Exxon Mobil Corporation	Hyundai Motor Company
Honda Motor Co Ltd	Total SA	China Ocean Shipping (Group) Company[e]
Iberdrola SA	GDF Suez	América Móvil SAB de CV
Pfizer Inc	Chevron Corporation	Tata Steel Ltd
ConocoPhillips	Eni SpA	Jardine Matheson Holdings Ltd
Daimler AG	Schlumberger Ltd	Noble Group Ltd
Ford Motor Company	Alcoa Inc	Petroleo Brasileiro SA
Johnson & Johnson	**Configuration 3 (HQ$_{AD}$, R$_{AD}$, P$_{EM}$, M$_{EM}$)**	Gerdau SA
Mitsubishi Corporation	SABMiller PLC	China National Petroleum Corporation
Sony Corporation	Telefonica SA	Tata Motors Ltd
Wal-Mart Stores Inc	Lafarge SA	New World Development Ltd
EADS N.V.	British American Tobacco PLC	Hindalco Industries Ltd
General Motors Co	Caterpillar Inc	First Pacific Company Ltd
Nissan Motor Co Ltd	AES Corporation	Sinochem Group
France Telecom S.A.	**Configuration 4 (HQ$_{AD}$, R$_{AD}$, P$_{AD}$, M$_{EM}$)**	CLP Holdings Ltd
BMW AG	Rio Tinto PLC	Axiata Group Bhd
RWE AG	Unilever PLC	Fomento Economico Mexicano SAB
Mitsui & Co Ltd	BHP Billiton Group Ltd	POSCO
Procter & Gamble Co	Japan Tobacco Inc	China Resources Enterprises Ltd
International Business Machines Corporation	**Configuration 6 (HQ$_{AD}$, R$_{EM}$, P$_{EM}$, M$_{AD}$)**	Severstal Group Holdings
Hewlett-Packard Co	Linde AG	China National Offshore Oil Corp
Kraft Foods Inc	BG Group plc	Sun Hung Kai Properties Ltd
GlaxoSmithKline PLC	**Configuration 7 (HQ$_{AD}$, R$_{EM}$, P$_{EM}$, M$_{EM}$)**	VimpelCom Ltd
Veolia Environnement SA	Anglo American plc	Swire Pacific Ltd
BASF SE	**Configuration 9 (HQ$_{EM}$, R$_{AD}$, P$_{AD}$, M$_{AD}$)**	Mechel OAO
Ferrovial SA	Suzlon Energy Ltd	Lenovo Group Ltd
Compagnie de Saint-Gobain SA	Techtronic Industries Co Ltd	Sime Darby Bhd
Carrefour SA	**Configuration 10 (HQ$_{EM}$, R$_{AD}$, P$_{EM}$, M$_{AD}$)**	MMC Norilsk Nickel
Deutsche Post AG	Hutchison Whampoa Limited	China Railway Construction Corporation Ltd
AstraZeneca PLC	**Configuration 11 (HQ$_{EM}$, R$_{AD}$, P$_{EM}$, M$_{EM}$)**	ZTE Corp
ThyssenKrupp AG	Petronas – Petroliam Nasional Bhd	Galaxy Entertainment Group Ltd
Fiat S.p.A.	Evraz Group SA	Mobile TeleSystems OJSC
Vivendi SA	Skyworth Digital Holdings Ltd	Reliance Communications Ltd
Tesco PLC	**Configuration 12 (HQ$_{EM}$, R$_{AD}$, P$_{AD}$, M$_{EM}$)**	Lee & Man Paper Manufacturing Ltd
National Grid PLC	Cemex S.A.B. de C.V.	TMK OAO
Merck & Co	**Configuration 13 (HQ$_{EM}$, R$_{EM}$, P$_{AD}$, M$_{AD}$)**	Tata Chemicals Ltd
Schneider Electric SA	Li & Fung Ltd	Sistema JSFC
Dow Chemical Company	Ternium SA	Oil and Natural Gas Corp Ltd
Repsol YPF SA	Tata Consultancy Services	**Configuration 16 (HQ$_{EM}$, R$_{EM}$, P$_{AD}$, M$_{EM}$)**
Sanofi-Aventis SA	Esprit Holdings Ltd	Genting Bhd
Liberty Global Inc	Doosan Corp	Grupo Bimbo SAB de CV

References

Adler, N., Hashai, N., 2007. Knowledge flows and the modelling of the multinational enterprise. Journal of International Business Studies 38 (4), 639–657.

Amsden, A.H., 2009. Does firm ownership matter? In: Ramamurti, R., Singh, V.S. (Eds.), Emerging Multinationals in Emerging Markets. Cambridge University Press, Cambridge, UK.

Amsden, A.H., Hikino, T., 1994. Project execution capability, organizational know-how and conglomerate corporate growth in late industrialization. Industrial and Corporate Change 3 (1), 111–147.

Amsden, A.H., Chu, W.W., 2003. Beyond late Development: Taiwan's Upgrading Policies. MIT Press, Cambridge, MA.

Archibugi, D., Coco, A., 2004. A new indicator of technological capabilities for developed and emerging countries (ArCo). World Development 32 (4), 629–654.

Archibugi, D., Coco, A., 2005. Measuring technological capabilities at the country level: a survey and a menu for choice. Research Policy 34, 175–194.

Athreye, S., Cantwell, J.A., 2007. Creating competition? Globalization and the emergence of new technology producers. Research Policy 36 (2), 209–226.

Aulakh, P.S., Kotabe, M., Teegan, H., 2000. Export strategies and the performance of firms from emerging economies. Academy of Management Journal 43 (3), 342–361.

Bonaglia, F., Goldstein, A., Mathews, J.A., 2007. Accelerated internationalization by emerging markets' multinationals: the case of the white goods sector. Journal of World Business 42 (4), 369–383.

Borensztein, E., Ostry, J.D., 1996. Accounting for China's growth performance. American Economics Review 86 (2), 224–228.

Brandz, 2010. Top 100 Most Valuable Global Brands 2010. Millward, Brown, Optimer.

Buckley, P.J., 2009. The impact of the global factory on economic development. Journal of World Business 44 (2), 131–143.

Buckley, P.J., Casson, M., 1976. The Future of the Multinational Enterprise. Macmillan, London.

Buckley, P.J., Casson, M.C., 1998. Models of the multinational enterprise. Journal of International Business Studies 29 (1), 21–44.

Buckley, P.J., Clegg, L.J., Cross, A.R., Zheng, P., Voss, H., Liu, X., 2007. The determinants of Chinese outward foreign direct investment. Journal of International Business Studies 38 (4), 499–518.

Buckley, P.J., Ghauri, P.N., 2004. Globalisation, economic geography and the strategy of multinational enterprises. Journal of International Business Studies 35 (2), 81–98.

Buckley, P.J., Hashai, N., 2004. A global system view of firm boundaries. Journal of International Business Studies 35 (1), 33–45.

Buckley, P.J., Hashai, N., 2009. Formalizing internationalization in the eclectic paradigm. Journal of International Business Studies 40 (1), 58–70.

Cantwell, J., Barnard, H., 2008. Do firms from emerging markets have to invest abroad? Outward FDI and the competitiveness of firms. In: Sauvant, K.P. (Ed.), The Rise of Transnational Corporations from Emerging Countries – Threat or Opportunity? Edward Elgar, Cheltenham, UK.

P.J. Buckley, N. Hashai / Research Policy 43 (2014) 423–437   437

Casson, M.C., 1985. Multinational monopolies and international cartels. In: Buckley, P.J., Casson, M. (Eds.), The economic theory of the multinational enterprise. Macmillan, London.

Casson, M.C., 1994. Why are firms hierarchical. Journal of the Economics of Business 1 (1), 47–76.

Casson, M.C., 2000. Enterprise and Leadership: Studies on Firms, Networks and Institutions. Edward Elgar, Cheltenham.

Coase, R.H., 1937. The nature of the firm. Economica 4, 386–405.

Contractor, F.J., 1990. Ownership patterns of US joint ventures abroad and the liberalization of foreign government regulations in the 1980s: evidence from the benchmark surveys. Journal of International Business Studies 21 (1), 55–73.

Cuervo-Cazzura, A., Genc, M., 2008. Transforming disadvantages into advantages: emerging countries MNEs in the least developed countries. Journal of International Business Studies 39, 957–979.

Demirbag, M., Glaister, K.W., 2010. Factors determining offshore location choice for R&D projects: a comparative study of developed and emerging regions. Journal of Management Studies 47 (8), 1534–1560.

Dunning, J.H., 1977. Trade, location of economic activity and the multinationals. In: Ohlin, B., Hesselborn, P., Wijkman, P. (Eds.), The International Allocation of Economic Activity. Macmillan.

Dunning, J.H., 1988. Changes in the level and structure of international production: the Last One Hundred Years. In: Dunning, J.H. (Ed.), Exploring International Production. Unwin Hyman, London, pp. 71–119.

Dunning, J.H., 1993. Multinational enterprises and the global economy. Addison Wesley, Wokingham.

Dunning, J.H., 2006. Comment on dragon multinationals: new players in 21st century globalisation. Asia Pacific Journal of Management 23, 139–141.

Dunning, J.H., Kim, C., Park, D., 2008. Old wine in new bottles: a comparison of emerging-market TNCs today and developed-country TNCs thirty years ago. In: Sauvant, K.P. (Ed.), The Rise of Transnational Corporations from Emerging Countries – Threat or Opportunity? Edward Elgar, Cheltenham, UK.

Dunning, J.H., Lundan, S.M., 2008. Multinational Enterprises and the Global Economy, 2nd edition. Edward Elgar, Cheltenham.

Duysters, G., Jacob, J., Lemmens, C., Jintian, Y., 2009. Internationalization and technological catching up of emerging multinationals: a comparative case study of China's Haier group. Industrial and Corporate Change 18, 325–349.

Filippetti, A., Peyrache, A., 2011. The patterns of technological capabilities of countries: a dual approach using composite indicators and data envelopment analysis. World Development 39 (7), 1108–1121.

Fisch, J.H., 2004. Allocating innovative activities in international R&D with fuzzy logic. Management International Review 44 (3), 147–166.

Flam, H., Helpman, E., 1987. Vertical product differentiation and north-south trade. American Economic Review 77 (5), 810–822.

Gassmann, O., Hann, Z., 2004. Motivations and barriers of foreign R&D activities in China. R&D Management 34 (4), 423–437.

Ghymn, K.I., 1980. Multinational enterprises from the third world. Journal of International Business Studies 11, 118–122.

Goldstein, A., 2007. Multinational Companies from Emerging Economies. Palgrave Macmillan, London.

Heather, P., 2013. The Restoration of Rome: Barbarian Popes and Imperial Pretenders. Macmillan, London.

Hirsch, S., 1976. An international trade and investment theory of the firm. Oxford Economic Papers 28, 258–270.

Hofstede, G., 1980. Culture's Consequences: International Differences in Work Related Values. Sage Publications, Beverly Hills.

Hoskisson, R.E., Eden, L., Lau, C.M., Wright, M., 2000. Strategy in Emerging Economies. Academy of Management Journal 43, 249–267.

Hummels, D., 2007. Transportation costs and international trade in the second era of globalization. Journal of Economic Perspectives 21 (3), 131–154.

Hymer, S., 1976. The International Operations of National Firms: A Study of Direct Foreign Investment. MIT Press, Cambridge, MA.

Khanna, T., Palepu, K., 2006. Emerging giants: building world class companies in emerging countries. Harvard Business Review 84 (1), 60–69.

Kogut, B., Singh, H., 1988. The effect of national culture on the choice of entry mode. Journal of International Business Studies 19 (3), 411–432.

Kogut, B., Zander, U., 1993. Knowledge of the firm and the evolutionary theory of the multinational corporation. Journal of International Business Studies 4, 625–645.

Lall, S. (Ed.), 1983. The New Multinationals: The Spread of Third World Enterprises. John Wiley, Chinchester, UK/New York.

Lawrence, R.Z., 1993. Japan's low levels of inward investment: the role of inhibitions on acquisitions. In: Froot, K. (Ed.), Foreign Direct Investment. University of Chicago for NBER, Chicago.

Lee, K., Kim, B.Y., Park, Y.Y., Sanidas, E., 2013. Big businesses and economic growth: identifying a binding constraint for growth with country panel analysis. Journal of Comparative Economics 31, 561–582.

Lewin, A., Massini, S., Peeters, C., 2009. Why are companies offshoring innovation? The emerging global race for talent. Journal of International Business Studies 40, 901–925.

Luo, Y., Tang, R.L., 2007. International expansion of emerging countries enterprises: a springboard perspective. Journal of International Business Studies 38, 481–498.

Li, J., Zhong, J., 2003. Explaining the growth of R&D alliances in China. Managerial and Decision Economics 24, 101–105.

Mahmood, I.P., Singh, J., 2003. Technological dynamism in Asia. Research Policy 32 (6), 1032–1054.

Martin, X., Salomon, R., 2003. Knowledge transfer capacity and its implications for the theory of the multinational corporation. Journal of International Business Studies 34 (4), 356–373.

Mathews, J.A., 2002. Dragon Multinational: A New Model for Global Growth. Oxford University Press, Oxford/New York.

Mathews, J.A., 2006. Dragon multinationals: new players in 21st century globalisation. Asia Pacific Journal of Management 23, 5–27.

Matsuyama, K., 2000. A Ricardian model with a continuum of goods under nonhomothetic preferences: demand complementarities, income distribution, and north-south trade. Journal of Political Economy 108 (6), 1093–1120.

Morck, R., Yeung, B., 1992. Internalization: an event study test. Journal of International Economics 33 (1–2), 41–56.

Mudambi, R., 2008. Location, control and innovation in knowledge-intensive industries. Journal of Economic Geography 8 (5), 699–725.

National Science Board, 2012. Research and Development, innovation and the science and engineering workforce. National Science Foundation, Arlington, Virginia.

Naughton, B., 2007. The Chinese Economy: Transitions and Growth. MIT Press Book.

Nelson, R.R., Pack, H., 1999. The Asian miracle and modern growth theory. The Economic Journal 109, 416–436.

Niosi, J., Tschang, F.T., 2009. The strategies of Chinese and Indian software multinationals: implications for internationalization theory. Industrial and Corporate Change 18 (2), 269–284.

Nolan, P., 2004. China at the Crossroads. Polity Press, Cambridge, UK.

Obstfeld, M., Taylor, A.M., 2002. Globalization and capital markets. NBER working paper 8846. National Bureau of Economic Research, Cambridge, MA.

Peng, M.W., Wang, D.Y.L., Jiang, Y., 2008. An institution-based view of international business strategy: a focus on emerging economies. Journal of International Business Studies 39 (5), 920–935.

Perez, C., 2002. Technological Revolutions and Financial Capital, The Dynamics of Bubbles and Golden Ages. Edward Elgar, Cheltenham, UK.

Porter, M.W., 1990. The Competitive Advantage of Nations. Free Press, New York.

Ramamurti, R., 2009a. Why study emerging country multinationals? In: Ramamurti, R., Singh, V.S. (Eds.), Emerging Multinationals in Emerging Markets. Cambridge University Press, Cambridge, UK.

Ramamurti, R., 2009b. What have we learned about emerging market MNEs? In: Ramamurti, R., Singh, V.S. (Eds.), Emerging Multinationals in Emerging Markets. Cambridge University Press, Cambridge, UK.

Ramamurti, R., Singh, V.S. (Eds.), 2009. Emerging multinationals in emerging markets. Cambridge University Press, Cambridge, UK.

Rugman, A.M., 1986. New theories of the multinational enterprise: an assessment of internalization theory. Bulletin of Economic Research 38 (2), 101–119.

Rugman, A.M., 2008. Theoretical aspects of MNEs from emerging economies. In: Ramamurti, R., Singh, V.S. (Eds.), Emerging Multinationals in Emerging Markets. Cambridge University Press, Cambridge, UK.

Rugman, A., 2009. How global are TNCs from emerging countries? In: Sauvant, K.P. (Ed.), The Rise of Transnational Corporations from Emerging Countries – Threat or Opportunity? Edward Elgar, Cheltenham, UK.

Rugman, A.M., Doh, J., 2008. Multinationals and Development. Yale University Press, New Haven, CT.

Sachs, J.D., 2008. The rise of TNCs from emerging markets: the global context. In: Sauvant, K.P. (Ed.), The Rise of Transnational Corporations from Emerging Countries – Threat or Opportunity? Edward Elgar, Cheltenham, UK.

Sauvant, K.P. (Ed.), 2008. The Rise of Transnational Corporations from Emerging Countries – Threat or Opportunity? Edward Elgar, Cheltenham, UK.

Teece, D.J., 1977. Technology transfer by multinational corporations: the resource cost of transferring technological know-how. Economic Journal 87, 242–261.

Teece, D.J., 1986. Profiting from technological innovation: implications for integration, collaboration, licensing and public policy. Research Policy 15, 285–305.

UNCTAD, 2011. World Investment Report, Geneva.

UNCTAD, 2009. Assessing the Impact of the Current Financial and Economic Crisis on Global FDI Flows. United Nations Publication, New York/Geneva.

Vernon, R., 1966. International investment and international trade in the product cycle. Quarterly Journal of Economics 80, 190–207.

Vernon, R., 1971. Sovereignty at Bay. Basic Books, New York.

Volrath, T.L., 1991. A theoretical evaluation of alternative trade intensity measures of revealed comparative advantage. Weltwirtschaftliches Archiv 130, 265–279.

Von Zedtwitz, M., 2004. Managing foreign R&D laboratories in China. R&D Management 34 (4), 439–452.

Wells, L.T., 1983. Third World Multinationals – The Rise of Foreign Investment from Emerging Countries. MIT Press, Cambridge, MA/London.

Williamson, O.E., 1985. The Economic Institutions of Capitalism. The Free Press, New York.

Williamson, P.J., Zeng, M., 2009. Chinese multinationals: emerging through new global gateways. In: Ramamurti, R., Singh, V.S. (Eds.), Emerging Multinationals in Emerging Markets. Cambridge University Press, Cambridge, UK.

WIPO, 2012. Global Brands Database.

World Bank, 2000, 2010, 2012. World Development Indicators Database, Washington, DC.

Yang, D., 2003. The development of intellectual property in China. World Patent Information 25 (2), 131–142.

Yang, D., Fryxell, G., Sie, A.K.Y., 2008. Anti-piracy effectiveness and managerial confidence: insights from MNCs in China. Journal of World Business 43 (3), 321–339.

Journal of Economic Geography 15 (2015) pp. 103–128
Advance Access Published on 13 December 2013

doi:10.1093/jeg/lbt040

The economic geography of offshore incorporation in tax havens and offshore financial centres: the case of Chinese MNEs

Peter J. Buckley*,**, Dylan Sutherland***,‡, Hinrich Voss**** and Ahmad El-Gohari†

*Centre for International Business, University of Leeds LS2 9JT, Leeds, UK
**Cheung Kong Scholar Chair Professor in the University of International Business and Economics (UIBE), Chaoyang District, Beijing, China
***Durham University Business School, University of Durham, DH1 3LB, Durham, UK
****Centre for International Business, University of Leeds LS2 9JT, Leeds, UK
†Cardiff School of Management, University of Wales Institute CF5 2YB, Cardiff, UK
‡Corresponding author: Dylan Sutherland, Durham University Business School, University of Durham, Mill Hill Lane, Durham, DH1 3LB, UK. *email* <dylan.sutherland@durham.ac.uk>

Abstract

A large share of the outward foreign direct investment (FDI) of emerging market MNEs is directed towards a small number of specific tax havens and offshore financial centres. The establishment of investment-holding companies for taxation related purposes is frequently adduced as a key motivation ('round-tripping') for these investments. This explanation, however, accounts for neither the concentration of such investments in specific havens nor the comparatively large national shares of such investments that originate from emerging markets. Here we draw from and build links between the geography of money and finance and international business literatures to conceptually and empirically explore this prominent, if somewhat disregarded, feature of global FDI flows.

Keywords: Offshore financial centres, tax havens, theory of FDI, PR China
JEL classification: f23
Date submitted: 20 January 2012   **Date accepted:** 13 November 2013

1. Introduction

The growth of outward foreign direct investment (OFDI) from emerging markets is an important force shaping international economic geography in the wake of the 2008 global financial crisis. This FDI growth has also stimulated interest in the characteristics, motivation and behaviour of emerging market multinational enterprises (EM MNEs) (Deng, 2012). This in turn has led to calls for new theoretical approaches to explain EM MNEs (Child and Rodrigues, 2005; Luo and Tung, 2007; Hennart, 2012). Useful conceptualisations stress the relative (dis-)advantages EM MNEs experience and how their home country institutional environment influences their development (Luo and Rui, 2009; Luo et al., 2011). Despite this interest, comparatively little theoretical or empirical consideration has been given to the most prominent destination of emerging market OFDI, namely certain specific tax havens and offshore financial centres (THOFCs) and the role they play in the global economy (Palan, 2009; Wójcik, 2013).

© The Author (2013). Published by Oxford University Press. All rights reserved. For Permissions, please email: journals.permissions@oup.com

Here we cross-fertilise ideas found in financial geography with those in internalisation theory, a cornerstone theory of the MNE within the International Business (IB) literature, to develop our explanatory framework. Because classic internationalisation theory lacks a specifically spatial dimension, its integration with economic geography allows us to extend the theory.

Brazil, Russia, India and China, for example, all record very significant FDI to such destinations. By 2007, one half of Brazil's OFDI stock was located in just three havens (Cuervo-Cazurra and Stahl, 2010) and by 2009, two thirds of Russia's FDI stock was found in four havens (Kuznetsov, 2011). In 2008 and 2009, 40% of Indian OFDI flows went to two havens (RBI, 2010). By 2011, 74% of all mainland Chinese OFDI stock was registered in three tax havens (MOFCOM, NBS, and SAFE, 2012). By comparison the share of FDI stock for developed market economies in tax havens, despite their generally higher rates of corporation tax, stood at around 25% to 33% (Palan et al., 2010). The high concentration of FDI by EM MNEs in a relatively small number of specific THOFCs requires further explanation. It is often suggested that tax-induced regulatory arbitrage (e.g. Fung et al., 2010; Shaxson, 2011; Palan, 2009; Lipsey, 2007) is the main driver for such investments. Accordingly, it is argued that 'most FDI into countries that serve as tax havens generate no actual productive activity' (Beugelsdijk et al., 2010, 1). The argument that THOFCs are 'fictitious spaces', however, does not explain the geographic concentration of such FDI in specific THOFCs, or why the average national OFDI shares to these jurisdictions are higher for many large emerging economies than for developed economies. In this article we explore this problem conceptually and empirically for FDI from mainland China, drawing from and building links between the geography of money and finance (Martin, 1999; Wrigley, 1999; Pollard, 2003; Wójcik, 2013) and IB literatures, and more specifically, internalisation theory (Buckley and Casson, 1976; McCann, 2011).

The article is organised into five further sections. Section 2 explains how internalisation theory, a mainstay of IB, provides a complementary firm-level perspective to the insights and approaches of financial geography for understanding FDI to THOFCs. Section 3 outlines our data and research methods. Section 4 presents the findings and interprets these through the approaches introduced in Section 2. We conclude by outlining frameworks for explaining FDI to THOFCs derived from the cross-fertilisation of internalisation theory and financial geography.

2. Financial geography and internalisation theory

Considerable shares of the world's FDI stocks, as well as financial capital, are held in THOFCs. These jurisdictions, at least on paper, are therefore important host and source countries for MNE activity. The high concentration of FDI to THOFCs (Sharman, 2012), particularly in the case of outward FDI from emerging markets, should make them of special interest to the IB research agenda, given its preoccupation with the MNE. This, however, has not been the case. Rather, economic geographers, and specifically financial geographers, have paid greater attention to financial centres (including THOFCs) (Hudson, 2000), albeit with a comparative lack of such research in the period leading up to the global financial crisis (Wójcik, 2013). We first explore the relevance of financial geography for understanding offshore incorporation in THOFCs before going on to explain how internalisation theory provides a complementary approach for thinking about FDI to THOFCs.

2.1. Financial geography, THOFCs and offshore incorporation

Financial geography emerged from a recognition among economic geographers that financial systems and services are 'lubricants' that are of fundamental importance to 'all production circuits', and therefore 'central to the operation of the economy' (Dicken, 2011, 368). It also grew from an acknowledgement that the assumptions of the early researchers within the field of financial geography, which borrowed heavily from neoclassical growth theory, were not realistic (Martin, 1999). With its assumptions of 'free and costless movement of capital and labour and perfect and ubiquitous information flows between regions, this theory essentially assumes away any regional role for money' (Martin, 1999, 3). In light of the global financial crisis and recognition that capital markets are often imperfect, however, 'money and finance have now moved from the fringes towards the centre of interest in economic geography' (Pryke, 2011, 298). This includes a growing recognition of the vital role of THOFCs (Wójcik, 2013; Wainwright, 2011).

In emerging markets financial systems are considered to be quite inefficient and their capital markets, in this neoclassical sense, also imperfect. One might, therefore, expect finance to be highly relevant to the economic geography of emerging markets. The capital markets of the People's Republic of China, for example, are generally considered not to be driven purely by market forces (and are imperfect, in this neoclassical sense) (Karreman and van der Knaap, 2012; Lai, 2011; Vlcek, 2013). And as Martin (1999, 8) points out, 'the institutional geography of the financial system is important because it can influence how money moves between locations and communities'. This is certainly true in China, where State Owned Enterprises, especially 'national champion' business groups, have privileged access to capital through the state banking sector at favourable rates and preferential access to capital markets owing to their embedded nature within the Communist Party system (Sutherland, 2009; Karreman and van der Knaap, 2012; Naughton, 2007). Private firms, by comparison, generally face acute challenges in securing bank loans because of state control over lending within Chinese banks and control over domestic stock markets (Shen et al., 2009; Lai, 2011). Consequently, except for the favoured few, private firms are often crowded out of the domestic capital market (Lu and Yao, 2009). As access to domestic capital is limited by regulation, discrimination by lenders and by the restricted range of outside funders, private firms search for alternative ways to augment their capital stock, sometimes outside of China.

Accessing international capital markets, particularly through international listings, is an increasingly popular alternative for Chinese businesses (Wójcik and Burger, 2010). Capital market imperfections have also been identified in financial geography as an important driver of these EM MNE offshore listings (Clark and Wójcik, 2007; Wójcik and Burger, 2010). To date, however, this literature has been comparatively silent on the firm-level corporate geography of FDI related to offshore incorporation in THOFCs that often precedes such listings. This is surprising, as the geography of money and finance has taken great interest in financial centres (Martin, 1999; Corbridge et al., 1994; Leyshon and Thrift, 1997; Hudson, 2000; Roberts, 1995; Mullings, 2004; Cobb, 1998). Pollard (2003), for example, emphasises that the study of specific financial centres is one of four major themes within this sub-discipline of economic geography (see also Martin (1999)). Until recently, however, the main focus within financial geography has been 'on what might be termed the "geography of financial institutions, systems and markets"' (Wrigley, 1999) and more generally 'the "supply" architectures of financial geographies' (Lee et al., 2009, 735). How firm-level financing has impacted on the spatial economy of firms, by contrast, has been somewhat overlooked (Wrigley, 1999; Lee et al., 2009; Pollard, 2003; Pryke, 2011). In one of the few studies of its kind, for example, Wrigley (1999) explored how firm-level financing decisions had significant impacts on the economic geography of US food retailers. From this study it was concluded that financial geographers had 'traditionally underemphasised types of restructuring which involve transformations of the capital structure and ownership configuration of firms', despite their important spatial consequences (Wrigley, 1999, 186). Investments to THOFCs, as we will later show, often involve these kinds of transformations.

This focus on the broader financial architecture and institutions, as opposed to firm-level financing and its impact on economic geography, also strongly manifests itself in the specific analysis of THOFCs by economic geographers (Cobb, 1998; Hudson, 2000; Roberts, 1994, 1995). Economic geographers, for example, have analysed the role of THOFCs in fostering regulatory competition between states (Hudson, 2000; Mullings, 2004); the way in which THOFCs develop their own competitive advantages (Cobb, 1998) and how THOFCs shape the global financial system (Roberts, 1994). The importance of THOFCs to the geography of the global financial system and architecture, including the growing volumes of offshore financial flows through THOFCs and their recent involvement in the global financial crisis, has been noted (French et al., 2009).

Interestingly, economists, in a somewhat similar fashion to economic geographers, have similarly taken a broadly macroeconomic approach to exploring THOFCs. This, for example, has involved undertaking modelling using national-level data (Rose and Spiegel, 2007; Dharmapala and Hines, 2009). To date, therefore, the ways in which firm-level financing via THOFCs impacts on corporate economic geography has received comparatively less attention, both within economics and economic geography, with only a few exceptions (Wójcik, 2013; Wainwright, 2011). Yet, as noted, very large shares of global FDI flows are channelled through THOFCs. They therefore constitute an important component in the geographical map of global FDI stocks and flows and MNE activity, a subject of perennial interest to economic geographers (Dicken, 2003, 2011; Coe and Yeung, 2001; McCann, 2011).

In certain ways, the approach of IB scholars has mirrored the trends found in financial geography. In particular, the extent and ways in which firm-level financing decisions specifically influence the location decisions of MNEs have been somewhat overlooked. This omission is surprising, given it is well known that large volumes of FDI pass through THOFCs and that significant MNE activity is undertaken offshore, including the raising of capital and property rights transactions. This type of FDI, however, is often not considered to be involved in physically 'productive activity' (Beugelsdijk et al., 2010). It also does not easily fit under the categories of market, efficiency or asset seeking investment motivations or horizontal and vertical investments (Shatz and Venables, 2003), that the IB literature often focuses upon. As a result, it is often dismissed. One result has been the tendency to consider FDI to THOFCs as mainly driven by tax induced regulatory arbitrage (Fung et al., 2010) and not to treat it as genuine MNE activity. It has been noted, for example, that empirical studies looking at the location choice of MNEs simply often exclude such FDI (Beugelsdijk et al., 2010). It is perhaps unsurprising then that Witt and Lewin (2007) have recently pointed out that all FDI seen purely as an 'escape response' to non-supportive home country institutional environments, including capital markets, remains a much neglected area in the IB research agenda.

To summarise, there are some interesting and close similarities between the ways in which economic geographers, and specifically those with an interest in money and finance, and IB scholars, have elided from their analysis the impact of firm-level financing decisions on economic geography and investment location decisions. Partly as a result of this, conceptual and empirical firm-level analysis of why MNEs use specific THOFCs, what they do in them, and the implications of their use, is still rather limited. Internalisation theory, with its specific focus at the micro-level, as well as its concern with imperfect markets, provides a complementary approach to those found in economic geography for further exploring offshore incorporation and FDI to THOFCs.

2.2. Internalisation theory and the economic geography of FDI to THOFCs

Despite the interest of economic geographers in both financial centres and the role of capital market imperfections in determining economic geography, there remains a dearth of firm-level analysis explaining offshore incorporation in THOFCs. Following from this, there are a number of reasons why the location choice of FDI as explained by internalisation theory (Buckley and Casson, 1976; McCann, 2011), provides a complementary approach to the financial geography literature looking at THOFCs. First, internalisation theory, which is based upon transaction cost economics and the theory of the firm, provides an explicit micro-level perspective with which to analyse offshore incorporation and the related FDI to THOFCs. As noted, financial geography has paid less attention to how firm-level financing decisions impact upon firm-level corporate economic geographies. Rather, its interest has been directed more towards the geography of financial supply architectures and systems (Wrigley, 1999). Secondly, financial geography grew, in part, from the recognition that imperfect capital markets shape economic geographies. Internalisation theory specifically deals with the role imperfect markets, including the impact of imperfect capital markets on FDI (Buckley and Casson, 2009), lending itself to cross-fertilisation with financial geography.

Thirdly, emerging markets, as noted, are renowned not only for their domestic capital market imperfections but also for their relatively poor domestic institutional environments and the high transactions costs that these can create (Khanna and Yafeh, 2007). Emerging market businesses are often forced to undertake a wide variety of innovative responses in an attempt to mitigate these high transactions costs. A considerable literature, for example, explains the formation of 'business groups' as preferred organisational forms in emerging markets as one such response mechanism (Khanna and Yafeh (2007) summarise this extensive literature). The most successful THOFCs, by contrast, are recognised for their well-developed legal and financial systems, particularly those havens that also act as offshore financial centres (OFCs) (Dharmapala and Hines, 2009; Rose and Spiegel, 2007; Roberts, 1995). The drive for offshore incorporation and FDI flows may, therefore, be driven not only by domestic capital market imperfections and the needs of EM MNEs to augment their existing capital structure, but also by access to a more favourable institutional environment.

Internalisation theory accounts for the impact of imperfect markets and also draws attention to these broader institutional misalignments, including how businesses exploit multi-country presence (Dicken, 2003). These may drive what has been referred to as 'institutional arbitrage' (Boisot and Meyer, 2008; Kedia and Mukherjee, 2009), in which EM MNEs use THOFCs to internalise institutional and market differences between countries, with the strategic intent of guaranteeing their long term economic viability. As such, firm-level financing and institutional arbitrage decisions may become an important determinant of where MNEs invest.

Finally, we note that economic geographers have seen MNEs as geographical constellations of social relationships (Dicken, 2003; Yeung, 2009) that invest along horizontal and vertical axes (Shatz and Venables, 2003). In addition, they have at times decried what they see as the 'methodological nationalism' of some IB scholars, in so far as they too closely follow the precepts of neoclassical economics (as exemplified by Yeung (2009, 204)). Neoclassical economic theories and IB variants that build on them, for example, assume free and costless movement of capital and labour and perfect and ubiquitous information flows. It is argued these theories, including internalisation theory, do not therefore explicitly address the role of territory in the case of financial flows and systems, or the spatially embedded nature of MNEs (Martin, 1999; Yeung, 2009; Seo, 2011). We look to address these criticisms here by arguing that localities and their specificities do matter, are location bound and are very difficult to transfer. As such, we regard the MNE as a locally embedded network of relationships, focussing here on financial relationships in particular. By doing so the article progresses our understanding of the globalisation of EM MNEs and their corporate financial geographies (Coe and Yeung, 2001). It also advances the theory of the MNE by focussing on the wider institutional framework of the global economy and relaxing the assumption that MNE's 'decision making and corporate behaviour are the same everywhere' (Yeung, 2009, 203). Geography is therefore conceptualised as a central component of the existence of MNEs (Beugelsdijk et al., 2010).

3. Research method, sample and analysis

We look at the specific case of the People's Republic of China to explore the use of THOFCs by EM MNEs in further detail, focusing in particular on the use of two of the more important THOFCs used by Chinese MNEs, the Cayman Islands and BVI, as well as their interaction with Hong Kong. China is a particularly interesting case because of the domestic institutional configuration and its evolution over time. Since 2000, mainland China's outward OFDI has grown at a faster rate than at any time in its history. This is the result of domestic policy liberalisation and state promotion (Buckley et al., 2007; Luo et al., 2010). The majority of Chinese OFDI, however, is destined for several specific THOFCs (see Table 1). These constituencies accounted for 69–87% of the annual outflow between 2003 and 2011 so that, as noted, the stock of Chinese investments in these locations now stands at around 80% of the total. In 2006, one tax haven alone, the Cayman Islands, had become the largest recipient of Chinese OFDI, with 44% of officially recognised flows (and 18% of its global OFDI stock). Subsequently, the THOFC Hong Kong became the lead recipient ahead of the Cayman Islands and British Virgin Islands (BVI) (MOFCOM, NBS, and SAFE, 2012). In addition, by 2006, 18% of China's utilised inward FDI originated from the BVI.

Table 1. FDI flows between China and the Cayman Islands, British Virgin Islands, Hong Kong and other THOFCs, 2003–2011 (US$ billion and %)

	2003		2004		2005		2006		2007		2008		2009		2010		2011		Stock, 2011	
	Billion	%	Billion	%	Billion	%	Billion	%	Billion	%	Billion	%	Billion	%	Billion	%	Billion	%	Billion	%
From China to:																				
Cayman Islands	0.8	28.3	1.3	23.4	5.2	42.1	7.8	44.4	2.6	9.8	1.5	2.7	5.4	9.5	3.5	5.1	4.9	6.6	21.7	5.1
BVI	0.2	7.3	0.4	7.0	1.2	10.0	0.5	3.1	1.9	7.1	2.1	3.8	1.6	2.9	6.1	8.9	6.2	8.3	29.3	6.9
Hong Kong	1.1	40.2	2.6	47.8	3.4	27.9	6.9	39.3	13.7	51.8	38.6	69.1	35.6	63.0	38.5	55.9	35.7	47.8	261.5	61.6
Other THOFCs	0.0	0.0	0.1	0.0	0.1	0.0	0.2	0.0	1.1	0.0	1.6	2.8	4.0	7.0	5.0	7.3	6.6	8.9	22.6	5.3
Total THOFCs	2.1	75.8	4.4	78.2	9.9	80.0	15.4	86.8	19.3	68.7	43.8	75.6	46.5	82.3	53.1	77.1	53.4	71.5	335.1	78.9
Total OFDI	2.9		5.5		12.3		17.6		26.5		55.9		56.5		68.9		74.7		424.8	
To China from:																				
Cayman Islands	0.9	1.6	2.0	3.4	1.9	3.2	2.1	3.3	2.6	3.4	3.1	3.4	2.5	2.9	2.5	2.4	2.2	1.9	n/a	n/a
BVI	5.8	10.8	6.7	11.1	9.0	15.0	11.2	17.8	16.6	22.1	16.0	17.3	11.3	12.5	10.5	9.9	9.7	8.4	n/a	n/a
Hong Kong	17.7	33.1	19.0	31.3	17.9	29.8	20.2	32.1	27.7	37.1	41.0	44.4	46.1	51	60.6	57.3	70.5	60.8	n/a	n/a
Other THOFCs	5.4	9.8	6.1	8.9	6	10.5	7.1	11.2	9.2	12.4	12.3	13.4	9.1	10.1	7.9	7.5	10.7	9.2	n/a	n/a
Total THOFCs	29.8	55.7	33.8	55.7	34.8	57.7	40.6	64.4	56.1	75.0	72.4	78.0	69.0	76.0	68.5	64.7	93.2	80.3	n/a	n/a
Total FDI	53.5		60.6		60.3		63.0		74.8		92.4		90.0		105.7		116.0		n/a	

Source: MOFCOM, NBS, & SAFE (2009, 2012); National Bureau of Statistics (various years).
Note: 'Other tax haven and OFCs' comprises 44 countries based on Zorome (2007). The *China Statistical Yearbook 2012* does not publish inward FDI stock data.

Indirect financial flows to the Cayman Islands and BVI, moreover, are often channelled via Hong Kong (another OFC and haven) and arguably remain very large. As such, the triad of the Cayman Islands, BVI and Hong Kong remain very important to understanding the characteristics, motivations and behaviour of Chinese MNEs (Vlcek, 2013). Or, as Kolstad and Wiig (2012, 33) note, the 'question of how to account for investment flows through tax havens is important for a more complete understanding of Chinese FDI'.

3.1. Sample selection

As noted, economists have employed aggregated OFDI data to explore the impacts of THOFCs on regional capital markets (Rose and Spiegel, 2007). Economic geographers have also used specific haven examples to explain 'bottom up' accounts of tax haven development (Roberts, 1994; Cobb, 1998; Hudson, 2000). Comparatively little research, owing to the inherent secrecy of havens, has been undertaken at the micro (firm)-level. This veil of secrecy makes it difficult to determine which firms have interests in THOFCs and what activities they engage in once offshore. One of the few windows through which to observe such behaviour is the publicly available data of firms that have raised capital on foreign stock markets. All businesses listed on stock markets in the USA, for example, must submit various formal documents to the US Securities Exchange Commission (SEC), including annual financial statements and reports. It is a requirement of the SEC that foreign private issuers complete a 20-F form annually (SEC, 2010). These submissions, owing to legal obligations, are generally candid in nature and provide detailed information on company accounts; capital raising activities and use of proceeds from such activities; information on the organisational structure; subsidiary information including the country in which any listing vehicle is incorporated and the use of offshore vehicles for such purposes. As such, the usage of 20-F forms is now well established in corporate governance and accounting research (e.g. La Porta et al., 2002).

Our sample of firms is taken from all firms listed on the US SEC EDGAR database classified as having their country location (i.e. primary business activities) in China (totalling 869 firms as of June 2010). The vast majority of Chinese firms listed in the USA are incorporated offshore. From these we then identify and select firms meeting the following criteria: all firms submitting 20-F forms in the period January 2009 through to June 2010, to ensure the sample included only operational firms; all firms incorporated in OECD recognised tax havens (excluding blank check companies, i.e. a development stage company that has no operating activities or specific business plan) and all firms originating in China as wholly Chinese owned entities. This left a final sample of 72 firms (Table 2).[1]

The data for each firm within our sample covers the time period from each firm's first 20-F submission until its latest submission, either in 2009 or 2010. Qiao Xing Universal Telephone was the first firm within our sample to submit a 20-F form to the SEC in 1999. Accordingly we analyse each of its 12 20-F form submissions and its two 20-F form amendment submissions which cover the time period 1999–2010. There are 13 firms within our sample which listed in the 2009–2010 period and have submitted

---

1   A detailed overview of our sample is available from the authors.

Table 2. Our sample of 20-F forms

Year	Total number of sample firms	Number of sample firms submitting first 20-F forms	Total number of sample 20-F submissions
1999	1	1	1
2000	0	0	2
2001	0	0	3
2002	3	2	6
2003	3	0	9
2004	4	1	13
2005	11	7	24
2006	22	11	46
2007	32	10	78
2008	59	27	137
2009	66	7	203
2010	72	6	275

Source: Securities and Exchange Commission (2010).

only one 20-F form to date, for example, 7 Days Group Holdings. Our analysis is therefore informed by its single submission. Section 4 ('company history') of each 20-F form, however, includes information on the origins of the firm within China and details of its incorporation process within the tax havens. The information provided covers the time period from the incorporation of the firm offshore until the present.

All of the firms we analyse, by definition, have raised foreign capital in the USA. This may limit the conclusions that we can draw, as we cannot compare our findings to firms that have used offshore vehicles to trade on non-American markets, or have invested in the havens to raise capital through venture capitalists or other means. This said, given the legal obligations to accurately report information in SEC submissions, the use of 20-F forms partially overcomes issues of reliability and credibility from which primary data often suffer.

3.2. Data analysis

Following from our approaches outlined in Section 2, we are concerned in the internalisation of arbitrage opportunities related to capital market imperfections and other institutional constraints and whether these activities take place within particular THOFC jurisdictions as well as the reasons why Chinese MNEs might use specific THOFCs. We are therefore interested in which offshore jurisdictions Chinese firms use to (i) access capital and (ii) to avail of a favourable institutional environment, including the legal institutional and regulatory environment conducive to doing business, as well as how they exploit this environment using multinational advanced business service (ABS) providers, including financial (i.e. investment banks) and professional service MNEs (i.e. legal and accounting firms). Our intention is therefore to explore some of the reasons, moving beyond taxation related reasons alone, for the use of THOFCs.

We note the jurisdiction of the listing vehicles and the amount that is raised in each company's initial public offerings (IPOs), also taking into account follow-on offerings and changes in bank borrowing following the IPOs, as proxies for capital raising activity in specific jurisdictions due to capital market imperfections in China. The jurisdiction of incorporation and magnitude of the capital raised in the IPO (to give a sense of the importance of this activity) is calculated from information within the 20-F's Section 4 ('company history'); Section 5 ('investing activities' and 'financing activities') and Section 14 ('material modifications to the rights of security holders and use of proceeds'). To gain insights into the influence of high transaction cost activities and the specific THOFCs used for reducing these (Naughton, 2007), we explore whether the firm has used the offshore market for property rights to acquire other China-based businesses that are held through offshore special purpose vehicles. Specifically, for each firm we check whether it has acquired controlling interests in any other Chinese company (either privately held or publicly listed) that itself is controlled through an offshore vehicle as well as the preferred THOFC of jurisdiction for this activity. We take this as a useful proxy for the use of offshore institutions and the favoured jurisdictions, as it explicitly reflects how Chinese businesses restructure their operations back in China through offshore vehicles. It therefore provides one further indicator of how offshore institutions are used for their benefit. Sections 3, 4 and 7 of the 20-F form, covering 'key information'; 'company history' and 'related party transactions', respectively, were used to identify such activities. For each firm we used all available 20-F submissions.

Our final area of investigation relates to the nature of China's OFDI to THOFCs vis-à-vis the domestic institutional environment as it changes over time. The new Enterprise Income Tax Law, introduced in mainland China in January 2008, has important implications for the use of offshore holding companies. It has harmonised corporate tax rates for foreign (i.e. including Chinese business owned via offshore holding-companies, as in our sample firms) and domestic businesses, as well as introducing new punitive withholding taxes for offshore companies. These tax changes potentially reduce the tax benefits of incorporating offshore. The new law, however, also provides that some foreign investors (i.e. including offshore holding-companies that own domestic mainland subsidiaries) may benefit from specific inter-governmental agreements on taxation (Buckley et al., 2008). Firms that are incorporated in a country or region with which China has a tax treaty may benefit from reduced rates of withholding taxes levied on dividends paid to offshore holding companies. Hong Kong has negotiated a highly favourable treaty (discussed later in Section 4.3). The deployment of a Hong Kong-based holding company directly holding mainland China subsidiaries, therefore, is used here as a proxy for responsiveness to institutional change. Sections 3 and 4 of the 20-F form covering 'risk factors' and 'organisational structure', respectively, were used to establish how institutional changes influence investment decisions and the type of holding company structures used to mitigate these effects.

We use three examples to illustrate our findings, supported by aggregate data from the sample. The selections were made on the basis that each case was representative of our sample firms (Yin, 2008). The examples provide richer detail (e.g. Eisenhardt, 1989) of the activities undertaken by Chinese firms within THOFCs, and particularly for the three most commonly used havens of the Cayman Islands, BVI and Hong Kong.

A limitation of our method is that it uses a sample of publicly listed businesses from one emerging market (mainland China) listed on US markets to gain insights into offshore incorporation. Further research could look at publicly listed Chinese companies on non-domestic stock markets, such as Hong Kong and Singapore, with primary business activities in China. It could also explore whether our arguments hold for other EM MNEs. Our preliminary investigations, however, suggest that Chinese MNEs are not singular in exploiting the access to capital markets and superior institutional environments of specific THOFCs.

4. Findings and discussion

Financial geographers have identified the important role of imperfect capital markets and firm-level financing decisions in driving the spatial decision-making of firms (Martin, 1999; Pollard, 2003; Wrigley, 1999). As with the IB literature, however, there is still limited firm-level research on FDI to THOFCs, albeit that such jurisdictions are gaining increasing recognition in economic geography (Wójcik, 2013; Wainwright, 2011). Addressing this gap, our findings show that one way in which Chinese businesses address domestic market imperfections that have been created and sustained by government policies and regulations, such as the markets for capital and property rights, is by establishing offshore companies. As a result, they are able to reduce the costs of raising capital, restructuring their domestic businesses, and can pursue short-term and long-term strategic goals via the use of offshore vehicles. The transaction cost approach of internalisation theory argues that FDI is determined by the internalisation of imperfect markets across different locations, enabling MNEs to control crucial intermediate markets in goods, factors and services (Buckley and Casson, 1976). It also provides a useful explanatory framework for understanding why such high levels of FDI are found in certain specific THOFCs, which we now discuss.

4.1. Capital market imperfections: the use of THOFCs for international listings

According to internalisation theory, outward investors seek locations that minimise the cost of their activities so as to achieve optimality in location for the firm. Buckley et al. (2007) applied this theory to Chinese OFDI and found that special determinants arising from imperfections in China's capital market were a major factor in Chinese FDI. The capital market in China, in the aforementioned neoclassical sense, is imperfect (Huang, 2003; Karreman and van der Knaap, 2012) and this in turn influences OFDI. A limited number of studies have also noted the importance of raising capital on foreign capital markets (Wójcik and Burger, 2010; Xiao, 2004). Xiao, for example, has noted that OFDI to tax havens and OFCs 'creates value added much like the financial sector's role for the real economy' (Xiao, 2004, 12). Xiao's argument is not well developed, though the implication is clear: registering as a company in a tax haven could enable Chinese companies to circumvent imperfections in the domestic Chinese capital market. This may create greater value than they could obtain by listing on domestic stock exchanges, if such an option were even available.[2] In the Chinese case, as access to domestic capital is limited by regulation, discrimination by lenders and by the restricted range of outside funders, private firms in particular must search for alternative ways to augment their capital stock, sometimes seeking capital outside of China. Financial geographers have also emphasised that the institutional geography of the financial system influences the

---

2   The Chinese government prevents companies (even some large SOEs) from listing on Chinese stock markets—thereby forcing them to go overseas for financing (Kung and Cheng, 2012).

---

movement of money between locations and different communities or groups (Martin, 1999). Investment in THOFCs via the creation of offshore holding companies is one such way of augmenting existing capital, particularly for private businesses. Of our sample of 72 firms, in total 66 were incorporated in the Cayman Islands (55), BVI (7) and Hong Kong (4), with the remaining six in other havens. It is of interest to note, therefore, that by far the most commonly used offshore listing vehicles also correspond to some of the main destinations of officially recorded Chinese OFDI (Table 1). For these firms, details of the largest five shareholders are provided in their 20-F forms. The majority are usually owned and controlled by their founders (either directly, or beneficially through further BVI companies). Many are prominent Chinese entrepreneurs. In our 72 sample firms we identify 42 in which the combined holdings of the three largest individual shareholders exceed 20% of their companies' ordinary shares, a threshold commonly considered sufficient to lock in control (La Porta et al., 2002). These individuals are identified as 'founders' in the 20-F submissions and are Chinese nationals. Nearly all of the other sample firms, moreover, have significant stakes owned by Chinese nationals, though sometimes these ownership shares have been diluted by other investors. Chinese OFDI to THOFCs can therefore be seen as a strong response to Chinese domestic capital market imperfections, particularly by private entrepreneurs.

Collectively, the 72 sample firms raised estimated gross IPO proceeds of US$11 billion and net proceeds of US$9.8 billion.[3] Major international investment banks, which all have significant operations in Hong Kong, acted as underwriters and co-ordinated the global offerings of our sample companies. This included CLSA, UBS, Credit Suisse First Boston, Morgan Stanley, JP Morgan and ABN AMRO Rothschild. It is striking that 55 sample firms were incorporated in one haven, the Cayman Islands.[4] Of these, moreover, 40 had one or more BVI holding companies owned by the Cayman Island listing vehicle, which usually in turn held the mainland subsidiaries. The sample firms commonly followed similar procedures of incorporation prior to listing, with 23 of the sample firms first registering in the BVI prior to incorporating their listing vehicle in the Cayman Islands.

Suntech Power provides us with a representative example of the listing process, illustrating the sequence whereby Chinese businesses develop their offshore corporate structures. Suntech was originally incorporated in Wuxi (Jiangsu province), China as Suntech China. It designs, develops and manufactures a variety of photovoltaic cells and modules and is one of the world's largest producers. The following quote, taken from Section 4 of its 20-F form submitted in 2006 illustrates the process whereby offshore vehicles are used to raise capital and uses language that is echoed by a majority of sample firms in their 20-F forms:

> Suntech China was incorporated in January 2001 and commenced business operations in May 2002. *To enable us to raise equity capital from investors outside of China, we established a holding*

---

3   This estimation is based on the average difference between gross and net IPO proceeds directed towards underwriting fees, advisory fees and related costs from firms returning both figures, applied to omitted IPO values from firms only returning either gross or net IPO proceeds in their 20-F statements.

4   Hong Kong symbolises well how advanced business services located here link the city with other important cities (in PRC: Shanghai), other offshore jurisdiction (CI, BVI) and the final country of business activity (China or elsewhere) (cf. Wójcik, 2013).

company structure by incorporating Power Solar System Co., Ltd., or Suntech BVI, in the British Virgin Islands on January 11, 2005. Suntech BVI acquired all of the equity interests in Suntech China through a series of transactions that have been accounted for as a recapitalization. In anticipation of our initial public offering, we incorporated Suntech Power Holdings Co., Ltd., or Suntech, in the Cayman Islands as a listing vehicle on August 8, 2005. Suntech became our ultimate holding company when it issued shares to the existing shareholders of Suntech BVI on August 29, 2005 in exchange for all of the shares that these shareholders held in Suntech BVI. We conduct a significant portion of our operations through Suntech China. (Suntech, 2006, 27) (emphasis added)

Suntech illustrates the typical processes and structures predominantly used by Chinese businesses when raising capital on foreign stock markets. Suntech raised net IPO proceeds of US$321.8mn on the New York Stock Exchange (NYSE) in 2005 (Suntech, 2010). CLSA Asia-Pacific Markets, based in Hong Kong, was an important underwriter of the IPO (which also included Credit Suisse First Boston and Morgan Stanley). Once in place, these offshore structures allow Chinese companies to raise further capital. In 2009, for example, Suntech closed a follow-on offering on the NYSE with net proceeds of US$277 million (Suntech, 2010). Suntech has made use of two corporate bond offerings to raise capital in 2007 and 2008, with net proceeds of US$485.6 million and US$560.1 million, respectively. Following its IPO in 2005 Suntech's access to short term bank borrowing dramatically improved, its net proceeds from short-term bank borrowing increased from US$15.3 million in 2005 to US$183.6 million in 2006 and to US$305.8 million by 2008 (Suntech, 2007, 2010). Suntech was able to realise net proceeds of US$294.1 million in longer term bank loans by 2009 (Suntech, 2010). Both Chinese and international banks lent to Suntech.

The capital raised has allowed Suntech to expand its production capacity, exploit its China based low-cost manufacturing model and to allow it to undertake a series of acquisitions in industrialised countries. For example, in 2006 Suntech acquired MSK in Japan (now Suntech Japan; see Figure 1)—a leader in the integrated photo-voltaic market (Suntech, 2006). In 2008, Suntech acquired one of its component suppliers, KSL-Kuttler, a leading German-based manufacturer of automation systems for the printed circuit board industry. In 2009 Suntech acquired a 76.6% interest in CSG Solar, a German company involved in developing, producing and marketing PV cells (Figure 1).

The strong preference to incorporate a listing vehicle in the Cayman Islands warrants further analysis. While zero rates of tax on income and capital gains and secrecy regulations are undoubtedly an attraction of the Cayman Islands, which can be exploited in numerous ways, such as via the use of complex transfer pricing and intra-corporate loan strategies, it is important to stress numerous other THOFCs would also meet these criteria (OECD, 2010). We believe the most important reason for Chinese firms to specifically favour the Cayman Islands as a base for their listing vehicles is that it allows them to minimise their costs of raising capital. The Cayman Islands is the world's fifth largest financial centre by asset size and an important adjunct to the North American capital markets (IMF, 2009; Roberts, 1995). The most recent comparisons show it had 464 offshore banks, compared with nine in the BVI, 30 in Cyprus and 77 in Guernsey (Hampton, 2002). As an OFC it also specialises in business related cross-border financial services, particularly in banking. It held total banking assets of US$1.7 trillion in 2009 (IMF, 2009). It has become jurisdiction to the largest number of investment funds in the world, with over 9,000 funds and net assets approaching US$2.3 trillion in 2007

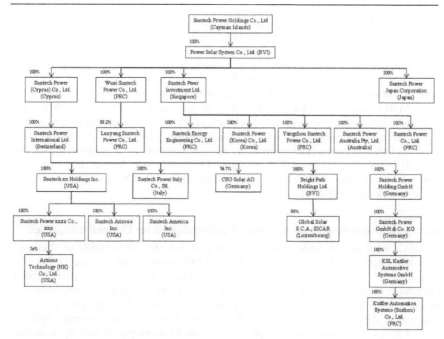

Figure 1. Suntech Power Holding Co.'s organisational structure, 2010.
Source: Suntech (2010: 47).

(IMF, 2009). The Cayman Islands also hosts 75% of the world's hedge funds and nearly half of the estimated US$1 trillion assets under management (HOC, n.d.). It therefore provides ready access to deep pools of international capital (IMF, 2009). Most importantly of all, however, by vertically locating a listing vehicle within the Cayman Islands, IPOs may also be undertaken on multiple stock exchanges, including both Hong Kong and US stock exchanges. Historically, no other havens have provided this facility (Greguras et al., 2008). Thus, the Cayman Islands is the jurisdiction of choice for listing vehicles and raising capital. As such, finance, accounting and legal professionals argue that 'in many, if not most cases, the use of a Cayman vehicle is not wholly or mainly for tax planning purposes' (Knowles, 2010, 1). This is not, of course, to say zero tax rates are unimportant, but simply that many other jurisdictions also offer such incentives.

Financial geographers have drawn attention to the role of imperfect capital markets in shaping economic geography (Martin, 1999) even if to date research showing how corporate financing affects firm location decisions has been limited (Pollard, 2003; Wrigley, 1999; Pryke, 2011). As noted above, economic geographers have 'traditionally underemphasised types of restructuring which involve transformations of the capital structure and ownership configuration of firms' (Wrigley, 1999, 186). Similarly, IB research has largely overlooked the importance of imperfect capital markets and firm-level financing on location choice (Witt and Lewin, 2007). The high concentration of EM MNE FDI in the Cayman Islands is a novel but important example of how firm-level financing decisions and responses to imperfect capital markets in the home country alter EM MNE corporate economic geography. The spatial consequences of the decisions that we have focused on here are related to incorporation in offshore jurisdictions. As Roberts (1994) puts it, in some senses these are 'fictitious spaces', as the businesses in question usually do not physically relocate there and no physical production is undertaken offshore. Nonetheless, the use of these jurisdictions does have very significant impacts on the more tangible, value-adding productive activities of these MNEs, somewhat akin to vertical FDI. In this light, Pollard's (2003, 446) comment that 'finance is a fundamental part of economic co-ordination that is not logically prior to or separate from production', is highly germane (see also Sarre (2007) for an elaboration on the links between finance and production). It has been shown, for example, how the capital raised offshore facilitates both further domestic and international expansion of Chinese businesses (Sutherland and Ning, 2011), illustrating its direct links to production.

4.2. Institutional misalignments: the offshore market for Chinese companies

THOFCs may also provide institutional support for the restructuring of domestic operations back in China. Boisot and Meyer (2008) conceive of Chinese OFDI as a means of 'institutional arbitrage', that is the strategic pursuit of an MNE to exploit differences in the configuration of the professional, administrative, cultural, economic or geographic environment between countries to their own advantage (Dicken, 2003; Ghemawat, 2003; Gaur and Lu, 2007; Zhao, 2006). The market for property rights of other Chinese businesses, for example, was late in its development and the domestic transactions costs are reportedly high (Jefferson and Rawski, 2002; Naughton, 2007). OFDI to THOFCs simultaneously allows Chinese firms to reduce costs arising from various types of institutional misalignments. Chinese firms, moreover, avail of administrative and professional institutions, and engage in a form of arbitrage whereby they exploit the other comparatively superior institutions of foreign markets. As noted, these superior offshore institutional environments are also exploited via the use of large multinational ABS providers which themselves typically have a significant offshore presence. For example, we found 23 of the 72 20-F submissions in our sample were directly audited via the Hong Kong registered affiliates of several large MNE accounting firms (with KPMG in the lead, followed by Deloitte Touche Tohmatsu and Price Waterhouse Coopers). A further 25 were audited by the local mainland subsidiaries of these MNEs (typically in Shanghai or Beijing). Our sample firms show that the use of established MNE business service providers, which typically have both a strong offshore and onshore presence, are used by our sample firms so as to fully exploit the benefits of offshore incorporation.

It is notable that important transactions involving the buying and selling of Chinese businesses take place via these offshore jurisdictions. In our sample firms we find evidence that 22 firms have acquired fully or partially one or more other China-based companies that are themselves held through offshore holding companies, supporting the idea that havens offer a supportive institutional environment for organisational restructuring. Chinese firms may also benefit from foreign banking and financial expertise, which can add value to the Chinese capital (Zhan, 1995), as well as more sophisticated and stable legal institutions (Huang, 2003). This allows businesses to undertake significant restructuring of their mainland operations via THOFCs and reduce their exposure to, and negotiation with, Chinese institutions in this process.

As with the high transactions costs incurred in domestic capital markets, transactions costs in the domestic market for property rights may force businesses to seek less costly and effective alternatives. More specifically, when transactions costs are high, as they are in China (Buckley et al., 2007), Chinese firms investing in the havens may follow diminution or escape strategies to reduce exposure to domestic institutional conditions (Witt and Lewin, 2007). The BVI, in contrast to the Cayman Islands, specialises in international business company (IBC) registrations and far outstrips all other havens in this regard (HOC, n.d.). In 2002, for example, it had around 400,000 IBCs compared, for example, to only 60,000 in the Cayman Islands or 24,000 in Cyprus and 30,000 in Netherlands Antilles (Hampton, 2002). Qualitative research on Chinese investors using the BVI shows they have particular regard for the BVI's legal system (Maurer and Martin, 2011). This may explain why the overwhelming majority of property rights transactions in our sample firms are undertaken in the BVI.

Xinhua Sports & Entertainment Limited (XSEL) provides an interesting example of how Chinese businesses use THOFCs for property rights transactions. It is a sports and media entertainment group that conducts all of its operations in mainland China. It has grown significantly since its inception, primarily through the acquisition of assets and businesses and development of its distribution channels (Xinhua, 2008). XSEL undertook a different sequence to most of the sample firms, by directly incorporating in the Cayman Islands. It completed its IPO on the NASDAQ in 2007, receiving net proceeds of US$200.3 million (Xinhua, 2008). XSEL has also raised capital via placements of convertible preferred shares (US$60 million in 2006 and US$29.2 million in 2008) and convertible bonds in 2008 (US$30.7 million) (Xinhua, 2009). Its access to bank borrowing has dramatically expanded since its IPO, from US$5.6 million in 2006 to US$48.7 million in 2007 and to US$40.3 million in 2008.

After XSEL secured access to international capital markets it has undertaken numerous acquisitions. The proceeds from the IPO were used, for example, to fully acquire at least seven privately held offshore holding companies that own (or control) other onshore Chinese media businesses (italics in Figure 2). It has established one new offshore company in the Cayman Islands (Xinhua Media Entertainment Ltd). Of these eight new businesses six were incorporated in the BVI, one in the Cayman Islands and one in Hong Kong. Seven of these companies in turn effectively control at least 29 mainland Chinese subsidiaries (compared to the sample average of 6.3) and a further eight offshore holding companies (sample average is 3.7). Through its 2007 acquisition of East Alliance Limited, a BVI holding company, XSEL now controls all of East Alliance's wholly owned subsidiaries and variable interest entities collectively known as M-Group, a mainland China-based mobile service provider. These are controlled via contractual agreements which include a secured loan agreement, exclusive equity purchase option agreement, an equity pledge agreement and a subrogation agreement entered into with Wuxianshijie (Figure 2). Through these acquisitions XSEL has 17 offshore holding companies in total (sample average is 3.3). As a result of these acquisitions XSEL has been able to expand aggressively into a range of different areas of media, as well as greatly expanding its geographical coverage of the Chinese market.

The flexible and integrated use of a triad of holding companies in the Cayman Islands, BVI and Hong Kong, involving exploitation of their individual strengths as well as their complementarities, moreover, is very popular among Chinese MNEs (see Figures 1, 2 and 3). The use of these regions is facilitated by their very close financial and legal integration (Vlcek, 2013). All have been or still are overseas British territories.

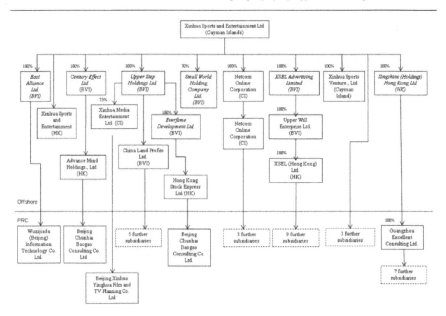

Figure 2.   Xinhua Sports and Entertainment Ltd.'s organisational structure, 2010.
Source: Xinhua Sports and Entertainment (2010, 56).

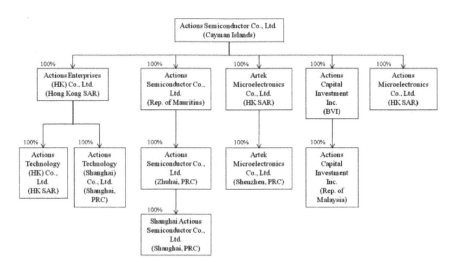

Figure 3.   Actions Semiconductor Co.'s organisational structure, 2010.
Source: Actions Semiconductor (2010, 36).

Their integration was also greatly promoted by Hong Kong's return to China in 1997. According to the IMF, the BVI sent a delegation to Hong Kong in 1989 to 'promote the use of IBCs to hold assets in anticipation of the 1997 return of the colony to Chinese sovereignty' (IMF, 2004, 16). This promotional visit was followed 'by a significant increase in the registration of IBCs by Hong Kong residents, and it is estimated that a significant number of IBCs continue to be formed by residents of Hong Kong' (IMF, 2004, 16). Indeed, the bi-directional flows of capital registered between the BVI and Hong Kong are unusually large and it is 'common practice for Hong Kong companies to set up non-operating companies in offshore financial centres' (Census and Statistics Department, 2004, FC3). In 2007 the BVI was the largest recipient of OFDI flows from Hong Kong, receiving 47.8%. It was also the second largest inward investor to Hong Kong (after mainland China), responsible for 36.6% of all inward investment (Census and Statistics Department, 2007). These large flows between Hong Kong and the BVI, moreover, were due to 'the popularity for Hong Kong enterprises in setting up non-operating companies to channel funds back to Hong Kong or to other places' (Census and Statistics Department, 2007, 6). Hong Kong, moreover, has historically been by far the largest holder of OFDI stock in the BVI—making it the BVI's largest inward and outward investor (UNCTAD, 2004). It is thus perhaps unsurprising that the BVI appears to be the preferred location for business registrations and property rights transactions and also explains its popularity with Chinese investors.

4.3. Responsiveness to domestic institutional change: China's taxation policy

An important explanation for the use of THOFCs has been the preferential tax rates afforded to foreign invested enterprises (FIEs) in China which leads to 'round-tripping', a form of tax-induced regulatory arbitrage that involves moving capital offshore only to bring back onshore again in the guise of FDI, so as to benefit from preferential tax treatment (e.g. Huang, 2003; Fung et al., 2010; Vlcek, 2013). A variety of measures, however, have also been introduced to restrict the registration of offshore holding companies by Chinese firms and discourage round-tripping. Since 2006, new regulations mandate that all Chinese nationals wishing to invest overseas must register with their local State Administration of Foreign Exchange (SAFE). More importantly, since January 2008 the new Enterprise Income Tax Law has harmonised tax rates for FIEs and Chinese businesses. This provides that enterprises established under the laws of foreign countries or regions but whose 'de facto management body' is located in the PRC be treated as a resident enterprise for PRC taxation purposes. This means offshore holding companies may now be subject to the PRC income tax at the rate of 25% for their global income. Such measures are, potentially, highly punitive to offshore holding companies. Indeed, under the law, dividends, interests, rent or royalties payable by a FIE to its foreign non-resident enterprise investors (and proceeds from the disposition of assets by a foreign enterprise investor) are also subject to an additional 10% withholding tax. As such the tax benefits of setting up offshore holding companies have been eliminated and replaced with disincentives. Looking at the most recent listings on US stock-markets, however, we find 40 of our sample firms filed their first 20-F form in 2008 or later (Table 2). Thirty-three of these incorporated their listing vehicle in the Cayman Islands (and 7 in the BVI). The sample firms have increasingly incorporated a Hong Kong holding company to directly hold their mainland businesses. Between January 2005 and December 2009, 46 of our 72 sample firms had established a Hong

Kong subsidiary, which, according to their annual reports, were established with a view to reducing their potential tax burdens. Every single one of the 330 20-F submissions made since the end of 2006 has specifically commented on the implications of new withholding taxes in China paid to offshore holding companies, including the preferential tax arrangements found in Hong Kong (that is a 5% instead of 10% rate). This demonstrates that offshore holding companies incorporated in THOFCs continued to be used even after the new enterprise income tax law, punitive to such offshore holding companies, took effect.

Actions Semiconductor provides us with a typical example (Figure 3). It is a leading semiconductor manufacturer specialising in the design and sale of portable media players. It was incorporated in the Cayman Islands in 2005 specifically to take advantage of, among other things, access to international capital markets: '[B]y incorporating our company in the Cayman Islands, we believe that we may have additional flexibility to pursue future business opportunities or financing alternatives' (Actions, 2010, 23). It completed its IPO on the NASDAQ in 2005, receiving net proceeds of US$43.6 million. Since its IPO, it has entered into a series of strategic investments, including equity acquisitions in other international companies incorporated in the BVI. Actions Semiconductor has also been active in the reorganisation of its offshore organisational structure, establishing holding companies as 'tax effective investment vehicles' to counter the new withholding taxes (Actions, 2010, 23). Shortly before the income tax law change was introduced Actions began to reconfigure the organisational structure of its offshore holding company and international and mainland China subsidiaries explicitly for tax purposes:

> We determined that it is advantageous for us to adjust our investment structure to use Hong Kong companies to hold our interests in our PRC [People's Republic of China] subsidiaries. On August 17, 2007 and September 6, 2007, we established two subsidiaries in Hong Kong.... which serve as the holding companies of our PRC subsidiaries. We wound up two BVI holding companies (Actions, 2010, 23).

Actions Semiconductor has changed its holding company structure so as to pre-empt the introduction of the new withholding taxes.

A common theme found in Sections 3 and 10 of the 20-F form (sections 'Risks' and 'PRC taxation', respectively) is the pending review of the tax status of our sample firms, particularly regarding the introduction of withholding taxes paid on dividends from mainland Chinese firms to offshore holding companies. Many of the sample firms clearly state that all necessary measures will be taken to mitigate the adverse impacts of any possible rescinding of preferential taxation rates currently applied, and cite the use of Hong Kong holding companies as a possible solution. In effect, disincentives to incorporate offshore (and round-trip) have been put in place. In this light, it is of interest that many of our sample firms still look to use offshore vehicles. In total 40 of our sample firms filed their first 20-F form in 2008 or later (Table 2), after the introduction of these withholding taxes. If these businesses were able to use alternative tax avoidance strategies to overcome the introduction of the new withholding taxes (such as transfer pricing strategies), it is not clear why they would go to the expense of incorporating these Hong Kong-based holding companies. This suggests that lower tax rates alone are unlikely to be the sole explanation for the extensive use of the specific THOFCs we have identified.

The internalisation theory of the MNE is based on the principle that firm boundaries are set at the margin where the benefits of further internalisation just offset the costs (Buckley and Casson, 1976). Our findings suggest that while the costs of going offshore have increased, the benefits, in terms of mitigating the high costs of domestic market imperfections, still outweigh these additional costs. If round-tripping for lower taxes was the primary explanation for the use of THOFCs, we might expect to see a reduction in their use, but this is not the case (Table 1). To date most attention on Chinese MNE's OFDI to THOFCs has been placed on how such investments are driven by tax-induced regulatory arbitrage (e.g. Fung et al., 2010; Dharmapala and Hines, 2009). Following from this, the consequences this may have for biasing FDI as a measure of MNE affiliate activity have also been raised. This line of thinking, focussing on the value-added generated in havens, assumes that tax haven related FDI generates no other productive activity (Beugelsdijk et al., 2010). Chinese businesses, however, also appear to use offshore companies to mitigate the high transactions costs of specific domestic market imperfections and institutional constraints. A degree of caution, therefore, is required when thinking about what type of productive or unproductive activities may take place in tax havens. While it is true, in the sense of physical production of goods or services, that no productive activities may take place in THOFCs, this is not to say that such multinational activity does not serve other important functions.

Interestingly, macroeconomic modelling looking at the impact of tax havens also shows they create significant capital market competition (Rose and Spiegel, 2007). So while Beugelsdijk et al. (2010) are right to draw our attention to the large volumes of FDI channelled through THOFCs, care is required in thinking about the exact ways in which they are used. Our sample of firms, for example, shows that tax havens provide important financial services that are not supplied domestically. While many countries aspire to become tax havens, moreover, it is only those with the best governance and institutions that actually succeed (Dharmapala and Hines, 2009). Low taxes, therefore, are only one, albeit important attraction, of THOFCs. Comparatively superior capital markets and more efficient institutions for property rights are also driving Chinese OFDI to THOFCs, facilitated by multinational ABS providers (Wójcik, 2013).

5. Conclusion

The growth of outward FDI from emerging markets has become an important force shaping international economic geography. To date, however, the relatively high concentrations of national OFDI shares from the largest emerging markets to specific THOFCs have been somewhat overlooked. While financial geographers have consistently drawn attention to the importance of THOFCs (e.g. Roberts, 1995; Hudson, 2000), far fewer have looked at firm-level motivations for FDI to these jurisdictions, despite the very large volumes of global FDI flowing to them. This gap exists, in part, because the way in which firm-level financing decisions affects corporate economic geographies has been somewhat overlooked (Martin, 1999; Wrigley, 1999; Pollard, 2003). Motivated by the calls of financial geographers for greater research on how financing affects corporate, firm-level economic geographies, we used internalisation theory as a complementary approach to further investigate the use of offshore incorporation in THOFCs (McCann, 2011). Based upon transaction costs and the theory of the firm, internalisation theory provides an explicitly firm-level perspective relevant to MNEs. As such, it can provide insights into FDI location decisions in THOFCs. And although it is sometimes criticised as too closely following the precepts of neoclassical economics (Buckley and Casson, 1976), as it does not explicitly address the role of territory in the case of financial flows and systems, or the spatially embedded nature of MNEs (Martin, 1999; Yeung, 2009; Seo, 2011), here we have taken these criticisms seriously. We have done so by casting 'location advantages' in terms of the institutional, legal institutional and social relationship setting of the source country (China), the proximate host countries (BVI and Cayman Islands) and the target countries, which include China (for 'round-tripping') or the USA (for capital augmentation) as well as the eventual destination of the capital. In doing so, despite the relatively conventional theoretical stance employed, we have extended internalisation theory and also contributed to areas of current interest in financial geography.

We argue that locality and its specificities do matter, are location bound, and also difficult to transfer. As such we take the MNE as an embedded network of relationships, focussing on financial relationships in particular. The spatial configurations of MNEs, moreover, are seen as the cause and agency of economic activity. The taxation and legal institutions of all the relevant locations are perceived of as parts of integrated global value chains, centred on individual (Chinese in our case) MNEs but also embedded in all the countries in which they have activities. Using this approach our findings show Chinese MNEs invest in THOFCs vertically in order to access certain markets and institutions that are not available to them domestically. As well as this, they also address capital market imperfections in and through particular THOFCs, taking advantage of the respective specialisations of these spaces, as well as the networks that these jurisdictions are embedded within. Even despite increased regulation and higher costs associated with offshore incorporation, this has meant Chinese MNEs continue to undertake FDI to THOFCs to address the significant domestic market imperfections they face (cf. McCann, 2011). The case of Chinese MNEs investing in THOFCs therefore provides an interesting, albeit novel example, of how corporate financing and institutional misalignments drive FDI location decisions and corporate economic geography. The integration of spatial aspects into internationalisation theory allows us to extend the conventional scope of internalisation theory and to provide pointers to future theoretical and empirical advances.

In light of the global financial crisis, there have been increasing calls by financial geographers for the impact of 'financialisation' to be better incorporated and given more prominence within economic geography (Pike and Pollard, 2010; Pryke, 2011). Among financial geographers, moreover, it has also been noted that in spite of the great importance of THOFCs, including their links to world cities, ABS and general financial system growth and development, there has been comparatively little research on them (Wójcik, 2013). Wójcik (2013, 338), for example, notes the irony of how in the lead up to the global financial crisis, 'offshore finance seems to have been treated as a mere footnote to financial geography'. The same charge can be even more strongly levelled at IB scholars, who have, with one or two exceptions (Beugelsdijk et al., 2010; Sutherland and Ning, 2011), almost entirely elided this topic from the remit of their analysis, despite the huge volumes of FDI flows and stocks held offshore. Financial geographers have called for more research (Wainwright, 2011), including for the type of firm-level study undertaken here, which also incorporates consideration of emerging market MNEs (Wójcik, 2013). These are now strongly shaping international economic geography and, increasingly, the offshore world (Maurer and Martin, 2011; Vlcek, 2013; Wójcik, 2013). By cross-fertilising ideas found in financial geography and mainstream IB and then applying them to how Chinese MNEs use THOFCs, we have made a start in addressing some of these prominent and important gaps highlighted by economic geographers (Wainwright, 2011; Wójcik, 2013).

In doing so we have provided some directions for a future research agenda for IB and economic geography scholars alike, pointing towards new directions in thinking about offshore incorporation and in turn the economic geography of the MNE. IB scholars can still do much more to learn from economic geographers and incorporate greater analysis of THOFCs in the study of the MNE. To repeat the words of Pollard (2003, 446), and an idea echoed by a number of other economic geographers (Dicken, 2011; Sarre, 2007), 'finance is a fundamental part of economic co-ordination that is not logically prior to or separate from production'. IB scholars can learn from these calls and do more to consider the relevance of their theories of the MNE to the case of FDI activity to THOFCs. By the same token, economic geographers can learn from the firm-level approaches often employed in IB, thus moving beyond study of 'financial architectures' and more towards how firm-level financing decisions influence corporate economic geographies (Wrigley, 1999). The approach we have employed here, moreover, with its detailed focus on firm-level data on offshore subsidiaries, provides a potentially useful method for further studies. In the first instance these could, for example, develop our opening paragraph further and look at other emerging market MNEs, such as those from Brazil, Russia and India, to see if our arguments regarding offshore incorporation are also useful in these cases.

Acknowledgements

Earlier versions of this article were presented at the 3rd China Goes Global Conference, 30 September to 2 October 2009, Harvard University, Cambridge, MA, USA.; the China and India Conference, 29–30 October 2009,University of Edinburgh, Edinburgh, UK; Emerging Market MNE conference, Copenhagen Business School, 25–26 November 2010. The authors wish to thank four anonymous reviewers and conference participants for their comments and suggestions.

References

Actions Semiconductor Co. Ltd. (Actions) (various years) Form 20-F. Annual and transition report of foreign private issuers. SEC EDGAR filing information. http://www.sec.gov/Archives/edgar/data/1342068/000114420410023516/0001144204-10-023516-index.htm [Accessed 27 June 2010].
Boisot, M., Meyer, M. W. (2008) Which way through the open door? Reflections on the internationalization of Chinese firms. *Management and Organization Review*, 4: 349–365.
Buckley, P. J., Casson, M. C. (1976) *The Future of the Multinational Enterprise*. London: McMillan.
Buckley, P. J., Casson, M. C. (2009) The internalization theory of the multinational enterprise: A review of the progress of a research agenda after 30 years. *Journal of International Business Studies*, 40: 1563–1580.
Buckley, P. J., Clegg, L. J., Cross, A. R., Liu, X., Voss, H., Zheng, P. (2007) The determinants of Chinese outward foreign direct investment. *Journal of International Business Studies*, 38: 499–518.
Buckley, P. J., Clegg, L. J., Cross, A. R., Voss, H., Rhodes, M., Zheng, P. (2008) Explaining China's outward FDI: an institutional perspective. In K. Sauvant (ed.) *The Rise of*

Transnational Corporations from Emerging Markets: Threat or Opportunity?, pp. 151–224. Cheltenham: Edward Elgar.

Beuglesdijk, S., Hennart, J. -F., Slangen, A., Smeets, R. (2010) Why and how FDI stocks are a biased measure of MNE affiliate activity. *Journal of International Business Studies*, 41: 980–995.

Beugelsdijk, S., McCann, P., Mudambi, R. (2010) Introduction: Place, space and organization - economic geography and the multinational enterprise. *Journal of Economic Geography*, 10: 485–493.

Census and Statistics Department. (2004) *Hong Kong Monthly Digest of Statistics, External Direct Investment Statistics*. Hong Kong: Census and Statistics Department.

Census and Statistics Department. (2007) *External Direct Investment Statistics of Hong Kong*. Hong Kong: Census and Statistics Department.

Child, J., Rodrigues, S. (2005) The internationalization of Chinese firms: a case for theoretical extension? *Management and Organization Review*, 1: 381–410.

Clark, G. L., Wójcik, D. (2007) *The Geography of Finance: Corporate Governance in the Global Marketplace*. Oxford: Oxford University Press.

Cobb, S. C. (1998) Global finance and the growth of offshore financial centres: the Manx experience. *Geoforum*, 29: 7–21.

Coe, N. C., Yeung, H. W. -C. (2001) Geographical perspectives on mapping globalisation. An introduction to the JEG Special Issue 'Mapping globalisation: geographical perspectives on international trade and investment'. *Journal of Economic Geography*, 1: 367–380.

Corbridge, S., Martin, R., Thrift, N. (1994) *Money Power and Space*. Oxford: Blackwell.

Cuervo-Cazurra, A., Stahl, E. (2010) Extending the investment development path explanation of outward foreign direct investment of developing countries: the role of pro-market reforms and regulatory escape. *The 2nd Copenhagen Conference on: 'Emerging Multinationals': Outward Investment from Emerging and Developing Economies*. Copenhagen Business School.

Dharmapala, D., Hines, J. R. (2009) Which countries become tax havens? Journal of Public Economics., 93: 1058–1068.

Deng, P. (2012) The internationalization of Chinese firms: a critical review and future research. *International Journal of Management Review*, 14: 408–427.

Dicken, P. (2003) Places and flows: situating international investment. In G. L. Clark, M. P. Feldman, M. S. Gertler (eds) *Oxford Handbook of Economic Geography*, pp. 125–145. Oxford: Oxford University Press.

Dicken, P. (2011) *Global Shift: Mapping the Changing Contours of the World Economy*. New York: Guilford Press.

Eisenhardt, K. M. (1989) Building theories from case study research. *Academy of Management Review*, 14: 532–550.

French, S., Leyshon, A., Thrift, N. (2009) A very geographical crisis: the making and breaking of the 2007-2008 financial crisis. *Cambridge Journal of Regions Economy and Society*, 2: 287–302.

Fung, H., Yau, J., Zhang, G. (2010) Reported trade figure discrepancy, regulatory arbitrage, and round-tripping: evidence from the China-Hong Kong trade data. *Journal of International Business Studies*, 42: 152–176.

Gaur, A. S., Lu, J. W. (2007) Ownership strategies and survival of foreign subsidiaries: impacts of institutional distance and experience. *Journal of Management*, 33: 84–110.

Ghemawat, P. (2003) Semiglobalization and international business strategy. *Journal of International Business Studies*, 34: 138–152.

Greguras, F., Bassett, B., Zhang, J. (2008) *Update to Doing Business in China via the Cayman Islands*. Fenwick and West LLP. Available online at: http://www.fenwick.com/docstore/Publications/Corporate/2007_Update_Business_China.pdf. [Accessed 8 August 2008].

Hampton, M. P., Christensen, J. (2002) Offshore Pariahs? Small island economics, tax havens, and the re-configuration of global finance. *World Development*, 30: 16.

Hennart, J. F. (2012) Emerging market multinationals and the theory of the multinational enterprise. *Global Strategy Journal*, 2: 168–187.

House of Commons. (HOC). (n.d.). Offshore financial centres. Written evidence (unapproved final record of evidence received by the committee). HOC: Treasury Committee, UK. Available online at: http://www.caymanfinances.com/pdf/OFCWrittenEvidence.pdf. [Accessed 3 July 2010].

Huang, Y. (2003) *Selling China: foreign direct investment during the reform era*. Cambridge, UK: Cambridge University Press.

Hudson, A. (2000) Offshoreness, globalization and sovereignty: a postmodern geo-political economy? *Transactions of the Institute of British Geographers*, 25: 269–283.

IMF. (2004) Volume I: Review of financial sector regulation and supervision. British Virgin Islands. *IMF Country Report*, No. 04/92. Available online at: http://www.imf.org/external/pubs/ft/scr/2004/cr0492.pdf. [Accessed 3 July 2010].

IMF. (2009) Cayman Islands: off-shore financial center assessment update-assessment of financial sector supervision and regulation. *IMF Country Report No. 09/323*: IMF.

Jefferson, G. H., Rawski, T. G. (2002) China's emerging market for property rights: Theoretical and empirical perspectives. *Economics of Transition*, 10: 586–617.

Karreman, B., van der Knaap, B. (2012) The geography of equity listing and financial centre competition in mainland China and Hong Kong. *Journal of Economic Geography*, 12: 899–922.

Kedia, B. L., Mukherjee, D. (2009) Understanding offshoring: A research framework based on disintegration, location and externalization advantages. *Journal of World Business*, 44: 250–261.

Khanna, T., Yafeh, Y. (2007) Business groups in emerging markets: Paragons or parasites? *Journal of Economic Literature*, 45: 331–372.

Knowles, G. (2010) Cayman and BVI – The benefit for China in times of regulatory change. *Offshore Review 2010*. Available online at: http://www.maplesandcalder.com/news/article/cayman-and-bvi-the-benefit-for-china-in-times-of-regulatory-change-86/ [Accessed 3 May 2011].

Kolstad, I., Wiig, A. (2012) What determines Chinese outward FDI? *Journal of World Business*, 47: 26–34.

Kung, F. -H., Cheng, C. -L. (2012) The determinants of overseas listing decisions: evidence from Chinese H-share companies. *Asian Business & Management*, 11: 591–613.

Kuznetsov, A. (2011) *Outward FDI from Russia and its policy context*, update 2011. Columbia FDI Profiles Country profiles of inward and outward foreign direct investment issued by the Vale Columbia Center on Sustainable International Investment, 2 August 2011.

La Porta, R., Lopez-De-Silanes, F., Shleifer, A., Vishny, R. (2002) Investor protection and corporate valuation. *Journal of Finance*, LVII: 1147–1170.

Lai, K. P. Y. (2011) Marketization through contestation: reconfiguring financial markets through knowledge networks. *Journal of Economic Geography*, 11: 87–117.

Lee, R., Clark, G., Pollard, J., Leyshon, A. (2009) The remit of financial geography-before and after the crisis. *Journal of Economic Geography*, 9: 723–747.

Leyshon, A., Thrift, N. (1997) *Money Space: Geographies of Monetary Transformation*. London: Routledge.

Lipsey, R. E. (2007) Defining and measuring the location of FDI output. *National Bureau of Economic Research Working Paper*, 12996.

Lu, F. S., Yao, Y. (2009) The effectiveness of law, financial development, and economic growth in an economy of financial repression: Evidence from China. *World Development*, 37: 763–777.

Luo, Y., Rui, H. (2009) An ambidexterity perspective toward multinational enterprises form emerging economies. *Academy of Management Perspectives*, 23: 49–70.

Luo, Y., Tung, R. L. (2007) International expansion of emerging market enterprises: A springboard perspective. *Journal of International Business Studies*, 38: 481–498.

Luo, Y., Xue, Q., Han, B. (2010) How emerging market governments promote outward FDI: Experience from China. *Journal of World Business*, 45: 68–79.

Luo, Y., Zhao, H., Wang, Y., Xi, Y. (2011) Venturing abroad by emerging market enterprises: a test of dual strategic intents. *Management International Review*, 51: 433–459.

Martin, R. (1999) The new economic geography of money. In R. Martin (ed.) *Money and the Space Economy*, pp. 3–27. New York: Wiley.

Maurer, B., Martin, S. J. (2011) Changes of state, spaces of equity: the aesthetics of value transformation and Chinese offshore incorporation in the British Virgin Islands. Unpublished manuscript.

McCann, P. (2011) International business and economic geography: knowledge, time and transactions costs. *Journal of Economic Geography*, 11: 309–317.

MOFCOM, NBS, SAFE. (2009) 2008 Statistical Bulletin of China's Outward Foreign Direct Investment. Available online at: http://hzs2.mofcom.gov.cn/aarticle/statistic/200909/20090906535723.html [Accessed 7 October 2011].

MOFCOM, NBS, SAFE. (2012) 2011 Statistical Bulletin of China's Outward Foreign Direct Investment. Beijing: China Statistics Press.

Mullings, B. (2004) Globalization and the territorialization of the new Caribbean service economy. *Journal of Economic Geography*, 4: 23.

National Bureau of Statistics of China (NBS). (various years) *China Statistical Yearbook*. Beijing: NBS.

Naughton, B. (2007) *The Chinese economy: transitions and growth*. Cambridge, Mass.: MIT Press.

OECD. (2010) Tax Haven Criteria. Available online at: http://www.oecd.org/document/23/0,3343,en_2649_33745_30575447_1_1_1_1,00.html. [Accessed 24 September 2012].

Palan, R. (2009) The history of tax havens. Available online at: http://www.historyandpolicy.org/papers/policy-paper-92.html [Accessed 24 September 2012].

Palan, R., Murphy, R., Chavagneux, C. (2010) *Tax Havens: How Globalization Really Works*. Ithaca and London: Cornell University Press.

Pike, A., Pollard, J. (2010) Economic geographies of financialization. *Economic Geography*, 86: 29–51.

Pollard, J. S. (2003) Small firm finance and economic geography. *Journal of Economic Geography*, 3: 429–452.

Pryke, M. (2011) Geographies of economic growth II: money and finance. In A. Leyshon, R. Lee, L. McDowell, P. Sunley (eds) *The SAGE Handbook of Economic Geography*, pp. 286–302. London: Sage.

RBI (Reserve Bank of India). (2010) Indian Investment Abroad in Joint Ventures and Wholly Owned Subsidiaries: 2009-10 (April-June). In: Division of International Trade, Department of Economic Analysis and Policy (ed). *RBI Bulletin*. Delhi: RBI.

Roberts, S. (1994) Fictitious capital, fictitious spaces: the geography of offshore financial flows. In S. Corbridge, N. J. Thrift, R. Martin (eds) *Money, Power and Space*, pp. 91–115. Oxford: Blackwell.

Roberts, S. M. (1995) Small place, big money: the Cayman Islands and the International Financial System. *Economic Geography*, 71: 237–256.

Rose, A. K., Spiegel, M. M. (2007) Offshore financial centres: parasites or symbionts? *The Economic Journal*, 117: 1310–1335.

Sarre, P. (2007) Understanding the geography of international finance. *Geography Compass*, 1: 1076–1096.

Securities and Exchange Commission. (SEC). (2010) EDGAR filer manual (volume 2), September 2009. Available online at: http://www.sec.gov/info/edgar/forms/edgform.pdf. [Accessed 27 June 2010].

Seo, B. (2011) Geographies of finance: centers, flows, and relations. *Hitotsubashi Journal of Economics*, 52: 69–86.

Sharman, J. C. (2012) Chinese capital flows and offshore financial centers. *Pacific Review*, 25: 317–337.

Shatz, H. J., Venables, A. J. (2003) The geography of international investment. In G. L. Clark, M. P. Feldman, M. S. Gertler (eds) *Oxford Handbook of Economic Geography*, pp. 125–145. Oxford: Oxford University Press.

Shaxson, N. (2011) *Treasure Islands: Tax Havens and the Men who Stole the World*. London: Bodley Head, Random House.

Shen, Y., Shen, M., Xu, Z., Bai, Y. (2009) Bank size and small- and medium-sized enterprise (SME) lending: Evidence from China. *World Development*, 37: 800–811.

Suntech Power Holdings Co. Ltd. (Suntech). (various years) Form 20-F - Annual and transition report of foreign private issuers. SEC EDGAR filing information. Available online at: http://www.sec.gov/Archives/edgar/data/1342803/000095012310047699/0000950123-10-047699-index.htm. [Accessed 27 June 2010].

Sutherland, D. (2009) China's 'national team' business groups in strategic-asset-seeking OFDI: Are they important? *Chinese Management Studies*, 3: 11–24.

Sutherland, D., Ning, L. (2011) Exploring onward-journey strategies in China's private sector businesses. *Journal of Chinese Economic and Business Studies*, 9: 43–65.

UNCTAD. (2004) *World Investment Directory*. Geneva: UNCTAD.

Vlcek, W. (2013) From road town to Shanghai: situating the Caribbean in global capital flows to China. *British Journal of Politics and International Relations*, 16: 534–553.

Wainwright, T. (2011) Tax doesn't have to be taxing': London's 'onshore' finance industry and the fiscal spaces of a global crisis. *Environment and Planning A*, 43: 1287–1304.

Witt, M. A., Lewin, A. Y. (2007) Outward foreign direct investment as escape response to home country institutional constraints. *Journal of International Business Studies*, 38: 579–594.

Wójcik, D. (2013) Where governance fails: advanced business services and the offshore world. *Progress in Human Geography*, 37: 330–347.

Wójcik, D., Burger, C. (2010) Listing BRICs: Stock Issuers from Brazil, Russia, India, and China in New York, London, and Luxembourg. *Economic Geography*, 86: 275–296.

Wrigley, N. (1999) Corporate finance, leveraged restructuring and the economic landscape: the LBO wave in US food retailing. In R. Martin (ed.) *Money and the Space Economy*, pp. 185–206. New York: Wiley.

Xiao, G. (2004) People's Republic of China's round-tripping FDI: Scale, causes and implications. *Asia Development Bank Institute, Discussion Paper No.7*. Available at: http://www.adbi.org/files/2004.06.dp7.foreign.direct.investment.people.rep.china.implications.pdf.   [Accessed 12 August 2008].

Xinhua Sports and Entertainment Ltd. (Xinhua). (various years). Form 20-F - Annual and transition report of foreign private issuers. SEC EDGAR filing information. Available at: http://www.sec.gov/Archives/edgar/data/1389476/000114554909000720/0001145549-09-000720-index.htm. [Accessed 27 June 2010].

Yeung, H. W.-C. (2009) Transnational corporations, global production networks, and urban and regional development: a geographer's perspective on multinational enterprises and the global economy. *Growth and Change*, 40: 197–226.

Yin, R. K. (2008) *Case Study Research: Design and Methods*, 4th edn. London: Sage.

Zhan, J. (1995) Transnationalization and outward investment: the case of Chinese firms. *Transnational Corporations*, 4: 67–100.

Zhao, M. (2006) Conducting R&D in countries with weak IPR protection. *Management Science*, 52(8): 1185–1199.

Zoromé, A. (2007) *Concept of Offshore Financial Centers: In Search of an Operational Definition*. IMF Working Paper/07/87, Available at: http://www.imf.org/external/pubs/ft/wp/2007/wp0787.pdf [Accessed 3 February 2011].

[12]

Journal of World Business 49 (2014) 611–632

Contents lists available at ScienceDirect

Journal of World Business

journal homepage: www.elsevier.com/locate/jwb

ELSEVIER

Acquisitions by emerging market multinationals: Implications for firm performance

Peter J. Buckley [a,1], Stefano Elia [b,c], Mario Kafouros [a,*]

[a] Centre for International Business, University of Leeds, Maurice Keyworth Building, Leeds LS2 9JT, United Kingdom
[b] DIG-Politecnico di Milano, Piazza Leonardo da Vinci 32, 20133 Milan, Italy
[c] Milano, Italy

ARTICLE INFO

Article history:
Available online 3 January 2014

Keywords:
Emerging countries
FDI
Acquisitions
Performance
Resources
Experience

ABSTRACT

This study develops and tests a framework about the resource- and context-specificity of prior experience in acquisitions. Although extant research has explained why multinational companies from emerging countries (EMNCs) acquire companies in developed countries, we have an incomplete and inconsistent understanding of the consequences of such acquisitions for the performance of target firms. First, we show that despite the concerns raised by politicians and the general public in developed countries, the acquisitions made by EMNCs often enhance the performance of target firms. Second, we examine whether the role of EMNCs' idiosyncratic resources (such as access to new markets and cheap production facilities) and investment experience in enhancing the performance of target firms differs across acquisition contexts. We demonstrate that not all types of resources and investment experience are equally beneficial and, in fact, some types of experience even have a negative effect on the performance of target firms. By contrast, other types of experience that EMNCs accumulate from prior investment enhance the performance of target firms by facilitating resource redeployment and the exploitation of complementarities.

© 2013 Elsevier Inc. All rights reserved.

1. Introduction

Although globalization was for several decades driven by firms from developed nations, multinational companies from emerging countries (EMNCs) are increasingly investing in developed countries by acquiring firms. This entry mode is strategically important because it gives EMNCs quick access to new markets, resources and capabilities. The rise of outward foreign direct investment (OFDI) from emerging economies is a phenomenon that has important theoretical and empirical implications, and has therefore recently attracted considerable scholarly attention. However, extant research on the subject has largely focused on either the characteristics and determinants of OFDI (Buckley et al., 2007; Gammeltoft, 2008; Kalotay, 2008; Li, 2007; Mathews, 2006; Rugman, 2008; Sauvant, 2005) or examined whether established theory can explain the recent internationalization of EMNCs. Hence, although prior studies have offered valuable insights into the determinants of OFDI from emerging economies, little research has analyzed its consequences for performance, leaving an interesting and important question less well understood: "How do the acquisitions of EMNCs influence the performance of target firms in developed countries?". The incomplete understanding of the performance consequences of OFDI not only limits theorizing on international business, but also influences EMNCs' acquisition strategy and the behavior of host-country governments. Indeed, the effectiveness of EMNCs' internationalization depends on how well they understand the conditions shaping the success of their acquisitions in developed countries. Equally, given that the general public and politicians in developed countries only rarely welcome EMNCs' acquisitions (Goldstein, 2007), host-country governments need to identify and attract the type of investors that have the potential to enhance the performance of domestic firms.

To address the above question, we examine how acquisitions from Brazil, Russia, India and China (BRIC) influence the performance of target firms in developed countries. Our analysis extends prior research in two important ways. First, established international business theory has largely been created with developed countries in mind. It thus relies on predictions and assumptions that are not always valid in situations where an EMNC acquires a firm in a developed country (Kuada, 2002). For example, whereas previous studies point to the importance of intangible resources in affecting the performance of target firms acquired by developed market firms (Delios & Beamish, 2001), prior research has shown that EMNCs only rarely possess strong intangible resources and may invest abroad precisely in order to access intangible assets (Ramamurti, 2009). To increase understanding of these differences, we develop and test a conceptual framework that explains the

* Corresponding author. Tel.: +44 0113 343 4588; fax: +44 0113 343 4754.
E-mail addresses: pjb@lubs.leeds.ac.uk (P.J. Buckley), stefano.elia@polimi.it (S. Elia), mk@lubs.leeds.ac.uk (M. Kafouros).
[1] Tel.: +44 0113 343 4588; fax: +44 0113 343 4754.

1090-9516/$ – see front matter © 2013 Elsevier Inc. All rights reserved.
http://dx.doi.org/10.1016/j.jwb.2013.12.013

mechanisms influencing the post-acquisition performance of developed country firms. Our contribution lies in demonstrating how variations in the performance of target firms is explained by the idiosyncratic resources possessed by the acquiring EMNC. More specifically, our analysis contributes to theory on the role of external resources (Lavie, 2006; Rui & Yip, 2008) by explaining how such acquisitions enable target firms to become part of a wider network, exploit complementarities and benefit from the resources owned by other parts of the organization (Capron, Dussauge, & Mitchell, 1998; Capron, 1999; Uhlenbruck, 2004). The findings of the study are surprising and differ significantly from studies that focused on acquisitions made by developed country MNCs (Conyon, Girma, Thompson, & Wright, 2002; Feys & Manigart, 2010, Chap. I; Kyoji, Ito, & Kwon, 2005; Piscitello & Rabbiosi, 2005) or the performance of the acquiring EMNC (Contractor, Kumar, & Kundu, 2007; Garg & Delios, 2007; Gaur & Kumar, 2009).

Our second contribution concerns the role of experience accumulated by EMNCs through previous acquisitions and green-field investment in developed and emerging markets. Inherent contextual properties map onto distinct learning processes and experiences (Muehlfeld, Rao Sahib, & van Witteloostuijn, 2012). Building on the notion of context-specific applicability, we examine whether the experience that EMNCs gain from various investment contexts influences subsequent outcomes in either different-context or similar-context acquisitions. This involves the analysis of whether the usefulness of experiential learning patterns associated with prior investments differs across contexts depending on the type of market entry (greenfield or acquisition) and the investment location (emerging or developed countries). Although prior research has acknowledged that experience influences the success of acquisitions (Barkema & Vermeulen, 1998; Muehlfeld et al., 2012), EMNCs originate from countries that differ significantly from developed countries in their political, economic, cultural and institutional environments (Goldstein, 2007). As such, their experience differs from that of developed country MNEs. We extend the literature on OFDI by demonstrating that not all *types* of experience are equally beneficial. Rather, we find that the performance-enhancing effects of investment experience depend on the context in which experience was gained. This differs from the general tenet that firms become more proficient at managing new investments with each additional investment experience.

The implication for theory and practice is that the direct and moderating role of EMNCs' experience is not equally effective for enhancing the performance of the EMNC's investment pattern. In fact, we find that some types of experience may even have negative consequences for the performance of target firms. Conversely, other types of EMNCs' experience (or a combination of different types of experience) positively moderate the relationship between their resources and the performance of target firms. Overall, the findings suggest that the idiosyncratic characteristics, experience and resources of EMNCs lead to significant differences in the potential synergies and complementarities that EMNCs may exploit when acquiring new firms. They also suggest that different types and locations of investment are associated with a given set of capabilities that is not transferable to other acquisition deals. These idiosyncrasies change the role that firm experience plays in managing resources and new acquisitions and in improving the performance of target firms.

2. Theoretical foundation and hypotheses development

2.1. The post-acquisition role of EMNCs' intangible and tangible resources

After an acquisition, the firms involved may transfer and use each other's resources, create new opportunities and benefit from

potential synergies and complementarities (Lavie, 2006). Nevertheless, firm resources can be used more efficiently or less efficiently. The nature and performance effects of these synergies depend on the type of resources possessed by the target and acquiring firms. Although developed country firms typically possess strong intangible resources such as technology, know-how and brand names (Delios & Beamish, 2001), EMNCs lag behind in this respect (Ramamurti, 2009). Indeed, it has long been established in the international business literature that there is an element of specialization in the global landscape because developed country firms typically have a good grasp of technology (Lane & Beamish, 1990). This view is also supported by a large volume of more recent studies indicating that EMNCs often engage in cross border acquisitions to address this comparative disadvantage, source new intangible resources and knowledge, and become more competitive in the global arena (Athreye & Kapur, 2009; Deng, 2009; Guillén & García-Canal, 2009; Luo & Tung, 2007; Mathews, 2006; Rui & Yip, 2008). Hence, EMNCs usually absorb, rather than transfer, technical and marketing knowledge from target firms located in developed countries. Consequently, EMNCs' intangible assets are likely to have a less significant effect on the performance of developed-country target firms. For these reasons, the theoretical prediction indicating that the performance of target firms is affected by the intangible assets of the acquiring company may not hold when the acquiring firm is an EMNC (Delios & Beamish, 2001).

Nevertheless, EMNCs often possess strong tangible resources because of various home-country-specific advantages including government support, access to cheap capital and oligopolistic market position (Kumar, 2007; Liu, Buck, & Shu, 2005; Morck, Yeung, & Zhao, 2008; Rui & Yip, 2008). The availability of such resources increases the likelihood of benefiting from complementarities between the tangible assets of EMNCs and the knowledge-, marketing- and technology-intensive resources of target firms in developed countries. We propose two mechanisms – *resource redeployment* and *asset divestiture* – through which these benefits occur (Capron et al., 1998; Capron, 1999). Resource redeployment refers to the extent to which the target firm may use the resources of the acquiring EMNC; and may involve the use or transfer of physical assets (e.g. production facilities). Asset divestiture refers to the extent to which the target firm improves its performance by disposing of some of its physical assets or by cutting back its personnel (Capron, 1999). Resource-based and cost-efficiency theories emphasize that resource redeployment and asset divestiture may enhance the performance of target firms by leading not only to revenue-enhancing improvements but also to cost-based synergies.

EMNCs usually have access and can rely on cheap intermediate materials, raw resources and production facilities in their home countries (Buckley et al., 2007; Goldstein, 2007). The low cost and abundance of these tangible resources derives not only from the macro-economic conditions (e.g. cheap wages, large populations, extensive primary resources), but also from the possibility to access cheap capital from EMNCs. Family firms, prevalent in many emerging markets, including India, can count on cheap capital from family members. State owned firms (and state-associated firms) may have capital allocated to them at below market rates – a key example is China. Conglomerate firms, again prevalent in many emerging economies, may operate a biased internal capital market favoring FDI (Buckley et al., 2007). For all these reasons, cheap capital may represent a formidable support to the procurement of cheap tangible resource for many EMNCs, thus providing them with a strong competitive advantage not only in labor-intensive but also in capital-intensive activities.

Hence, target firms in developed countries can become more cost effective by accessing the tangible resources of EMNCs through resource redeployment (i.e. transfer or utilization of such resources). Furthermore, access to EMNCs' tangible resources

P.J. Buckley et al./Journal of World Business 49 (2014) 611–632   613

enables target firms to cut down the amount of manufacturing investment (or concentrate production in one location), sell off less efficient or excess physical assets and eliminate redundant activities, thus increasing efficiency. It also enables target firms that use contracting to bypass markets with high transaction costs and lower the managerial burden associated with off-shoring activities. As a result, they can free up resources, focus on their core competences and pursue new strategic initiatives to enhance their performance.

Beyond gains from cost cutting, access to EMNCs' tangible resources may also increase the ability of target firms to enhance revenues. According to extant research (e.g., Capron, 1999), such revenue-enhancing activities are facilitated by resource redeployment (i.e. by sharing complementary resources). Resource complementarities arise when, for example, the target firm can increase the sales and returns of its new products and innovations by accessing chain stores and other distribution assets and channels owned by the acquiring EMNC in other countries (Schweizer, 2005). Access to tangible resources, such as chain stores and distribution points abroad, may also increase the market coverage of target firms, thus leading to economies of scale and higher market and bargaining power (Gugler, Mueller, Yurtoglu, & Zulehner, 2003). Given that EMNCs' home markets are growing quickly, this is a strong advantage for developed country firms, whose economies are often saturated. This practice may also lead to economies of scope as the target firm can integrate its technologies and know-how across several business units (Feys & Manigart, 2010). In summary, access to EMNCs' tangible resources enables target firms from developed countries to create value and enhance their performance by exploiting cost-based and revenue-enhancing synergies through resource redeployment and asset divestiture. Hence:

Hypothesis 1. EMNCs' tangible resources (rather than intangible resources) enhance the post-acquisition performance of target firms in developed economies.

2.2. The direct and moderating effect of different types of experience

We further argue that the performance of the target firm depends on the experience that the acquiring EMNC accumulates through foreign investment. The overarching argument here is that because prior investment experience facilitates the development of the EMNC's managerial and coordination capabilities, it influences the performance of target firms both *directly* and *indirectly* (i.e., through moderating effects). The direct effect on the performance of target firms occurs when the experience accumulated from previous investments helps EMNCs to manage new deals, avoid pre- and post-acquisition mistakes and challenges, and increase the probability of success. Pre-acquisition challenges and mistakes include the over-valuation of the target company and the difficulty to assess the value of the resources possessed by the target company. Post-acquisition challenges include the strategic integration of the two companies – a process that may lead to conflicts and slow down the performance of target firms (Buckley & Ghauri, 2002). Prior experience may also increase the degree of clarity in the causal relationships between the actions of the EMNC and the performance of the target firm (Zollo & Winter, 2002).

Beyond these direct effects, experience may also moderate the relationship between the resources of the acquiring EMNC and the performance of the target firm through various indirect mechanisms. The availability of resources alone is not a sufficient condition for increasing firm competitiveness (Barney, 1997; Eisenhardt & Martin, 2000; Hitt, Uhlenbruck, & Shimizu, 2006; Winter, 1995). To identify and benefit from potential synergies and complementarities, firms need the organizational capabilities (Newbert, 2007;

Teece, Pisano, & Shuen, 1997) required to re-allocate resources (Leiblein, 2011). Previous investment experience moderates the relationship between EMNCs' resources and target firms' performance by increasing EMNCs' ability to exploit the cost-based and revenue-enhancing synergies discussed in the previous section through resource redeployment and asset divestiture. It also enables EMNCs to appreciate the potential contribution of the target firm (Saxton, 1997), develop coordination capabilities, and more readily identify redundant activities. As well, it enhances the EMNC's institutional capital and international market knowledge, allowing the firm to adapt its resources to the local context and respond to institutional variations and market specificities (Brouthers, Brouthers, & Werner, 2008; Sun & Tse, 2009).

Nevertheless, not all types of investment experience are equally beneficial to all firms. Different types of experience may facilitate the development of different capabilities (Brouthers et al., 2008). The usefulness of prior learning and experience is determined by the context or the configuration of stimuli attached to certain activities (e.g. foreign investment). Hence the context in which experience is accumulated affects the success or failure of subsequent investments and transactions (Muehlfeld et al., 2012). This prompts the need to investigate how variations in the modes of investment experience and the locations in which the acquiring EMNC has invested influence the performance of target firms in developed markets. Accordingly, we distinguish between greenfield and acquisition investment experience, and between investment experience in developed and emerging markets.

Fig. 1 summarizes these two dimensions (i.e., the entry mode dimension and the geographic dimension). Although the cells in Fig. 1 present four key combinations of entry mode and location choices, these combinations are not mutually exclusive – i.e., it is possible that some firms have experience in both greenfield investment and acquisitions or have invested in both emerging and developed markets. Our modeling allows for such variations. In the following sections, we demonstrate how and why some types of investment experience are more effective than others in improving the capability of EMNCs to reallocate and use their resources in a way that enhances the performance of target firms in developed economies. It is important to note that prior experience may influence the effectiveness of both tangible and intangible resources. However, given that the context of our analysis is the acquisitions of EMNCs, the next sections build on Hypothesis 1 and focus on how experience moderates the performance effects of tangible resources.

	Experience in Emerging Markets (59)	Experience in Developed Markets (61)
Acquisition Experience (47)	3 (41)	4 (23)
Greenfield Experience (42)	1 (18)	2 (38)

Fig. 1. EMNCs with different types of experience.

2.2.1. Investment experience associated with the entry mode

Our central argument in Hypothesis 1 is that the tangible resources of EMNCs facilitate ease of takeover, revenue-enhancing improvements and cost-based synergies. Although EMNCs that have previously engaged in foreign investment will be better able to employ their tangible resources to enhance the performance of target firms, we posit that their ability to do so differs depending on whether they have experience in acquisitions (rather than greenfield investment). The challenges associated with acquisitions differ significantly from these associated with greenfield investment. In the case of acquisitions, the EMNC has to integrate carefully the operations and resources of the target firm with its own (Buckley & Ghauri, 2002). As the culture and routines of acquiring and target firms differ, the post-acquisition resource integration process can be time consuming, challenging and costly. EMNCs that have engaged in acquisitions before are familiar with these problems and are better equipped to deal with these issues. By contrast, because firms that have previously only engaged in greenfield investment are less familiar with these challenges, they are less efficient in identifying complementary or supplementary resource combinations. Consequently, the post-acquisition mistakes associated with resource redeployment and asset divestiture are likely to be more pronounced when the acquiring firm has only greenfield experience than when it has acquisition experience.

Furthermore, different entry modes involve different strategies. Greenfield investment is undertaken by firms that want to exploit advantages that are not firm-specific (Harzing, 2002). Conversely, as acquisitions aim at accessing complementary or supplementary resources, they require significant organizational changes in order to achieve synergies (Estrin & Meyer, 2011; Haspeslagh & Jemison, 1991; Hitt, Ireland, Camp, & Sexton, 2001; Jemison & Sitkin, 1986; Zollo & Singh, 2004) and resource redeployment (Capron, 1999; Capron et al., 1998). Such capabilities can be accumulated only through a series of acquisition investments. This argument is also supported by the transaction cost studies that suggest that the more frequently a firm transacts with a specific type of organization, the more its knowledge stock regarding the efficacy and reliability of a given set of practices is likely to increase (Ring & Van de Ven, 1992). On the other hand, whilst firms that focus on greenfield investment learn to operate in a foreign environment, this entry mode does not offer firms the opportunity to learn about a foreign partner (Barkema, Shenkar, Vermeulen, & Bell, 1997). Therefore, EMNCs relying exclusively on greenfield investment are less likely to be able to create value by exploiting cost-based and revenue-enhancing synergies through resource redeployment and asset divestiture. Hence, the acquiring and target firms may become misaligned, thus decreasing the strategic fit of the two companies. Given that a better strategic fit is associated with superior performance (Datta, 1991; Ramaswamy, 1997; Shelton, 1988), target firms acquired by EMNCs that only have greenfield experience are likely to achieve lower performance levels than target firms acquired by EMNCs that have acquisition experience. Hence:

Hypothesis 2. The positive effects of EMNCs' tangible resources on the post-acquisition performance of target firms in developed economies are enhanced when EMNCs have experience in acquisitions (rather than in greenfield investment).

2.2.2. Investment experience in developed and emerging markets

Although some EMNCs, conforming to traditional theory (e.g. Johanson & Vahlne, 1977), start their internationalization in other emerging nations where they can exploit home-country experience and advantages (Ramamurti, 2009), others internationalize in a way that differs from this and invest in developed countries (Mitchell, Shaver, & Yeung, 1994; Mathews, 2006). We argue that EMNCs engaging in the latter internationalization path are better

off by being able to accumulate experience that assists them in undertaking new deals in developed countries. By contrast, the experience that EMNCs accumulate by investing in emerging countries does not sufficiently improve the skills needed to benefit from resource redeployment and asset divestiture in target firms in developed countries. This argument is supported by Madhok (1997) who argued that when there is a lack of experience in a new field of activity, the difficulty of knowledge acquisition is substantially higher, as well as by Barkema et al. (1997) who suggested that a different context erodes the applicability of the acquiring firm's competencies. Hence, when EMNCs do not have investment experience in developed countries, we expect the role of their tangible resources in increasing target firms' performance to work less well in terms of increasing the performance of firms in developed country firms.

Because the economic, political, cultural and social conditions of EMNCs' environments differ fundamentally from the ways in which developed country firms operate (Goldstein, 2007), the experience accumulated from investment in emerging countries may not be particularly useful for target firms in developed economies. Empirical work informed by transaction cost economics suggests that a recurring source of risk in new ventures is the uncertainty of accomplishing activities that require cooperation from others (Ring & Van de Ven, 1992). Whereas uncertainty leads to risk, prior related experience in developed countries facilitates organizational learning and a better understanding of how cost-based and revenue-enhancing synergies can be achieved. The central argument in this literature is that the familiarity and predictability emerging from prior similar acquisitions alters the transaction costs associated with new investments (Gulati, 1995). As firms engage in multiple acquisitions in developed countries, the emergent processes associated with resource redeployment and asset divestiture become more efficient.

In a similar vein, several case studies point to the difficulties arising when developed and emerging country firms cooperate or interact. Hence, although resource redeployment and asset divestiture require the acquiring and target firms to work together, these activities are negatively affected when the acquiring EMNC does not understand the different values, systems and practices adopted by developed market firms (Lane & Beamish, 1990). Conversely, familiarity with these differences helps EMNCs that have investment experience in developed countries to change, use their resources more efficiently and thus improve the performance of target firms. Therefore an important consequence of being familiar with investment in developed countries is that it can alter the value that EMNCs create from new acquisitions in these economies. As Gulati (1995) put it, related experience can engender trust among firms, and trust can limit the transaction costs associated with similar investments in the future.

In summary, we expect EMNCs that have invested in developed countries in the past to have built the capabilities and skills needed for using their resources in ways that will lead to cost-based and revenue-enhancing improvements. We therefore expect that the performance of target firms increases more when they are acquired by EMNCs which already have experience in developed countries. By contrast, EMNCs' experience in emerging countries will have a less significant effect on the performance of target firms in developed markets. This discussion leads us to the following hypothesis:

Hypothesis 3. The positive effects of EMNCs' tangible resources on the post-acquisition performance of target firms in developed economies are enhanced when EMNCs have experience in developed countries (rather than in other countries).

Furthermore, although the resources of firms that have experience in either acquisition investment or investment in developed

P.J. Buckley et al. / Journal of World Business 49 (2014) 611–632   615

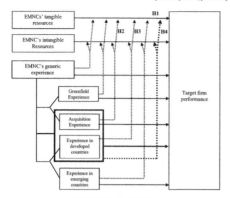

Fig. 2. Conceptual framework.

countries (i.e. cells 2 and 3 in Fig. 1) will positively influence the post-acquisition performance of target firms, we expect these performance-enhancing effects to be higher when EMNCs have acquisition experience in developed countries (i.e. cell 4 in Fig. 1). Hence:

Hypothesis 4. The positive effects of EMNCs' tangible resources on the post-acquisition performance of target firms in developed economies are stronger for EMNCs' that have acquisition experience in developed countries (as opposed to acquisition experience in other countries or greenfield experience in developed or other countries).

Fig. 2 summarizes our conceptual framework. EMNCs' tangible and intangible assets might affect the performance of target firms. However, because of the mechanisms discussed in the previous sections, we expect that only tangible resources have a positive and significant impact on the performance of target firms (H1). Prior investment experience may moderate the effects that EMNCs' tangible resources have on the performance of target firms, but different types of experience have different moderating effects (see the dotted arrows). More specifically, we expect that the positive moderating effect of investment experience is more pronounced when EMNCs have invested in acquisitions (H2) and in developed countries (H3). This effect is likely to be even stronger when the EMNC have both acquisition experience and investment experience in developed countries (H4).

3. Methods

3.1. The sample

The data collection process includes three steps. First, we collected data from Thomson One Banker concerning acquisitions[2] undertaken by EMNCs from BRIC countries into 27 EU countries, USA, Canada and Japan between 2000 and 2007. The final dataset is the result of a careful screening conducted on a large population of deals. To be specific, we excluded (1) deals that were part of 'round tripping',[3] (2) acquisitions undertaken by single investors because they are structurally different from, and hence not comparable

with, acquisitions undertaken by corporate investors[4] and (3) acquisitions undertaken by BRIC firms that were controlled by non-BRIC firms. Given that the parent company is a non-BRIC firm and that international investments decisions are made at the headquarters, this type of investment cannot be classified as acquisition from a BRIC country.

Second, we collected additional firm-level panel data for both the acquiring and target companies for the 1999–2008 period (from Thomson One Banker and Orbis). This enabled us to observe the target and acquiring companies for at least one year before and one year after the deals. The use of a second database also allowed us to increase the number of observations as in some cases data were available in one database only. Finally, we downloaded the balance sheets of the target and acquiring companies from the companies' websites for the period 1999–2008. This was necessary for our analysis because in several cases target firms stopped providing independent and unconsolidated data after the acquisition. Nevertheless, parent companies often provide financial data concerning their subsidiaries within their balance sheets. We were therefore able to examine the performance of target firms after the acquisition even if data were not available from Thomson OneBanker or Orbis.

The final sample includes 79 deals that occurred between 2000 and 2007.[5] The target and acquiring firms are observed for a period of 10 years (1999–2008). Due to missing data, the panel data are composed of 570 observations,[6] but each firm is observed both before and after the acquisition. In our sample, China, India and Russia are responsible for 21, 38 and 18 acquisitions, respectively, while only 2 deals originate from Brazil. Investments are directed towards Western Europe (52 deals), North America (16), Eastern Europe (8) and Japan (3). The predominance of Western Europe is due to the high number of acquisitions (18) undertaken by India in the UK. As for the industries involved in acquisitions, both acquiring and target firms are from a variety of industries ranging from Metal Mining (SIC Code 10) to Engineering, Accounting, Research, Management and Related Services (SIC Code 87).

3.2. Measures

3.2.1. Dependent variables

To capture both the financial and market aspects of firm performance, we take into account the profitability and sales of target firms. Examining different aspects of performance is important since an increase in sales might not lead to higher profitability due to increased costs (e.g. labor, marketing or distribution). The first dependent variable accounts for the profitability of the firm, which is typically operationalized in the literature using either a direct measure of profitability (e.g. Bertrand & Zitouna, 2008) or a profitability index such as ROE or ROS (Capar & Kotabe, 2003; Contractor, Kundu, & Hsu, 2003a,b; Hitt, Hoskisson, & Hicheon, 1997; Lu & Beamish, 2004). We employ the first method because it provides a direct measure of the profit of the firm that can be more easily linked to other performance measure such as sales. Specifically, we employ the variable *Target Firm Profit Variation*, which is measured as the target firm's net income (before taxes) annual difference (i.e. between t and $t - 1$). The second dependent variable that we use, *Target Firm Sales Variation*, is based on sales and is measured using the difference between time t and $t - 1$ of the turnover of the target firms. These two measures enable us to investigate the effect of explicative

---

[2] All deals involve the acquisition of a share of equity of the target firm higher than 50%.

[3] The round-tripping phenomenon occurs when companies undertake investments abroad in order to offshore funds and to bring them back to their home country as inward foreign direct investments. This phenomenon occurs due to financial reasons such as tax avoidance, access to financial incentives that has been allocated to inward FDI. Such investments cannot be considered as foreign direct investments because they involve a temporary transfer of funds.

[4] Some investments were undertaken by individuals (e.g. "Mr. Smith") who purchased large shares (or the entire equity) of the target company. These are therefore portfolio investments rather than foreign direct investment.

[5] 78 when using sales as dependent variables because in one case we had data on profitability but not on sales.

[6] 559 when using sales as dependent variable.

variables on the target firm profit and sales differences rather than on their absolute value, and thus avoid biases associated with the size of the firm. The data have been collected from Thomson One Banker, Orbis and firms' balance sheets.[7]

3.2.2. EMNCs' resources

We measure *EMNCs' Tangible Resources* using the ratio of Tangible Fixed Net Assets to Total Assets of the EMNCs. This proxy is not affected by firm size and thus captures the effective intensity of Tangible Resources. Tangible Fixed Assets refer to "the current value of assets with physical form, such as land, buildings, property and equipment", whereas the Total Assets measure is defined as "the sum of total current assets, long term receivables, investment in unconsolidated subsidiaries, other investments, net property plant, equipment and other assets". We operationalize *EMNCs' Intangible Resources* using the ratio of Intangible Assets to Total Assets of EMNCs. Intangible Assets are defined as "assets not having a physical existence", such as goodwill, patents and trademarks etc.[8] These data were collected from Thomson One Banker, Orbis and firms' balance sheets.

3.2.3. EMNCs foreign direct investments experience

In our conceptual framework we take into account foreign investment experience in developed economies vs. rest of the world, and greenfield vs. acquisitions experience. The generic *EMNCs' Experience* is accounted for through a dummy, taking the value of 1 if the EMNC has, in the year of acquisition in our sample, at least one investment abroad regardless of the nature (greenfield or acquisition) and geographic location. In our sample, 66 out of 79 firms had prior investment experience. To distinguish between greenfield and acquisitions experience, we employed two dummies, namely *EMNCs' Acquisition Experience* and *EMNCs' Greenfield Experience*. The first variable takes the value of 1 if the EMNC has acquired at least one firm before the present acquisition, while the second variable takes the value of 1 if the EMNC has at least one greenfield investment before the acquisition. The two dummies are not mutually exclusive as the EMNC might have engaged in both greenfield investment and acquisitions.

To capture foreign investment experience in developed economies vs. rest of the world we employed two other dummy variables, namely *EMNCs' Experience in Developed Countries* and *EMNCs' Experience in other Countries*. The first variable takes the value of 1 if the EMNCs has invested in developed countries in the past.[9] Similarly, the second variable takes value of 1 if the EMNC has invested in other (emerging or less developed) countries. These two variables, once again, are not mutually exclusive. Finally, to account for the combination of different types of experience as shown in Fig. 1, we introduced four different dummies, i.e. (i) *EMNCs' Acquisition Experience in Developed Countries* (cell 4 in Fig. 1), (ii) *EMNCs' Acquisition Experience in Other Countries* (cell 3 in Fig. 1), (iii) *EMNCs' Greenfield Experience in Developed Countries* (cell 2 in Fig. 1), (iv) *EMNCs' Greenfield Experience in Other Countries* (cell 1 in Fig. 1). These dummies take the value of 1 when foreign investment

occurred in (i) developed countries and is an acquisition, (ii) other countries and is an acquisition, (iii) developed countries and is a greenfield, and (iv) other countries and is a greenfield. To test our hypotheses, we interact different acquisition experience variables with the EMNCs' tangible and intangible resources. Information about the number of firms that have each of the different types of experience at the year of acquisition is reported in Fig. 1.

3.2.4. Control variables

Our estimates take into account several control variables at different levels of analysis, i.e. the target firm's control variables, acquiring firm's control variables, deal-specific control variables and fixed-effects. For the target firm, we control for their tangible and intangible resources as they rely not only on EMNCs' resources but also on their own assets to increase performance. Specifically, we introduce two variables, *Target Firms Tangible Resources* and *Target Firms Intangible Resources*, which are measured in terms of Tangible Fixed Net Assets to Total Assets and Intangible Assets to Total Assets of target firms, respectively. These data were collected from Thomson One Banker and Orbis.[10] Second, we control for the size of the target firm. Large firms perform better because they can exploit economies of scale and scope, and have higher bargaining power (Mansfield, 1962). Nevertheless, small firms have flexible non-hierarchical structures and can adapt better to environmental changes (Yang & Chen, 2009). Although size can be measured in a number of ways (e.g., annual sales, employment and assets), we use the target firms' Total Assets as we do not have detailed data on employment; and we use sales as one of our dependent variables. This operationalization is commonly used in the literature (Dhawan, 2001).[11]

For the acquiring firms, we control for the availability of any of the EMNCs' other resources that might affect the performance of target firms. Public companies typically rely on the stock exchange. Hence, they might be able to undertake larger investment in target firms with a strong impact on performance. Therefore, we employ the variable *EMNCs' Public Company*, a dummy which takes the value of 1 if the company is public. In our sample, 63 EMNCs are public companies. The data are sourced from Thomson OneBanker.

Further, we employ deal-specific control variables. First, we control for the ownership involved in the acquisition. We considered all deals involving the acquisition of more than 50% of the equity of the target firm. Nevertheless, in our sample, 63 transactions refer to full ownership acquisition (i.e. 100% of the equity). Since these two different types of acquisitions might differ in the drivers and mechanisms (i.e. redeployment and divesture, as described above) through which acquiring and target firms use each other's resources, we introduced the variable *Full Ownership*, a dummy taking the value of 1 if the deal involves the takeover of the whole equity of the target firm.

Second, we develop a variable to control for differences in the determinants of acquisitions. Each subsidiary fulfills a specific role and an EMNC might not want to prioritize profitability and sales growth in all the subsidiaries. For instance, an acquisition might help a firm to pursue a supply chain integration strategy through vertical investment. Conversely, horizontal or related investments extend activity in similar or complementary products and markets. A higher degree of overlap between the acquiring and target firm may involve

[7] Net income and sales are expressed in millions of dollars. The values have been deflated through the Consumer Price Indexes provided by the OECD database (we use 2005 as our baseline year).
[8] Specifically, Intangible Assets provided by Thomson OneBanker and Orbis include: Goodwill/Cost in excess of net assets purchased, Patents, Copyrights, Trademarks, Formulae, Franchises of no specific duration, Capitalized software development costs/Computer programs, Organizational costs, Customer lists, Licenses of no specific duration, Capitalized advertising cost, Mastheads (newspapers), Capitalized servicing rights, Purchased servicing right.
[9] We consider in this category the host countries of our sample. Australia and New Zealand have been included in the dummy accounting for previous investments in developed economies even though they have not been taken into account to draw our sample. However, previous investments in these two countries were rare.

[10] Since in most cases data on target firms were available only up to the year of acquisition, and since balance sheets of the acquiring EMNCs tend to report only data on subsidiaries' sales, performance and total assets, we controlled for tangible and intangible resources of target firms by using the value of target firms' tangible and intangible assets (over total assets) in the year of acquisition for the whole period.
[11] Data on the tangible, intangible and total assets of target firms have been collected in U.S. dollars and have been deflated through the Consumer Price Index provided by the OECD database.

P.J. Buckley et al./Journal of World Business 49 (2014) 611–632   617

lower integration costs, efficiency gains through the exploitation of potential synergies and a better strategic fit (Buckley & Ghauri, 2002; Dunning & Lundan, 2007; Rabbiosi, Elia, & Bertoni, 2012). Following Rabbiosi et al. (2012), we control for this using the concept of industrial relatedness between the industries of the acquiring and target firm. We introduce three dummy variables to account for *Horizontal, Vertical* and *Conglomerate* investments, using horizontal investment (which would be expected to result into higher performance) as a benchmark. Our operationalization of industrial relatedness relies on the well-established measure of acquirer-to-target relatedness (Haunschild, 1994; Haleblian & Finkelstein, 1999). Specifically, we consider investments as horizontal if the acquiring and target firms have at least one two-digit SIC code in common. Conversely, we define an acquisition as vertical when the industry of the acquiring firm sells more than 5 per cent of its output to the industry of the target firm or when the industry of the acquiring firm receives more than 5 per cent of its input from the industry of the target firm.[12] The remaining acquisitions have been considered to be conglomerate. In our sample, 40 investments have been classified as horizontal, 31 as conglomerates and the remaining 8 as vertical.

We finally control for fixed effects that may arise from host and home countries, from the industries of the target firms and from year-specific idiosyncrasies. We have controlled for host countries through four dummy variables: *Host Western Europe, Host Eastern Europe, Host North America* (USA + Canada), and *Host Japan*, by using the former as a benchmark. Home countries have been controlled for through three dummy variables for *India, China* and *Russia-Brazil* (we use the former as benchmark). Russia and Brazil have been treated jointly since Brazil accounts only for two observations. These two countries share similar country-specific characteristics driving their foreign direct investments, since they are both resource-abundant countries (Bertoni, Elia, & Rabbiosi, 2012). We finally control for target firms' industry and time fixed-effects using dummy variables.[13]

3.3. Models and estimation method

To test how the explanatory variables affect target firms' performance, we employ the difference between t and $t - 1$ of target firm performance measures as dependent variables, as explained above. The explanatory variables are one-year lagged because EMNCs' resources and experience may take some time before manifesting their effects on target firms. Furthermore, the lagged values of the independent variables allow mitigation of any possible reverse causality problems that may arise from the interaction between the dependent and independent variables.[14] Furthermore, all variables that refer to the EMNCs have been interacted with a deal-specific dummy variable that takes a value of 0 until the year before the acquisition and 1 from the acquisition year onwards. This reflects the fact that, before the acquisition, the target and acquiring firms had no economic relationship. Hence, any apparent relationship between the performance of the target firm and the resources and experience of the EMNC would be spurious in the years before the acquisition. The interaction of the EMNCs'

variables with the dummy that accounts for acquisition ensures that the performance of the target firm depends on the resources and experience of EMNCs only since the year of the acquisition.

Eq. (1) accounts for the relationship between the performance of the target firm and the independent variables:

$$\Delta Target\ Firm\ Performance_d^t = \alpha + \beta_1 EMNCs'\ Resources_d^{t-1}$$
$$+ \beta_2 EMNCs'\ Experience_d^{t-1}$$
$$+ \beta_3 Controls\ d + \epsilon_d^t \qquad (1)$$

where $d = 1, 2, \ldots, 79$ is the deal, t is the year, and $t-1$ accounts for the lagged value of the variables; $\Delta TargetFirmPerformance_d^t$ represents the variation of the performance of the target firm, i.e. *Target Firm Profit Variation* and *Target Firm Sales Variation*; $EMNCs'Resources_d^{t-1}$ is the lagged value of the resources of the EMNCs, which has been distinguished in terms of tangible and intangible resources; $EMNCs'Experience_d^{t-1}$ is the lagged value of experience of the EMNCs, which has been separated into the four types of experience and their possible combinations; $Controls_d$ represents the control variables, and ϵ_d^t is the error term. To examine the moderating effect of EMNCs' experience, we extend Eq. (1) by introducing interaction terms:

$$\Delta Target\ Firm\ Performance_d^t = \alpha + \beta_1 EMNCs'\ Resources_d^{t-1}$$
$$+ \beta_2\ EMNCs'\ Experience_d^{t-1}$$
$$+ \beta_3\ Controls$$
$$+ \beta_4 (EMNCs'Resources_d^{t-1}$$
$$\times \beta_2 EMNCs'\ Experience_d^{t-1})$$
$$+ \epsilon_d^t \qquad (2)$$

To estimate Eqs. (1) and (2), we employ the Feasible Generalized Least Square (FGLS) approach, which produces a matrix-weighted average of the "random effect" and "within" results. Unlike the Generalized Least Square, the FGLS model makes use of an estimate of a variance-covariance matrix instead of assuming that it is known. We adopted the FGLS approach since, as suggested by Petersen (2009), it produces efficient estimates and unbiased standard errors. It also negates the need to introduce the firm dummies that are typically employed to control for fixed effect whenever the independence assumption of the regression can be violated (e.g. in case firms undertake more than one investment). Prior research shows that "including firm dummies or estimating a random effect model with GLS eliminates the biases in the ordinary standard errors only when the firm effect is fixed" (Petersen, 2009, p. 437). These studies distinguish between the fixed and the non-fixed firm effect (the latter arises when the data structure includes a component that is assumed to be a first-order autoregressive process) and show that "the GLS estimates are more efficient than the OLS estimates both with and without firm dummies when the residuals are correlated [...]. The standard errors produced by GLS, however, are unbiased only when the firm effect is permanent" (Petersen, 2009, p. 465). Hence, to assess whether our dependent variables (i.e. the variation between t and $t - 1$ of profit and sales) rely on a first-order autoregressive process, we performed two Wooldridge tests. Both tests do not reject the null hypothesis of absence of autocorrelation (F-test = 1.721 with Prob > F = 0.1935 for the *Target Firm Profit Variation* measure and F-test = 0.094 with Prob > F = 0.7595 for the variable *Target Firm Sales Variation*). Hence, although our performance measures are not affected by temporary firm effects, they might be affected by fixed firm effects. This suggests that the use of FGLS comes with three major advantages (Petersen, 2009): (i) the estimated coefficients are more efficient than the OLS model, (ii) there are unbiased standard errors, and (iii) we can avoid

---

[12] This percentage has been estimated by looking at the input/output tables published annually by the Bureau of Economic Analysis of the US Department of Commerce. Since we used the US input/output, while having a sample that include also other home countries, we assumed that industrial ties are not country-specific and that they reflect cross-country characteristics of the production technology, as it is commonly assumed in other empirical studies (see e.g. Bowen, Leamer, & Sveikauskas, 1987; Mariotti, Piscitello, & Elia, 2010; Rabbiosi et al., 2012).

[13] The industry dummies have been introduced by taking into account the SIC codes of the industry of the target company at 2 digit level. A total of 25 dummies have been introduced for industries, by using SIC Code 10 (metal mining) as benchmark. The time dummies amounts to 10, being the year 1999 the benchmark.

[14] The issue of endogeneity will be discussed in the Robustness Check section.

P.J. Buckley et al. / Journal of World Business 49 (2014) 611–632

Table 1
Correlation matrix of the dependent and explicative variables.

	1)	2)	3)	4)	5)	6)	7)	8)	9)	10)	11)	12)	13)	14)	15)	16)	17)	18)	19)	20)	21)
1) Target Firm Profit Variation	1.000																				
2) Target Firm Sales Variation	0.573	1.000																			
3) EMNCs' Tangible Resources	0.045	0.124	1.000																		
4) EMNCs' Intangible Resources	-0.003	-0.016	0.229	1.000																	
5) EMNCs' Experience	0.034	0.079	0.734	0.407	1.000																
6) EMNCs' Acquisition Experience	0.035	0.097	0.592	0.386	0.785	1.000															
7) EMNCs' Greenfield Experience	0.003	0.009	0.544	0.414	0.776	0.431	1.000														
8) EMNCs' Experience in Developed Countries	0.031	0.106	0.670	0.433	0.935	0.687	0.830	1.000													
9) EMNCs' Experience in Other Countries	0.035	0.084	0.697	0.390	0.953	0.794	0.734	0.882	1.000												
10) EMNCs' Acquisition Experience in Developed Countries	0.041	0.157	0.312	0.169	0.494	0.630	0.060	0.528	0.477	1.000											
11) EMNCs' Acquisition Experience in Other Countries	0.039	0.099	0.594	0.332	0.710	0.905	0.322	0.598	0.745	0.416	1.000										
12) EMNCs' Greenfield Experience in Developed Countries	0.005	0.004	0.543	0.376	0.714	0.322	0.921	0.764	0.665	-0.145	0.380	1.000									
13) EMNCs' Greenfield Experience in Other Countries	0.003	0.000	0.286	0.161	0.520	0.040	0.670	0.556	0.546	0.184	-0.152	0.508	1.000								
14) Target Firms' Tangible Resources	0.038	0.100	0.037	-0.156	-0.066	0.001	-0.124	-0.028	-0.060	0.132	0.016	-0.133	-0.109	1.000							
15) Target Firms' Intangible Resources	-0.008	-0.037	-0.106	0.014	-0.051	-0.024	-0.052	-0.048	-0.087	-0.007	-0.054	-0.051	-0.061	-0.294	1.000						
16) Target Firms Size	0.251	0.359	0.022	-0.004	0.048	0.102	-0.001	0.052	0.060	0.124	0.080	-0.033	-0.011	0.218	-0.094	1.000					
17) EMNCs Public Company	-0.030	0.013	0.529	0.168	0.550	0.479	0.442	0.406	0.531	0.572	0.361	0.345	0.298	-0.051	-0.055	0.038	1.000				
18) Full Ownership	-0.060	-0.020	0.385	0.298	0.423	0.232	0.266	0.370	0.391	0.223	0.431	0.262	0.039	-0.135	-0.064	-0.094	0.522	1.000			
19) Conglomerate Investment	-0.075	-0.034	0.249	0.182	0.284	0.232	0.087	0.185	0.238	0.122	0.249	0.123	0.041	-0.079	0.005	-0.009	0.229	0.388	1.000		
20) Horizontal Investment	0.044	0.057	0.343	0.249	0.440	0.366	0.436	0.469	0.437	0.267	0.281	0.343	0.295	-0.106	-0.027	0.049	0.590	0.374	-0.271	1.000	
21) Vertical Investment	-0.002	-0.014	0.268	-0.011	0.144	0.058	0.160	0.163	0.158	0.007	0.081	0.184	0.132	0.019	-0.070	-0.056	0.300	0.136	-0.113	-0.136	1.000

Table 2
Descriptive statistics of the dependent and explicative variables.

Variable	Observations	Mean	Std. Dev.	Min	Max
1) Target Firm Profit Variation	570	0.000	0.032	−0.296	0.469
2) Target Firm Sales Variation	559	0.058	0.650	−4.421	11.471
3) EMNCs' Tangible Resources	570	0.132	0.224	0.000	0.971
4) EMNCs' Intangible Resources	570	0.029	0.085	0.000	0.527
5) EMNCs' Experience	570	0.286	0.452	0.000	1.000
6) EMNCs' Acquisition Experience	570	0.198	0.399	0.000	1.000
7) EMNCs' Greenfield Experience	570	0.195	0.396	0.000	1.000
8) EMNCs' Experience in Developed Countries	570	0.260	0.439	0.000	1.000
9) EMNCs' Experience in Other Countries	570	0.267	0.443	0.000	1.000
10) EMNCs' Acquisition Experience in Developed Countries	570	0.089	0.286	0.000	1.000
11) EMNCs' Acquisition Experience in Other Countries	570	0.168	0.375	0.000	1.000
12) EMNCs' Greenfield Experience in Developed Countries	570	0.170	0.376	0.000	1.000
13) EMNCs' Greenfield Experience in Other Countries	570	0.098	0.298	0.000	1.000
14) Target Firms' Tangible Resources	570	0.273	0.220	0.000	0.869
15) Target Firms' Intangible Resources	570	0.051	0.114	0.000	0.658
16) Target Firms Size	570	0.006	0.975	−0.274	11.232
17) EMNCs Public Company	570	0.379	0.486	0.000	1.000
18) Full Ownership	570	0.305	0.461	0.000	1.000
19) Conglomerate Investment	570	0.188	0.391	0.000	1.000
20) Horizontal Investment	570	0.240	0.428	0.000	1.000
21) Vertical Investment	570	0.053	0.223	0.000	1.000

controlling for fixed effects through firms' dummies, a process which would generate a degree of freedom problems.

4. Results

Tables 1 and 2 provide the correlation matrix and the descriptive statistics. The highest correlations refer to variables that are used alternatively in the model (e.g. *EMNCs' Experience* and the other more specific types of experience, i.e. Acquisition, Greenfield, Developed Countries, Other countries). However, given that there are still some high correlations, we estimated the Variance Inflation Factors (VIF) to control for potential multi-collinearity problems, as specified below. Furthermore, following the usual practice, the variables of the interaction terms have been mean centered to mitigate any multicollinearity problems.

The results of the FGLS regressions are reported in Tables 3, 4a, 4b, 5a and 5b. The results of Table 3 rely on the generic experience of EMNCs without specifying the geographic and entry mode dimensions.[15] Columns 1 and 4 report the results for the main model, whereas columns 2, 3, 5 and 6 report the interaction effects of EMNCs' experience with EMNCs' tangible and intangible resources. *EMNCs' Tangible Resources* have a positive and significant effect on the sales performance of target firms, but not on their profitability. These results provide partial support for H1. By contrast, the effects of intangible resources are statistically insignificant. In addition, EMNCs' (generic) experience does not exhibit any statistically significant moderating effect, prompting the need to take a more detailed account of EMNCs' experience.

Tables 4a and 4b distinguish between different types of investment experience, and report the effects on target firm profitability and sales performance, respectively.[16] Column 1 in both Tables 4a and 4b displays the results of the main model, while the other columns report the interactions between the tangible

and intangible resources and the four different types of experience. Sales performance is directly affected by EMNCs' tangible resources, thus partially confirming H1. Investment experience in developed countries, regardless of whether it is greenfield or acquisition, has a positive direct effect on the sales of target firms. Conversely, EMNCs' greenfield experience has a negative and significant direct impact on both profitability and sales performance, even though the effect is stronger on the latter than the former. As for the moderating effect of EMNCs' experience, the results provide partial support for H2. Column 2 in Table 4b indicates that EMNCs' acquisition experience positively moderates the relationship between EMNCs' tangible resources and target firms' sales. Yet, the opposite is true regarding the moderating effect of EMNC's greenfield experience, which exhibits a negative moderating effect on EMNCs' tangible resources with sales. Also, the interaction effect of acquisition experience and tangible resources is not significant when considering target firm profitability. Therefore H2 is only partially confirmed. Furthermore, the results do not support H3. As column 3 in both Tables 4a and 4b indicates, the effects of tangible resources on firm performance (as well as that of intangible resources in columns 5) are not moderated by EMNCs' acquisition experience in developed countries. Conversely, EMNCs' experience in other countries has a slightly positive moderating effect ($p < 0.10$) on EMNCs' tangible resources when considering sales variation as a performance measure.

Finally, Tables 5a and 5b introduce the combination of different types of experience as described in Fig. 1.[17] Tables 5a and 5b refer to target firms' profitability and sales performance, respectively. Table 5b shows that EMNCs' tangible resources still have a positive and significant impact on the sales performance of target firms. The corresponding effect on profit variation in Table 5a is not equally strong, thus providing a partial support for H1. It is worth noting that EMNCs' acquisition experience in developed countries (cell 4 in Fig. 1) has a positive and statistically significant effect on sales. The same variable displays a positive moderating effect on EMNCs' tangible resources with both target firm profitability and sales as can be seen in column 2. By contrast, EMNCs' intangible resources do not influence target performance, neither directly nor through moderating effects. The results therefore fully support our predictions and H4. The results also show that the greenfield

---

[15] The highest VIF of this specification is 6.86 and is due to the variable *Target Firms' Tangible Resources*, while the average VIF is 2.53, thus both values are below the threshold of 10 (O'Brien, 2007).

[16] The highest VIFs of this specification are 14.57 and 14.09 and refer to the variables accounting for previous investments in developed countries and previous investments in other countries. Given that these values are above the threshold of 10, we run additional regressions by introducing firstly only the two variables accounting for experience in developed and in other countries, and then only the two variables accounting for the acquisition and greenfield experience. The results were confirmed when we used these alternative specifications separating experience in developed and in other countries from acquisition and greenfield experience.

[17] In this specification, the variable Greenfield Experience in Developed Countries displays the highest VIF, being equal to 7.48, while the average VIF amounts to 2.79, thus below the threshold of 10.

P.J. Buckley et al./Journal of World Business 49 (2014) 611–632

Table 3
Results of the FGLS regressions: the role of generic experience.

Explicative variables	Target firm profit variation			Target firm sales variation		
	1)	2)	3)	4)	5)	6)
H1: EMNCs' Tangible Resources	0.014	0.018	0.012	0.574***	0.286	0.567***
	(1.36)	(1.13)	(1.13)	(2.80)	(0.92)	(2.63)
EMNCs' Intangible Resources	−0.012	−0.014	0.015	−0.462	−0.321	−0.345
	(−0.61)	(−0.67)	(0.27)	(−1.19)	(−0.79)	(−0.31)
EMNCs' Experience	0.005	0.006	0.005	0.025	−0.029	0.026
	(0.94)	(0.99)	(0.95)	(0.23)	(−0.24)	(0.23)
Target Firms' Tangible Resources	0.014	0.015	0.015	−0.071	−0.096	−0.070
	(1.26)	(1.28)	(1.29)	(−0.31)	(−0.42)	(−0.31)
Target Firms' Intangible Resources	0.013	0.014	0.013	0.100	0.059	0.101
	(0.66)	(0.68)	(0.67)	(0.26)	(0.15)	(0.26)
Target Firms Size	0.011***	0.011***	0.011***	0.244***	0.244***	0.244***
	(7.09)	(7.10)	(7.10)	(8.01)	(8.01)	(8.01)
EMNCs Public Company	−0.003	−0.003	−0.003	−0.155	−0.146	−0.155*
	(−0.65)	(−0.67)	(−0.66)	(−1.64)	(−1.54)	(−1.65)
Full Ownership	−0.003	−0.003	−0.003	0.058	0.067	0.058
	(−0.74)	(−0.76)	(−0.77)	(0.72)	(0.82)	(0.71)
Conglomerate Investment	−0.008	−0.008	−0.008	−0.147	−0.137	−0.148
	(−1.48)	(−1.50)	(−1.53)	(−1.46)	(−1.35)	(−1.46)
Vertical Investment	−0.003	−0.003	−0.003	−0.131	−0.118	−0.131
	(−0.35)	(−0.37)	(−0.34)	(−0.90)	(−0.81)	(−0.90)
Host Eastern Europe	−0.002	−0.002	−0.002	−0.047	−0.046	−0.047
	(−0.32)	(−0.32)	(−0.33)	(−0.37)	(−0.37)	(−0.38)
Host Japan	−0.005	−0.005	−0.005	−0.001	−0.024	−0.001
	(−0.61)	(−0.57)	(−0.61)	(−0.01)	(−0.15)	(−0.01)
Host North America	−0.004	−0.004	−0.004	0.041	0.047	0.041
	(−0.94)	(−0.96)	(−0.95)	(0.49)	(0.56)	(0.49)
Russia-Brazil	−0.006	−0.005	−0.006	0.197*	0.175	0.198*
	(−0.93)	(−0.88)	(−0.93)	(1.67)	(1.47)	(1.67)
China	0.003	0.003	0.003	0.034	0.039	0.034
	(0.50)	(0.49)	(0.51)	(0.31)	(0.36)	(0.31)
EMNCs' Tangible Resources × EMNCs' Experience		−0.007			0.522	
		(−0.31)			(1.23)	
EMNCs' Intangible Resources × EMNCs' Experience			−0.032			−0.135
			(−0.52)			(−0.11)
Constant	−0.034***	−0.034***	−0.034***	−0.168	−0.146	−0.168
	(−2.84)	(−2.86)	(−2.85)	(−0.72)	(−0.63)	(−0.72)
Dummy Year	Yes	Yes	Yes	Yes	Yes	Yes
Dummy Target Industry	Yes	Yes	Yes	Yes	Yes	Yes
Number of groups	79	79	79	78	78	78
Number of observations	570	570	570	559	559	559
Chi-square	81.096***	81.204***	81.403***	135.426***	137.297***	135.442***

* $p < 0.1$.
** $p < 0.05$.
*** $p < 0.01$.

experience in developed countries (cell 2 in Fig. 1) negatively moderates the effect of EMNCs' tangible resources on performance. Further, EMNCs' public companies and conglomerate investments perform slightly worse in terms of sales.

5. Robustness checks

We performed several tests to assess the robustness of the results. First, endogeneity might arise from some independent variables being correlated with unobserved factors that affect performance. A higher level of EMNCs' tangible and intangible resources, for instance, might be correlated with a higher ability to search, find and make a better deal that might result in a better post-acquisition performance. Moreover, because EMNCs and target firms might set up their resources with a specific performance outcome in mind, performance might not be the consequence but the determinant of the resources.[18] To deal with this issue, we employed the GMM-SYS approach suggested by Blundell and Bond (1998). This provides a GMM estimator as a result of both first-differenced and levels equations. We trans-

formed the main model accordingly (see Eq. (3)) by setting the level of performance at time t as the dependent variable and by including the lagged value of the dependent variable as an explanatory variable. As shown by prior studies (e.g., Chesher, 1979), such modelling under the presence of autocorrelation can provide evidence on the dynamics of target firm performance (rather than the absolute level). Endogenous variables have been instrumented using their lagged absolute and first-differenced values as well as using exogenous variables such as time and EMNCs' industry dummies[19]

$$Target\ Firm\ Performance_d^t = \alpha + \beta_1\ Target\ Firm\ Performance_d^{t-1}$$
$$+ \beta_2\ EMNCs'\ Resources_d^{t-1}$$
$$+ \beta_3\ EMNCs'\ Experience_d^{t-1}$$
$$+ \beta_4\ Controls\ d + \epsilon_d^t \qquad (3)$$

---

[18] The use of lagged values of both EMNC's and target firms' variables is likely to mitigate this problem, but the variables could still be predetermined.

[19] The industry dummies that have been used as external exogenous variables refer to EMNCs' 2 digit sectors, which are likely to be more correlated with the endogenous variables related to EMNCs than target firm's industry dummies. Given the high amount of horizontal and vertical investments, EMNCs' industry dummies are likely to be good instruments also for the endogenous variables referring to target firm.

P.J. Buckley et al./Journal of World Business 49 (2014) 611–632

621

Table 4a
Results of the FGLS regressions: acquisition vs. greenfield experience and experience in developed countries vs. other countries – target firm profit variation.

Explicative variables	Target firm profit variation				
	1)	2)	3)	4)	5)
H1: EMNCs' Tangible Resources	0.017* (1.67)	0.018 (1.31)	0.014 (0.98)	0.017* (1.65)	0.015 (1.45)
EMNCs' Intangible Resources	−0.007 (−0.33)	−0.007 (−0.34)	−0.005 (−0.23)	−0.014 (−0.31)	0.011 (0.20)
EMNCs' Acquisition Experience	−0.002 (−0.26)	−0.005 (−0.61)	−0.002 (−0.27)	−0.002 (−0.23)	−0.002 (−0.28)
EMNCs' Greenfield Experience	−0.014* (−1.89)	−0.006 (−0.59)	−0.014* (−1.91)	−0.015* (−1.92)	−0.013* (−1.77)
EMNCs' Experience in Developed Countries	0.009 (1.00)	0.010 (1.04)	0.008 (0.71)	0.010 (1.07)	0.008 (0.89)
EMNCs' Experience in Other Countries	0.006 (0.70)	0.002 (0.19)	0.007 (0.58)	0.006 (0.62)	0.007 (0.77)
Target Firms' Tangible Resources	0.016 (1.39)	0.015 (1.33)	0.016 (1.36)	0.016 (1.36)	0.017 (1.43)
Target Firms' Intangible Resources	0.011 (0.56)	0.010 (0.48)	0.011 (0.54)	0.012 (0.60)	0.011 (0.56)
Target Firms Size	0.011*** (7.13)	0.011*** (7.10)	0.011*** (7.13)	0.011*** (7.13)	0.011*** (7.12)
EMNCs Public Company	−0.003 (−0.68)	−0.003 (−0.61)	−0.003 (−0.68)	−0.003 (−0.65)	−0.003 (−0.60)
Full Ownership	−0.003 (−0.82)	−0.004 (−1.05)	−0.003 (−0.78)	−0.003 (−0.73)	−0.004 (−0.86)
Conglomerate Investment	−0.008 (−1.49)	−0.008 (−1.61)	−0.007 (−1.45)	−0.008 (−1.53)	−0.008 (−1.60)
Vertical Investment	−0.001 (−0.19)	−0.000 (−0.02)	−0.001 (−0.16)	−0.002 (−0.22)	−0.002 (−0.24)
Host Eastern Europe	−0.003 (−0.45)	−0.002 (−0.26)	−0.003 (−0.45)	−0.003 (−0.41)	−0.003 (−0.46)
Host Japan	−0.005 (−0.61)	−0.003 (−0.37)	−0.005 (−0.64)	−0.005 (−0.58)	−0.005 (−0.59)
Host North America	−0.004 (−0.85)	−0.003 (−0.71)	−0.004 (−0.84)	−0.003 (−0.82)	−0.004 (−0.88)
Russia-Brazil	−0.009 (−1.42)	−0.009 (−1.39)	−0.009 (−1.45)	−0.009 (−1.45)	−0.009 (−1.38)
China	0.002 (0.36)	0.005 (0.79)	0.002 (0.36)	0.002 (0.39)	0.002 (0.41)
H2: EMNCs' Tangible Resources × EMNCs' Acquisition Experience		0.027 (1.33)			
EMNCs' Tangible Resources × EMNCs' Greenfield Experience		−0.028 (−1.27)			
H3: EMNCs' Tangible Resources × EMNCs' Experience in Developed Countries			0.007 (0.21)		
EMNCs' Tangible Resources × EMNCs' Experience in Other Countries			−0.001 (−0.02)		
EMNCs' Intangible Resources × EMNCs' Acquisition Experience				−0.012 (−0.27)	
EMNC' Intangible Resources × EMNC' Greenfield Experience				0.021 (0.44)	
EMNCs' Intangible Resources × EMNCs' Experience in Developed Countries					0.037 (0.34)
EMNCs' Intangible Resources × EMNCs' Experience in Other Countries					−0.060 (−0.63)
Constant	−0.036*** (−3.01)	−0.037*** (−3.09)	−0.035*** (−2.97)	−0.036*** (−3.01)	−0.036*** (−3.04)
Dummy Year	Yes	Yes	Yes	Yes	Yes
Dummy Target Industry	Yes	Yes	Yes	Yes	Yes
Number of groups	79	79	79	79	79
Number of observations	570	570	570	570	570
Chi-Square	85.418***	88.781***	85.511***	85.674***	85.993***

* $p < 0.1$.
** $p < 0.05$.
*** $p < 0.01$.

The results of the GMM-SYS analysis are reported in Tables 6, 7a, 7b, 8a and 8b in the appendix. In all these tables, the null hypothesis of no first-order autocorrelation is rejected (unlike the hypothesis of second-order autocorrelation), thus confirming the presence of an autoregressive relationship between the dependent variable and its lagged value. The Hansen test confirms the validity of the instruments. The new results are similar to those reported earlier. Hypothesis 1 is still partially confirmed as EMNCs' tangible

resources have a positive effect on target firms' sales performance. The results also confirm H2, as regards to the interaction effect of EMNCs' acquisition experience with EMNCs' tangible resources on sales performance (Tables 7a and 7b). By contrast, H3, regarding the moderating effect of EMNCs' experience in developed countries on EMNC's tangible resources, is not confirmed for any of the performance measures. Finally, Tables 8a and 8b show that the effect of EMNCs' tangible resources on both profitability and sales

P.J. Buckley et al./Journal of World Business 49 (2014) 611–632

Table 4b
Results of the FGLS regressions: acquisition vs. greenfield experience and experience in developed countries vs. other countries – target firm sales variation.

Explicative variables	Target firm sales variation				
	1)	2)	3)	4)	5)
H1: EMNCs' Tangible Resources	0.557***	0.441*	0.151	0.573***	0.561***
	(2.82)	(1.70)	(0.54)	(2.83)	(2.70)
EMNCs' Intangible Resources	−0.423	−0.328	−0.124	−0.865	−0.382
	(−1.06)	(−0.79)	(−0.30)	(−0.99)	(−0.35)
EMNCs' Acquisition Experience	−0.075	−0.255*	−0.088	−0.072	−0.066
	(−0.56)	(−1.72)	(−0.65)	(−0.53)	(−0.48)
EMNCs' Greenfield Experience	−0.451***	−0.155	−0.481***	−0.486***	−0.457***
	(−3.16)	(−0.82)	(−3.35)	(−3.29)	(−3.17)
EMNCs' Experience in Developed Countries	0.448**	0.497***	0.554**	0.494***	0.455**
	(2.47)	(2.74)	(2.47)	(2.65)	(2.48)
EMNCs' Experience in Other Countries	0.010	−0.186	−0.214	−0.015	−0.001
	(0.06)	(−1.02)	(−0.91)	(−0.08)	(−0.01)
Target Firms' Tangible Resources	−0.066	−0.114	−0.142	−0.079	−0.071
	(−0.29)	(−0.50)	(−0.62)	(−0.34)	(−0.31)
Target Firms' Intangible Resources	−0.061	−0.165	−0.170	−0.025	−0.061
	(−0.15)	(−0.42)	(−0.43)	(−0.06)	(−0.15)
Target Firms Size	0.247***	0.244***	0.245***	0.246***	0.247***
	(8.14)	(8.17)	(8.12)	(8.14)	(8.15)
EMNCs Public Company	−0.146	−0.125	−0.128	−0.141	−0.154
	(−1.55)	(−1.35)	(−1.36)	(−1.50)	(−1.61)
Full Ownership	0.038	−0.012	0.048	0.053	0.040
	(0.47)	(−0.15)	(0.59)	(0.64)	(0.49)
Conglomerate Investment	−0.156	−0.178*	−0.161	−0.167*	−0.146
	(−1.57)	(−1.80)	(−1.61)	(−1.66)	(−1.43)
Vertical Investment	−0.098	−0.031	−0.106	−0.107	−0.090
	(−0.68)	(−0.22)	(−0.73)	(−0.74)	(−0.62)
Host Eastern Europe	−0.080	−0.024	−0.061	−0.071	−0.080
	(−0.64)	(−0.19)	(−0.49)	(−0.57)	(−0.64)
Host Japan	−0.015	0.058	−0.049	−0.007	−0.016
	(−0.10)	(0.38)	(−0.32)	(−0.05)	(−0.10)
Host North America	0.054	0.083	0.069	0.060	0.055
	(0.65)	(1.01)	(0.83)	(0.73)	(0.66)
Russia–Brazil	0.079	0.072	0.035	0.070	0.075
	(0.65)	(0.59)	(0.28)	(0.57)	(0.62)
China	−0.008	0.114	0.023	0.001	−0.011
	(−0.07)	(1.00)	(0.21)	(0.01)	(−0.10)
H2: EMNCs' Tangible Resources × EMNCs' Acquisition Experience		1.431***			
		(3.71)			
EMNCs' Tangible Resources × EMNCs' Greenfield Experience		−1.049**			
		(−2.48)			
H3: EMNCs' Tangible Resources × EMNCs' Experience in Developed Countries			−0.116		
			(−0.19)		
EMNCs' Tangible Resources × EMNCs' Experience in Other Countries			1.092*		
			(1.84)		
EMNCs' Intangible Resources × EMNCs' Acquisition Experience				−0.359	
				(−0.43)	
EMNCs' Intangible Resources × EMNCs' Greenfield Experience				0.946	
				(1.04)	
EMNCs' Intangible Resources × EMNCs' Experience in Developed Countries					−1.017
					(−0.49)
EMNCs' Intangible Resources × EMNCs' Experience in Other Countries					0.998
					(0.54)
Constant	−0.219	−0.253	−0.149	−0.219	−0.209
	(−0.95)	(−1.11)	(−0.64)	(−0.95)	(−0.90)
Dummy Year	Yes	Yes	Yes	Yes	Yes
Dummy Target Industry	Yes	Yes	Yes	Yes	Yes
Number of groups	78	78	78	78	78
Number of observations	559	559	559	559	559
Chi-Square	149.796***	172.111***	157.789***	151.206***	150.177***

* $p < 0.1$.
** $p < 0.05$.
*** $p < 0.01$.

is positively moderated by EMNCs' acquisition experience in developed countries, thus fully confirming H4.

Second, we tried to assess whether the effects of the model are consistent over longer time lags. Specifically, we re-ran the FGLS regressions, lagging our explicative variables by either 1 or 2 years. The results, which are not shown in the tables but are available

upon request, indicate that the effects of lagged EMNC's resources on target firms' performance measures become insignificant after the second lagged year.

Third, we checked the sensitivity of our results to industrial sectors that exhibit common characteristics. Specifically, we explored variations across manufacturing (in which we included

P.J. Buckley et al./Journal of World Business 49 (2014) 611–632

Table 5a
Results of the FGLS regressions: acquisition experience in developed countries vs. other types of experience – target firm profit variation.

Explicative variables	Target firm profit variation				
	1)	2)	3)	4)	5)
H1: EMNCs' Tangible Resources	0.015	0.010	0.028**	0.014	0.016
	(1.53)	(0.81)	(2.32)	(1.32)	(1.52)
EMNCs' Intangible Resources	−0.012	−0.013	−0.022	0.008	−0.013
	(−0.60)	(−0.62)	(−1.05)	(0.22)	(−0.37)
EMNCs' Acquisition Experience in Developed Countries (cell 4 in Fig. 1)	0.005	−0.004	0.005	0.005	0.005
	(0.56)	(−0.45)	(0.62)	(0.60)	(0.56)
EMNCs' Acquisition Experience in Other Countries (cell 3 in Fig. 1)	0.006	0.008	0.003	0.006	0.006
	(0.75)	(0.87)	(0.44)	(0.77)	(0.73)
EMNCs' Greenfield Experience in Developed Countries (cell 2 in Fig. 1)	−0.001	0.001	0.009	−0.001	−0.001
	(−0.12)	(0.08)	(0.85)	(−0.11)	(−0.13)
EMNCs' Greenfield Experience in Other Countries (cell 1 in Fig. 1)	0.000	−0.001	−0.004	−0.000	0.001
	(0.04)	(−0.06)	(−0.30)	(−0.02)	(0.07)
Target Firms' Tangible Resources	0.015	0.015	0.016	0.015	0.015
	(1.31)	(1.27)	(1.39)	(1.30)	(1.31)
Target Firms' Intangible Resources	0.010	0.012	0.013	0.011	0.010
	(0.51)	(0.61)	(0.65)	(0.57)	(0.51)
Target Firms Size	0.011***	0.011***	0.011***	0.011***	0.011***
	(7.05)	(7.15)	(7.11)	(7.04)	(7.04)
EMNCs Public Company	−0.004	−0.004	−0.004	−0.004	−0.004
	(−0.79)	(−0.83)	(−0.76)	(−0.74)	(−0.80)
Full Ownership	−0.004	−0.004	−0.005	−0.003	−0.003
	(−0.84)	(−0.87)	(−1.12)	(−0.73)	(−0.78)
Conglomerate Investment	−0.007	−0.008	−0.008*	−0.008	−0.008
	(−1.47)	(−1.52)	(−1.65)	(−1.59)	(−1.47)
Vertical Investment	−0.001	0.001	−0.001	−0.001	−0.001
	(−0.14)	(0.14)	(−0.07)	(−0.19)	(−0.15)
Host Eastern Europe	−0.003	−0.002	−0.002	−0.003	−0.003
	(−0.47)	(−0.28)	(−0.33)	(−0.44)	(−0.47)
Host Japan	−0.004	−0.005	−0.003	−0.004	−0.004
	(−0.56)	(−0.59)	(−0.31)	(−0.51)	(−0.56)
Host North America	−0.004	−0.003	−0.003	−0.004	-0.004
	(−0.87)	(−0.70)	(−0.80)	(−0.83)	(−0.87)
Russia-Brazil	−0.007	−0.010	−0.007	−0.007	−0.007
	(−1.20)	(−1.59)	(−1.17)	(−1.23)	(−1.20)
China	0.004	0.005	0.005	0.004	0.004
	(0.66)	(0.85)	(0.82)	(0.70)	(0.66)
H4: EMNCs' Tangible Resources × EMNCs' Acquisition Experience in Developed Countries		0.057**			
		(2.26)			
EMNCs' Tangible Resources × EMNCs' Acquisition Experience in Other Countries		−0.010			
		(−0.41)			
EMNCs' Tangible Resources × EMNCs' Greenfield Experience in Developed Countries			−0.039*		
			(−1.81)		
EMNCs' Tangible Resources × EMNCs' Greenfield Experience in Other Countries			0.001		
			(0.03)		
EMNCs' Intangible Resources × EMNCs' Acquisition Experience in Developed Countries				−0.026	
				(−0.51)	
EMNCs' Intangible Resources × EMNCs' Acquisition Experience in Other Countries				−0.024	
				(−0.59)	
EMNCs' Intangible Resources × EMNCs' Greenfield Experience in Developed Countries					0.003
					(0.07)
EMNCs' Intangible Resources × EMNCs' Greenfield Experience in Other Countries					−0.004
					(−0.09)
Constant	−0.034***	−0.036***	−0.036***	−0.034***	−0.034***
	(−2.89)	(−3.03)	(−3.04)	(−2.90)	(−2.89)
Dummy Year	Yes	Yes	Yes	Yes	Yes
Dummy Target Industry	Yes	Yes	Yes	Yes	Yes
Number of groups	79	79	79	79	79
Number of observations	570	570	570	570	570
Chi-Square	83.223***	89.561***	87.563***	83.879***	83.237***

* $p < 0.1$.
** $p < 0.05$.
*** $p < 0.01$.

mining) and service industries as well as across high-tech and low-tech industries.[20] We re-estimated the results after adding new dummy variables and triple interactions in the model. Although the effects on target firms' profitability are statistically insignifi-

cant, this distinction is important when considering sales performance. More specifically, they suggest that the moderating effect that EMNCs' acquisition experience has on the relationship between EMNCs' tangible resources and target firms' sales performance is more significant for manufacturing industries than for services sectors. There is also a (weak) positive moderating effect of EMNCs' experience in developed countries on the relationship between EMNCs' intangible resources and target

---

[20] The distinction between high- and low-tech industries is based upon Eurostat-OECD classification (2007), which identifies high-tech manufacturing sectors and knowledge-intensive services.

Table 5b
Results of the FGLS regressions: acquisition experience in developed countries vs. other types of experience – target firm sales variation.

Explicative variables	Target firm sales variation				
	1)	2)	3)	4)	5)
H1: EMNCs' Tangible Resources	0.523***	0.081	0.883***	0.510**	0.557***
	(2.65)	(0.35)	(3.76)	(2.50)	(2.77)
EMNCs' Intangible Resources	−0.583	−0.371	−0.913**	−0.328	−1.096
	(−1.49)	(−0.90)	(−2.25)	(−0.49)	(−1.54)
EMNCs' Acquisition Experience in Developed Countries (cell 4 in Fig. 1)	0.356**	0.055	0.382**	0.398**	0.392**
	(2.05)	(0.29)	(2.20)	(2.25)	(2.20)
EMNCs' Acquisition Experience in Other Countries (cell 3 in Fig. 1)	−0.038	−0.131	0.109	−0.055	−0.060
	(−0.25)	(−0.72)	(−0.72)	(−0.36)	(−0.40)
EMNCs' Greenfield Experience in Developed Countries (cell 2 in Fig. 1)	0.063	0.137	0.378*	0.049	0.058
	(0.39)	(0.87)	(1.95)	(0.30)	(0.36)
EMNCs' Greenfield Experience in Other Countries (cell 1 in Fig. 1)	−0.121	−0.144	−0.321	−0.102	−0.108
	(−0.67)	(−0.81)	(−1.35)	(−0.55)	(−0.57)
Target Firms' Tangible Resources	−0.099	−0.152	−0.083	−0.092	−0.096
	(−0.43)	(−0.68)	(−0.36)	(−0.40)	(−0.42)
Target Firms' Intangible Resources	−0.116	−0.142	−0.025	−0.068	−0.090
	(−0.29)	(−0.36)	(−0.06)	(−0.17)	(−0.22)
Target Firms Size	0.242***	0.244***	0.243***	0.240***	0.241***
	(7.97)	(8.23)	(8.10)	(7.94)	(7.94)
EMNCs Public Company	−0.166*	−0.158*	−0.161*	−0.167*	−0.164*
	(−1.76)	(−1.72)	(−1.72)	(−1.77)	(−1.74)
Full Ownership	0.044	0.037	0.010	0.074	0.066
	(0.54)	(0.46)	(0.12)	(0.86)	(0.77)
Conglomerate Investment	−0.155	−0.165*	−0.183*	−0.178*	−0.164
	(−1.56)	(−1.69)	(−1.85)	(−1.75)	(−1.64)
Vertical Investment	−0.084	0.013	−0.077	−0.099	−0.095
	(−0.58)	(0.09)	(−0.53)	(−0.68)	(−0.65)
Host Eastern Europe	−0.086	−0.023	−0.058	−0.081	−0.082
	(−0.69)	(−0.19)	(−0.47)	(−0.65)	(−0.65)
Host Japan	−0.008	−0.007	0.038	−0.001	−0.006
	(−0.05)	(−0.04)	(0.24)	(−0.01)	(−0.04)
Host North America	0.050	0.089	0.060	0.055	0.053
	(0.60)	(1.10)	(0.72)	(0.66)	(0.64)
Russia-Brazil	0.117	0.014	0.109	0.102	0.108
	(0.97)	(0.11)	(0.90)	(0.84)	(0.89)
China	0.040	0.121	0.062	0.046	0.044
	(0.36)	(1.11)	(0.57)	(0.42)	(0.40)
H4: EMNCs' Tangible Resources × EMNCs' Acquisition Experience in Developed Countries		2.045***			
		(4.21)			
EMNCs' Tangible Resources × EMNCs' Acquisition Experience in Other Countries		0.433			
		(0.92)			
EMNCs' Tangible Resources × EMNCs' Greenfield Experience in Developed Countries			−1.257***		
			(−2.99)		
EMNCs' Tangible Resources × EMNCs' Greenfield Experience in Other Countries			0.345		
			(0.57)		
EMNCs' Intangible Resources × EMNCs' Acquisition Experience in Developed Countries				−1.288	
				(−1.30)	
EMNCs' Intangible Resources × EMNCs' Acquisition Experience in Other Countries				−0.044	
				(−0.06)	
EMNCs' Intangible Resources × EMNCs' Greenfield Experience in Developed Countries					0.777
					(0.91)
EMNCs' Intangible Resources × EMNCs' Greenfield Experience in Other Countries					−0.093
					(−0.10)
Constant	−0.176	−0.225	−0.226	−0.189	−0.186
	(−0.76)	(−0.99)	(−0.97)	(−0.82)	(−0.80)
Dummy Year	Yes	Yes	Yes	Yes	Yes
Dummy Target Industry	Yes	Yes	Yes	Yes	Yes
Number of groups	78	78	78	78	78
Number of observations	559	559	559	559	559
Chi-Square	145.756***	180.076***	157.458***	147.878***	146.804***

* $p < 0.1$.
** $p < 0.05$.
*** $p < 0.01$.

firms' sales performance in services sectors. Finally, when we examined how the results differ across high- and low-tech industries, the results did not indicate any significant differences for target firms' profitability. However, when we considered the effects on sales performance, we found that the moderating effects of EMNCs' acquisition experience in developed countries on EMNCs' tangible resources is more important for low-tech industries.

Finally, we explored the role of other combinations of experience. To do this, we introduced two new dummies to account for situations in which EMNCs have (1) both greenfield and acquisition experience (regardless of the geographic diversification), and (2) experience in both developed and other countries (regardless of the entry mode type). The results show that only EMNCs' experience in developed and other countries has a positive and significant moderating effect on the relationship between EMNCs' tangible resources and target firm sales.

6. Discussion and conclusion

6.1. Theoretical implications

The emergence of new global players from BRIC countries and their investments in developed countries are changing the global landscape. In this study, we examined a phenomenon that remains under-theorized: "how do such acquisitions influence the performance of target firms in developed countries?" More specifically, building on the notion of context-specific applicability, we developed and tested a framework about the resource- and context-specificity of prior experience in acquisitions. We demonstrate that variations in the performance of target firms in developed markets can be explained by differences in (1) the resources of the acquiring EMNC and (2) the experience accumulated by the EMNC from previous acquisitions and investments in developed and emerging countries. Our conceptualization highlights the need to consider not only the characteristics of current acquisitions and investments, but also patterns in the previous ones. This approach is useful because it enables us to explain why some acquisitions generate greater benefits than others, even though the resources of the firms might be similar in their characteristics. It is also useful in showing that different types of experience may lead to different types of learning and capabilities and, in turn, influence different aspects of performance.

Our findings have a number of theoretical implications. First, an interesting pattern emerges concerning the role of experience. The results indicate that prior investment experience is not always beneficial for the performance of target firms, and that it might even have negative consequences. In fact, only specific types of investment experience enhance the performance of target firms. For instance, acquisition experience assists the acquiring firm in managing the resources of the organization as a whole and in identifying synergies and complementarities that improve the performance of the target firm through two key mechanisms – resource redeployment and asset divestiture (Capron et al., 1998; Lavie, 2006; Newbert, 2007). Interestingly, EMNCs that are most effective in enhancing the performance of target firms are those that have investment experience in *both* acquisitions and developed countries.

Overall, our analysis suggests that because inherent contextual properties map onto distinct learning processes (Muehlfeld et al., 2012), the experience that EMNCs gain from a given context is unlikely to influence subsequent acquisition outcomes in different contexts. Different investments are associated with a given set of capabilities and organizational routines that are not always transferable to other situations. This may also explain why multinationals often choose to follow a similar investment pattern over time. The theoretical implication for the OFDI literature is that that not all *types* of experience are equally beneficial. The usefulness of experiential learning differs across contexts depending on the type of market entry (greenfield or acquisition) and the investment location (emerging or developed countries). These findings differ from the general tenet that each additional investment experience makes firms better at managing future investments.

It seems that investment experience is so type- and location-specific that when EMNCs that only have greenfield investment experience engage in acquisitions, there is a negative effect on the performance of the target companies because greenfield experience is less useful in providing acquisition-specific knowledge. Greenfield investment involves a different logic and dynamic to acquisitions because it often focuses on asset-exploitation, rather than asset-exploration. Hence, the target firm might run the risk of

not being well embedded in the strategy of the parent company, thus decreasing the performance of both firms (Datta, 1991; Ramaswamy, 1997; Shelton, 1988). We also provide evidence that the performance of target firms, especially in the manufacturing sector, is largely driven by EMNCs' tangible assets. This finding stands in contrast with the established resource-based notion that intangible resources are usually more important. By contrast, while studies on developed market MNCs suggest that their intangible resources enhance the performance of target firms, we find that this does not hold in the case of EMNCs as the performance consequences of their intangible resources turn out to be insignificant. This finding is consistent with the view that EMNCs invest in developed countries to source rather than to transfer knowledge-intensive and intangible assets.

Furthermore, we show that both the direct and the moderating effects of experience differ in the case of EMNCs. Emerging country environments have different characteristics compared to developed countries. They are grounded in informal ties and democracies that are not always completely accomplished (Goldstein, 2007). These differences limit EMNCs' ability to undertake investments in developed economies, increasing the probability of making pre- and post-acquisition mistakes. This might explain our finding showing that previous investments in developed countries have a positive and significant direct effect on the performance of target firms. This type of experience provides EMNCs with the necessary knowledge to manage new deals in similar (i.e. developed) countries. An analysis of acquiring firms from developed countries might yield different results since such MNCs have a better understanding of the environments that can be found in other developed countries.

6.2. Managerial relevance

Our results have two implications for practice. First, developed countries often raise concerns about the acquisitions of EMNCs, suggesting that EMNCs will eventually control part of these economies. Although the international press focuses on high-visibility large acquisitions and raises concerns, we show that the performance effects of EMNCs' investments on target firms can be positive. This is consistent with the view that resource-based and cost-efficiency strategies can improve the performance of target firms by leading to revenue-enhancing and cost-based synergies. Nevertheless, our findings also imply that host-country governments should set up policies that attract not just experienced EMNCs (as generic experience is not always useful), but EMNCs with the right type of experience. Alternatively, they could choose to assist less experienced EMNCs to gain local knowledge before completing the takeover in the host country.

Second, performance outcomes depend not only on the characteristics of current acquisitions, but also on patterns in the previous ones. Hence, managers of EMNCs should carefully evaluate their experience before undertaking foreign investment. This significantly influences the success of the acquisition and the performance of new subsidiaries in developed countries. In this respect, what matters is not merely the "degree" of experience but its relevance and type. EMNCs with investment experience in acquisitions and in developed countries are likely to be more successful in their future international expansion plans. These firms are also more likely to have accumulated the capabilities required to manage new acquisitions and generate valuable post-acquisition synergies and complementarities. This may assist target firms in increasing their performance and expansion (Yaprak & Karademir, 2011). By contrast, it may be more beneficial for firms that have either no experience or experience that is less specific to a developed market to consider a cooperative strategy (e.g. joint-ventures) when investing in a developed country.

Our analysis is subject to a number of limitations, some of which offer opportunities for future research. First, the analysis is based on EMNCs. This group of firms has different idiosyncratic characteristics compared to multinationals from developed economies. A similar analysis for MNCs from developed countries may yield different results. For instance, a counterfactual analysis will allow future research to examine whether the resources of the acquiring firm and the direct or moderating effects of experience have different impacts when firms are acquired by EMNCs or developed country MNCs. Second, our analysis focused on the distinction between tangible and intangible resources. A useful research avenue for extending this approach would be to either examine the role of other resources (e.g. financial) or adopt a more fine-grained approach and consider what types of tangible or intangible resources contribute to the performance of target firms. Experience could be further disentangled by accounting for a more fine-grained distinction among entry modes (e.g. by including joint-ventures) and by considering more disaggregated geographic areas. Future research should also investigate the direct and moderating effect of experience intensity by using a continuous variable (rather than a dummy variable) because the effect between a single experience and multiple experiences might be different. Furthermore, as the strategic objectives of EMNCs vary widely, an investigation of other performance indicators, such as innovation and knowledge acquisition, is needed. Future research should also try to open up the "black box" of target firms in order to understand whether and how they gain access to new production, technology and markets when they are acquired by EMNCs. Another fruitful avenue for future research is to investigate the effects of acquisitions from emerging countries on the rest of the host economy. This will increase understanding of whether the positive effects on firm performance are limited to target firms or they extend to their supply chain.

Appendix

Table 6
Results of the GMM-SYS analysis: the role of generic experience.

Explicative variables	Target firm profit variation			Target firm sales variation		
	1)	2)	3)	4)	5)	6)
Lagged value of performance measure	0.627	0.632	0.632	0.213	0.209	0.213
	(1.33)	(1.33)	(1.32)	(0.63)	(0.63)	(0.64)
H1: EMNCs' Tangible Resources	0.008	0.011	0.008	0.875*	−0.064	0.586
	(0.91)	(0.93)	(0.97)	(1.68)	(−0.33)	(1.55)
EMNCs' Intangible Resources	−0.026	−0.024	0.030	−0.598	−0.443	−1.695
	(−1.29)	(−1.28)	(0.64)	(−1.14)	(−0.90)	(−1.49)
EMNCs' Experience	0.011	0.010	0.009	0.016	0.035	0.203
	(1.27)	(1.28)	(1.31)	(0.08)	(0.24)	(1.33)
Target Firms' Tangible Resources	0.051	0.048	0.053	−0.479	−0.640	−0.335
	(1.22)	(1.20)	(1.31)	(−0.83)	(−1.11)	(−0.68)
Target Firms' Intangible Resources	0.040	0.042	0.035	−0.587	−0.201	−0.093
	(0.73)	(0.81)	(0.76)	(−0.60)	(−0.25)	(−0.12)
Target Firms Size	0.016**	0.016**	0.016**	0.677***	0.677***	0.675***
	(2.20)	(2.21)	(2.22)	(2.75)	(2.77)	(2.80)
EMNCs Public Company	0.001	0.000	0.001	−0.149	−0.116	−0.123
	(0.14)	(0.02)	(0.19)	(−0.91)	(−0.80)	(−0.81)
Full Ownership	−0.008	−0.008	−0.008	0.182	0.187	0.164
	(−1.02)	(−1.04)	(−1.11)	(1.42)	(1.42)	(1.24)
Conglomerate Investment	−0.018	−0.017	−0.014	−0.412**	−0.403**	−0.446**
	(−1.23)	(−1.27)	(−1.19)	(−2.08)	(−2.01)	(−2.17)
Vertical Investment	−0.012	−0.013	−0.013	−0.721**	−0.569*	−0.720**
	(−0.79)	(−0.91)	(−0.92)	(−2.26)	(−1.95)	(−2.25)
Host Eastern Europe	−0.010	−0.009	−0.010	−0.171	−0.253	−0.327
	(−0.74)	(−0.76)	(−0.83)	(−0.40)	(−0.84)	(−0.95)
Host Japan	−0.021	−0.020	−0.016	0.046	0.070	0.130
	(−1.11)	(−1.18)	(−0.93)	(0.11)	(0.20)	(0.42)
Host North America	−0.006	−0.006	−0.003	0.327	0.401*	0.312
	(−0.35)	(−0.40)	(−0.19)	(1.34)	(1.65)	(1.32)
Russia-Brazil	−0.001	0.001	−0.001	0.481*	0.409	0.500*
	(−0.03)	(0.03)	(−0.05)	(1.67)	(1.45)	(1.71)
China	0.014	0.013	0.009	0.102	0.132	0.155
	(1.09)	(1.12)	(0.89)	(0.43)	(0.63)	(0.72)
EMNCs' Tangible Resources × EMNCs' Experience		−0.002			1.186**	
		(−0.15)			(2.55)	
EMNCs' Intangible Resources × EMNCs' Experience			−0.058			1.096
			(−1.11)			(1.00)
Constant	0.103	0.105	0.098	−0.488	−0.422	−0.532
	(0.44)	(0.45)	(0.42)	(−0.77)	(−0.73)	(−0.87)
Dummy Year	Yes	Yes	Yes	Yes	Yes	Yes
Dummy Target Industry	Yes	Yes	Yes	Yes	Yes	Yes
Number of groups	79	79	79	78	78	78
Number of observations	570	570	570	559	559	559
AR1	−1.764*	−1.749*	−1.742*	−1.919*	−1.915*	−1.915*
AR2	−1.017	−1.016	−1.019	−0.916	−0.954	−0.890
HANSEN TEST	18.946	17.610	20.882	28.425	30.134	41.044
Chi-Square	7487.793***	13085.803***	12800.607***	98199.186***	83986.432***	89743.142***

$^{*}p < 0.1$, $^{**}p < 0.05$, $^{***}p < 0.01$. Resources and experience of EMNCs and resources of target firms have been considered endogenous. Lagged values and first-differences of (i) endogenous variables, (ii) time dummies and (iii) EMNCs' industrial dummies have been used as instruments.

Table 7a
Results of the GMM-SYS analysis: acquisition vs. greenfield experience and experience in developed countries vs. other countries – target firm profit variation.

Explicative variables	Target firm profit variation				
	1)	2)	3)	4)	5)
Lagged value of performance measure	0.655	0.675	0.664	0.662	0.659
	(1.36)	(1.37)	(1.35)	(1.35)	(1.34)
H1: EMNCs' Tangible Resources	0.030*	0.023	0.019	0.024*	0.023*
	(1.92)	(1.46)	(1.06)	(1.76)	(1.76)
EMNCs' Intangible Resources	−0.004	−0.004	−0.002	−0.013	0.036
	(−0.27)	(−0.30)	(−0.18)	(−0.35)	(0.76)
EMNCs' Acquisition Experience	−0.001	−0.006	0.000	−0.002	−0.004
	(−0.13)	(−0.66)	(0.01)	(−0.21)	(−0.37)
EMNCs' Greenfield Experience	−0.022	−0.012	−0.025	−0.024	−0.023
	(−1.35)	(−1.25)	(−1.63)	(−1.55)	(−1.56)
Target Firms' Tangible Resources	0.009	0.014	0.009	0.012	0.007
	(0.58)	(0.97)	(0.53)	(0.88)	(0.45)
Target Firms' Intangible Resources	0.008	−0.002	0.010	0.010	0.014
	(0.67)	(−0.17)	(0.60)	(0.91)	(1.10)
Target Firms Size	0.070	0.054	0.054	0.057	0.061
	(1.47)	(1.35)	(1.37)	(1.42)	(1.39)
EMNCs Public Company	0.041	0.032	0.019	0.035	0.033
	(0.69)	(0.72)	(0.42)	(0.84)	(0.64)
Full Ownership	0.018**	0.017**	0.017**	0.017**	0.018**
	(2.23)	(2.25)	(2.24)	(2.25)	(2.31)
Conglomerate Investment	0.007	0.005	0.005	0.006	0.007
	(0.91)	(0.87)	(0.75)	(0.70)	(0.87)
Vertical Investment	−0.020	−0.016	−0.017	−0.017	−0.017
	(−1.33)	(−1.38)	(−1.28)	(−1.25)	(−1.34)
Host Eastern Europe	−0.001	−0.007	−0.005	−0.004	−0.005
	(−0.08)	(−0.81)	(−0.47)	(−0.50)	(−0.53)
Host Japan	−0.011	−0.003	−0.004	−0.007	−0.008
	(−0.66)	(−0.26)	(−0.34)	(−0.51)	(−0.56)
Host North America	0.001	−0.004	−0.009	−0.004	−0.007
	(0.05)	(−0.35)	(−0.80)	(−0.31)	(−0.52)
Russia-Brazil	−0.038	−0.021	−0.036	−0.035	−0.027
	(−1.18)	(−0.91)	(−1.22)	(−1.39)	(−1.13)
China	−0.014	−0.006	−0.014	−0.015	−0.012
	(−0.63)	(−0.38)	(−0.66)	(−0.73)	(−0.60)
EMNCs' Experience in Developed Countries	−0.010	−0.010	−0.006	−0.007	−0.005
	(−0.41)	(−0.50)	(−0.29)	(−0.33)	(−0.21)
EMNCs' Experience in Other Countries	0.011	0.012	0.008	0.010	0.005
	(0.79)	(1.19)	(0.74)	(0.91)	(0.56)
H2: EMNCs' Tangible Resources × EMNCs' Acquisition Experience		0.057			
		(1.56)			
EMNCs' Tangible Resources × EMNCs' Greenfield Experience		−0.045			
		(−1.50)			
H3: EMNCs' Tangible Resources × EMNCs' Experience in Developed Countries			0.013		
			(0.54)		
EMNCs' Tangible Resources × EMNCs' Experience in Other Countries			−0.001		
			(−0.04)		
EMNCs' Intangible Resources × EMNCs' Acquisition Experience				0.001	
				(0.02)	
EMNCs' Intangible Resources × EMNCs' Greenfield Experience				0.010	
				(0.29)	
EMNCs' Intangible Resources × EMNCs' Experience in Developed Countries					0.074
					(0.82)
EMNCs' Intangible Resources × EMNCs' Experience in Other Countries					−0.121
					(−1.08)
Constant	0.066	0.066	0.075	0.076	0.070
	(0.28)	(0.28)	(0.32)	(0.33)	(0.30)
Dummy Year	Yes	Yes	Yes	Yes	Yes
Dummy Target Industry	Yes	Yes	Yes	Yes	Yes
Number of groups	79	79	79	79	79
Number of observations	570	570	570	570	570
AR1	−1.775*	−1.741*	−1.740*	−1.758*	−1.760*
AR2	−1.040	−1.070	−1.039	−1.033	−1.032
Hansen test	19.596	11.477	17.996	17.405	17.628
Chi-Square	12230.669***	13930.041***	11514.572***	11003.927***	9394.409***

*$p < 0.1$, ** $p < 0.05$, *** $p < 0.01$. Resources and experience of EMNCs and resources of target firms have been considered endogenous. Lagged values and first-differences of (i) endogenous variables, (ii) time dummies and (iii) EMNCs' industrial dummies have been used as instruments.

P.J. Buckley et al. / Journal of World Business 49 (2014) 611–632

Table 7b

Results of the GMM-SYS analysis: acquisition vs. greenfield experience and experience in developed countries vs. other countries – target firm sales variation.

Explicative variables	Target firm profit variation				
	1)	2)	3)	4)	5)
Lagged value of performance measure	0.207	0.221	0.262	0.251	0.209
	(0.69)	(0.80)	(0.91)	(0.83)	(0.68)
H1: EMNCs' Tangible Resources	0.711**	0.441	0.087	0.600*	0.700*
	(2.08)	(1.57)	(0.62)	(1.89)	(1.94)
EMNCs' Intangible Resources	−0.261	−0.215	−0.082	−0.905	−1.293
	(−0.62)	(−0.57)	(−0.26)	(−1.25)	(−1.19)
EMNCs' Acquisition Experience	−0.139	−0.300	−0.128	−0.122	−0.175
	(−0.71)	(−1.42)	(−0.80)	(−0.74)	(−0.84)
EMNCs' Greenfield Experience	−0.719	−0.253	−0.643	−0.613	−0.679
	(−1.59)	(−0.82)	(−1.57)	(−1.49)	(−1.60)
Target Firms' Tangible Resources	0.734*	0.833**	0.926**	0.656*	0.695*
	(1.76)	(2.06)	(2.07)	(1.81)	(1.72)
Target Firms' Intangible Resources	0.065	−0.438*	−0.437	0.021	0.129
	(0.24)	(−1.87)	(−1.31)	(0.10)	(0.42)
Target Firms Size	−0.035	−0.082	−0.277	−0.018	0.025
	(−0.08)	(−0.22)	(−0.78)	(−0.05)	(0.06)
EMNCs Public Company	−0.850	−0.869	−0.822	−0.385	−0.688
	(−0.89)	(−0.98)	(−1.26)	(−0.67)	(−0.74)
Full Ownership	0.693***	0.674***	0.664***	0.672***	0.701***
	(3.07)	(3.35)	(3.10)	(3.00)	(3.15)
Conglomerate Investment	0.033	0.072	0.020	−0.042	0.000
	(0.21)	(0.53)	(0.18)	(−0.31)	(0.00)
Vertical Investment	−0.037	−0.055	0.083	0.094	0.002
	(−0.22)	(−0.37)	(0.74)	(0.76)	(0.01)
Host Eastern Europe	−0.245	−0.403*	−0.299*	−0.276*	−0.279
	(−1.14)	(−1.95)	(−1.88)	(−1.71)	(−1.25)
Host Japan	−0.636**	−0.450**	−0.407**	−0.466**	−0.648**
	(−2.19)	(−2.14)	(−2.08)	(−2.11)	(−2.35)
Host North America	−0.422	−0.266	−0.373	−0.446	−0.494
	(−0.98)	(−0.73)	(−1.50)	(−1.61)	(−1.37)
Russia-Brazil	0.115	0.372	0.144	0.146	0.154
	(0.32)	(1.21)	(0.62)	(0.69)	(0.49)
China	0.345	0.547***	0.433***	0.274*	0.275
	(1.41)	(2.64)	(2.93)	(1.79)	(1.29)
EMNCs' Experience in Developed Countries	0.282	0.211	0.196	0.321	0.327
	(1.13)	(0.98)	(0.87)	(1.26)	(1.35)
EMNCs' Experience in Other Countries	−0.032	0.173	−0.055	−0.014	−0.027
	(−0.13)	(0.92)	(−0.34)	(−0.09)	(−0.14)
H2: EMNCs' Tangible Resources × EMNCs' Acquisition Experience		2.456***			
		(2.84)			
EMNCs' Tangible Resources × EMNCs' Greenfield Experience		−1.598**			
		(−2.50)			
H3: EMNCs' Tangible Resources × EMNCs' Experience in Developed Countries			−0.758		
			(−1.10)		
EMNCs' Tangible Resources × EMNCs' Experience in Other Countries			2.114**		
			(2.49)		
EMNCs' Intangible Resources × EMNCs' Acquisition Experience				−0.631	
				(−1.01)	
EMNCs' Intangible Resources × EMNCs' Greenfield Experience				1.150	
				(1.55)	
EMNCs' Intangible Resources × EMNCs' Experience in Developed Countries					2.151
					(1.15)
EMNCs' Intangible Resources × EMNCs' Experience in Other Countries					−1.186
					(−0.80)
Constant	−0.944	−1.102	−0.766	−0.798	−0.949
	(−1.20)	(−1.49)	(−1.16)	(−1.23)	(−1.20)
Dummy Year	Yes	Yes	Yes	Yes	Yes
Dummy Target Industry	Yes	Yes	Yes	Yes	Yes
Number of groups	78	78	78	78	78
Number of observations	559	559	559	559	559
AR1	−2.010**	−2.169**	−2.063**	−1.997**	−2.018**
AR2	−0.922	−1.026	−0.936	−0.890	−0.892
Hansen test	30.344	18.183	15.876	15.374	23.139
Chi-Square	93473.845***	153000***	167000***	389000***	127000***

*p < 0.1, ** p < 0.05, ***p < 0.01. Resources and experience of EMNCs and resources of target firms have been considered endogenous. Lagged values and first-differences of (i) endogenous variables, (ii) time dummies and (iii) EMNCs' industrial dummies have been used as instruments.

P.J. Buckley et al./Journal of World Business 49 (2014) 611–632

Table 8a
Results of the GMM regressions: acquisition experience in developed countries vs. other types of experience – target firm profit variation.

Explicative variables	Target firm profit variation				
	1)	2)	3)	4)	5)
Lagged value of performance measure	0.662	0.689	0.669	0.662	0.658
	(1.36)	(1.33)	(1.37)	(1.36)	(1.36)
H1: EMNCs' Tangible Resources	0.018*	0.000	0.046*	0.022*	0.020
	(1.84)	(0.02)	(1.67)	(1.67)	(1.59)
EMNCs' Intangible Resources	−0.013	0.001	−0.056	−0.001	0.004
	(−1.01)	(0.02)	(−1.63)	(−0.01)	(0.08)
EMNCs' Acquisition Experience in Developed Countries (cell 4 in Fig. 1)	0.006	−0.048	0.010	0.010	0.010
	(0.60)	(−1.41)	(0.63)	(0.63)	(0.53)
EMNCs' Acquisition Experience in Other Countries (cell 3 in Fig. 1)	0.005	0.044	0.013	0.011	0.013
	(1.10)	(1.22)	(1.14)	(1.14)	(1.12)
EMNCs' Greenfield Experience in Developed Countries (cell 2 in Fig. 1)	−0.000	−0.034	0.018	−0.000	0.000
	(−0.08)	(−1.50)	(1.14)	(−0.04)	(0.03)
EMNCs' Greenfield Experience in Other Countries (cell 1 in Fig. 1)	−0.003	0.031	−0.006	−0.003	0.000
	(−0.52)	(0.98)	(−0.40)	(−0.22)	(0.03)
Target Firms' Tangible Resources	0.038	0.181*	0.080	0.071	0.072
	(0.99)	(1.80)	(1.42)	(1.21)	(1.25)
Target Firms' Intangible Resources	0.018	0.187	0.045	0.024	0.032
	(0.39)	(1.34)	(0.87)	(0.38)	(0.56)
Target Firms Size	0.016**	0.020**	0.017***	0.017**	0.017**
	(2.28)	(2.40)	(2.21)	(2.18)	(2.19)
EMNCs Public Company	0.003	0.010	0.005	0.005	0.002
	(0.48)	(0.64)	(0.48)	(0.42)	(0.15)
Full Ownership	−0.011	−0.022	−0.021	−0.020	−0.020
	(−1.01)	(−1.28)	(−1.47)	(−1.34)	(−1.33)
Conglomerate Investment	−0.004	−0.008	−0.012	−0.005	−0.006
	(−0.64)	(−0.44)	(−0.85)	(−0.42)	(−0.54)
Vertical Investment	−0.013	0.003	−0.016	−0.014	−0.010
	(−0.96)	(0.10)	(−0.56)	(−0.56)	(−0.42)
Host Eastern Europe	−0.003	−0.010	−0.011	−0.014	−0.021
	(−0.34)	(−0.34)	(−0.74)	(−0.96)	(−1.37)
Host Japan	−0.018	−0.017	−0.028	−0.040	−0.040
	(−1.08)	(−0.35)	(−0.97)	(−1.34)	(−1.44)
Host North America	−0.015	0.034	−0.018	−0.022	−0.023
	(−0.88)	(0.75)	(−0.68)	(−0.88)	(−0.91)
Russia-Brazil	−0.006	−0.028	−0.008	−0.006	−0.004
	(−0.24)	(−0.87)	(−0.31)	(−0.24)	(−0.16)
China	0.005	0.020	0.020*	0.015	0.018*
	(0.82)	(1.20)	(1.85)	(1.50)	(1.73)
H4: EMNCs' Tangible Resources × EMNCs' Acquisition Experience in Developed Countries		0.238**			
		(2.09)			
EMNCs' Tangible Resources × EMNCs' Acquisition Experience in Other Countries		−0.042			
		(−0.45)			
EMNCs' Tangible Resources × EMNCs' Greenfield Experience in Developed Countries				−0.098*	
				(−1.87)	
EMNCs' Tangible Resources × EMNCs' Greenfield Experience in Other Countries				0.014	
				(0.29)	
EMNCs' Intangible Resources × EMNCs' Acquisition Experience in Developed Countries				0.005	
				(0.10)	
EMNCs' Intangible Resources × EMNCs' Acquisition Experience in Other Countries				−0.035	
				(−0.66)	
EMNCs' Intangible Resources × EMNCs' Greenfield Experience in Developed Countries					−0.034
					(−0.60)
EMNCs' Intangible Resources × EMNCs' Greenfield Experience in Other Countries					−0.054
					(−1.25)
Constant	0.100	−0.089	0.060	0.075	0.076
	(0.41)	(−0.34)	(0.25)	(0.30)	(0.31)
Dummy Year	Yes	Yes	Yes	Yes	Yes
Dummy Target Industry	Yes	Yes	Yes	Yes	Yes
Number of groups	79	79	79	79	79
Number of observations	570	570	570	570	570
AR1	−1.706*	−1.798*	−1.924*	−1.826*	−1.839*
AR2	−1.025	−1.064	−1.016	−1.040	−1.034
Hansen test	12.762	21.926	13.318	17.548	17.298
Chi-Square	18124.616***	8607.777***	19281.279***	22744.007***	13664.865***

* $p < 0.1$, ** $p < 0.05$, *** $p < 0.01$. Resources and experience of EMNCs and resources of target firms have been considered endogenous. Lagged values and first-differences of (i) endogenous variables, (ii) time dummies and (iii) EMNCs' industrial dummies have been used as instruments.

P.J. Buckley et al./Journal of World Business 49 (2014) 611–632

Table 8b
Results of the GMM regressions: acquisition experience in developed countries vs. other types of experience – target firm sales variation.

Explicative variables	Target firm profit variation				
	1)	2)	3)	4)	5)
Lagged value of performance measure	0.256	0.257	0.178	0.197	0.194
	(0.84)	(1.02)	(0.62)	(0.64)	(0.64)
H1: EMNCs' Tangible Resources	0.540**	−0.598	2.012**	0.797*	1.034**
	(2.00)	(−1.12)	(2.01)	(1.82)	(1.99)
EMNCs' Intangible Resources	−0.599	0.261	−1.456	0.085	−1.467
	(−1.59)	(0.25)	(−1.59)	(0.13)	(−1.34)
EMNCs' Acquisition Experience in Developed Countries (cell 4 in Fig. 1)	0.451	0.835	1.140	0.725	0.834*
	(1.60)	(1.37)	(1.53)	(1.59)	(1.66)
EMNCs' Acquisition Experience in Other Countries (cell 3 in Fig. 1)	−0.068	−0.794	−0.178	0.020	−0.158
	(−0.41)	(−1.19)	(−0.28)	(0.06)	(−0.45)
EMNCs' Greenfield Experience in Developed Countries (cell 2 in Fig. 1)	0.212	0.432	1.186**	0.287	0.359
	(1.28)	(1.25)	(2.21)	(0.96)	(1.16)
EMNCs' Greenfield Experience in Other Countries (cell 1 in Fig. 1)	−0.261	−0.542	−0.988	−0.313	−0.452
	(−1.35)	(−1.06)	(−1.64)	(−0.75)	(−1.04)
Target Firms' Tangible Resources	−0.122	−0.827	−0.200	0.051	−0.176
	(−0.36)	(−1.03)	(−0.24)	(0.11)	(−0.37)
Target Firms' Intangible Resources	−0.567	−1.445	0.268	−0.091	−0.377
	(−0.86)	(−0.75)	(0.22)	(−0.09)	(−0.38)
Target Firms Size	0.645***	0.695***	0.714***	0.688***	0.686***
	(2.88)	(3.92)	(3.67)	(3.17)	(3.18)
EMNCs Public Company	−0.038	0.013	0.035	−0.092	−0.078
	(−0.30)	(0.06)	(0.17)	(−0.49)	(−0.42)
Full Ownership	0.041	0.175	0.057	0.148	0.126
	(0.30)	(0.67)	(0.21)	(0.78)	(0.72)
Conglomerate Investment	−0.218	−0.707**	−0.715*	−0.468**	−0.386*
	(−1.50)	(−2.00)	(−1.91)	(−2.01)	(−1.67)
Vertical Investment	−0.533**	−0.615	−0.828*	−0.630**	−0.676**
	(−2.02)	(−1.45)	(−1.92)	(−2.05)	(−2.24)
Host Eastern Europe	−0.329	−0.369	−0.341	−0.617*	−0.526
	(−1.27)	(−0.77)	(−0.61)	(−1.72)	(−1.40)
Host Japan	0.195	0.664	0.592	−0.010	−0.052
	(0.79)	(0.71)	(0.81)	(−0.03)	(−0.14)
Host North America	0.339**	1.115	0.884*	0.255	0.269
	(1.97)	(1.45)	(1.95)	(1.17)	(1.24)
Russia-Brazil	0.320	0.024	0.200	0.333	0.315
	(1.41)	(0.07)	(0.59)	(1.20)	(1.15)
China	0.051	0.233	0.322	0.192	0.134
	(0.32)	(0.68)	(1.01)	(0.78)	(0.51)
H4: EMNCs' Tangible Resources × EMNCs' Acquisition Experience in Developed Countries		4.180**			
		(2.48)			
EMNCs' Tangible Resources × EMNCs' Acquisition Experience in Other Countries		2.438			
		(1.56)			
EMNCs' Tangible Resources × EMNCs' Greenfield Experience in Developed Countries			−3.591***		
			(−2.98)		
EMNCs' Tangible Resources × EMNCs' Greenfield Experience in Other Countries			1.166		
			(1.01)		
EMNCs' Intangible Resources × EMNCs' Acquisition Experience in Developed Countries				−1.542	
				(−1.08)	
EMNCs' Intangible Resources × EMNCs' Acquisition Experience in Other Countries				−0.752	
				(−0.91)	
EMNCs' Intangible Resources × EMNCs' Greenfield Experience in Developed Countries					1.055
					(1.03)
EMNCs' Intangible Resources × EMNCs' Greenfield Experience in Other Countries					0.757
					(0.78)
Constant	−0.664	−1.285	−1.243	−0.783	−0.633
	(−1.11)	(−1.15)	(−1.25)	(−1.17)	(−1.00)
Dummy Year	Yes	Yes	Yes	Yes	Yes
Dummy Target Industry	Yes	Yes	Yes	Yes	Yes
Number of groups	78	78	78	78	78
Number of observations	559	559	559	559	559
AR1	−1.931*	−2.232**	−2.336**	−2.028**	−2.044**
AR2	−0.888	−1.433	−1.032	−1.003	−0.994
Hansen test	19.385	27.530	22.782	23.481	27.202
Chi-Square	585000***	121000***	166000***	233000***	172000***

$^* p < 0.1$, $^{**}p < 0.05$, $^{***}p < 0.01$. Resources and experience of EMNCs and resources of target firms have been considered endogenous. Lagged values and first-differences of (i) endogenous variables, (ii) time dummies and (iii) EMNCs' industrial dummies have been used as instruments.

P.J. Buckley et al. / Journal of World Business 49 (2014) 611–632   631

References

Athreye, S., & Kapur, S. (2009). Introduction: The internationalisation of Chinese and Indian firms – Trends, motivations and strategy. *Industrial and Corporate Change*, 18(2): 209–221.

Barkema, H. G., Shenkar, O., Vermeulen, F., & Bell, J. H. J. (1997). Working abroad, working with others: How firms learn to operate international joint ventures. *Academy of Management Journal*, 40(2): 426–442.

Barkema, H. G., & Vermeulen, F. (1998). International expansion through start up or acquisition: A learning perspective. *Academy of Management Journal*, 41(1): 7–26.

Barney, J. B. (1997). *Gaining and sustaining competitive advantage*. Reading, MA: Addison-Wesley.

Bertoni, F., Elia, S., & Rabbiosi, L. (2012). Outward FDI from the BRICs: Trends and patterns of acquisitions in advanced countries. In M. A. Marinov & S. T. Marinova (Eds.), *Emerging economies and firms in the global crisis* (pp. 47–82). New York: Palgrave Macmillan.

Bertrand, O., & Zitouna, H. (2008). Domestic versus cross-border acquisitions: Which impact on the target firms' performance? *Applied Economics*, 40(17): 2221–2238.

Blundell, R., & Bond, S. (1998). Initial conditions and moment restrictions in dynamic panel data models. *Journal of Econometrics*, 87(1): 115–143.

Bowen, H. P., Leamer, E. E., & Sveikauskas, L. (1987). Multicountry, multifactor tests of the factor abundance theory. *American Economic Review*, 77(5): 791–809.

Brouthers, K. D., Brouthers, L. E., & Werner, S. (2008). Resource-based advantages in an international context. *Journal of Management*, 34(2): 189–217.

Buckley, P. J., Clegg, L. J., Cross, A. R., Liu, X., Voss, H., & Zheng, P. (2007). The determinants of Chinese outward foreign direct investment. *Journal of International Business Studies*, 38(4): 499–518.

Buckley, P. J., & Ghauri, P. N. (2002). *International mergers and acquisitions: A reader*. London: Thomson.

Capar, N., & Kotabe, M. (2003). The relationship between international diversification and performance in service firms. *Journal of International Business Studies*, 34(4): 345–355.

Capron, L., Dussauge, P., & Mitchell, W. (1998). Resource redeployment following horizontal acquisitions in Europe and North America, 1988–1992. *Strategic Management Journal*, 19(7): 631–661.

Capron, L. (1999). The long-term performance of horizontal acquisitions. *Strategic Management Journal*, 20(11): 978–1018.

Chesher, A. (1979). Testing the law of proportionate effect. *Journal of Industrial Economics*, 27(4): 403–411.

Contractor, F., Kundu, S., & Hsu, C. C. (2003). A three-stage theory of international expansion: The link between multinationality and performance in the service sector. *Journal of International Business Studies*, 34(1): 5–18.

Contractor, F. J., Kundu, S. K., & Hsu, C. C. (2003). A three-stage theory of international expansion: The link between multinationality and performance in the service sector. *Journal of International Business Studies*, 1(1): 5–18.

Contractor, F. J., Kumar, S. K., & Kundu, S. K. (2007). Nature of the relationship between international expansion and performance: The case of emerging market firms. *Journal of World Business*, 42(4): 401–417.

Conyon, M. J., Girma, S., Thompson, S., & Wright, P. W. (2002). The productivity and wage effect of foreign acquisition in the United Kingdom. *Journal of Industrial Economics*, 50(1): 85–102.

Datta, D. K. (1991). Organizational fit and acquisition performance: Effects of post-acquisitions integration. *Strategic Management Journal*, 12(4): 281–297.

Delios, A., & Beamish, P. W. (2001). Survival and profit: The roles of experience and intangible assets in foreign subsidiary performance. *Academy of Management Journal*, 44(5): 1028–1038.

Deng, P. (2009). Why do Chinese firms tend to acquire strategic assets in international expansion? *Journal of World Business*, 44(1): 74–84.

Dhawan, R. (2001). Firm size and productivity differential: Theory and evidence from a panel of US firms. *Journal of Economic Behavior & Organization*, 44(3): 269–293.

Dunning, J. H., & Lundan, S. (2007). *Multinational enterprises and the global economy* (2nd ed.). Cheltenham: Elgar.

Eisenhardt, K. M., & Martin, J. A. (2000). Dynamic capabilities: What are they? *Strategic Management Journal*, 21(10–11): 1105–1121.

Estrin, S., & Meyer, K. E. (2011). Brownfield acquisitions: A reconceptualization and extension. *Management International Review*, 51(4): 483–509.

Eurostat-OECD. (2007). *Science, technology and innovation in Europe*. Eurostat Pocketbooks. ISSN 1725-5821.

Feys, C., & Manigart, S. (2010). The post-acquisition performance of acquired entrepreneurial firms. *Frontiers of Entrepreneurship Research30*(1). Harvest Article 2.

Gammeltoft, P. (2008). Emerging multinationals: Outward FDI from the BRICS countries. *International Journal Technology and Globalization*, 4(1): 5–22.

Garg, M., & Delios, A. (2007). Survival of the foreign subsidiaries of TMNCs: The influence of business group affiliation. *Journal of International Management*, 13(3): 278–295.

Gaur, A. S., & Kumar, V. (2009). International diversification, business group affiliation and firm performance: Empirical evidence from India. *British Journal of Management*, 20(2): 172–186.

Goldstein, A. (2007). *Multinational companies from emerging economies: Composition, conceptualization and direction in the global economy*. New York: Palgrave Macmillan.

Gugler, K., Mueller, D. C., Yurtoglu, B. B., & Zulehner, C. (2003). The effects of mergers: An international comparison. *International Journal of Industrial Organization*, 21(5): 625–653.

Guillén, M. F., & García-Canal, E. (2009). The American model of the multinational firm and the "new" multinationals from emerging economies. *Academy of Management Perspectives*, 23(2): 23–25.

Gulati, R. (1995). Does familiarity breed trust? The implications of repeated ties for contractual choice in alliances. *Academy of Management Journal*, 38(1): 85–112.

Haleblian, J., & Finkelstein, S. (1999). The influence of organizational acquisition experience on acquisition performance: A behavioral learning perspective. *Administrative Science Quarterly*, 44(1): 29–56.

Harzing, A. W. K. (2002). Acquisitions versus greenfield investments: International strategy and management of entry modes. *Strategic Management Journal*, 23(3): 211–227.

Haunschild, P. R. (1994). How much is that company worth? Interorganization relationships, uncertainty and acquisition premiums. *Administrative Science Quarterly*, 39(3): 391–411.

Haspeslagh, P. C., & Jemison, D. B. (1991). *Managing acquisitions: Creating value through corporate renewal*. New York: The Free Press.

Hitt, M. A., Hoskisson, R. E., & Hicheon, K. (1997). International diversification: Effects on innovation and firm performance in product-diversified firms. *Academy of Management Journal*, 40(4): 767–798.

Hitt, M. A., Ireland, D. R., Camp, M. S., & Sexton, D. L. (2001). Guest Editors' introduction to the special issue: Strategic entrepreneurship, entrepreneurial strategies for wealth creation. *Strategic Management Journal*, 22(Special issue): 479–491.

Hitt, M. A., Uhlenbruck, K., & Shimizu, K. (2006). The importance of resources in the internationalization of professional service firms: The good, the bad, and the ugly. *Academy of Management Journal*, 49(6): 1137–1157.

Jemison, D., & Sitkin, S. B. (1986). Corporate acquisitions: A process perspective. *Academy of Management Review*, 11(1): 145–163.

Johanson, J., & Vahlne, J. E. (1977). The internationalisation process of the firm: A model of knowledge development and increasing foreign market commitments. *Journal of International Business Studies*, 8(1): 23–32.

Kalotay, K. (2008). Russian transnational and international investments paradigms. *Research in International Business and finance*, 22(2): 85–107.

Kuada, J. E. (2002). Collaboration between developed and developing country-based firms: Danish-Ghanaian experience. *Journal of Business and Industrial Marketing*, 17(6): 538–557.

Kumar, N. (2007). Emerging multinationals: Trends, patterns and determinants of outward investment by Indian Enterprises. *Transnational Corporations*, 16(1): 1–26.

Kyoji, F., Ito, K., & Kwon, H. U. (2005). Do out-in M&As bring higher TFP to Japan? An empirical analysis based on micro-data on Japanese manufacturing firms. *Journal of the Japanese and International Economies*, 19(2): 272–301.

Lane, H. W., & Beamish, P. W. (1990). Cross-cultural cooperative behavior in joint ventures in LCD's. *Management International Review*, 30(Special issue): 87–102.

Lavie, D. (2006). The competitive advantage of interconnected firms: An extension of the resource-based view. *Academy of Management Review*, 31(3): 638–658.

Leiblein, M. J. (2011). What do resource- and capability-based theories propose? *Journal of Management*, 37(4): 909–932.

Li, P. P. (2007). Toward an integrated theory of multinational evolution: The evidence of Chinese multinational enterprises as latecomers. *Journal of International Management*, 13(3): 296–318.

Liu, X., Buck, T., & Shu, C. (2005). Chinese economic development, the next stage: Outward FDI? *International Business Review*, 14(1): 97–115.

Lu, J. W., & Beamish, P. W. (2004). International diversification and firm performance: The S-curve hypothesis. *Academy of Management Journal*, 47(4): 598–609.

Luo, Y., & Tung, R. L. (2007). International expansion of emerging market enterprises: A springboard perspective. *Journal of International Business Studies*, 38(4): 481–498.

Madhok, A. (1997). Cost, value and foreign market entry mode: The transaction and the firm. *Strategic Management Journal*, 18(1): 39–61.

Mansfield, E. (1962). Entry, Gibrat's law, innovation, and the growth of firms. *American Economic Review*, 52(5): 1023–1051.

Mariotti, S., Piscitello, L., & Elia, S. (2010). Spatial agglomeration of multinational enterprises: The role of information externalities and knowledge spillovers. *Journal of Economic Geography*, 10(4): 519–538.

Mathews, J. A. (2006). Dragon multinationals: New players in 21th century globalization. *Asia Pacific Journal of Management*, 23(1): 5–27.

Mitchell, W., Shaver, J. M., & Yeung, B. (1994). Foreign entrant survival and foreign market share: Canadian companies experience in United States medical sector markets. *Strategic Management Journal*, 15(7): 555–567.

Morck, R., Yeung, B., & Zhao, M. (2008). Perspectives on China's outward foreign direct investment. *Journal of International Business Studies*, 39(3): 337–350.

Muehlfeld, K., Rao Sahib, P., & van Witteloostuijn, A. (2012). A contextual theory of organizational learning from failures and successes: A study of acquisition completions in the global newspaper industry 1981–2008. *Strategic Management Journal*, 33(8): 938–964.

Newbert, S. L. (2007). Empirical research on the resource-based view of the firm. *Strategic Management Journal*, 28(2): 121–146.

O'Brien, M. R. (2007). A caution regarding rules of thumb for variance inflation factors. *Quality & Quantity*, 41(5): 673–690.

Petersen, M. A. (2009). Estimating standard errors in finance panel data sets: Comparing approaches. *Review of Financial Studies*, 22(1): 435–480.

Piscitello, L., & Rabbiosi, L. (2005). The impact of inward FDI on local companies' labour productivity: Evidence from the Italian case. *International Journal of the Economics of Business*, 12(1): 35–51.

Rabbiosi, L., Elia, S., & Bertoni, F. (2012). Acquisitions by EMNCs in developed markets: An organisational learning perspective. *Management International Review*, 52(2): 193–212.

Ramamurti, R. (2009). What have we learned about emerging-market MNEs? In R. Ramamurti & J. V. Singh (Eds.), *Emerging multinationals in emerging markets* (pp. 399–426). New York: Cambridge University Press.

Ramaswamy, K. (1997). The performance impact of strategic similarity in horizontal mergers: Evidence from the U.S. Banking industry. *Academy of Management Journal, 40*(3): 697–715.

Ring, P. S., & Van de Ven, A. (1992). Structuring cooperative relationships between organizations. *Strategic Management Journal, 13*(7): 483–498.

Rugman, A. M. (2008). How global are TNCs from emerging markets? In K. P. Sauvant (Ed.), *The rise of transnational corporations from emerging markets. Threat or opportunity?* (pp. 86–106). Cheltenham, UK/Northampton, MA, USA: Edward Elgar.

Rui, H., & Yip, G. (2008). Foreign acquisitions by Chinese firms: A strategic intent perspective. *Journal of World Business, 43*(2): 213–226.

Sauvant, K. P. (2005). New sources of FDI: The BRICs. Outward FDI from Brazil, Russia, India and China. *Journal of World Investment and Trade, 6*(5): 639–709.

Saxton, T. (1997). The effects of partner and relationship characteristics on alliance outcomes. *Academy of Management Journal, 40*(2): 443–461.

Schweizer, L. (2005). Concept and evolution of business models. *Journal of General Management, 31*(2): 37–56.

Shelton, L. M. (1988). Strategic business fits and corporate acquisition: Empirical evidence. *Strategic Management Journal, 9*(3): 279–287.

Sun, M., & Tse, E. (2009). The resource-based view of competitive advantage in two-sided markets. *Journal of Management Studies, 46*(1): 45–64.

Teece, D., Pisano, G., & Shuen, A. (1997). Dynamic capabilities and strategic management. *Strategic Management Journal, 18*(7): 509–533.

Uhlenbruck, K. (2004). Developing acquired foreign subsidiaries: The experience of MNEs in transition economies. *Journal of International Business Studies, 35*(2): 109–123.

Winter, S. G., Jr. (1995). Four r's of profit: Rents, resources, routines and replication. In C. A. Montgomery (Ed.), *Resource-based and evolutionary theories of the firm: Towards a synthesis* (pp. 147–178). Boston: Kluwer.

Yang, C. H., & Chen, K. H. (2009). Are small firms less efficient? *Small Business Economics, 32*(4): 375–395.

Yaprak, A., & Karademir, B. (2011). Emerging market multinationals' role facilitating developed country multinationals' regional expansion: A critical review of the literature and Turkish MNC examples. *Journal of World Business, 46*(4): 438–446.

Zollo, M., & Winter, S. G. (2002). Deliberate learning and the evolution of dynamic capabilities. *Organization Science, 13*(3): 339–351.

Zollo, M., & Singh, H. (2004). Deliberate learning in corporate acquisitions: Post-acquisition strategies and integration capability in U.S. bank mergers. *Strategic Management Journal, 25*(13): 1233–1256.

[13]

International Business Review 25 (2016) 130–140

Contents lists available at ScienceDirect

International Business Review

journal homepage: www.elsevier.com/locate/ibusrev

ELSEVIER

Do foreign resources assist or impede internationalisation? Evidence from internationalisation of Indian multinational enterprises[☆]

Peter J. Buckley[a], Surender Munjal[a,d,*], Peter Enderwick[a,b], Nicolas Forsans[c]

[a] Centre for International Business, Leeds University Business School, University of Leeds, Leeds LS2 9JT, United Kingdom
[b] Auckland University of Technology, Auckland, New Zealand
[c] University of Exeter Business School, Exeter EX4 4PU, United Kingdom
[d] James E. Lynch India and South Asia Business Centre, Leeds University Business School, University of Leeds, Leeds LS2 9JT, United Kingdom

ARTICLE INFO	ABSTRACT
Article history: Available online 10 July 2015 Keywords: Acquisitions Emerging country multinational enterprise India Internationalisation	Cross-border acquisitions (CBAs) by emerging country multinational enterprises (EMNEs) have attracted considerable scholarly attention in recent years. However, researchers have not yet thoroughly investigated the effects of combining external resources accessed from abroad with resources owned and possessed by the EMNE when undertaking acquisitions. Against the general supposition in the Resource Based View (RBV) that all resources facilitate acquisitions, the paper shows that external foreign resources can impede, as well as assist, cross-border acquisitions. Their effect depends on the nature of interactions between external and internally owned resources within the EMNE. This study offers managerial implications for EMNEs planning to use external resources to accelerate their internationalisation. Crown Copyright © 2015 Published by Elsevier Ltd. All rights reserved.

1. Introduction

The paper analyses the effects of combining external resources with resources owned and possessed by multinationals from emerging economies (EMNEs) when undertaking cross-border acquisitions (CBAs). It is an important topic in international business for three related reasons: *first*, EMNEs are rapidly growing in the world economy. According to the latest World Investment Report, 2014 the share of emerging economies in world outward foreign direct investment (FDI) flows has now reached 39 percent. *Second*, a significant part of their FDI is utilised in undertaking CBAs (UNCTAD, 2014). *Third*, the EMNE's internationalisation using CBAs creates an interesting theoretical conundrum that is worth exploring.

Scholars have attempted to explain the accelerated internationalisation of EMNEs using novel ideas, for instance the Linkage, Leverage and Learning (LLL) framework (Mathews, 2006) which

suggest that the EMNE seeks external resources from abroad to internationalise. The idea is in contrast to the implicit assumption in the general theory of internationalisation, which assumes that resources are available in the firm's home market (Dunning & Lundan, 2008). However, for some firms, and particularly for multinationals from emerging markets, such an assumption may be difficult to support. Emerging markets may lack the sorts of resources – technological, managerial, and organisational – that underpin the success of established multinational enterprises (MNEs) (Deng, 2009; Kumar, 1988; Lecraw, 1993; Makino, Lau, & Yeh, 2002; Ramamurti, 2009). Furthermore, as latecomers to world markets, EMNEs may find that the most attractive resources are possessed by firms located outside their home country. Thus, EMNEs access external resources from abroad and exploit them together with their own resources to accelerate its internationalisation and overcome barriers of internationalisation, such as psychic distance (Johanson & Vahlne, 1977) and the liabilities of both foreignness (Zaheer, 1995), and origin (Pant & Ramachandran, 2012).

The idea of amassing and exploiting external resources along with own resources relates to literature on combinative capabilities which suggests that the firm accessing external resources can fruitfully combine them with its own resources to build competitive advantages (Kogut & Zander, 1992). However, we argue that the current understanding seems to be impaired because, in the context of EMNEs, we do not know how far the EMNE can

[☆] Acknowledgement: We thank the guest editors and three anonymous reviewers for their constructive comments, which helped us to improve the manuscript.
[*] Corresponding author at: Centre for International Business, Leeds University Business School, Maurice Keyworth Building, University of Leeds, Leeds LS2 9JT, United Kingdom. Tel.: +44 113 343 8080; fax: +44 113 343 4754.
E-mail addresses: P.J.Buckley@lubs.leeds.ac.uk (P.J. Buckley), S.Munjal@lubs.leeds.ac.uk (S. Munjal), Peter.enderwick@aut.ac.nz (P. Enderwick), N.Forsans@exeter.ac.uk (N. Forsans).

http://dx.doi.org/10.1016/j.ibusrev.2015.04.004
0969-5931/Crown Copyright © 2015 Published by Elsevier Ltd. All rights reserved.

P.J. Buckley et al./ International Business Review 25 (2016) 130–140 131

successfully combine external resources with its own resources. In other words, how do external foreign resources impact on home-based resources?

In this paper, we examine this important question utilising a data set based on acquisitions by a sample of Indian firms. We define internal resources as domestically sourced resources owned and possessed by the EMNE, while resources sourced by the EMNE from abroad are referred to as external resources. Although similar resources can be accessed by the EMNE from the home country, as indicated above, it is unlikely that domestically available resources, alone, will be sufficient in building competitive advantages that can enable accelerated internationalisation of the EMNE. The extant literature often suggests that given the operating conditions in emerging economies (Wang, Clegg, & Kafouros, 2009) the EMNE may lack the typical resources required to succeed in foreign markets (Child & Rodrigues, 2005; Isobe, Makino, & Montgomery, 2000; Mathews, 2006). For instance, emerging economies are often characterised by weak human and entrepreneurial resources (Khanna & Palepu, 2000; Meyer, Estrin, Bhaumik, & Peng, 2009; Peng, 2003), weak technological and managerial resources (Bartlett & Ghoshal, 2000; Dunning, Kim, & Park, 2008), and underdeveloped marketing resources (Duysters, Jacob, Lemmens, & Jintian, 2009). Therefore, the EMNE seeks to utilise external resources from abroad to compensate for the competitive advantages it typically lacks (Dierickx & Cool, 1989; Mathews, 2006).

We use the resource based view (RBV) (Barney, 1991; Lavie, 2006; Wernerfelt, 1984) to explore the effect of external resources on the EMNE's own resources in making acquisitions. Use of the RBV is apposite because cross-border acquisitions help the EMNE to accelerate its internationalisation and catch-up with peers, but requires the acquiring firm to possess the right kind of resources (Anand & Delios, 2002). Studies using the resource-based theories (Tseng, Tansuhaj, Hallagan, & Mccullough, 2007) conclude that the availability of both internal and external resources is a key factor for the EMNE's internationalisation (Lavie, 2006; Mathews, 2006). Extending this stream of literature, we argue that not all external resources facilitate the EMNE in undertaking cross-border acquisitions. The effect depends upon the interaction of external resources with internal resources possessed by the EMNE.

We show that external foreign resources not only assist in making acquisitions but can also impede acquisitions. More specifically, we find that external technological resources complement the domestic resources of Indian firms. Our argument is that external technological resources are important given that EMNEs are (generally) technologically poorer in comparison to their counterparts from advanced economies. Access to advanced foreign technology augments the EMNE's technological know-how, enabling it to undertake CBAs to exploit rapidly economic rent arising from the use of advanced foreign technology before it becomes obsolete. This is consistent with research that suggests that firms that enjoy accelerated internationalisation are those most able to utilise intangible resources, such as technology and network relations (Etemad, 2005). Access to foreign technology improves the internal technological capabilities of the firm and builds absorptive capacity that allows the accretion of increasingly sophisticated external technological resources (Kogut & Zander, 1992).

On the other hand, we suggest that financial resources drawn from abroad may impede the internationalisation process where, for example, investors exercise a preference for expansion in what are often large and rapidly developing domestic markets, as opposed to more risky overseas ventures. Our hypotheses are tested using a sample of 315 Indian MNEs that undertook foreign acquisitions in the period 2000–2007. The dataset covers 623 foreign acquisitions in 65 host countries with a combined value of almost US$50 billion.

Our findings broaden the boundary conditions of the RBV by combining external and internal resources. They suggest that this interaction may lead to optimum combinations of resources across technology and finance. This aspect is particularly important for EMNEs that lack technological resources, but seek accelerated internationalisation through CBAs. We leave open the possibility that the moderating effects can be negative as well as positive. We contribute to the stream of literature on the resource-based antecedents of cross-border acquisition by EMNEs. We challenge the fundamental assumption, embedded within the RBV (Lavie, 2006) and the LLL framework (Mathews, 2006), that all resources, including external resources, are beneficial for the firm. The existing literature on the value of external resources is overly optimistic, as it has not fully considered the effect of external resources on the competitive strength of the EMNE. Reconciling our findings with existing studies, we present a general model for analysing the effects of external resources on internal resources during the process of CBAs, and suggest that EMNE managers need to exercise caution when accessing external resources.

The paper is organised into five substantive sections. The following section provides a brief review of the relevant literature and hypotheses development. This is followed by a discussion of the research methods used in the study. The results and a discussion of findings are provided in section four. The final section offers concluding comments.

2. Literature review and hypotheses development

Traditionally, the RBV considers the firm as a 'bundle of resources' (Penrose, 1959/2005). It suggests that internal resources, i.e. resources owned or at least fully controlled by the firm, determine the firm's competitive advantages (Barney, 1991; Grant, 1991, 1996; Rubin, 1973; Wernerfelt, 1984). The RBV proposes that these resources are immobile across firms. This results in heterogeneity among firms, with different configurations of competitive advantages within an industry (Barney, 1991; Peteraf, 1993). The firm devises its strategies depending on the quantity and quality of resources possessed, with the aim of optimum utilisation of its proprietary assets (Barney, 1996; Oliver, 1997; Tallman & Li, 1996). Thus, the main idea underlying the RBV is exploitation of internal resources which ultimately determine the firm's strategic choices (Madhok, 1997), performance (Barney, 1986), degree of multinationality (Tseng et al., 2007) and the mode of entry into foreign markets (Isobe et al., 2000; Madhok, 1997).

Scholars (e.g. Anand & Delios, 2002; Tseng et al., 2007) agree that the significance of resources becomes even more important in the case of cross-border acquisitions because acquisitions usually demand a higher degree of resource commitment by the firm. The resources are needed right from the pre acquisition phase that requires target identification and valuation, until the post acquisition phase that deals with the integration of the acquired firm. The need for more resources arises because the cost of acquiring an existing firm is usually more than that of setting up a new venture and the acquiring firm may use the acquisition to diversify into a new business.

Firms, however, face constraints both in terms of the quantity and type of resources required in making CBAs (Tseng et al., 2007). The resource constraint problem is more serious in relation to EMNEs. Prior research suggests that firms originating from emerging economies may lack the resources that underpin success in foreign markets (e.g. Dunning et al., 2008; Gammeltoft, Barnard, & Madhok, 2010; Isobe et al., 2000; Miller, Thomas, Eden, & Hitt, 2009; Rui & Yip, 2008). Facing serious resource limitations, the EMNE needs external resources that not only compensate for existing resource deficiencies, but also accelerate its internationalisation (Dierickx & Cool, 1989; Luo & Rui, 2009; Mathews, 2006).

132   *P.J. Buckley et al./International Business Review 25 (2016) 130–140*

Thus, amassing external resources is a crucial business strategy for EMNEs. It can result in variation in the resource endowment that explains the heterogeneity among firms. Firms that are better endowed are more likely to engage in acquisition than others (Bernard, Eaton, Jensen, & Kortum, 2003; Knight & Cavusgil, 2004; Peteraf, 1993; Tseng et al., 2007). However, a careful selection and deployment of external resources is needed that "permit [the] investing firm to efficiently exploit and enhance existing competitive advantages" (Anand & Delios, 2002, p. 121). Firms that combine resources more efficiently than others are likely to accelerate their internationalisation.

The literature on combinative capabilities suggests that the firm not only accumulate resources but also learns "new skills" by combining external resources with the internal resources possessed by the firm (Kogut & Zander, 1992, p. 383). Furthermore, external resources may increase the firm's production capacity (Ernst & Kim, 2002), marginal rate of return, and economies of scale (Cassiman & Veugelers, 2006) if they complement and/or supplement the firm's internal resources (Kumar, 2009; Luo and Tung, 2007; Murray, Kotabe, & Zhou, 2005). Thus, in a variety of ways, external resources enhance the firm's competitiveness, which may be exploited by the firm through further expansion into foreign markets, including the acquisition of host country firms.

Moreover, accessing and combining external resources with internal resources over time helps the firm learn and become a mature player. Within the context of CBAs, this learning and experience facilitates the firm in identifying appropriate target firms in host countries and exploiting its resources in acquiring foreign firms (Mathews, 2006; Rabbiosi, Elia, & Bertoni, 2012). Further, prior experience of conducting acquisitions increases the likelihood of subsequent acquisitions, sometimes triggering more resource rich firms to engage in serial acquisitions (Elango & Pattnaik, 2011; Haleblian, Kim, & Rajagopalan, 2006).

The literature seems to have largely concluded that internal and external resources are key inputs in undertaking cross-border acquisitions believing that external resources positively combine with the internal resources. To investigate this assumption, we use a systematic classification of resources developed by Miller and Shamsie (1996) which categorises resources into two types: *first*,

knowledge-based resources, and *second* property-based resources. Knowledge-based resources are intangible resources, which refer to know-how and skills. In contrast, property-based resources are tangible resources, which take the form of physical assets. Thus, knowledge-based resources are collective goods that do not diminish in volume when shared with others. However, property-based resources are private goods that dissipate when shared with others.

Miller and Shamsie (1996) classification of knowledge-based resources and property-based resources has been used in similar studies, such as Tseng et al. (2007), following which we use technological know-how as a knowledge-based resource, and financial reserves as a property-based resource when testing our hypotheses. We include external resources, in both categories, to explore their facilitative and obstructive effects. Our conceptual model is given in Fig. 1, which shows four hypotheses that are developed in the following sections. Solid lines represent the direct effect of internal resources on CBAs, and doted lines represent the moderation effect of external resources.

The conceptual model shows that the internal financial and technological resources have a direct positive effect on CBAs. These direct effects are negatively moderated by external financial resources, and positively moderated by external technological resources. Our explanations follow.

2.1. External financial resources and internal financial resources

Our conceptual model shows that internal financial resources have a direct positive effect on CBAs conducted by the firm. Finance is a key resource for the firm's growth (Grant, 1991). The firm's decision on cross-border expansion into foreign markets primarily depends upon its internal financial resources. These give the firm a high degree of freedom in exploiting opportunities for acquisition of foreign firms (Ito & Rose, 2002) and the basis for survival and competition in international markets (Hitt, Dacin, Levitas, Arregle, & Borza, 2000). Further, own financial resources also indirectly influence the firm's ability to undertake a CBA by increasing the endowment of other resources (Doukas & Lang, 2003). For example, a financially affluent firm can hire the talented pool of

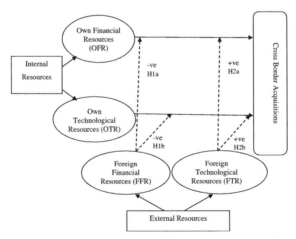

Fig. 1. Conceptual model. Notes: (1) broken arrows (‑ ‑ ‑ ‑▶) represent moderation effect; (2) solid arrows (──▶) represent direct effects.
Source: Authors.

P.J. Buckley et al./International Business Review 25 (2016) 130–140   133

managers and consultants needed for making an acquisition. Thus, own financial resources have a positive relationship with the cross-border expansion of the firm.

Studies (cf. Claessens & Schmukler, 2007; Gozzi, Levine, & Schmukler, 2010) show that multinational enterprises often raise finance externally from international capital markets especially when undertaking foreign direct investment. This might be linked with the growing ease of rising finance internationally. Among the labour, product and capital markets, the capital market is the most globalised and most easily accessed (Buckley, Clegg, Forsans, & Reilly, 2003). Theoretically, external finance is as good a resource as internal finance because it enables the firm to grow and build its competitive advantages. Investors are, by default, interested in the growth of the firm. Therefore, external finance is likely to positively combine with the firm's internal financial resources (Khanna & Palepu, 2004). In the context of internationalisation, the literature suggests several ways in which external financial resources affect the firm's internationalisation. For instance, external finance providers may bring market knowledge that many emerging economy firms lack. It reduces the level of risk faced by the firm in foreign markets (Aitken & Harrison, 1999) and may trigger the firm's internationalisation (Gupta & Govindarajan, 2002). Further, by providing finance an external financer shares risk in foreign markets, which is usually higher than risk in the home market (Johanson & Vahlne, 1977; Welch & Luostarinen, 1993). All these effects can motivate the firm and remove its lassitude in investing abroad (Bhaumik, Driffield, & Pal, 2010). Thus, availability of external finance is likely to positively influence the CBAs undertaken by the firm having own financial resources.

However, in relation to EMNEs, external finance may negatively affect the cross-border expansion of the firm. Given that investment decisions are influenced by rate of return on investment, a foreign investor investing in an EMNE, is likely to maximise economic rent from the thriving home economy of the EMNE. Therefore, foreign investors may prefer the EMNE to focus on its domestic business and exploit domestic growth rather than divert its efforts to foreign markets by undertaking CBA. Hence, contrary to the theoretical benefits of foreign partners – such as orientation towards foreign market and sharing of risk which can positively influence foreign acquisitions undertaken by the EMNE – we hypothesise that a foreign finance provider may impede the EMNE in undertaking CBAs even if the EMNE has its own financial resources.

Hypothesis 1a. Foreign financial resources (FFR) negatively moderate the positive effect of own financial resources (OFR) on cross-border acquisitions undertaken by Indian MNEs.

2.2. External financial resources and internal technological resources

Our conceptual model shows that internal technological resources have a direct positive effect on CBAs. The extant literature suggests that own technological resources help the firm to generate technological assets and capability (Caves, 1971, 2007; Martin & Salomon, 2003). These facilitate growth by bringing operational efficiency, optimising existing processes, and developing innovative capabilities, e.g. the development of new products (Knight & Cavusgil, 2004). A firm with technological resources is therefore likely to be more competitive and ready to undertake FDI so as to maximise the economic returns from exploiting its operational efficiencies and sales of new innovative products (Kafouros, 2008; Tsang, Yip, & Toh, 2008).

The decision of a technologically intensive firm to undertake FDI is positively moderated by a foreign investor. First, a foreign financial partner may provide the capital required for undertaking cross-border acquisitions, for example, in establishing a sales

subsidiary through which the technologically intensive firm can maximise its income by selling its innovative products in foreign markets (Kafouros, 2008; Tsang et al., 2008). In addition, foreign financial partners share the inherent risks in foreign markets and the risk involved in research and development projects, which can facilitate the technologically intensive firm to become more research active and internationalise. Finally, a foreign financial partner providing finance to the technologically intensive firm may also improve the creditworthiness of the firm (Ferris & Park, 2005) because the market presumes that foreign investors monitor the progress of the firm and govern it in a more efficient way (Douma, George, & Kabir, 2006). This may enhance the firm's legitimacy (Pant & Ramachandran, 2012) and raise the trust of lenders and creditors in the market (Ramaswamy, Li, & Veliyath, 2002) enabling the firm to secure more finance to exploit foreign acquisition opportunities.

However, in the context of EMNEs, the application of these general theoretical benefits of a foreign financial investor is debatable for two main reasons. *First*, the impeding argument, stated earlier, is also applicable to the technological intensive EMNE, that is, the foreign investor may want the EMNE to concentrate on exploiting domestic growth by supporting research and development (R&D) projects that have greater applicability to the domestic market. *Second*, given the lower level of technological capability of the EMNE (Dierickx & Cool, 1989; Dunning et al., 2008), the foreign investor may prefer not to risk their funds by supporting cross-border acquisitions undertaken by the EMNE. Thus, we hypothesise that:

Hypothesis 1b. Foreign financial resources (FFR) negatively moderate the positive effect of own technological resources (OTR) on cross-border acquisitions undertaken by Indian MNEs.

2.3. External technological resources and internal financial resources

As earlier discussed in Section 2.1, internal finance is a vital resource for undertaking acquisitions. It directly, as well as indirectly, accelerates the firm's internationalisation (Doukas & Lang, 2003). We argue that the effect of internal financial resources is positively moderated by the availability of external technological resources available to the firm. In the context of EMNEs, we can support our argument by drawing on Penrose's (1959/2005) idea that the limitation of knowledge-based resources put constraints on the firm. Since EMNEs are generally technology deficient (Dierickx & Cool, 1989), acquiring technological resources from an external source can help overcome the EMNE's technological weaknesses (Giroud, Jindra, & Marek, 2012). Thus, the EMNE having its own financial resources can source complementary technological resources to build competitive advantages for internationalisation. Cuervo-Cazurra and Un (2007) argue that many EMNEs are cash rich but in the absence of sufficient technological capabilities they fail to exploit internationalisation opportunities. Thus, we hypothesise that foreign technological resources are likely to have a positive impact on the cross-border acquisitions undertaken by a financially affluent EMNE.

Hypothesis 2a. Foreign technological resources (FTR) positively moderate the positive effect of own financial resources (OFR) on the cross-border acquisitions undertaken by Indian MNEs.

2.4. External technological resources and internal technological resources

As discussed in section 2.2, technological resources have a positive effect on CBAs. Technological resources are recognised as an important factor in the foreign direct investment decisions of the firm (Buckley & Casson, 1976; Chen & Hennart, 2004) because they improve the firm's competitive advantages and facilitate its internationalisation (Kafouros & Buckley, 2008; Tsang et al., 2008). Scholars argue (e.g. Liu, Hodgkinson, & Chuang, 2014) that the effect of own technological resources is supplemented by the availability of external technological resources. Own technological resources can contribute to absorptive capacity (Cohen & Levinthal, 1990; Kogut & Zander, 1992) which enables the firm to assimilate external technological know-how (Liu, Lu, Fila-totchev, Buck, & Wright, 2010). By integrating external technological resources with internal ones, the firm can unlock its potential for innovation (Kafouros & Forsans, 2012) and develop technology based competitive advantages, such as new knowledge, new products, and innovative production processes (Kafouros & Buckley, 2008; Kyläheiko, Jantunen, Puumalainen, Saarenketo, & Tuppura, 2011; Silverman, 1999). This accelerates the firm's internationalisation for market seeking purposes (Diamantopoulos & Inglis, 1993). In other words, technologically intensive firms aim to maximise profits by selling their innovative products in foreign markets (Kafouros, 2008; Tsang et al., 2008). In addition, technologically intensive firms often acquire other technologically intensive firms to broaden and boost their own technological efforts (Kogut & Chang, 1991), for instance by geographically dispersing their R&D (Papanastassiou & Pearce, 1994; Pearce, 1999). Literature on organisational learning also suggests that exposure to external technological resources can enhance the speed of internationalisation (Doz & Prahalad, 1991; Hamel, 1991). Thus, we hypothesise that access to foreign technological resources will have a positive impact on the foreign acquisitions undertaken by a technologically intensive firm.

Hypothesis 2b. Foreign technological resources (FTR) positively moderate the positive effect of own technological resources (OTR) on the cross-border acquisitions undertaken by Indian MNEs.

3. Methods

3.1. The use of Indian MNEs as a test-bed for a research on foreign acquisitions

We examine cross-border acquisitions undertaken by Indian MNEs to test our hypotheses. Indian MNEs offer a good test case for a number of reasons. First, acquisition is a popular internationa-lisation strategy among Indian MNEs. Unlike multinationals from other emerging countries, the majority of India's outward FDI occurs through acquisition of foreign firms by Indian MNEs. In fact, multinationals from India stand out from multinationals from other emerging economies due to their distinctive preference for CBAs (Athreye & Kapur, 2009). Second, recent research suggests that Indian MNEs are building their competencies for foreign expansion by securing strategic foreign resources from abroad (Buckley, Enderwick, Forsans, & Munjal, 2013). Finally, in recent years, Indian MNEs have undertaken some high profile acquisitions that have not only attracted the attention of scholars and policy makers but have also transformed some of these firms into industry leaders. Examples include Infosys and Tata Consultancy Services (TCS) in the Information Technology (IT) industry; Bharti Airtel in the telecommunication industry; Ranbaxy, Dr. Reddy's and The Chemical, Industrial & Pharmaceutical Laboratories (CIPLA) in the pharmaceutical industry; Suzlon, and state owned Oil and Natural Gas Corporation (ONGC) in the power and energy industry; Tata Motors and Mahindra & Mahindra in the automobile industry; and Tata Steel in the steel industry. Tata Steel, after the acquisition of Corus, became the fifth largest steel producer in the world in terms of revenue (UNCTAD, 2007); Bharti Airtel, after

acquiring the African business of Zain Telecom, became the fourth largest telecommunication company in the world in terms of number of mobile phone subscribers; and Tata Motors, after the acquisition of Land Rover and Jaguar, has become the third most innovative company in India (MIT, 2012).

Due to the rising importance of Indian MNEs, questions regarding their ability to undertake CBAs are frequently debated; for instance, what internal and external resources do these MNEs exploit? and how far do external resources impact on the internal resources in acquiring foreign firms? The core motivation of this paper is to answer these intriguing questions.

3.2. Data

Our data on cross-border acquisitions is drawn from Thomson One Banker (TOB) which reports data for both Indian MNEs and Indian subsidiaries of foreign MNEs engaged in acquiring domestic firms in foreign countries. TOB is a reputed and widely used dataset on CBAs in international business, accounting, finance and economics research (Daniels, Krug, & Trevino, 2007; Lara, Osma, & Noguer, 2006; Ma, Pagan, & Chu, 2010; Zou & Ghauri, 2008). We excluded Indian subsidiaries of foreign MNEs from our analysis because they are likely to follow significantly different internationalisation strategies (Fisman & Khanna, 2004). Our final data set incorporates 315 Indian firms that made 623 acquisitions, valued at around US$ 50 bn. in 65 host countries during the period 2000–2007. We created a panel of 315 firms during the eight years from 2000 to 2007, with 2520 observations but after accounting for missing values and lags were left with 1959 observations.

We selected the period 2000–2007 because before the year 2000, Indian acquisitions abroad were negligible while the period after 2007 is affected by the global financial crisis. Therefore, the period 2000–2007 provides an excellent canvas to investigate the CBAs undertaken by Indian MNEs.

We combined the TOB data with Prowess, which is a recognised database on Indian MNEs. Prowess provided financial and background information on Indian MNEs. The Prowess database is substantially richer than other global corporate databases, such as Worldscope (Oura et al., 2009), and has been used in similar recent research (Banga, 2006; Bhaumik et al., 2010; Elango & Pattnaik, 2007). We identified the firms in both data sets by matching their names. Our data set is credible because TOB covers the entire population of Indian firms making foreign acquisitions while Prowess provides extensive information about each of these firms.

3.3. Dependent variable

As stated earlier, our dependent variable is foreign acquisitions undertaken by Indian MNEs. Thomson One Banker provides information on the value of acquisition for each deal. We aggregated acquisitions undertaken by each firm for each year under examination. Consequently, we had two measures of acquisition: first, the number of acquisitions conducted by each firm in each year; and second, the value of these acquisitions. Thomson One Banker provides the value of acquisitions in US dollars rather than the local currency where the deal is made. This is helpful because it brings uniformity in the measurement of the dependent variable.

Measuring acquisitions in two different ways enables us to test two models, one based on the number of foreign acquisitions (NFA), and the other estimating the value of foreign acquisitions (VFA). Estimating acquisitions in two ways is a good practise in research as it provides robustness to results and has been followed in previous studies (Buckley, Forsans, & Munjal, 2012).

P.J. Buckley et al. / International Business Review 25 (2016) 130–140 135

3.4. Independent variables

Own financial resources (OFR) are measured by retained earnings of the firm. Retained earnings means the profits accumulated from previous years after paying dividends to shareholders. It represents free reserves available to the firm that can be ploughed back into the business for future growth, e.g. by acquiring firms abroad. In contrast, foreign financial resources (FFR) are measured by the equity capital contribution of foreign investors. The capital contributed by the foreign investor is usually freely disposable by the firm. However, in the context of EMNEs, it is likely that foreign investors may put covenants and exert pressures on the EMNE decision of internationalisation, which is a focal point under examination in this paper. Both of these measures, OFR and FFR, are standard and have been used in earlier studies (e.g. Bhaumik et al., 2010; Tseng et al., 2007).

Technological resources are measured by the firm's research intensity because, as suggested earlier, research intensive firms are more likely to undertake acquisitions, e.g. for market seeking purposes. Own technological resources (OTR) are represented by the ratio of internal R&D spending to total sales. The ratio represents the research intensity of the firm. This is also a standard measure and follows previous studies, such as Gatignon and Anderson (1988), Erramilli, Agarwal, and Kim (1997), and Tseng et al. (2007). Foreign technological resources (FTR) are measured by the amount of royalty expenditure paid to foreign licensors for technological know-how. Royalty expenditure is a good proxy because royalty payments are directly related to the quantity and quality of technological resources available to the firm, e.g. more royalties are likely to be paid for more advanced technology. Further, royalty payment also captures time period because technological licenses are valid for a specific time period for which the royalty is paid. Moreover, external technological resources, not owned by the firm, cannot be measured in any other way.

3.5. Control variables

We control for both time effects and firm heterogeneity. Time effects are controlled by incorporating time dummies for each year, while firm heterogeneity is controlled by introducing factors such as firm size, firm age, business group affiliation, and experiential learning. All of these variables – size, age and group ownership are standard control variables (Tseng et al., 2007; Bhaumik et al., 2010). Firm size (SIZE) is measured by the capital of the firm and firm age (AGE) is calculated by the number of years that the firm has been in existence, i.e. the number of years since its incorporation. Business group (BG) affiliation is measured using a dummy variable, which takes the value 1 if the firm belongs to an Indian conglomerate business house and 0 otherwise. We also used two extra controls–foreign trade experience (FT), and foreign direct investment experience (FDI). These controls are necessary as a firm engaged in foreign trade is likely to have better knowledge of foreign markets and this can influence foreign acquisition behaviour (Johanson & Vahlne, 1977). The same logic applies to prior foreign direct investment experience (Collins, Holcomb, Certo, Hitt, & Lester, 2009). The international trade variable was created by adding together the yearly value of imports and exports made by the firm, and foreign direct investment experience is measured using the aggregated value of foreign direct investments made by the firm.

3.6. Model and modelling strategy

As discussed earlier, acquisitions are measured in two ways: (1) numbers of deals; and (2) value of deals. Therefore, we have developed two models, which are expressed as follows:

$$\ln VFA_{it} = a + b_1 \ \ln OTR_{it-1} + b_2 \ \ln FTR_{it-1} + b_3 \ \ln OFR_{it}$$
$$+ b_4 \ \ln FFR_{it} + b_5 \ \ln SIZE_{it} + b_6 \ \ln AGE_{it} + b_7 \ BG_{it}$$
$$+ b_8 \ \ln FT_{it} + b_9 \ \ln FDI_{it} + b_{10}I_1 + b_{11}I_2 + b_{12}I_3 + b_{13}I_4$$
$$+ u_{it}$$

$$NFA_{it} = a + b_1 \ \ln OTR_{it-1} + b_2 \ \ln FTR_{it-1} + b_3 \ \ln OFR_{it}$$
$$+ b_4 \ \ln FFR_{it} + b_5 \ \ln SIZE_{it} + b_6 \ \ln AGE_{it} + b_7 \ BG_{it}$$
$$+ b_8 \ \ln FT_{it} + b_9 \ \ln FDI_{it} + b_{10}I_1 + b_{11}I_2 + b_{12}I_3 + b_{13}I_4$$
$$+ u_{it}$$

where i stands for the ith firm and t for time; a is the constant term, b_1 to b_{13} are regression coefficients, and u is the stochastic random error term. The prefix ln indicates the natural log. Thus, NFAit is number of foreign acquisitions by the ith firm in t time and so on. I_1, I_2, I_3 and I_4 are interaction effects; where I_1 is the interaction between FFR and OFR; I_2 is the interaction between FFR and OTR; I_3 is the interaction between FTR and OFR; and I_4 is the interaction between FTR and OTR.

Our hypotheses have the following inference for the coefficient estimates of I_1, I_2, I_3 and I_4.

Hypotheses 1a and 1b imply b_{10}, $b_{11} < 0$
Hypotheses 2a and 2b imply b_{12}, $b_{13} > 0$

Since we have external resources from foreign sources our model may suffer from endogeneity, i.e. overestimation due to reverse causation. In order to address the possibility of endogeneity we have used lags. We used one year lags for foreign technological resources. Lags of foreign financial resources were not used because observation of the data suggests that the foreign investors share has generally remained constant over time. Further, we have also taken one year lag of own technological resources because it is a flow variable and it is likely that the effect of research activities on the firm's decision to internationalise may takes place in the later years.

In estimating our model on value of CBAs we could use the pooled ordinary least square (POLS) method. However, in that case our estimates may be biased for lack of independence and unobserved heterogeneity. This means that the standard errors may be underestimated inflating the significance of variables. In order to address these biases, we used the random effect generalised least square (GLS) method for estimating our model on value of foreign acquisitions. In estimating the model on number of foreign acquisitions we used the random effect negative binomial (NB) method because in this case the dependent variable is a non-continuous variable. The negative binomial model also accounts for the likely over-dispersion of zeros in the dependent variable (Greene, 2003; Hilbe, 2011).

4. Results

Our results are presented in Tables 1 and 2. Table 1 shows GLS random effect estimation results when CBAs are measured in terms of value of acquisitions, and Table 2 shows NB random effect estimation results when CBAs are measured in terms of count of acquisitions. The results are robust and consistent across both number and value of foreign acquisitions. Table 3 includes descriptive statistics, variance inflation factor tests (VIF) and the correlation matrix. We do not envisage multicollinearity in our results because our sample size is large, and all correlation coefficients are below the 0.70 benchmark. The correlation between OFR and SIZE, OFR and FT and FTR and FT are a little

136   P.J. Buckley et al./International Business Review 25 (2016) 130–140

Table 1
GLS random effect results for value of foreign acquisitions (VFA).

	Model 1	Model 2	Model 3	Model 4	Model 5	Model 6
	B (SE)	B (SE)	B (SE)	B (SE)	B (SE)	B (SE)
Time and industry dummies	Yes	Yes	Yes	Yes	Yes	Yes
Firm age (AGE)	−0.442** (0.214)	−0.483** (0.213)	−0.456** (0.214)	−0.494** (0.214)	−0.429** (0.214)	−0.511** (0.213)
Firm size (SIZE)	−0.076 (0.056)	−0.065 (0.056)	−0.072 (0.056)	−0.045 (0.057)	−0.078 (0.056)	−0.038 (0.056)
Business group (BG)	−0.004 (0.244)	−0.057 (0.243)	−0.033 (0.246)	−0.04 (0.244)	0.019 (0.244)	−0.051 (0.2448)
Foreign trade (FT)	0.066** (0.031)	0.081** (0.031)	0.065** (0.031)	0.064** (0.031)	0.073** (0.031)	0.087*** (0.0318)
Foreign direct investment (FDI)	0.094*** (0.02)	0.077*** (0.021)	0.092*** (0.021)	0.091*** (0.02)	0.092*** (0.02)	0.073*** (0.021)
Own technological resources (OTR)	0.04 (0.029)	0.033 (0.029)	0.047 (0.03)	0.043 (0.029)	0.019 (0.031)	0.008 (0.032)
Own financial resources (OFR)	0.173*** (0.06)	0.274*** (0.064)	0.178*** (0.06)	0.133*** (0.061)	0.174*** (0.06)	0.224*** (0.065)
Foreign technological resource (FTR)	0.06** (0.03)	0.052* (0.03)	0.062** (0.03)	−0.043 (0.042)	0.091*** (0.034)	−0.012 (0.044)
Foreign financial resource (FFR)	0.005 (0.023)	0.006 (0.022)	0.041 (0.043)	0.003 (0.023)	0.005 (0.023)	−0.006 (0.044)
OFR*FFR		−0.227*** (0.052)				−0.206*** (0.055)
OTR*FFR			−0.061 (0.063)			0.018 (0.065)
OFR*FTR				0.327*** (0.094)		0.329*** (0.096)
OTR*FTR					0.108** (0.052)	0.136** (0.053)
Constant	−7.191*** (0.821)	−7.5*** (0.82)	−7.195*** (0.821)	−7.976*** (0.849)	−7.093*** (0.822)	−8.137*** (0.847)
R^2	7.37	8.23	7.41	7.93	7.56	8.96
χ^2	154.64***	174.45***	155.58***	162.42***	159.08***	191.05***

Note: Standard errors are reported in parenthesis.
Observations = 1959.
* Significant at 10%.
** Significant at 5%.
*** Significant at 1%.

Table 2
Negative binomial random effect result for number of foreign acquisitions (NFA).

	Model 1	Model 2	Model 3	Model 4	Model 5	Model 6
	B (SE)	B (SE)	B (SE)	B (SE)	B (SE)	B (SE)
Time and industry dummies	Yes	Yes	Yes	Yes	Yes	Yes
Firm age (AGE)	−0.157 (0.098)	−0.152 (0.098)	−0.159 (0.098)	−0.167* (0.098)	−0.153 (0.098)	−0.159 (0.098)
Firm size (SIZE)	0.042 (0.035)	0.056 (0.034)	0.044 (0.035)	0.051 (0.035)	0.041 (0.035)	0.059* (0.034)
Business group (BG)	−0.263** (0.117)	−0.3** (0.118)	−0.274** (0.118)	−0.271** (0.117)	−0.253** (0.117)	−0.2941** (0.119)
Foreign trade (FT)	0.024* (0.014)	0.033** (0.014)	0.023 (0.014)	0.021 (0.014)	0.026 (0.014)	0.0319** (0.015)
Foreign direct investment (FDI)	0.04*** (0.009)	0.036*** (0.009)	0.04*** (0.009)	0.04*** (0.009)	0.039*** (0.009)	0.035*** (0.009)
Own technological resources (OTR)	0.004 (0.012)	0.002 (0.012)	0.007 (0.012)	0.005 (0.012)	−0.002 (0.013)	−0.004 (0.013)
Own financial resources (OFR)	0.116*** (0.032)	0.157*** (0.034)	0.117*** (0.032)	0.098*** (0.032)	0.117*** (0.032)	0.138*** (0.035)
Foreign technological resources (FTR)	0.015 (0.012)	0.008 (0.012)	0.015 (0.012)	−0.017 (0.019)	0.026** (0.013)	−0.007 (0.019)
Foreign financial resources (FFR)	−0.008 (0.011)	−0.029** (0.013)	0.003 (0.02)	−0.008 (0.011)	−0.008 (0.011)	−0.02 (0.022)
OFR*FFR		−0.13*** (0.037)				−0.108*** (0.039)
OTR*FFR			−0.02 (0.03)			−0.009 (0.031)
OFR*FTR				0.085** (0.037)		0.074* (0.039)
OTR*FTR					0.044* (0.024)	0.049** (0.025)
Constant	0.924* (0.474)	0.777 (0.493)	0.909* (0.474)	0.668 (0.489)	0.966* (0.475)	0.616 (0.507)
Log likelihood	−1193.90	−1188.10	−1193.66	−1192.33	−1192.20	−1184.79
χ^2	148.87***	173.41***	149.87***	164.5***	152.66***	184.19***

Note: Standard Errors are reported in parenthesis.
Observations = 1959.
* Significant at 10%.
** Significant at 5%.
*** Significant at 1%.

Table 3
Multicollinearity indices, descriptive statistics and correlation.

	VIF	Mean	S.D.	1	2	3	4	5	6	7	8	9	10	11
1. VFA				1										
2. NFA				0.17	1									
3. AGE	1.39	30.05	19.82	0.09	0.05	1								
4. SIZE	5.35	76.35	208.99	0.10	0.11	0.15	1							
5. BG	1.23	0.64	0.48	0.04	0.06	0.28	0.22	1						
6. FT	2.95	789.88	6186.45	0.05	0.07	0.09	0.41	0.08	1					
7. FDI	1.48	78.24	459.44	0.04	0.08	0.18	0.24	0.11	0.04	1				
8. OTR	1.56	0.61	2.03	0.01	0.12	0.01	−0.04	0.05	−0.01	0.05	1			
9. OFR	6.86	119.22	562.74	0.16	0.13	0.18	0.65	0.14	0.68	0.25	−0.02	1		
10. FTR	1.6	2.12	20.79	0.10	0.04	0.11	0.32	0.07	0.69	0.01	−0.01	0.54	1	
11. FFR	1.27	13.68	16.82	0.01	0.06	−0.02	0.09	0.10	−0.01	0.05	−0.02	0.02	0.01	1

high but the VIF for all variables are within the acceptable level of 10 (Belsley, Kuh, & Welsch, 1980; Field, 2010; Hair, Black, Babin, & Anderson, 2010). The highest VIF is 6.8 for OFR. Furthermore, normal probability distribution and residual plots do not suggest violation of the regression assumptions of normality and homoscedasticity.

In both Tables 1 and 2, our results show six models. The first model is the control model while models 2, 3, 4, 5 and 6 show the

P.J. Buckley et al./International Business Review 25 (2016) 130–140   137

interaction effects between internal and external resources. Models 2, 3, 4 and 5 show individual interactions, while model 6 shows all interactions together. It may be noted that our results are not only consistent across models but they are also consistent across Tables 1 and 2. This shows that our models are robust and reliable.

Overall, the results show foreign financial resources negatively moderate the effect of the firm's financial resources on cross-border acquisitions; while, foreign technological resources positively moderate the effect of both own financial resources and own technological resources on acquisitions of foreign firms undertaken by Indian MNEs. Thus, our Hypotheses 1a, 2a and 2b are fully supported but Hypothesis 1b is not supported. These are interesting results and our interpretations follow.

5. Discussion

The results broadly show that the direct effect of own financial resources on both value (Table 1) and number (Table 2) of cross-border acquisitions undertaken by Indian MNEs are positive and significant. The significance of own financial resources confirm previous studies that EMNEs have significant financial reserves. They have lower levels of debt and higher free cash flows than their counterparts (Knowledge@Wharton, 2006; Staney, Ramarathinam, & Bhoir, 2008; Kumar, 2010) and their internal financial reserves help them to undertake cross-border acquisitions. However, as expected in Hypothesis 1a, the interaction of own financial resources with foreign financial resources (see model 2 in Tables 1 and 2) is significant at the 1% level of significance, with a negative sign. This shows that the combination of own financial resources with foreign financial resources has a negative effect both on the value *(beta = −0.22)* and number *(beta = −0.13)* of cross border acquisitions undertaken by Indian MNEs. This means EMNEs receiving investment from foreign investors engage less in cross-border acquisitions. We have two explanations for this.

First, the negative sign signifies the presence of a substitution effect between the firm's own finance and foreign finance. The availability of own financial resources negates the need for foreign finance because the firm having its own financial resources, in the form of local currency, can convert it into foreign currency for acquiring firms abroad. The second explanation is that, in the context of emerging economies, the foreign finance provider may impede the EMNE's decision to undertake the acquisition of a foreign firm. In terms of combinative capabilities it can be inferred that the EMNE does not have the capabilities to effectively combine foreign financial resources with their own resources. It is important to note that the main effect of the FFR is insignificant which shows that foreign investors do not appear to promote the internationalisation EMNEs. Foreign investors curb the EMNE's decision for internationalisation because one of the main attractions for investing in an emerging economy is the growth potential of the local economy. In the context of the Indian economy, institutional reforms and the large size of the economy have attracted many foreign investors into India (Munjal, Buckley, Enderwick, & Forsans, 2013). Hence, foreign investors prefer the EMNE to expand within its growing domestic market rather than overseas because the foreign investor seeks to capture economic rents arising from rapid growth in the home market of the EMNE. Further, the EMNE is required to invest more in the foreign market because risks in the foreign market are higher than those in the home economy, e.g. due to the presence of psychic distance (Johanson & Vahlne, 1977; Zaheer, 1995). Thus, in terms of combinative capabilities, we argue that foreign finance negatively combines with the internal financial resources of the EMNE.

Model 3 shows the interaction of foreign finance with the firm's own technological resources (Hypothesis 1b). In both Tables 1 and

2, though the coefficient has the expected negative sign it does not reach expected significance levels. Thus, we cannot infer that foreign financial resources do not negatively moderate the effect of own technological resources on CBAs undertaken by Indian MNEs. In other words, the EMNE may lack the capability to combine foreign finance with its own technological resources in order to build its competitive advantages for cross-border expansion. We argue that because the direct effect of own technological resources in our sample is not significant therefore, the negative effect of the interaction term has also not reached significance. This can be a subject for further investigation. The insignificance of own technological resources is consistent with the extant literature that suggests EMNEs lack technology based competitive advantages (Dunning et al., 2008; Duysters et al., 2009). It can be further inferred that the EMNE does not have capabilities to combine foreign financial resources with its own resources or to leverage from foreign investors in making CBA decisions.

The interaction effects of foreign technological resources on the firm's own financial resources are shown in the model 4. According to our expectations, foreign technological resources positively moderate the effect of Indian MNEs' own financial resources on the value *(beta = 0.32)* and number of CBAs *(beta = 0.08)*, at 1% and 5% level of significance, respectively (Hypothesis 2a). This indicates that foreign technology complements Indian MNEs own financial resources, promoting cross border acquisitions. We argue that the firm having its own finance can effectively utilise advanced foreign technology to build competitive advantages required to acquire firms abroad. Having accessed foreign technological resources, the EMNE is likely to undertake acquisitions for market-seeking purposes so that it can quickly realise economic gains before the advanced foreign technology becomes obsolete (Kafouros, 2008; Tseng et al., 2007). In this regard, we argue that the EMNE not only utilises its own financial resource in buying foreign firms but also in undertaking investment to commercially exploit foreign technological resources, e.g. by producing new products (Tsang et al., 2008).

Model 5, shows the interaction effects of foreign technological resources on the firm's own technological resources. As expected, foreign technological resources also positively moderate the effect of Indian MNEs' own technological resources on the value *(beta = 0.10)* and number of CBAs *(beta = 0.04)*, at 5% and 10% level of significance, respectively CBAs (Hypothesis 2b). This indicates that foreign technological resources supplement the firm's own technological resources. The firm's own technological efforts create absorptive capacity to assimilate foreign technology, and in return, foreign technological know-how creates synergy that boosts the firm's own technological efforts (Gentile-Lüdecke & Giroud, 2012; Kogut & Zander, 1992). The literature also suggests that the integration from combining own and foreign technological resources can lead to economies of scale in research and development (Cassiman, Colombo, Garrone, & Veugelers, 2005) and increases the marginal return on the use of own technological resources (Cassiman & Veugelers, 2006). All of these have a positive impact on the performance and technological competitive advantages of the firm that enables the firm to acquire foreign firms, e.g. for market-seeking purposes (Kafouros & Forsans, 2012; Kafouros et al., 2008).

Acquisition also gives the EMNE a pre-emptive advantage by preventing the accelerated internationalisation of competing technologically intensive firms (Tseng et al., 2007; Madhok & Keyhani, 2012). Moreover, it allows the EMNE to concentrate on its core competency in developing technology by utilising advanced foreign technology. Our finding is consistent with a range of studies that highlight the importance of technological resources (cf. Dhanaraj & Beamish, 2003), in explaining the rapid internationalisation of the firm. It also indicates that the EMNE

138   *P.J. Buckley et al. / International Business Review 25 (2016) 130–140*

effectively combines its own resources with foreign technological resources and exploits them in making foreign acquisitions.

6. Conclusions

This paper analyses the combination of internal and external resources in explaining acquisitions undertaken by Indian MNEs. It broadens the boundary conditions of the RBV by examining the interrelationship between external and internal resources. The contribution of the paper lies in exploring how external resources accessed from abroad moderate the effect of internal resources on the EMNE's accelerated internationalisation through CBAs.

Our findings suggest that foreign technological resources positively moderate the effect of both own financial and technological resources in facilitating acquisitions of foreign firms by Indian MNEs. However, foreign financial resources negatively moderate the effect of Indian MNEs financial resources in conducting CBAs. The moderation effect of foreign financial resources on the firm's own technological resources was not significant.

Our interpretation of these results emphasises the domestic economic conditions in the home economy and the Indian firm's (weak) technological, and (strong), financial capability. The positive impact of foreign technology on CBAs suggests that a financially affluent EMNE taps foreign markets by undertaking acquisitions to exploit the potential commercial gains from the use of foreign technological resources. The negative impact of foreign finance on the firm's cross border expansion is interpreted as an incompatibility of external and internal finance combined with the (foreign) investor's preference to focus on growth opportunities within the home market, as well as an indication of substitution of resources. Thus, the financially affluent Indian firm has little need for, and is unlikely to benefit from, external foreign finance.

Our results have implications for the resource seeking motives of EMNEs, and suggest that technological resources provide the strongest impetus to accelerated internationalisation through acquisition. There may be a robust correlation between technological capability and a subsequent desire to secure market resources, such as brand names, distribution networks and local customer knowledge, which complement the effective exploitation of technology in foreign markets. There is also an important trade-off implied by our results. It may be that EMNEs need to balance their desire for rapid international growth against their need to attract additional overseas finance. Foreign investor's preferences for strong domestic growth in emerging economies, certainly in the case of India, appear to impede cross-border expansion.

The study contributes to our understanding on the combinative capabilities of resources for EMNEs' accelerated internationalisation through CBAs, and raises interesting implications for managers. While managers of EMNEs may focus on the quantity of resources as a means of overcoming barriers to internationalisation, our findings suggest that the nature of resources, particularly when foreign and own sources are combined, is also important. Managers need to undertake a careful assessment of resource selection and utilisation in understanding the contribution of a firm's resource base to its competitive strength. Where strong complementarity is apparent, as in the case of foreign technology and the firm's own resources, strong leveraging may facilitate internationalisation through CBAs.

Our results also suggest that CBAs are not driven simply by the availability of resources. Successful assimilation of external resources, in particular, also requires combinative capabilities – technological, organisational and managerial. This suggests that EMNE managers may face trade-offs. One is between time and resources. The firm may benefit from delaying internationalisation to build up its own assets if it wishes to avoid the constraints that

come with foreign resources. Some managerial discretion is sacrificed when growth is underpinned by foreign resources. In the case of foreign technological resources the restrictions are likely to be operational, for example restrictions on side selling or a requirement to source inputs from the licensor. In the case of foreign finance the boundaries appear to be more strategic with asset owners (foreign investors) expressing market preferences. A second trade-off may be internal, particularly in the case of India's larger conglomerates, where 'internal' funds could be sourced from other divisions of the organisation. While this overcomes the home market preference, it imposes a cost on those divisions denied funds and such funds may not convey the additional benefits (foreign market knowledge, experience etc.) that foreign investors provide. Finally, it is worth noting that our results relate only to internationalisation achieved through CBAs and further work to examine the interaction effects of different types of resources on greenfield investment would be most valuable.

In common with most research, our paper suffers a number of limitations that suggest the need for future research. We restrict our analysis only to Indian EMNEs and the extent to which these findings can be generalised to firms in other emerging markets is not clear. Future research could test our propositions in the context of other emerging economies. Institutional differences in funding, forms of ownership (family owned, state owned) and governance are also likely to impact on resource use. This is an area worthy of further study. We did not model local economic conditions to provide empirical support to our argument that foreign investors may impede CBA. Empirical tests incorporating market growth rates and the pace and degree of reforms in local host economies could provide useful corroborating findings. Further, it would also be useful to improve our understanding of the relationship between internal and external resources, i.e. the mechanisms through which the moderation effect takes place, e.g. complementarity and substitution between internal and external resources. Further work might also attempt to examine the relationships between the antecedent conditions we have identified and subsequent CBAs. Finally, we have suggested that the utilisation of technological resources in foreign markets provides an incentive for the EMNE to undertake CBAs and we might expect to see complementarities between the current resources of the investing firm and the resources provided by acquisition targets.

References

Aitken, B. J., & Harrison, A. E. (1999). Do domestic firms benefit from direct foreign investment? Evidence from Venezuela. *American Economic Review, 89*, 605–618.
Anand, J., & Delios, A. (2002). Absolute and relative resources as determinants of international acquisitions. *Strategic Management Journal, 23*, 119–134.
Athreye, S. S., & Kapur, S. (2009). The internationalization of Chinese and Indian firms: Trends, motivations and strategy. *Industrial and Corporate Change, 18*, 209.
Banga, R. (2006). The export-diversifying impact of Japanese and US foreign direct investments in the Indian manufacturing sector. *Journal of International Business Studies, 37*, 558–568.
Barney, J. (1986). Strategic factor markets: Expectations, luck, and business strategy. *Management Science, 32*, 1231–1241.
Barney, J. (1991). Firm resources and sustainable competitive advantage. *Journal of Management, 17*, 99–120.
Barney, J. (1996). The resource-based theory of the firm. *Organization Science, 7*, 469.
Bartlett, C. A., & Ghoshal, S. (2000). Going global: Lessons from late movers. *Harvard Business Review, 78*, 132–142.
Belsley, D. A., Kuh, E., & Welsch, R. E. (1980). *Regression diagnostics: Identifying influential observations and sources of collinearity.* New York: John Wiley and Sons.
Bernard, A. B., Eaton, J., Jensen, J. B., & Kortum, S. (2003). Plants and productivity in international trade. *American Economic Review, 93*, 1268–1290.
Bhaumik, S. K., Driffield, N., & Pal, S. (2010). Does ownership structure of emerging-market firms affect their outward FDI? The case of the Indian automotive and pharmaceutical sectors. *Journal of International Business Studies, 41*, 437–450.
Buckley, P. J., & Casson, M. (1976). *The future of the multinational enterprise.* London: Macmillan.
Buckley, P. J., Clegg, J., Forsans, N., & Reilly, K. T. (2003). Evolution of FDI in the United States in the context of trade liberalisation and regionalisation. *Journal of Business Research, 56*, 853–857.

Buckley, P. J., Forsans, N., & Munjal, S. (2012). Host–home country linkages and host–home country specific advantages as determinants of foreign acquisitions by Indian firms. *International Business Review, 21*, 878–890.

Buckley, P. J., Enderwick, P., Forsans, N., & Munjal, S. (2013). Country linkages and firm internationalisation: Indian MNEs within economic-political alliances of nations. In G. Cook & J. Johns (Eds.), *The changing geography of international business*. Basingstoke: Palgrave MacMillan.

Cassiman, B., Colombo, M. G., Garrone, P., & Veugelers, R. (2005). The impact of M&A on the R&D process: An empirical analysis of the role of technological-and-market-relatedness. *Research Policy, 34*, 195–220.

Cassiman, B., & Veugelers, R. (2006). In search of complementarity in innovation strategy: Internal R&D and external knowledge acquisition. *Management Science*, , 68–82.

Caves, R. E. (1971). International corporations: The industrial economics of foreign investment. *Economica, 38*, 1–27.

Caves, R. E. (2007). *Multinational enterprise and economic analysis*. Cambridge: Cambridge University Press.

Chen, S.-F.S., & Hennart, J.-F. (2004). A hostage theory of joint ventures: Why do Japanese investors choose partial over full acquisitions to enter the United States? *Journal of Business Research, 57*, 1126–1134.

Child, J., & Rodrigues, S. B. (2005). The internationalisation of Chinese firms. *Management and Organisation Review, 1*, 381–410.

Claessens, S., & Schmukler, S. L. (2007). International financial integration through equity markets: Which firms from which countries go global? *Journal of International Money and Finance, 26*, 788–813.

Cohen, W. M., & Levinthal, D. A. (1990). Absorptive capacity: A new perspective on learning and innovation. *Administrative Science Quarterly, 35*, 128–152.

Collins, J. D., Holcomb, T. R., Certo, S. T., Hitt, M. A., & Lester, R. H. (2009). Learning by doing: Cross-border mergers and acquisitions. *Journal of Business Research, 62*, 1329–1334.

Cuervo-Cazurra, A., & Un, A. C. (2007). Types of difficulties in internationalization and their consequences. In S. Tallman (Ed.), *A new generation in international strategic management*. Cheltenham: Edward Elgar.

Daniels, J. D., Krug, J. A., & Trevino, L. (2007). Foreign direct investment from Latin America and the Caribbean. *Transnational Corporations, 16*, 27.

Deng, P. (2009). Why do Chinese firms tend to acquire strategic assets in international expansion? *Journal of World Business, 44*, 74–84.

Dhanaraj, C. A., & Beamish, P. W. (2003). Resource-based approach to the study of export performance. *Journal of Small Business Management, 41*, 242–261.

Diamantopoulos, A., & Inglis, K. (1993). Identifying differences between high-and low-involvement exporters. *International Marketing Review, 5*, 52–60.

Dierickx, I., & Cool, K. (1989). Asset stock accumulation and sustainability of competitive advantage. *Management Science, 35*, 1504–1511.

Doukas, J. A., & Lang, L. H. P. (2003). Foreign direct investment, diversification and firm performance. *Journal of International Business Studies, 34*, 153–172.

Douma, S., George, R., & Kabir, R. (2006). Foreign and domestic ownership, business groups, and firm performance: Evidence from a large emerging market. *Strategic Management Journal, 27*, 637–657.

Doz, Y. L., & Prahalad, C. K. (1991). Managing DMNCs: A search for new paradigm. *Strategic Management Journal, 12*, 145–164.

Dunning, J. H., Kim, C., & Park, D. (2008). Old wine in new bottles: A comparison of emerging-markets TNCs today and developed country TNCs thirty years ago. In K. P. Sauvant (Ed.), *The rise of transnational corporations from emerging markets: Threat or opportunity?* Cheltenham: Edward Elgar.

Dunning, J. H., & Lundan, S. (2008). *Multinational enterprises and the global economy*. Cheltenham: Edward Elgar.

Duysters, G., Jacob, J., Lemmens, C., & Jintian, Y. (2009). Internationalization and technological catching up of emerging multinationals: A comparative case study of China's Haier group. *Industrial and Corporate Change, 18*, 325–349.

Elango, B., & Pattnaik, C. (2007). Building capabilities for international operations through networks: A study of Indian firms. *Journal of International Business Studies, 38*, 541–555.

Elango, B., & Pattnaik, C. (2011). Learning before making the big leap. *Management International Review, 51*, 461–481.

Ernst, D., & Kim, L. (2002). Global production networks, knowledge diffusion, and local capability formation. *Research policy, 31*, 1417–1429.

Erramilli, M. K., Agarwal, S., & Kim, S.-S. (1997). Are firm-specific advantages location-specific too? *Journal of International Business Studies, 28*, 735–757.

Etemad, H. (2005). SMEs' Internationalization strategies based on a typical subsidiary evolutionary life cycle in three distinct stages. *Management International Review, 45*, 145–186.

Ferris, S. P., & Park, K. (2005). *Foreign ownership and firm value: Evidence from Japan*. *Advances in Financial Economics*. Bingley: Emerald (MCB UP).

Field, A. (2010). *Discovering statistics using SPSS*. London: SAGE Publications.

Fisman, R., & Khanna, T. (2004). Facilitating development: The role of business groups. *World Development, 32*, 609–628.

Gammeltoft, P., Barnard, H., & Madhok, A. (2010). *Emerging multinationals, emerging theory: Macro- and micro-level perspectives*. Oxford: Elsevier.

Gatignon, H., & Anderson, E. (1988). The multinational corporation's degree of control over foreign subsidiaries: An empirical test of a transaction cost explanation. *Journal of Law, Economics, & Organization, 4*, 305–336.

Gentile-Lüdecke, S., & Giroud, A. (2012). Knowledge transfer from TNCs and upgrading of domestic firms: The Polish Automotive Sector. *World Development, 40*, 796–807.

Giroud, A., Jindra, B., & Marek, P. (2012). Heterogeneous FDI in transition economies – A novel approach to assess the developmental impact of backward linkages. *World Development, 40*, 2206–2220.

Gozzi, J. C., Levine, R., & Schmukler, S. L. (2010). Patterns of international capital raisings. *Journal of International Economics, 80*, 45–57.

Grant, R. M. (1991). The resource-based theory of competitive advantage: Implications for strategy formulation. *California Management Review, 33*, 114–135.

Grant, R. M. (1996). Toward a knowledge-based theory of a firm. *Strategic Management Journal, 17*, 109–122.

Greene, W. H. (2003). *Econometric analysis*. New York: Prentice Hall.

Gupta, A. K., & Govindarajan, V. (2002). Cultivating a global mindset. *Academy of Management Executive, 16*, 116–126.

Hair, J. F., Black, W. C., Babin, B. J., & Anderson, R. E. (2010). *Multivariate data analysis: A global perspective*. New Jersey: Pearson Prentice Hall.

Haleblian, J., Kim, J. Y. J., & Rajagopalan, N. (2006). The influence of acquisition experience and performance on acquisition behaviour: Evidence from the US commercial banking industry. *Academy of Management Journal, 49*, 357–370.

Hamel, G. (1991). Competition for competence and inter-partner learning within international strategic alliances. *Strategic Management Journal, 12*, 83–103.

Hilbe, J. M. (2011). *Negative binomial regression*. New York: Cambridge University Press.

Hitt, M. A., Dacin, M. T., Levitas, E., Arregle, J. L., & Borza, A. (2000). Partner selection in emerging and developed market contexts: Resource-based and organizational learning perspectives. *Academy of Management Journal, 43*, 449–467.

Isobe, T., Makino, S., & Montgomery, D. B. (2000). Resource commitment, entry timing, and market performance of foreign direct investments in emerging economies: The case of Japanese international joint ventures in China. *Academy of Management Journal, 43*, 468–484.

Ito, K., & Rose, E. L. (2002). Foreign direct investment location strategies in the tire industry. *Journal of International Business Studies, 33*, 593–602.

Johanson, J., & Vahlne, J. E. (1977). The internationalization process of the firm—a model of knowledge development and increasing foreign market commitments. *Journal of International Business Studies, 8*, 23–32.

Kafouros, M. I., & Buckley, P. J. (2008). Under what conditions do firms benefit from the research efforts of other organizations? *Research Policy, 37*, 225–239.

Kafouros, M. I., & Forsans, N. (2012). The role of open innovation in emerging economies: Do companies profit from the scientific knowledge of others? *Journal of World Business, 47*, 362–370.

Kafouros, M. I. (2008). *Industrial innovation and firm performance: The impact of scientific knowledge on multinational corporations*. Cheltenham: Edward Elgar Publishing.

Khanna, T., & Palepu, K. G. (2000). Is group affiliation profitable in emerging markets? An analysis of diversified Indian business groups. *Journal of Finance, 55*, 867–891.

Khanna, T., & Palepu, K. G. (2004). Globalization and convergence in corporate governance: Evidence from Infosys and the Indian software industry. *Journal of International Business Studies, 35*, 484–507.

Knight, G. A., & Cavusgil, S. T. (2004). Innovation, organizational capabilities, and the born-global firm. *Journal of International Business Studies, 35*, 124–141.

Knowledge@Wharton (2006). *How Indian companies fund their overseas acquisitions*. Published India KnowledgeWharton [Online] [accessed 130110].

Kogut, B., & Chang, S. J. (1991). Technological capabilities and Japanese foreign direct investment in the United States. *Review of Economics and Statistics, 73*, 401–413.

Kogut, B., & Zander, U. (1992). Knowledge of the firm, combinative capabilities, and the replication of technology. *Organization Science, 3*, 383–397.

Kumar, K. (2009). The role of local entrepreneurship and multinational firms in the growth of the IT sector. *South Asian Journal of Management, 16*, 24–41.

Kumar, N. (1988). Globalization. In *Foreign direct investment and technology transfers: Impacts on and prospects for developing countries*. New York: Routledge.

Kumar, S. R. (2010, January 4). Indian firms high on equity, low on debt. *Financial Chronicle*.

Kyläheiko, K., Jantunen, A., Puumalainen, K., Saarenketo, S., & Tuppura, A. (2011). Innovation and internationalization as growth strategies: The role of technological capabilities and appropriability. *International Business Review, 20*, 508–520.

Lara, J. M. G., Osma, B. G., & Noguer, B. G. D. A. (2006). Effects of database choice on international accounting research. *Abacus, 42*, 426–454.

Lavie, D. (2006). The competitive advantage of interconnected firms: An extension of the resource-based view. *Academy of Management Review, 31*, 638–658.

Lecraw, D. J. (1993). Outward direct investment by Indonesian firms: Motivation and effects. *Journal of International Business Studies, 24*, 589–600.

Liu, X., Lu, J., Filatotchev, I., Buck, T., & Wright, M. (2010). Returnee entrepreneurs, knowledge spillovers and innovation in high-tech firms in emerging economies. *Journal of International Business Studies, 41*, 1183–1197.

Liu, X., Hodgkinson, I. R., & Chuang, F. M. (2014). Foreign competition, domestic knowledge base and innovation activities: Evidence from Chinese high-tech industries. *Research Policy, 43*, 414–422.

Luo, Y., & Rui, H. (2009). An ambidexterity perspective toward multinational enterprises from emerging economies. *Academy of Management Perspectives, 23*, 49–70.

Luo, Y., & Tung, R. L. (2007). International expansion of emerging market enterprises: A springboard perspective. *Journal of International Business Studies, 38*, 481–498.

Ma, J., Pagan, J. A., & Chu, Y. (2010). Abnormal returns to mergers and acquisitions in ten Asian stock markets. *International Journal of Business, 14*, 235–250.

Madhok, A., & Keyhani, M. (2012). Acquisitions as entrepreneurship: Asymmetries, opportunities, and the internationalization of multinationals from emerging economies. *Global Strategy Journal, 2*, 26–40.

Madhok, A. (1997). Cost, value and foreign market entry mode: The transaction and the firm. *Strategic Management Journal, 18*, 39–61.

Makino, S., Lau, C.-M., & Yeh, R.-S. (2002). Asset-exploitation versus asset-seeking: Implications for location choice of foreign direct investment from newly industrialized economies. *Journal of International Business Studies, 33*, 403–421.

Martin, X., & Salomon, R. (2003). Knowledge transfer capacity and its implications for the theory of the multinational corporation. *Journal of International Business Studies, 34*, 356–373.

Mathews, J. A. (2006). Dragon multinationals: New players in 21st century globalization. *Asia Pacific Journal of Management, 23*, 5–27.

Meyer, K. E., Estrin, S., Bhaumik, S. K., & Peng, M. W. (2009). Institutions, resources, and entry strategies in emerging economies. *Strategic Management Journal, 30*, 61–80.

Miller, D., & Shamsie, J. (1996). The resource-based view of the firm in two environments: The Hollywood film studios from 1936 to 1965. *Academy of Management Journal, 39*, 519–543.

Miller, S. R., Thomas, D. E., Eden, L., & Hitt, M. (2009). Knee deep in the big muddy: The survival of emerging market firms in developed markets. *Management International Review, 48*, 645–666.

MIT (2012, October 6). *MIT India conference: Entrepreneurship panel.* Boston: Massachusetts Institute of Technology.

Murray, J. Y., Kotabe, M., & Zhou, J. N. (2005). Strategic alliance-based sourcing and market performance: Evidence from foreign firms operating in China. *Journal of International Business Studies, 36*, 187–208.

Munjal, S., Buckley, P. J., Enderwick, P., & Forsans, N. (2013). The growth trajectory of Indian MNEs. In C. Brautaset & C. Dent (Eds.), *The great diversity – Trajectories of Asian development.* Wagening, Netherlands: Wageningen Academic Press.

Oliver, C. (1997). Sustainable competitive advantage: Combining institutional and resource-based views. *Strategic Management Journal, 18*, 697–713.

Oura, H., Hume, A. R., Papi, L., Saxegaard, M., Petia, T., Peiris, S. J., & Alejandro, S. (2009). *India: Selected issues.* Washington, DC: International Monetary Fund.

Pant, A., & Ramachandran, J. (2012). Legitimacy beyond borders: Indian software services firms in the United States, 1984 to 2004. *Global Strategy Journal, 2*, 224–243.

Papanastassiou, M., & Pearce, R. D. (1994). The internationalisation of research and development by Japanese enterprises. *R&D Management, 24*, 155–165.

Pearce, R. D. (1999). Decentralised R&D and strategic competitiveness: Globalised approaches to generation and use of technology in multinational enterprises. *Research Policy, 28*, 157–178.

Peng, M. W. (2003). Institutional transitions and strategic choices. *Academy of Management Review, 28*, 275–296.

Penrose, E. T. (1959/2005). *The theory of the growth of the firm.* Oxford: Oxford University Press.

Peteraf, M. A. (1993). The corner stones of competitive advantage: A resource-based view. *Strategic Management Journal, 14*, 179–191.

Rabbiosi, A. P. L., Elia, A. P. S., & Bertoni, A. P. F. (2012). Acquisitions by EMNCs in developed markets. *Management International Review, 52*, 193–212.

Ramamurti, R. (2009). Why study emerging-market multinationals? In R. Ramamurti & J. V. Singh (Eds.), *Emerging multinationals from emerging markets.* Cambridge: Cambridge University Press.

Ramaswamy, K., Li, M., & Veliyath, R. (2002). Foreign investors, foreign directors and corporate diversification: An empirical examination of large manufacturing companies in India. *Strategic Management Journal, 23*, 345–358.

Rubin, P. H. (1973). The expansion of firms. *Journal of Political Economy, 81*, 936–949.

Rui, H., & Yip, G. S. (2008). Foreign acquisitions by Chinese firms: A strategic intent perspective. *Journal of World Business, 43*, 213–226.

Silverman, B. S. (1999). Technological resources and the direction of corporate diversification: Toward an integration of the resource-based view and transaction cost economics. *Management Science, 45*, 1109–1124.

Staney, N., Ramarathinam, A., & Bhoir, A. (2008, June 26). Low debt to cushion Indian cos from higher borrowing costs. *Livemint.*

Tallman, S., & Li, J. (1996). Effects of international diversity and product diversity on the performance of multinational firms. *Strategic Management Journal, 39*, 196–197.

Tsang, E. W. K., Yip, P. S. L., & Toh, M. H. (2008). The impact of R&D on value added for domestic and foreign firms in a newly industrialized economy. *International Business Review, 17*, 423–441.

Tseng, C.-H., Tansuhaj, P., Hallagan, W., & Mccullough, J. (2007). Effects of firm resources on growth in multinationality. *Journal of International Business Studies, 38*, 961–974.

UNCTAD (2007). *Transnational corporations, extractive industries and development* (World Investment Report) Geneva and New York, United Nations.

UNCTAD (2014). *Investing in the SDGs: An action plan* (World Investment Report) Geneva and New York, United Nations.

Wang, C., Clegg, J., & Kafouros, M. (2009). Country-of-origin effects of foreign direct investment. *Management International Review, 49*, 179–198.

Welch, L. S., & Luostarinen, R. (1993). Internationalization: Evolution of a concept. In P. J. Buckley & P. N. Ghauri (Eds.), *The internationalization of the firm: A reader.* Oxford: Thomson Learning.

Wernerfelt, B. (1984). A resource-based view of the firm. *Strategic Management Journal, 5*, 171–180.

Zaheer, S. (1995). Overcoming the liability of foreignness. *Academy of Management Journal, 38*, 341–363.

Zou, H., & Ghauri, P. (2008). Learning through international acquisitions: The process of knowledge acquisition in China. *Management International Review, 48*, 207–226.

[14]

International Business Review 25 (2016) 986–996

Contents lists available at ScienceDirect

International Business Review

journal homepage: www.elsevier.com/locate/ibusrev

ELSEVIER

Cross-border acquisitions by Indian multinationals: Asset exploitation or asset augmentation?

Peter J. Buckley[a], Surender Munjal[a,d,*], Peter Enderwick[a,b], Nicolas Forsans[c]

[a] Centre for International Business, Leeds University Business School, University of Leeds, Leeds LS2 9JT, United Kingdom
[b] Auckland University of Technology, Auckland, New Zealand
[c] University of Exeter Business School, Exeter EX4 4PU, United Kingdom
[d] James E. Lynch India and South Asia Business Centre, Leeds University Business School, University of Leeds, Leeds LS2 9JT, United Kingdom

ARTICLE INFO

Article history:
Received 15 April 2014
Received in revised form 7 October 2015
Accepted 16 October 2015
Available online 6 November 2015

Keywords:
Firm specific assets
Asset augmentation
Cross-border acquisitions
India
Multinationals from emerging countries
Asset seeking foreign direct investment

ABSTRACT

This paper examines cross-border acquisitions by Indian multinationals and places them in the context of Emerging Country Multinationals. It tests hypotheses based on internalisation theory and the resource based view to ask if these firms are asset exploiting or asset augmenting in their takeover behaviour. Internal financial and technological resources are found to be important explanatory variables, as is asset seeking; of brands, technology and market access. The home environment in India allows firms to amass profits, to manage in a culturally diverse setting and to develop asset bundling skills. All these factors are significant in determining cross-border acquisitions.

© 2015 Elsevier Ltd. All rights reserved.

1. Introduction

Cross-border acquisitions (CBAs) undertaken by emerging country multinational enterprises (EMNEs) have increased significantly over time (UNCTAD, 2011). Though the phenomenon of EMNE's internationalisation using CBAs has been investigated (Luo, 2010), the lack of theoretical and empirical attention to the determinants of CBAs by EMNEs is particularly surprising (Haleblian, Devers, McNamara, Carpenter, & Davison, 2009; Tseng, Tansuhaj, Hallagan, & McCullough, 2007).

Traditionally, internationalisation of the firm is explained by the asset-exploitation perspective (Caves, 1971; Hymer, 1976) which along with internalisation theory (Buckley & Casson, 1976) became the foundation for the popular 'eclectic framework' of internationalisation (Dunning, 1977, 1981). According to the framework, the firm successfully undertakes foreign direct investment (FDI) by exploiting its ownership advantages and out-competing local firms in foreign markets. Thus in this

framework, possession of ownership advantages is a necessary pre-condition of which the firm is not able to overcome the liabilities of foreignness (Zaheer, 1995).

Increasing internationalisation of EMNEs through acquisitions has significant implications for theory building (Peng, 2012). It presents an excellent opportunity to revisit theories, provide new empirical evidence, and find new theoretical explanations (Ramamurti, 2012). For instance, Hennart (2012) suggests that home country specific advantages push EMNE's to undertake acquisitions of foreign firms for asset augmentation purposes. In this respect, Hoskisson, Wright, Filatotchev, and Peng (2013) argue that new multinationals from the mid-range emerging economies, such as India, present an interesting case study because they break the dichotomy between the internationalisation behaviour of MNEs originating from emerging and developed economies. Market institutions in emerging economies provide an important contextualised perspective that explains the competitive advantages that EMNEs realise at home, and their need to attain complementary assets through internationalisation.

Hennart (2012) argues that Dunning's OLI framework (1977, 1981, 1988) does not explain the pattern of EMNEs because it does not account for the 'bundling' of assets that an MNE requires to internationalise. Hennart's view is that the approach built within the OLI framework overlooks the skills that all MNEs need to

---

* Corresponding author at: Centre for International Business, Leeds University Business School, University of Leeds, Leeds LS2 9JT, United Kingdom.
E-mail addresses: P.J.Buckley@lubs.leeds.ac.uk (P.J. Buckley), S.Munjal@lubs.leeds.ac.uk (S. Munjal), Peter.enderwick@aut.ac.nz (P. Enderwick), N.Forsans@exeter.ac.uk (N. Forsans).

http://dx.doi.org/10.1016/j.ibusrev.2015.10.006
0969-5931/© 2015 Elsevier Ltd. All rights reserved.

P.J. Buckley et al./International Business Review 25 (2016) 986–996   987

combine the locational attributes ("Country specific advantages" (CSAs)) with their own complementary assets ("Firm specific advantages" (FSAs)) (see also, Hennart, 2009). Moreover, the OLI approach does not explain why some emerging country firms manage to convert their home CSAs into FSAs while others do not. The evolving literature on the internationalisation of EMNEs suggests that firms originating from emerging economies aim to augment home country strategic assets with foreign ones (Child & Rodrigues, 2005; Mathews, 2002b, 2006; Rui & Yip, 2008; Santangelo, 2009). This view, known as the asset-augmentation perspective, argues that EMNEs lack the competitive advantages required to out-compete local firms in foreign markets. EMNEs internationalise in order to build competitive advantages by augmenting strategic assets and resources. Thus asset-seeking internationalisation is a 'spring-board' for growth and further internationalisation (Luo & Tung, 2007).

In this respect, the extant literature does not provide sufficient understanding of how the EMNE internationalises to augment its assets if it does not have sufficient pre-existing competitive advantages. Thus, the literature presents a 'chicken or egg' puzzle on the subject of EMNE's internationalisation. The contribution of this paper lies in addressing this puzzle by examining the foreign acquisitions undertaken by Indian MNEs. These firms represent a good case study given: (1) Indian MNEs have made some prominent acquisitions in recent years; (2) by making foreign acquisitions many Indian MNEs such as Bharti Airtel, Tata Steels, and Suzlon have become industry leaders (Airtel, 2012; MIT, 2012; Suzlon, 2012; UNCTAD, 2007); (3) India stands out in comparison to other emerging economies in terms of the number of foreign acquisitions undertaken by Indian MNEs (KPMG, 2012) and (4) the majority of Indian outward FDI occurs through foreign acquisitions (Athukorala, 2009).

The development of Indian firms into domestic giants and then EMNEs is first and foremost a product of home country factors and, in particular, Indian government policy. Many Indian firms grew domestically and diversified because of a protected home market (Khanna & Palepu, 2010; Munjal, Buckley, Enderwick, & Forsans, 2013). They were unable to import technology (Desai, 1972) and so the 'catch-up' process involved the acquisition of foreign technology, largely through the purchase of foreign firms (Duysters, Jacob, Lemmens, & Jintian, 2009; Narayanan & Bhat, 2010). We argue that these acquisitions were financed by the accumulation of funds arising from super-normal profits in the large, protected Indian economy. Furthermore, diversities within India (on almost every dimension – language, religion, culture) enabled domestic Indian firms to build skills that aided internationalisation, such as managing a diverse workforce (Pereira & Malik, 2015). Marketing strategies too, had to provide for a fragmented consumer market. There are, therefore, grounds for believing that, even prior to internationalisation, Indian firms had internalised the skills, attributes and resources necessary to successfully undertake foreign acquisitions. This accords with Hennart's (2012) analysis of the management skills needed to 'bundle' assets and to convert latent country specific advantages into firm specific advantages. One further factor of note is that many Indian firms are part of large, diversified business groups and this too, may impact their pattern of internationalisation.

We also contribute to literature, especially the 'Goldilocks' debate (Cuervo-Cazurra, 2012), by integrating the asset exploitation and asset augmentation views, suggesting that no new theory is required for explaining the internationalisation of EMNEs. EMNEs are growing rapidly and some of these firms have emerged as world leaders in their industries. The study of EMNEs has generated significant academic interest and generated the 'Goldilocks debate' regarding the need to analyse their distinctiveness in relation to theory. The debate has three perspectives: (1) EMNEs

behave differently and there is a need to have new theories and models to analyse their behaviour; (2) EMNEs are not a new species and existing theories can adequately explain their behaviour and (3) the analysis of EMNEs does not require new theories but some modification or extension to existing theories and models (Cuervo-Cazurra, 2012). EMNEs seek to compensate for their weaknesses by using network-based resources emerging from institutional and industrial characteristics of their home countries (Cuervo-Cazurra & Genc, 2008; Elango & Pattnaik, 2007). However, these firms do possess firm specific ownership advantages and 'bundling' skills (Hennart, 2012) shaped by home country conditions.

2. Literature review

2.1. Internationalisation by asset exploitation

In order to resolve the puzzle, we draw on the internalisation/market imperfection perspective (Buckley & Casson, 1976; Caves, 1971; Hymer, 1976) and the resource based view (Barney, 1991; Wernerfelt, 1984). According to the market imperfection perspective, structural market imperfections lead to monopolistic powers of the MNE. These monopolistic powers or advantages take various forms including proprietary technology, ownership or control of factors of production, economies of scale, privileged access to inputs, control of distribution networks and the ability to achieve product differentiation (Kalfadellis & Gray, 2002; Sullivan, 1994).

In imperfect markets, firms are "unequal in their ability to operate in a particular industry. A firm with advantages over other firms in the production of a particular product may find it profitable to undertake the production of this product in a foreign country as well." (Hymer, 1960, p. 25–26, 1976). Thus, the firm internationalises by exploiting its firm specific advantage (Dunning, 1977, 1981). The role of FSAs is to provide competitive advantage to the firm, sufficient enough to compete successfully with local firms in a foreign market and to overcome the liabilities of foreignness (Zaheer, 1995). However, it is important to note that FSAs are embedded within resources, tied 'semi-permanently' to the firm (Caves, 1980).

According to Wernerfelt (1984), resources can be tangible or intangible and include everything that could be thought of as a strength of a given firm and which allow the MNE to appropriate rent by undertaking FDI (Hymer, 1960, 1976). However, the extant literature suggests that firms originating from emerging economies may typically lack the FSAs required to succeed in foreign markets (Child & Rodrigues, 2005; Gammeltoft, Barnard, & Madhok, 2010; Isobe, Makino, & Montgomery, 2000; Mathews, 2006; Miller, Thomas, Eden, & Hitt, 2009). This deficiency is attributed to the country of origin effect (Wang, Clegg, & Kafouros, 2009) because emerging economies are typically characterised by weak human and entrepreneurial resources (Khanna & Palepu, 2000; Meyer, Estrin, Bhaumik, & Peng, 2009; Peng, 2003), inferior technological resources (Dunning, Kim, & Park, 2008), and less effective marketing resources (Duysters et al., 2009). Therefore, the EMNE seeks to augment its strategic assets by acquiring the compensating competitive advantages it generally lacks (Dierickx & Cool, 1989; Mathews, 2006). It sees internationalisation as a "springboard" in its growth (Luo & Tung, 2007, p. 481).

Bartlett and Ghoshal (2000, p. 134) observed that multinational firms in emerging economies not only lack the usual resources possessed by their "first world" multinational competitors, but are also distinguished by their "strategic, organisational and management diversity". EMNEs usually operate in low value adding activities because of weak technological and managerial capabilities and generally internationalise by exploiting home country specific advantages (Lall, 1983; Lecraw, 1983, 1993; Wells Jr., 1983).

Rugman (2009) argued that EMNEs internationalise by exploiting home CSAs since these firms may not have significant FSAs to assure success in international markets. However, such an argument seems unsatisfactory because internationalisation based on home CSAs, available to all firms located in that source country, may not be sustainable (Lessard & Lucea, 2009; Ramamurti, 2012). This is where the bundling of assets argument becomes important, as an explanation of why some emerging country firms can transform CSAs into FSAs.

2.2. Internationalisation for Asset Augmentation

Many other studies (for example, Anand & Delios, 2002; Child & Rodrigues, 2005; Isobe et al., 2000; Mathews, 2006) argue that in order to compensate for deficiencies in resources required for building competitiveness in foreign markets, the EMNE seeks strategic assets. "An acquisition can be seen as the purchase of a bundle of resources in a highly imperfect market", through which the acquiring firm *ceteris paribus* can boost its growth (Wernerfelt, 1984, p. 172). Dunning (1998, 2006, p. 1) also acknowledged that EMNEs are often prompted to acquire businesses, "in more advanced countries to access or augment, rather than to exploit their ownership advantages", with an aim to enhance capability, to acquire knowledge and resources.

EMNEs use internationalisation as a "springboard" in the trajectory of growth by "acquiring foreign companies or their subunits that possess knowledge-based assets, such as sophisticated technologies or advanced manufacturing know-how" (Luo & Tung, 2007, p. 485). The motive of acquisition is to build competitive advantages within the acquiring firm. MNEs from the 'Newly Industrialised Countries' (NIC) also followed asset augmentation strategies in their internationalisation during the 1980s (Makino, Lau, & Yeh, 2002; Mathews, 2006).

Acquisitions are generally undertaken for the purpose of acquiring technology (Mutinelli & Piscitello, 1998), strategic resources (Deng, 2009), and globally known brands (Sauvant, 2005). As stated earlier, the EMNE is deficient in such strategic assets and capabilities since these are not generally available in their developing home markets which are typically characterised by surplus labour, lower operating costs, and large unsaturated markets (Lecraw, 1983; Wells Jr., 1983).

We argue that the above-mentioned economic conditions at home offer opportunities to grow and develop FSAs, for example lower operating cost and large unsaturated markets allow local firms to earn rents by serving the home market. The EMNE utilises its domestically developed FSAs to acquire strategic assets, including knowledge-based resources and globally known brands to catch-up and become an internationally competitive and known firm.

Acquisition of foreign firms, to seek strategic assets, is a preferred strategy amongst EMNEs because they originate in an economy that has limited availability of such assets at home. Thus, internationalisation of the EMNE is not triggered by push factors but by pull factors, such as a desire to acquire advanced technology and managerial skills (Luo & Tung, 2007). As a result, acquisitions from emerging economies, Brazil, Russia, India and China (also called BRIC countries), targeted towards developed countries are significant (KPMG, 2012; Stucchi, 2012).

Acquisition of strategic assets by EMNEs allows them to leapfrog and establish rapidly in globally competitive industries (Athreye & Kapur, 2009; Mathews, 2002b). Sometimes the strategic assets and capabilities required by EMNEs are not available through market transactions (Gubbi, Aulakh, Ray, Sarkar, & Chittoor, 2009). Thus, for many EMNEs acquisition is the preferred route for augmenting strategic assets.

We argue that recent developments in the extant literature present various explanations for the asset augmentation strategies of the EMNE but do not offer a plausible explanation as to what types of ownership advantages are possessed by the EMNE that enable it to undertake an acquisition in the first place. As it is difficult to internationalise in the absence of competitive advantages, the literature presents a 'chicken or egg' puzzle.

In recent years EMNEs have grown strongly in both number and size. The number of EMNEs in the Global 500 list has doubled in the last few years and the capitalisation of many EMNEs runs into billions of dollars (PWC, 2010). Ramamurti (2009a, 2012, p. 42) argues that it is not plausible that EMNEs will "have market capitalisations of tens of billions of dollars" without having ownership advantages. Thus, the EMNE is likely to possess ownership advantages of some kind that may be different from the typical ownership advantages possessed by the so-called "first world" MNEs. This view is also supported by Dunning et al. (2008).

2.3. Development of hypotheses

In the context of Indian MNEs, we argue that they possess firm specific ownership advantages that are an outcome of imperfections in the home economy. Market imperfections can provide significant opportunities for the creation of novel technologies and business models (Cohen & Winn, 2007). The preponderance of business groups and family firms in emerging economies is largely attributed to high degrees of market imperfection and the existence of institutional voids (Khanna & Palepu, 1999, 2000, 2005, 2010; Meyer et al., 2009; Peng, 2003). Furthermore, protectionist policies and a slow pace of liberalisation in the home economy provide growth opportunities to domestic firms able to serve a large unsaturated domestic market (Munjal et al., 2013). These arguments are developed in the several hypotheses that are presented in the later part of this section where our basic premise remains that EMNEs may possess FSAs that enable them to undertake acquisitions. FSAs emerge out of different kinds of resources available to the firm (Barney, 1991; Daft, 1983; Luo, 2000; Sun, Peng, Ren, & Yan, 2012). These resources could be tangible or intangible, such as of financial resources, managerial resources, marketing resources, technological resources, or ownership by conglomerate business group (Dunning, 1988). Using these different types of resources identified in the extant literature we build six hypotheses, the first five of which represent the resource base of the firm, including its membership (usually leadership) of a business group, and the last hypothesis covers the asset augmentation motive.

2.4. Financial resources

Ownership of financial resources is critical for the firm's growth (Doukas & Lang, 2003). Finance is the most flexible resource a firm can possess. A financially rich firm has a high degree of freedom in exploiting opportunities for growth (Ito & Rose, 2002). A firm possessing financial resources can build competitive advantages; for instance, by spending on research and development, marketing campaigns, and recruiting skilled human resources.

Finance can be raised externally from the capital market or internally from operations. External financing is associated with cost and redemption constraints attached to it, while finance from internally generated profits are free of such costs and redemption constraints (Jensen, 1986). Further, the corporate finance literature suggests that low leveraged firms are usually associated with higher profits and financial surpluses (Baker, 1973)

Thus, a profitable firm that generates financial resources internally is likely to benefit in its internationalisation plans. Internal financing gives more freedom to the firm to undertake

P.J. Buckley et al./International Business Review 25 (2016) 986–996   989

riskier projects in foreign markets. Indian MNEs are considered to have low debt levels (Kumar, 2010; Staney, Ramarathinam, & Bhoir, 2008), and to be cash rich (Knowledge@Wharton, 2006). It is reasonable to expect that the internationalisation of Indian MNEs will be positively influenced by the availability of the firm's own financial resources.

The hypothesis stated below is fundamentally derived from internalisation theory (Buckley & Casson, 1976). Imperfections in external markets and their substitution by the internal allocation of capital (including across business groups) lead to the ability to invest abroad.

Hypothesis 1. Cross-border acquisitions by Indian MNEs are positively related to the firm's own financial resources.

2.5. Technological resources

Technological resources are generally referred to as technological assets, such as technical know-how, patents, and designs. A firm may generate technological resources by engaging in research and development (Caves, 1971, 2007; Martin & Salomon, 2003). Technological resources help the firm to upgrade products, improve operational efficiency, and develop innovative capabilities (Knight & Cavusgil, 2004). They may also enhance the firm's internationalisation and performance; for example, a firm which has produced an innovative product may undertake export or FDI to maximise revenue streams (Kafouros, 2008; Tsang, Yip, & Toh, 2008).

The firm can augment the technological assets it lacks (Luo & Tung, 2007) but to benefit from acquired technology it must have absorptive capacity. Technological resources also represent the firm's absorptive capacity, i.e. the firm's own capabilities which enable it to integrate external technological assets into its operations (Cohen & Levinthal, 1990).

Chittoor, Sarkar, Ray, and Aulakh (2009) argue that Indian MNEs possess essential absorptive capacity. The research and innovation capacity available in India (Contractor, Kumar, Kundu, & Pedersen, 2010) is supported by the availability of skilled human resources in some sectors (Forbes, 2002; Kapur & Ramamurti, 2001), capabilities of engineering and adopting existing technology, excellent infrastructure, such as availability of US FDA approved labs, and positive changes in the domestic regulatory institutional landscape (Athreye & Godley, 2009; Athreye & Kapur, 2009). Thus, it is anticipated that Indian MNEs have technological resources that can facilitate the firm's internationalisation. Hence, the hypothesis is:

Hypothesis 2. Cross-border acquisitions by Indian MNEs are positively related to the firm's own technological resources.

2.6. Managerial resources

Managerial and entrepreneurial abilities are key factors in the internationalisation of a firm (Buckley, 1996; Ibeh, 2004). International entrepreneurship is often driven by high levels of managerial skills and research (Crick & Jones, 2000). Ibeh (2004, p. 94) highlights the importance of managerial and entrepreneurial resources for the MNE originating from developing countries by suggesting that good decision makers could lead the firm to "procure and develop other advantage-creating competencies" that can enhance the firm's prospects for internationalisation. Furthermore, managerial experience facilitates the entrepreneurial decision to internationalise.

Though internationalisation strategies devised by the entrepreneur are influenced by the resources available to the firm (Andersson, 2000), an effective manager seeks to make the best use

of resources available to the firm through efficient utilisation and appropriate allocation. In this process, the development of bundling the necessary assets together is crucial. This skill is transferable internationally.

Emerging economies are typically characterised by weak human and entrepreneurial resources (Khanna & Palepu, 2000; Meyer et al., 2009; Peng, 2003). It is also argued that EMNEs usually operate in low value adding activities because of their shortage of technological and managerial capabilities (Bartlett & Ghoshal, 2000). However, in recent years some Indian MNEs are competing successfully in dynamic modern technology-intensive industries. In a recent study, Chittoor, Aulakh, & Ray, 2015 reported that foreign education and experience of Chief Operating Officers of Indian MNEs have enabled them to undertake acquisitions of foreign firms. It is further argued that Indian managers and entrepreneurs have the ability to deliver "value for money" and the skills to succeed despite India's geographic and cultural diversity (Kumar, 2008, p. 251) and that this is an important internationally transferable skill. Thus it is hypothesised that:

Hypothesis 3. Cross-border acquisitions by Indian MNEs are positively related to the managerial resources of the firm.

2.7. Marketing resources

Marketing resources are used to build brand reputation, customer loyalty, market orientation, and product differentiation (Hooley, Greenley, Cadogan, & Fahy, 2005). They also help in the firm's internationalisation (Erramilli, Agarwal, & Kim, 1997; Kotabe, Srinivasan, & Aulakh, 2002). The impact of marketing resources on internationalisation has become more important with recent technological advancements, increasing levels of globalisation, and market integration across countries and regions (Chung, 2003).

Furthermore, strong marketing campaigns may also help the firm to establish its brand in a foreign market. An internationally recognised brand often acts as a vehicle for further internationalisation of the firm when the firm can transfer its known brand from one market to another (Douglas, Craig, & Nijssen, 2001). Conventional internationalisation wisdom further suggests that the market experience gained in a foreign market also helps the firm to further internationalise (Eriksson, Johanson, Majkgard, & Sharma, 1997; Johanson & Vahlne, 1977).

Marketing resources enable the MNE to cope with the pressures for localisation (Bartlett & Ghoshal, 1989) and overcome the liabilities of foreignness (Zaheer, 1995), for instance by undertaking product adaptation. Indian MNEs experience of operating in a multicultural setting at home provides them with marketing capability that is valuable in foreign markets (Kumar, 2008). Thus, it can be hypothesised that:

Hypothesis 4. Cross-border acquisitions by Indian MNEs are positively related to the firm's own marketing resources.

2.8. Business group affiliation

A business group or enterprise group is a diversified enterprise generally owned and managed by a family. Business groups are normally considered as a pool of resources which can promote internationalisation of the affiliated firms (Yiu, Bruton, & Lu, 2005). Business groups provide an internal financial market (in principle) to channel capital to those parts of the group able to marshal the resources to expand abroad. It can also transfer other resources internally, such as knowledge, needed to operate internationally. The literature indicates that a firm may internationalise by leveraging group resources (Douma, George, & Kabir, 2006; Guillén, 2003; Tan & Meyer, 2010; Yiu et al., 2005).

Besides the potential pool of resources, synergy between different subsidiaries of a business group can facilitate internationalisation of the firm; for instance, there are strong synergies between some subsidiaries of the Tata group (for details see, Mukherjee & Radhakrishnan, 2002). Business groups are dominant in many emerging economies (Tan & Meyer, 2010). Research finds that the emergence of business groups is related to market imperfections and other institutional characteristics of a country (Khanna & Palepu, 1999; Peng & Heath, 1996). In India, various business groups are active including the Tata group. Most Indian business groups are diversified across various industries and highly internationalised at the same time; for example, the Tata group operates in 28 industries with a presence in about 80 countries (Tata, 2012). Therefore, it is hypothesised that:

Hypothesis 5. Cross-border acquisitions by Indian MNEs are positively related to the firm's affiliation to a business group.

2.9. Asset augmentation and EMNEs' internationalisation

In contrast to the asset exploitation view, the internationalisation of multinationals from emerging economies is viewed as a strategy for augmenting resources and assets (Luo & Tung, 2007; Yiu, Lau, & Bruton, 2007). Ramamurti (2009b) suggests that acquisition is an appropriate and popular strategy for asset augmentation activities particularly among EMNEs acquiring technological know-how (Yeoh, 2011) because acquisitions can provide full control and ownership of strategic assets (Barney, 1991, 1996; Dunning & Lundan, 2008). Buckley, Clegg and Tan (2003, p. 67) argued that ownership based entry strategy binds "foreign firms into constraints" which ensures transfer of technological know-how. Internalisation theory (Buckley & Casson, 1976) emphasises the role of ownership based control in FDI decisions. Furthermore, strategic assets are often not available through market transactions because of embeddedness in firms (Gubbi, Aulakh, Ray, Sarkar, & Chittoor, 2009).

The move to acquire strategic assets allows the EMNE to leapfrog competition and establish rapidly in the global market (Athreye & Godley, 2009; Mathews, 2002a). This further enables EMNEs to geographically disperse their production units and laboratories in ways that can increase the likelihood of generating knowledge-based competitive advantages (Pearce, 1999). Luo and Tung (2007, p. 485) further argue that the EMNE uses internationalisation as a "springboard" in its growth trajectory by "acquiring foreign companies or their subunits that possess knowledge-based assets, such as sophisticated technologies or advanced manufacturing know-how".

During the1980s many MNEs from the 'Newly Industrialised Countries'; for example Samsung, LG, and Haier, followed asset augmentation strategies to leapfrog the competition (Makino, Lau, & Yeh, 2002). Today these multinationals are able to compete successfully with traditional MNEs (Mathews, 2006). Like other EMNEs, Indian MNEs are also actively seeking different types of strategic assets from foreign markets. Buckley, Enderwick, Forsans, and Munjal (2013), Sauvant (2005) and Kumar (2008) argue that Indian MNEs are actively seeking technology and brands aboard. The acquisition of Land Rover and Jaguar (in the UK) by Tata Motors and the acquisition of Tetley tea (in the UK) and Eight O'clock coffee (in the USA) by Tata Beverages are classic examples of acquisitions by Indian MNEs seeking technological and market based strategic assets. Thus, it is hypothesised that:

Hypothesis 6. Cross-border acquisitions by Indian MNEs are positively related to the asset augmentation activities of the firm.

3. Research methods

Data for this study was taken from two different sources – Thomson One Banker (TOB) and Prowess. TOB provides data on foreign acquisitions while Prowess provides the supplementary financial information for firms engaged in making foreign acquisitions. Where TOB covers the entire population of Indian firms making foreign acquisitions, Prowess provides extensive financial and background information on the firm. Both the Thomson One Banker and Prowess databases are widely used in the IB literature. Prowess is considered substantially richer than other global corporate databases, such as Worldscope (Oura et al., 2009).

TOB provides data on foreign acquisitions which consists of both Indian companies and non-Indian firms (Indian subsidiaries of foreign MNEs) making foreign acquisitions from India. Acquiring firms were identified by name across the two databases to match the dependent and independent variables. For the purpose of this study we identified and separated the cases of Indian MNEs making foreign acquisitions. Hence, our dependent variable here is foreign acquisitions made by Indian MNEs measured by the value of acquisitions and the number of acquisitions. Thus, we have two dependent variables, to be explained by a set of FSAs and the motive for acquisition. Our models are as follows, which are explained below:

$$VFA_{it} = a + b_1FR_{it} + b_2TI_{it} + b_3MI_{it} + b_4MS_{it} + b_5GroupD_{it}$$
$$+ b_6AA_{it} + b_7FDI_{it} + b_8IT_{it} + b_9SIZE_{it} + b_{10}AGE_{it}$$
$$+ b_{11}TimeD + b_{12}IndD + u_{it} \qquad (1)$$

$$NFA_{it} = a + b_1FR_{it} + b_2TI_{it} + b_3MI_{it} + b_4MS_{it} + b_5GroupD_{it}$$
$$+ b_6AA_{it} + b_7FDIExp_{it} + b_8IT_{it} + b_9SIZE_{it} + b_{10}AGE_{it}$$
$$+ b_{11}TimeD + b_{12}IndD + u_{it} \qquad (2)$$

$$NFA_{it} = \exp(a + b_1FR_{it} + b_2TI_{it} + b_3MI_{it} + b_4MS_{it}$$
$$+ b_5GroupD_{it} + b_6AA_{it} + b_7FDIExp_{it} + b_8IT_{it}$$
$$+ b_9SIZE_{it} + b_{10}AGE_{it} + b_{11}TimeD + b_{12}IndD + u_{it}) \qquad (3)$$

where, VFA_{it} is the value of foreign acquisitions by ith firm in t time and NFA_{it} is the number (count) of foreign acquisitions by ith firm in t time; FR_{it} is the financial resources of ith firm in t time; TI_{it} is the technological intensity of ith firm in t time; MI_{it} stands for marketing intensity of ith firm in t time; MS_{it} stands for managerial skills of ith firm in t time; $GroupD_{it}$ represents a dummy variable for group affiliation for ith firm in t time (which takes value 1 if the firm belongs to a group, else 0); IT_{it} represents international trade of the ith firm in t time; FDI_{it} represents FDI stock of the ith firm in t time; AA_{it} represents a dummy variable for motive of strategic asset augmentation of ith firm in t time (which takes value 1 if the firm makes acquisition for seeking strategic assets, else 0); $SIZE_{it}$ is a variable controlling the size of the ith firm in t time; AGE_{it} is another control representing age of ith firm in t time; TimeD represent Time Dummy (takes value 1 for the year to be controlled, else 0); IndD represent Industry Dummy; and finally, u_{it} is a stochastic random error for ith firm in t time; $a, b_1, b_2, b_3, \ldots, b_{11}$ are the usual regression coefficients.

We control for firm and time heterogeneity. Firm heterogeneity is controlled through age and size of the firm; both are standard controls and have been previously used in similar studies. We controlled for industry effects by incorporating industry dummies (IndD). For industry classification we used the OECD's International Standard Industry Classification (ISIC) REV. 3. We extend this control by incorporating the international business network and

222   *The Global Factory*

Table 1
Independent variables and data sources.

Variable and proxy	Proxy	Data source
Financial resource (FR)	Retained earnings	Prowess
Technical intensity (TI)	Ratio of R&D expenditure to sales	
Managerial skills (MS)	Ratio of managerial salary to sales	
Marketing intensity (MI)	Ratio of marketing expenditure to sales	
Business group (GroupD)	Dummy variable (equal to 1 if firm *i* is affiliated to a business group and 0 otherwise)	
Strategic assets Augmentation (AA)	Dummy variable (equal to 1 if the motive for making acquisition is to acquire strategic asset and 0 otherwise)	Thomson One Banker
Firm size	Capital of the firm	Prowess
Firm age	Total years since incorporation	
Previous FDI	Value of FDI	Thomson One Banker
International trade	Value of foreign trade	

Note: The data on motives of acquisition is coded from the synopsis of acquisition deals given in the Thomson One Banker database.

experience of the firm through international trade, and existing overseas investment, because these are likely to influence the internationalisation of the firm (Johanson & Mattson, 1988; Johanson & Vahlne, 1977, 2009). The measures used to proxy independent variables are provided in Table 1.

The effect of time is controlled by incorporating time dummies for each year under study. Control for the time effect was necessary because: (1) the acquisitions are on a rising trend; and (2) various changes that occurred over time may have impacted the firm's acquisition capabilities. For example, gradual changes in the overseas investment policies of India are likely to have an effect on acquisitions made by Indian MNEs. Controlling for time effects automatically controls for all time related changes. Fig. 1 gives the conceptual framework.

According to the dataset complied from TOB, during 2000–2007, 315 Indian multinational firms made 623 acquisitions in 70 countries valued at about US$ 48.55 billion. We accumulated the acquisitions made by these 315 firms by year and created a pooled data set. Generally, acquisition is not a regular activity for the firm. Foreign acquisitions are usually made once every few years, in our data sample the average acquisition by a firm is about 2 (623 acquisition by 315 firms) over an 8 year period. This kind of dispersion in the data is not best captured by panel data estimation techniques, such as the random effects, because panel data estimation procedures assume both cross-sectional and time series relationships within the data. In this situation, the best estimation technique for our data set is pooled OLS (POLS). However, for comparison we also run random effect regression[1] and found that the pooled OLS estimations were more efficient than panel data estimates. We further use negative binomial regression to estimate the number of acquisitions because it is a discrete variable. Our POLS models are expressed in Eqs. (1) and (2) and negative binomial regression is expressed in Eq. (3) above.

4. Results and discussion

The POLS estimates, correlation matrix and descriptive statistics of dependent and independent variables are presented in Tables 2 and 3. It can be seen from Table 2 that results for two regression models used to test the hypotheses are consistent and robust. It can be noted that regressions models fits well with the data as the *Chi* Square and the *F* test statistics are all significant at 1% level of significance. Our Hypotheses 1, 2 and 6 are fully supported and Hypothesis 3 is tentatively supported, but Hypotheses 4 and 5 are not supported.

These results suggest that financial resources support the foreign acquisitions made by EMNEs (Hypothesis 1). Indian MNEs

are able to undertake foreign acquisitions because they accumulate their own financial resources and often enjoy low debt levels, high profitability and strong cash flows (Knowledge@Wharton, 2006). In a globalising world, many opportunities arise where investment can be made from the home economy and a firm that has its own financial resources can exploit such opportunities promptly by undertaking outward FDI.

Mathews (2006) sees EMNEs as 'latecomers' in the world economy due to the recent liberalisation of their home economies. Until these economies followed liberalisation policies, their EMNEs did not face much international competition at home. This suggests that, as a result, these EMNEs could not build or accumulate FSAs that can provide them with global competitiveness. However, the protectionist policies followed at home (before liberalisation) allowed the EMNE to serve their domestic markets in a monopolistic way. Typically, emerging markets, such as Brazil, India, Russia and China, have large domestic markets. As a result of servicing large domestic markets, most of these EMNEs have grown at home and accumulated the necessary financial resources required for making foreign acquisitions. In some cases, these firms have also emerged as conglomerate business groups by internalising markets (Khanna & Palepu, 1999; Khanna, Palepu, & Sinha, 2005) so that an internal financial market is potentially available to their subsidiaries. Thus, many of these firms have acquired financial resources generated from their domestic operations but still lack the competitive advantages in marketing, managerial skills and technological know-how which are pursued through acquisition of foreign MNEs.

In line with earlier research (such as, Chen, Chen, & Ku, 2004; Elango & Pattnaik, 2007), this study tested managerial (Hypothesis 3) and marketing resources (Hypothesis 4) as sources of competitive advantages. Managerial skills show tentative significance. We argue that Indian MNEs have some degree of managerial skills that enable them to expand internationally. This may be the result of Indian managers' vast experience of managing within a diverse home country (Kumar, 2008) and foreign education and experience of working abroad (Chittoor, Aulakh, & Ray, 2015). We acknowledge that our measurement for managerial skills is based on manager's salary. It does not cover managers' experience and education as used in other studies. However, it seems that the managerial salary accounts for the variation in managerial skills arising due to experience and foreign education.

Our tests did not capture the significance of marketing resources. This indicates that Indian MNEs may not have marketing resources that can support their internationalisation. This is consistent with Madhok and Keyhani (2012) view that EMNEs do not possess resources such as globally recognised brands that "underpin a monopolistic firm-specific advantage" and "that have traditionally been considered as the source of extraordinary rents". However, they do have internalised skills

---
[1] Random effect results are not reported. Results are available upon request to the corresponding author.

P.J. Buckley et al./International Business Review 25 (2016) 986–996

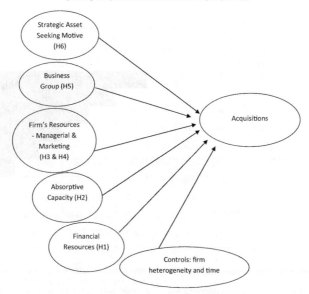

Fig. 1. Conceptual model.

Table 2
Results.

Independent variables	Coefficients		
	Acquisitions no. (negative binomial)	Acquisitions no. (POLS)	Acquisitions value (POLS)
Financial resources (H1)	0.092**	0.014*	0.158**
	(0.029)	(0.006)	(0.053)
Technological intensity (H2)	3.802*	1.73**	14.893**
	(1.697)	(0.601)	(4.895)
Managerial skills (H3)	0.140	0.00011***	0.0008***
	(0.149)	(0.00003)	(0.0002)
Marketing intensity (H4)	0.00033	0.00006	0.0006
	(0.0003)	(0.0001)	(0.001)
Business group (H5)	−0.135	−0.017	0.13
	(0.115)	(0.027)	(0.221)
Strategic asset seeking (H6)	0.422***	0.125***	0.78**
	(0.118)	(0.032)	(0.267)
Firm age	−0.098	−0.036	−0.396*
	(0.093)	(0.023)	(0.191)
Firm size	0.086**	0	−0.052
	(0.032)	(0.006)	(0.05)
Previous outward FDI	0.016	0.006**	0.038
	(0.009)	(0.002)	(0.02)
International trade	0	0	0.037
	(0.011)	(0.002)	(0.022)
Time and industry control	Included	Included	Included
Constant	−1.179***	0.4955	−7.030
	(0.328)	(0.0841)***	(0.685)***
(Pseudo) R^2	0.1181	0.1279	0.1195
F	–	13.48***	12.47***
LR *Chi* Square	332.17***	–	–
Observations	2230	2230	2230

Standard errors are reported in parenthesis.
* Significant at 0.05
** Significant at 0.01
*** Significant at 0.001

P.J. Buckley et al./International Business Review 25 (2016) 986–996

Table 3
Descriptive statistics.

		N	Mean	SD	VIF	Tolerance	1	2	3	4	5	6	7	8	9	10
	NFA	2513	0.24	0.572												
	VFA	2513	19.31	294.55												
1	Firm Age	2513	30.05	19.81	1.41	0.711	1									
2	Capital	2513	76.34	208.98	5.61	0.178	0.152	1								
3	Marketing Intensity	2513	10.11	117.15	1.02	0.984	-0.031	0.007	1							
4	Technology Intensity	2513	0.61	2.029	1.16	0.865	0.004	-0.041	-0.010	1						
5	Financial Resources	2230	119.21	562.73	7.06	0.141	0.181	0.646	-0.005	-0.015	1					
6	Int'l Trade	2513	251.52	1622.92	2.22	0.450	0.071	0.311	-0.009	0.021	0.633	1				
7	Business group	2513	0.64	0.47	1.28	0.781	0.275	0.222	0.040	0.036	0.135	0.075	1			
8	Managerial Skills	2513	0.59	2.66	1.21	0.826	0.094	0.211	-0.004	0.148	0.415	0.584	0.111	1		
9	Previous outward FDI	2513	78.23	459.43	1.71	0.585	0.184	0.238	-0.008	0.034	0.248	0.060	0.113	0.018	1	
10	Strategic Asset Seeking	2513	0.19	0.39	1.33	0.752	0.239	0.064	-0.022	0.074	0.118	0.140	0.239	0.121	-0.012	1

that enable them to realise benefits from the integration of foreign assets.

Hypothesis 6 on strategic asset augmentation is supported with the expected positive sign. In this study, strategic assets represent marketing and technological assets. Thus, the significance of Hypothesis 6 supports the view that Indian MNEs seek to acquire marketing and technological assets by acquiring companies abroad.

Post-independence Indian MNEs were not allowed to import technology (Desai, 1972), a factor that restricted the modernisation of Indian MNEs. Further, protection during the post-independence period also constrained the ability of Indian MNEs to develop globally known brands. In the post liberalisation period, when Indian MNEs are allowed to invest overseas, strategic asset seeking FDI seems to be used to overcome deficiencies in technological and marketing assets. The rising number of acquisitions targeting the industrially advanced economies also indicates that Indian MNEs are seeking marketing and technological strategic assets that are usually found in developed countries (Athreye & Kapur, 2009; Buckley, Forsans, & Munjal, 2012; Ramamurti & Singh, 2009).

Earlier research suggests that strategic assets, such as foreign technological assets improve performance, competitive advantage and internationalisation of the firm (Kafouros, Buckley, Sharp, & Wang, 2008; Tsang, Yip, & Toh, 2008) which seems to be the rationale for acquiring such assets by EMNEs. Augmentation of strategic assets through foreign acquisitions is of particular importance for the EMNE's internationalisation because such assets are generally not found in the EMNE's home country. Therefore it can be concluded that FDI by Indian MNEs is influenced by country of origin effect (Duysters et al., 2009; Wang et al., 2009).

Foreign knowledge is a key success factor in the internationalisation of Indian firms in many knowledge intensive industries, such as information technology, pharmaceuticals, automobiles and telecommunications. There are several examples where acquisition is undertaken to augment strategic assets; for instance, Wockhardt, a leading Indian pharmaceutical firm bought Rhein Biotech, a German firm, to acquire the technological capabilities it needed to be successful in the global pharmaceutical industry

(Athreye & Godley, 2009; Stucchi, 2012). Augmentation of strategic assets, such as technology, research and development skills, and international brands through acquisition, is not only a faster route to build competitive advantages (Barkema & Vermeulen, 1998) but "it can also deny them to competitors" (Child & Rodrigues, 2005, p. 392).

Further, acquisitions have given Indian MNEs global status, larger production scale, and capability to build "new competitive advantages" by combining foreign technology with a low cost production base at home (Satyanand & Raghavendran, 2010). Tata and Suzlon are examples of this. Tata Steel, after acquiring Corus, gained significant production capacity and became the fifth largest steel producer (by revenue) in the world (UNCTAD, 2007). Tata Motors, after acquiring Land Rover and Jaguar, is planning to start production of high performance engines in India (ENS Economic Bureau, 2012). Suzlon, after acquiring RE Power and Hansen, has become the fifth largest wind turbine manufacturer in the world and is offering "the most comprehensive product portfolios – ranging from sub-megawatt on-shore turbines at 600 kilowatts (kW), to the world's largest commercial 6.15 megawatt (MW) offshore turbine – built on a vertically integrated, low-cost, manufacturing base (Suzlon, 2012).

However, in order to gain from the foreign technology, the firm must have absorptive capacity (Cohen & Levinthal, 1990; Zahra, Matherne, & Carleton, 2003). Since this study finds support for the firm's own technological resources (Hypothesis 2), it is argued that Indian MNEs may have absorptive capacity, which helps them assimilate foreign technological assets. The significance of the motive to acquire know-how based strategic assets along with the importance of the firm's own technological resources, supports the view that many Indian MNEs augment and exploit foreign know-how along with their own research and development capabilities. This has also resulted in the success of many Indian MNEs in the pharmaceutical industry (for details see, Chittoor, Sarkar, Ray, & Aulakh, 2009; Pradhan & Sahu, 2008).

The acquisition strategies of Indian MNEs seem to be consistent with the strategies of traditional multinational enterprises, which establish foreign subsidiaries to build competitive advantages. For example, in the context of Japanese multinational enterprises, Papanastassiou and Pearce (1994, p. 155) found that Japanese

994   P.J. Buckley et al./International Business Review 25 (2016) 986–996

MNEs have "established a large number of R&D labs outside Japan which play particular roles in global-innovation strategies". In contrast, Indian MNEs establish subsidiaries through acquisitions for establishing 'global-production' and 'global-innovation' strategies.

The firm's affiliation to a business group (Hypothesis 5) is found to be insignificant. Though this is not expected, we argue that since business groups are pool of resources (Khanna & Palepu, 2000) and their main role is to channel resources to the firm to aide its internationalisation, it appears that the significance of business groups has been offset by the separate inclusion of resources (financial, technological, managerial and marketing) in the model. Furthermore, in the context of Indian business groups, a study by Gaur and Kumar (2009) indicates that the diversification strategy of a business groups can hold back the international expansion of the firm because the group lacks market expertise and specialisation.

Control variables included firm age, size, and international business experience. Among them, only age of firm and previous OFDI experience are significant. This indicates that younger firms are more inclined to use acquisitions for foreign expansion than older firms. This might be because younger firms have less competitive advantages than older firms and therefore acquisition is a preferred strategy for internationalisation. Learning from previous outward FDI positively affects acquisition activities but previous international trade experience is insignificant.

5. Summary and conclusion

This paper analysed the asset exploitation and asset augmentation motives of the EMNE in the context of the growing phenomenon of EMNEs internationalisation through cross-border acquisitions. Taking a sample of acquisitions made by Indian MNEs, it finds support for the conventional asset exploitation perspective. It finds that the financial capabilities and the absorptive capacity of Indian MNEs have enabled them to undertake foreign acquisitions to acquire technology and marketing related strategic assets.

The availability of financial resources to Indian MNEs is an outcome of imperfections in the home economy, such as late liberalisation and the large home market size (Munjal et al., 2013), which allowed many Indian MNEs to earn monopolistic rents. Thus, home market conditions shape the FSAs of EMNEs (Elango & Pattnaik, 2007; Tan & Meyer, 2010; Yiu et al., 2007) and allow the development of bundling skills – some prior to internationalisation.

We also found that Indian MNEs augment foreign technological know-how to supplement their own technological resources (Lall, 1983; Tolentino, 1993). The lack of strong technological resources of Indian MNEs is also an outcome of market imperfections at home (Desai, 1972) which triggers catch-up strategies. Acquisition is an appropriate mode through which EMNEs can augment strategic assets and catch-up mature MNEs because, in many cases, strategic assets such as technology are not available through market transactions (Gubbi et al., 2009; Kumaraswamy, Mudambi, Saranga, & Tripathy, 2012).

The contribution of the paper rests in identifying and resolving the 'chicken or egg' puzzle by untangling the entwined relationships between the asset exploitation and asset augmentation perspectives. It is the firm's own financial resources that support the asset augmentation strategy of the EMNE to build competitive advantages for further internationalisation. Structural imperfections and a large, rapidly growing market at home generate competitive advantages for some EMNEs.

This paper also provides a framework for analysing EMNEs' internationalisation and finds support for Dunning's (2006) argument that asset exploitation and asset augmentation activities can be complementary. It supports the view that no new theory is required for explaining the internationalisation of EMNEs. They are not different from traditional MNEs, since both internationalise by exploiting FSAs and aim to augment the resources they lack (Narula, 2006). This aligns with the view that the MNEs strategies not only exploit existing resources but also aim to develop new ones (Wernerfelt, 1984). Thus, asset augmentation is not a new and unique strategy idiosyncratic to EMNEs.

The contribution of this paper also lies in enlarging the market imperfection perspective (Buckley & Casson, 1976; Caves, 1971; Hymer, 1976) that can also be used to explain asset augmentation strategies. It is imperfections in the home market that provide the core explanation of asset augmentation strategies. In addition, we support Hennart's (2009) view that some firms are capable of transferring latent country specific advantages into firm specific advantages and that they develop bundling skills at home that can enable them to exploit foreign located assets by internationalisation and cooperation. Acquisitions are the route to this combination of firm specific and foreign located assets.

The paper has important implications for managers of EMNEs. It suggests that managers should try to explore grounds for growth within their home economy and take advantage of rapid growth at home before venturing abroad. Furthermore, it suggests that firms need not have variegated competitive advantages. Having just one FSA might be sufficient to venture out – and other strategic assets can then be accumulated by judicious bundling. The first step to successful internationalisation is to recognise the skills already internalised within the firm. The second is to identify and to acquire the necessary complementary skills that the firm needs, at home or abroad.

We acknowledge that though the findings may be generalisable for other emerging economies with a large home market, Indian MNEs could present a special case. Therefore, future research should examine the FSAs of firm's originating from other emerging economies. Finally, qualitative research could also shed more light on some of the findings offered by this study.

References

Airtel. (2012). *The website of Bharti Aritel*. New Delhi.
Anand, J., & Delios, A. (2002). Absolute and relative resources as determinants of international acquisitions. *Strategic Management Journal, 23*(2), 119–134.
Andersson, S. (2000). The internationalization of the firm from an entrepreneurial perspective. *International Studies of Management & Organization, 30*(1), 63–92.
Athreye, S. S., & Godley, A. (2009). Internationalization and technological leapfrogging in the pharmaceutical industry. *Industrial and Corporate Change, 18*(2), 295–323.
Athreye, S. S., & Kapur, S. (2009). The internationalization of Chinese and Indian firms: Trends, motivations and strategy. *Industrial and Corporate Change, 18*(2). 209-209.
Athukorala, P. C. (2009). Outward foreign direct investment from India. *Asian Development Review, 26*(2), 26–56.
Baker, S. H. (1973). Risk, leverage and profitability: An industry analysis. *The Review of Economics and Statistics, 55*(4), 503–507.
Barkema, H. G., & Vermeulen, F. (1998). International expansion through start up or acquisition: A learning perspective. *The Academy of Management Journal, 41*(1), 7–26.
Barney, J. (1991). Firm resources and sustainable competitive advantage. *Journal of Management, 17*(1), 99–120.
Barney, J. (1996). The resource-based theory of the firm. *Organization Science, 7*(5), 469.
Bartlett, C. A., & Ghoshal, S. (1989). *Managing across borders: The transnational solution*. London: Harvard Business School Press.
Bartlett, C. A., & Ghoshal, S. (2000). Going global: Lessons from late movers. *Harvard Business Review, 78*(2), 132–142.
Buckley, P. J. (1996). The role of management in international business theory: A meta-analysis and integration of the literature on international business and international management. *Management International Review, 36*(1), 7–54.
Buckley, P. J., & Casson, M. (1976). *The future of the multinational enterprise*. London: Macmillan.
Buckley, P. J., Clegg, J., & Tan, H. (2003). The art of knowledge transfer: Secondary and reverse transfer in China's telecommunications manufacturing industry. *Management International Review, 43*(2), 67–93.
Buckley, P. J., Enderwick, P., Forsans, N., & Munjal, S. (2013). Country linkages and firm internationalisation: Indian MNEs within economic-political alliances of

nations. In G. Cook & J. Johns (Eds.), *The changing geography of international business* (pp. 79–94). Basingstoke: Palgrave MacMillan.

Buckley, P. J., Forsans, N., & Munjal, S. (2012). Host-home country linkages and host-home country specific advantages as determinants of foreign acquisitions by Indian firms. *International Business Review, 21*(5), 878–890.

Caves, R. E. (1971). International corporations: The industrial economics of foreign investment. *Economica, 38*(149), 1–27.

Caves, R. E. (1980). Industrial organization, corporate strategy and structure. *Journal of Economic Literature, 58*, 64–92.

Caves, R. E. (2007). *Multinational enterprise and economic analysis*. Cambridge: Cambridge University Press.

Chen, T.-J., Chen, H., & Ku, Y.-H. (2004). Foreign direct investment and local linkages. *Journal of International Business Studies, 35*(4), 320–333.

Child, J., & Rodrigues, S. B. (2005). The internationalisation of Chinese firms. *Management and Organisation Review, 1*(3), 381–410.

Chittoor, R., Aulakh, P. S., & Ray, S. (2015). What drives overseas acquisitions by indian firms?. A behavioral risk-taking perspective. *Management International Review, 55*(2), 255–275.

Chittoor, R., Sarkar, M. B., Ray, S., & Aulakh, P. S. (2009). Third-world copycats to emerging multinationals: Institutional changes and organizational transformation in the Indian pharmaceutical industry. *Organization Science, 20*(1), 187–205.

Chung, H. F. L. (2003). International standardization strategies: The experiences of Australian and New Zealand firms operating in the Greater China markets. *Journal of International Marketing, 11*(3), 48–82.

Cohen, B., & Winn, M. I. (2007). Market imperfections, opportunity and sustainable entrepreneurship. *Journal of Business Venturing, 22*(1), 29–49.

Cohen, W. M., & Levinthal, D. A. (1990). Absorptive capacity: A new perspective on learning and innovation. *Administrative Science Quarterly, 35*(1), 128–152.

Contractor, F. J., Kumar, V., Kundu, S. K., & Pedersen, T. (2010). Reconceptualizing the firm in a world of outsourcing and offshoring: The organizational and geographical relocation of high value company functions. *Journal of Management Studies, 47*(8), 1417–1433.

Crick, D., & Jones, M. V. (2000). Small high-technology firms and international high-technology markets. *Journal of International Marketing, 8*(2), 63–85.

Cuervo-Cazurra, A. (2012). Extending theory by analyzing developing country multinational companies: Solving the goldilocks debate. *Global Strategy Journal, 2*(3), 153–167.

Cuervo-Cazurra, A., & Genc, M. (2008). Transforming disadvantages into advantages: Developing-country MNEs in the least developed countries. *Journal of International Business Studies, 39*(6), 957–979.

Daft, L. R. (1983). *Organizational theory and designs*. St. Paul West Publishing Company.

Deng, P. (2009). Why do Chinese firms tend to acquire strategic assets in international expansion? *Journal of World Business, 44*(1), 74–84.

Desai, A. V. (1972). Technology management in Indian companies. *Long Range Planning, 5*(4), 70–72.

Dierickx, I., & Cool, K. (1989). Asset stock accumulation and sustainability of competitive advantage. *Management Science, 35*(12), 1504–1511.

Douglas, S. P., Craig, C. S., & Nijssen, E. J. (2001). Integrating branding strategy across markets: Building international brand architecture. *Journal of International Marketing, 9*(2), 97–114.

Doukas, J. A., & Lang, L. H. P. (2003). Foreign direct investment, diversification and firm performance. *Journal of International Business Studies, 34*(2), 153–172.

Douma, S., George, R., & Kabir, R. (2006). Foreign and domestic ownership, business groups, and firm performance: Evidence from a large emerging market. *Strategic Management Journal, 27*(7), 637–657.

Dunning, J. H. (1977). Trade, location of economic activity and the multinational enterprise: A search for an eclectic approach. In B. Ohlin, P. O. Hesselborn, & P. J. Wijkmann (Eds.), *The international allocation of economic activity* (pp. 395–416). London: McMillan.

Dunning, J. H. (1981). *International production and the multinational enterprise*. London: Allen & Unwin.

Dunning, J. H. (1988). The eclectic paradigm of international production: A restatement and some possible extensions. *Journal of International Business Studies, 19*(1), 1–31.

Dunning, J. H. (1998). *Globalization, trade, and foreign direct investment*. Oxford: Elsevier.

Dunning, J. H. (2006). Comment on dragon multinationals: New players in 21st century globalization. *Asia Pacific Journal of Management, 23*(2), 139–141.

Dunning, J. H., Kim, C., & Park, D. (2008). Old wine in new bottels: A comparison of emerging-markets TNCs today and developed country TNCs thirty years ago. In K. P. Sauvant (Ed.), *The rise of transnational corporations from emerging markets: Threat or opportunity?* (pp. 158–180). Cheltenham: Edward Elgar.

Dunning, J. H., & Lundan, S. M. (2008). *Multinational enterprises and the global economy*. Cheltenham: Edward Elgar.

Duysters, G., Jacob, J., Lemmens, C., & Jintian, Y. (2009). Internationalization and technological catching up of emerging multinationals: A comparative case study of China's Haier group. *Industrial and Corporate Change, 18*(2), 325–349.

Elango, B., & Pattnaik, C. (2007). Building capabilities for international operations through networks: A study of Indian firms. *Journal of International Business Studies, 38*(4), 541–555.

ENS Economic Bureau (2012). *Tata Motors may produce high performance engines in India, UK*. Delhi: Indian Express.

Eriksson, K., Johanson, J., Majkgard, A., & Sharma, D. D. (1997). Experiential knowledge and cost in the internationalization process. *Journal of International Business Studies, 28*(2), 337–360.

Erramilli, M. K., Agarwal, S., & Kim, S.-S. (1997). Are firm-specific advantages location-specific too? *Journal of International Business Studies, 28*(4), 735–757.

Forbes, N. (2002). *Doing business in India: Economic policy reforms and the indian economy*. New Delhi: Oxford University Press.

Gammeltoft, P., Barnard, H., & Madhok, A. (2010). *Emerging multinationals, emerging theory: Macro- and micro-level perspectives*. Oxford: Elsevier.

Gaur, A. S., & Kumar, V. (2009). International diversification, business group affiliation and firm performance: Empirical evidence from India. *British Journal of Management, 20*(2), 172–186.

Gubbi, S. R., Aulakh, P. S., Ray, S., Sarkar, M. B., & Chittoor, R. (2009). Do international acquisitions by emerging-economy firms create shareholder value?. The case of Indian firms. *Journal of International Business Studies, 41*(3), 397–418.

Guillén, M. F. (2003). Experience, imitation, and the sequence of foreign entry: Wholly owned and joint-venture manufacturing by South Korean firms and business groups in China, 1987–1995. *Journal of International Business Studies, 34*(2), 185–198.

Haleblian, J., Devers, C. E., McNamara, G., Carpenter, M. A., & Davison, R. B. (2009). Taking stock of what we know about mergers and acquisitions: A review and research agenda. *Journal of Management, 35*(3), 469–502.

Hennart, J.-F. (2009). Down with MNE-centric theories! Market entry and expansion as the bundling of MNE and local assets *Journal of International Business Studies, 40*(8), 1432–1454.

Hennart, J.-F. (2012). Emerging market multinationals and the theory of the multinational enterprise. *Global Strategy Journal, 2*(3), 168–187.

Hooley, G. J., Greenley, G. E., Cadogan, J. W., & Fahy, J. (2005). The performance impact of marketing resources. *Journal of Business Research, 58*(1), 18–27.

Hoskisson, R. E., Wright, M., Filatotchev, I., & Peng, M. W. (2013). Emerging multinationals from mid range economies: The influence of institutions and factor markets. *Journal of Management Studies, 50*(7), 1295–1321.

Hymer, S. A. (1960). *The international operations of national firms: A study of direct foreign investment*. Cambridge, MA, Boston: MIT.

Hymer, S. H. (1976). *The international operations of national firms: A study of direct foreign investment*. Lexington, MA: Lexington Books.

Ibeh, K. I. N. (2004). Furthering export participation in less performing developing countries: The effects of entrepreneurial orientation and managerial capacity factors. *International Journal of Social Economics, 31*(1/2), 94–110.

Isobe, T., Makino, S., & Montgomery, D. B. (2000). Resource commitment, entry timing, and market performance of foreign direct investments in emerging economies: The case of Japanese international joint ventures in China. *The Academy of Management Journal, 43*(3), 468–484.

Ito, K., & Rose, E. L. (2002). Foreign direct investment location strategies in the tire industry. *Journal of International Business Studies, 33*(3), 593–602.

Jensen, M. C. (1986). Agency costs of free cash flow, corporate finance, and takeovers. *The American Economic Review, 76*(2), 323–329.

Johanson, J., & Mattson, L. G. (1988). Internationalisation in industrial systems – Network approach. In N. Hood & J. E. Vahlne (Eds.), *Strategies in Global Competition* (pp. 287–314). London: Croom Helm.

Johanson, J., & Vahlne, J. E. (1977). The internationalization process of the firm – A model of knowledge development and increasing foreign market commitments. *Journal of International Business Studies, 8*(1), 23–32.

Johanson, J., & Vahlne, J. E. (2009). The Uppsala internationalization process model revisited: From liability of foreignness to liability of outsidership. *Journal of International Business Studies, 40*, 1411–1431.

Kafouros, M. I. (2008). *Industrial innovation and firm performance: the impact of scientific knowledge on multinational corporations*. Edward Elgar Publishing.

Kafouros, M. I., Buckley, P. J., Sharp, J. A., & Wang, C. (2008). The role of internationalization in explaining innovation performance. *Technovation, 28*(1–2), 63–74.

Kalfadellis, P., & Gray, J. (2002). Are proxies valued measures of internationalization? "Regional integration, agglomeration and international business". *28th European International Business Academy Conference*.

Kapur, D., & Ramamurti, R. (2001). India's emerging competitive advantage in services. *The Academy of Management Executive, 15*(2), 20–32.

Khanna, T., & Palepu, K. (1999). *Emerging market business groups, foreign investors, and corporate governance*. NBER working paper.

Khanna, T., & Palepu, K. (2000). Is group affiliation profitable in emerging markets? An analysis of diversified Indian business groups. *The Journal of Finance, 55*(2), 867–891.

Khanna, T., & Palepu, K. (2005). The evolution of concentrated ownership in India: Broad patterns and a history of the Indian software industry. In R. K. Morck (Ed.), *A history of corporate governance around the world: Family business groups to professional managers* (pp. 283–324). Chicago: University of Chicago Press.

Khanna, T., & Palepu, K. (2010). *Winning in emerging markets*. Boston: Harvard Business Press.

Khanna, T., Palepu, K., & Sinha, J. (2005). Strategies that fit emerging markets. *Harvard Business Review, 83*(6), 63–76.

Knight, G. A., & Cavusgil, S. T. (2004). Innovation, organizational capabilities, and the born-global firm. *Journal of International Business Studies, 35*(2), 124–141.

Knowledge@Wharton, I. (2006). *How Indian companies fund their overseas acquisitions*. Philadelphia: India Knowledge@Wharton.

Kotabe, M., Srinivasan, S. S., & Aulakh, P. S. (2002). Multinationality and firm performance: The moderating role of R&D and marketing capabilities. *Journal of International Business Studies, 33*(1), 79–97.

KPMG (2012). *Emerging market international acquisition tracker KPMG*.

Kumar, N. (2008). Internationalization of Indian enterprises: Patterns, strategies, ownership advantages, and implications. *Asian Economic Policy Review, 3*(2), 242–261.

Kumar, S. R. (2010). Indian firms high on equity, low on debt. *Financial Chronicle*.

Kumaraswamy, A., Mudambi, R., Saranga, H., & Tripathy, A. (2012). Catch-up strategies in the Indian auto components industry: Domestic firms' responses to market liberalization. *Journal of International Business Studies, 43*(4), 368–395.

Lall, S. (1983). Multinationals from India. In S. Lall (Ed.), *The new multinationals: The spread of third world enterprises* (pp. 21–87). New York: John Wiley and sons.

Lecraw, D. J. (1983). Performance of transnational corporations in less developed countries. *Journal of International Business Studies, 14*(1), 15–33.

Lecraw, D. J. (1993). Outward direct investment by Indonesian firms: Motivation and effects. *Journal of International Business Studies, 24*(3), 589–600.

Lessard, D., & Lucea, R. (2009). Mexican multinationals: Insights from CEMEX. In R. Ramamurti & J. V. Singh (Eds.), *Emerging multinationals in emerging markets* (pp. 280–311). Cambridge: Cambirdge University Press.

Luo, Y. (2000). Dynamic capabilities in international expansion. *Journal of World Business, 35*(4), 355–378.

Luo, Y. (2010). *Administrative Science Quarterly*.

Luo, Y., & Tung, R. L. (2007). International expansion of emerging market enterprises: A springboard perspective. *Journal of International Business Studies, 38*(4), 481–498.

Madhok, A., & Keyhani, M. (2012). Acquisitions as entrepreneurship: Asymmetries, opportunities, and the internationalization of multinationals from emerging economies. *Global Strategy Journal, 2*(1), 26–40.

Makino, S., Lau, C.-M., & Yeh, R.-S. (2002). Asset-exploitation versus asset-seeking: Implications for location choice of foreign direct investment from newly industrialized economies. *Journal of International Business Studies, 33*(3), 403–421.

Martin, X., & Salomon, R. (2003). Knowledge transfer capacity and its implications for the theory of the multinational corporation. *Journal of International Business Studies, 34*(4), 356–373.

Mathews, J. A. (2002a). Competitive advantages of the latecomer firm: A resource-based account of industrial catch-up strategies. *Asia Pacific Journal of Management, 19*(4), 467–488.

Mathews, J. A. (2002b). *Dragon multinational: A new model for global growth*. Oxford and New York: Oxford University Press.

Mathews, J. A. (2006). Dragon multinationals: New players in 21st century globalization. *Asia Pacific Journal of Management, 23*(1), 5–27.

Meyer, K. E., Estrin, S., Bhaumik, S. K., & Peng, M. W. (2009). Institutions, resources, and entry strategies in emerging economies. *Strategic Management Journal, 30*(1), 61–80.

Miller, S. R., Thomas, D. E., Eden, L., & Hitt, M. (2009). Knee deep in the big muddy: The survival of emerging market firms in developed markets. *Management International Review, 48*(6), 645–666.

MIT (2012). *MIT India conference: Entrepreneurship panel*. Boston: Massachusetts Institute of Technology.

Mukherjee, S., & Radhakrishnan, R. (2002). The Tata re-engineering co: The winds of change are sweeping through Bombay House. In *Get prepared to be swept away* (Vol. 2008). Tata.com.

Munjal, S., Buckley, P. J., Enderwick, P., & Forsans, N. (2013). The growth trajectory of Indian MNEs. In C. Brautaset & C. Dent (Eds.), *The great diversity – Trajectories of Asian development* (pp. 191–203). Wageningen, Netherlands: Wageningen Academic Press.

Mutinelli, M., & Piscitello, L. (1998). The entry mode choice of MNEs: An evolutionary approach. *Research Policy, 27*(5), 491–506.

Narayanan, K., & Bhat, S. (2010). Technology sourcing and outward FDI: A study of IT industry in India. *Technovation*.

Narula, R. (2006). Globalization, new ecologies, new zoologies, and the purported death of the eclectic paradigm. *Asia Pacific Journal of Management, 23*(2), 143–151.

Oura, H., Hume, A. R., Papi, L., Saxegaard, M., Petia, T., Peiris, S. J., et al. (2009). *India: selected issues*. Washington, D.C International Monetary Fund.

Papanastassiou, M., & Pearce, R. D. (1994). The internationalisation of research and development by Japanese enterprises. *R&D Management, 24*(2), 155–165.

Pearce, R. D. (1999). Decentralised R&D and strategic competitiveness: globalised approaches to generation and use of technology in multinational enterprises. *Research Policy, 28*(2–3), 157–178.

Pereira, V., & Malik, A. (2015). Making sense and identifying aspects of Indian culture(s) in organisations: Demystifying through empirical evidence. *Culture and Organization, 21*(5), 355–365.

Peng, M. W. (2003). Institutional transitions and strategic choices. *The Academy of Management Review, 28*(2), 275–296.

Peng, M. W. (2012). The global strategy of emerging multinationals from China. *Global Strategy Journal, 2*(2), 97–107.

Peng, M. W., & Heath, P. S. (1996). The growth of the firm in planned economies in transition: Institutions, organizations, and strategic choice. *The Academy of Management Review*, 492–528.

Pradhan, J. P., & Sahu, P. P. (2008). *Transnationalization of Indian pharmaceutical SMEs*. Delhi: Bookwell.

PWC (2010). Emerging multinationals: The rise of new multinational companies from emerging economies. *Economic Letters, 8*. London: Price Water House Coopers.

Ramamurti, R. (2009a). What have we learned about emerging-market MNEs? In R. Ramamurti & J. V. Singh (Eds.), *Emerging multinationals in emerging markets* (pp. 399–426). Cambridge: Cambrdige University Press.

Ramamurti, R. (2009b). Why study emerging-market multinationals? In R. Ramamurti & J. V. Singh (Eds.), *Emerging multinationals from emerging markets*. Cambridge: Cambridge University Press.

Ramamurti, R. (2012). What is really different about emerging market multinationals? *Global Strategy Journal, 2*(1), 41–47.

Ramamurti, R., & Singh, J. V. (2009). Indian multinationals: Generic internationalization strategies. In R. Ramamurti & J. V. Singh (Eds.), *Emerging multinationals in emerging markets* (pp. 110–165). Cambridge: Cambridge University Press.

Rugman, A. M. (2009). Theoretical aspects of MNEs from emerging markets. In R. Ramamurti & J. V. Singh (Eds.), *Emerging multinationals in emerging markets* (pp. 42–63). Cambridge: Cambridge University Press.

Rui, H., & Yip, G. S. (2008). Foreign acquisitions by Chinese firms: A strategic intent perspective. *Journal of World Business, 43*(2), 213–226.

Santangelo, G. D. (2009). MNCs and linkages creation: Evidence from a peripheral area. *Journal of World Business, 44*(2), 192–205.

Satyanand, P. N., & Raghavendran, P. (2010). *Outward FDI from India and its policy context, country profiles of inward and outward foreign direct investment: 16*. Columbia: Vale Columbia Center on Sustainable International Investment.

Sauvant, K. P. (2005). New sources of FDI: The BRICs – Outward FDI from Brazil, Russia, India and China. *The Journal of World Investment & Trade, 6*(5), 639–709.

Staney, N., Ramarathinam, A., & Bhoir, A. (2008). Low debt to cushion Indian cos from higher borrowing costs. *Livemint*.

Stucchi, T. (2012). Emerging market firms' acquisitions in advanced markets: Matching strategy with resource-, institution- and industry-based antecedents. *European Management Journal, 30*(3), 278–289.

Sullivan, D. (1994). Measuring the degree of internationalization of a firm. *Journal of International Business Studies, 25*(2), 325–342.

Sun, S. L., Peng, M. W., Ren, B., & Yan, D. (2012). A comparative ownership advantage framework for cross-border M&As: The rise of Chinese and Indian MNEs. *Journal of World Business, 47*(1), 4–16.

Suzlon (2012). *The website of Suzlon, 2012*.

Tan, D., & Meyer, K. E. (2010). Business groups' outward FDI: A managerial resources perspective. *Journal of International Management, 16*(2), 154–164.

Tata. (2012). *The website of Tata group*. Mumbai.

Tolentino, P. E. (1993). *Technological innovation and third world multinationals*. London: Routledge.

Tsang, E. W. K., Yip, P. S. L., & Toh, M. H. (2008). The impact of R&D on value added for domestic and foreign firms in a newly industrialized economy. *International Business Review, 17*(4), 423–441.

Tseng, C.-H., Tansuhaj, P., Hallagan, W., & McCullough, J. (2007). Effects of firm resources on growth in multinationality. *Journal of International Business Studies, 38*(6), 961–974.

UNCTAD (2007). *World investment report: Transnational corporations, extractive industries and development*. In *World investment report* (pp. 1–323). Geneva and New York: United Nations.

UNCTAD (2011). *World investment report: Non-equity modes of international production and development*. New York and Geneva: United Nation.

Wang, C., Clegg, J., & Kafouros, M. (2009). Country-of-origin effects of foreign direct investment. *Management International Review, 49*(2), 179–198.

Wells, L. T., Jr. (1983). *Third world multinationals: The rise of foreign investment from developing countries*. Cambridge, MA: MIT Press.

Wernerfelt, B. (1984). A resource-based view of the firm. *Strategic Management Journal, 5*(2), 171–180.

Yeoh, P. L. (2011). Location choice and the internationalization sequence: Insights from Indian pharmaceutical companies. *International Marketing Review, 28*(3), 291–312.

Yiu, D., Bruton, G. D., & Lu, Y. (2005). Understanding business group performance in an emerging economy: Acquiring resources and capabilities in order to prosper. *SSRN eLibrary, 42*(1), 183–206.

Yiu, D. W., Lau, C., & Bruton, G. D. (2007). International venturing by emerging economy firms: The effects of firm capabilities, home country networks, and corporate entrepreneurship. *Journal of International Business Studies, 38*(4), 519–540.

Zaheer, S. (1995). Overcoming the liability of foreignness. *The Academy of Management Journal, 38*(2), 341–363.

Zahra, S. A., Matherne, B. P., & Carleton, J. M. (2003). Technological resource leveraging and the internationalisation of new ventures. *Journal of International Entrepreneurship, 1*(2), 163–186.

PART IV

THE GLOBAL FACTORY

© Academy of Management Perspectives
2015, Vol. 29, No. 2, 237–249.
http://dx.doi.org/10.5465/amp.2013.0113

A R T I C L E S

THE GOVERNANCE OF THE GLOBAL FACTORY: LOCATION AND CONTROL OF WORLD ECONOMIC ACTIVITY

PETER J. BUCKLEY
University of Leeds

ROGER STRANGE
University of Sussex

Recent years have witnessed major changes in the global location of economic activity, with the emerging economies assuming greater shares relative to the advanced economies. These developments have led many authors to refer to the idea of the global factory. But little attention has been given to who has control over the geographically dispersed activities—or, to put it another way, about the governance of the global factory. Have the changes in the global location of economic activity come about primarily through the growth of locally owned firms in the emerging economies, or through increased FDI by MNEs from the advanced economies, or through the proliferation of outsourcing arrangements coordinated by firms in the advanced economies? These control/governance issues have profound implications for the capture of the profits/rents earned in global value chains, and hence for the global distribution of income. This paper explores these issues, and considers who has benefited most from the contemporary phase of globalization.

The basic proposition of this paper is that the location and internalization strategies of multinational enterprises (MNEs) are changing, with implications for the *global factory*—that is, where various activities are located and how they are controlled—and for the distribution of income among countries. We explore different conceptions of the global factory and consider the implicit consequences of each. In short, our research question is this: Who has benefited (and, in particular, who has benefited most) from the development of the global factory?

Over the past 30 years, we have witnessed major changes in the global location of economic activity. The major drivers of these changes are well documented and include the following: economic restructuring and market liberalization in many countries in Eastern Europe, Asia, and elsewhere; financial deregulation and the integration of world financial markets; trade and investment liberalization—including the proliferation of preferential trading arrangements (multilateral and bilateral); and technological

advances, particularly in information and communication technologies (ICT) and transportation. In particular, technological advances have allowed the value chains[1] for many goods and services to become more disaggregated ("fine-sliced") into distinct stages that can be carried out in different locations. Some of these stages involve labor-intensive activities and/or modest skill requirements, and hence are suited for location in emerging and/or developing economies where labor costs are generally lower, while other stages are located in more advanced economies. A greater international fragmentation of production (IFP) has been the outcome, one corollary of which has been the increased importance of intermediate goods traded in the global economy (Baldwin & Lopez-Gonzalez, 2013; Baldwin & Venables, 2013). Trade in intermediate goods now dominates global trade flows, accounting

---

[1] The value chain concept refers to the range of activities required in the production of a good or service, including design, procurement of inputs, production, marketing, distribution, and after-sales service.

Copyright of the Academy of Management, all rights reserved. Contents may not be copied, emailed, posted to a listserv, or otherwise transmitted without the copyright holder's express written permission. Users may print, download, or email articles for individual use only.

238   *Academy of Management Perspectives*   May

for over 60% of world exports, although this overall figure masks marked differences among countries and products (UNCTAD, 2013). The expansion of the market for market transactions (Liesch et al., 2012) has brought more nations into the viable set of production and service locations.

The shifts in the global location of economic activity have been dramatic, whatever indicators are considered, and have excited much interest not just in the academic literature but also in the popular press and in civil society. This has led various authors to propose the idea of the global factory. For example, Gereffi (1989, p. 97) used the term "global factory" to represent "the emergence of a global manufacturing system in which production capacity is dispersed to an unprecedented number of developing as well as industrialized countries." He suggested that different nations are thus able to specialize in distinct industrial sectors, and even in different stages within value chains in the same industry. Furthermore, Gereffi asserted that this greater dispersion of activity has been associated with a widening of corporate ownership on a global scale, with many more firms controlled by a more diverse set of owners in many different countries.

In contrast, Grunwald and Flamm's (1985) conception of the global factory focused on the growth of foreign assembly facilities, drawing on earlier theoretical ideas by Raymond Vernon (1966, 1979) on the product life cycle. The authors highlighted the fact that MNEs have established offshore assembly operations to meet the competition of low-cost imports. Many value-chain activities have been relocated to emerging economies, but these activities are still integrated (internalized) under common ownership within MNEs headquartered in advanced economies.

A third possible conception of the global factory is that this offshoring of activities has been accompanied by an outsourcing (externalization) of some of the value-chain activities to independent suppliers (Buckley, 2004, 2007, 2009a, 2009b, 2011; Buckley & Ghauri, 2004).[2] Such

externalization involves not only a physical "slicing up" of the value chain but also a change in its ownership. Here the global factory is seen as a complex strategy by MNEs to reduce location and transaction costs, with global value chains linked together by international flows of intermediate products. Importantly, the MNEs are assumed to still control the resultant distributed networks of activities even though they have relinquished equity ownership. In short, this model suggests that knowledge will be increasingly internalized, while operations are increasingly externalized.

Each of these three models of the global factory envisages a greater global dispersion of economic activity, but each makes different assumptions about who maintains control over these dispersed activities—or, to put it another way, each makes different assumptions about the governance of the global factory (see Table 1). These control/governance issues have profound implications for the capture of the profits/rents earned in global value chains (GVCs), and hence for the global distribution of income.[3] On one hand, if the shifts in the location of activity reflect the rise in the global importance of firms owned and controlled in emerging/developing economies, then it is likely that these economies will grow in terms of absolute gross domestic product (GDP) and GDP relative to other economies, and in terms of living standards (GDP per capita). On the other hand, if the shifts in the location of activity reflect offshoring and/or outsourcing initiatives by firms from the advanced economies, then both the absolute and relative impacts on GDP in the host economies will be smaller, and there will be smaller increases in living standards.

The key questions addressed in this paper, thus, are these: Which of these three models of the global factory is most important in practice, and who has benefited (and, in particular who has benefited most) from the emergence of the global factory? We bring together insights from the literatures on the strategies of emerging economy multinational enterprises (EMNEs), on GVCs, and on the motives and consequences of outsourcing arrangements.

---

[2] *Outsourcing* is a process that involves the firm externalizing elements of its value chain—that is, there is an organizational fragmentation of production. *Offshoring* refers to the relocation of the production of goods and/or services overseas—that is, there is an international fragmentation of production. *Outsourcing* and *offshoring* are conceptually different and have different determinants. Outsourced activities may take place within the same country or involve the relocation of production overseas. Offshored activities may take place under the control of the lead firm (FDI) or independently (Strange, 2011).

---

[3] As Nissanke and Thorbecke (2006, pp. 1340–1341) explained, various concepts can be used to identify trends in the global distribution of income. Here we refer to the between-country income distribution and do not consider the within-country distribution or vertical/horizontal inequalities.

TABLE 1
Key Issues in the Analysis of the Global Factory: Location, Ownership, and Governance

	Gereffi (1989)	Grunwald and Flamm (1985)	Buckley/Buckley and Ghauri (2004)
Location	Dispersion of manufacturing but national specialization in distinct industrial sectors and stages of the value chain	Relocation of assembly activities to developing countries	"Fine-slicing" and relocation of activities
Ownership and control	Widening of corporate ownership	Largely internalized in MNEs	Increased externalization of control of operations; increased internalization of knowledge
Governance	Growth of locally owned firms; more varied governance modes	Offshoring; MNE control	Increased control of focal firm through internalization of knowledge and contractual control of operations

Recent work on EMNEs suggests that their strategies manifest important differences in comparison to established Western MNEs, although there are many similarities. For instance, Peng (2012, p. 97) noted that "While sizeable components of their strategy and behaviour are consistent with what we observe of MNEs from other countries, Chinese MNEs are characterised by three relatively unique features." These are (1) the important role of the home country government, (2) the challenge of going abroad in the absence of superior technological and managerial resources, and (3) the rapid adoption of acquisitions as a primary mode of entry. Points 2 and 3 also apply strongly to Indian MNEs (Munjal et al., 2013). This is reinforced by Sun et al. (2012), who examined the international mergers and acquisitions (M&A) strategies of Indian and Chinese MNEs, and by Hoskisson et al. (2013), who emphasized the role of home country institutions. The route to global factory status may be shortened by M&As in the strategy of EMNEs, but the end point is substantially the same structure.

In addition, we consider how the governance of the global factory affects the appropriation of the value added within spatially dispersed GVCs, and hence the distribution of income within the world income. Such income-distribution issues are clearly important in their own right, but are also a potential trigger for policy initiatives undertaken by governments eager to secure greater value capture from GVC participation—which, in turn, affects MNE strategies (UNCTAD, 2013). As Anand and Segal (2008, p. 57) noted in their comprehensive review of the literature on global income inequality,

Controversy centers on whether inequality has increased or decreased in the recent past. The direction and magnitude of change have been highly charged questions with some authors arguing that globalization has benefited the rich disproportionately, while others argue that it has reduced global income inequalities. Various findings are cited in the media, including the financial press, typically to support one or other position on globalization.

Anand and Segal (2008) also reported a range of estimates in the literature for the direction and magnitude of changes in global inequality, and concluded that there was insufficient evidence to establish whether there had been a (positive or negative) change in global income inequality over the last three decades of the 20th century. This finding contrasts starkly with the data on changes in the global location of economic activity, and provides a compelling rationale for our consideration of governance issues.

This paper is organized as follows. We first present data illustrating the changes in the global location of economic activity between 1985 and 2012, and highlight that emerging economies are steadily becoming more important relative to the advanced economies. We next consider the empirical evidence for each of the three models. We find that the greater global dispersion of economic activity has been accompanied by the rise of locally owned production capacity in emerging economies, but also that MNEs worldwide have increasingly offshored activities so that a substantial amount of activity that had previously been internalized within MNEs is now taking place under outsourcing contracts in the emerging economies. In other words, it appears that each of the three models captures a part of the contemporary reality. We then turn to the governance issue and consider the implications of each of the three models of the global factory for who has effective control of the globally dispersed economic activity and the implications for the global distribution of income. The final section summarizes our conclusions and points out some avenues for future research.

THE GLOBAL LOCATION OF ECONOMIC
ACTIVITY

It is a common perception that the emerging economies account for a large and growing share of global economic activity. There are several difficulties in trying to validate this perception, not least in deciding which countries should be defined as emerging, which as advanced, and which as developing. There is no universally agreed-upon set of criteria[4] for membership of each of these groupings, and there exist many different categorization schemes. This basic definitional difficulty is compounded by the fact that some countries might well be best categorized into one grouping at one point in time but merit a different categorization at a later date.

These problems notwithstanding, we have categorized the countries of the world into three broad groups (advanced, emerging, and developing), broadly following the 2012 International Monetary Fund (IMF) categorizations (IMF, 2012) but including both South Korea and Taiwan, which the IMF does not include. These two countries are both clear examples of the historical problem identified above, in that few would argue that both fit into the emerging category some years ago but might well have been more appropriately placed in the advanced category by 2012. We have thus categorized 26 emerging economies and 32 advanced economies in our statistical analysis, with the other 156 economies all classified as developing:

- *Emerging economies*: Argentina, Brazil, Bulgaria, Chile, China, Colombia, Hungary, India, Indonesia, Latvia, Lithuania, Malaysia, Mexico, Pakistan, Peru, Philippines, Poland, Romania, Russian Federation, South Africa, South Korea, Taiwan, Thailand, Turkey, Ukraine, Venezuela
- *Advanced economies*: Australia, Austria, Belgium, Canada, Cyprus, the Czech Republic, Denmark, Estonia, Finland, France, Germany, Greece, Hong Kong SAR, Iceland, Ireland, Israel, Italy, Japan, Luxembourg, Malta, the Netherlands, New Zealand, Norway, Portugal, Singapore,

---

[4] In broad terms, the advanced economies are those with relatively high levels of GDP per capita and significant levels of industrialization. The emerging economies are those that have lower levels of GDP per capita than the advanced economies, though typically higher growth rates, and are in the process of industrialization. The developing economies are those with low levels of GDP per capita, stagnating growth, and low levels of industrialization (IMF, 2012).

Slovakia, Slovenia, Spain, Sweden, Switzerland, the United Kingdom, the United States

In Table 2 we present illustrative data for four years: 1985, 2000 (the start of the new millennium), 2006 (before the global financial crisis of 2007–2008), and 2012 (the latest year for which data are available). Data are presented via five indicators: population, GDP, merchandise exports, inward foreign direct investment (FDI) flows, and outward FDI flows. One problem with presenting annual data for selected years is that some economic variables (e.g., annual FDI flows) vary considerably from one year to the next. Nevertheless, Table 2 is useful in highlighting some broad historical trends. Here we look at each of the five indicators in turn.

- *Population*: The population of the world increased from 4.86 billion in 1985 to 6.12 billion in 2000, 6.6 billion in 2006, and 7.05 billion in 2012. Meanwhile, the proportion residing in the emerging economies stayed relatively constant at about 60%, while the share in the advanced economies fell (from 17.1% to 13.7%) and that of the developing economies rose (from 22.1% to 27.1%) from 1985 to 2012.
- *GDP*: World GDP rose more than fivefold from US$13,078 billion in 1985 to US$71,435 billion in 2012. In terms of GDP distribution, the advanced economies' share grew from 71.9% in 1985 to 76.9% in 2000—at the expense of the developing economies, whose share fell from 11.3% to 4.7%. But the most dramatic changes have occurred since the start of the 21st century. The advanced economies' share of the GDP fell by 17 percentage points, from 76.9% in 2000 to 70.9% in 2006 and to 59.8% in 2012. Meanwhile, the emerging economies' share rose markedly, from 18.4% in 2000 to 23.1% in 2006 and to 31.7% in 2012, while the developing economies' share recovered to 8.5% by 2012.
- *Exports*: The aggregate world figure for merchandise exports (i.e., exports of goods but not services) grew strongly through the period, from US$1964 billion in 1985 to US$6449 billion in 2000 and US$18,402 billion in 2012. But while exports from the advanced economies increased sevenfold (in nominal terms) between 1985 and 2012, those from the emerging economies went up 17-fold. As a result, the share of exports from the advanced economies fell over 16 percentage points, from 70.1% of the global total in 1985 to 53.6% in 2012, while exports from the emerging economies almost doubled, from 18% to 33.5%, over the same period.

TABLE 2
The Rise of the Emerging Economies

	Year	Advanced economies	Emerging economies	Developing economies
Population	1985	17.1%	60.8%	22.1%
	2000	14.6%	60.4%	25.0%
	2006	14.2%	60.0%	25.9%
	2012	13.7%	59.3%	27.1%
GDP	1985	71.9%	16.8%	11.3%
	2000	76.9%	18.4%	4.7%
	2006	70.9%	23.1%	6.0%
	2012	59.8%	31.7%	8.5%
Merchandise exports	1985	70.1%	18.0%	11.9%
	2000	69.8%	22.8%	7.4%
	2006	61.5%	28.4%	10.1%
	2012	53.6%	33.5%	12.9%
Inward FDI	1985	76.0%	15.9%	8.1%
	2000	85.8%	11.2%	3.0%
	2006	68.8%	21.0%	10.2%
	2012	49.5%	33.5%	17.0%
Outward FDI	1985	95.5%	3.3%	1.2%
	2000	94.0%	2.3%	3.7%
	2006	84.4%	11.0%	4.6%
	2012	79.7%	21.3%	−1.0%

(1) All figures are expressed as percentages of the world totals.

(2) The annual GDP, exports, and FDI data were all expressed in current prices at current exchange rates. The population data refer to July 1st in the year indicated.

(3) The following 32 countries are classified as *advanced* economies: Australia, Austria, Belgium, Canada, Cyprus, Czech Republic, Denmark, Estonia, Finland, France, Germany, Greece, Hong Kong SAR, Iceland, Ireland, Israel, Italy, Japan, Luxembourg, Malta, Netherlands, New Zealand, Norway, Portugal, Singapore, Slovakia, Slovenia, Spain, Sweden, Switzerland, United Kingdom, United States.

(4) The following 26 countries are classified as *emerging* economies: Argentina, Brazil, Bulgaria, Chile, China, Colombia, Hungary, India, Indonesia, Latvia, Lithuania, Malaysia, Mexico, Pakistan, Peru, Philippines, Poland, Romania, Russian Federation, South Africa, South Korea, Taiwan, Thailand, Turkey, Ukraine, Venezuela.

(5) The following 156 countries are classified as *developing* economies: Afghanistan, Albania, Algeria, American Samoa, Andorra, Anguilla, Antigua and Barbuda, Armenia, Aruba, Azerbaijan, Bahamas, Bahrain, Bangladesh, Barbados, Belarus, Belize, Benin, Bermuda, Bhutan, Bolivia, Bonaire, Bosnia and Herzegovina, Botswana, British Virgin Islands, Brunei Darussalam, Burkina Faso, Burundi, Cambodia, Cape Verde, Cayman Islands, Central African Republic, Chad, Congo, Cook Islands, Costa Rica, Croatia, Cuba, Curaçao, Democratic Republic of the Congo, Djibouti, Dominican Republic, Ecuador, Egypt, El Salvador, Equatorial Guinea, Eritrea, Ethiopia, Falkland Islands, Faroe Islands, Fiji, French Polynesia, Gabon, Gambia, Georgia, Ghana, Gibraltar, Greenland, Grenada, Guam, Guatemala, Guinea, Guinea-Bissau, Guyana, Haiti, Honduras, Iran, Iraq, Ivory Coast, Jamaica, Jordan, Kazakhstan, Kenya, Kiribati, Kuwait, Kyrgyzstan, Laos, Lebanon, Lesotho, Liberia, Libya, Macao SAR, Macedonia, Madagascar, Malawi, Maldives, Mali, Marshall Islands, Mauritania, Mauritius, Micronesia, Moldova, Mongolia, Montenegro, Montserrat, Morocco, Mozambique, Myanmar, Namibia, Nauru, Nepal, Netherlands Antilles, New Caledonia, Nicaragua, Niger, Nigeria, Niue, North Korea, Oman, Palau, Palestine, Panama, Papua New Guinea, Paraguay, Qatar, Rwanda, Saint Helena, Saint Kitts and Nevis, Saint Lucia, Saint Pierre and Miquelon, Saint Vincent and the Grenadines, Samoa, San Marino, São Tomé and Príncipe, Saudi Arabia, Senegal, Serbia, Seychelles, Sierra Leone, Solomon Islands, Somalia, South Sudan, Sri Lanka, Sudan, Suriname, Swaziland, Syria, Tajikistan, Timor-Leste, Togo, Tokelau, Tonga, Trinidad and Tobago, Tunisia, Turkmenistan, Turks and Caicos Islands, Tuvalu, Uganda, United Arab Emirates, Uruguay, Uzbekistan, Vanuatu, Vietnam, Wallis and Futuna Islands, Yemen, Zambia, Zimbabwe.

Source: Authors' calculations based on country data extracted from UNCTADSTAT.

• *Inward FDI*: The aggregate annual world inflow of inward FDI rose from a mere US$55 billion in 1985 to US$1413 billion in 2000, before the inflow first stabilized and then fell back to US$1351 billion in 2012. The FDI inflows were largely (76%) targeted at the advanced economies in 1985, and this proportion actually rose to almost 86% by 2000 at the expense of both the emerging and the developing economies. Since then, however, the share directed to the advanced economies fell to under 50% by 2012, while the share going to the emerging economies rose dramatically to over a third (33.5%) of the global total; that going to the developing economies also increased to 17%. These data hint at significant cross-border flows of investment, though it should be stressed again that annual FDI data are very volatile and provide an imperfect indication of increases in foreign productive capacity (Beugelsdijk et al., 2010).

• *Outward FDI*: In principle, world FDI inflows and outflows should be equal, though timing differences and varying reporting procedures mean that the recorded data never match exactly. The aggregate annual world outflow rose from US$62 billion in 1985 to US$1240 billion in 2000, before the inflow first stabilized and then fell back to US$1391 billion in 2012. The advanced economies accounted for an overwhelming proportion (95%) of global flows in both 1985 and 2000, while the emerging economies provided only 2% to 3%. But the situation was quite different in 2012, when the emerging economies were the provenance of over 20% of global FDI flows and the share provided by the developed economies had fallen to less than 80%.

These four years paint a picture of significant changes in the global distribution of economic activity, even with the important caveats mentioned above. In particular, there has been a clear shift since 1985 in the locus of activity away from the advanced economies toward the emerging economies,[5] and this shift has been very pronounced since the turn of the century. Furthermore, as Abiad, Bluedorn, Guajardo, and Topalova (2012) argued, these shifts are likely to continue, as the economic performance of the emerging (and developing) economies is showing increased resilience, largely due to improved policy-making.

CONTROL AND OWNERSHIP OF ACTIVITIES THROUGH THE GLOBAL FACTORY

What is the empirical evidence for each of the three models of the global factory? The main evidence in support of a rise in locally owned production

---

[5] It might be argued that both South Korea and Taiwan should not be categorized as emerging economies, and that their inclusion in this category will have an undue effect on the total for emerging economies and thus on conclusions reached above. These two countries accounted for 7.4% of the aggregate GDP in the emerging economies in 1985, 14.4% in 2000, and 7.2% in 2012. The corresponding figures for merchandise exports and outward FDI in 2012 were higher at 13.8% and 15.5%, respectively, while the figure for inward FDI was lower at 2.9% for both countries combined.

capacity in emerging economies (the Gereffi concept of the global factory) is provided by the data on outward direct investment (Table 1), and by the rising growth and economic influence of EMNEs (Guillén & García-Canal, 2013; Sauvant, Govitrikar, & Davies, 2011). EMNEs were responsible for outward FDI flows of US$296 billion in 2012, or 21.3% of the global outward FDI total. The corresponding figures just 12 years earlier in 2000 were US$28 billion and 2.3%. These aggregate figures highlight an important trend, but they reveal nothing about the ownership of the firms undertaking the investment. In some emerging economies (e.g., Taiwan, South Korea), private corporate ownership has been the norm, although (see below) the ownership structures have often been complex. In others (e.g., China, Russia), there is evidence of significant state interest both through sovereign wealth funds (SWFs) and state-owned enterprises (SOEs). It has been estimated that state-owned MNEs accounted for over one-tenth of global FDI flows in 2012 (UNCTAD, 2013). Furthermore, as Guillén and García-Canal (2013, pp. 1–2) noted:

[A]t the end of the twentieth century, few emerging market multinationals had successfully challenged their European, North American, and Japanese counterparts. Long-established brands such as Sony, Gulfstream, and Hewlett-Packard were still golden. The world corporate pecking order was mostly a game of musical chairs among the same two dozen firms. When *Forbes* published its first Global 2000 list in March 2003, no one could have been surprised by the top 10 entries—Citigroup, GE, AIG, and ExxonMobil among them. Almost 40 percent of the top 2,000 corporations were US based. More than 60 percent of the corporations were headquartered in three countries alone: the United States, Japan, and the United Kingdom. *Forbes'* more recent Global 2000 list—in April 2012—tells a radically different story. A third of its top 25 businesses are from nations barely represented in the listing only eight years earlier. China, of course, leads the way with oil companies and banks; but Brazil's Petrobas and Russia's Gazprom are right in the mix as well. Break down the world economic order by sector, and the list of global leaders from emerging economies … becomes still more impressive.

Meanwhile, the evidence for increased involvement in emerging economies by MNEs from the advanced economies (the Grunwald and Flamm concept of the global factory) is provided by the data on inward direct investment provided in Table 1.

Inward FDI into the emerging economies amounted to US$453 billion in 2012, or 33.5% of global inward FDI—figures that are rather larger than those cited above for outward FDI. The corresponding inward FDI figures just 12 years earlier, in 2000, were US$157 billion and 11.1%. The majority of this inward investment emanates from MNEs in advanced economies, as the inward investment profiles for selected emerging economies (i.e., Argentina, China, Colombia, India, Pakistan, Peru, Russia, and Ukraine) clearly demonstrate (Sauvant et al., 2013). Inward FDI accounted for only 0.4% of GDP in the emerging economies in 1985, but this figure had risen to 2.0% by 2012, suggesting that foreign MNEs are becoming ever more important in these economies.

It should be emphasized, especially in the context of the discussion below about the income distribution effects, that FDI inflows are followed—albeit with a lag of some years—by outflows of income associated with those investments (Economic Commission for Latin America, 2013). As Pérez Ludeña (2014) noted,

Multinational enterprises (MNEs) multiplied their profits made in developing countries by four between 2002 and 2011 (at current prices). In Latin America and the Caribbean, they rose from US$20 billion in 2002 to US$113 billion in 2011. The growth rate has been even higher in Africa and China, but much lower in developed countries. ... FDI income is now higher than portfolio or other investment income and one of the largest items in the balance of payments as a whole. Between 2008 and 2011, FDI income originating in Latin America was almost double the surplus in goods trade.

Finally, we turn to the evidence for greater outsourcing initiatives by firms from the advanced economies (the Buckley and Ghauri model of the global factory). UNCTAD (2011) provided data showing that manufacturing and services outsourcing was worth $1100 billion to $1300 billion in 2010. Furthermore, firms from emerging economies such as the People's Republic of China, India, Taiwan, and Chile figure prominently in the lists of most important providers of outsourced goods. Data by industry (UNCTAD 2011) show that the most active sectors are garments (with $200 billion of cross-border outsourced sales and 7 million employees), footwear ($50 billion sales, 2 million employees), toys ($15 billion sales, 0.5 million employees), electronics ($240 billion sales, 1.7 million employees), auto components ($220 billion sales, 1.4 million

employees), and pharmaceuticals ($30 billion sales, 0.2 million employees). The figure of $1100 billion to $1300 billion for cross-border outsourcing activity may be compared to the $6000 billion exports by the foreign affiliates of MNEs in 2010, though it should be stressed that the outsourcing activity takes place largely in emerging/developing economies, while global FDI stocks tend to be concentrated in advanced economies (UNCTAD, 2011).

In short, and taking into account the fragmented nature of the evidence, it appears as though the observed shift in the global distribution of economic activity toward the emerging economies has been accompanied not only by a rise of locally owned production capacity within those economies, but also by an increasing presence of MNEs from advanced economies, and by increasing amounts of activity within the emerging economies taking place under cross-border outsourcing contracts.

THE GOVERNANCE OF THE GLOBAL FACTORY AND ITS IMPACT ON ECONOMIC DEVELOPMENT

As noted above, each of the three models of the global factory has quite different implications for who has effective control of the globally dispersed economic activity—that is, the governance of the global factory—and hence for the global distribution of income.

A rise in production capacity, owned and controlled by locally owned firms (the Gereffi model) means that not only will there be greater employment opportunities and higher labor remuneration within the emerging economies, but also that substantial proportions of any profits from the domestic value-chain activities will accrue to the shareholders of those firms. This should give rise to a more equitable distribution of income across countries.

In contrast, the Grunwald and Flamm model of the global factory envisages much of the increased economic activity in emerging economies as accruing from offshoring strategies pursued by MNEs from more advanced economies. Various stages of the MNEs' value chains may be offshored to more cost-effective locations, as long as the costs of coordinating across locations and transporting the intermediate goods are low enough to make the process economically viable (Deardorff, 2001). However, MNEs are the lead firms in these GVCs and retain (internalize) explicit ownership and control of the offshored activities though FDI. This is the traditional domain of much IB theory and empirical analysis. Within this model then, what are the implications for the global distribution of income? Certainly there will be greater employment opportunities and higher labor remuneration within the host emerging economies, but the (increased) profits from the dispersed value-chain activities will accrue to the shareholders of the MNEs. The overall impact on income in the host emerging economies will be limited, while the MNEs' shareholders (predominantly in the advanced economies) will generally profit from these overseas ventures in the long term, even considering the risks they incur in making the capital investments in the host countries. Global inequalities in the distribution of income may thus be exacerbated as a result of the development of the global factory. Nevertheless, many host countries view such inward FDI as a key element of their economic development strategies and welcome its potential employment and value-added and technology transfer benefits while downplaying any concerns about foreign domination of local productive capacity (Reich, 1990, 1991; UNCTAD, 2003). Other host countries are more circumspect about inward FDI and highlight the associated loss of national sovereignty and alleged problems such as transfer price manipulation and the "footloose" nature of many foreign investments.

In the Buckley and Ghauri model the shifts of economic activity from the advanced economies to the emerging economies not only reflect offshoring imperatives but are accompanied by a reduction in the ownership of global productive capacity by MNEs from the advanced economies as they outsource (externalize) elements of their value chains to independent suppliers in the host economies. The motives for offshoring to more cost-effective locations are obvious, but why might the MNEs (the lead firms in GVCs) choose to externalize (outsource) these activities rather than internalize them through FDI? Most theoretical explanations argue that firms embrace outsourcing as an efficient response to changing economic conditions (in particular, ICT advances), and emphasize that firms are either concentrating on their core competencies (Prahalad & Hamel, 1990), taking advantage of complementary resources and capabilities owned by external suppliers (Gottfredson, Puryear, & Phillips, 2005), or taking advantage of more efficient external suppliers (Abraham & Taylor, 1996). However, such explanations neglect the power asymmetries between the lead firms and their independent suppliers in outsourcing relationships (Hymer, 1972; Strange & Newton, 2006).

ICT advances have reduced the costs of searching for potential suppliers and increased competition among suppliers at various stages of the value chain (Strange, 2011). This has shifted power within value chains away from suppliers toward lead firms, which are able to control the interface with the final customers through a variety of "isolating mechanisms" (Rumelt, 1984, 1987) such as branding, product customization, and preferential access. The firms that control these interfaces with the final customer are able to relinquish ownership and externalize the production of various intermediate goods and/or services within their value chains, while crucially still retaining effective control over the chains. In this conceptualization of the global factory, "the control or orchestration of these activities remains very firmly within the metropolitan (advanced) countries" (Buckley, 2009b, p. 131), notwithstanding the absence of central ownership.

The strategy of internalization followed by global factories is of a particular type: knowledge internalization. This is distinct from operational internalization (Buckley & Casson, 1976, 2009). Gains from knowledge internalization arise from asymmetric information, whereby the global factory is in possession of a wider and deeper range of knowledge than potential partners. Consequently, knowledge-intensive activities—those intensive in the fruits of R&D—are internalized, while more routine activities (including production) are more frequently outsourced.

What are the implications of such outsourcing arrangements for the global distribution of income, given that lead firms based in advanced economies are retaining effective control of the value chains? The lead firms will be able to leverage their power over their suppliers to appropriate all the rents along the chain from a smaller asset base while enjoying increased flexibility of supply. To illustrate this point, consider the following simple numerical example (see Table 3). Suppose widget manufacture involves three stages of production, the first two of which are for cost reasons best undertaken in emerging economies. The technology is such that the three stages are capable of being carried out independently, and the marginal costs of production (excluding the costs of inputs) at each stage are $20, $30, and $40 respectively. Markets do exist for the intermediate products from stages one and two, and the prices are $25 and $60, but transaction costs are initially such that it makes economic sense to vertically integrate the three stages and internalize the transfer of the intermediate

TABLE 3
The Economics of Widget Production

Vertically integrated production

	Stage 1	Stage 2	Stage 3
Required assets	40	40	80
Cost of inputs	0	25	60
Marginal costs of production	20	30	40
Price of output	25	60	110
Profit	5	5	10

Externalized production

	Stage 1	Stage 2	Stage 3
Required assets	40	40	80
Cost of inputs	0	20	50
Marginal costs of production	20	30	40
Price of output	20	50	110
Profit	0	0	20

products. The widget manufacturer is thus a multinational enterprise (MNE) with direct investments overseas, and there will be substantial intrafirm international flows of intermediate goods. The final widgets may be sold for $110 in the advanced economy in which the MNE resides. The net result is that the MNE earns a total profit of $20 on an asset base of $160, and hence shows a 12.5% return.

Now assume that the marginal costs of production at each stage remain the same, as do the required resources, but that the markets for the intermediate products become more competitive—though the firm still retains its monopoly power in the final widget market. If the firm externalizes the production in stages one and two, it will be able to leverage its external contractors to supply the intermediate goods at cost (i.e., at the cost of inputs plus the marginal costs of production) and then appropriate all the profit ($20) for itself. The firm will thus earn the full $20 profit but on a smaller asset base, and its rate of return will rise to 25%.[6]

Three points about this example are worth noting. The first is that the key to the improved performance of the lead firm has not been greater efficiency, but rather the firm's leverage of power over its suppliers. Certainly the firm enjoys increased flexibility of supply, but this is a happy by-product of externalization rather than the root cause. Second, it would be misleading to suggest that externalization is

the result of the firm's focusing on its core competencies, or taking advantage of external competencies, or reducing costs by taking advantage of suppliers' potential economies of scale or their ability to provide better service quality. As the example shows, the firm will opt to externalize its production when the circumstances permit the appropriation of the total rents from a smaller asset base, even if there are no direct cost advantages. One could couch this proposition from a resource-based perspective that the firm is simply taking advantage of its capabilities in coordinating the activities along the production chain, but this is close to being a tautological statement. Third, the lead firm is no longer an MNE in the legal sense, as the firm now undertakes production in only one country. There will still be the same international flows of intermediate goods, but they will constitute interfirm rather than intrafirm trade.

There are thus substantial potential gains from externalization to the shareholders of the lead firms, whom we assume reside primarily in the advanced economies, over and above the profits to be made from internalizing production though FDI. In such circumstances, critics often claim that the suppliers in the emerging countries are being exploited, with no contractual security and constant pressures to reduce costs. Indeed, there is a substantial literature (see, e.g., Bartlett et al., 2008; UNCTAD, 2011) highlighting low wage levels, poor working conditions, and environmental abuses by the suppliers of various infamous lead firms (e.g., Nike, Apple).

On the positive side, the international fragmentation of production (IFP) increases the opportunities for countries that are not efficient producers of the final good to benefit from trade through specialization in the labor-intensive stages of a production process that, as a whole, may be capital or technology intensive (Yeats, 1997). Participation in global value chains provides local firms with access to overseas markets at lower cost than would otherwise be possible, and may give rise to technology transfer and/or benefits from organizational learning (Bair & Gereffi, 2003; Gereffi, 1999; Gibbon, 2001; Humphrey & Schmitz, 2000). The challenge for local firms is not so much to participate in global value chains as to upgrade their positions within such chains from that of simple assembly to OEM, and ultimately to original brand-name manufacturing (OBM).

There is evidence across a range of industries, including garments, automobiles, and electronics, of an evolving tiered structure of suppliers, wherein the first tier may undertake relatively sophisticated

---

[6] There will be the additional transaction costs associated with using the market mechanism, but the firm will save on the costs associated with coordinating a vertically integrated multinational operation.

activities and lower-tier positions typically involve lower-skilled activities that are relatively easy to imitate but provide little scope for learning and growth. In practice, upgrading is beset with obstacles such as transactional dependence vis-à-vis the lead firms and various isolating mechanisms around the profitable activities within the chains (Palpacuer & Parisotto, 2003; UNCTAD, 2013).

Nevertheless, there are success stories. The Taiwanese component supplier Foxconn Technology Group has evolved from humble beginnings to become a major MNE in its own right, employing more than 600,000 people[7] in 2010 at manufacturing locations in more than 20 countries and supplying electronic components to an array of major clients including Apple, Dell, Sony, Nintendo, Hewlett-Packard, and Samsung (Denicolai et al., 2015; UNCTAD, 2011). Furthermore, as the example of Foxconn clearly demonstrates, the very process of outsourcing undermines the power asymmetries that were inherent in the original externalized relationship, as Foxconn is now a powerful intermediary within the value chains of all of its clients.

In short, the global income distribution implications of the Buckley and Ghauri model of the global factory are likely to change over time. Initially, the likelihood is that income inequalities will widen as the outsourcing arrangements enrich the shareholders of the lead firms while simultaneously suppressing wages/profits in the emerging economies. Thereafter, however, the implications are less obvious, and depend on the extent to which locally owned firms in the emerging economies are able to embark upon successful upgrading strategies (UNCTAD, 2013).

CONCLUSIONS

It is clear that there have been major changes in the global location of economic activity over the past 30 years, with the emerging economies assuming greater shares relative to the advanced economies over a range of indicators. Far less obvious, however, is the impact of these changes on the global distribution of income, especially as the empirical evidence is inconclusive about whether global income inequalities are rising or falling (Anand & Segal, 2008). Has the emergence of the "global factory" reduced global income inequalities, or has it benefited disproportionately those in the advanced economies? We do not have a definitive

answer to this question, but, as we have argued in this paper, the answer will depend in large part on who has control over the geographically dispersed activities—in other words, the governance of the global factory.

More specifically, the global income distribution implications depend crucially on whether the changes in the global location of economic activity have come about primarily through (1) the growth of locally owned firms in the emerging economies, (2) increased FDI by MNEs from the advanced economies, or (3) the proliferation of outsourcing arrangements coordinated by firms in the advanced economies. The available evidence is piecemeal, yet we have shown that there is empirical support for each of the three conceptual models of the global factory. For example, there has been an increase in locally owned production capacity in emerging economies, MNEs from advanced economies have increased their FDI activity, and many firms are outsourcing various activities that were previously internalized within vertically integrated operations. This is no doubt one reason why the extant literature has failed to report conclusive empirical support for either global income convergence or divergence.

The academic literature contains (1) many papers on the growth and strategies of firms from emerging economies,[8] (2) many papers on the causes and consequences of inward FDI in emerging economies,[9] and (3) many papers on the motives for outsourcing and non-equity modes of international production.[10] However, there is little empirical work on the relative empirical importance of each of these three phenomena, and also little work on the different implications for economic development and the global distribution of income. The contribution of this paper is to draw attention to these deficiencies, and to emphasize that further academic research is required on the governance of the global factory. This might well combine the insights of internalization theory (Buckley & Strange, 2011), GVC analysis (Gereffi et al., 2005), and corporate governance research (Wright et al., 2005).

---

[7] This figure had risen to 1.6 million by the end of 2012.

[8] See, for instance, Gammeltoft et al. (2010), Guillén and García-Canal (2009, 2013), Hoskisson et al. (2000), Hoskisson et al. (2013), Meyer (2004), Munjal et al. (2013), Peng (2012), Sauvant et al. (2011), Sun et al. (2012), and Wright et al. (2005).

[9] See Dunning and Lundan (2008, part III) for a comprehensive review.

[10] See UNCTAD (2011) for a comprehensive review.

Our analysis also has important implications for policymakers. Governments of emerging economies should be aware of the differential benefits that accrue as a result of activities being organized within different governance structures. It is not enough to provide an attractive low-cost location for value-chain activities; governments should also encourage local firms to upgrade their positions within the value chains and also ensure that as much as possible of the value-chain rents are retained within the economy. This message is echoed by UNCTAD (2013, p. 175), which noted that:

> Participation in GVCs can generate considerable economic development benefits but also involve risks. The potential social and environmental consequences of GVCs, and the experience of some countries with local value capture from GVCs, have led many developing-country policymakers to ask the legitimate question: are active promotion of GVCs and GVC-led development strategies the only available options or are there alternatives? [The alternative] is an industrial development strategy aimed at building domestic productive capacity, including for exports, in all stages of production ... to develop a vertically integrated industry that remains relatively independent from the key actors of GVCs for its learning and upgrading processes.

Our objective in this paper has been to note the significant changes in the global location of economic activity over the past 30 years, and to highlight some important conceptual and empirical issues about who controls these activities and the implications for the global distribution of income. We believe these issues are of great importance, not least because they address the conundrum posed by Anand and Segal (2008) about whether globalization has benefited the rich disproportionately or reduced global income inequalities, but also because they have received too little attention in the academic literature and elsewhere.

Our empirical evidence is necessarily partial and fragmented, and this is a limitation of the paper. Further research should be devoted to uncovering the patterns of (domestic and foreign) corporate ownership in emerging economies, and to cataloging the extent of cross-border outsourcing contracts. We have focused on the possible implications for the intercountry distribution of income, yet there are also important questions about the effects on the distribution of income within economies, and especially within emerging economies—namely, have the benefits of the global factory been equitably distributed, or have they been retained by powerful elites?

REFERENCES

Abiad, A., Bluedorn, J., Guajardo, J., & Topalova, P. (2012). *The rising resilience of emerging market and developing economies* (IMF Working Paper WP/12/300). Washington, DC: International Monetary Fund.

Abraham, K., & Taylor, S. (1996). Firms' use of outside contractors: Theory and evidence. *Journal of Labor Economics, 14*(3), 394–424.

Anand, S., & Segal, P. (2008). What do we know about global income inequality? *Journal of Economic Literature, 46*(1), 57–94.

Bair, J., & Gereffi, G. (2003). Upgrading, uneven development, and jobs in the North American apparel industry. *Global Networks, 3*(2), 143–169.

Baldwin, R., & Lopez-Gonzalez, J. (2013). *Supply-chain trade: A portrait of global patterns and several testable hypotheses* (NBER Working Paper 18957). Cambridge, MA: National Bureau of Economic Research.

Baldwin, R., & Venables, A. J. (2013). Spiders and snakes: Offshoring and agglomeration in the global economy. *Journal of International Economics, 90*(2), 245–254.

Bartlett, C., Ghoshal, S., & Beamish, P. (Eds.). (2008). *Transnational management: Text, cases, and readings in cross-border management.* New York: McGraw-Hill.

Beugelsdijk, S., Hennart, J.-F., Slangen, A., & Smeets, R. (2010). Why and how FDI stocks are a biased measure of MNE affiliate activity. *Journal of International Business Studies, 41*(9), 1444–1459.

Buckley, P. J. (2004). The role of China in the global strategy of multinational enterprises. *Journal of Chinese Economic and Business Studies, 2*(1), 1–25.

Buckley, P. J. (2007). The strategies of multinational enterprises in the light of the rise of China. *Scandinavian Journal of Management, 23*(2), 107–126.

Buckley, P. J. (2009a). Internalization thinking: From the multinational enterprise to the global factory. *International Business Review, 18*(3), 224–235.

Buckley, P. J. (2009b). The impact of the global factory on economic development. *Journal of World Business, 44*(2), 131–143.

Buckley, P. J. (2011). International integration and coordination in the global factory. *Management International Review, 51*(2), 121–127.

Buckley, P. J., & Casson, M. C. (1976). *The future of the multinational enterprise.* London: Macmillan.

Buckley, P. J., & Casson, M. C. (2009). The internalization theory of the multinational enterprise: A review of the progress of a research agenda after 30 years. *Journal of International Business Studies, 40*(9), 1563–1580.

Buckley, P. J., & Ghauri, P. N. (2004). Globalization, economic geography and the strategy of multinational enterprises. *Journal of International Business Studies, 35*(2), 81–98.

Buckley, P. J., & Strange, R. (2011). The governance of the multinational enterprise: Insights from internalization theory. *Journal of Management Studies, 48*(2), 460–470.

Deardorff, A. V. (2001). Fragmentation across cones. In S. Arndt & H. Kierzkowski (Eds.), *Fragmentation: New production patterns in the world economy* (pp. 35–51). Oxford, UK: Oxford University Press.

Denicolai, S., Strange, R., & Zucchella, A. (2015). The dynamics of the outsourcing relationship. In R. Ven Tulder, A. Verbeke, & R. Drogendijk (Eds.), *Multinational enterprises and their organizational challenges. Progress in international business research* (Vol. 10). Bingley, UK: Emerald.

Dunning, J. H., & Lundan, S. M. (2008). *Multinational enterprises and the global economy* (2nd ed.). Cheltenham, UK: Edward Elgar.

Economic Commission for Latin America. (2013). *Foreign direct investment in Latin America and the Caribbean, 2012.* Santiago, Chile: Author.

Gammeltoft, P., Barnard, H., & Madhok, A. (2010). Emerging multinationals, emerging theory: Macro- and micro-level perspectives. *Journal of International Management, 16*(2), 95–101.

Gereffi, G. (1989). Development strategies and the global factory. *Annals of the American Academy of Political and Social Science, 505,* 92–104.

Gereffi, G. (1999). International trade and industrial upgrading in the apparel commodity chain. *Journal of International Economics, 48*(1), 37–70.

Gereffi, G., Humphrey, J., & Sturgeon, T. (2005). The governance of global value chains. *Review of International Political Economy, 12*(1), 78–104.

Gibbon, P. (2001). Upgrading primary production: A global commodity chain approach. *World Development, 29*(2), 345–363.

Gottfredson, M., Puryear, R., & Phillips, S. (2005). Strategic sourcing: From periphery to the core. *Harvard Business Review, 83*(2), 132–139.

Grunwald, J., & Flamm, K. (1985). *The global factory: Foreign assembly in international trade.* Washington, DC: Brookings Institution.

Guillén, M., & García-Canal, E. (2009). The American model of the multinational firm and the "new" multinationals from emerging economies. *Academy of Management Perspectives, 23*(2), 23–35.

Guillén, M., & García-Canal, E. (2013). *Emerging markets rule: Growth strategies of the global giants.* New York: McGraw-Hill.

Hoskisson, R. E., Eden, L., Lau, C. M., & Wright, M. (2000). Strategy in emerging economies. *Academy of Management Journal, 43*(3), 249–267.

Hoskisson, R. E., Wright, M., Filatotchev, I., & Peng, M. W. (2013). Emerging multinationals from mid-range economies: The influence of institutions and factor markets. *Journal of Management Studies, 50*(7), 1295–1321.

Humphrey, J., & Schmitz, H. (2000). *Governance and upgrading: Linking industrial cluster and global value-chain research* (IDS Working Paper #120). Sussex, UK: University of Sussex.

Hymer, S. H. (1972). The United States multinational corporation and Japanese competition in the Pacific. *Chuokoron-sha* (spring). Reprinted in R. B. Cohen, N. Felton, M. Nkosi, & J. van Liere (Eds.), *The multinational corporation: A radical approach — Papers by Stephen Herbert Hymer* (pp. 239-255). Cambridge, UK: Cambridge University Press, 1979.

IMF. (2012). *World economic outlook 2012: Coping with high debt and sluggish growth.* Washington, DC: International Monetary Fund.

Liesch, P. W., Buckley, P. J., Simonin, B. L., & Knight, G. (2012). Organizing the worldwide market for market transactions. *Management International Review, 52,* 3–21.

Meyer, K. E. (2004). Perspectives on multinational enterprises in emerging economies. *Journal of International Business Studies, 35*(4), 259–276.

Munjal, S., Buckley, P. J., Enderwick, P., & Forsans, N. (2013). The growth trajectory of Indian MNEs. In C. Brautaset & C. Dent (Eds.), *The great diversity: Trajectories of Asian development* (pp. 191–203). Wageningen, Netherlands: Wageningen Academic Press.

Nissanke, M., & Thorbecke, E. (2006). Channels and policy debate in the globalization-inequality-poverty nexus. *World Development, 34*(8), 1338–1360.

Palpacuer, F., & Parisotto, A. (2003). Global production and local jobs: Can global enterprise networks be used as levers for local development? *Global Networks, 3*(2), 97–120.

Peng, M. W. (2012). The global strategy of emerging multinationals from China. *Global Strategy Journal, 2*(2), 97–107.

Pérez Ludeña, M. (2014). *The rise of FDI income, and what it means for the balance of payments of developing countries* (Columbia FDI Perspectives no. 122). New York: Columbia University.

Prahalad, C. K., & Hamel, G. (1990). The core competence of the corporation. *Harvard Business Review, 28*(3), 79–91.

Reich, R. B. (1990). Who is us? *Harvard Business Review, 68*(1), 53–64.

Reich, R. B. (1991). Who is them? *Harvard Business Review, 69*(2), 77–88.

Rumelt, R. P. (1984). Towards a strategic theory of the firm. In R. Lamb (Ed.), *Competitive strategic management* (pp. 566–570). Englewood Cliffs, NJ: Prentice Hall.

Rumelt, R. P. (1987). Theory, strategy and entrepreneurship. In D. J. Teece (Ed.), *The competitive challenge: Strategies for industrial innovation and renewal* (pp. 137–158). Cambridge, MA: Ballinger.

Sauvant, K. P., Govitrikar, V. P., & Davies, K. (2011). *MNEs from emerging markets: New players in the world FDI market*. New York: Vale Columbia Center on Sustainable International Investment.

Sauvant, K. P., Mallampally, P., & McAllister, G. (2013). *Inward and outward FDI profiles*. New York: Vale Columbia Center on Sustainable International Investment.

Strange, R. (2011). The outsourcing of primary activities: Theoretical analysis and propositions. *Journal of Management & Governance, 15*(2), 249–269.

Strange, R., & Newton, J. (2006). Stephen Hymer and the externalization of production. *International Business Review, 15*(2), 180–193.

Sun, S. L., Peng, M. W., Ren, B., & Yan, D. (2012). A comparative ownership advantage framework for cross-border M&As: The rise of Chinese and Indian MNEs. *Journal of World Business, 47*(1), 4–16.

UNCTAD. (2003). *World investment report 2003: FDI policies for development: National and international perspectives*. New York, Geneva: United Nations.

UNCTAD. (2011). *World investment report 2011: Non-equity modes of international production and development*. New York, Geneva: United Nations.

UNCTAD. (2013). *World investment report 2013: Global value chains: Investment and trade for development*. New York, Geneva: United Nations.

Vernon, R. (1966). International investments and international trade in the product life cycle. *Quarterly Journal of Economics, 80*(2), 190–207.

Vernon, R. (1979). The product cycle hypothesis in a new international environment. *Oxford Bulletin of Economics and Statistics, 41*(4), 255–267.

Wright, M., Filatotchev, I., Hoskisson, R., & Peng, M. (2005). Strategy research in emerging economies: Challenging the conventional wisdom. *Journal of Management Studies, 42*(1), 1–34.

Yeats, A. J. (1997). *Just how big is global production sharing?* (World Bank Policy Research Paper no. 1871). Washington, DC: World Bank.

Peter Buckley, OBE, FBA (P.J.Buckley@lubs.leeds.ac.uk), is a professor of international business, founder director of the Centre for International Business at the University of Leeds, founder director of the Business Confucius Institute at the University of Leeds, and Cheung Kong Scholar Chair Professor at the University of International Business and Economics in Beijing. He was president of the Academy of International Business from 2002 to 2004.

Roger Strange (R.N.Strange@sussex.ac.uk) is a professor of international business at the University of Sussex. His research focuses on the effects of corporate governance factors on FDI decisions; the determinants of MNE subsidiary location; and the reasons for, and the implications of, the trend toward the outsourcing of primary activities.

[16]

Global Strategy Journal
Global Strat. J., **5**: 27–47 (2015)
Published online in Wiley Online Library (wileyonlinelibrary.com). DOI: 10.1002/gsj.1088

IN THE RIGHT PLACE AT THE RIGHT TIME!: THE INFLUENCE OF KNOWLEDGE GOVERNANCE TOOLS ON KNOWLEDGE TRANSFER AND UTILIZATION IN MNEs

ULF ANDERSSON[12], PETER J. BUCKLEY[34], and
HENRIK DELLESTRAND[5*]
[1]*School of Business, Society and Engineering, Mälardalen University, Västerås, Sweden*
[2]*Department of Strategy and Logistics, BI Norwegian Business School, Oslo, Norway*
[3]*Centre for International Business, Leeds University Business School, University of Leeds, Leeds, U.K.*
[4]*University of International Business and Economics, Beijing, China*
[5]*Department of Business Studies, Uppsala University, Uppsala, Sweden*

This article examines the utilization of knowledge transferred between sending and receiving subsidiaries within multinational enterprises. A model was developed and tested on 169 specific knowledge transfer projects. The model explains the utilization of knowledge subject to transfer in terms of hierarchical governance tool efficacy and lateral relationships within the multinational enterprise. The results show that headquarters' involvement during knowledge development does not have any significant impact on subsequent knowledge utilization in the receiving units and, in fact, hierarchical governance forms have a negative impact on knowledge utilization. However, lateral relationships are positive stimuli to building subsidiary capabilities in the knowledge transfer process that enhance receiving unit knowledge utilization. Copyright © 2015 Strategic Management Society.

INTRODUCTION

In this article, we analyze knowledge transfer effectiveness between sending and receiving subsidiaries within multinational enterprises (MNEs) in terms of utilization of transferred knowledge at the receiving unit. Viewing and measuring knowledge transfer as a discrete event, rather than an aggregate of knowledge in- and outflows enables teasing out the knowledge transfer effectiveness in terms of use and

adoption at the receiver.[1] This is an important contribution of our study, as only knowledge that has been adopted and is used can have a genuine impact on capability development. The conceptual framework of this article builds on the knowledge-based view and integrates both hierarchical governance tools and lateral relationships for understanding

Keywords: headquarter-subsidiary roles and relations; knowledge governance; knowledge management; multinational enterprise; relationships
*Correspondence to: Henrik Dellestrand, Department of Business Studies, Uppsala University, Box 513, SE-751 20, Uppsala, Sweden. E-mail: henrik.dellestrand@fek.uu.se

[1] Effectiveness reflects the utilization of knowledge that has been transferred to a receiving unit. As the adoption and use of transferred knowledge is what influences organizational learning, this is the goal when transferring knowledge between units in an MNE. The 'cost efficiency,' that is, the number of people, hours, and amount of financial resources employed in the transfer process, can, of course, compromise the benefits of adopting and using the transferred knowledge, but it does not in itself influence organizational capabilities. Previous research has found that knowledge transfer drives performance, but the issue of use and adoption has been left relatively unexplored.

Copyright © 2015 Strategic Management Society

28   *U. Andersson, P. J. Buckley, and H. Dellestrand*

knowledge transfer effectiveness. The knowledge-based view highlights integrating isolated knowledge (Almeida, Song, and Grant, 2002; Foss and Pedersen, 2004; Song, Almeida, and Wu, 2003). We contribute to the knowledge-based view by making manifest hierarchical and lateral factors facilitating, or impeding, firms' *de facto* knowledge integration. Put differently, the knowledge-based view is extended by explaining antecedents to the use and adoption of geographically dispersed knowledge by focusing on effective knowledge transfer.

Given knowledge's prominence as a fundamental competitive resource, a key firm activity is knowledge governance, that is, the development and leverage of knowledge throughout the firm (Argote and Ingram, 2000; Foss, 2007). Managers at different firm levels orchestrate knowledge processes with varying degrees of difficulty: for example, the more geographically dispersed the firm is, and the more dissimilar the activities of its subsidiaries are, the greater the obstacle to knowledge transfer (Agrawal, Kapur, and McHale, 2008; Tallman and Phene, 2007). The MNE, which can be viewed as a bundle of resources that are geographically dispersed (Bartlett and Ghoshal, 1989; Penrose 1959), therefore constitutes a particularly important laboratory in which to study knowledge governance (Foss, 2006). Geographically dispersed knowledge and associated sources may benefit the MNE due to location heterogeneity, but, at the same time, it may be difficult to integrate (Foss and Pedersen, 2004). However, a core idea of the knowledge-based view is that MNEs can transfer this knowledge efficiently (Kogut and Zander, 1993), but at the same time it may be difficult for the recipient to utilize the transferred knowledge effectively (Barney, 1991). This conundrum is rarely discussed within the knowledge-based view; by focusing on the use and adoption of transferred knowledge, we address this gap in the literature.

The struggle between internal consistency and local adaptation is apt to be more pronounced in MNEs as compared to domestic firms, thus complicating the knowledge transfer process. MNE managers at both the subsidiary and the headquarters level can employ different governance mechanisms to influence knowledge transfer processes (Foss, Husted, and Michailova, 2010)—hence, the need to understand the various tools at the managers' disposal. We focus on specific knowledge transfer projects with particular reference to the role of headquarters in the process—the relationship between subsidiaries and specific managerial actions

taken to ensure effective knowledge transfer (Foss and Pedersen, 2004; Grant, 1996; Kogut and Zander, 1992, 1993; Martin and Salomon, 2003; Szulanski and Jensen, 2006).

Firms are not only important and efficient governance structures, but are also a locus for learning (Ghoshal and Moran, 1996; Madhok 1996, 1997; Tallman and Chacar, 2011; Teece, 1990) and cultivate routines as coordinative devices (Nelson and Winter, 1982; Williamson, 1999). Previous research has primarily focused on characteristics of the knowledge transferred or subsidiaries' absorptive capacity , that is, cognitive aspects (Mahnke and Pedersen, 2004), whereas hierarchical intervention has attracted less attention, especially at the subsidiary level. Relational governance, defined as, 'a social institution that governs and guides exchange partners on the basis of cooperative norms and collaborative activities' (Poppo, Zhou, and Zenger, 2008: 1197) seems to be a promising perspective in analyzing the utilization of transferred knowledge, i.e., transfer effectiveness, as it encompasses hierarchical governance tools and lateral relationships.

This article also addresses the important question, discussed by Foss and Pedersen (2004), of how MNE managers at both the subsidiary and headquarters level can orchestrate knowledge transfer activities in the MNE network and how this affects knowledge transfer effectiveness. The link between organizational processes and knowledge transfer is still under-researched (Foss, 2006). This article connects actions taken by headquarters with more micro-features associated with subsidiaries engaged in knowledge transfer, that is, the social structures of inter-subsidiary relationships (Szulanski, Cappetta, and Jensen, 2004) that can help explain knowledge transfer effectiveness. While extant research has looked at knowledge transfer in MNEs from different viewpoints, most has looked at 'flows of knowledge' as an aggregated quota that is transferred, which makes it inherently difficult to tease out the actual effect of the knowledge transfer effort at the recipient unit. The focus on flows of knowledge obscures the success of individual transfer projects in terms of adoption and use in the receiving units. It also makes the influence of different knowledge governance tools on knowledge transfer effectiveness ambiguous. In the present study, we address this important gap in the existing knowledge transfer literature.

The findings are based on a questionnaire administered through structured face-to-face interviews

Copyright © 2015 Strategic Management Society

Global Strat. J., **5**: 27–47 (2015)
DOI: 10.1002/gsj.1088

with subsidiary managers involved in 169 specific intra-MNE knowledge transfer projects. The knowledge transaction was used as the unit of analysis (Foss, 2007). The specificity of the data from these 169 transfer projects adds to the quality of the findings, since research has found that MNEs apply different control strategies depending on the context in which the subsidiaries operate (Nohria and Ghoshal, 1994). By looking at specific transfer projects, a fine-grained understanding of both hierarchical and lateral relationships is attained, thereby contributing to an increased understanding of knowledge governance and the knowledge-based view. This is directly related to Grant's (1996) conceptualization of the firm as a knowledge integrator.

The remainder of the article is organized as follows: the theoretical background is outlined in the next section. This is followed by a section outlining five hypotheses that address how hierarchical governance tools and lateral relationships affect the utilization of transferred knowledge. Subsequently, the data and methods are presented, followed by the results of the study. The results are then discussed with limitations pointed out and suggestions made for future research.

THEORETICAL BACKGROUND

Transfer of knowledge

Knowledge management is at the forefront of MNE research (cf. Agrawal *et al.*, 2008; Grant, 1996; Gupta and Govindarajan, 2000; Kogut and Zander, 1992, 1993; Szulanski, 1996; Tallman and Phene, 2007). The MNE is conceptualized as a superior vehicle for knowledge development and transfer because it is a social community (Kogut and Zander, 1993) rather than a market transactor of knowledge. Teece (1986) conceptualized innovations as bearers of knowledge. Thus, in this article, knowledge is captured by analyzing different innovations that embody knowledge. The transfer of knowledge is an attempt to close gaps between what is known and what is currently being used throughout the organization (Cool, Dierickx, and Szulanski, 1997; Pfeffer and Salancik, 1978; Pfeffer and Sutton, 2000; Repenning, 2002). This may be described as 'additive complementarity' (Buckley and Carter, 1999). Still, the knowledge transfer activity needs to be managed and coordinated, that is, governed. In essence, this suggests a framework where both the formal power of headquar-

ters and the informal social relationships formed by subsidiaries—where much of the actual network influence may reside (Forsgren, Holm, and Johanson, 2005)—are taken into account.

The rationale behind knowledge transfer in MNEs arises because it is costly to develop new knowledge and the organization has an interest in making use of existing knowledge elsewhere in the MNE, although transfer also has a cost (Teece, 1977). This is in accordance with Penrose's (1959) assertion that the competence of a firm is connected to its ability to leverage its resources. By transferring knowledge, the performance observed at one location in the organization can potentially be enhanced in another location, either by generating new knowledge or by economizing on existing knowledge (Schulz, 2001; Szulanski *et al.*, 2004). This implies that there is both cost and gain from knowledge transfer. The cost-benefit balance is dependent on the transfer process performance; more specifically, echoing Teece (1977) and Penrose (1959), the transferred knowledge has to be *utilized* at the recipient. If transferred knowledge is not used, it seems inept to engage in transfer at all, since costs are incurred but no effect is achieved in terms of upgrading the competencies and competitive advantage in the receiving unit. Making sure that what is developed in one location is transferred to another is core for knowledge governance and the knowledge-based view, and usage may lead to an improved competitive position for the receiving unit.

Knowledge transfer performance

Extant research has by and large focused on knowledge transfer measured as an outflow from a sender or inflow to a receiver (Gupta and Govindarajan, 2000; Haas and Hansen, 2005; Noorderhaven and Harzing, 2009; Schulz, 2001). However, this literature offers limited insights as to whether the knowledge transferred is being implemented and used at the receiving subsidiary. There have been some voices arguing that this might not be the case (Argote and Ingram, 2000; Kostova, 1999), for example, knowledge being ceremonially adopted (Kostova and Roth, 2002). Hence, our knowledge is limited regarding whether or not knowledge really is adopted by the receiving subsidiary. In this respect, our understanding of knowledge transfer effectiveness is underdeveloped.

Studying knowledge transfer performance requires investigating individual transfer projects.

We capture individual project performance variance and elucidate the associated underlying reasons in an approach similar to Szulanski (1996) and Kostova and Roth (2002), where knowledge transfer was suggested to be a distinct experience related to specific projects. In this article, knowledge transfer effectiveness is defined as a distinct measure related to the receiving subsidiary's knowledge implementation and usage (Ciabuschi, Dellestrand, and Kappen, 2011a; Kostova, 1999; Leonard-Barton and Sinha, 1993). As proposed by Foss (2007), we use the specific knowledge transaction as the unit of analysis in this study.

Organizational processes at different levels can affect MNE knowledge transfer performance in general. Though efficiency and effectiveness are inter-related, this article focuses on effectiveness rather than efficiency, that is, the transfer cost (Daft, 1992). Knowledge that is used by the recipient is key, since it is only then that the transferred knowledge has implications for the functioning of the recipient subsidiary. The following two sections elaborate on hierarchical governance and lateral relationships by focusing on the discrete event of individual knowledge transfer projects. Both are distinct organizational governance dimensions and do not exclude the other—rather they are complementary forces influencing the degree of the receiving unit's transferred knowledge utilization.[2] The variables included in this analysis are associated with key concepts in the discussion of hierarchy and lateral relationships and illuminate the emerging knowledge governance approach (Foss, 2007; Grandori, 2001). Our approach is also consistent with the horizontal and vertical dimensions of the knowledge-based view (Grant, 1996).

HYPOTHESIS DEVELOPMENT

Hierarchical governance and knowledge transfer

Ghoshal and Bartlett (1990) and Birkinshaw (2001) argued that headquarters is potentially very influen-

tial in managing knowledge flows between MNE units. Headquarters can be thought of as a knowledge webmaster (Tallman and Koza, 2010), occupying a special position within the MNE network as the unit with formal authoritative power. Headquarters has a holistic role that entails a strategic responsibility to identify needs and solutions in the organization, i.e., top management has an important role in identifying, creating, and sharing knowledge (Markides, 2002; Markides and Williamson, 1994), which relates to the transfer process in filling gaps where knowledge resides at other organization locations. For headquarters, this involves participating in subsidiary-level activities, as well as using formal monitoring and evaluation criteria. The level of hierarchical involvement in subsidiary activities is not equal for all organizations and, even within one organization, the degree to which governance mechanisms are employed can vary (Nohria and Ghoshal, 1994); that is, there is a unique configuration of the headquarters-subsidiary control problem in every relationship.

Headquarters' role during innovation development

Headquarters' involvement can affect how knowledge—and the subsidiary developing the knowledge—is perceived within the organization. If headquarters pays attention to specific innovation projects (Williamson, 1992), a corollary is that the subsidiaries related to this project gain visibility, receive legitimacy (Ambos, Andersson, and Birkinshaw, 2010), and are perceived to be important players (Andersson, Forsgren, and Holm, 2007). This is also true for the specific knowledge developed, i.e., not only is the subsidiary developing the knowledge perceived as important, but so is the specific knowledge *per se*. Consequently, innovations subject to transfer that have received headquarters' attention through its direct involvement during the development stage are, by definition, allocated resources and prioritized by headquarters (Ciabuschi, Dellestrand, and Martín Martín, 2011b). By involving itself in the innovation's development, for instance by specifying requests, the outcome of the development process is affected and the developed innovation is more suitable for other MNE subsidiaries. Headquarters' involvement in development also encompasses adding specific competencies and knowledge as well as actively participating in the development process (Ciabuschi *et al.*, 2011b).

---

[2] Indeed, there is a multitude of knowledge management tools available, but for our model, we emphasize the direct interventions linked to a specific knowledge transfer project and not other activities that may be ongoing within the MNE, such as employee training, conferences, acculturation, etc. These are activities that may be initiated by headquarters for fostering a general positive knowledge-sharing environment, but since they do not directly relate to the transfer project, we do not consider these activities in this study.

Copyright © 2015 Strategic Management Society

Global Strat. J., 5: 27–47 (2015)
DOI: 10.1002/gsj.1088

By doing so, headquarters steers knowledge development toward internal consistency with the result that it is easier for a receiving subsidiary to adopt and integrate the knowledge transferred to it (Schulz, 2001; Yang, Mudambi, and Meyer, 2008). For headquarters, involvement in development indicates a commitment that is likely to be reflected in the subsequent transfer and signals that the innovation should be utilized at a recipient once transferred. Also, if headquarters has influenced the outcome of the development process via its involvement by, for instance, specifying requests, this will increase the perceived relevance of the knowledge subject to transfer (Yang *et al.*, 2008) and, as a corollary, positively influence the adoption and use of the transferred knowledge. Consequently, the following hypothesis is proposed:

Hypothesis 1 (H1): Greater headquarters involvement in the development of an innovation will positively affect the utilization of the transferred knowledge.

Headquarters control and monitoring of knowledge transfer processes

One of headquarters' objectives in upgrading subsidiary capabilities is to make sure that knowledge is transferred between them (Dellestrand and Kappen, 2012). If knowledge is not transferred within the MNE, opportunities may be lost and the organization may lose an advantage. The role of headquarters in MNEs has been conceptualized as avoiding the negative (losses), as well as taking on an entrepreneurial role (value creation) (Foss, 1997). Headquarters can be thought of as an MNE network orchestrator (Dhanaraj and Parkhe, 2006), where it identifies critical knowledge and points out transfer opportunities to subsidiaries. This resonates with headquarters taking action and becoming a visible hand within the MNE by issuing commands without directly controlling the transfer process (Tallman and Koza, 2010). Such hierarchical governance can create ill feelings among the subsidiaries and instigate ceremonial adoption of knowledge (Ghoshal and Moran, 1996; Kostova and Roth, 2002). The parties engaged in the transfer process may feel forced into a costly and time-consuming activity and, consequently, perceive little value in it, which negatively influence the process of adoption and integration at the receiving unit.

Moreover, the knowledge that headquarters possesses regarding the subsidiaries' local business network is often shallow (Forsgren *et al.*, 2005). If headquarters actively involves itself in knowledge transfer and governs this process by formal demands and evaluation systems, it can be perceived as ignorant because of its lack of relationship-specific knowledge This can create a negative disposition toward adopting and using the knowledge at the subsidiary level (Forsgren, 2008). Hence, the effects of headquarters governance mechanisms may be detrimental and social activities at the subsidiary level become important for knowledge transfer (Kostova and Roth, 2003). This negative side of headquarters' governance could be mitigated by the fact that it possesses formal power to exert influence over subsidiaries, and direct transactional involvement of headquarters can mean additional resources for the subsidiary. However, even if headquarters provides a knowledge-directing function within the MNE, it may be biased toward cost efficiency and not effectiveness of the transfer processes. This is because cost efficiency is a dimension more easily measured and monitored at a distance (Kostova and Roth, 2002). A focus on efficiency can be detrimental for utilization of the transferred knowledge since adoption takes more time and understanding than simply transferring knowledge in a cost-efficient manner (Ciabuschi *et al.*, 2011a). In line with this reasoning, the following is suggested:

Hypothesis 2 (H2): Greater use of formal hierarchical governance tools by headquarters in the innovation transfer process will negatively affect the utilization of the transferred knowledge.

Subsidiary control mechanisms in knowledge transfer

One way to govern the transfer process is by using expatriates from the sending subsidiary to the receiving subsidiary, which can facilitate lateral relationship building (Minbaeva, 2008). The use of expatriates can further facilitate knowledge flows between the technology-sending subsidiary and other MNE units (Gupta and Govindarajan, 2000) and is one way of governing knowledge transfer processes laterally (Edström and Galbraith, 1977). Expatriates from the sending subsidiary collaborate with colleagues at the receiving subsidiary, and this will facilitate the creation of communities of practice and the establishment of social ties that facilitate

Copyright © 2015 Strategic Management Society

Global Strat. J., **5**: 27–47 (2015)
DOI: 10.1002/gsj.1088

learning (Tallman and Chacar, 2011). Consequently, expatriates can facilitate the process of integrating new knowledge at the receiving subsidiary and help overcome problems during the transfer phase (Tsang, 1999). Using expatriates specifically for a knowledge transfer project is costly and can be seen as an investment by the organization, but should have a positive impact on the understanding and adoption of the knowledge subject to transfer. Put differently, the communities of practice established by individuals (e.g., expatriates) also have implications for establishing networks of practices between subsidiaries (Tallman and Chacar, 2011). This is likely to positively influence knowledge transfer.

Furthermore, expatriates can understand the value added of the transferred knowledge, have direct experience in handling the knowledge, and help explain complicated tacit knowledge dimensions when it is used at the receiving unit (Björkman, Barner-Rasmussen, and Li, 2004; Moran 2005). Hence, the following hypothesis can be formulated:

Hypothesis 3 (H3): Greater use of expatriates from the sending subsidiary to the receiving subsidiary during the transfer will positively affect the utilization of transferred knowledge.

Subsidiary networks and knowledge transfer

In the intraorganizational MNE network, indistinct formal boundaries exist between subsidiaries (Ghoshal and Bartlett, 1990), and subsidiaries develop (more informal) collaborations and cooperate with each other (Andersson *et al.*, 2007; Forsgren *et al.*, 2005). Previous (voluntarily) developed relationships between subsidiaries have, due to prior exchange and collaboration, enhanced the social capital between them (Tsai, 2000). Social capital provides cohesiveness and makes the firm strive toward a common goal (Adler and Kwon, 2002). Value is generated by building social capital due to the facilitation of the exchange process of resources and through providing access to extended network relationships (Inkpen and Tsang, 2005; Moran, 2005; Nahapiet and Ghoshal, 1998). This implies that social capital entails both personal connections and network structures at the unit level that often transcend organizational boundaries (Granovetter, 1985; Moran, 2005; Mäkelä, Andersson, and Seppäle, 2012) and help govern knowledge transfer.

In established relationships, where the actors have previously cooperated, the perceived risk of engag-

ing in a new project is decreased since knowledge pertaining to the functioning of the relationship has already been built, behavior has been experienced, and trust has been developed (Inkpen and Tsang, 2005; Uzzi, 1997). Further, processes and routines are in place for future interaction, which will facilitate collaboration and cooperation (Kostova and Roth, 2003) and thereby knowledge transfer, connecting to what constitutes 'relational governance' (Poppo *et al.*, 2008). Through social ties, a common identity is created (Håkansson and Snehota, 1995) and since many knowledge transfer processes are complicated to explain during the transfer phase, this will take time and is more likely to be effective in a relationship where a closeness between the individuals partaking in the transfer exists (Moran, 2005). Expressed differently, social ties between a sender and a receiver will facilitate the utilization of the knowledge transferred. Moreover, in a relationship where the actors know each other, the search process for relevant knowledge is facilitated. Consequently, the knowledge transferred in such a relationship will entail more relevant knowledge for the receiver; and the sender will be more understanding of the needs of the receiver. This will affect the utilization of transferred knowledge positively (Szulanski *et al.*, 2004; Yang *et al.*, 2008). This line of reasoning implies that social capital can be built by repeated interaction (Buckley and Casson, 1988); if the transfer partners are experienced, their capabilities for conducting such processes are enhanced (Cyert and March, 1963; Eisenhardt and Martin, 2000; Zollo and Winter, 2002) and routines are established for transferring and incorporating knowledge. Therefore, the following hypothesis is postulated:

Hypothesis 4 (H4): An established relationship between the sending and receiving subsidiaries will positively affect the utilization of transferred knowledge.

From the logic about relationships, it follows that relationship building between the sending and the receiving units enhances social capital, where social capital is understood as, 'the relational resources attainable by individual actors through networks of social relationships' (Tsai, 2000: 927). More specifically, relationship building within MNEs corresponds to knowledge management tools such as temporary training, forming task forces, and face-to-face meetings. However, it is important to keep in mind that this study focuses on actions related to specific knowledge transfer projects and associated relationship-building efforts. This relates to utilization and effectiveness because the opportunity to explain complex issues and reduce errors during the transfer process increases. As such, building relationships will facilitate the learning and the understanding of the knowledge transferred (Lane and Lubatkin, 1998; Tallman and Phene, 2007). In other words, the actors have a common basic understanding of the knowledge subject to transfer, which facilitates adoption and use of the transferred knowledge (Kogut and Zander, 1992, 1993). Social interaction will also increase the knowledge transparency, which further facilitates integration and adoption of knowledge (Tallman and Phene, 2007). Consequently the following hypothesis is proposed:

Hypothesis 5 (H5): Relationship building between the sending and receiving subsidiary will positively affect the utilization of transferred knowledge.

DATA AND METHODS

The data used in this research was collected from 2002 to 2005 and covers 169 intra-MNE innovation transfer projects in great detail. Innovations in subsidiaries were identified through snowball sampling, which is appropriate when the population is difficult to define and no comprehensive listing exists (Hair *et al.*, 2006). The data can be traced back to 72 innovation development projects hosted by 63 subsidiaries belonging to 23 different MNEs headquartered in the U.S. and Europe. The sending subsidiaries span 14 countries and the receivers 31 countries.[3] Different industries are represented in the sample, for example, manufacturing, telecommunications, transportation, and the steel industry. The innovation selection criterion was based on the novelty and specific value to the organization. This follows the 2005 OECD definition of innovations, that is, 'the implementation of a new or significantly improved product (good or service), or process, a new marketing method, or a new organizational method in business practices, workplace organization or external

relations' (OECD, 2005: 47). This selection was done by the innovating/developing subsidiary. Moreover, the innovations had to have the potential of being transferred and they also had to have been completed one to 10 years prior to the interview. Sampling innovations that have transfer potential means that the dataset contains some innovations that have not been subject to transfer. These innovations are excluded in the present analysis.

One potential sample bias is that it only contains successful innovations, in terms of having been developed. However, given the question at hand, this bias is almost intrinsic since the transfer of unsuccessful innovations is highly unlikely and would not add anything to the MNE's competitive advantage. 'Successful' in this sense does not imply subsequent market success.

The data was collected through face-to-face interviews on site at the subsidiaries where the respondent answered a structured questionnaire—an approach similar to surveys, but with the advantage of being able to target the respondent in person and knowing exactly who answers the questionnaire. The respondents had been involved in the innovation development and were usually R&D managers, project managers, or subsidiary CEOs. In relation to the transfer projects, even if the data was collected at the sending subsidiary, the innovations had been transferred to more than one receiver (on average, the innovations in our sample were transferred to 2.35 receivers). This allows respondents to compare, for instance, transfer effectiveness across projects. The questionnaire had been pretested in two pilot interviews, and minor changes were made in order to eliminate ambiguous questions and phrasings as well as to exclude erroneous indicators. By having access to managers with detailed knowledge of the specific innovations, a deeper understanding could be gained (Denrell, Arvidsson, and Zander, 2004), and we could discuss the questions with the respondents. This approach allows targeting the appropriate respondent and detecting inconsistencies in the answers during the interview, hence increasing reliability and face validity of the data.

Measures

The advice of Boyd, Gove, and Hitt (2005) was followed and single-measure indicators were avoided. Multiple indicators were used in both the dependent and independent variables. This approach minimizes measurement error, is parsimonious, and

---

[3] More specifically, the senders are located in: Sweden, Taiwan, Italy, France, the U.K., the U.S., Germany, Belgium, Finland, Austria, Czech Republic, Denmark, the Netherlands, and Switzerland.

Copyright © 2015 Strategic Management Society

Global Strat. J., **5**: 27–47 (2015)
DOI: 10.1002/gsj.1088

offers a multifaceted representation of the underlying construct (Hair et al., 2006). Additionally, as recommended by Cox (1980), seven-point Likert-type scales were used to obtain the data on innovation transfer in MNEs. Besides the subjective estimations by the respondents, distance measures using secondary data, patenting, and size were included as control variables. The constructs were identified in an iterative process, where coefficient alphas as well as theoretical issues were considered (Churchill, 1979; Nunnally, 1978). The constructs were theoretically valid and empirically verified. Subsequently, factor analysis was used in order to confirm the constructs' discriminant validity.

Dependent variable

The dependent variable—knowledge transfer effectiveness—reflects the adoption and use of the transferred knowledge within the receiving unit. The responses focused on circumstances related to completeness, ease, and timeliness of the adoption and use and follows previous recommendations and discussions in the literature (Kostova and Roth, 2002; Leonard-Barton and Sinha, 1993; Repenning, 2002; Szulanski 1996). Compared to earlier studies concentrating on the *extent* of knowledge flows between firm subsidiaries, our method of depicting transfer performance is the degree of transfer *effectiveness* in terms of investigating the actual adoption and use of the innovation at the receiving subsidiary (Ciabuschi et al., 2011a). This reflects key ideas in the knowledge-based view (Grant, 1996) and reflects utilization of transferred knowledge.

Transfer performance effectiveness is measured as a four-item construct where the respondents were asked to indicate on a scale from 1 (totally disagree) to 7 (totally agree) whether: (1) the performance of the innovation transfer was very satisfactory; (2) the counterpart adopted the innovation very quickly; and (3) the innovation has been very easy to adopt by this counterpart. One final item was included in this construct and was measured on a similar scale from 1 (not at all) to 7 (very high): (4) to what extent the innovation transfer has been completed. The internal construct reliability was good, with a coefficient alpha of 0.817, exceeding the recommended level of 0.7 (Nunnally, 1978). These four items were summed and averaged to form the dependent variable in the statistical analysis. The dependent

variable is distinct from other variables in the analysis, as Table 1 shows.[4]

Independent variables

The first dimension of headquarters' subsidiary-level influence is whether or not they have been involved in the innovation development of the innovation subject to transfer and build on and extend the attention-based view (Bouquet, Morrison, and Birkinshaw, 2009; Ocasio, 1997). *Headquarters' involvement in innovation development* is captured in a four-item construct where the respondents were asked to indicate, on a scale from 1 (totally disagree) to 7 (totally agree) whether: (1) the MNE HQ has participated closely in developing this innovation; (2) the MNE HQ has brought competence of use for the development of this innovation; (3) the MNE HQ has been important through specifying requests; and (4) the MNE HQ has taken important initiatives for developing the innovation. The four indicators were summed and averaged in order to form the construct used in the regression analysis. Internal construct reliability was high, with a coefficient alpha of 0.908.

The use of formal hierarchical governance tools and sanctions by headquarters is captured by four items and is similar to measures employed by Gates and Egelhoff (1986) and Tsai (2002). The respondents were asked to indicate, on a scale from 1 (totally disagree) to 7 (totally agree), to what extent: (1) the MNE HQ has formally instructed you to share this innovation with the counterpart; and (2) the transfer of the innovation has occurred without any sanctions by HQ with the counterpart (reversed). Moreover, the respondents were asked to indicate on a scale from 1 (not at all) to 7 (very much) whether the transfer of the innovation was driven by: (1)

---

[4] Since the research project and data collection effort aimed at capturing both MNE subsidiary development and transfer activities, the primary data collection target was the developing/sending subsidiary. We worked under the assumption that respondents involved in development and transfer of the specific projects will have a good knowledge of associated structures and processes, and the face-to-face data collection increased data quality. Subsequent to the initial data collection, we collected data from 23 receivers. We have matched data corresponding to the item 'the performance of the innovation transfer was very satisfactory,' and when performing a t-test between answers, no significant differences can be found. This signals that senders and receivers estimate the transfer performance similarly.

Copyright © 2015 Strategic Management Society

Global Strat. J., **5**: 27–47 (2015)
DOI: 10.1002/gsj.1088

Table 1.   Factor analysis with varimax rotation

Variable	Factor loading	Communality
Factor 1: HEADQUARTERS INVOLVEMENT IN DEVELOPMENT		
The MNE HQ has participated closely in developing this innovation	0.913	0.872
The MNE HQ has brought competence of use for the development of this innovation	0.864	0.814
The MNE HQ has been important through specifying requests	0.899	0.832
The MNE HQ has taken important initiatives for developing the innovation	0.785	0.678
Eigenvalue	3.790	
% Variance	19.950	
Factor 2: TRANSFER PERFORMANCE EFFECTIVENESS		
The counterpart adopted the innovation very quickly	0.649	0.512
The innovation has been very easy to adopt by this counterpart	0.836	0.720
The performance of the innovation transfer was very satisfactory	0.811	0.692
To what extent the innovation transfer has been completed	0.813	0.688
Eigenvalue	3.154	
% Variance	16.600	
Factor 3: HEADQUARTERS HIERARCICHAL GOVERNANCE TOOLS		
The MNE HQ has formally instructed you to share this innovation with the counterpart	0.526	0.519
The transfer of the innovation has occurred without any sanctions by HQ with the counterpart (Reversed)	0.561	0.610
Requirement from HQ	0.811	0.716
HQ evaluation system	0.686	0.575
Eigenvalue	2.350	
% Variance	12.367	
Factor 4: RELATIONSHIP BUILDING		
Temporary training at partner sites	0.790	0.729
Cross-unit teams, project groups, etc.	0.806	0.764
Face-to-face meetings	0.761	0.679
Eigenvalue	1.847	
% Variance	9.720	
Factor 5: ESTABLISHED RELATIONSHIP		
They previously cooperated with the receiver	0.867	0.811
They previously had shared knowledge	0.823	0.801
Eigenvalue	1.284	
% Variance	6.757	
Factor 6: SUBSIDIARY EXPATRIATES		
To what extent, with regard to the transfer of the innovation, exchange of managers, was used	0.881	0.837
To what extent the transfer of the innovation was driven by moving personnel between the developer and the receiver	0.817	0.802
Eigenvalue	1.225	
% Variance	6.446	
Total variance explained	71.840	

36   U. Andersson, P. J. Buckley, and H. Dellestrand

requirement from HQ; and (2) HQ evaluation system. These four items were summed and averaged to form the construct. The coefficient alpha of this construct is 0.632, which is below the recommendation as set by Nunnally (1978). Since this construct employs relatively few indicators, it is not uncommon to find that alpha tests, given that they generally are conservative, return a lower coefficient than the recommended level. Reliability increases the more items a scale contains (Nunnally, 1978). With the same average inter-item correlation and the inclusion of additional variables, the alpha value will increase (Carmines and Zeller, 1979). When a low alpha is found, it is appropriate to check the mean inter-item correlation (MIC). The optimal range for the MIC is 0.2 to 0.4 (Briggs and Cheek, 1986). The MIC for this construct was 0.295, thus meeting the stipulated criterion. This, plus the construct being identified as distinct from others in a principal component factor analysis (see Table 1), where both the factor loadings and communalities extracted for the items were adequate, indicate the appropriateness of using this construct.

The use of *subsidiary expatriates* is reflected in a two-item construct and builds on Gupta and Govindarajan's (2000) measure and Galbraith's (1973) integrative mechanisms. The respondents were asked to indicate, on a scale ranging from 1 (not at all) to 7 (very high): to what extent, with regard to the transfer of the innovation, exchange of managers was used. The respondents were also asked to indicate, on a scale from 1 (not at all) to 7 (very much): to what extent the transfer of the innovation was driven by moving personnel between the developer and the receiver. The indicators were added and averaged to form the scale. A coefficient alpha of 0.743 indicates good internal construct reliability.

Established relationships, that is, dyadic transfer experience in the sender-receiver relationship, is a two-item construct where the respondents indicated to what extent, (besides the focal innovation discussed during the data collection) on a scale from 1 (not at all) to 7 (very much): (2) they previously had cooperated with the receiver; and (2) they previously had shared knowledge. The indicators were summed and averaged in order to form the construct, which had a coefficient alpha of 0.738. This construct builds on literature highlighting experience's role in knowledge transfer (Ingram and Baum, 1997).

Finally, *relationship building* between the sending and receiving subsidiaries during the innovation

transfer was captured using a three-item construct drawing on Ghoshal and Bartlett's (1988) framework concerning socialization mechanisms, as well as on the indicators used by Persson (2006). The respondents were asked to indicate on a scale from 1 (not at all) to 7 (very high) the level of use of: (1) temporary training at partner sites; (2) cross-unit teams, project groups, etc.; and (3) face-to-face meetings. The indicators were summed and averaged. The construct has adequate internal reliability, with a coefficient alpha of 0.732.

Control variables

In order to more fully specify the model, a number of control variables were introduced. *Age* was included since older subsidiaries are more established in their business networks and have a tendency to be more autonomous (Forsgren, 1990); they can also exhibit a higher innovative capability (Cohen and Levinthal, 1990; Foss and Pedersen, 2002). To control for age, the logarithm of the number of years the subsidiary had been operating on the market was included in the regression equation.

Size, measured as the natural logarithm of the number of developing subsidiary employees, is used as a proxy for many subsidiary-related characteristics. Research has shown that large subsidiaries have greater intrafirm bargaining power (Mudambi and Navarra, 2004), and size can also affect knowledge transfer even if the knowledge has a low relevance (Yang *et al.*, 2008). Research has also used size as one indicator for valuable knowledge stock, which can be of greater overall value for the MNE (Gupta and Govindarajan, 2000).

Basic research is captured with the help of a dummy variable. If the subsidiary conducted research considered to be core, the variable was coded '1;' if the subsidiary did not conduct any basic research, the observation was coded '0.' Knowledge developed by a subsidiary performing core activities is likely to be more easily adopted, building on absorptive capacity logic. In order to control whether *knowledge-sharing* activities are stimulated in the MNE, this was included as a single-item variable. The respondents were asked to indicate, on a scale of 1 to 7, how important knowledge sharing was in the performance evaluation made of them. This has been shown to have a positive impact on knowledge transfer flows in previous studies (Björkman *et al.*, 2004). To control for the target subsidiary's knowledge-receiving ability, we employed a measure capturing

Copyright © 2015 Strategic Management Society

Global Strat. J., **5**: 27–47 (2015)
DOI: 10.1002/gsj.1088

unit similarity of the innovation transfer partners. This is a two-item construct capturing how similar the sender and receiver are regarding technological and organizational features. The respondents were asked to indicate, with regard to the receiver, on a scale of 1 (totally disagree) to 4 (neither) to 7 (totally agree) whether: (1) technical difference makes the transfer problematic; and (2) organizational difference makes the transfer problematic.[5] The indicators were summed and averaged to form the construct. Internal reliability was good, with a coefficient alpha of 0.738. A dummy variable indicating whether the innovation subject to transfer was *patented* or not was included in the model. The potential ease with which the knowledge might be transferred connects to codification, which can be proxied by patenting (Tallman and Chacar, 2011). Additionally, distances and differences between countries in which subsidiaries are located may influence knowledge transfer. Therefore, we controlled for distances in a number of dimensions. The *geographic distance* between the locations was calculated for each transfer project. The number of kilometers was calculated using MapCrow. This measure was transformed into the natural log of the distance measure and is consistent with the approach of other studies using geographic distance (e.g., Hansen and Lovås, 2004). Cultural distance was controlled for by using Kogut and Singh's 1988 index, expressed as:

$$CD_j = \sum_{i=1}^{4}\left\{(I_{ij} - I_{iN})^2 / V_i\right\}/4, \qquad (1)$$

where CD is the cultural distance between the subsidiary host countries, I_{ij} is the score of the receiving subsidiary's country on the ith dimension, and I_{iN} is the score of the sending subsidiary's country in this dimension. V_i represents the score variance in the specific dimension. *Institutional distance* was measured building on the approach of Gaur *et al.* (2007) and Xu, Pan, and Beamish (2004). The institutional dimensions found in the Executive Opinion Survey of the Global Competitiveness Report (2005) were explored, and a factor analysis was conducted (principal component with varimax rotation and Kaiser normalization). The institutional

environment is captured by a seven-item construct that loaded on a single factor having a coefficient alpha of 0.961. This data was matched to our data calculating the institutional distance between the host countries of the sending and receiving subsidiaries. The relative *economic differences* were captured by estimating differences in GDP per capita between the host countries of the subsidiaries (Tsang and Yip, 2007). Data was obtained through the Total Economy Database (2006). Following Tsang and Yip (2007), we created a measure for relatively more developed countries in relation to the other part of the dyad. This measure can be expressed as:

$$\ln(GDP_{sender}) - \ln(GDP_{reciever}) \text{ if } GDP_{sender} \geq GDP_{reciever} \text{ and } = 0 \text{ if } GDP_{sender} < GDP_{receiver} \qquad (2)$$

Common method bias and multicollinearity

The use of perceptual measurements can be problematic because of social desirability and self-assessment bias. This is mitigated by the face-to-face interviews. In order to check for common method bias augmenting the relationships, Harman's one-factor test was used (Podsakoff and Organ, 1986). All relevant indicators were included in a principal component factor analysis (principal component with varimax rotation and Kaiser normalization, see Table 1). The 0.638 KMO value exceeded the recommended 0.6 level (Tabachnick and Fidell, 2001). The Bartlett's test of sphericity was at a 0.001 significance level, indicating sufficient correlations between the indicators (Hair *et al.*, 2006) and factor analysis procedure appropriateness. The factor analysis indicated data validity and reported good properties. If high common method variance is a problem, only one factor will emerge with an eigenvalue exceeding 1 or, alternatively, one of the factors extracted will account for a majority of the variance. In the principal component analysis, six factors were extracted with eigenvalues above 1. The seventh factor returned with an eigenvalue of 0.837, thus being far from meeting the latent root criterion and, consequently, not included in the analysis.

None of the factors explain a majority of the variance, ranging from 6.446 percent to 19.950 percent. The cumulative variance explained by the seven factors was 71.840 percent. In the rotated factor solution, a cutoff value of 0.32 was used, and only two cross-loadings appeared above this level. Factor loadings below 0.32 can be considered poor since

---

[5] These items were reverse coded in order to capture the similarities between the subsidiaries involved in the knowledge transfer.

Copyright © 2015 Strategic Management Society

Global Strat. J., **5**: 27–47 (2015)
DOI: 10.1002/gsj.1088

the overlapping variance then is below 10 percent; and a factor loading of 0.45 represents 20 percent of the overlapping variance and can be considered fair (Comrey and Lee, 1992). The first cross-loading occurred for the item of headquarters' instruction to share the innovation with the counterpart on the construct of headquarters' participation during the development with a value of 0.436. The second cross-loading relates to the respondents reporting whether the innovation transfer occurred without any sanctions from headquarters (reversed), with a value of 0.324 on the construct of headquarters' participation during the development. However, both items loaded with higher values on the headquarters hierarchical governance tool construct. These two cross-loadings do not factor when interpreting the data, even though the presence of common method bias cannot entirely be ruled out.

Following Lindell and Whitney (2001), we introduced a marker variable to further test for common method variance,. This technique has been argued to be an effective tool for accounting for common method variance (Malhotra, Kim, and Patil, 2006). The marker variable should be measured by the same questionnaire as for the other variables. However, the marker variable should be theoretically unrelated to the relevant perceptual variables. From the questionnaire, the respondents' answer to the following question was used: rate the level of usage of logistics data during the development of the innovation (on a scale ranging from 1 (not at all) to 7 (very high)). This question was selected since there did not seem to be any theoretical reason why it should be related to the variables in the conceptual model. Additionally, this variable was measured in the same way as the other perceptual measures. We controlled for any effect of the marker variable on the partial correlations of the perceptual variables. All significant correlations remained the same, and the marker variable did not significantly correlate with any of the perceptual measures. Thus, this additional test for common method variance ensures that it is not likely to affect the estimation outcomes.

To investigate whether there is a correlation between two or more predictor variables augmenting the estimated R^2 of the model, the variance inflation factor (VIF) was calculated. Different acceptable VIF value sizes have been proposed, and there does not seem to be a consensus of what cutoff value to use, although 5 has been suggested as a reasonable number (Studenmund, 1992). No VIF values in any of the models exceeded 5. In Model 2, the highest calculated VIF value was 1.963, with a mean of 1.450. Consequently, multicollinearity does not seem to threaten the model estimates, and this should not distort the regression model results.

RESULTS

The mean values, standard deviations, and correlation matrix for all the variables are presented in Table 2. The highest correlation is 0.635 ($p < 0.01$) between physical and cultural distance. However, it is to be expected that the distance dimensions are highly correlated.

The article examines how different organizational mechanisms affect knowledge transfer effectiveness. In order to estimate the models, ordinary least squares regressions were used. In the second specification, all independent variables were entered. In Table 3, the standardized parameter estimates of all models are reported. The first model returned significant with an F-value of 3.519 ($p < 0.01$), and the control variables explained 24.9 percent of the variance. Model 2 is significant with an F-value of 3.915 ($p < 0.01$) and an R^2-value of 0.368. Hence, both models are significant and the explanatory value increases between model specifications (see diagnostics in Table 3). In order to control for potential industry effects, we ran a *post hoc* analysis including industry dummies. This analysis suggests that industry differences are not influencing estimate outcomes.

This supports the chosen model specifications and no VIF values are abnormally large in any of the models, indicating that multicollinearity does not augment the R^2 value or the model's predictive capability. We employed the Ramsey reset test to investigate whether nonlinear alterations of the independent variables would yield a higher adjusted R^2. The outcome suggested that the models are better without introducing power alterations. Additionally, we plotted the residuals to see if nonconstant variance was present across different independent variable values. No heteroskedasticity problem was detected.

The findings indicate a very small influence of headquarters' involvement during the development of the innovation, and the relationship is insignificant. Hence, no support is found for Hypothesis 1. Hypothesis 2, which relates to whether the transfer was driven by headquarters' hierarchical governance tools, showed a significant ($p < 0.01$) negative

Table 2.   Correlation and descriptive statistics

	MEAN	S.D.	1.	2.	3.	4.	5.	6.	7.	8.	9.	10.	11.	12.	13.	14.	15.	16.
1. Transfer performance effectiveness	5.211	1.312	1															
2. Age	3.528	0.903	0.036	1														
3. Size	5.414	1.590	0.041	0.112	1													
4. Basic research	0.555	0.498	0.132	0.402**	0.224**	1												
5. Knowledge sharing	4.148	1.774	0.147	0.081	0.272**	0.173*	1											
6. Unit similarity	5.557	1.55271	0.465**	-0.213**	-0.158	-0.060	0.002	1										
7. Patent	0.569	0.496	-0.111	-0.102	-0.212**	0.019	-0.240**	0.093	1									
8. Physical distance	5.735	3.578	-0.001	-0.008	0.024	-0.035	-0.062	0.016	0.051	1								
9. Cultural distance	0.618	0.809	0.015	0.049	-0.148	-0.012	-0.023	0.052	0.106	0.635**	1							
10. Institutional distance	0.491	0.572	0.041	-0.114	0.059	-0.025	-0.147	-0.057	-0.070	0.464**	0.379**	1						
11. Economic differences	0.052	0.124	0.067	-0.067	0.060	-0.008	0.209**	0.052	-0.007	0.391**	0.270**	-0.042	1					
12. Headquarters involvement in dev.	2.110	1.580	-0.147	-0.350**	-0.149*	-0.182*	0.005	0.099	0.024	0.073	0.080	-0.057	0.150	1				
13. Headquarters hierarchical tools	2.601	1.569	-0.039	0.056	0.324**	0.228**	0.169	-0.054	-0.180*	0.048	0.123	-0.020	0.150	0.348**	1			
14. Subsidiary expatriates	1.893	1.472	-0.390**	-0.042	-0.064	-0.137	0.032	-0.264**	0.034	-0.049	-0.037	-0.026	-0.150	0.081	-0.098	1		
15. Established relationship	4.777	1.660	0.289**	0.085	0.046	0.007	0.151	0.255**	0.074	-0.110	0.009	-0.202**	0.002	-0.039	0.108	-0.028	1	
16. Relationship building	4.025	1.753	-0.004	0.000	-0.016	-0.020	-0.056	-0.037	0.012	-0.138	-0.167*	-0.059	-0.185*	0.241**	0.093	0.175*	0.256**	1
VIF value	1.450	—		1.597	1.629	1.433	1.277	1.310	1.271	1.963	1.585	1.409	1.478	1.508	1.528	1.185	1.336	1.246

Spearman's correlation
**Correlation is significant at the 0.01 level (two tailed).
*Correlation is significant at the 0.05 level (two tailed).

Copyright © 2015 Strategic Management Society

Global Strat. J., **5**: 27–47 (2015)
DOI: 10.1002/gsj.1088

40   *U. Andersson, P. J. Buckley, and H. Dellestrand*

Table 3.   Results from the ordinary least squares regression analysis[a]

Regressor	Model 1		Model 2	
	β	s.e.	β	s.e.
Age	0.068	0.143	−0.006	0.145
Size	0.038	0.079	0.085	0.083
Basic research	0.129	0.256	0.114	0.250
Knowledge sharing	0.055	0.070	0.062	0.066
Patent	−0.153[†]	0.244	−0.202*	0.236
Unit similarity	0.471***	0.075	0.368***	0.077
Physical distance	0.015	0.042	−0.019	0.041
Cultural distance	−0.065	0.166	−0.010	0.162
Institutional distance	0.011	0.224	0.071	0.216
Economic differences	0.053	1.035	0.075	1.020
Headquarters involvement in development	—	—	−0.002	0.081
Headquarters hierarchical governance tools	—	—	−0.240**	0.082
Subsidiary expatriates	—	—	−0.239**	0.077
Established relationship	—	—	0.211*	0.072
Relationship building	—	—	0.039	0.066
Diagnostics				
N	169		169	
R^2	0.249		0.368	
Adj.R^2	0.178		0.274	
ΔR^2	0.249		0.118	
F-statistics	3.519***		3.915***	

[a]Values are standardized parameter estimates.
[†]$p < 0.1$, *$p < 0.05$, **$p < 0.01$, ***$p < 0.001$.

relationship to transfer performance effectiveness in Model 2. Thus, Hypothesis 2 is supported. Contrary to what was postulated in Hypothesis 3, using subsidiary expatriates indicates a significant ($p < 0.01$) negative relationship to transfer performance in Model 2. Hence, Hypothesis 3 is not supported.[6] Established relationships are positively ($p < 0.05$) related to knowledge transfer effectiveness, thus lending support to Hypothesis 4. Finally, relationship building has a small positive effect on transfer

effectiveness. However, this relationship is not significant and Hypothesis 5 is consequently not supported.

DISCUSSION

This article set out to fill the research gap on the influence of formal hierarchical governance tools and lateral relationships on transferred knowledge utilization, that is, transfer effectiveness. A major contribution of this study is the focus on effectiveness in specific transfer projects related to hierarchy and relationships within the MNE. This allows for a better understanding of hierarchical and lateral tools for effective knowledge governance. The knowledge governance approach (Foss, 2007) holds that an organizational action to influence knowledge transfer should start with formal mechanisms since these are readily available to managers. However, informal mechanisms also affect the transfer. The idea is that the formal mechanisms influence behavior, thus enabling satisfactory transfer performance. Building

[6] The result pertaining to subsidiary expatriates is especially notable and opposed to our expectations. In order to further understand this result from an empirical point of view, we ran additional models as *post hoc* tests with the subsidiary expatriates variable interacting with the patenting variable, as well as with the established relationship variable. This is based on the reasoning that since expatriates may be more useful for transferring tacit knowledge, patents might moderate their value. Moreover, expatriates from a familiar source might be more useful and may, consequently, also moderate their effect. However, when running additional tests for these effects, the moderations return insignificant. Additionally, the model does not get significantly better with any of the moderation effects included. This is consistent with the results from the Ramsey reset test.

Copyright © 2015 Strategic Management Society

Global Strat. J., **5**: 27–47 (2015)
DOI: 10.1002/gsj.1088

on this approach, our article deals with two formal tools employed by headquarters, one formal control tool employed in the sending-receiving relationship, and two lateral relationship characteristics of a more informal nature that may govern the knowledge transfer process. The results suggest that, in general, hierarchical and formal governance tools are not positively related to transfer effectiveness, but that lateral relationships affect transfer effectiveness positively. This enables us to advance the understanding of headquarters' role and function in knowledge transfer projects and the benefits of using lateral relationship building. This informs us about the role of headquarters and subsidiaries within the knowledge-based view and how this relates to knowledge governance. Moran and Ghoshal (1999: 395) highlighted the importance of facilitating, 'the continual reallocation of resources to more productive uses.' This study emphasize effective knowledge governance for realizing the value of knowledge exchange between units and, thereby, contributes to the knowledge-based view by analyzing antecedents to effective use of transferred knowledge.

Hierarchy in the MNE

In line with our expectations, a significant negative effect on knowledge utilization is found when headquarters drives the transfer process through formal tools. This may be due to actors feeling forced into action without any real motivation, and it might be irrelevant knowledge that is being transferred to the receiver, i.e., the motivational disposition of the subsidiaries toward the transfer is low, which impedes integration and use. Thus, a transfer process between subsidiaries that is initiated and required by headquarters is going to be less effective.

Even though headquarters may have both value creation and cost control in mind, its focus is more likely to be on efficiency rather than effectiveness because it is easier to measure and follow-up, thus offering one explanation of the negative result vis-à-vis effectiveness (Daft, 1992; Kostova and Roth, 2002). Another explanation may be that headquarters involves itself in problematic transfers. For managers, this points out that classical, easily available control tools may not always be appropriate in ensuring that knowledge is adopted, integrated, and used at the receiving subsidiary. Thus, our results indicate that the role of headquarters as a knowledge webmaster tasked with assembling the global company and enabling self-renewal is indeed challenging

(Tallman and Koza, 2010). Command and control seems to be an ineffective headquarters strategy with respect to knowledge transfer effectiveness.

A surprising finding is the insignificant effect of headquarters' involvement during the knowledge development on the subsequent utilization of the knowledge when transferred to another unit. The involvement of headquarters can be perceived as a distinctly different governance tool compared to monitoring and control with a different rationale and performance effect. In some cases, headquarters needs to be involved and to support promising subsidiary developments (Rugman and Verbeke, 2001). Even though involvement does not have a direct effect on transfer performance effectiveness, the indirect effects of headquarters involvement may be great. For example, the foundations for organizational influence can potentially be traced back to headquarters' involvement in subsidiary-level activities. Also, the perception of the subsidiary as an important player in the MNE network is increased as a result of headquarters involvement (Ciabuschi *et al.*, 2011b). Our model does not consider this political power balance and evolution within the MNE, but it at least indicates that no significant detrimental effect of involvement during development can be found with respect to transfer effectiveness. Thus, with respect to headquarters' tools for effective knowledge governance, our findings indicate that there may be a difference between formal policy and support for innovative activities within subsidiaries compared to direct transactional governance. In some cases, headquarters interference in subsidiary operations is likely to create, rather than solve, knowledge transfer problems (Tallman and Chacar, 2011; Tallman and Koza, 2010).

Subsidiary expatriates

A surprising finding relates to the negative effect of expatriates for the utilization of transferred knowledge. In fact, correlating the individual items making up the expatriate construct with transfer effectiveness shows significant and negative correlations for both items. As discussed by Björkman *et al.* (2004), the expatriate role needs to be further researched. In their study, they found no effect of expatriates on knowledge outflow. One reason behind the current negative transfer effect may be that it is easier to evaluate financial performance and cost, that is, efficiency, than the extent to which knowledge is used and integrated, that is, effectiveness. Hence, expatri-

Copyright © 2015 Strategic Management Society

Global Strat. J., **5**: 27–47 (2015)
DOI: 10.1002/gsj.1088

42   *U. Andersson, P. J. Buckley, and H. Dellestrand*

ates are more likely to have a focus similar to that of headquarters rather than a subsidiary focus on implementing and using the knowledge in order to improve the operations in the long run at the recipient (Björkman *et al.*, 2004). Moreover, as suggested by Tallman and Chacar (2011), knowledge transfer mechanisms should be considered at the level of communities and networks of practice, implying that social ties facilitate learning. However, the conditions for a positive outcome of such social ties are that individuals have, for instance, similar training and objectives, as well as shared professional norms. In our setting, this may translate into considering whether the 'right' or 'wrong' expatriates are used for the specific knowledge utilization setting.

As argued by Tallman and Chacar (2011), it is easy to disrupt social ties; if that is the case, a problematic situation for knowledge utilization may emerge. Our results indicate that expatriate managers do not always facilitate transfer effectiveness, as they often lack sufficient understanding about how the transferred knowledge should be implemented and used at the receiving unit. Instead, path dependencies, in terms of established relationships and unit similarity, lead to transfer effectiveness. This highlights the importance of organizational and personal relationships that are established over time (Buckley and Carter, 1999, 2004). Parachuting 'strangers' into a social process does not appear to be successful. Our *post hoc* test does not, however, indicate a significant positive moderation effect between expatriates and established relationships. For research on expatriates, it seems important to consider what an appropriate expatriate in a particular setting is in order to create communities and networks of practices that facilitate conditions for learning (Tallman and Chacar, 2011).

Another explanation of this notable finding might be the receiving subsidiary's increasing (perceived) dependence on the sending unit when expatriates are used. In their seminal study of organizational practice transfers, Kostova and Roth (2002) found a negative relation between subunits' perceived headquarters dependence and practice implementation. Along somewhat similar lines of reasoning, expatriates from the sending subsidiary increase the receiving subsidiary's dependence on this unit and, therefore, make the adaption and utilization of the transferred knowledge more arduous than otherwise. As the utilization and adoption of transferred knowledge normally entail some modification and adaptation to work smoothly in a new setting, the increased

dependence, implying subordination and control from the expatriates, might circumscribe the needed flexibility for utilizing and adopting the knowledge fully and, thereby, produce the negative relation between expatriates and transfer effectiveness (Kostova and Roth, 2002).

Finally, it may be that subsidiaries make use of expatriates only in transfer processes they believe will be very difficult to carry out. Thus, it may be that the additional cost of using expatriates in a transfer process for adopting and utilizing the transferred knowledge is incurred only in cases that are expected to be difficult. It is then natural to receive a negative result on performance, but we can only speculate that the negative result would have been even stronger if expatriates had not been used. This remains open for future research.

Subsidiary lateral relationships

Turning to lateral relationships, the results indicate that the utilization of transferred knowledge is achieved in situations where the transfer occurs in established relationships. It is important to cooperate with partners that the actors already know and trust and with whom they have working experience. Our results indicate that this facilitates knowledge adoption and use. Highlighting the importance of already-established relationships compared to building relationships contributes to understanding how knowledge can be governed effectively. This supplements reasoning highlighting the importance of long-standing relationships and the accumulation of specific exchange process experiences (Mayer and Argyres, 2004; Zollo, Reuer, and Singh, 2002). Hence, it becomes a matter of selecting the transfer counterparts carefully if success is to be achieved, not to transfer the knowledge to just anyone.

Selecting the transfer counterparts carefully makes better use of available resources and will help the subsidiaries govern their knowledge transfer processes. Looking at transfer performance effectiveness allows for a deeper understanding that is not gained by viewing successful transfer simply as the extent of flows between units. By cooperating with known counterparts, the subsidiary builds specific dyadic knowledge transfer experience and knowledge. The relationship partners learn how to organize and conduct knowledge transfer within the dyadic relationship, i.e., an evolutionary process of tacit capability development takes place (Nelson and Winter, 1982). This capability is connected to spe-

Copyright © 2015 Strategic Management Society

Global Strat. J., **5**: 27–47 (2015)
DOI: 10.1002/gsj.1088

cific relationships and lends support to the idea of the MNE as a social community (Kogut and Zander, 1992, 1993). These findings connect well with the relational governance approach discussed by Poppo *et al.* (2008), where exchange is governed by cooperative norms and collaborative activities. Organizational economics also acknowledges informal social relationships as governance tools, often in the form of trust (Williamson, 1994; Woolthius, Hillebrand, and Nooteboom, 2005). Hierarchical governance can sometimes be substituted by or complemented with relational arrangements (Woolthius *et al.*, 2005); in the current framework, this translates as subsidiaries' governing knowledge. Thus, relational governance can be an effective process aimed at increasing subsidiary-level capabilities, i.e., knowledge transfer effectiveness.

The disappointing nonsignificant result for relationship building may have occurred because the variables that make up this construct (temporary training, cross-units teams, and face-to-face meetings) can all be seen as precursors of long-standing relationships and may pay off only in the future. These may be considered investments in strengthening and establishing relationships that pay off in future knowledge transfer effectiveness as our result for 'established relationships' show. This has to remain an important conjecture requiring careful longitudinal investigation.

Limitations and directions for future research

One major limitation of the study is that the data originates only from the sending subsidiary. In order to estimate transfer performance in a more holistic way, dyadic data needs to be collected. However, since the sending subsidiary is actively involved during the transfer, it is reasonable to assume that the targeted respondents gave an accurate estimation of both headquarters' role, the dyadic relationship, and how well the knowledge was implemented and adopted at the receiving subsidiary.[7] Moreover, the respondent had usually been involved in multiple transfer projects (encompassing the same innovation), which allowed for cross-project comparison. Some of the measurements consist of subjective estimations made by the respondents, which can be problematic because of social desirability and self-

assessment biases. However, this is mediated by the fact that our data is collected from key informants through face-to-face interviews.

In terms of future research, the interplay between efficiency and effectiveness needs to be better understood, as does the indirect effects of headquarters' involvement in subsidiary-level activities. The role of expatriates and incentive systems and their potential contribution to transfer performance needs to be further investigated since prior studies found mixed results (Björkman *et al.*, 2004; Gupta and Govindarajan, 2000). This study is cross-sectional, and longitudinal research is required to test the dynamic proposition that relationship building leads to future knowledge transfer effectiveness through establishing strong relationships.

CONCLUDING REMARKS

The contribution of this article is twofold; first, a more in-depth knowledge transfer performance measure (effectiveness in terms of adoption and use) is employed compared to previous studies that have focused more on aggregated knowledge flows (Agrawal *et al.*, 2008; Gupta and Govindarajan, 2000; Haas and Hansen, 2005; Schulz 2001). We have analyzed the performance variation in individual knowledge transfer projects and shed light on the reasons for this variation. Second, we show the importance of considering both hierarchical governance tools and lateral relationships, as they influence knowledge utilization simultaneously and in different ways. This directly contributes to an enhanced understanding of knowledge governance and the knowledge-based view.

The results indicate that headquarters' involvement during knowledge development does not have any impact on subsequent transfer effectiveness, whereas more formal hierarchical governance forms have a negative impact. We suggest that relational characteristics are preferable for building subsidiary capabilities in knowledge transfers. Similarly, the use of expatriates may be disruptive to an essentially social process. Consequently, this article augments the understanding of knowledge governance and integration in large international organizations.

ACKNOWLEDGEMENTS

This article was developed when Dellestrand was a visiting researcher at CIBUL, Leeds University

---

[7] In fact, our t-test of one item from the dependent variable where we have dyadic data confirms this notion.

Copyright © 2015 Strategic Management Society

Business School. The authors would like to thank the World Universities Network (WUN) and Handelsbankens research foundation for supporting the research.

REFERENCES

Adler PS, Kwon S-W. 2002. Social capital: prospects for a new concept. *Academy of Management Review* **27**(1): 17–40.

Agrawal A, Kapur D, McHale J. 2008. How do spatial and social proximity influence knowledge flows? Evidence from patent data. *Journal of Urban Economy* **64**(2): 258–269.

Almeida P, Song J, Grant R. 2002. Are firms superior to alliances and markets? An empirical test of cross-border knowledge building. *Organization Science* **13**(2): 147–161.

Ambos T, Andersson U, Birkinshaw J. 2010. What are the consequences of initiative-taking in multinational subsidiaries? *Journal of International Business Studies* **41**(7): 1099–1118.

Andersson U, Forsgren M, Holm U. 2007. Balancing subsidiary influence in the federative MNC: a business network perspective. *Journal of International Business Studies* **38**(5): 802–818.

Argote L, Ingram P. 2000. Knowledge transfer: a basis for competitive advantage. *Organizational Behavior and Human Decision Processes* **82**(1): 150–169.

Barney JB. 1991. Firm resources and competitive advantage. *Journal of Management* **17**(1): 99–122.

Bartlett CA, Ghoshal S. 1989. *Managing Across Borders: The Transnational Solution*. Harvard Business School Press: Boston, MA.

Birkinshaw J. 2001. Strategies for managing internal competition. *California Management Review* **44**(1): 24–38.

Björkman I, Barner-Rasmussen W, Li L. 2004. Managing knowledge transfers in MNCs: the impact of headquarters control mechanisms. *Journal of International Business Studies* **35**(5): 443–455.

Bouquet C, Morrison A, Birkinshaw J. 2009. International attention and multinational enterprise performance. *Journal of International Business Studies* **40**(1): 108–131.

Boyd BK, Gove S, Hitt MA. 2005. Construct measurement in strategic management research: illusion or reality? *Strategic Management Journal* **26**(3): 239–257.

Briggs SR, Cheek JM. 1986. The role of factor analysis in the development and evaluation of personality scales. *Journal of Personality* **54**(1): 106–148.

Buckley PJ, Carter MJ. 1999. Managing cross-border complementary knowledge: conceptual developments in the business process approach to knowledge management in multinational firms. *International Studies of Management & Organization* **29**(1): 80–104.

Buckley PJ, Carter MJ. 2004. A formal analysis of knowledge combination in multinational enterprises. *Journal of International Business Studies* **35**(5): 371–384.

Buckley PJ, Casson M. 1988. A theory of cooperation in international business. In *Cooperative Strategies in International Business*, Contractor FJ, Lorange P (eds). Lexington Books: Lexington, MA; 31–54.

Carmines EG, Zeller RA. 1979. *Reliability and Validity Assessment*. SAGE Publications: Beverly Hills, CA.

Churchill GAJ. 1979. A paradigm for developing better measures of marketing constructs. *Journal of Marketing Research* **16**(1): 64–73.

Ciabuschi F, Dellestrand H, Kappen P. 2011a. Exploring the effects of vertical and lateral mechanisms in international knowledge transfer projects. *Management International Review* **51**(2): 129–155.

Ciabuschi F, Dellestrand H, Martín Martín O. 2011b. Internal embeddedness, headquarters involvement, and innovation importance in multinational enterprises. *Journal of Management Studies* **48**(7): 1612–1639.

Cohen WM, Levinthal DA. 1990. Absorptive capacity: a new perspective on learning and innovation. *Administrative Science Quarterly* **35**(1): 128–152.

Comrey AL, Lee HB. 1992. *A First Course in Factor Analysis* (2nd edn). Lawrence Erlbaum: Hillsdale, NJ.

Cool KO, Dierickx I, Szulanski G. 1997. Diffusion of innovations within organizations: electronic switching in the Bell system, 1971–1982. *Organization Science* **8**(5): 543–559.

Cox EP. 1980. The optimal number of response alternatives for a scale: a review. *Journal of Marketing Research* **17**(4): 407–422.

Cyert RM, March JG. 1963. *A Behavioral Theory of the Firm*. Prentice Hall: Englewood Cliffs, NJ.

Daft RL. 1992. *Organization Theory and Design* (4th edn). West Publishing: St. Paul, MN.

Dellestrand H, Kappen P. 2012. The effects of spatial and contextual factors on headquarters resource allocation to MNE subsidiaries. *Journal of International Business Studies* **43**(3): 219–243.

Denrell J, Arvidsson N, Zander U. 2004. Managing knowledge in the dark: an empirical study of the reliability of capability evaluations. *Management Science* **50**(11): 1491–1503.

Dhanaraj C, Parkhe A. 2006. Orchestrating innovation networks. *Academy of Management Review* **31**(3):659–669.

Edström A, Galbraith JR. 1977. Transfer of managers as a coordinating and control strategy in multinational corporations. *Administrative Science Quarterly* **22**(2): 248–263.

Eisenhardt KM, Martin JA. 2000. Dynamic capabilities: what are they? *Strategic Management Journal* **21**(10/11): 1105–1121.

Forsgren M. 1990. Managing the international multi-centre firm: case studies from Sweden. *European Management Journal* **8**(2): 261–267.

Forsgren M. 2008. Are multinationals superior or just powerful? A critical review of the evolutionary theory of the MNC. In *Foreign Direct Investment, Location and Competitiveness*, Dunning J, Gugler P (eds). Elsevier: Amsterdam, Netherlands; 29–50.

Forsgren M, Holm U, Johanson J. 2005. *Managing the Embedded Multinational*. Edward Elgar Publishing: Cheltenham, U.K.

Foss N. 1997. On the rationales of corporate headquarters. *Industrial and Corporate Change* 6(2): 313–338.

Foss N. 2006. Knowledge and organization in the theory of the multinational corporation: some foundational issues. *Journal of Management and Governance* 10(1): 3–20.

Foss N. 2007. The emerging knowledge governance approach: challenges and characteristics. *Organization* 14(1): 27–50.

Foss N, Husted K, Michailova S. 2010. Governing knowledge sharing in organizations: levels of analysis, governance mechanisms, and research directions. *Journal of Management Studies* 47(3): 455–482.

Foss N, Pedersen T. 2002. Transferring knowledge in MNCs: the role of sources of subsidiary knowledge and organizational context. *Journal of International Management* 8(1): 49–67.

Foss N, Pedersen T. 2004. Organizing knowledge processes in the multinational corporation: an introduction. *Journal of International Business Studies* 35(5): 340–349.

Galbraith J. 1973. *Designing Complex Organizations*. Addison-Wesley: Reading, MA.

Gates SR, Egelhoff WG. 1986. Centralization in headquarters-subsidiary relationships. *Journal of International Business Studies* 17(1): 71–92.

Gaur AS, Delios A, Singh K. 2007. Institutional environments, staffing strategies, and subsidiary performance. *Journal of Management* 33(4): 611–636.

Ghoshal S, Bartlett CA. 1988. Creation, adoption and diffusion of innovations by subsidiaries of multinational corporations. *Journal of International Business Studies* 19(3): 365–388.

Ghoshal S, Bartlett CA. 1990. The multinational corporation as an interorganizational network. *Academy of Management Review* 15(4): 603–625.

Ghoshal S, Moran P. 1996. Bad for practice: a critique of the transaction cost theory. *Academy of Management Review* 21(1): 13–47.

Grandori A. 2001. Neither hierarchy nor identity: knowledge-governance mechanisms and the theory of the firm. *Journal of Management and Governance* 5(3/4): 381–399.

Granovetter MS. 1985. Economic action and social structure: the problem of embeddedness. *American Journal of Sociology* 91(3): 481–510.

Grant RM. 1996. Towards a knowledge-based theory of the firm. *Strategic Management Journal*, Winter Special Isssue 17: 109–122.

Gupta AK, Govindarajan V. 2000. Knowledge flows within multinational corporations. *Strategic Management Journal* 21(4): 473–496.

Haas MR, Hansen MT. 2005. When using knowledge can hurt performance: the value of organizational capabilities in a management consulting company. *Strategic Management Journal* 26(1): 1–24.

Hair JF, Black WC, Babin BJ, Anderson RE, Tatham RL. 2006. *Multivariate Data Analysis* (6th edn). Prentice Hall: Upper Saddle River, NJ.

Håkansson H, Snehota I. 1995. *Developing Relationships in Business Networks*. Routledge: London, U.K.

Hansen MT, Lovås B. 2004. How do multinational companies leverage technological competencies? Moving from single to interdependent explanations. *Strategic Management Journal* 25(8–9): 801–822.

Ingram P, Baum JAC. 1997. Opportunity and constraint: organizational learning from the operating and competitive experience of industries. *Strategic Management Journal* 18(1): 75–98.

Inkpen A, Tsang EW. 2005. Networks, social capital, and learning. *Academy of Management Review* 30(1): 146–165.

Kogut B, Singh H. 1988. The effect of national culture on the choice of entry mode. *Journal of International Business Studies* 19(3): 411–432.

Kogut B, Zander U. 1992. Knowledge of the firm, combinative capabilities, and the replication of technology. *Organization Science* 3(3): 383–397.

Kogut B, Zander U. 1993. Knowledge of the firm and the evolutionary theory of the multinational corporation. *Journal of International Business Studies* 24(4): 625–645.

Kostova T. 1999. Transnational transfer of strategic organizational practices: a contextual perspective. *Academy of Management Review* 24(2): 308–324.

Kostova T, Roth K. 2002. Adoption of an organizational practice by subsidiaries of multinational corporation: institutional and relational effects. *Academy of Management Journal* 45(1): 215–233.

Kostova T, Roth K. 2003. Social capital in multinational corporations and a micro-macro model of its formation. *Academy of Management Review* 28(2): 297–317.

Lane PJ, Lubatkin M. 1998. Relative absorptive capacity and interorganizational learning. *Strategic Management Journal* 19(5): 461–477.

Leonard-Barton D, Sinha DK. 1993. Developer-user interaction and user satisfaction in internal technology transfer. *Academy of Management Journal* 36(5): 1125–1139.

Lindell MK, Whitney DJ. 2001. Accounting for common method variance in cross-sectional research designs. *Journal of Applied Psychology* 86(1): 114–121.

Madhok A. 1996. The organization of economic activity: transaction costs, firm capabilities and the nature of governance. *Organization Science* 7(5): 577–590.

Copyright © 2015 Strategic Management Society

Global Strat. J., 5: 27–47 (2015)
DOI: 10.1002/gsj.1088

Madhok A. 1997. Cost, value and foreign market entry mode: the transaction and the firm. *Strategic Management Journal* 18(1): 39–62.

Mahnke V, Pedersen T. 2004. Knowledge governance and value creation. In *Knowledge Flows, Governance and the Multinational Enterprise*, Mahnke V, Pedersen T (eds). Palgrave MacMillan: New York; 3–17.

Mäkelä K, Andersson U, Seppälä T. 2012. Interpersonal similarity and knowledge sharing within multinational organizations. *International Business Review* 21(3): 439–451.

Malhotra NK, Kim SS, Patil A. 2006. Common method variance in IS research: a comparison of alternative approaches and a reanalysis of past research. *Management Science* 52(12): 1865–1883.

Markides CC. 2002. Corporate strategy: the role of the centre. In *Handbook of Strategy and Management*, Pettigrew A, Thomas H, Whittington R (eds). SAGE Publications: London, U.K.; 98–112.

Markides CC, Williamson PJ. 1994. Related diversification, core competencies and corporate performance. *Strategic Management Journal* 15(2): 149–165.

Martin X, Salomon R. 2003. Knowledge transfer capacity and its implications for the theory of the multinational enterprise. *Journal of International Business Studies* 34(4): 356–373.

Mayer K, Argyres N. 2004. Learning to contract: evidence from the personal computer industry. *Organization Science* 15(4): 394–410.

Minbaeva DB. 2008. HRM practices affecting extrinsic and intrinsic motivation of knowledge receivers and their effect on intra-MNC knowledge transfer. *International Business Review* 17(6): 703–713.

Moran P. 2005. Structural vs. relational embeddedness: social capital and managerial performance. *Strategic Management Journal* 26(12): 1129–1151.

Moran P, Ghoshal S. 1999. Markets, firms, and the process of economic development. *Academy of Management Review* 24(3): 390–412.

Mudambi R, Navarra P. 2004. Is knowledge power? Knowledge flows, subsidiary power and rent-seeking within MNCs. *Journal of International Business Studies* 35(5): 385–406.

Nahapiet J, Ghoshal S. 1998. Social capital, intellectual capital, and the organizational advantage. *Academy of Management Review* 23(2): 242–266.

Nelson RR, Winter SG. 1982. *An Evolutionary Theory of Economic Change*. Harvard University Press: Cambridge, MA.

Nohria N, Ghoshal S. 1994. Differentiated fit and shared values: alternatives for managing headquarters-subsidiary relations. *Strategic Management Journal* 15(6): 491–502.

Noorderhaven NG, Harzing AWK. 2009. Factors influencing knowledge flows within MNCs. *Journal of International Business Studies* 40(5): 719–745.

Nunnally J. 1978. *Psychometric Theory* (2nd edn). McGraw-Hill: New York.

Ocasio W. 1997. Towards an attention-based view of the firm. *Strategic Management Journal*, Summer Special Issue 18: 187–206.

OECD (Organisation for Economic Co-operation and Development). 2005. *Oslo Manual: Guidelines for Collecting and Interpreting Innovation Data* (3rd edn). OECD Publishing: Paris, France.

Penrose ET. 1959. *The Theory of the Growth of the Firm*. Oxford University Press: New York.

Persson M. 2006. The impact of operational structure, lateral integrative mechanisms and control mechanisms on intra-MNE knowledge transfer. *International Business Review* 15(5): 547–569.

Pfeffer J, Salancik GR. 1978. *The External Control of Organizations: A Resource Dependency Perspective*. Stanford Business Books: New York.

Pfeffer J, Sutton RI. 2000. *The Knowing-Doing Gap: How Smart Companies Turn Knowledge Into Action*. Harvard Business School Press: Boston, MA.

Podsakoff PM, Organ D. 1986. Self-reports in organizational research: problems and prospects. *Journal of Management* 12(4): 531–544.

Poppo L, Zhou KZ, Zenger T. 2008. Examining the conditional limits of relational governance: specialized assets, performance ambiguity, and long-standing ties. *Journal of Management Studies* 45(7): 1195–1216.

Repenning NP. 2002. A simulation-based approach to understanding the dynamics of innovation implementation. *Organization Science* 13(2): 109–127.

Rugman AM, Verbeke A. 2001. Subsidiary-specific advantages in multinational enterprises. *Strategic Management Journal* 22(3): 237–250.

Schulz M. 2001. The uncertain relevance of newness: organizational learning and knowledge flows. *Academy of Management Journal* 44(4): 661–681.

Song J, Almeida P, Wu G. 2003. Learning-by-hiring: when is mobility more likely to facilitate interfirm knowledge transfer? *Management Science* 49(4): 351–365.

Studenmund AH. 1992. *Using Economics. A Practical Guide* (2nd edn). HarperCollins: New York.

Szulanski G. 1996. Exploring internal stickiness: impediments to the transfer of best practice within the firm. *Strategic Management Journal*, Winter Special Issue 17: 27–43.

Szulanski G, Cappetta R, Jensen RJ. 2004. When and how trustworthiness matters: knowledge transfer and the moderating effect of causal ambiguity. *Organization Science* 15(5): 600–613.

Szulanski G, Jensen RJ. 2006. Presumptive adaptation and the effectiveness of knowledge transfer. *Strategic Management Journal* 27(10): 937–957.

Tabachnick BG, Fidell LS. 2001. *Using Multivariate Statistics* (4th edn). HarperCollins: New York.

Tallman S, Chacar A. 2011. Knowledge accumulation and dissemination in MNEs: a practice-based framework. *Global Strategy Journal* **48**(2): 278–304.

Tallman S, Koza MP. 2010. Keeping the global in mind: the evolution of the headquarters' role in global multibusiness firms. *Management International Review* **50**(4): 433–448.

Tallman S, Phene A. 2007. Leveraging knowledge across geographic boundaries. *Organization Science* **18**(2): 252–260.

Teece DJ. 1977. Technology transfer by multinational firms: the resource cost of transferring technological know-how. *Economic Journal* **87**(346): 242–261.

Teece DJ. 1986. Profiting from technological innovation: implications for integration, collaboration, licensing and public policy. *Research Policy* **15**(6): 285–305.

Teece DJ. 1990. Contribution and impediments of economic analysis to the study of strategic management. In *Perspectives on Strategic Management*, Fredrickson JW (ed). Harper: New York; 39–80.

Tsai W. 2000. Social capital, strategic relatedness, and the formation of intraorganizational linkages. *Strategic Management Journal* **21**(9): 925–939.

Tsai W. 2002. Social structures of 'coopetition' within a multiunit organization: coordination, competition, and intraorganizational knowledge sharing. *Organization Science* **13**(2): 179–190.

Tsang EW. 1999. The knowledge transfer and learning aspects of international HRM: an empirical study of Singapore MNCs. *International Business Review* **8**(5/6): 591–609.

Tsang EWK, Yip PS. 2007. Economic distance and the survival of foreign direct investments. *Academy of Management Journal* **50**(5): 1156–1168.

Uzzi B. 1997. Social structure and competition in interfirm networks: the paradox of embeddedness. *Administrative Science Quarterly* **42**(1): 35–67.

Williamson OE. 1992. Market, hierarchies, and the modern corporation: an unfolding perspective. *Journal of Economic Behavior & Organizations* **17**(3): 335–352.

Williamson OE. 1994. Visible and invisible governance. *American Economic Review* **84**(2): 323–326.

Williamson OE. 1999. Strategy research: governance and competence perspectives. *Strategic Management Journal* **20**(12): 1087–1108.

Woolthius RK, Hillebrand B, Nooteboom B. 2005. Trust, contract and relationship development. *Organization Studies* **26**(6): 813–840.

Xu D, Pan Y, Beamish PW. 2004. The effect of regulative and normative distances on MNE ownership and expatriate strategies. *Management International Review* **44**(3): 285–307.

Yang Q, Mudambi R, Meyer K. 2008. Conventional and reverse knowledge flows in multinational corporations. *Journal of Management* **34**(5): 882–902.

Zollo M, Reuer J, Singh H. 2002. Inter-organizational routines and performance in strategic alliances. *Organization Science* **13**(6): 701–713.

Zollo M, Winter SG. 2002. Deliberate learning and the evolution of dynamic capabilities. *Organization Science* **13**(3): 339–351.

Copyright © 2015 Strategic Management Society

Global Strat. J., **5**: 27–47 (2015)
DOI: 10.1002/gsj.1088

Journal of Management
1–25
DOI: 10.1177/0149206315592030 ©
The Author(s) 2015
Reprints and permissions:
sagepub.com/journalsPermissions.nav

The Performance Implications of Speed, Regularity, and Duration in Alliance Portfolio Expansion

Niron Hashai

Hebrew University of Jerusalem

Mario Kafouros

Peter J. Buckley

University of Leeds

Extant research on the management of time shows that the speed of undertaking new strategic moves has negative consequences for firm profitability. However, the literature has not distinguished whether this outcome results from the effects of speed on firms' revenues or from the effects of speed on firms' costs, or examined how firms can become more profitable by reducing the negative consequences of speed. We address these gaps for a specific strategic move: alliance portfolio expansion. We show that the speed at which firms expand their alliance portfolios increases managerial costs disproportionately relative to revenues, leading to an overall negative effect on firm profitability. However, a more regular rhythm of expansion and a longer duration of existing alliances reduce the negative profitability consequences of expansion speed by moderating the increase in managerial costs. These findings suggest that firms that make strategic moves, such as alliances, may reduce the negative profitability consequences of speed when they maintain a regular expansion rhythm and when their existing strategic engagements require modest managerial resources.

Keywords: *alliance portfolio; expansion speed; pace; regularity; alliance duration; firm profitability*

Acknowledgments: The authors wish to thank Antoney Goerzen, Patricia Klarner, Dovev Lavie, editor Catherine Maritan, and two anonymous reviewers for their comments on this study. Niron Hashai would like to acknowledge the financial support of the Asper Center for Entrepreneurship at the Hebrew University.

Corresponding author: Niron Hashai, Jerusalem School of Business Administration, Hebrew University of Jerusalem, Mount Scopus, Jerusalem 91905, Israel.

E-mail: nironH@huji.ac.il

Alliance portfolio expansion is a major strategic move that can have a profound effect on firm profitability. Prior research has shown that interfirm profitability variations are driven by attributes such as the size of alliance portfolios, partner quality, redundancy among partners, and partner diversity (Ahuja, 2000; Baum, Calabrese, & Silverman, 2000; Goerzen & Beamish, 2005; Lavie & Miller, 2008). However, the development of alliance portfolios is not an isolated event, and firm profitability is driven not only by the attributes of alliance portfolios but also by the temporal variations and patterns through which they are built (Das & Teng, 2002; Shi & Prescott, 2011). A key temporal dimension that may affect firm profitability is the speed at which firms expand their alliance portfolios (Shi, Sun, & Prescott, 2012). However, the extant research has not investigated how the expansion speed of alliance portfolios affects firm profitability.

To enhance our understanding of the effect of expansion speed on profitability, we investigate how speed of alliance portfolios' expansion influences firm-level revenue generation, "managerial costs," and, thereby, profitability. By analyzing both the revenue-generating and cost-escalating consequences of alliance portfolio expansion speed, we offer a finer-grained view of the factors affecting firm profitability when expansion speed is increased. Furthermore, this distinction allows us to investigate how two additional temporal dimensions—the rhythm of expansion and the duration of alliances in existing portfolios—influence the ability of firms that expand their alliance portfolios quickly to accelerate revenue generation while minimizing the increase in managerial costs associated with rapid expansion.

Managerial costs are a particularly salient feature in alliance portfolio expansion that is associated with the time and effort invested in creating, nurturing, and managing alliances (White & Lui, 2005). Managerial costs do not depend just on transaction costs (i.e., the costs associated with partners behaving opportunistically; Williamson, 1985). Creating and sustaining alliance portfolios is a managerially challenging and costly endeavor. Even when firms do not face transaction costs, alliance portfolio expansion may still increase managerial costs because of the need to identify and interact with new partners, to maintain an effective interorganizational interface, and to implement changes in response to partners' actions (White & Lui, 2005). Alliance portfolio expansion therefore requires partner firms to commit substantial managerial time to developing partner-specific capabilities, to building trust and reputation, to identifying synergies, and to creating positions in networks of alliances (Dyer & Singh 1998; Schilke & Goerzen, 2010).

Our analysis of 147 high-tech firms engaged in 1,043 alliances reveals that alliance portfolio expansion speed is positively associated with both firm-level revenue generation and managerial costs. However, managerial costs increase disproportionately more than revenues, leading to a negative net effect on firm profitability. Subsequently, we show how firms can expand quickly while avoiding, or at least reducing, the disadvantages of rapid expansion. This analysis underscores the moderating role of the regularity with which firms expand their alliance portfolio and the duration of existing alliances in the firm's portfolio. Firms that expand their alliance portfolio in a more regular rhythm and firms that sustain their existing alliances for longer durations can limit the negative implications that expansion speed has on managerial costs. In other words, a constant alliance portfolio expansion speed and lower managerial resource demands resulting from maintaining alliances for longer durations help firms to reduce the disproportionate increase in managerial costs, thus improving their profitability.

We extend prior research on the speed, regularity, and duration of expansion and provide insights for firms undertaking new strategic moves, in general, and those expanding their alliance portfolio, in particular. Prior research has focused on the overall profitability consequences of speed as it pertains to strategic moves, such as entry into new countries and business sectors (Klarner & Raisch, 2013; Vermeulen & Barkema, 2002). Engaging in strategic moves at greater speeds has been shown to have negative profitability implications (Klarner & Raisch, 2013; Vermeulen & Barkema, 2002). Yet these studies have not explicitly considered whether and why profitability variations are driven by differences in revenue generation or differences in the managerial costs involved in making strategic moves. The current study highlights that the reason for such profitability reduction is the disproportionate increase in managerial costs relative to revenues, rather than a decrease in revenues due to firms' limited capacity of capturing the benefits of fast-paced strategic moves (Vermeulen & Barkema, 2002). Clearly, each type of strategic move differs in its context and in its revenue-generating and cost-escalating patterns. Yet we expect the direction of the hypothesized effects to remain similar.

Our analysis further identifies the circumstances in which firms that expand quickly can succeed in reducing the negative effects of this strategy. These results show that firms that make strategic moves at high but constant speed manage to moderate the negative consequences of rapid expansion. Hence, whereas previous studies have focused on the direct effect of regularity on firm performance (Klarner & Raisch, 2013; Laamanen & Keil, 2008; Shi & Prescott, 2012; Vermeulen & Barkema, 2002), we show that a regular expansion rhythm enables firms that make fast-paced strategic moves to reduce the acceleration of managerial costs. Furthermore, although research on the profitability implications of expansion speed has considered the role of regularity or rhythm, it has not sufficiently explored the duration of existing strategic engagements. Our analysis suggests that because existing strategic engagements of longer duration place lower managerial demands compared to "younger" strategic engagements, they increase firms' capacity to direct managerial resources to new strategic moves, thus reducing the negative effect of expansion speed on managerial costs.

Overall, our findings suggest that two firms may end up undertaking similar strategic moves but experience different profitability outcomes because they have expanded at different speeds, with different regularities, and for different durations. The remainder of this study is organized as follows: The next section presents our theoretical framework and specifies our hypotheses. We then present our data, measures, and methods and follow with a presentation of our results. Finally, we present the conclusions and elaborate upon the theoretical and practical implications of the study.

Theoretical Framework

The Performance Consequences of Speed

The extant research on time management and its consequences (Shi et al., 2012) suggests that new strategic moves may accelerate organizational learning and facilitate the acquisition of new capabilities and the adoption of new routines and processes (Klarner & Raisch, 2013; Vermeulen & Barkema, 2002). Fast-paced strategic moves may also help firms avoid competency traps, implement new initiatives, and pursue new opportunities by facilitating the

4   Journal of Management

implementation of "change" routines that support subsequent strategic moves (Amburgey, Kelly, & Barnett, 1993; Barkema & Schijven, 2008; Beck, Brüderl, & Woywode, 2008). Fast-paced strategic moves can further help firms adapt to changing environments (Teece, 2007).

Although these benefits may assist firms in generating revenues, fast-paced strategic moves also require managerial attention, time, and resources and may disrupt existing organizational operations (Klarner & Raisch, 2013; Vermeulen & Barkema, 2002). Because establishing new organizational routines takes time, firms that engage in new strategic initiatives face substantial adaptation costs in seeking to exploit new resources and capabilities (Dierickx & Cool, 1989; Zollo & Winter, 2002). Rapid strategic moves also require senior managers to make many decisions within a short time, which raises the risk of information overload (Huber, 1991) and may lead to ineffective decision making and costly mistakes (Hambrick, Finkelstein, & Mooney, 2005). Prior studies have shown that the speed of strategic moves negatively affects firm profitability (e.g., Klarner & Raisch, 2013; Vermeulen & Barkema, 2002) and other performance measures, such as market returns (Laamanen & Keil, 2008), but this literature has not examined whether the negative effects on firm profitability result from increases in managerial costs, difficulties in capturing new streams of revenues, or a combination of the two.

The extant research also shows that firm profitability depends on the regularity at which firms make strategic moves, with regular expansion having positive effects on profitability (Klarner & Raisch, 2013; Vermeulen & Barkema, 2002). Whereas this observation has its own merits, the literature is silent regarding the question of whether regularity also has a moderating effect on the relationship between the speed of strategic moves and firm profitability. As a result, it remains unclear how fast-paced strategic moves affect profitability differently depending on whether they are made regularly or irregularly. Similarly, we know very little about how the temporal characteristics of firms' existing strategic engagements, such as their duration (Child & Yan, 2003; Shi et al., 2012), affect the profitability consequences of fast-paced strategic moves. We confront the unresolved issues concerning the effect of speed and its interaction with regularity and the duration of existing strategic engagements on revenue generation, managerial costs, and firm profitability in the context of alliance portfolio expansion.

Clearly, there are variations in the revenue-generating and cost-increasing patterns within and across different types of strategic moves, such as alliances, acquisitions, entry into new foreign markets and business segments, and other types of investment. For example, managerial costs in alliances result from monitoring and interacting with partners, managerial costs in foreign market entries result from the need to identify new locations and analyze their characteristics, and managerial costs in acquisitions result from the complexities of integrating firms with different structures and cultures into a unified entity. Yet we expect the relationship between the speed of undertaking new strategic moves and firm-level revenue generation and managerial costs to be similar, where fast-paced strategic moves are expected to increase both the benefits and costs of firms (Pacheco de Almeida, Hawk, & Yeung, 2015).

In the following subsections, we define the nature of the benefits of building a portfolio of alliances, the effect of building such a portfolio on revenue generation, and the associated managerial costs firms face. Then, we hypothesize how the speed of alliance portfolio expansion and its interactions with the regularity of alliance portfolio expansion and the duration of existing alliances affect revenue generation, managerial costs and, subsequently, firm profitability.

Revenue Generation and Managerial Costs of Alliance Portfolios

It has long been recognized that firms do not have to fully own resources to enjoy their benefits (Das & Teng, 2000; Kale, Dyer, & Singh, 2002; Lavie, 2006; Zaheer & Bell, 2005). Rather, they can exploit rent-generating resources residing outside the firm's boundaries (Dyer, 1996; Gulati, 1999; Gulati, Nohria, & Zaheer, 2000) that are embedded in interfirm routines and processes (Dyer & Singh, 1998). Hence, firm performance is directly linked to the alliances in which firms participate, where idiosyncratic interfirm linkages may result in economic benefits generated through the joint contributions of alliance partners. Such benefits may take the form of greater product differentiation and faster product development cycles (Dyer & Singh, 1998; Vasudeva & Anand, 2011). In turn, greater differentiation and faster development cycles allow firms to improve competitive positions, expand customer bases, and increase their revenues (Belderbos, Carree, & Lokshin, 2004; Singh & Mitchell, 2005; Stuart, 2000).

Engagement in alliances, however, may also lead to increased managerial costs. These costs are associated with the managerial time and effort required to generate and maintain new relationships, develop partner-specific learning capabilities, monitor alliance outcomes, build trust and reputation, and identify synergies and complementarities (Dyer & Singh, 1998; Levinthal & Fichman, 1988; Schilke & Goerzen, 2010; Zaheer, McEvily, & Perrone, 1998). Managerial costs not only result from the transaction costs associated with partners that behave opportunistically (Williamson, 1985) but also stem from the need to collaborate with alliance partners to achieve certain strategic objectives. Even in the absence of transaction costs, managerial costs may be incurred. Such costs can be classified into "task-related" and "social" dimensions (White & Lui, 2005). Task-related dimensions involve the difficulties of coordinating interdependent projects, changing internal routines, and addressing conflicts and complexities in knowledge transfer. Social dimensions involve the need to establish an effective interorganizational interface and to overcome cultural and social differences (White & Lui, 2005).

Because managers need a stream of supporting services to operate effectively, managerial costs do not merely refer to managers' direct compensation. Managerial costs include the costs related to the time and effort invested by existing managers, the costs related to the acquisition of additional managerial resources, and the costs of supporting managerial resources, such as administrative assistance, legal and financial consulting, communication, and travel.

The Effects of the Speed of Alliance Portfolio Expansion

We expect the speed with which firms expand their alliance portfolios to have a substantial impact on revenue generation, managerial costs, and, subsequently, firm profitability. Rapid alliance portfolio expansion is likely to positively affect the generation of firm revenues by accelerating organizational learning and the adaptation of new routines and processes from alliance partners (Dyer & Nobeoka, 2000; Hoffmann, 2007). As in the case of acquisitions (Barkema & Schijven, 2008; Laamanen & Keil, 2008), a faster expansion rate can help firms to more rapidly access new resources, capitalize on external knowledge, and learn from their alliance partners how to develop more efficient structures (Kale, Singh, & Perlmutter, 2000). A faster alliance portfolio expansion also enhances firm flexibility, which is particularly important in volatile competitive environments (Teece, 2007). In turn, these mechanisms enable firms that expand their alliance portfolios quickly to enjoy advantages, such as greater product differentiation and faster product development cycles (Dyer & Singh, 1998). A faster alliance portfolio expansion allows firms to widen their customer base and increase revenues (Singh & Mitchell, 2005; Stuart, 2000) more than firms that expand their alliance portfolios slowly.

However, given that integrating partners' resources with firms' existing routines and processes takes time and consumes substantial managerial resources (Barkema & Schijven, 2008; Miller, Fern, & Cardinal, 2007), a higher speed of alliance portfolio expansion may challenge existing managerial capacity to identify synergies, change organizational routines, and create interfaces with partners (Huber, 1991; Laamanen & Keil, 2008). A rapid alliance portfolio expansion therefore requires significant effort from existing managers, the acquisition of additional managerial resources, and a stream of administrative support services, which in turn significantly increase the firm's managerial costs.

When firms rapidly expand their alliance portfolios within a short time span, they are constrained by time compression diseconomies (Dierickx & Cool, 1989). According to asset accumulation theory (Dierickx & Cool, 1989), time compression diseconomies pertain to the additional costs incurred by firms seeking to quickly reach a given level of asset stock when this stock could be accumulated more economically over a longer duration. In the current context, this theory implies that creating many alliances within a short time requires a larger increase in the commitment of managerial resources (and consequently in related administrative support) than does establishing the same number of alliances over a longer period. Rapid alliance portfolio expansion requires substantial investments of managerial resources to avoid costly mistakes due to information overload (Huber, 1991) and to ensure that existing processes are appropriately adapted to those of partners. Such investments are accompanied with convex adjustment costs; that is, the cost of the investments increases disproportionally when the speed of expansion is accelerated (Knott, Bryce, & Posen, 2003). Time compression diseconomies are less likely to arise when alliance portfolios are developed gradually because the organization can handle the associated complexities without overstretching its existing managerial resources and administrative support services (Barkema & Schijven, 2008).

Because expansion speed increases both firm revenues and managerial costs, the net effect of speed on firm profitability will depend on whether the effect of rapid expansion on revenues is greater than the increase in managerial costs. We argue that although fast-paced expansion may enhance revenue generation, the disproportionate increase in managerial costs will lead to lower profitability. This prediction derives directly from the notion of time compression diseconomies, which predicts that a higher speed of conducting a given process will lead to a nonlinear increase in the costs of such a process (Dierickx & Cool, 1989). Overall, we expect disproportionate increases in managerial costs when firms expand their alliance portfolios rapidly to outweigh the positive effects of a rapid alliance portfolio expansion on revenues, which will negatively affect profitability:

Hypothesis 1: A higher expansion speed of the alliance portfolio (a) enhances revenue generation, (b) disproportionately increases managerial costs, and therefore (c) reduces profitability.

Given the predicted effects of alliance portfolio expansion speed on firms' revenues and managerial costs, an important strategic question is to determine when firms can expand quickly and at the same time reduce the negative effects of a rapid expansion. We argue that two important factors that may make such an expansion possible are (a) the regularity with which firms conduct a rapid alliance portfolio expansion and (b) the duration of firms' existing alliances when making a rapid alliance portfolio expansion. The regularity with which strategic moves are made is often studied together with the speed of making such moves (e.g., Klarner & Raisch, 2013; Laamanen & Keil, 2008; Vermeulen & Barkema, 2002). However, the duration of existing strategic engagements has been overlooked in this literature. Yet it is a key construct in studying temporal aspects of alliance portfolios (Shi et al., 2012) and has implications for both managerial costs and revenue generation. Since both the regularity of alliance portfolio expansion and the duration of the existing alliances are closely associated with the managerial demands placed on firms (Shi et al., 2012), they are both likely to play a significant role in facilitating a rapid alliance portfolio expansion.

The Moderating Effect of Alliance Expansion Regularity

Regularly paced alliance portfolio expansion is likely to enhance revenue generation while reducing managerial costs. By contrast, time periods between the establishment of alliances that are either too short or too long are likely to negatively affect the skills, structures, and processes a firm draws upon (Klarner & Raisch, 2013; Laamanen & Keil, 2008) when establishing new alliances. In turn, these effects will likely lead to lower revenues and higher managerial costs.

Regularity in alliance portfolio expansion increases predictability. As a result, firms can interpret their experiences in establishing alliances in the past and relate these experiences to similar organizational routines and operations (Klarner & Raisch, 2013; Laamanen & Keil, 2008; Vermeulen & Barkema, 2002) that are required for future alliances. Predictability therefore makes the process of alliance building more efficient (Gulati, 1995). Firms become accustomed to a given rate of new alliance engagement. Hence, they can effectively plan, implement, and adapt to new collaboration agreements because they are accustomed to the routines and structures required to assign responsibilities, take the required actions, and make appropriate resources available (Shi & Prescott, 2012). In turn, this enables firms to better leverage their alliance portfolios to increase revenues. It further allows firms to use their managerial capacities more effectively to reduce the managerial costs involved in meeting the requirements of the chosen rhythm (Klarner & Raisch, 2013).

Conversely, firms that expand at a highly irregular pace face complexities in creating new alliances—both during periods of expansion peaks and during periods of inactivity—because organizational structures and systems are seldom sufficiently flexible to manage the resulting complexities of abrupt and discontinuous changes (Klarner & Raisch, 2013; Laamanen & Keil, 2008; Shi & Prescott, 2012). During peaks of rapid expansion, firms will find it difficult to assimilate knowledge and resources from their partners to reap the benefits of engaging in alliances and increasing revenues. Such peaks represent an extreme case of time compression diseconomies and will therefore also increase managerial costs significantly.

Alternatively, periods of inactivity may lead firms to gradually forget the practices they have learned in previous alliances (Darr, Argote, & Epple, 1995). This is frequently the result of the overturn of personnel who engaged in previous alliances, marked by managers leaving the firm or switching positions within it, leading to the loss of valuable knowledge and experience (Laamanen & Keil, 2008), hampering future alliance formation. Such inactivity may become detrimental to the ability of firms to reap the benefits of new alliances and increase their revenues. It may also result in additional managerial costs, as firms will need to redevelop the necessary skills, routines, and structures to effectively reengage in new alliances.

Hence, maintaining a regular expansion rhythm is likely to allow firms to avoid some of the negative effects of rapid alliance expansion.[1] A rapid but constant pace of alliance expansion may help firms leverage the advantages of predictability when establishing alliances. It also allows them to use their knowledge of similar organizational routines and operations to become more efficient at building new alliances (Gulati, 1995; Laamanen & Keil, 2008). This efficiency further enhances firms' ability to leverage rapid alliance portfolio expansions to generate revenues while reducing time compression diseconomies and their associated managerial costs. By contrast, the combination of rapid alliance portfolio expansion and irregular expansion rhythm is likely to stretch a firm's managerial capacity even further. This combination limits firms' ability to rely on past experiences due to the severe time constraints and the limited predictability that the combination of high speed and irregular expansion pace imposes. This combination will therefore further increase managerial costs and constrain firms' ability to use previously learned skills and processes to generate revenues.

We therefore expect firms that follow both rapid and constant alliance portfolio expansion to generate higher returns and incur lower managerial costs than firms that adopt a rapid expansion but irregular rhythm. In other words, firms that choose to expand their alliance portfolio rapidly but keep their expansion rhythm regular are likely to further increase their revenues (over and above the revenue generation effect of rapid alliance portfolio expansion). In turn, these firms reduce their managerial costs and improve their profitability. By contrast, firms that expand their alliance portfolios rapidly but irregularly will find it difficult to exploit their alliance portfolio expansion to generate revenues. These firms will further face higher managerial costs because of time compression diseconomies. As a result of this combination, they will achieve lower profitability. Accordingly, we propose the following:

> *Hypothesis 2:* A regular alliance portfolio expansion rhythm (a) enhances the positive effects of a higher expansion speed on revenue generation, (b) decreases the positive effects of a higher expansion speed on managerial costs, and therefore (c) decreases the negative effects of a higher expansion speed on profitability.

The Moderating Effect of Alliance Portfolio Duration

The average duration of the alliances in alliance portfolios varies across firms. We expect such variations and the associated challenges that firms face when their portfolios consist of younger alliances (relative to more mature alliances) to have a profound impact on the revenue, managerial costs, and profitability consequences of a fast-paced alliance portfolio expansion. Younger alliances are characterized by limited trust, because partners are unfamiliar with one another's processes and systems (Dyer & Singh 1998; Kale et al., 2002; Lavie, 2006). A portfolio consisting of shorter-duration alliances requires firms to invest substantial managerial time and effort in developing partner-specific learning capabilities, to monitor alliance outcomes, to build trust and reputation, and to identify synergies. These developments result in increased managerial resource demands and, hence, higher managerial costs. Mature alliances enable firms to become more familiar with their partners' needs and practices (Kale et al., 2002; Lavie, 2006). Thus, less managerial effort is required for mature alliances than for younger alliances, in both the task-related and social dimensions of managerial costs (White & Lui, 2005).

Because the managerial resource demands of managing mature alliances tend to be lower than those of managing younger alliances, such firms have a higher capacity to expand their alliance portfolios rapidly while avoiding the pitfalls of time compression diseconomies faced by firms engaged in less-established alliances. Furthermore, the greater availability of managerial resources in firms that sustain a portfolio of longer-duration alliances is likely to make them more capable of reaping the benefits of rapidly expanding their alliance portfolios. Subsequently, this will enable such firms to increase their revenue generation relative to firms that manage less-established alliances. Altogether, we expect these mechanisms to allow firms that have a portfolio of alliances of longer duration to be able to enhance the benefits of speed to increase their revenues, reduce associated managerial costs, and thus achieve higher profitability. Accordingly, we propose the following:

> *Hypothesis 3:* A longer alliance portfolio duration (a) enhances the positive effects of a higher expansion speed on revenue generation, (b) decreases the positive effects of a higher expansion speed on managerial costs, and therefore (c) decreases the negative effects of a higher expansion speed on profitability.

Method

Data and Sample

Our hypotheses were tested on a sample of randomly selected, Israel-based, private and public high-technology firms. High-technology firms are suitable for the current research because the alliance literature frequently focuses on such firms (Kumar & Nti, 1998; Lavie & Miller, 2008; Phelps, 2010; Stuart, 2000). The use of high-technology firms is particularly important for our analysis because the dynamic and intensive alliance formation in this sector enhances the meaningfulness, reliability, and variability of the relationships we wish to test. The sample was derived from the full list of Israel-based high-technology firms constructed by the consulting firm Dolev and Abramovitz Ltd. for the year 2007. The Dolev and Abramovitz data set is recognized as a comprehensive resource for this sector in Israel and includes approximately 400 high-technology firms that have reached the stage at which they sell their products. The data set represents the vast majority of high-tech sectors.[2] We collected data both at the firm and at the alliance level. This approach is essential for testing our framework because it allows us to link revenues, managerial costs, and profitability variations at the firm level to variations related to firms' alliance portfolios. It further allows controlling for both firm- and alliance portfolio–level effects.

Firm-level data—including revenues, number of employees, firm age, and investments attracted—were collected from the Dolev and Abramovitz data set and the Israel Venture Capital (IVC) data set. Dolev and Abramovitz Ltd. is a private company that collects and publishes annual information on Israeli high-tech firms. The IVC data set is another comprehensive source for Israeli high-technology industries.[3] We further used annual financial reports to collect firm-level financial data. These data are readily available for public firms. We were also granted access to key figures in the financial reports of private firms that represent 72% of the sample. Such financial figures include the following: general and administrative (G&A) expenditures; operational expenses; earnings before interest, taxes, and depreciation (EBITDA); and fixed assets. Finally, we also collected patent data from the U.S. Patent and Trademark Office (USPTO). Because all the sampled firms had substantial sales in the United States, it was important to collect patent data from the USPTO.[4]

Alliance-specific data were collected from the LexisNexis Academic archive and the archives of leading Israeli financial newspapers, such as TheMarker and Globes. These archival sources were used to identify announcements of alliance formation, to identify the governance mode of each alliance agreement, and to find announcements of alliance terminations. LexisNexis Academic was further used to identify the country of origin of each alliance partner. Overall, firm-level data were collected for 147 firms over the 2000-to-2007 period. Basic *t* test comparisons of the 147 participating firms and the 253 nonparticipating firms did not show evidence of nonresponse bias in terms of the average numbers for firm revenues, number of employees, firm age, firm valuation, and industrial classification. Because the sampled firms may have been engaged in alliances established prior to 2000 and to avoid right-censoring bias, our alliance-level data also included data on active alliances established before 2000.

The firm year was used as the unit of analysis because our dependent variables were defined at the firm level (Goerzen & Beamish, 2005; Lavie & Miller, 2008). Data for 1,043 alliance announcements were transformed to alliance year records by replicating alliance records for active periods of alliance duration and by updating all time-variant variables. These records were used to form 895 firm year observations for the 147 analyzed firms by pooling the data for all alliances in a firm's alliance portfolio in a given year.

Measures

The variables required for the current study and their measures are detailed in Appendix Table A1 and are further described below.

Dependent variables. To capture firm-level revenues, we used each firm's income in a given year. To capture firm-level managerial costs, we used each firm's G&A expenditures.[5] G&A expenditures consist primarily of senior managers' compensation and of other administrative costs incurred at the head office for supporting the senior management (e.g., administrative employees, legal and accounting consulting, communication and travel costs). To further examine the extent to which this measure indeed captures managerial costs, we interviewed the CFOs of 10 random firms in our sample. These CFOs indicated that the costs related to senior managers' compensation and the direct costs of administrative support for such managers typically range between 65% and 80% of the overall G&A expenditures. Hence, the use of G&A expenditures as a proxy for firm-level managerial costs is consistent with our earlier observation that alliance portfolio engagement involves the time and effort of managers as well as administrative support services for such managers. Finally, we captured each firm's profitability through each firm's EBITDA. This measure allows us to avoid potential biases that might arise from different financing strategies, tax treatments, and depreciation rules in different industries.[6]

Independent variables. The expansion speed of a firm's alliance portfolio is operationalized as the number of new alliances that the firm has established in a given year (derived from alliance announcements) divided by the alliance portfolio size (i.e., the number of part-ner firms a focal firm has) in that year. This metric has the advantages of capturing a nor-malized measure of alliance portfolio establishments in a given year relative to the firm's alliance portfolio size, which has been shown in past alliance portfolio research to affect firm performance (Wassmer, 2010).[7] It is noteworthy that firms are less consistent in reporting on alliance termination, whereas many announce alliance creation. We used two alternative ways to overcome this problem.

For 584 alliances (out of the total of 1,043 alliance announcements), we obtained alliance termination dates either from secondary sources or by directly approaching the relevant firms. The average duration of this subset of alliances was 2 years and 10 months. Regarding those alliances for which we could not establish a precise termination date, we followed the procedure conducted by Ahuja (2000) and Phelps (2010) to estimate alliance duration when termination dates were missing. This procedure distinguishes between joint venture (JV) alli-ances and non-JV alliances. We assumed that JVs with no termination announcements existed until the end of 2007, the last year of our study. Non-JV alliances with no termination announcements were presumed to exist until the end of the last year in which they were docu-mented (in secondary sources) or until the end of the year after the year they were founded, whichever was later (Phelps, 2010). This procedure led to an average alliance duration of 2 years and 8 months. Given that the *t* test of the difference in mean alliance portfolio size when using the two alternative methods of calculating alliances' duration found no signifi-cant difference between these alternatives, we followed the second approach for all data in calculating alliance portfolio size in each year.

We followed Laamanen and Keil (2008) and used the standard deviation of alliance engagement speed within the analyzed time frame to measure alliance portfolio expansion regularity. More specifically, we used the inverse of the standard deviation ($1/s$, where $s =$ standard deviation) as our measure. High peaks in a firm's alliance portfolio expansion com-bined with periods of inactivity result in a relatively high standard deviation and, therefore, low values of the engagement regularity measure. A regular pace of alliance portfolio expan-sion results in low standard deviation and, therefore, high values of the expansion regularity measure. Given that Hypothesis 2 concerns the advantages of regularity for rapid alliance portfolio expansion, this measure allows us to have a straightforward interpretation of regu-larity and to estimate its direct effects.

The alliance portfolio duration is measured as the average duration (in years) of each firm's alliance portfolio in a given year (i.e., all alliances that have not been terminated—or deemed to have been terminated—up to the end of a given year). It is computed as the sum of the duration of each firm's existing alliances divided by the number of alliances. The dura-tion of each alliance is calculated as the time elapsed (in years) between the announcement of the alliance and the end of year *t*.[8] The alliance portfolio duration is expected to moderate the effect of the alliance portfolio expansion speed on profitability—as predicted in Hypothesis 3—and may also have a positive direct effect on the dependent variables.

Control variables. Our analysis controls for an extensive number of firm-level and alli-ance portfolio–level factors that might impact our dependent variables.

We control for firm size (Ahuja, Lampert, & Tandon, 2008), which is operationalized as the log of the number of employees to reduce its skewness. To control for the effects of the firm's tangible resources, our regression models also include a measure of fixed assets.

12   Journal of Management

Another factor that might affect revenues, G&A expenditures, and profitability represents the financial investments made in a firm. We therefore control for total investments (in millions of U.S. dollars) made in each firm by private investors, venture capital funds, corporate venture capitalists, or acquisitions and/or through public offerings. This measure is log-transformed to reduce its skewness.

The yearly numbers of patents for which firms applied (and that were granted at a later stage) are used as a proxy for the possible impact of firms' technological innovations on their revenues, managerial costs, and profitability. The number of patents reflects high-technology firms' innovation output. The literature highlights the superiority of the number of patent citations compared to merely the number of patents as an innovation output measure, because the former reflects the patents' value (Ahuja & Katila, 2001; Grilliches, 1990). However, because patent citations are likely to lag behind the act of technological innovation, we choose the number of patents as our main proxy for innovation output.[9] A firm's level of technological innovation is expected to increase its revenues and profitability, but it may also increase managerial costs.

The degree of diversification may also affect firm profitability (Goerzen & Beamish, 2005). Because the firms in our sample are mostly single-business firms, we control for intraindustry product diversification by calculating the cumulative number of product lines that a firm has in a given year. We also control for the geographic diversification of firms. This measure is operationalized as an entropy measure of their sales across six foreign regions: North America, South and Central America, the European Union, the rest of Europe, Asia, and the rest of the world (Hitt, Hoskisson, & Kim, 1997; Kim, Hwang, & Burgers, 1993). This classification builds on the observation that regional considerations play a significant role in firms' internationalization (Rugman & Verbeke, 2004). It has the further advantage of capturing diversity between regions in terms of geographic, institutional, and cultural distances (Delios & Henisz, 2003; Ronen & Shenkar, 1985). A further control is firm age. This measure captures interfirm heterogeneity in revenues, managerial costs, and profitability that result from maturity differences. Firm age may also account for the observation that high-technology firms reach profitability at relatively late stages of their life cycle (Hart, 1995; Lee, Lee, & Pennings, 2001). Intertemporal trends are controlled for by year effects. Industry effects, representing 11 principal high-technology sectors, are used to control for interindustry variances in revenues, managerial costs, and profitability.

We control for the potential effect of prior alliance portfolio experience on revenues, managerial costs, and profitability (Anand & Khanna, 2000). Following Gulati, Lavie, and Singh (2009), we use the number of alliances in which each firm was engaged up to the beginning of each year as a proxy for prior alliance experience. In addition, alliance function diversity measures the dispersion of existing alliances across R&D, production, marketing, and customer support activities (Jiang, Tao, & Santoro, 2010). Alliance function diversity should be positively correlated with revenues and profitability because of greater learning and resource complementarity potential (Dyer & Singh, 1998; Gulati, 1999; Jiang et al., 2010; Kale et al., 2002). This measure should also be positively correlated with managerial costs due to greater coordination complexity (Goerzen & Beamish, 2005). Accounting for these alliance portfolio–level measures is likely to increase the reliability of our results because they allow us to test the possible effects of alliance portfolio–level heterogeneity on our dependent variables.

Statistical Method

To overcome potential endogeneity issues, we first take differences in our regression models to control for unobservable model-specific effects and then estimate the model using a generalized-method-of-moments (GMM) approach, thus applying panel random-effect methods. Arellano and Bond (1991) show that the most efficient set of instruments in the absence of serial correlation are found using the lagged values of the dependent variable and the potentially endogenous explanatory variables (i.e., expansion speed, expansion regularity, and duration) from t –2. Therefore, these are the instruments we adopt. Arellano and Bond's dynamic panel model has been shown to produce poor results when there are many independent variables and few periods. In such cases, fewer instruments are available (i.e., because the Arellano and Bond framework uses lags and combinations of time periods and lags to produce instruments), and the number of periods analyzed consequently decreases. Building on the work of Arellano and Bover (1995), who used lagged differences as potential instruments, Blundell and Bond (1998) exploit additional moment restrictions, which substantially improve the performance of the Arellano and Bond GMM estimator in circumstances in which the number of time series observations is relatively small (e.g., in which there are relatively few years of data). Because we have a maximum of eight periods per firm (2000–2007), we adopt the Blundell and Bond extension.

Results

Descriptive statistics and correlations are presented in Table 1. The firms in our sample are fairly young (less than 6 years old on average); they are small to medium sized in terms of their numbers of employees (131 employees on average) and revenues (US$30 million on average). On average, each firm has approximately 10 patents. Because Israel is a fairly small economy, 74% of the alliances are with foreign partners, mainly with U.S. and European firms. Firms have engaged in approximately 1.3 new alliances per year, on average, and the average alliance portfolio engagement regularity is approximately 2.7. The average duration of alliances is 2 years and 8 months (2.66). In a given year, firms have been engaged in an average of over five alliances.

The results of the GMM regressions are presented in Table 2, in which revenues, managerial costs and profitability are tested against the independent and control measures. Models 1 through 4 test the effects on revenues, Models 5 through 8 test the effects on managerial costs, and Models 9 through 12 test the effects on profitability. Models 2 through 4 show that expansion speed has a significant positive effect on revenues, supporting Hypothesis 1a. Models 6 through 8 show a significant negative effect for expansion speed on managerial cost, thus lending support to Hypothesis 1b. Models 10 through 12 show a significant negative effect of expansion speed on profitability, thus supporting Hypothesis 1c. Importantly, we also investigate whether the increase in managerial costs is indeed disproportionate to the increase in revenues, which would lead to a reduction in profitability growth. When comparing the coefficients of expansion speed in Models 2 through 4 (predicting revenues) and Models 6 through 8 (predicting managerial costs), Wald tests show the coefficients for managerial costs are consistently significantly larger than those for revenues ($p > \chi^2 = 0.001$ for all models).[10] Furthermore, when comparing the marginal effect of expansion speed on revenues and managerial costs for the average firm in absolute terms, it is clear that the increase in

Table 1
Descriptive Statistics and Pearson Correlations (*N* = 895)

Variable	M (SD)	1	2	3	4	5	6	7	8	9	10	11	12	13	14	15
1. Revenues (in Million $US)	30.24 (80.12)	—														
2. G&A expenditures (in Million $US)	3.93 (6.15)	0.13**	—													
3. EBITDA (in Million $US)	3.3 (5.17)	.07	.25***	—												
4. Expansion speed	1.29 (0.37)	.08*	.10*	-.07	—											
5. Expansion regularity	2.70 (125)	-.05	-.01*	-.08**	.05	—										
6. Firm size	130.7 (91.15)	.31***	.22***	.23***	.06	.05	—									
7. Tangible resources (in Million $US)	42.57 (59.09)	.14**	.05	.09*	.02	.02	.24***	—								
8. Total investments (in Million $US)	21.07 (16.32)	.32***	.11**	.23***	.03	.02	.15**	.01	—							
9. Patents	10.12 (16.21)	.19***	.13*	.24***	.00	.01	.02	-.09*	.09*	—						
10. Product diversification	6.62 (19.13)	.15**	.15**	.04	.04	.03	.08*	-.01	.01	.07*	—					
11. Geographic diversification	0.82 (0.35)	.09**	.13**	.12**	.01	.02	.15**	.07*	.07*	.01	.02	—				
12. Firm age	5.67 (5.02)	.23***	.11**	.26***	.00	.01	-.16**	.03	.10*	.02	.06	.12**	—			
13. Duration	2.66 (1.01)	.17**	.01	.21**	.03	.02	.18**	-.01	.01	-.05	.02	.00	.26***	—		
14. Alliance portfolio size	5.32 (7.47)	.25***	.19**	.01*	-.07*	.05	.01	-.04	.03	.06	.03	.02	.22***	.25**	—	
15. Alliance experience	5.96 (4.91)	.19**	.18**	.08*	.19**	.17**	.29***	.18**	.09*	.08*	.30***	.06	.02	.26**	.00	—
16. Alliance function diversity	0.49 (0.21)	.11*	.08*	.05	.08*	.00	.14**	0.03	.04	.03	-.02	.01	-.12**	.17**	.18***	-.10*

*p ≤ .05.
**p ≤ .01.
***p ≤ .001.

14

Table 2
Arellano and Bond (1991) GMM Regression Models (*N* = 895)

Variable	Revenues				Managerial Costs				Profitability			
	(1)	(2)	(3)	(4)	(5)	(6)	(7)	(8)	(9)	(10)	(11)	(12)
Expansion speed		.03** (.01)	.03*** (.01)	.03** (.01)		.35*** (.10)	.35** (.08)	.35*** (.11)		−.03*** (.01)	−.03*** (.01)	−.03** (.01)
Expansion regularity		.06** (.02)	.06** (.02)	.05** (.02)			−.38** (.11)	−.38*** (.11)			.04*** (.01)	.04** (.01)
Duration			.08* (.04)	.08* (.03)			−.21*** (.07)	−.22*** (.06)			.11** (.03)	.11** (.04)
Expansion Regularity × Expansion Speed				.12 (.10)				−.21* (.08)				.01* (.00)
Duration × Expansion Speed				.04 (.05)				−.12* (.05)				.01* (.00)
Firm size	.22* (.09)	.22* (.08)	.23* (.09)	.22* (.08)	.12 (.12)	.15 (.13)	.12 (.10)	.13 (.13)	.06 (.06)	.05 (.04)	.05 (.05)	.06 (.06)
Tangible resources	.14 (.08)	.14 (.09)	.13 (.08)	.14 (.108)	.05 (.11)	.05 (.11)	.06 (.10)	.06 (.01)	.12 (.09)	.12 (.09)	.12 (.11)	.12 (.10)
Total investments	.25*** (.04)	.24** (.05)	.28*** (.06)	.26*** (.04)	.35** (.09)	.36** (.1)	.37** (.12)	.36** (.12)	.06** (.02)	.06** (.02)	.07** (.02)	.07** (.02)
Patents	.30*** (.07)	.30** (.07)	.30** (.07)	.33** (.07)	.02 (.05)	.02 (.05)	.02 (.03)	.02 (.02)	.22** (.07)	.21** (.06)	.21** (.07)	.21** (.06)
Product diversification	.26* (.12)	.25* (.12)	.25* (.12)	.27* (.13)	.51*** (.12)	.50** (.13)	.49** (.13)	.50** (.13)	.05 (.10)	.05 (.09)	.05 (.09)	.04 (.08)
Geographic diversification	.20*** (.04)	.21*** (.04)	.21*** (.06)	.20*** (.04)	.20** (.06)	.20** (.06)	.20** (.06)	.21** (.06)	.02** (.00)	.02** (.00)	.02** (.00)	.02** (.00)
Firm age	.13* (.06)	.14* (.06)	.14* (.06)	.15* (.06)	.21* (.09)	.21* (.09)	.21* (.09)	.21* (.08)	.15 (.10)	.15 (.09)	.15 (.09)	.15 (.10)
Alliance experience	.17 (.10)	.16 (.09)	.17 (.10)	.16 (.09)	−.13 (.10)	−.13 (.10)	−.14 (.08)	−.14 (.08)	.13 (.10)	.13 (.08)	.13 (.09)	.14 (.01)
Alliance function diversity	.13*** (.02)	.13*** (.02)	.12*** (.02)	.13*** (.02)	.10** (.05)	.11** (.04)	.11** (.04)	.118** (.04)	.02* (.01)	.03* (.01)	.03* (.01)	.02* (.01)
Industry	+	+	+	+	+	+	+	+	+	+	+	+
Year	+	+	+	+	+	+	+	+	+	+	+	+
Sargan test (Prob > χ^2)	.30	.34	.31	.33	.30	.40	.33	.36	.21	.32	.31	.36
Second-order serial correlation (Pr > Z)	.27	.32	.50	.51	.29	.41	.49	.56	.40	.44	.59	.57
Wald test	402.15	417.30	469.85	471.28	362.44	455.76	478.69	504.41	366.81	467.34	479.96	508.21

Note: Intercept is not shown. Standard errors in parentheses. GMM = generalized method of moments.
*$p \leq .05$.
**$p \leq .01$.
***$p \leq .001$.

15

sales in Model 4 ($0.04 \times 30.24 =$ US\$1.21 million) is always smaller than the increase in managerial costs in Model 8 ($0.35 \times 3.93 =$ US\$1.37 million). Together, these results indicate that increases in expansion speed lead to greater increases in managerial costs than revenues. This outcome substantiates our point that it is the increase in managerial costs that hampers profitability, despite the increase in revenues.

Next, Models 3 and 4 indicate that a more regular expansion of alliance portfolios positively affects revenues, but the interaction between regularity and expansion speed (Model 4) is insignificant, indicating that Hypothesis 2a is not supported.[11] Models 7 and 8 show that a more regular expansion of alliance portfolios negatively affects managerial cost, and its interaction with expansion speed (Model 8) is negative and significant, thus supporting Hypothesis 2b. Finally, Models 11 and 12 show that a more regular expansion of alliance portfolios positively affects profitability, and its interaction with expansion speed (Model 12) is also positive and significant, thus supporting Hypothesis 2c. Overall, these results show that greater regularity does not allow firms that rapidly expand their alliance portfolios to increase their revenues more than firms that also expand their alliance portfolio rapidly but not in a regular way. Yet greater regularity enables firms that expand rapidly to reduce their managerial costs more than firms that expand their alliance portfolios rapidly but irregularly. This phenomenon, in turn, enables the former group of firms to have higher profitability than the latter group of firms.

Finally, Models 3 and 4 further indicate that longer duration of alliance portfolios positively affects revenues, but the interaction of longer duration and expansion speed (Model 4) is insignificant. Hence, Hypothesis 3a is not supported. Models 7 and 8 show that duration negatively affects managerial cost, and its interaction with expansion speed (Model 8) is negative and significant, which supports Hypothesis 3b. Finally, Models 11 and 12 show that duration positively affects profitability, and its interaction with expansion speed (Model 12) is also positive and significant, thus supporting Hypothesis 3c. As in the case of alliance expansion regularity, these results indicate that firms with more mature alliances that expand their alliance portfolios rapidly are not able to increase their revenues more than firms with younger alliances that rapidly expand their alliance portfolios. Yet the former group of firms may expand rapidly and bear lower costs than the latter group and subsequently increase their profitability.

Overall, we conclude that both alliance portfolio expansion regularity and duration can reduce the managerial costs resulting from rapid alliance portfolio expansion. Yet they do not contribute to an increase in revenues when alliance portfolios are rapidly expanded. A possible explanation for the fact that Hypotheses 2a and 3a are not supported may be that, unlike managerial costs (which are under the firm's control), revenues depend on external factors, such as market conditions and competitors' actions. Because it is difficult to control for the effects of a multiplicity of external factors, they may mask the moderation effects of engagement regularity and duration.

Models 1, 5, and 8 present the effects of firm- and alliance-level control variables on the dependent variables. Total investments, patents, geographic diversification, and alliance function diversity are found to be significantly associated with all the dependent variables. Firm size is also positively associated with revenues. The models provide support for our regression specifications in terms of their Wald statistics. The Sargan tests (Blundell & Bond, 1998) confirm the validity of the instruments, and the null hypothesis of no serial autocorrelation of the residuals is also retained. Wald tests further show that all models that include our independent variables are more significant than those models that include only the control measures (Models 1, 5, and 8) at the $p > F = 0.01$ level.

Robustness Tests

To test the robustness of our results, we conduct several additional analyses, the first of which is a more direct test of our argument that managerial costs increase more than revenues as a result of rapid alliance portfolio expansion. Although we use profitability to capture the effects of speed, regularity, and duration on revenues deducted from costs, this measure also includes additional cost components that make profitability cruder for this paper's purpose. We therefore construct a measure that deducts managerial costs from revenues per firm and year and run all our models with this measure as the dependent variable.[12] The new results remain consistent with those presented in Models 9 through 12 in Table 2. We also use market value and return on sales as alternative operationalizations for firm performance (Farjoun 1998; Goerzen & Beamish, 2003, 2005).[13] The results using these alternative performance measures remain similar to those presented in Models 9 through 12 in Table 2.

Second, to further test the argument that faster expansion generates revenues through the enhanced effect of alliance portfolios on product differentiation and product scope expansion, we use patents and product diversification as dependent variables rather than as controls. The results of these models show that expansion speed is indeed positively associated with both product diversification and patents, thus corroborating our argument. When we use expansion regularity and duration as moderators for the effect of expansion speed on product diversification, we find positive and significant moderating effects. These results are in line with Hypothesis 2a, which was not supported when revenues was used as the dependent variable. When we use expansion regularity and duration as moderators for the effect of expansion speed on patents, we find no significant moderating effects, consistent with our core results.

Third, we examine the existence of curvilinear effects by squaring the key constructs (expansion speed, expansion regularity, and duration). Among other considerations, this investigation is conducted due to the study of Shi and Prescott (2012) showing that the expansion regularity of acquisitions and alliances has an inverted U-shaped relationship with firm performance (Tobin's Q). We find insignificant effects for all squared measures. Moreover, we examine whether some effects of expansion speed, expansion regularity, and duration might be mitigated when repeated alliances are included (Goerzen, 2007; Goerzen & Beamish, 2005). We therefore reestimate the models while excluding repeated alliances from the sample. This reestimation does not change the results. We also test whether the number of repeated alliances moderates the effects of expansion speed. The rationale for this is that when firms have many repeated alliances, their enhanced familiarity with their partners may reduce managerial costs. The role of repeated alliances, however, is insignificant both for its main and moderating effects, most likely because of the low number of repeated alliances in our sample (only 0.72 on average). Tests of the moderating effect of alliance experience also yield no significant results.

Furthermore, we replace our measure of technological innovation with the number of patent citations in each period as reported by the USPTO and with the level of R&D expenditures. These alternative measures, once again, yield similar results. Next, we test whether the results are affected by the governance mode of alliances (licensing, JV, outsourcing, distribution agreements, and OEM agreements) and specific functions of alliances (R&D, production, marketing, and customer support) by running separate regressions for such sub-groups. No significant effects are found. We also add controls for the share of alliances in the alliance portfolios of firms with specific governance modes and for the share of alliances pertaining to a given function. This allows us to examine whether alliance portfolios that are biased toward a specific governance mode or function affect our results. No significant effects are found in these cases either.

In addition, we test whether additional alliance portfolio diversity measures—such as partner industry, partner nationality, or governance mode diversity (Jiang et al., 2010)—affect our results. The effects are insignificant for these measures. Additionally, given the possible effect of uncertainty on alliance portfolio expansion moves (Koka, Madhavan, & Prescott, 2006), we follow the procedure described in Beckman, Haunschild, and Phillips (2004: 265) for the subsample of public firms (41 firms represented by 251 firm year obser-vations). Here, we test whether the addition of firm-specific uncertainty and market uncer-tainty might also affect our results. The results remain consistent for this subsample, while the significance of the independent variables is approximately 5%, most likely due to the smaller sample size. Finally, we lag all independent variables and controls by 1, 2, and 3 years relative to the dependent variables. This allows us to test for whether time lags change the effects of expansion speed, regularity, and duration. The results remain consistent with those presented in Table 2, although the significance level decreases as the time lag increases.

Discussion and Conclusion

Theoretical Contributions and Implications

This study advances the view that the speed at which firms make strategic moves (such as alliances, mergers, acquisitions, and new market entry) has a significant direct effect on their profitability over and above the actual outcome of the strategic moves themselves. Although firms' ability to enhance their profitability should be positively related to their ability to respond rapidly to changing environments by quickly making new strategic moves (Teece, 2007), the emerging literature on temporal effects and time management largely suggests that fast-paced strategic moves have negative profitability consequences (Klarner & Raisch, 2013; Vermeulen & Barkema, 2002). The present study distinguishes between the effects of expansion speed on revenue generation, managerial costs, and profitability. It therefore con-tributes to prior research that has not explicitly considered whether decreases in profitability are driven by the effects of speed on the firm's ability to capture new revenue streams or by its effects on managerial costs.

This distinction allows us to examine the exact factors that determine how quickly firms should make new strategic moves and identify how firms that undertake strategic moves quickly can accelerate revenue generation while minimizing costs. Although a higher speed of strategic moves, such as alliance portfolio expansion, increases both revenues and mana-gerial costs, our findings reveal that the increase in managerial costs is disproportionately high relative to contemporaneous increases in revenues, leading to an overall reduction in firm profitability. Therefore, ignoring the distinction between the effects of fast-paced strate-gic moves on revenue generation and managerial costs could be a major shortcoming in understanding what factors allow firms to make rapid strategic moves in a manner that maximizes their profitability. This view is consistent with recent work on temporal effects that suggests scholars should focus on time management and its underlying performance consequences (Shi & Prescott, 2011).

We further advance the literature on the speed of strategic moves by explaining how the profitability consequences of such speed are influenced by the moderating effects of expansion regularity and the duration of existing strategic engagements. The extant literature (Laamanen & Keil, 2008; Shi & Prescott, 2012; Vermeulen & Barkema, 2002) has treated rhythm separately from speed but has neglected the role of duration. Instead, we show that expansion speed should be considered alongside expansion regularity and the duration of existing strategic engagements when firms make new strategic moves. A key insight of our study is that firms that combine rapid and regular strategic moves profit more than firms whose expansion is irregular. We argue that firms can become more profitable by being better prepared for such moves, by reducing the possibility of overstretching resources and capabilities in peaks of expansion, and by improving their responsiveness and adaptation. A more regular expansion may enable firms to create a temporal map and manage the expansion process more efficiently (Klarner & Raisch, 2013; Shi & Prescott, 2011). More regular expansion thus allows firms that make fast-paced strategic moves to increase revenue generation, control managerial costs, and become more profitable.

Furthermore, although the importance of time compression diseconomies has long been recognized in the literature (Dierickx & Cool, 1989), our study explains how regularity helps firms to make rapid strategic moves while reducing the negative consequences of time compression diseconomies. This finding is consistent with recent insights into the role of regularity (Klarner & Raisch, 2013; Laamanen & Keil, 2008; Shi & Prescott, 2012). It further contributes to the "change-stability" debate (Beckman et al., 2004; Klarner & Raisch, 2013) by suggesting that an effective way to balance a firm's need for fast-paced strategic moves and optimal profitability is to regularly undertake such moves.

The negative profitability consequences of speed are also moderated by the duration of the existing strategic engagements of firms. We argue that existing strategic engagements that are mature place fewer demands on managerial resources. They therefore reduce managerial costs and allow a higher capacity for fast-paced expansion. These results, together with the findings regarding the role of regularity, underscore important contingencies that enable firms to expand quickly while reducing negative profitability consequences. In both cases, the effect on managerial costs enables a more rapid expansion (compared with the effect on revenues, which is insignificant), further emphasizing the importance of distinguishing between the revenue generation and managerial costs of strategic moves.

Our findings challenge the established view that fast-paced strategic moves negatively influence profitability because firms cannot quickly absorb the benefits associated with such moves (Vermeulen & Barkema, 2002). This view typically suggests that constraints on absorptive capacity and cognitive scope (Cohen & Levinthal, 1990; Zahra & George, 2002) limit firms' ability to capture the benefits of fast-paced strategic moves and to identify complementarities that will increase revenues. By contrast, our findings indicate that a higher speed of strategic moves, such as alliance portfolio expansion, increases the benefits that firms can get out of their alliance portfolio in terms of expanding their product differentiation and product scope and, in turn, generates more revenue.[14] Making strategic moves at a higher speed increases revenues by enabling firms to accumulate new resources, achieve greater flexibility, and adapt to changing environments. The overall effect of speed on firm profitability is indeed negative, but this result is driven not by the firm's inability to capture the revenue generation benefits of fast-paced strategic moves but by the significant increases in managerial costs that accompany this faster pace.

In that respect, another key contribution of this study is examining how temporal constructs, such as speed, regularity, and duration, affect a fundamental problem in alliances: the cost of managing such agreements. Even when alliance partners trust one another and are not confronted with the opportunistic behavior of their partners (Williamson, 1985), alliances involve significant managerial costs in terms of coordination and integration mechanisms (White & Lui, 2005). Managerial costs are therefore a salient feature of hybrid forms of governance. Although our analysis focused on the context of alliances, managerial costs may, in fact, be a crucial component when firms make other types of strategic moves. For instance, acquisitions require managerial efforts in identifying and evaluating target firms, reaching acquisition agreements, and integrating acquired firms with the parent company. Entering foreign markets requires substantial managerial effort in selecting target markets, deciding the appropriate timing and entry mode, and establishing collaborations in the target country. Likewise, diversification into new business areas can consume significant managerial time and effort to establish new operations in an unfamiliar industry. Our findings therefore indicate that when fast-paced strategic moves are considered, the role of managerial costs is pivotal in determining whether such moves will enhance or reduce firm performance.

This study also contributes to the literature on the profitability implications of alliances (e.g., Ahuja, 2000; Baum, Calabrese, & Silverman, 2000; Goerzen & Beamish, 2005; Lavie & Miller, 2008). A significant insight offered by this study is that the benefits and costs of alliances depend not only on the attributes of alliance portfolios but also on differences in the alliance portfolio expansion process. This finding suggests that two firms may end up with apparently similar portfolios of alliances and collaborate with similar partners but experience different profitability because they build their portfolios at different speeds, with different regularities, and for different durations. A key implication is that understanding how differences in firm-level profitability consequences of alliances involves considering how alliance portfolios are developed over time. Slower alliance portfolio expansion speeds enable firms to achieve higher profitability because they avoid sharp increases in the managerial costs associated with such expansion. By contrast, a fast buildup of alliance portfolios results in time compression diseconomies, thereby increasing the managerial costs associated with alliance portfolio expansion. Yet, although a higher alliance portfolio expansion speed by itself will most likely hamper firm profitability, firms that keep a regular expansion rhythm and sustain mature alliances in their portfolio can reap the benefits of a higher speed (in terms of revenue generation) while substantially reducing the cost disadvantages of speed. Because the buildup speed, regularity, and duration of alliance portfolios vary significantly across firms, empirical analyses that ignore the time-dependent processes in which alliance portfolios are developed may be incomplete explanations of profitability outcomes.

Managerial Implications

Our study demonstrates how and why the speed at which strategic moves are made influences the returns of these moves. The speed of new strategic moves cannot be rushed, because new initiatives require significant managerial attention and resources over a limited time frame. Prior research has suggested that managers of firms that expand quickly should be concerned with their ability to absorb and appropriate the benefits associated with such new strategic moves (Cohen & Levinthal, 1990; Vermeulen & Barkema, 2002; Zahra & George, 2002). Instead, our findings show that managers should shift their attention to controlling managerial costs. This shift is in fact largely what determines the extent to which firms will profit (or not) from their new strategic moves.

Managers should bear in mind that it is not only speed that must be monitored but also the regularity of new strategic moves and the duration of existing ones. Greater regularity allows firms not only to prepare successfully and adapt to new moves but also to limit the over-stretching of managerial resources. Managers can benefit from a more rapid speed in their strategic moves by maintaining a regular pace. Likewise, strategic endeavors of longer dura-tion require less attention, thus giving firms the opportunity to better pursue rapid expansion without substantially increasing managerial costs. In so doing, they may reap the revenue-enhancing benefits of rapid strategic moves while reducing the negative cost consequences associated with such moves.

These contingencies are particularly important for firms that compete in dynamic indus-tries and have little choice with respect to slowing down their rates of expansion. Institutional pressures for rapid expansion can be strong in dynamic sectors, but managers should bear in mind that firm profitability depends on the careful timing of their strategic moves rather than solely on their ability to keep up with their competitors' expansion. This timing may enable managers to build new sources of competitive advantage that derive from the effective man-agement of time. As Shi and Prescott (2011) suggest, managers engaged in new strategic moves should behave as experienced chess players who visualize the game as a series of well-timed sequential moves.

Limitations and Future Research Avenues

Our analysis has a number of limitations, some of which may lead to opportunities for future research. First, all firms in the data set originate from a single country. Thus, coun-try-specific characteristics, such as the cultural distance from foreign alliance partners and the costs implied by such distance (Lavie & Miller, 2008), may affect the results. Likewise, specific socioeconomic factors, such as business culture and managerial backgrounds, may also affect our findings by influencing firms' expansion speed. In addition, the sectorial distribution of Israeli high-technology industries is biased toward specific areas, such as capital equipment, medical devices, telecommunications, and information technology. The revenues and managerial costs of alliance portfolio expansion in these sectors do not nec-essarily represent those found in other sectors. Moreover, the fact that our sample consists of fairly young and relatively small high-technology firms implies that the profitability implications of these firms' alliance portfolios might differ from those for more established firms that can use their experience and size to weather the negative effects of greater alli-ance portfolio expansion speeds. Thus, future analyses of larger and more mature firms originating in multiple countries and industries should enhance the external validity of our results.

From a broader perspective, this study has focused on the effects of a specific strategic move (alliances) on revenue generation, managerial costs, and profitability. Each strategic move differs from others in terms of revenue-generating and cost-escalating patterns, resource demands, and the durability of its effects. It is therefore important to replicate the current study to cover other strategic moves, such as mergers and acquisitions, and entry into new markets and business segments. In addition, although we have focused on the speed and moderating effects associated with new strategic initiatives, future studies can extend the analysis to capture the effect of speed on revenue generation, managerial costs, and profitability when strategic initiatives are dissolved (see Klarner & Raisch, 2013). It is also worth examining alternative measures of performance as means to enhance our understanding of the variability in the consequences of the speed of making new strategic moves. Finally, although our analysis focused on each firm's own speed of making strategic moves, its effects may also depend on competitors' speed. An interesting avenue for future research would be to collect data to examine the effect of a given firm's speed of making strategic moves relative to the average speed of its competitors.

Appendix

Table A1
Description of Variables and Measures

Variable Name	Variable Description
Revenues	For each firm i at year t, revenues is measured using the following logarithmic function: $\ln(\text{revenues}_{i,t})$, where $\text{revenues}_{i,t}$ represents the overall income of firm i in year t.
Managerial costs	For each firm i at year t, managerial costs is measured using the following logarithmic function: $\ln(\text{G\&A}_{i,t})$, where $\text{G\&A}_{i,t}$ represents the general and administrative expenditures of firm i in year t.
Profitability	For each firm i at year t, profitability is measured by $\text{EBITDA}_{i,t}$ which represents the earnings before interest, tax, and depreciation of firm i in year t.
Expansion speed	The number of new alliances that the firm has established in a given year t divided by the total number of partner firms in its alliance portfolio.
Expansion regularity	$1/s$, where s = standard deviation of the number of alliance portfolio expansions in the analyzed time frame.
Duration	The average duration (in years) of each firm's existing alliances in a given year t.
Firm size	Ln(LAN) of the number of employees at the end of year t.
Tangible resources	Firm i's fixed assets in year t (in millions of U.S. dollars).
Total investments	Ln(LAN) of total investments (in millions of U.S. dollars) made up to a given year t.
Patents	Number of patents applied at year t (granted patents only).
Product diversification	Number of products marketed by firm i in year t.
Geographic diversification	Sales dispersion across different regions. The entropy measure is defined as $\Sigma[P_j * \ln(1/P_j)]$ where in each year t P_j is the proportion of sales attributed to region j (out of total sales) and $\ln(1/P_j)$ is the weight given to each region.
Firm age	Age of firm i.
Alliance experience	The number of alliances in which the firm has participated prior to year t (since the firm's inception).
Alliance function diversity	The dispersion of existing alliances across R&D, production, marketing, and customer support activities in a given year t. The entropy measure is defined as $\Sigma[P_j * \ln(1/P_j)]$, where P_j is the proportion of alliances of a given function j (out of total existing alliances) and $\ln(1/P_j)$ is the weight given to each function.

Notes

1. As Shi and Prescott (2012) show, overregularity may also hamper performance. We address this issue in the robustness tests.

2. These sectors include the following: capital equipment, medical devices, telecommunications, enterprise software, storage and data centers, homeland security, multimedia and broadcasting, cellular, chip design, the Internet, and electronics.

3. As such, formal publications of the Israeli Central Bureau of Statistics concerning high-tech industries in Israel are based on data from this source.

4. With respect to the total sales of firms in our sample, 58% were in the United States.

5. We used logarithmic transformations to reduce the skewness of our measures for revenues and managerial costs.

6. Alternative measures of firm performance, namely, returns on sales (ROS) and market value, were also used in the robustness tests for comparison purposes.

7. This approach reflects the view that adding two alliances to a portfolio of 10 alliances is likely to have different effects than adding two alliances to an alliance portfolio of three alliances.

8. Per the methodology of Ahuja (2000) and Phelps (2010) described previously.

9. We did use patent citations as an alternative proxy for innovation output in the robustness tests.

10. In Models 4 and 8, we also account for the fact that expansion speed also has an interaction term.

11. Note that larger values of expansion rhythm represent a more regular expansion rhythm of alliance portfolios.

12. We are indebted to an anonymous reviewer for this suggestion.

13. Market value depends on the investments that were made in the firm (either by private investors, venture capital funds, corporate venture capitalists, acquisitions, or public offerings) and the resulting ownership percentages ("after-the-money" valuation). For instance, if an investor has invested US$1 million in a firm and has received 10% ownership, this firm's market value is US$10 million. ROS represents the ratio of firm earnings before interest, tax, and depreciation to its revenues in a given year *t*.

14. In our robustness tests, we explicitly show that alliance portfolio expansion speed is positively associated with greater product diversification and patent output.

References

Ahuja, G. 2000. Collaboration networks, structural holes and innovation: A longitudinal study. *Administrative Sciences Quarterly*, 45: 425-455.

Ahuja, G., & Katila, R. 2001. Technological acquisitions and the innovation performance of acquiring firms: A longitudinal study. *Strategic Management Journal*, 22: 197-220.

Ahuja, G., Lampert, C.M., & Tandon, V. 2008. Moving beyond Schumpeter: Managerial research on the determinants of technological innovation. *Academy of Management Annals*, 2: 1-98.

Amburgey, T. L., Kelly, D., & Barnett, W. P. 1993. Resetting the clock: The dynamics of organizational change and failure. *Administrative Science Quarterly*, 38: 51-73.

Anand, B. N., & Khanna, T. 2000. Do firms learn to create value? The case of alliances. *Strategic Management Journal*, 21: 295-317.

Arellano, M., & Bond, S. R. 1991. Some tests of specification for panel data: Monte Carlo evidence and an application to employment equations. *Review of Economic Studies*, 58: 277-297.

Arellano, M., & Bover, O. 1995. Another look at the instrumental variable estimation of error-components models. *Journal of Econometrics*, 68: 29-51.

Barkema, H. G., & Schijven, M. 2008. Toward unlocking the full potential of acquisitions: The role of organizational restructuring. *Academy of Management Journal*, 51: 696-722.

Baum, J. A. C., Calabrese, T., & Silverman, B. S. 2000. Don't go it alone: Alliance network composition and start-ups' performance in Canadian biotechnology. *Strategic Management Journal*, 21: 267-294.

Beck, N., Brüderl, J., & Woywode, M. 2008. Momentum or deceleration? Theoretical and methodological reflections on the analysis of organizational change. *Academy of Management Journal*, 51: 413-435.

Beckman, C. M., Haunschild, P. R., & Phillips, D. J. 2004. Friends or strangers? Firm-specific uncertainty, market uncertainty, and network partner selection. *Organization Science*, 15: 259-275.

Belderbos, R., Carree, M., & Lokshin, B. 2004. Cooperative R&D and firm performance. *Research Policy*, 33, 1477-1492.

Blundell, R., & Bond, S. R. 1998. Initial conditions and moment restrictions in dynamic panel data models. *Journal of Econometrics*, 87: 115-143.

Child, J., & Yan, Y. 2003. Predicting the performance of international joint ventures: An investigation in China. *Journal of Management Studies*, 40: 283-320.

Cohen, W. M., & Levinthal, D. A. 1990. Absorptive capacity: A new perspective on learning and innovation. *Administrative Sciences Quarterly*, 35: 128-152.

Darr, E. D., Argote, L., & Epple, D. 1995. The acquisition, transfer and depreciation of knowledge in service organizations: Productivity in franchises. *Management Science*, 42: 1750-1762.

Das, T. K., & Teng, B. S. 2002. The dynamics of alliance conditions in the alliance development process. *Journal of Management Studies*, 39: 725-746.

Delios, A., & Henisz, W. J. 2003. Policy uncertainty and the sequence of entry by Japanese firms. 1980-1998. *Journal of International Business Studies*, 34: 227-241.

Dierickx, I., & Cool, K. 1989. Asset stock accumulation and sustainability of competitive advantage. *Management Science*, 35: 1504-1511.

Dyer, J. 1996. Specialized supplier networks as a source of competitive advantage: Evidence from the auto industry. *Strategic Management Journal*, 17: 271-291.

Dyer, J. H., & Nobeoka, K. 2000. Creating and managing a high-performance knowledge-sharing network: The Toyota case. *Strategic Management Journal*, 21: 345-367.

Dyer, J. H., & Singh, H. 1998. The relational view: Cooperative strategy and sources of interorganizational competitive advantage. *Academy of Management Review*, 23: 660-679.

Farjoun, M. 1998. The independent and joint effects of the skill and physical bases of relatedness in diversification. *Strategic Management Journal*, 19: 611-630.

Goerzen, A. 2007. Alliance networks and firm performance: The impact of repeated partnerships. *Strategic Management Journal*, 28: 487-509.

Goerzen, A., & Beamish, P. W. 2003. Geographic scope and multinational enterprise performance. *Strategic Management Journal*, 24: 1289-1306.

Goerzen, A., & Beamish, P. W. 2005. The effect of alliance network diversity on multinational enterprise performance. *Strategic Management Journal*, 26: 333-354.

Grilliches, Z. 1990. Patent statistics as economic indicators: A survey. *Journal of Economic Literature*, 28: 1661-1707.

Gulati, R. 1995. Does familiarity breed trust? The implications of repeated ties for contractual choice in alliances. *Academy of Management Journal*, 38: 85-112.

Gulati, R. 1999. Network location and learning: The influence of network resources and firm capabilities on alliance formation. *Strategic Management Journal*, 20: 397-420.

Gulati, R., Lavie, D., & Singh, H. 2009. The nature of partnering experience and the gains from alliances. *Strategic Management Journal*, 30: 1213-1233.

Gulati, R., Nohria, N., & Zaheer, A. 2000. Strategic networks. *Strategic Management Journal*, 21: 203-215.

Hambrick, D. C., Finkelstein, S., & Mooney, A. C. 2005. Executive job demands: New insights for explaining strategic decisions and leader behaviors. *Academy of Management Review*, 30: 472-491.

Hart, S. 1995. *New product development: A reader*. London: Dryden Press.

Hitt, M. A., Hoskisson, R. E., & Kim, H. 1997. International diversification: Effects on innovation and firm performance in product-diversified firms. *Academy of Management Journal*, 40: 767-798.

Hoffmann, W. H. 2007. Strategies for managing a portfolio of alliances. *Strategic Management Journal*, 28: 827-856.

Huber, G. 1991. Organizational learning: The contributing processes and literatures. *Organization Science*, 2: 88-115.

Jiang, R. J., Tao, Q. T., & Santoro, M. D. 2010. Alliance portfolio diversity and firm performance. *Strategic Management Journal*, 31: 1136-1144.

Kale, P., Dyer, J. H., & Singh, H. 2002. Alliance capability, stock market response, and long term alliance success: The role of the alliance function. *Strategic Management Journal*, 23: 747-767.

Kale, P., Singh, H., & Perlmutter, H. 2000. Learning and protection of proprietary assets in strategic alliances: Building relational capital. *Strategic Management Journal*, 21: 217-237.

Kim, W. C., Hwang, P., & Burgers, W. P. 1993. Multinationals' diversification and the risk-return trade-off. *Strategic Management Journal*, 14: 275-286.

Klarner, P., & Raisch, S. 2013. Move to the beat: Rhythms of change and firm performance. *Academy of Management Journal*, 56: 160-184.

Knott, A. M., Bryce, D. J., & Posen, H. E. 2003. On the strategic accumulation of intangible assets. *Organization Science*, 14: 192-207.

Koka, B. R., Madhavan, J., & Prescott, J. E. 2006. The evolution of interfirm networks: Environmental effects on patterns of network change. *Academy of Management Review*, 31: 721-737.

Kumar, R., & Nti, K. O. 1998. Differential learning and interaction in alliance dynamics: A process and outcome discrepancy model. *Organization Science*, 9: 356-367.

Laamanen, T., & Keil, T. 2008. Performance of serial acquirers: Toward an acquisition program perspective. *Strategic Management Journal*, 29: 663-672.

Lavie, D. 2006. The competitive advantage of interconnected firms: An extension of the resource-based view. *Academy of Management Review*, 31: 638-658.

Lavie, D., & Miller, S. 2008. Alliance portfolio internationalization and firm performance. *Organization Science*, 19: 623-646.

Lee, C., Lee, K., & Pennings, J. M. 2001. Internal capabilities, external networks, and performance: A study on technology-based ventures. *Strategic Management Journal*, 22: 615-640.

Levinthal, D. A., & Fichman, M. 1988. Dynamics of interorganizational attachments: Auditor-client relationships. *Administrative Science Quarterly*, 33: 345-369.

Miller, J. D., Fern, M. J., & Cardinal, L. B. 2007. The use of knowledge for technological innovation within diversified firms. *Academy of Management Journal*, 50: 308-326.

Pacheco de Almeida, G., Hawk, A., & Yeung, B. 2015. The right speed and its value. *Strategic Management Journal*, 36: 159-176.

Phelps, C. C. 2010. A longitudinal study of the influence of alliance network structure and composition on firm exploratory innovation. *Academy of Management Journal*, 53: 890-913.

Ronen, S., & Shenkar, O. 1985. Clustering countries on attitudinal dimensions: A review and synthesis. *Academy of Management Review*, 10: 435-454.

Rugman, A. M., & Verbeke, A. 2004. A perspective on regional and global strategies of multinational enterprises. *Journal of International Business Studies*, 35: 3-18.

Schilke, O., & Goerzen, A. 2010. Alliance management capability: An investigation of the construct and its measurement. *Journal of Management*, 36: 1192-1219.

Shi, W. S., & Prescott, J. E. 2011. Sequence patterns of firms' acquisition and alliance behavior and their performance implications. *Journal of Management Studies*, 48: 1044-1070.

Shi, W. S., & Prescott, J. E. 2012. Rhythm and entrainment of acquisition and alliance initiatives and firm performance: A temporal perspective. *Organizational Studies*, 33: 1281-1310.

Shi, W. S., Sun, J., & Prescott, J. E. 2012. A temporal perspective of merger and acquisition and strategic alliance initiatives: Review and future direction. *Journal of Management*, 38: 164-209.

Singh, K., & Mitchell, W. 2005. Growth dynamics: The bidirectional relationship between interfirm collaboration and business sales in entrant and incumbent alliances. *Strategic Management Journal*, 26: 497-521.

Stuart, T. E. 2000. Interorganizational alliances and the performance of firms: A study of growth and innovation rates in a high-technology industry. *Strategic Management Journal*, 21: 791-811.

Teece, D. J. 2007. Explicating dynamic capabilities: The nature and microfoundations of (sustainable) enterprise performance. *Strategic Management Journal*, 28: 1319-1350.

Vasudeva, G., & Anand, J. 2011. Unpacking absorptive capacity: A study of knowledge utilization from alliance portfolios. *Academy of Management Journal*, 54: 611-623.

Vermeulen, F., & Barkema, H. 2002. Pace, rhythm and scope: Process dependence in building a profitable multinational corporation. *Strategic Management Journal*, 23: 637-653.

Wassmer, U. 2010. Alliance portfolio: A review and research agenda. *Journal of Management*, 36: 141-171.

White, S., & Lui, S. S. Y. 2005. Distinguishing costs of cooperation and control in alliances. *Strategic Management Journal*, 26: 913-932.

Williamson, O. E. 1985. *The economic institutions of capitalism: Firms, markets, relational contracting.* New York, NY: Free Press.

Zaheer, A., & Bell, G. G. 2005. Benefiting from network position: Firm capabilities, structural holes, and performance. *Strategic Management Journal*, 26: 809-825.

Zaheer, A., McEvily, B., & Perrone, V. 1998. Does trust matter? Exploring the effects of interorganizational and interpersonal trust on performance. *Organization Science*, 9: 1-20.

Zahra, S. A., & George, J. 2002. Absorptive capacity: A review, reconceptualisation, and extension. *Academy of Management Review*, 27: 185-203.

Zollo, M., & Winter, S. G. 2002. Deliberate learning and the evolution of dynamic capabilities. *Organization Science*, 13: 339-351.

Printed and bound by CPI Group (UK) Ltd, Croydon, CR0 4YY

23/04/2025

14660989-0002